T0212417

Lecture Notes in Computer Science   8815

Commenced Publication in 1973
Founding and Former Series Editors:
Gerhard Goos, Juris Hartmanis, and Jan van Leeuwen

More information about this series at http://www.springer.com/series/7412

Aurélio Campilho · Mohamed Kamel (Eds.)

Image Analysis and Recognition

11th International Conference, ICIAR 2014
Vilamoura, Portugal, October 22–24, 2014
Proceedings, Part II

 Springer

Editors
Aurélio Campilho
Faculty of Engineering
University of Porto
Porto
Portugal

Mohamed Kamel
Department of Electrical and Computer
  Engineering
University of Waterloo
Waterloo, ON
Canada

ISSN 0302-9743   ISSN 1611-3349   (electronic)
ISBN 978-3-319-11754-6   ISBN 978-3-319-11755-3   (eBook)
DOI 10.1007/978-3-319-11755-3

Library of Congress Control Number: 2014950801

LNCS Sublibrary: SL6 – Image Processing, Computer Vision, Pattern Recognition, and Graphics

Springer Cham Heidelberg New York Dordrecht London

Printed on acid-free paper

Springer is part of Springer Science+Business Media (www.springer.com)

Preface

This is the 11th edition of the ICIAR series of annual conferences offering an opportunity for the participants to interact and present their latest research in theory, methodology, and applications of image analysis and recognition. ICIAR 2014, the International Conference on Image Analysis and Recognition, was held in Vila Moura, Portugal, October 22–24, 2014. ICIAR is organized by AIMI – Association for Image and Machine Intelligence, a not-for-profit organization registered in Ontario, Canada.

For ICIAR 2014, we received a total of 177 full papers from 39 countries. Before the review process all the papers were checked for similarity using a comparison database of scholarly work. The review process was carried out by members of the Program Committee and other reviewers. Each paper was reviewed by at least two reviewers, and checked by the conference chairs. A total of 107 papers were finally accepted and appear in the two volumes of this proceedings. We would like to sincerely thank the authors for responding to our call, and we thank the reviewers for the careful evaluation and feedback provided to the authors. It is this collective effort that resulted in the strong conference program and high-quality proceedings.

Each year we attempt to focus on a specific topic for the keynote speeches and conduct a panel discussion on the topic.

This year, the conference theme was focused on the topic "Sparse Representations for Image Analysis and Recognition." We were very pleased to include three outstanding keynote talks on this topic: "Optimization Algorithms for Sparse Representations: Some History and Recent Developments" by Mário Figueiredo, Instituto Superior Técnico Portugal; "Morphological Diversities in Astrophysics" by Jean-Luc Starck, CosmoStat Laboratory, France; and "Sparse Stochastic Processes with Application to Biomedical Imaging" by Michael Unser, Ecole Polytechnique Fédérale de Lausanne, Switzerland. The keynote speakers also participated in the panel "Sparse Representation for Image Analysis and Recognition: Trends and Applications." We would like to express our gratitude to the keynote speakers for accepting our invitation to share their vision and recent advances in their areas of expertise, which are at the core of the topics of the conference.

We would like to thank Khaled Hammouda, the webmaster of the conference, for maintaining the Web pages, interacting with the authors, and preparing the proceedings.

As all conferences, the success of ICIAR 2014 is attributed to the effort and work of many people, including members of the Organizing Committee, staff, and volunteers. We gratefully acknowledge their support and efforts.

We are also grateful to Springer's editorial staff for supporting this publication in the LNCS series. We also would like to acknowledge the professional service of Viagens Abreu in taking care of the registration process and the special events of the conference.

Finally, we are very pleased to welcome all the participants to ICIAR 2014. For those who were not able to attend, we hope this publication provides a good view into the research presented at the conference, and we look forward to meeting you at the next ICIAR conference.

October 2014   Aurélio Campilho
                                                                     Mohamed Kamel

ICIAR 2014 – International Conference on Image Analysis and Recognition

General Chairs

Aurélio Campilho	University of Porto, Portugal
Mohamed Kamel	University of Waterloo, Canada

Local Organizing Committee

Ana Maria Mendonça	University of Porto, Portugal
Jorge Alves Silva	University of Porto, Portugal
João Rodrigues	University of the Algarve, Portugal
José Rouco Maseda	Biomedical Engineering Institute, Portugal
Jorge Novo Buján	Biomedical Engineering Institute, Portugal

Conference Secretariat

Viagens Abreu	SA, Portugal

Webmaster

Khaled Hammouda	Waterloo, Ontario, Canada

Advisory Committee

M. Ahmadi	University of Windsor, Canada
P. Bhattacharya	Concordia University, Canada
T.D. Bui	Concordia University, Canada
M. Cheriet	University of Quebec, Canada
E. Dubois	University of Ottawa, Canada
Z. Duric	George Mason University, USA
G. Granlund	Linköping University, Sweden
L. Guan	Ryerson University, Canada
M. Haindl	Institute of Information Theory and Automation, Czech Republic
E. Hancock	University of York, UK
J. Kovacevic	Carnegie Mellon University, USA
M. Kunt	Swiss Federal Institute of Technology (EPFL), Switzerland

J. Padilha	University of Porto, Portugal
K.N. Plataniotis	University of Toronto, Canada
A. Sanfeliu	Technical University of Catalonia, Spain
M. Shah	University of Central Florida, USA
M. Sid-Ahmed	University of Windsor, Canada
C.Y. Suen	Concordia University, Canada
A.N. Venetsanopoulos	University of Toronto, Canada
M. Viergever	Utrecht University, Netherlands
B. Vijayakumar	Carnegie Mellon University, USA
R. Ward	University of British Columbia, Canada
D. Zhang	Hong Kong Polytechnic University, Hong Kong

Program Committee

A. Abate	University of Salerno, Italy
M. Ahmed	Wilfrid Laurier University, Canada
L. Alexandre	University of Beira Interior, Portugal
J. Alirezaie	Ryerson University, Canada
G. Andreu-Garcia	Universitat Politècnica de València, Spain
H. Araújo	University of Coimbra, Portugal
Emilio Balaguer-Ballester	Bournemouth University, UK
T. Barata	University of Coimbra, Portugal
J. Barbosa	University of Porto, Portugal
J. Batista	University of Coimbra, Portugal
R. Bernardes	University of Coimbra, Portugal
A. Bezerianos	National University of Singapore, Singapore
J. Bioucas	Technical University of Lisbon, Portugal
I. Bloch	Télécom ParisTech, France
T.D. Bui	Concordia University, Canada
C. Busch	Gjøvik University College, Norway
F. Camastra	University of Naples Parthenope, Italy
J. Cardoso	University of Porto, Portugal
G. Carneiro	University of Adelaide, Australia
M. Coimbra	University of Porto, Portugal
M. Correia	University of Porto, Portugal
J. Debayle	Ecole Nationale Supérieure des Mines de Saint-Étienne, France
J. Dias	University of Coimbra, Portugal
G. Doretto	West Virginia University, USA
H. du Buf	University of the Algarve, Portugal
J. Fernandez	Centro Nacional de Biotecnología – CSIC, Spain
I. Fondón	University of Seville, Spain
A. Fred	Technical University of Lisbon, Portugal
G. Freeman	University of Waterloo, Canada

Reviewers

M. Al-Rawi	University of Aveiro, Portugal
R. Araujo	University of Waterloo, Canada
E. Bhullar	South Asian University, India
M. Camplani	University of Bristol, UK
C. Caridade	Instituto Superior de Engenharia de Coimbra, Portugal
J. Chen	Lehigh University, USA
L. Fernandez	University of León, Spain
J. Ferreira	University of Porto, Portugal
E. Fidalgo	University of León, Spain
M. Gangeh	University of Toronto, Canada
M. Garcia	University of León, Spain
V. Gonzalez	Ecole Nationale Supérieure des Mines de Saint-Étienne, France
H. Haberdar	University of Houston, USA
M. Hortas	Universidade da Coruña, Spain
N. Lori	University of Coimbra, Portugal
S. Mahmoud	University of Waterloo, Canada
J. Marcos	Spanish National Research Council, Spain
Y. Miao	University of Waterloo, Canada
F. Monteiro	IPB – Instituto Politécnico de Bragança, Portugal
P. Moreno	Instituto Superior Técnico, Portugal
J. Novo	INESC TEC – INESC Technology and Science, Portugal
H. Oliveira	INESC TEC, Portugal
A. Ragab	University of Waterloo, Canada
L. Reis	University of Minho, Portugal
R. Rocha	INESC TEC – INESC Technology and Science, Portugal
J. Rodrigues	University of the Algarve, Portugal
N. Rodriguez	Universidade da Coruña, Spain
J. Rouco	INESC TEC – INESC Technology and Science, Portugal
P. Trigueiros	Polytechnic Institute of Porto, Portugal

Supported by

AIMI – Association for Image and Machine Intelligence

Center for Biomedical Engineering Research
INESC TEC – INESC Technology and Science
Portugal

Department of Electrical and Computer Engineering
Faculty of Engineering
University of Porto
Portugal

CPAMI – Centre for Pattern Analysis and Machine Intelligence
University of Waterloo
Canada

Contents – Part II

Medical Image Processing and Analysis

Medical Image Segmentation

3D Imaging

Contents – Part I

Image Restoration and Enhancement

Feature Detection and Image Segmentation

Classification and Learning Methods

Document Image Analysis

Image and Video Retrieval

Remote Sensing

Applications

Action, Gestures and Audio-Visual Recognition

Audio-Visual Emotion Analysis Using Semi-Supervised Temporal Clustering with Constraint Propagation

Rodrigo Araujo$^{(\boxtimes)}$ and Mohamed S. Kamel

Department of Electrical and Computer Engineering, Centre for Pattern Analysis and Machine Intelligence, University of Waterloo, 200 University Ave W, Waterloo, ONN2L 3G1, Canada
{raraujo,mkamel}@uwaterloo.ca

Abstract. In this paper, we investigate applying semi-supervised clustering to audio-visual emotion analysis, a complex problem that is traditionally solved using supervised methods. We propose an extension to the semi-supervised aligned cluster analysis algorithm (SSACA), a temporal clustering algorithm that incorporates pairwise constraints in the form of *must-link* and *cannot-link*. We incorporate an exhaustive constraint propagation mechanism to further improve the clustering process. To validate the proposed method, we apply it to emotion analysis on a multimodal naturalistic emotion database. Results show substantial improvements compared to the original aligned clustering analysis algorithm (ACA) and to our previously proposed semi-supervised approach.

Keywords: Semi-supervised · Facial expression · Speech emotion recognition · Clustering · Temporal segmentation · Kernel k-means

1 Introduction

Analysis of naturally occurring human emotions has become the main focus of recent research in the field of affective computing. Emotional analysis is considered a vital step towards building efficient and more realistic intelligent human-computer interfaces. The focus is now directed towards recognition in terms of dimensional and continuous description, rather than a small number of discrete emotion categories. Numerical representation of emotions in a multi-dimensional space is considered a more appropriate representation that can reflect the gradated nature of emotions. Moreover, human natural affective behavior is multimodal, subtle, and complex, which makes it challenging to map the affective human state into a single label or discrete number of classes [4].

Facial expressions and speech are the two modalities most commonly used to analyze emotions in human interaction. While facial expressions are considered the major modality in human communication, according to [8], speech is the fastest and most natural method of communication between humans.

A. Campilho and M. Kamel (Eds.): ICIAR 2014, Part II, LNCS 8815, pp. 3–11, 2014.
DOI: 10.1007/978-3-319-11755-3_1

The bulk of the approaches found in the literature are on supervised learning, despite the fact that the labeling process is demanding. With the abundance of data available in this domain and the burdensome nature of the labeling process, it is understandable that unsupervised methods should be pursued more intensively. However, purely unsupervised methods may not produce desirable results due to the complexity of the problem at hand. This need to balance the demands of process and accuracy of results motivated us to pursue a semi-supervised approach.

In this paper, we extend our previously proposed Semi-Supervised Aligned Cluster Analysis (SSACA) method [1] by using an exhaustive constraint propagation approach and apply it to the AVEC audio-visual database.

2 Related Work

Very few works have applied unsupervised methods to emotion analysis in general. This observation is true for both of the two most-used modalities: facial expressions and speech. A possible reason for the shortage of unsupervised work is due to the lack of the temporal aspect of the traditional clustering algorithms. The bulk of the methods are supervised, with HMM being the most used method in terms of audio. In terms of visual features, Relevance Vector Machine (RVM) has shown very good results [7].

Some supervised works that tackle the problem as a dimensional and continuous emotion recognition are [11] [7] [3]. Wollmer et al. [11] have studied the estimation of emotions from speech in the valence and activation dimensions using Long- Short-Term Recurrent Neural Networks. Nicolaou et al. [7] have proposed the use of Output-Associative Relevance Vector Machine (OA-RVM) for dimensional and continuous estimation of emotions from facial expressions. Grimm et al. [3] have compared the performance of Support Vector Regression, Fuzzy k-Nearest Neighbor, and Rule-based Fuzzy Logic classifiers as estimators of spontaneously expressed emotions in speech from three continuous-valued emotion primitives.

In terms of unsupervised methods for emotion analysis, one recent publication is the work of De la Torre *et al.* [2], who have proposed a temporal segmentation method of facial gestures to cluster similar facial actions. Zhou *et al.* [13] have examined facial events directly from naturally occurring videos, using temporal clustering. They use two algorithms for this task: Aligned Cluster Analysis (ACA) and a multi-subject correspondence for matching expressions.

Both of these works, however, analyze only one modality, and they use either categorical labels or action units. In the case of speech and unsupervised methods, most of the research is on speech segmentation for speech recognition or on speech separation.

Recently, we proposed a semi-supervised method, SSACA [1], which uses pairwise constraints in the form of *must-links* and *cannot-links* as a way to add side information to help the clustering process, and to boost its performance with minimal supervised information. We applied this method to a naturalistic database, and the results showed improvements compared to the original approach. In this paper, we build on our previous approach, adding an exhaustive constraint propagation artifact to the framework, and we apply the proposed method to a larger multimodal naturalistic database, using audio-visual features.

3   Model Description

The emotional behavior of a person can be treated as a time series, wherein the specific emotion primitive being evaluated varies over time. The goal is to factorize (segment) multiple time series into disjointed segments that belong to k temporal clusters. Essentially, we have a temporal clustering problem. The idea is to have frames within a segment that are similar to each other and non-overlapping segments that belong to k temporal clusters.

3.1   Semi-Supervised Aligned Cluster Analysis (SSACA)

This section describes SSACA [1], a transformation of the temporal clustering algorithm ACA into a semi-supervised temporal clustering method. In contrast to ACA, SSACA adds some side information to its framework in the form of pairwise constraints, improving the accuracy and performance of the temporal clustering. ACA is a combination of kernel k-means and Dynamic Time Alignment Kernel (DTAK).

The goal of ACA is to decompose a segment $\mathbf{X} = [\mathbf{x}_1, \ldots, \mathbf{x}_n] \in \mathbb{R}^{d \times n}$ into m disjoint segments, where each segment belongs to a single cluster. Each segment is constrained by a maximum length n_{max}, which also serves as a way to control the temporal granularity of the segmentation. The segments begin at position s_i and end at $s_{i+1} - 1$, such that $n_i = s_{i+1} - s_i \leq n_{max}$. An indicator matrix $\mathbf{G} \in \{0,1\}^{k \times m}$ assigns each segment to a cluster; $g_{ci} = 1$ if $\mathbf{Z}_i$ belongs to cluster c.

ACA combines kernel k-means with DTAK to achieve temporal clustering by minimizing:

$$J_{aca}(\mathbf{G}, \mathbf{s}) = \sum_{c=1}^{k} \sum_{i=1}^{m} g_{ci} \underbrace{\left\| \psi(\mathbf{X}_{[\mathbf{s_i}, \mathbf{s_{i+1}}]}) - \mathbf{z_c} \right\|^2}_{dist^2_\psi(\mathbf{Y}_i, \mathbf{z}_c)} = \left\| [\psi(\mathbf{Y}_1, \ldots, \psi(\mathbf{Y}_m) - \mathbf{ZG} \right\|^2_F ,$$

$$s.t. \mathbf{G}^T \mathbf{1}_k = \mathbf{1}_m \text{ and } s_{i+1} - s_i \in [1, n_{max}],$$

$$(1)$$

where $\mathbf{G} \in \{0,1\}^{k \times m}$ is a cluster indicator matrix, and $s \in \mathbb{R}^{m+1}$ is the segment vector $\mathbf{Y} = \mathbf{X}_{[s_i, s_{i+1}]}$, which is one of the differences between ACA and kernel k-means. In the case of ACA, the $dist^2_\psi(\mathbf{Y}_i, \mathbf{z}_c)$ is the squared distance between the ith segment and the center of cluster c in the nonlinear mapped feature space represented by $\psi(.)$.

In order to add the semi-supervised component to the proposed method, we rely on the discovery of Kulis et al. [5], which has shown that the objective function for semi-supervised clustering, based on Hidden Markov Random

Fields (HMRF), with squared Euclidean distance and a certain class of constraint penalty function, can be expressed as a special case of the weighted kernel k-means. SSACA, which is based on kernel k-means, may use the same framework of HMRF semi-supervised clustering. Thus, we can write the SSACA objective function as:

$$
J_{ssaca}(\mathbf{G}, \mathbf{s}) = \sum_{c=1}^{k} \sum_{i=1}^{m} g_{ci} \underbrace{\left\| \psi(\mathbf{X}_{[\mathbf{s_i}, \mathbf{s_{i+1}}]}) - \mathbf{z_c} \right\|^2}_{dist_\psi^2(\mathbf{Y}_i, \mathbf{z}_c)} - \sum_{\substack{\mathbf{x}_i, \mathbf{x}_j \in \mathcal{M} \\ g_i = g_j}} w_{ij} + \sum_{\substack{\mathbf{x}_i, \mathbf{x}_j \in \mathcal{C} \\ g_i = g_j}} w_{ij} \quad (2)
$$

where $\mathcal{M}$ is the set of *must-link* constraints, $\mathcal{C}$ is the set of *cannot-link* constraints, w_{ij} is the penalty cost for violating a constraint $\mathbf{x}_i$ and $\mathbf{x}_j$, and g_i refers to the cluster label of $\mathbf{x}_i$. There are three terms in this objective function. The first term is the unsupervised k-means term of the objective function. Note that the distance $dist_\psi^2(\mathbf{Y}_i, \mathbf{z}_c)$ can be represented as a matrix of pairwise squared Euclidean distances among the data points (see proof in [5]). We refer later to this distance matrix as $\mathbf{S}$. The second term is based on the *must-link* constraints, and states that for every *must-link* $\mathbf{x}_i$ and $\mathbf{x}_j$ that are in the same cluster, the objective function is rewarded by subtracting some pre-specified weight. Similarly, the third term in the objective function states that for every *cannot-link* $\mathbf{x}_i$, $\mathbf{x}_j$ in the same cluster has violated that constraint, so the objective function is penalized by some pre-specified penalty weight. We will refer later to the second and third term of the function as $\mathbf{W}$.

Kulis *et al.* [5] have also shown that, for the equivalence of the HMRF k-means and the weighted kernel k-means to hold, it is necessary to construct a certain kernel matrix and set weights in a specific way. A kernel matrix $\mathbf{K}$ should have two components: $\mathbf{K} = \mathbf{S} + \mathbf{W}$. $\mathbf{S}$ is the similarity matrix, and comes from the unsupervised term, while $\mathbf{W}$ is the constraint matrix. This matrix $\mathbf{W}$ has a pre-specified w_{ij} weight for *must-link* and $-w_{ij}$ for *cannot-link*, and zero otherwise. Thus, this objective function is mathematically equivalent to the weighted kernel k-means objective function. In other words, we can run weighted kernel k-means to decrease the objective function.

Because the constraints are held in the segment level, we have two kernel matrices, $\mathbf{K}$ and $\mathbf{T}$. $\mathbf{K}$ is the frame kernel matrix, which defines the similarity between two frames, $\mathbf{x_i}$ and $\mathbf{x_j}$. $\mathbf{T} = [\tau_{ij}]_{m \times m} \in \mathbb{R}^{m \times m}$ is the segment kernel matrix that represents the similarity of the segments $\mathbf{X}_{[\mathbf{s_i}, \mathbf{s_{i+1}}]}$ and $\mathbf{X}_{[\mathbf{s_j}, \mathbf{s_{j+1}}]}$ using the distance DTAK. The segment kernel matrix $\mathbf{T}$ is be constructed as the sum of $\mathbf{T} + \mathbf{W}$. To avoid excessive notation we will also use $\mathbf{T}$ to designate the result of $\mathbf{T} + \mathbf{W}$.

In ACA, the method adopted to solve this optimization problem is a dynamic programming (DP)-based algorithm, which has a complexity of $O(n^2 n_{max})$ to exhaustively examine all possible segmentations. In SSACA, we adapt the DP-based search to a semi-supervised framework, incorporating the pairwise constraints into the algorithm. We call the new algorithm SS DPSearch (See Algorithm 1). SS DPSearch optimizes SSACA w.r.t $\mathbf{G}$ and s, as well as rewarding or penalizing the distance between segments $\tau(X_{[i,v]}, \dot{Y}_j)$ according to constraints.

Algorithm 1. SS DPSearch

---

parameter: n_{max}, k, n_{ml}, n_{cl}
input: $G \in \{0,1\}^{k \times \dot{m}}$, $\dot{s} \in \mathbb{R}^{(\dot{m}+1)}$, $K \in \mathbb{R}^{n \times n}$, $T \in \mathbb{R}^{m \times m}$, $\mathcal{M} \in \mathbb{Z}^{n_{ml} \times 2}$, $\mathcal{C} \in \mathbb{Z}^{n_{cl} \times 2}$
output: $G \in \{0,1\}^{k \times m}$, $\dot{s} \in \mathbb{R}^{(m+1)}$
1: headTail = getHeadTails($\mathcal{M}, \mathcal{C}$);
2: **for** $v = 1$ **to** n **do**
3:    $J(v) \leftarrow \infty$;
4:    **if** $v \geq$ headTail(:,1) **and** $v <$ headTail(:,2) **then**
5:       continue;
6:    **end if**
7:    **if** isTail(v) **then**
8:       **for** $j = 1$ **to** $\dot{m}$ **do**
9:          *Retrieve directly from* $T(X_{[i,v]}, \dot{Y}_j)$;
10:      **end for**
11:      $c^* \leftarrow \arg\min_c dist_\psi(X_{[i,v]}, \dot{z}_c)$;
12:      $J \leftarrow dist_\psi(X_{[i,v]}, \dot{z}_{c^*})$;
13:      $J([i,v]) \leftarrow J$, $g^*_{[i,v]} \leftarrow e^*_c$, $i^*_{[i,v]} \leftarrow i$;
14:   **else**
15:      **for** $n_v = 1$ **to** $min(n_{max}, v)$ **do**
16:         { *Same as DPSearch*}
17:      **end for**
18:   **end if**
19: **end for**
    {*Perform backward segmentation*}

3.2   Exhaustive and Efficient Constraint Propagation

The pairwise constraints are used to adjust the similarity matrix for the kernel k-means clustering algorithm. However, using this technique, only the constrained segment similarities are affected. In order to make the propagation of constraints more efficient, we borrow the idea of exhaustive and efficient constraint propagation from Lu and Ip [6] and adapt it to our framework. The rationale behind this method is to spread the effects of the constraints throughout the whole similarity matrix S.

Exhaustive and Efficient Constraint Propagation (E^2CP) tackles the problem of constraint propagation by decomposing it into sets of label propagation subproblems. Given the dataset $X = [x_1, \ldots, x_n] \in \mathbb{R}^{d \times n}$, a set of *must-link* $\mathcal{M}$ and a set of *cannot-link* $\mathcal{C}$, we can represent all the pairwise constraints in a single matrix $W = Z_{ij N \times N}$:

$$W_{ij} = \begin{cases} +1, & (x_i, x_j) \in \mathcal{M} \\ -1, & (x_i, x_j) \in \mathcal{C} \\ 0, & \text{otherwise} \end{cases} \tag{3}$$

Each j-th column of $W_{.j}$ can now be seen as a two-class semi-supervised learning problem, in which the *positive class* ($W_{ij} > 0$) represents the segments that should be on the same cluster, and the *negative class* ($W_{ij} < 0$) represents the segments that should not be in the same cluster. If ($W_{ij}) = 0$, x_i x_j are not constrained. Then, each column is solved by label propagation in parallel [12]. The same process is repeated for the rows, ensuring that all the segments will be affected by the propagation. The algorithm can be described as follows:

1. Create the similarity matrix T or a symmetric k-NN graph.
2. Create the matrix $\bar{\mathcal{L}} = D^{\frac{-1}{2}} T D^{\frac{-1}{2}}$, where D is a diagonal matrix with its (i,i)-element equal to the sum of the i-th row of T.
3. Iterate $F_v(t+1) = \alpha \bar{\mathcal{L}} F_v(t) + (1-\alpha)W$ for vertical constraint propagation until convergence, where $F_v(t) \in \mathcal{F}$ and α is a parameter in the range of $(0, 1)$.
4. Iterate $F_h(t+1) = \alpha F_h(t)\bar{\mathcal{L}} + (1-\alpha)F_v^*$ for horizontal constraint propagation until convergence, where $F_h(t) \in \mathcal{F}$ and F_v^* is the limit of $\{F_{v(t)}\}$.
5. Output $F^* = F_h^*$ as the final representation of the pairwise constraints, where F_h^* is the limit of $\{F_{h(t)}\}$.

Intuitively, the algorithm receives information from its neighbor at each iteration, and the parameter α controls the relative amount of information passed from the neighbors. The final label of segments is set to be the cluster from which it has received the most information during the iteration process.

Without loss of generality, [12] shows that $\{F(t)\}$ can be calculated in a closed form. The output F^* represents an exhaustive set of pairwise constraints with the associated confidence scores $|F^*|$. Now, we can adjust the similarities in T with the output scores of F^*, as described in Equation 4.

$$\tilde{T}_{ij} = \begin{cases} 1 - (1 - F_{ij}^*)(1 - W_{ij}), & F_{ij}^* \geq 0 \\ (1 + F_{ij}^*)W_{ij}, & F_{ij}^* < 0 \end{cases} \tag{4}$$

Algorithm 2 shows SSACA with the exhaustive propagation.

Algorithm 2. SSACA + Exhaustive propagation (EP)

---

input: $S \in \mathbb{R}^{n \times n}$: input frame kernel matrix, $T \in \mathbb{R}^{n \times n}$: input segment kernel matrix, $W \in \mathbb{R}^{n \times n}$: constraint penalty, k: number of clusters, $\mathcal{M}$: set of must-link constraints, $\mathcal{C}$: set of cannot-link constraints, $\dot{s}$: initial segmentation.
output: $G \in \{0, 1\}^{k \times n}$: Final partitioning of the points
1: Propagate the constraints $F^* \leftarrow W$
2: Form the matrix $\tilde{T}$ according to equation 4.
3: Diagonal-shift $\tilde{T}$ by adding σI to guarantee positive definiteness of $\tilde{T}$.
4: Get initial clusters $G^{(0)}$ using constraints.
5: Return $s = \text{SSDPSearch}(G^{(0)}, \dot{s}, S, \tilde{T}, \mathcal{M}, \mathcal{C}, k)$.

---

4   Experiments

We performed experiments on a naturalistic emotion speech database, and compared the performance of the exhaustive propagation SSACA (SSACA+EP) with SSACA and ACA. The accuracy evaluation criterion is the same used in [1], and is based on the Hungarian algorithm.

4.1   AVEC Database

AVEC[10] is an audio-visual emotion recognition database created for the emotion recognition challenge (AVEC 2012). It consists of conversations between participants and four stereotyped characters. Each character has a specific emotion stereotype: sensible, happy, angry, and sad. The train partition of the database contains 31 sections, wherein each session contains one dialogue with a specific character. The database is labeled for arousal, valence, power, and expectancy.

We used the Word-Level Sub-Challenge (WLSC) portion of the database. Because we used a temporal-clustering-based approach, we categorized the continuous values of the affective dimensions, which range from [-1, +1], in 6 categories: [-1,-0.66], [-0.66, -0.33], [-0.33, 0], [0, 0.33], [0.33, 0.66], and [0.66, 1].

The audio features used consist of 1871 features, including 25 energy and spectral related low-level descriptors (LLD) x 42 functionals, 6 voicing related LLD x 32 functionals, and 10 voiced/unvoiced durational features. Details for LLD and functionals can be found in [10]. For visual features, we extracted Local Binary Patterns (LBP), based on the approach described in [9]. For arousal, we used audio features, since it has been shown consistently in other works [9] that audio features are more suitable for this type of affect dimension. For valence, power, and expectancy, we used visual features.

Figure 1 shows the average results of 20 random initializations on the train portion of the AVEC database for three different methods on arousal, valence, power, and expectancy, respectively. Note that both SSACA and SSACA+EP had superior performance compared to the baseline algorithm, ACA, in almost all of the sessions, with the addition of only 5% percent of the possible constraints as side information. SSACA+EP and SSACA showed very similar results; however, for the sessions with higher number of segments and high variability, SSACA+EP showed significantly better results, (*e.g.*, session 22, Figure 1(a)).

Emotion variability seems to play a big role in influencing the results of SSACA+EP. We define variability in this context as the variation of emotions. When there are a lot of transitions from one category to another, we say we have a high variability; when there are few transitions, we say we have low variability. In order to observe this aspect on the AVEC database, we set up another experiment. In this experiment, we used the dialogue of a participant with 4 different characters and combined them, so we had a longer conversation with the possibility of a high variability. Table 1 shows the average result of 20 random initializations.

Note that in this setup, SSACA+EP improved the results in all emotion dimensions. For arousal, it improved from 0.74 to 0.78 with a lower standard

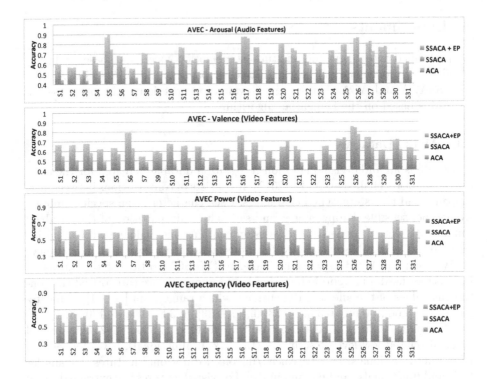

Fig. 1. Average accuracy of SSACA+EP, SSACA and ACA on the AVEC dataset for all sessions, at approximately 5% of the total number of possible constraints

deviation, using the same amount of constraints. Similar improvement was observed for valence, which improved from 0.71 to 0.75. For power, we observed improvements from 0.75 to 0.77. Finally, expectancy improved from 0.81 to 0.84. In terms of the baseline algorithm, the proposed method had a very significant increase in performance, in some cases doubling the accuracy with the addition of only 5% of the possible number of constraints.

Table 1. Average accuracy results on high variance segments

	Average Accuracy			
	Arousal	Valence	Power	Expectancy
SSACA+EP	0.78 ± 0.07	0.75 ± 0.08	0.77 ± 0.11	0.84 ± 0.08
SSACA	0.74 ± 0.09	0.71 ± 0.08	0.75 ± 0.12	0.81 ± 0.07
ACA	0.46 ± 0.02	0.51 ± 0.05	0.40 ± 0.12	0.40 ± 0.02

5 Conclusion

In this work, we propose SSACA+EP, a temporal clustering algorithm that extends SSACA. SSACA+EP incorporates a mechanism for constraint propagation into its framework, spreading the *must-link* and *cannot-link* constraints throughout the similarity matrix and making the process more efficient. Results on an audio-visual naturalistic emotion conversation database show improvement in all four dimensional emotions. One of the drawbacks of our approach is its complexity, which is quadratic in the number of frames. In future work, we plan on extending this approach to other temporal clustering methods and applying these methods to other temporal clustering problems.

References

1. Araujo, R., Kamel, M.: A semi-supervised temporal clustering method for facial emotion analysis. In: 2014 IEEE International Conference on Multimedia and Expo Workshops (ICMEW) (to appear, July 2014)
2. De La Torre, F., Campoy, J., Ambadar, Z., Conn, J.F.: Temporal segmentation of facial behavior. In: International Conference on Computer Vision, pp. 1–8 (2007)
3. Grimm, M., Kroschel, K.: Emotion estimation in speech using a 3d emotion space concept. In: Grimm, M., Kroschel, K. (eds.) Robust Speech Recognition and Understanding, pp. 281–300. I-Tech Education and Publishing, Vienna (2007)
4. Gunes, H., Pantic, M.: Automatic, dimensional and continuous emotion recognition. Int. J. Synth. Emot. **1**(1), 68–99 (2010)
5. Kulis, B., Basu, S., Dhillon, I.S., Mooney, R.J.: Semi-supervised graph clustering: a kernel approach. Machine Learning **74**(1), 1–22 (2009)
6. Lu, Z., Ip, H.H.S.: Constrained spectral clustering via exhaustive and efficient constraint propagation. In: Daniilidis, K., Maragos, P., Paragios, N. (eds.) ECCV 2010, Part VI. LNCS, vol. 6316, pp. 1–14. Springer, Heidelberg (2010)
7. Nicolaou, M.A., Gunes, H., Pantic, M.: Output-associative rvm regression for dimensional and continuous emotion prediction. Image Vision Comput. **30**(3), 186–196 (2012)
8. Pantic, M., Member, S., Rothkrantz, L.J.M.: Automatic analysis of facial expressions: The state of the art. IEEE Transactions on Pattern Analysis and Machine Intelligence **22**, 1424–1445 (2000)
9. Sayedelahl, A., Araujo, R., Kamel, M.: Audio-visual feature-decision level fusion for spontaneous emotion estimation in speech conversations. In: 2013 IEEE International Conference on Multimedia and Expo Workshops, pp. 1–6 (July 2013)
10. Schuller, B., Valstar, M., Cowie, R., Pantic, M.: Avec 2012: The continuous audio/visual emotion challenge - an introduction. In: Proceedings of the 14th ACM International Conference on Multimodal Interaction, ICMI 2012, pp. 361–362. ACM, New York (2012)
11. Wöllmer, M., Eyben, F., Reiter, S., Schuller, B., Cox, C., Douglas-cowie, E., Cowie, R.: Abandoning emotion classes - towards continuous emotion recognition with modelling of long-range dependencies. In: Proceedings Interspeech (2008)
12. Zhou, D., Bousquet, O., Lal, T.N., Weston, J., Schölkopf, B.: Learning with local and global consistency. In: Advances in Neural Information Processing Systems 16, pp. 321–328. MIT Press (2004)
13. Zhou, F., De la Torre, F., Cohn, J.F.: Unsupervised discovery of facial events. In: IEEE Conference on Computer Vision and Pattern Recognition (CVPR) (2010)

Exemplar-Based Human Action Recognition with Template Matching from a Stream of Motion Capture

Daniel Leightley[1]([✉]), Baihua Li[1], Jamie S. McPhee[2],
Moi Hoon Yap[1], and John Darby[1]

[1] School of Computing, Mathematics and Digital Technology,
Manchester Metropolitan University, Manchester M1 5GD, UK
[2] School of Healthcare Science,
Manchester Metropolitan University, Manchester M1 5GD, UK
d.leightley@ieee.org, {b.li,j.s.mcphee,m.yap,j.darby}@mmu.ac.uk
http://www.mmu.ac.uk

Abstract. Recent works on human action recognition have focused on representing and classifying articulated body motion. These methods require a detailed knowledge of the action composition both in the spatial and temporal domains, which is a difficult task, most notably under real-time conditions. As such, there has been a recent shift towards the exemplar paradigm as an efficient low-level and invariant modelling approach. Motivated by recent success, we believe a real-time solution to the problem of human action recognition can be achieved. In this work, we present an exemplar-based approach where only a single action sequence is used to model an action class. Notably, rotations for each pose are parameterised in Exponential Map form. Delegate exemplars are selected using k-means clustering, where the cluster criteria is selected automatically. For each cluster, a delegate is identified and denoted as the exemplar by means of a similarity function. The number of exemplars is adaptive based on the complexity of the action sequence. For recognition, Dynamic Time Warping and template matching is employed to compare the similarity between a streamed observation and the action model. Experimental results using motion capture demonstrate our approach is superior to current state-of-the-art, with the additional ability to handle large and varied action sequences.

Keywords: Human action recognition · Motion capture · Exponential map · Online recognition · Template matching · Dynamic time warping

1 Introduction

Human action recognition is an active and challenging field of research that has received wide attention in computer vision due to the number of applications.

This research is funded by the John Dalton Institute.

© Springer International Publishing Switzerland 2014
A. Campilho and M. Kamel (Eds.): ICIAR 2014, Part II, LNCS 8815, pp. 12–20, 2014.
DOI: 10.1007/978-3-319-11755-3_2

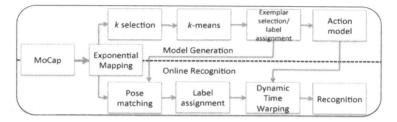

Fig. 1. Flowchart of the proposed approach. Top row denotes the process for generating an action model. Bottom row denotes the online recognition framework.

There is an ever-increasing demand for more robust, accurate and practical solutions for recognising human action online in areas such as healthcare, human-computer interaction, security and gaming.

Recognising and classifying human action is a difficult task. This is in a large part due to large variations among subjects, overlap of poses between actions and data noise [1]. It is important to have a sufficient number of training samples to allow for each action to be represented effectively. Thereby, a large number of training samples are common for many recognition approaches. However, it is not always practical to utilise a large number of training samples due to the size and complexity in computing classification. Therefore, we propose the use of the exemplar paradigm as an effective approach to modelling human action. For our approach, we use the exemplar paradigm to reduce an action sequence to its most descriptive *key* elements. Elgammal *et al.* [2] sought to capture the dynamics of human gesture with an exemplar-based recognition system. The approach represented each gesture as a sequence of key exemplars. The exemplars were selected based on a non-parametric estimation framework. Then, a probabilistic framework is employed for matching testing sequences with the exemplar model. Most recently, for exemplar-based approaches, Barnachon *et al.* [3] proposed an integral histogram approach for human action recognition evaluated against motion capture data (MoCap). They extend the concept of histograms to characterise action sequences, where similar poses are clustered to characterise the action phase with multiple exemplar histograms. Finally, for recognition, they decompose a stream of MoCap into integral histograms based on Dynamic Time Warping (DTW) to compute a confidence score based on distance. There are limitations with this approach, such as manual selection of k for k-medoids, ability to classify individual poses and recognition is undertaken on a limited dataset with *known* subjects and *known* test sequences.

The use of MoCap as a data medium presents a number of challenges, namely high degrees-of-freedom (DOF) and data consisting of complex non-linear relations, singularities that are difficult to model and interpret. To handle these challenges, parametrisation of the rotations in Exponential Map form (EMP) has been proposed [4]. EMP is more robust than other forms of rotation parametrisation, such as Euler angles or Quaternions. Bregler and Malik [5] were among the first to utilise traditional Exponential Maps for gradient-based recognition of complex human action based on complete MoCap sequences. They propose a novel method for computing the product of an Exponential Map to solve a simple linear problem. Their proposed method is capable of handling multiple DOF that may contain noise, singularities and discontinuities. More recently, Taylor *et al.* [6] proposed a non-linear generative approach by pre-processing MoCap poses into EMP form. Then, learn the local constraints and global dynamics of each sequence by a conditional Restricted Boltzmann Machine. The approach is able to capture complex non-linearities in the data and distinguish between different motion styles, as well as the transition between action classes.

We introduce a combined template-based exemplar approach for online action recognition evaluated by using streamed motion sequences provided by two popular MoCap datasets (as demonstrated in Fig. 1). To construct an exemplar-based action model we select a single action sequence to represent each action class. Where each pose is represented in EMP form. k-means clustering is used to group action poses based on similarity. An exemplar is selected for each cluster based on a ranking scheme. As a product of the clustering process, we are able to order the exemplars into a time-ordered sequence of labels, to reflect the different *phases* of the action sequence. For recognition, we evaluate and classify each pose in the observed motion sequence individually. Each pose is represented in EMP form, and then compared against the exemplar model based on the City Block metric, which returns a prediction of the most similar exemplar. Finally, we utilise DTW to perform template matching and recognition by analysing the labels associated with each classified pose and a corresponding exemplar.

The remainder of this paper is organised as follows; Section 2 describes the selection criteria to construct a action model. Section 3 outlines the approach for comparing exemplars and observations based on a distance and label matching. Experimental results and conclusion are provided in section 4 and 5 respectively.

2   Exemplar-Based Action Model

Human motion, typically captured by a marker-based MoCap system, is modelled using a *kinematic chain*. A kinematic chain consists of *body segments* that are connected to various body *joints*. Whereby a sequence can be seen as a time-sequential sequence of 3D joint coordinates that relate to the fixed kinematic chain. In our work, a motion sequence is a series of frames (otherwise denoted as poses), with each frame specifying the 3D coordinates of the joints at a certain time period. Thus, a sequence is denoted as $\mathcal{P} = \{p_t^j | t = 1, \ldots, T; j = 1, \ldots, J\}$, where t denotes the time and j is the joint index.

2.1   Pose Representation

There is no single solution to parametrisation of rotation that is suitable for all application domains. In our approach, we take each pose of a MoCap sequence and parametrise the 3D angle of each joint in Exponential Map form, as proposed in [4]. This allows us to avoid "gimbal" lock, discontinuities and ball-and-socket joints complications that are associated with using MoCap data. The Exponential Map is formulated from the corresponding Quaternion representation of each joint rotation. For clarity, the parametrisation can be expressed as

$$EMP(p_t^j) \mapsto \bar{p}_t^j \tag{1}$$

Thus, a set of transformed poses is denoted as $\bar{\mathcal{P}}$.

2.2   Exemplar Selection

A challenge to overcome is that certain poses may be semantically similar but not necessarily numerically, yet, represent the same time instance within an action sequence. To further complicate matters, to identify and group similar poses manually is a time consuming and arduous task. In our approach, we have selected a centroid method, namely k-means clustering [7] to group $\bar{\mathcal{P}}$ into k cluster based on similarity. The selection of k-means over other approaches, is due to the way in which the selection criteria of the median element is performed. Further, k-means is computationally faster when dealing with a large number of observations when compared to hierarchical clustering methods making it ideal for clustering MoCap data.

For our application, the objective is to cluster an action sequence in to k clusters, with each cluster containing similar poses. Hence, as a by-product of k-means process, each cluster characterises a phase of the action. Fig. 2 demonstrates the clustering process for two distinctively difference action sequences. Observe that for each cluster, similar poses are grouped together, making it ideal for our application. However, the difficulty with k-means is the selection of k. The Elbow method [8], which uses percentage of variance determined as a function is implemented to select the appropriate k based on automatic selection of the Elbow criterion.

In order to select a delegate for each cluster, we deploy a ranking scheme for each pose according to the City Block metric (also referred to as Manhattan

Fig. 2. Example clustering of MoCap data, where each cluster is denoted by a specific colour. Left: *Running in a circle*. Right: *Sitting in a chair*.

distance). The equivalence D between any two poses $\bar{p}_m$ and $\bar{p}_n$ in a cluster is measured using the total distance amongst corresponding joints, defined as

$$D(\bar{p}_m, \bar{p}_n) = \sum_{j=1}^{J} |\bar{p}_m^j - \bar{p}_n^j| \tag{2}$$

The delegate exemplar, denoted as $E_{e,k}$, is a pose which has the lowest distance average between a cluster grouping of poses. k-means provides an elegant method for segmenting an action sequence. For our proposed method, a unique label is assigned to each exemplar based on where it appears in the action sequence. This enables our recognition framework to perform template matching based on the action phase. Thus, for each action model we retain k number of exemplars and a time-ordered unique label sequence to represent each action class. For simplicity, let $C = \{c_e | e = 1, \ldots, E\}$ be the action set, where $c_e = \{E_{e,k} | k = 1, \ldots, K_e\}$ be the action model which is composed by K number of exemplars for action class e.

3   Recognition

Given a test sequence, $\mathcal{A} = \{a_t^j | t = 1, \ldots, T; j = 1, \ldots, J\}$, where t can be of any length. We treat each t-th pose individually and assume that the sequence forms an action in time order. Further, we expect that each pose correlates to an action class in our action set.

Firstly, we parameterise each pose in exponential form, as described in Eq. 1. Secondly, using the distance function (Eq. 2) to determine the similarity between the current observation and the delegate exemplars for each action model. We compute the minimum of the summation of distances defined by

$$L_t := min\{D(\bar{a}_t, E_{e,k}) | e = 1, \ldots, E; k = 1, \ldots, K\} \tag{3}$$

Therefore L_t is the winning exemplar label assigned to the observed pose. Recall, for each delegate exemplar we assign a unique label, using the selected exemplar and the associated label for each time instance we perform template matching to determine the action class of the current observation. Thus, over time a sequence of unique labels describing the action is constructed. We consider the temporal domain, as classifying poses individually will not provide the context to allow for robust recognition. An observed sequence can be of any length, to handle this we employ DTW as the action unfolds to match the observed label sequence to one of our previously learnt label sequences for each action model.

Given an observed label $L_1, \ldots, L_t$ derived above, we compare the sequence with each action model c_e to find the best pattern match. The winning class $\mathcal{L}_t$ is determined by the minimum DTW cost with respect to the Itakura constraint, given as

$$\mathcal{L}_t := min\{DTW(L_{1 \sim t}, c_e) |_{e=1, \ldots, E}\} \tag{4}$$

Finally, by having each pose classified, recognition of the sequence up to any time period is defined based on the accumulative voting indicated in $\mathcal{L}$. The recognition rate is computed by the total number of correctly classified frames divided by the total number of frames up to point t.

4   Experimental Results

All experiments were conducted on *unknown subject actions*, meaning that we include no data from the subject being tested. All results presented were computed based on average accumulation of classification results. We have tested the proposed approach on CMU [9] and HDM05 [10] datasets. These two datasets consist of single action sequences making them suitable for evaluating our proposed approach. For the CMU dataset we use 9 trials, with each trial representing

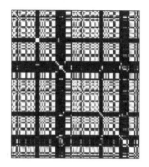

(a) Confusion matrix for CMU.

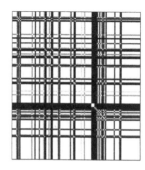

(b) Confusion matrix for HDM05.

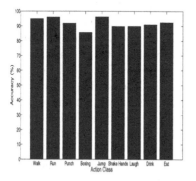

(c) Action class recognition rate for the CMU dataset.

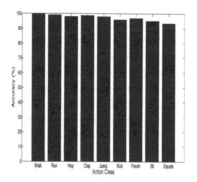

(d) Action class recognition rate for the HDM05 dataset.

Fig. 3. Confusion Matrix for two popular motion capture datasets using our proposed template-based exemplar approach

Table 1. Pose classification accuracy, average k selection and recognition rate of our proposed template-based exemplar approach

Dataset	Accuracy	Avg k	Per pose (ms)
CMU	91.89%	21 (± 18)	$17ms$
HDM05	97.95%	9 (± 4)	$9ms$

a single action class to generate our action model and 49 trials for testing (as used in [3]). For the HDM05 dataset 9 trials were used, each representing a single action to generate our action model and 144 trials for testing.

As a pre-processing task, six joint angles contained within CMU and five from the HDM05 consisted of constant values, so they were removed from our training and testing sequences. The remaining joints had between two and three DOF. For testing, the conversion process was undertaken on a per pose basis. We have achieved respectable recognition rates, inclusive of computational costs, as shown in Table 1. This demonstrates the ability of the proposed method to handle frames presented by a continuous sequence of MoCap in an online real-time setting at high-speed.

For the CMU dataset, we achieved a recognition rate of **91.89%** using our proposed framework. The average k obtained reflected complexity of each action class (as shown in Table 1). The difficulty is to overcome these variations, thus the exemplar paradigm is effective by generalisation of variations in the data. *Walking* and *Run* classes were relatively easy to distinguish between due to relatively small variation amongst subjects. However, difficulties were encountered, as demonstrated in Fig. 3(a) & Fig. 3(c) for *Laugh* class due to pose similarity between *Boxing* and *Punching* classes. In other work, Barnachon *et al.* [3] reported an accuracy of 90.92% which is comparable to our proposed method. Yet, we acknowledge our approach requires more exemplars to handle action complexity.

For the HDM05 dataset, a recognition rate of **97.95%** (as shown in Table 1) was achieved using our proposed framework. As with the CMU dataset, k was dependent on complexity and pose variation of each action class. *Walking* and *Running* classes were once again clearly identifiable. However confusion was observed for *Sit* and *Squat*, as demonstrated in Fig. 3(b) & Fig. 3(d) . Confusion observed was due to similar poses being performed in other action classes. Overall, interclass confusion remained limited reflecting the strength of our approach to correctly model action sequences using the exemplar paradigm. In other works tested on the HDM05 dataset, Muller *et al.* [11] reported an accuracy of 80% when using their *key-frames* approach. While this was a good recognition rate, the process cannot be performed online due to complex data processing.

Our approach achieved overall recognition results that are superior to other approaches, when using the CMU (91.89%) and HDM05 (97.95%) datasets. This is significant advance on current approaches, with the added benefit of being a more straight-forward approach for analysing highly complex datasets and also the small number of exemplars retained (avg. $k = 15$). For online application,

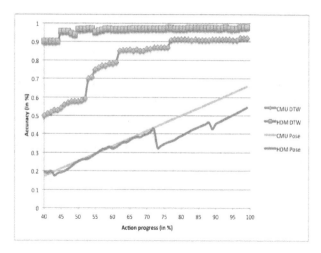

Fig. 4. Early recognition rate using our proposed method compared with individual pose results

there is a need to detect actions early on in a sequence. Fig. 4 demonstrates the potential of our approach for early action recognition. In addition, the use of the exemplar paradigm has reduced the need to use complete action sequences by approximately 98% while remaining efficient in representing each action class. Further, observe in Fig. 4 that by using the proposed approach we have achieved superior results when compared with classifying poses individually without template matching.

This work has focused on pose classification and template matching of real number sequences, which has presented a number of challenges. It has been difficult to distinguish certain actions due to poses being indistinguishable for a period resulting in class confusion. One solution may be to focus on adjacent poses in the temporal domain to aid in identification of the correct action class as they progress through time. The results we have achieved, as shown in Table. 1, present our baseline results for future exemplar-based approaches. Finally, the results are comparable to current exemplar-based approach, namely Barnachon *et al.* [3], in terms of accuracy and recognition time per pose ($17ms$). There is scope for further improvement in stabilising class confusion, classification and recognition of action(s) as they unfold.

5   Conclusion

In this paper, we propose a template-based exemplar approach for human action recognition evaluated using a stream of MoCap. The use of an action model to represent each action class, where each model is characterised by a small number of exemplars, has reduced the need to use whole motion sequences for action representation by an average of 98%. Ultimately this leads to a significant computational saving for recognition which then transforms the problem into a relativity simple distance/template matching task. Yet emphasis is placed on the importance of selecting *ideal* actions for each action class. By using MoCap action sequences, our work seeks to present a baseline study for future exemplar-based recognition approaches. To our knowledge, this paper is the first to propose an exemplar approach for MoCap sequences represented in exponential map form. By utilising EMP we have been able to effectively model key characteristics for each action sequences but also handle singularities and discontinuities. Further work is required to address issues related to similarity in poses shared between multiple action classes, possibly analysing temporal occurrence. With further experiments undertaken on a wider and varied testing set while handling more complex action(s) and diverse motion datasets (*e.g.* Microsoft Kinect).

References

1. Poppe, R.: A survey on vision-based human action recognition. Image and Vision Computing **28**(6), 976–990 (2010)
2. Elgammal, A., Shet, V., Yacoob, Y., Davis, L.S.: Learning dynamics for exemplar-based gesture recognition. In: CVPR, pp. 571–578. IEEE Computer Society, Washington, DC (2003)
3. Barnachon, M, Bouakaz, S., Boufama, B., Guillou, E.: Ongoing human action recognition with motion capture. Pattern Recognition (2013)
4. Grassia, F.S.: Practical parameterization of rotations using the exponential map. Journal of Graphics Tools **3**(3), 29–48 (1998)
5. Bregler, C., Malik, J.: Tracking people with twists and exponential maps. In: CVPR, pp. 8–15 (1998)
6. Taylor, G.W., Hinton, G.E., Roweis, S.: Modeling human motion using binary latent variables. In: NIPS, p. 2007 (2006)
7. MacQueen, J.: Some methods for classification and analysis of multivariate observations. In: Proc. of the Fifth Berkeley Symposium on Mathematrical Statistics and Probability, pp. 281–297. University of California Press (1967)
8. Ketchen, D., Shook, C.: The application of cluster analysis in strategic management research: An analysis and critique. Strategic Management Journal **17**(6), 441–458 (1996)
9. Carnegie Mellon University Motion Capture Dataset. The data used in this project was obtained from mocap.cs.cmu.edu. The database was created with funding from NSF EIA-0196217
10. Müller, M., Röder, T., Clausen, M., Eberhardt, B., Krüger, B., Weber, A.: Documentation mocap database HDM05. Universität Bonn, Tech. Rep. CG-2007-2 (2007)
11. Müller, M., Baak, A., Seidel, H.-P.: Efficient and robust annotation of motion capture data. In: ACM SIGGRAPH/Eurographics Symposium on Computer Animation, New Orleans, LA, pp. 17–26 (August 2009)

A New Visual Speech Recognition Approach for RGB-D Cameras

Ahmed Rekik[1]([⊠]), Achraf Ben-Hamadou[2], and Walid Mahdi[1]

[1] Multimedia Information Systems and Advanced Computing Laboratory (MIRACL),
Sfax University Pôle technologique de Sfax, route de Tunis Km 10, BP 242, 3021 Sfax, Tunisia
[2] Valeo Driving Assistance Research Center, 34 rue St-André Z.I. des Vignes,
93012 Bobigny, France
rekikamed@gmail.com, achraf.ben-hamadou@valeo.com,
walid.mahdi@isimsf.rnu.tn

Abstract. Visual speech recognition remains a challenging topic due to various speaking characteristics. This paper proposes a new approach for lipreading to recognize isolated speech segments (words, digits, phrases, *etc.*) using both of 2D image and depth data. The process of the proposed system is divided into three consecutive steps, namely, mouth region tracking and extraction, motion and appearance descriptors (HOG and MBH) computing, and classification using the Support Vector Machine (SVM) method. To evaluate the proposed approach, three public databases (MIRALC, Ouluvs, and CUAVE) were used. Speaker dependent and speaker independent settings were considered in the evaluation experiments. The obtained recognition results demonstrate that lipreading can be performed effectively, and the proposed approach outperforms recent works in the literature for the speaker dependent setting while being competitive for the speaker independent setting.

Keywords: Visual speech recognition · Lip-reading · Visual communication · Face tracking · Human-computer-interaction

1 Introduction

Visual Lip-Reading (LR) systems play an important role for Human-Machine-Interation applications in noisy environments where audio speech recognition still very challenging (*i.e.,* overcoming signals alternate the recognition). However, visual LR systems face their own challenges. Indeed, there is an important variation in terms of lip shapes, skin colors, speaking speeds and intensities *etc.* which make difficult to develop generative LR systems. Consequently, most of works in this research field are restricted to limited number of classes (*i.e.,* words, phrases, commands, *etc.*) and speakers [14, 15].

We can divide LR systems into two categories. The first category includes methods where a non-rigid tracking of the mouth region is needed. After performing the lips boundaries tracking, different features are extracted from the tracking results and used in the recognition process. For example, [12] applied an AAM (Active Appearance

© Springer International Publishing Switzerland 2014
A. Campilho and M. Kamel (Eds.): ICIAR 2014, Part II, LNCS 8815, pp. 21–28, 2014.
DOI: 10.1007/978-3-319-11755-3_3

Model) for deformable face tracking (including lips) and then used directly the animation units of the AAM as a descriptor of the lips deformations. Features like angles and distances computed between reference points located on the lips boundaries are also used with a KNN classifier in [14]. Recently, [9] used a combination of descriptors like HOG (Histogram of Oriented Gradients) [5] and LBP (Local binary patterns) [6] computed on small patches centred on reference points of the tracked lip boundaries. The advantage of such approaches is that lips deformation trajectory is directly modelized from the lips non-rigid tracking. However, lips deformation tracking is a complex task and very sensitive to illumination and texture variations. In opposition to these methods, the second category of LR systems gathers methods that do not rely on non-rigid tracking of the speaker's lips. In these methods, a rectangular mouth region is cropped from input data, then, features are computed on the cropped data to describe the mouth shape. For example, Zhao et al. [15] proposed a spatio-temporal version of LBP descriptor for lipreading. This descriptor is computed on the extracted mouth regions and used as input for an SVM classifier. Shaikh and Kumar [11], used optical flow for extracting the whole word features from the mouth region. These methods are characterized by their simplicity where no deformable lip tracking is needed. However, usually they are sensitive to the orientation of the speaker's face and assume a limited face motion.

In this paper, we propose a new LR system using both of 2D images and depth maps. We describe a rectification process to handle the motion of the speaker's face for a robust mouth region extraction. Also, we introduce an effective combination of appearance and motion descriptors to be used for the classification process.

The remaining of this paper is organized as follows. First, a general system overview is presented in section 2.1. A 3D face tracking and mouth region extraction process will be described in section 2.2. The appearance and motion descriptors used in the recognition step are presented in section 2.3. Experimental results will be shown in section 3. Finally, a conclusion and some perspectives and future work are given in section 4.

2   Lip-Reading System

2.1   System General Overview

As illustrated in Figure 1, the proposed LR system takes a multi-modal video clip (*i.e.,* 2D images and depth maps) representing a speech portion to recognize (*e.g.,* a word, a command, a phrase, *etc.*). The system is then divided in three main steps, namely, mouth region extraction, descriptors computing, and classification. In the first step, the user's face is detected and its 3D pose is tracked over the input sequence. This step allows to robustly extract the mouth region yielding a sequence of rectified patches centred on the user's mouth. Then, the second step takes the rectified patches as input to compute both of appearance and motion descriptors which serve for the final SVM classification step. All of these steps will be detailed in the following sections.

2.2   Mouth Region Extraction

Since an LR system user can obviously move his head while speaking, it is mandatory to track the position and the orientation of the user's face over the input sequence to

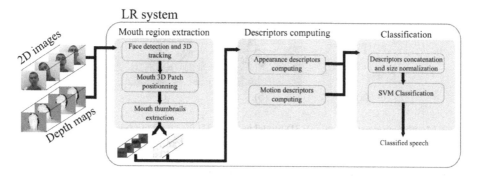

Fig. 1. General overview of our LR system

robustly extract the mouth region. To this end, we used a 3D rigid face tracking method [10]. This tracking method handles illumination changes and offers a very low jitter. The face tracking is modelized as an optimization problem to find the optimal 3D rigid motion between two consecutive video frames. We denote the optimal face pose of a given frame from the input sequence, by $\widehat{x} \in \mathbb{R}^6$ involving the 6 degree of freedom (*i.e.*, 3 translations and 3 rotation angles) of a 3D rigid motion. We presented the mouth region by a 3D rectangular patch (see figure 2(a)). This patch rigidly follows the face motion by means of the estimated face poses (*i.e.*, the 3D patch is rigidly fixed to the 3D face model). The size of the mouth patch is automatically scaled to adapt the user's face size using the tracking initialization parameters [10]. The patch is densely sampled to $n_h \times n_w$ 3D points $\{P_{i,j} | i = 1, \ldots, n_h, j = 1, \ldots, n_w\}$. For a given instant of the input sequence, the new position $\widehat{P}_{i,j}$ of each point $P_{i,j}$ is computed by applying the face pose as follows:

$$\widehat{P}_{i,j} = \mathbf{R} \, P_{i,j} + \mathbf{t} \tag{1}$$

where $\mathbf{R}$ and $\mathbf{t}$ are respectively the 3×3 rotation matrix and the 3D translation vector generated in a standard way from $\widehat{x}$. The definition of the mouth patch in 3D simplifies the mouth thumbnails rectification in terms of position, orientation, and size. Indeed, for a given face pose, the patch points $\widehat{P}_{i,j}$ are simply projected into the 2D image and the depth map yielding two rectified thumbnails (see figures 2(b), 2(c), and 2(d) for an example). Let denote by $p_{i,j}^c$ and $p_{i,j}^d$ the projection of $\widehat{P}_{i,j}$ in the 2D image and the depth map respectively. These projection points are computed as follows:

$$p_{i,j}^c = \mathcal{H}\left(\mathcal{K}_c \, \widehat{P}_{i,j}\right) \tag{2}$$

$$p_{i,j}^d = \mathcal{H}\left(\mathcal{K}_d \, \mathbf{T} \begin{bmatrix} \widehat{P}_{i,j} \\ 1 \end{bmatrix}\right) \tag{3}$$

In equation (2) and (3), $\mathcal{K}_c$ and $\mathcal{K}_d$ stand for the intrinsic matrix of the color and the depth cameras, respectively. Also, $\mathcal{H} : \mathbb{R}^3 \longmapsto \mathbb{R}^2$ is the homogeneous coordinate function where $\mathcal{H}\left([X\ Y\ Z]^T\right) \triangleq [X/Z\ Y/Z]^T$, and $\mathbf{T}$ is a 3×4 matrix corresponding to the global 3D transformation between the color and depth cameras. $\mathbf{T}$, $\mathcal{K}_c$, and $\mathcal{K}_d$ are known when calibrating the acquisition system [2,3]. Since $p_{i,j}^c$ and $p_{i,j}^d$ are not

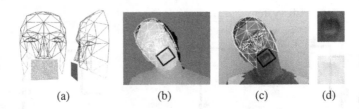

(a)   (b)   (c)   (d)

Fig. 2. Mouth region extraction. (a): 3D model used for 3D face tracking (viewed from two points of view). The rectangular mesh corresponds to the mouth patch rigidly fixed to the face model. (b) and (c): Projection of the 3D face model and the 3D mouth patch in the depth map and the 2D image, respectively. (d): Extracted 2D and depth rectified mouth thumbnails.

necessarily round coordinates, we perform a bilinear interpolation to fill pixel values of the 2D image and the depth thumbnails.

2.3 Motion and Appearance Descriptors Computing

To describe the mouth shape and deformation during a speech segment, we need to compute descriptors on the extracted mouth thumbnails. We combined both of appearance and motion descriptors to modelize temporal deformations of the mouth.

Appearance Descriptor: We consider the well known Histogram of Oriented Gradient (HOG) descriptor [4]. It is worth to notice that we tested other descriptors like Local Binary Patten (LBP) [7], but the best performance were provided using HOG descriptor. The HOG method tiles the mouth thumbnails with a dense grid of cells, with each cell containing a local histogram over orientation bins. At each pixel of the thumbnail, the image gradient vector is calculated and converted to an angle, voting into the corresponding orientation bin with a vote weighted by the gradient magnitude. Votes are accumulated over the pixels of each cell. The cells are grouped into blocks and a robust normalization process is run on each block to provide strong illumination invariance. The normalized histograms of all of the blocks are concatenated to give the window-level visual descriptor vector for learning. In the remaining sections, we denote by HOG_c and HOG_d the HOG descriptor computed on the 2D and depth thumbnail respectively.

Motion Descriptor: The motion descriptor allows somehow to modelize the lips movement. In [5], motion descriptors like Internal Motion Histograms (IMH) and Motion Boundary Histograms (MBH) were used for pedestrian detection in video sequences. A IMH variant gave the best recognition rates. However, in our case, the lips motion is much less complex than pedestrians motions. We tested both of the IMHcd (variant of IMH) and the MBH descriptors for our LR system. Briefly, the MBH computes the optical flow between two consecutive mouth thumbnails. Then, each flow component is treated as an independent thumbnail, takes their local gradients separately, find the corresponding gradient magnitudes and orientations, and use these as weighted votes into local orientation histograms in the same way as for the standard gray scale HOG.

2.4   Classification

Given an input sequence of N frames, the computed appearance and motion descriptors for each frame are concatenated to generate a single descriptor vector (denoted by $\mathcal{D}_i|_{i=1,\dots,N}$). Then, following [12], all $\mathcal{D}_i$ are interpolated to squeeze them in a fixed length vector. To give an example, in our experiments on words recognition we fixed the size of the final descriptor vector to 20 frames $\times$ size of $\mathcal{D}_i$.

This paper investigates the use of support vector machines (SVMs) [13]. SVMs are selected due to their ability to find a globally optimum decision function to separate the different classes of data. In this work, we compared the linear, the polynomial, and the RBF kernels for our LR system. The best performance was given by linear kernel.

3   Experiments and Results

3.1   Evaluation Datasets

To evaluate our LR system we used several datasets with different kind of input data (2D images, RGB-D sequences) and different configurations (distance of face from acquisition vision system) mouth resolution in the images. One of the contributions of this paper is the construction of a new dataset MIRACL-VC.

MIRACL-VC: It consists of 1500 word data (15 persons$\times$10 words$\times$10 times/word) and 1500 phrases (15 persons$\times$10 phrases$\times$10 times/phrase). The dataset covers words like *navigation, connection, etc.*. We took also phrases like *Nice to meet you, I love this game, etc.*. We used the Kinect sensor to acquire 2D images and depth maps with a resolution of 640×480 and at an acquisition rate of 15 fps. The distance between the speaker and the Kinect is about $1m$.

OuluVS: [15] It consists of ten different everyday phrases. Each phrase is uttered by 20 subjects up to five times. The frame rate was set to 25 fps at a resolution of 720×576. Only color images are provided for each phrase sequence.

CUAVE: [8] It consists of a speaker-independent corpus of over 7,000 utterances of both connected and isolated digits spoken by 37 subjects. The database was recorded at a resolution of 720×480 with a frame rate of 29.97 fps where only color images are provided for each sequence.

3.2   Visual Speech Recognition Results

We adopt two test settings for visual speech recognition: speaker independent and speaker dependent.

Speaker Independent (SI): In this experiment, the training and the query data are from different speakers. We employ the leave-one-out strategy where data from a single speaker are used as the validation data, and the remaining speakers are used as the training data. This is repeated for each speaker in the dataset.

Speaker Dependent(SD): In this experiment, the training and the testing data are from the same speaker.

MIRACL-VC Results. To evaluate our system on the MIRACL-VC dataset, we have applied our method to compute different descriptors on the extracted mouth thumbnails. Then, we have compared different combination of descriptors HOG_c, HOG_d and MBH. Table 1 illustrates the obtained recognition rates. For **SD** settings, the best performance is obtained for the combination HOG_c+HOG_d (96.0% for phrases and 95.4% for words). That is, when we added MBH (*i.e.*, HOG_c+HOG_d+MBH), we ameliorate the **SI** setting results (*i.e.*, gain of 12.5% and 3.3% of recognition rate) while keeping the same recognition rates for **SD** setting. We can see also in table 1 that the performance of our LR system is better for phrases than words. This is can be explained by the fact that a phrases contains a longer series of visemes than words. Thus, it is easier to discriminate between phrases than between words.

Table 1. Lipreading performances of speaker dependent (SD) and speaker independent (SI) experiments on MIRACL-VC dataset

	Phrases		Words	
Descriptors	**SD**	**SI**	**SD**	**SI**
HOG_c	95.4%	54.4%	92.8%	48.1%
HOG_d	94.2%	64.7%	94.2%	54.5%
HOG_c+HOG_d	96.0%	66.7%	95.4%	59.8%
MBH_c	87.4%	49.4%	86.2%	45.1%
$HOG_c+HOG_d+MBH_c$	96.0%	79.2%	95.3%	63.1%

OuluVS Results. We have compared our method with the recent lipreading works [1],[15],[16] on OuluVS dataset, where we combined only HOG_c and MBH_c descriptors since depth maps are not provided in this dataset. Table 2 shows the recognition rates of our method (first row) and recent works in the literature. Our method outperforms all the other works for **SD** configuration with 93.2% against 64.2%, 73.5%, 85.1% for [15], [1], and [16] respectively. However, we all obtained roughly a comparable results for **SI** configuration (*i.e.*, between 58.6% and 70.6%). Additionally, we can see that our system perform better in MIRACL-VC (see results for phrases in table 1). This difference of performance can be explained by the absence of the depth data in the OuluVS dataset.

Table 2. Lipreading performances of speaker dependent (SD) and speaker independent (SI) experiments on OuluVS dataset and comparison with other recent works

	SD	**SI**
Our method	93.2%	68.3%
[15]	64.2%	58.6%
[1]	73.5%	62.3%
[16]	85.1%	70.6%

CUAVE Results. In [9], only two sample on CUAVE where used for evaluation. They obtained 100% of recognition rate for the **SD** setting. For the same two sample and the same setting, we obtained 97.0%. We decided to perform more representative evaluation with CUAVE dataset and we used all the available samples (36 samples). We obtained 90% for **SD** setting and 70.1% for **SI** setting.

4 Conclusion

We proposed a new visual speech recognition system using both of 2D images and depth maps acquired typically with RGB-D cameras. Our approach is based on 3D rigid tracking of the speaker's face to robustly extract image and depth thumbnails. These are then used to compute motion and appearance descriptors which are used as input for an SVM classifier. For the evaluation of our system, we construct a new dataset (MIRACL-VC) and we used also two other public datasets (CUAVE and OuluVS). The obtained evaluation results on these three datasets show that our system is very competitive with other recent works in the literature. Additionally, we showed also that depth data ameliorate sensibly the LR system performance and the combination of the appearance and motion descriptors improve the **SI** performance.

In our future work, we will try to ameliorate the **SI** performance by considering other descriptors. Also, we would like to investigate the speech spotting in continuous speech flow.

References

1. Bakry, A., Elgammal, A.: Mkpls: Manifold kernel partial least squares for lipreading and speaker identification. In: CVPR, pp. 684–691. IEEE (2013)
2. Ben-Hamadou, A., Soussen, C., Daul, C., Blondel, W., Wolf, D.: Flexible projector calibration for active stereoscopic systems. In: 2010 IEEE International Conference on Image Processing, pp. 4241–4244 (September 2010)
3. Ben-Hamadou, A., Soussen, C., Daul, C., Blondel, W., Wolf, D.: Flexible calibration of structured-light systems projecting point patterns. Computer Vision and Image Understanding 117(10), 1468–1481 (2013)
4. Dalal, N., Triggs, B.: Histograms of oriented gradients for human detection. In: IEEE Computer Society Conference on Computer Vision and Pattern Recognition, CVPR 2005, vol. 1, pp. 886–893. IEEE (2005)
5. Dalal, N., Triggs, B., Schmid, C.: Human detection using oriented histograms of flow and appearance. In: Leonardis, A., Bischof, H., Pinz, A. (eds.) ECCV 2006. LNCS, vol. 3952, pp. 428–441. Springer, Heidelberg (2006)
6. Huang, D., Shan, C., Ardabilian, M., Wang, Y., Chen, L.: Local binary patterns and its application to facial image analysis: a survey. IEEE Transactions on Systems, Man, and Cybernetics, Part C: Applications and Reviews 41(6), 765–781 (2011)
7. Nanni, L., Lumini, A., Brahnam, S.: Survey on lbp based texture descriptors for image classification. Expert Syst. Appl. 39(3), 3634–3641 (2012)
8. Patterson, E.K., Gurbuz, S., Tufekci, Z., Gowdy, J.: Cuave: A new audio-visual database for multimodal human-computer interface research. In: 2002 IEEE International Conference on Acoustics, Speech, and Signal Processing (ICASSP), vol. 2, pp. II-2017-II-2020. IEEE (2002)

9. Pei, Y., Kim, T.K., Zha, H.: Unsupervised random forest manifold alignment for lipreading. In: ICCV, pp. 129–136 (2013)
10. Rekik, A., Ben-Hamadou, A., Mahdi, W.: Face pose tracking under arbitrary illumination changes. In: VISAPP (2014)
11. Shaikh, A.A., Kumar, D.K., Yau, W.C., Che Azemin, M., Gubbi, J.: Lip reading using optical flow and support vector machines. In: 2010 3rd International Congress on Image and Signal Processing (CISP), vol. 1, pp. 327–330. IEEE (2010)
12. Shin, J., Lee, J., Kim, D.: Real-time lip reading system for isolated korean word recognition. Pattern Recognition 44(3), 559–571 (2011)
13. Vapnik, V.: The nature of statistical learning theory. Springer (2000)
14. Yargic, A., Dogan, M.: A lip reading application on ms kinect camera. In: 2013 IEEE International Symposium on Innovations in Intelligent Systems and Applications (INISTA), pp. 1–5. IEEE (2013)
15. Zhao, G., Barnard, M., Pietikainen, M.: Lipreading with local spatiotemporal descriptors. IEEE Transactions on Multimedia 11(7), 1254–1265 (2009)
16. Zhou, Z., Zhao, G., Pietikainen, M.: Towards a practical lipreading system. In: 2011 IEEE Conference on Computer Vision and Pattern Recognition (CVPR), pp. 137–144. IEEE (2011)

2D Appearance Based Techniques for Tracking the Signer Configuration in Sign Language Video Recordings

Ville Viitaniemi$^{(\boxtimes)}$, Matti Karppa, and Jorma Laaksonen

Department of Information and Computer Science,
Aalto University School of Science, Espoo, Finland
{ville.viitaniemi,matti.karppa,jorma.laaksonen}@aalto.fi

Abstract. Current linguistic research on sign language is often based on analysing large corpora of video recordings. The videos must be annotated either manually or automatically. Automatic methods for estimating the signer body configuration—especially the hand positions and shapes—would thus be of great practical interest. Methods based on rigorous 3D and 2D modelling of the body parts have been presented. However, they face insurmountable problems of computational complexity due to the large sizes of modern linguistic corpora. In this paper we look at an alternative approach and investigate what can be achieved with the use of straightforward local 2D appearance based methods: template matching-based tracking of local image neighbourhoods and supervised skin blob category detection based on local appearance features. After describing these techniques, we construct a signer configuration estimation system using the described techniques among others, and demonstrate the system in the video material of Suvi dictionary of Finnish Sign Language.

1 Introduction

In automatic analysis of sign language videos it is necessary to detect and keep track of the configuration of the signer's body. On the coarsest level, the configuration modelling might correspond to roughly estimating the locations of the signer's hands. Estimates of handshapes, body poses, head poses and facial expressions add more details to the configuration modelling. However, estimating the configuration of the body, which is inherently three-dimensional, from a single 2D projection is not an easy task. The estimation can be done by fitting rendered complex 3D models to the observed image, as is done for example in [3] for a detailed model of the hand. Unfortunately these methods tend to be

This work has been funded by the following grants of the Academy of Finland: 140245, Content-based video analysis and annotation of Finnish Sign Language (CoBaSiL); 251170, Finnish Centre of Excellence in Computational Inference Research (COIN).

A. Campilho and M. Kamel (Eds.): ICIAR 2014, Part II, LNCS 8815, pp. 29–38, 2014.
DOI: 10.1007/978-3-319-11755-3_4

computationally far too expensive for amounts of video data that would need to be analysed in the context of automatic analysis of sign language corpora of any practical significance. After all, there are 25 frames in every second of video footage.

Models based on *pictorial structures* [5] come closer to appearance-based modelling by operating directly in two dimensions. The model of [1] rather accurately manages to estimate the configuration of a 2D arm model with three joints—shoulders, elbows and wrists. However, estimating pictorial structure models is computationally quite heavy, too. The application of [1] to practical analysis is hindered also by another serious issue: the estimation needs extensive manually annotated training data, separately for each person to be modelled, and for each imaging condition, for example each clothing of the signer. [10] solves the issues of run-time computational complexity, but with the price of even more extreme training data requirements. Actually the method was demonstrated by training it with a huge video collection first processed with [1].

In this paper we go further in the 2D appearance based direction where the underlying models get simpler and simpler. The philosophy here is that simple methods should be preferred over more complicated ones if they are able to perform the same tasks. In this spirit we investigate whether techniques based on straightforward detection and tracking of local 2D appearance primitives would be sufficient for deducing the signer configuration in video material—at least in most cases. In such cases one could omit the more advanced and computationally complex modelling, which can be prohibitively cumbersome in practice.

This work studies the application of two kinds of local appearance based techniques. In the first technique (Section 2) we consider tracking of constellations of nearby small local image neighbourhoods. In sign language videos the objects of interest—primarily hands—are not rigid, but their shape and projection constantly changes. Furthermore, their appearance may vary also for technical reasons: in the video material we have cosidered, motion blur and coding artifacts are often quite severe. This quality is not unrealistically poor as the videos are from the Suvi online dictionary of Finnish Sign Language (FinSL) and offer perfectly naturalistic viewing experience for human viewers. The model of the object that is tracked thus consists of nearby image neighbourhoods that may gradually change their appearance from frame to frame and whose relative positions may also change. This technique was originally described in [16].

In the second technique (Section 3) we model the objects of interest as blobs of skin-coloured pixels. We categorise the skin blobs in the image into a small set of categories using standard off-the-shelf 2D visual descriptors combined with standard supervising learning algorithms: support vector machines (SVM) and extreme learning machines (ELM). In particular, we investigate whether these standard methods of 2D visual analysis can discriminate between right and left hand blobs, or tell which end of a blob depicting an arm is the end with the hand and the fingers. The left-right separation task has the practical motivation that in our video material, skin blob detection works rather well in identifying the skin areas that may be either hands or the face. In configuration estimation, the next task would then be to decide which skin blobs correspond to which body part. Locating facial details is relatively easy, but hands are more problematic, especially deciding which hand is right and which one is left. In the video, the skin blobs can often be associated together by kinematic grounds when the movements are smooth, thus making the category estimation easier. A helpful clue is also provided by the areas where a skin blob moves: the right hand usually moves right of the left hand. However, these cues alone are not reliable enough to always correctly determine the configuration. Sometimes the movement is so fast that between subsequent frames the skin blobs have moved so much that associating the blobs in different frames is not straightforward. It may even be so that right hand appears nearly in the place where the left hand was previously and vice versa, throwing the kinematic analysis completely off the scent. Sometimes the image becomes temporarily unintelligible because of motion blur or the hands combine in a single blob with each other and/or the face, making it difficult to keep track of the position of each individual body part. Occasionally these factors combine. All in all, at times the tracking of configuration gets invalidated. Appearance-based blob categorisation can then come to help and re-establish the tracking.

After detailing the two techniques of main interest, we describe in Section 4 how we construct a system that performs signer body part identification and labelling in sign language videos. The system applies the two proposed techniques in several of its processing steps, as well as other image processing techniques. Section 5 demonstrates the system in labelling of videos of the Suvi dictionary. Section 6 discusses the findings and presents conclusions that can be drawn from this study.

2   Tracking of Local Image Neighbourhoods

Template matching based tracking of local image neighbourhoods—small rectangular patches in particular—is an important ingredient in our signer configuration tracking system. This elementary tracking method has been chosen because preliminary experiments with the video material at our disposal have indicated that some more advanced descriptors such as SIFT do not remain stable enough between the frames to make it possible to base the tracking on them. Partly this is because the appearance of the tracked objects keeps changing due to them being non-rigid, and also due to viewpoint changes. Image compression artifacts and motion blur are additional factors in our video material. In order to make the tracking more reliable, instead of tracking individual visual features we tie together a collection of multiple nearby points and track them collectively.

In the following we consider tracking a set of M points from a reference frame r to a target frame t. Let the coordinates of the tracked points be $\{\mathbf{r}_i\}_{i=1}^{M}$ in the reference frame. We impose a topology $\{N(i)\}_{i=1}^{M}$ upon the points. Here the set $N(i)$ specifies the indices of points that are neighbours of the ith point. There is no necessity of the topology to reflect any specific geometric notion of adjacency in the original image plane. In our formulation, the goal of the tracking is to find the coordinates $\{\mathbf{t}_i\}_{i=1}^{M}$ in the target frame so that the tracking cost function C is minimised:

$$\min_{\{\mathbf{t}_i\}_{i=1}^{M}} C = \sum_{i=1}^{M} \left(A\big(I_r(\mathbf{r}_i), I_t(\mathbf{t}_i)\big) + \alpha \sum_{j \in N(i)} B\big(|\|\mathbf{t}_i - \mathbf{t}_j\| - \|\mathbf{r}_i - \mathbf{r}_j\||\big) \right). \quad (1)$$

Here $I_r(\mathbf{r}_i)$ and $I_t(\mathbf{t}_i)$ are the image neighbourhoods of the points $\mathbf{r}_i$ and $\mathbf{t}_i$ in the reference and target frames, respectively, and $A(\cdot, \cdot)$ is the template matching distance. α is a weight parameter of the method and $B(\cdot)$ is a scalar weighting function of distance differences. The cost function thus balances the sum of template matching costs of individual points with a measure how much the inter-point distances in the target frame differ from the corresponding distances in the reference frame. In this paper, the following iterative algorithm has been used for the approximate minimisation of the cost function:

1. Initialise tracking, i.e. select initial values for $\{\mathbf{t}_i\}_{i=1}^{M}$ e.g. on the basis of the estimated motion field.
2. Denote the set of indices of the target points requiring update with R. Initialise R by inserting all the indices $1, \ldots, M$ into it.
3. Repeat until R is empty or some external stopping criterion is met (e.g. number of iterations reaches a set maximum):
   (a) Randomly select an index j from R.
   (b) Set $\mathbf{t}_{old} = \mathbf{t}_j$ and remove j from R.
   (c) Search a new location for the point $\mathbf{t}_j$ that minimises C of Eq. (1).
   (d) If $\mathbf{t}_j \neq \mathbf{t}_{old}$, add indices in $N(j)$ into R.

3   Skin Blob Category Detection

For category detection, the object of interest is modelled as a blob, i.e. some contiguous sub-area of an image. Set of standard 2D visual features is extracted from the blob. Based on the features, the blob is assigned to one out of a pre-specified set of categories by supervised learning, i.e. using classifiers that have been trained previously with manually labelled data. In practice, the blobs we consider in our system result from skin colour detection. Here we consider assigning the blobs into two sets of categories that 1) distinguish between left and right hands, and 2) determine which end of an arm blob is the hand end. In [15] we have used similar methods for recognising pre-specified classes of handshapes.

The rest of this section describes an experiment that we performed in left-right hand separation in order to see which visual features are suitable as input to classifiers. Based on these results and those reported in [15], we have selected the sPACT statistical texture feature [19] for use in our system. In addition to classifier accuracy, also the computational lightness and ease of extracting the feature was a factor in the decision as we perform feature extraction and classification on-line for each video frame in our analysis system. For the same reason we also want to re-use the same features for all categorisation tasks, including handedness detection and handshape classification. sPACT provides decent performance in both tasks.

Table 1. The extracted features

Shape	Fourier descriptors of the contour
	Zernike moments of the blob silhoutte
Texture statistics (BOV)	SIFT [7] histograms (Harris-Laplace interest points)
	Opponent colour ColorSIFT [13] histograms (dense sampling)
Texture statistics (non-BOV)	Edge co-occurrence matrix
	Edge histogram variants
	Fourier transform of edges
	Directional local brightness variation
	Spatial PCA of Census Transform histograms (sPACT) [19]
	Various Local Binary Pattern (LBP) histograms [9]
	Various Histogram of Oriented Gradients (HoG) features [2]

3.1 Right and Left Hand Discrimination Experiment

Our experiments were performed on a set of 7022 right hand blobs extracted from a number of sign language videos of the S-pot benchmark [14] that uses the material of the Suvi video dictionary [12] of Finnish Sign Language (FinSL). The blobs were mirrored to produce an artificial set of left hands. Half of the blobs was used for training and the other half for testing. In the experiment, a large set of visual features was extracted from the blobs (Table 1). A couple of features measure the shape of the extracted hand silhouettes (Fourier descriptors, Zernike moments). The remaining majority of features statistically describe the content of the blob area. When calculating statistical features, two independent design choices were explored: 1) extracting the feature from the actual skin blob area or its bounding box, and 2) calculating one feature vector for the whole blob or sub-dividing the blob area into parts and form the feature vector by concatenating the sub-part feature vectors.

In the experiment we systematically evaluated a large number of feature extraction parameter combinations. An SVM detector was trained for each of them, and the detector performance was then measured in the test set. For our on-line analysis system (Section 4), however, we use optimally pruned extreme learning machine (OP-ELM) classifiers [8] instead of SVMs because of the computational lightness of ELMs. Their classification accuracy almost equals that of SVMs. Table 2 highlights some of the SVM results. There we have included our best results for each feature type, as well as results that demonstrate some specific aspect of parameter selection. In the table, the first performance measure is the average precision (AP) in the task of ranking all the blobs in the test set according to their individual likelihood of showing a right hand. The pairwise error percentage measures the error in such a classification where the blob is compared with its mirror image and classified to be a right hand if the unmirrored blob has greater estimated right hand probability.

From the table we see that the handedness can be decided with a quite high accuracy based on the best of the blob appearance features. However, the accuracy drops markedly when instead of the complex texture features simpler elementary feature extraction methods are used (exemplified by the line

Table 2. Selection of left/right hand separation results

Feature	skin/bbox	sub-divisions	AP	pairwise error-%	extraction time/ blob
random guess			0.5	50	
Fourier descriptors	skin		0.844	24.1	20 ms
Edge co-occurrence	skin		0.646	32.2	21 ms
matrix	bbox	5-part	0.852	21.1	22 ms
Edge	skin	4×4	0.907	14.8	18 ms
histogram	bbox	4×4	0.903	14.5	18 ms
	bbox	5-part $\otimes$ (4×4)	0.924	12.6	22 ms
sPACT	skin		0.966	9.6	11 ms
	bbox		0.977	7.1	11 ms
LBP	skin		0.873	18.4	8 ms
	bbox		0.890	18.2	8 ms
	bbox	5×5	0.980	7.3	9 ms
HoG	skin	1×1	0.884	17.1	13 ms
	bbox	1×1	0.883	17.8	13 ms
	bbox	2×2	0.950	10.0	13 ms
	bbox	(2×2) $\otimes$ (2×2)	0.956	8.9	13 ms
ColorSIFT	bbox		0.975	7.3	380 ms
(512 bin codebook)	bbox	3×3 soft	0.983	6.2	390 ms

"Edge co-occurrence"). Overall the best performing feature is the most complex ColorSIFT feature we tested, the one with 3×3 soft spatial sub-division of the image area [17]. However, this feature implements the bag-of-visual-words (BOV) paradigm, making the feature extraction process computationally too heavy for on-line use in our system. We thus turn our attention to the best of other statistical texture features: LBP and sPACT. Subdividing the image area appears to be very beneficial in case of the LBP features (the sPACT feature already includes this internally). The 3×3 and 5×5 partitionings both appear to work well. Combining several different partitionings to a spatial pyramid does not bring further gains. The HoG features provide decent accuracy but are still clearly worse than LBP and sPACT. In case of LBP and sPACT, features extracted from the whole bounding box of the hand work better than limiting to the exact skin area of the hand. These results can be contrasted to the handshape recognition experiment [15] where HoG features extracted from the exact skin area worked best.

4 System for Signer Configuration Detection

We have devised a system for estimating the configuration of the signer in video recordings of sign language. More specifically, the system labels the skin pixels that correspond to the left and right hands of the signer and also identifies a single representative point for each hand. The videos have the constraint that they must portray a single signer filmed in a nearly frontal angle, without too distracting background objects. In practice this is the video format used in the material of the Suvi dictionary. Our system utilises the techniques of Sections 2 and 3 among others and consists of the following processing steps:

1. Face detection with the Viola-Jones method [18]
2. Colour-based skin detection with an ELM detector
3. Overall skin blob progression tracking
4. Identification and elimination of unoccluded facial areas
5. Seed hand blob identification
6. Hand area tracking forward and backward in time from the seed blobs
7. Representative point selection for hand blobs
8. Normalisation of detected hand coordinates according to the shoulders

The system has been implemented in the SLMotion video analysis software framework [6]. Steps 1–4 refine the methods of [16] and are not described any closer here for space reasons. It may be said, however, that the steps 3 and 4 build heavily on point constellation tracking.

Hand seed selection in step 5 considers the hand blobs that are separate from head and the other hand and decides, which of the blobs corresponds to which hand. Seed selection divides into two cases by the sleeve length of the signer, which is detected automatically by considering the skin blob shape statistics. For short-sleeved signers, identification can be performed rather reliably on geometric grounds as the visible elbows constrain how far left the rightmost point in the right hand can be found, and similarly for the left hand. For long-sleeved signers, geometric cues are no longer reliable enough as only small areas of skin are visible. Hands often cross and the left hand appears right of the right hand. The decision of which hand is which is thus done by the methods of Section 3: sPACT features of the hand blobs are extracted and fed into pre-trained ELM classifiers. The temporal consistency of the handedness labelling is additionally improved by temporal smoothing.

In step 6 point constellations are selected from the identified seed hand blobs and tracked using the method of Section 2. The tracking is performed through the video both forward and backward in time until the next seed hand blob is encountered. The points that are tracked are selected among the output of a salient point detector [11], augmented with evenly spaced points in otherwise untracked areas. In a typical case approximately 100 constellations of 4 points each are tracked for each seed hand blob. After this step each detected skin pixel is labelled as either unoccluded face, right hand or left hand, based on the spatial distribution of the tracked point constellations.

Step 7 is performed differently for different sleeve lengths. For long-sleeved signers, the mass centre of the right hand pixels is used as the representative point for the right hand, and similarly for the left hand. For short-sleeved signers the hand blobs include also the visible arms and elbows, which makes the mass centre a bad choice. Instead, the hand end of the arm is identified with an ELM classifier based on the sPACT features (Section 3) and the reference point is chosen near the hand end. Before feature extraction, the principal axis of the arm is identified and rotated to be vertical.

In the final step 8 the coordinates of the labelled skin pixels and selected reference points of the hands are normalised within each video frame against translation and scaling by using a signer-centred coordinate system. To this end, the shoulder positions of the signer are estimated in each video frame. This involves colour-based torso mask estimation, shoulder template matching in the mask, and temporal filtering. The mean point between the two detected shoulders is chosen as the coordinate system origin and the inter-shoulder distance as the length unit.

5   Experimental Demonstration

We are routinely running versions of our system on the whole Suvi dictionary material (5539 videos) using a cluster of PC workstations. This shows that our analysis methods come to the level of computational complexity that they can be practically applied for relatively large linguistic corpora. Visual inspection of the results shows that in most cases, the hand detections are rather successful from the human observer's point of view. Figure 1 shows some detections. However, problems do sometimes occur in all the stages of the system, starting from the skin detections being erroneous. Generally, long-sleeved signers present more problems to our system than the short-sleeved ones.

Fig. 1. Sample signer configuration detections in Suvi videos. The green mask denotes estimated right hand area, the blue mask the left hand area, and the red mask the unoccluded parts of face. The circles are the representative points selected for the hands.

Quantitative evaluation of the hand detection accuracy is challenging as we would need to measure the performance in a task that is known to be solvable well if the hand coordinates are known. Some benchmarking has been done [4] by the distance between automatic detections and manually estimated hand point locations. However, this task seems rather artificial in itself as it is difficult to say, what would the accuracy level need to be in order it to be useful in solving practical tasks. In contrast, we have tried to solve the sign spotting benchmark task [14] using the automatically estimated hand coordinates. The problem here is that it is not yet known how well the task can be solved even with perfect hand location estimates. When we replaced the skin distribution histograms of our earlier DTW-based solution with the estimated hand coordinates, the accuracy remained on the same 48% level, which can be considered a good result since the two hand coordinate points are a much more compact representation of the signer configuration than the full spatial skin histograms.

6   Conclusions and Discussion

In this paper we have described two straightforward 2D appearance based techniques for tracking the signer configuration in video recordings of sign language: template matching-based tracking of local image neighbourhoods and skin blob category detection using appearance features and supervised learning. For the category detection, we have evaluated several types of visual features and found that rather complicated statistical texture features work the best, despite the typically small size of the skin blobs.

We described how to construct a system for signer configuration—here mainly the hand location—detection and tracking using the above mentioned techniques among others. The system has turned out to be practically feasible for investigating linguistic corpora of large size. The configuration detection accuracy is not perfect, but seems acceptable in the majority of cases. We plan to use the system in applications where it would not be important to get each and every detection absolutely right, but where information of more statistical nature would already be beneficial, such as information retrieval type of tasks. One can—for example—combine the hand detection with the handshape recognition techniques of [15] and look at the statistics of handshape distribution in signed material, which is a linguistically interesting question. On the other hand, the combination of hand locations and hand shapes might be used for addressing the sign spotting benchmark task of [14].

References

1. Buehler, P., Everingham, M., Huttenlocher, D.P., Zisserman, A.: Long term arm and hand tracking for continuous sign language TV broadcasts. In: Proceedings of the British Machine Vision Conference (2008)
2. Dalal, N., Triggs, B.: Histograms of oriented gradients for human detection. In: Proceedings of the Conference on Computer Vision and Pattern Recognition, vol. 1, pp. 886–893 (2005)
3. de La Gorce, M., Fleet, D., Paragios, N.: Model-based 3D hand pose estimation from monocular video. IEEE Transactions on Pattern Analysis and Machine Intelligence 33(9), 1793–1805 (2011)
4. Dreuw, P., Forster, J., Ney, H.: Tracking benchmark databases for video-based sign language recognition. In: Kutulakos, K.N. (ed.) ECCV 2010 Workshops, Part I. LNCS, vol. 6553, pp. 286–297. Springer, Heidelberg (2012)

5. Felzenszwalb, P.F., Huttenlocher, D.P.: Pictorial structures for object recognition. Int. J. Comput. Vision **61**(1), 55–79 (2005)
6. Karppa, M., Viitaniemi, V., Luzardo, M., Laaksonen, J., Jantunen, T.: SLMotion - an extensible sign language oriented video analysis tool. In: Proceedings of 9th Language Resources and Evaluation Conference (LREC 2014), Reykjavík, Iceland. European Language Resources Association (May 2014)
7. Lowe, D.G.: Distinctive image features from scale-invariant keypoints. International Journal of Computer Vision **60**(2), 91–110 (2004)
8. Miche, Y., Sorjamaa, A., Bas, P., Simula, O., Jutten, C., Lendasse, A.: OP-ELM: Optimally-pruned extreme learning machine. IEEE Transactions on Neural Networks **21**(1), 158–162 (2010)
9. Ojala, T., Pietikäinen, M., Harwood, D.: A comparative study of texture measures with classification based on feature distributions. Pattern Recognition **29**(1), 51–59 (1996)
10. Pfister, T., Charles, J., Everingham, M., Zisserman, A.: Automatic and efficient long term arm and hand tracking for continuous sign language TV broadcasts. In: British Machine Vision Conference (2012)
11. Shi, J., Tomasi, C.: Good features to track. In: Proceedings of IEEE Computer Society Conference on Computer Vision and Pattern Recognition (CVPR 1994), pp. 593–600 (June 1994)
12. Suvi, the on-line dictionary of Finnish Sign Language (2013), http://suvi.viittomat. net, The online service was opened in 2003 and the user interface has been renewed in 2013
13. van de Sande, K.E.A., Gevers, T., Snoek, C.G.M.: Evaluation of color descriptors for object and scene recognition. In: Proc. of IEEE CVPR 2008, Anchorage. Alaska, USA (June 2008)
14. Viitaniemi, V., Jantunen, T., Savolainen, L., Karppa, M., Laaksonen, J.: S-pot - a benchmark in spotting signs within continuous signing. In Proceedings of 9th Language Resources and Evaluation Conference (LREC 2014), Reykjavík, Iceland. European Language Resources Association (May 2014)
15. Viitaniemi, V., Karppa, M., Laaksonen, J.: Experiments on recognising the handshape in blobs extracted from sign language videos. In: Proceedings of 22th International Conference on Pattern Recognition (ICPR), Stockholm, Sweden (August 2014)
16. Viitaniemi, V., Karppa, M., Laaksonen, J., Jantunen, T.: Detecting hand-head occlusions in sign language video. In: Kämäräinen, J.-K., Koskela, M. (eds.) SCIA 2013. LNCS, vol. 7944, pp. 361–372. Springer, Heidelberg (2013)
17. Viitaniemi, V., Laaksonen, J.: Spatial extensions to bag of visual words. In: Proceedings of ACM International Conference on Image and Video Retrieval (CIVR 2009), Fira, Greece (July 2009)
18. Viola, P., Jones, M.: Rapid object detection using a boosted cascade of simple features. In: IEEE Computer Society Conference on Computer Vision and Pattern Recognition (CVPR 2001), pp. I:511–I:518 (2001)
19. Wu, J., Rehg, J.M.: CENTRIST: A visual descriptor for scene categorization. IEEE Transactions on Pattern Analysis and Machine Intelligence **33**(8), 1489–1501 (2011)

Computer Aided Hearing Assessment: Detection of Eye Gesture Reactions as a Response to the Sound

A. Fernández$^{(\boxtimes)}$, Marcos Ortega, and Manuel G. Penedo

Departamento de Computación, Uiversidade da Coruña, A Coruña, Spain
{alba.fernandez,mortega,mgpenedo}@udc.es

Abstract. A methodology for the detection of eye gestural reactions as a response to auditory stimuli is presented in this work. A precise hearing evaluation is important to improve the quality of life of those who suffer from hearing loss. In the case of patients with cognitive decline or other communication disorders this evaluation becomes much more complicated. The audiologist needs to focus his attention on spontaneous gestural reactions that might indicate some sort of perception. The detection of this gestural reactions is sometimes imprecise and it requires a broad experience from the audiologist. To facilitate this task, we present a fully automated method that analyzes video sequences recorded during the audiometric evaluation and identifies these unconscious gestural reactions. The presented methodology achieves an accuracy of the 94.21 % in the detection of these reactions to the auditory stimuli, which makes of it an interesting tool to assist the audiologists in the hearing assessment of this specific group of patients.

Keywords: Hearing assessment · Gesture information · Eye movement analysis

1 Introduction

Hearing plays a key role on everyday living for every one of us. Among older adults, hearing loss is one of the most common self-reported conditions [1], which is also one of the most widely under-treated. Different studies [2] have demonstrated the considerable negative effects that untreated hearing loss may have on the physical, social, psychological and cognitive well-being of a person. In fact, those who suffer from hearing loss can experience an incomplete communication that impacts negatively to their social lives, at times leading to isolation, withdrawal and lack of independence.

Hearing loss can occur at all ages, but it is more common among the elderly adults. Approximately one in three people between ages of 65 and 74, and nearly half of those older than 75, suffer hearing loss. Age-related hearing loss, or presbyacusis, is the cumulative effect of aging on hearing, the consequence is the slow

© Springer International Publishing Switzerland 2014
A. Campilho and M. Kamel (Eds.): ICIAR 2014, Part II, LNCS 8815, pp. 39–47, 2014.
DOI: 10.1007/978-3-319-11755-3_5

loss of hearing that occurs as people gets older. For all these, regular hearing tests are totally necessary for elderly adults and highly recommended in case of any doubt about the ability of hearing at any age. Pure Tone Audiometry (PTA) is a behavioral test for the evaluation of the hearing sensitivity. This exam is one of the "gold standard" tests for the measuring the hearing capacity.

Since the PTA is a behavioral test, it involves some operational limitations, specially among patients with special needs or disabilities. Co-pathology is a major complication for the diagnosis of hearing problems. Almost all elderly adult will develop some degree in cognitive capacity as time progresses. This slow decline oftentimes progress into more serious conditions such as dementia or Alzheimer's disease. In these cases, the standard protocol of a PTA becomes unenforceable since the interaction between the audiologist and the patient is almost impossible. Since aging is highly related to both hearing loss and age related cognitive decline, the coexistence these two conditions is substantially likely, and it represents a challenge for the audiologists. With these specific group of patients, the audiologist needs to focus his attention on unconscious eye gestural movements that indicate some kind of perception. The proper detection of these spontaneous reactions requires broad experience since each patient may show different gestures as a reaction All the subjectivity involved make of this evaluation an imprecise problem, difficult to reproduce and very prone to errors.

In [3] an initial approach was proposed to provide an automatic solution for the detection and identification of these eye gestural reactions. This first approximation was developed in order to confirm the viability of the proposed methodology but, as pointed out in the conclusions, more studies need to be conducted in order to obtain a fully automated computer-driven system capable of solving this specific problem. The experimental results of this initial and novel solution showed the possibility of reliably distinguishing between the different categories of eye movement established by the experts, however, these categories have later been extended which makes necessary the development of new experiments.

It is important to note that, due to the nature of these patients and the features of the eye gestural reactions that they show, a typical method for the detection and classification of gestural reactions is not applicable. In this case, the reactions manifested by the patients are fully opened and can not be stereotyped into typical gestures associated to the classical emotions.

The scope of this paper is to extend and corroborate the results previously obtained and to define the complete methodology that receives as input a video sequence recorded during the performance of an audiometric evaluation and obtains as result the identification of the precise moments when an spontaneous eye gestural reaction may have happened. The initial proposal classified the detected eye moments into one of the established categories, but in order to obtain a fully automated solution it is necessary to give meaning to these movements and identify those that really correspond with a reaction to the sound.

The remainder of this paper is organized as follows: Section 2 is devoted to explain the clinical protocol.Section 3 explains the methodology for the automatic detection of the eye gestural reactions. Section 4 shows the experimental results. And finally, conclusions and future work lines are presented in Section 5.

2   Clinical Protocol for Pure Tone Audiometry

As mentioned before, the Pure Tone Audiometry (PTA) is the standard test for the evaluation of the hearing capacity. It allows the audiologist to determine the hearing threshold levels of the patient, and thus, to determine if hearing loss exists. The setup is this test is quite consistent (see Fig. 1): the patient is seated in front of the audiologist wearing earphones connected to the audiometer. Through this device, the audiologist delivers pure tone sounds at different frequencies and intensities. In the case of patients without any communication disorder, they are asked to raise their hands when they perceive the sound.

Fig. 1. Typical setup of the video sequences

There is a need of communication between the audiologist and the patient. Firstly, the audiologist needs to explain to the patient the protocol for the audiometric test, and it is highly important that the patient understands the instructions given. Also, during the performance of the test, the patient needs to indicate when he perceives the auditory stimuli, so there is a question-answer communication during all the procedure. This need of communication is what makes unenforceable the assessment of patients with a high degree of cognitive impairment. The evaluation of this patients is much more complex, but it is still possible if the audiologist is experienced enough and he focuses his attention of unconscious and spontaneous eye gesture reactions that represent some kind of perception for these patients, and they can be considered as a response to assess the hearing. The proper assessment of these patients is important, since the detection of hearing loss may allow its correction by the use of hearing aids, thus, achieving a decrease in the feeling of isolation of these patients.

3   Analysis of Eye-Based Gestural Reactions

The development of an automated solution for the identification of eye gestural movements as a reaction to the auditory stimuli may be of great relevance between the audiologist community. In order to analyze the assessments, the audiometries are recorded using a video camera located behind the audiologist. This way, the recorded video sequence has a viewpoint similar to the one observed by the expert during the test. This location ensures recording the audiometer (which is going to be necessary in order to correlate the stimuli and the reactions), and also that the face of the patient is recorded in frontal position.

Using computer vision techniques over the video sequences we propose a methodology for the detection and interpretation of the eye gestural reactions. The main scheme of this methodology is detailed in Fig. 2. The more complex stage is the *Eye Movement Classification*, which is presented more in detail in Fig. 4. Each stage is going to be explained next.

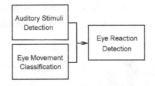

Fig. 2. General representation of the methodology

3.1   Auditory Stimuli Detection

In order to correlate the reactions with the delivery of the auditory stimuli it is necessary to know when an stimulus is being sent. In our particular case, experts are working with analogical audiometers, so this information can not be automatically extracted. It is necessary to develop a solution that analyzes the video sequence and provides this information. There are two devices employed by the experts, one of them (Fig. 3(a)) has a single light that turns on when the auditory stimulus is being sent; and the other one (Fig. 3(b)) has two lights, one light represents the left channel, and the other one the right channel.

Template matching is used to locate this light indicators, after that, in the HSV color space H and S components are thresholded in order to determine whether the lights are on or off, and consequently, if an auditory stimulus is being delivered or not.

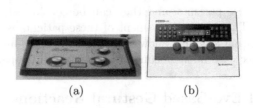

(a)   (b)

Fig. 3. Analogical audiometers: (a) Beltone Electronics and (b) Madsen Otometrics

3.2   Eye Movement Classification

The main stage of the methodology is the *Eye movement classification*. It analyzes the video sequences in order to detect eye movements and classify them into one of the categories established by the audiologists. The main steps of this stage are detailed in Fig. 4.

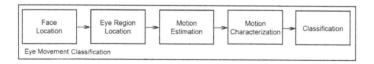

Fig. 4. Main steps of the *Eye Movement Classification*

Face Location. An initial face location facilitates the subsequently step. Due to the stability of the domain, it is possible to ensure that faces will always be in frontal position. Thanks to this particularity, the Viola-Jones [4] face detector is highly appropriate, since it is low computational cost and very accurate.

Eye Region Location. In order to obtain the location of the eye region, we specifically trained a Viola-Jones cascade. This new detector was built using more that 1000 images of the eye area.

Motion Estimation. Global movement analysis is now applied in order to estimate the movements produced within the detected eye region. The use of a global viewpoint justified in previous works. The motion is estimated by applying the iterative Lucas-Kanade [5] optical flow method with pyramids [6]. Since our frame rate is 25 FPS, the optical flow is computed between frame i and frame $i+3$. In Figure 5 a sample of the optical flow results is showed. Fig. 5(a) and Fig. 5(b) are the images to be compared and Fig. 5(d) represents the final vectors to be considered in the next step of the methodology.

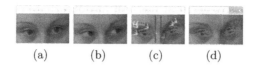

(a)   (b)   (c)   (d)

Fig. 5. Sample optical flow images. Optical flow is calculated between (a) and (b). Optical flow results in (c): green vectors for the softer movements, yellow for intermediate and red for strongest movements. Stronger vectors in (d) after filtering the rest.

Motion Characterization. Once the significant movement are detected, it is necessary to characterize them in order to lately classify them. When no significant movement occurs, the classification does not take place, but in other case it is necessary to have some descriptors that allow the movement categorization. To that end, a set of descriptors is going to be extracted.

The movement features considered for the descriptors are: orientation, magnitude and dispersion. Orientation provides information about changes in the gaze direction. Magnitude provides information about the intensity of the movement. Dispersion allows to discriminate between localized an global movements. According to this, the descriptor is comprised of a vector of 24 values: 8 for orientation, 8 for the average length for each orientation and, 8 for the dispersion. These descriptors are described with detail in previous works.

Classification. After new meetings with the experts, six typical movements are considered: no significant movement (Class NM), eye opening (Class EO), eye closure (Class EC), gaze shift to the left (class GL), gaze shift to the right (Class GR) and global movement (Class GM). It must be noted that a new category was introduced since the previous version of this work: Class NM (no significant movement), in order to classify vectors that represent a slight movement which should not be considered as a relevant reaction. More samples are included in this new training and also a new classifier has been tested obtaining better results. The results of this new training are detailed in Section 4.

3.3   Eye Reaction Detection

Finally, after detecting the auditory stimuli delivery and having all the movements classified, it is necessary to identify those movements that correspond with a reaction to the stimuli. To that end, both information are correlated and we consider as a positive reaction any significant movement produced after the beginning of an auditory stimuli. To consider a significant movement as a positive reaction it has to last at least two frames, since it is considered that with a frame rate of 25 FPS a one frame reaction would be too fast to correspond with a real positive reaction. In Fig. 6 it can be observed a visual example where, on the one hand the auditory stimulus has been detected, and on the other hand, an eye movement has been detected and classified as relevant moment (Class GR). The result of the conjunction of these two situations allows the system to determine that a positive gestural reaction has occurred. This correlation also allow to measure the reaction times, which is another important information in the assessment of the hearing.

4   Experimental Results

In order to conduct this experiment a total number of 820 movement descriptors were considered. A new classifier was included in this experiment, the Support Vector Machine (SVM). A summary of the results obtained from this new experiment is detailed in Table 1. Ten different trainings were conducted in order to generalize the results, all of them were quite consistent, thus, in order to be brief, only the results of one of them is detailed here. From these experiments it can

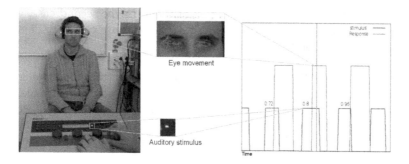

Fig. 6. Correlation between the stimulus and the reaction. Red signal for the stimuli (up when delivered) and green for reaction (up when reaction occurs). The response time is measured from the beginning of the stimulus until the beginning of the reaction.

Table 1. Accuracy of the classifiers by classes for the training dataset number 10

	Naive Bayes	Random Tree	Logistic	LMT	Perceptron	Random Forest	Random Committee	SVM
Class NM	47.1%	67.6%	55.9%	55.9%	61.8%	64.7%	58.8%	**69.1%**
Class EO	35.5%	67.1%	65.8%	67.1%	61.8%	**73.7%**	**73.7%**	73.6%
Class EC	73.7%	57.9%	76.3%	76.3%	77.6%	69.7%	75.0%	**92.5%**
Class GL	**90.6%**	73.4%	76.6%	76.6%	79.7%	78.1%	82.8%	76.9%
Class GR	64.7%	55.9%	38.2%	38.2%	50.0%	58.8%	61.8%	**85.0%**
Class GM	44.7%	80.3%	78.9%	81.6%	89.5%	86.8%	85.5%	**89.9%**
Average	59.2%	68.1%	69.2%	70.0%	73.1%	74.2%	75.6%	**81.4%**

be concluded that the new classifier, SVM, is the one which offers the higher accuracy, so it will be the one considered into our final methodology.

The final evaluation of the methodology is complicated due to the difficulties in obtaining video sequences of this particular group of patients. Most of them are entered in senior centers, and special permissions are required in order to record them. For this reason, and in order of being able to evaluate the accuracy of the proposed methodology two video sequences were recorded with two volunteers from our research group. These volunteers were instructed to reproduce the eye gestural reactions that the target patients show spontaneously.

In this experiment, the eye movements considered as a positive reaction are: gaze shift to the left and gaze shift to the right. This is because the audiologists have established that changes in the gaze direction are the most common reaction. In most of the cases, these patients are in a static attitude, and when they perceive an auditory stimulus through one if their ears, they slightly change the direction of their gaze to the side of where they have perceived the sound. This change on the gaze direction is totally spontaneous and unconscious, but our volunteers are going to reproduce it so we can test the methodology.

The correlation of the auditory stimuli delivery and the eye movement classification allow the identification of the eye movements considered as positive reactions to the auditory stimuli. The results of the evaluation of the method are depicted in Table 2. In the first experiment 31 positive reactions occur, and the method is able of reliably detecting 29 of them. In the second case, a total number of 39 positive reactions occur, and 37 of them are correctly identified. These results offer a total accuracy of the 94.21%.

It is important to note, that the previous results besides of being objectively good (almost a 95% of accuracy), are greatly important since the ground truth was obtained by labeling the images frame by frame, which makes easier the detection of the eye moments. However, in the traditional protocol, the detection of the positive reactions is conducted in real time while the audiologist handles the audiometer, what makes highly likely that the he misses any of these reactions.

Table 2. Accuracy of the methodology in the detection of eye gestural reactions

	Experiment 1	Experiment 2
Detected reactions	29	37
Lost reactions	2	2
Accuracy	93.55%	94.87%
Combined accuracy	**94.21%**	

5   Conclusions

This work evaluates the suitability of a novel approach for the detection of eye gestural reactions as a response to the auditory stimuli. It facilitates the hearing assessment of patients with cognitive decline or communication disorders that do not interact with the audiologist in the standard way. More samples, a new movement category and a new classifier were tested with regard to previous works. Due to the difficulties in the obtaining of video sequences of this particular group of patients, the evaluation was conducted with volunteers. The obtained results show an accuracy of the 94.21% for the detection of the eye gestural reactions, which is a promising result. This study demonstrates the possible contribution that this work would have for the audiologists, since nowadays not all the audiologist are trained for the evaluation of these patients and it is a very subjective task. This methodology would provide objectivity and reproducibility to the process. As future works it would be important to obtain the required permissions for recording real patients and test the methodology with them.

References

1. Cruickshanks, K.J., Wiley, T.L., Tweed, T., et al.: Prevalence of hearing loss in older adults in beaver dam, wisconsin: The epidemiology of hearing loss study. American Journal of Epidemiology **148**(9), 879–886 (1998)
2. Davis, A.: The prevalence of hearing impairment and reported hearing disability among adults in great britain. Int. J. Epidemiol. **18**, 911–917 (1989)
3. Fernandez, A., Ortega, M., Penedo, M.G., Cancela, B., Gigirey, L.M.: Automatic eye gesture recognition in audiometries for patients with cognitive decline. In: Kamel, M., Campilho, A. (eds.) ICIAR 2013. LNCS, vol. 7950, pp. 27–34. Springer, Heidelberg (2013)

4. Viola, P., Jones, M.: Robust real-time object detection. Int. J. Comput. Vision **57**, 137–154 (2004)
5. Lucas, B.D., Kanade, T.: An iterative image registration technique with an application to stereo vision. In: Proceedings of the 7th International Joint Conference on Artificial Intelligence, IJCAI 1981, vol. 2, pp. 674–679 (1981)
6. Bouguet, J.Y.: Pyramidal implementation of the Lucas-Kanade feature tracker: Description of the algorithm. Intel Corporation, Microprocessor Research Labs (2000)

Multi-sensor Acceleration-Based Action Recognition

Florian Baumann[1][✉], Irina Schulz[2], and Bodo Rosenhahn[1]

[1] Institut für Informationsverarbeitung (TNT), Leibniz Universität Hannover,
Hannover, Germany
baumann@tnt.uni-hannover.de
[2] Institute for Systems Engineering (RTS), Leibniz Universität Hannover,
Hannover, Germany

Abstract. In this paper, a framework to recognize human actions from acceleration data is proposed. An important step for an accurate recognition is the pre-processing of input data and the following classification by the machine learning algorithm. In this paper, we suggest to combine Dynamic Time Warping (DTW) with Random Forest. The intention of using DTW is to pre-process the data to eliminate outliers and to align the time series. Many applications require more than one inertial sensor for an accurate prediction of actions. In this paper, nine inertial sensors are deployed to ensure an accurate recognition of actions. Further, sensor fusion approaches are introduced and the most promising strategy is shown. The proposed framework is evaluated on a self-recorded dataset consisting of six human actions. Each action was performed three times by 20 subjects. The dataset is publicly available for download.

1 Introduction

In recent years, the use of inertial sensors has become a popular topic in machine learning. One reason for the growing interest is the improved quality and the reduced costs of the hardware [9]. Another reason is the rising number of applications. For instance, sonification of movements [8,10], analysis of sports-, rehabilitation-, and healthcare sessions [14,21,22,32] as well as applications within the clinical and veterinary field [18,24]. These applications require an accurate and precise recognition of actions and movements leading to a challenging topic in machine learning. For instance, each actor has the own style of performing an action and many variations in the subject's movement are possible. Thus, a large intra-class variation is inevitable. These problems are also reflected in the recorded data: the gathered acceleration-based time series strongly differ in their amplitude and length.

Contribution. In this paper, a combination of Dynamic Time Warping (DTW) with the well-known machine learning algorithm Random Forest is proposed. DTW is used as a pre-processing step to eliminate outliers, to align different time series and to compensate large intra-class variations. For classification, a Random Forest is learned on the aligned, raw acceleration values.

This work has been partially funded by the ERC within the starting grant Dynamic MinVIP.

A. Campilho and M. Kamel (Eds.): ICIAR 2014, Part II, LNCS 8815, pp. 48–57, 2014.
DOI: 10.1007/978-3-319-11755-3_6

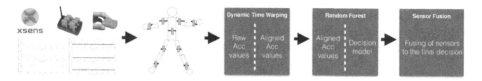

Fig. 1. An overview about the proposed framework. Acceleration data of six actions are obtained by nine inertial sensors. A Dynamic Time Warping is used in a pre-processing step to prepare the input data. The aligned acceleration time series are directly used to learn a Random Forest classifier. The final decision is determined by using sensor fusion methods.

The proposed approach is applied to a self-recorded dataset. Inspired by the KTH dataset for single human action recognition [29], six actions were defined: *walking, running, jogging, boxing, clapping and waving*. Each action was performed three times by 20 subjects. The acceleration data was gathered by nine Xsens motion wireless tracker (MTw). Each subject was equipped with sensors on the left/right wrist, left/right upper arm, left/right thigh, left/right ankle and one MTw on the waist, also see Figure 1. To combine multiple sensors, fusion methods are presented and evaluated. The dataset is publicly available for download. Thus, other researchers can evaluate their methods and algorithms and publish competing results.

The paper is structured as follows. Section 2 gives a short overview about related work. Section 3 briefly describes Dynamic Time Warping, Random Forest and sensor fusion strategies. Section 4 presents the dataset and the experimental results. Section 5 concludes the paper and gives an overview about future work.

2   Related Work

Action recognition has been playing an important role in many areas of medicine, in the industrial domain, in the automotive area, for scene understanding or in the surveillance area [1,25]. Many works use acceleration-based sensors, referred to as Xsens-sensors for ambulatory measurement [23] or for clinical gait analysis [12]. These works reveal that physical activities can be well-recognized by inertial sensors.

Chambers et al. [11] used one inertial sensor that was attached to the wrist of a subject for complex gesture recording by using Hidden Markov Models. Wang et al. [34] attached sensors to subjects and learned a Support Vector Machine to recognize daily activities. Karantonis et al. [17] explained a basic decision tree method using a single sensor on the waist of subjects for real-time classification. Tautges et al. [33] reconstructed whole body motions from the data taken by as few as one, two and four inertial sensors for several classes of motions. They use the acceleration data from some Xsens inertial sensors attached to the hands and feet of some subjects to reconstruct the performed motions. These motions are compared to a video that was taken during the capturing. Further information and a detailed survey about the current research using inertial sensors is presented by Avci et al. [3].

In comparison to the above mentioned works, a framework based on Random Forest in combination with Dynamic Time Warping is proposed. Six typical actions are defined and a self-recorded dataset is provided to the community. By using this dataset, nine inertial sensors can be utilized to recognize and analyze human actions. Finally, the most promising sensor fusion strategy is presented.

3 Approach

Figure 1 presents an overview of the proposed framework. The acceleration time series in (x, y, z)-direction are gathered by nine inertial sensors. For aligning the time series to each other a Dynamic Time Warping is applied to every training and testing example. Instead of deploying a specific feature extraction method, the aligned (x, y, z)-acceleration values are directly used to learn a Random Forest classifier. The final decision is computed by a sensor fusion method.

This Section briefly describes Dynamic Time Warping for pre-processing, Random Forest for classification and the sensor fusion strategies.

3.1 Dynamic Time Warping

Dynamic Time Warping (DTW) was introduced by Bellman and Kalaba [4]. DTW has been applied to several fields of applications like video or audio data for measuring the similarity of two temporal sequences. For instance, Myers et al. and Sakoe et al. applied DTW to the task of speech recognition [20, 27]. Generally, DTW is an algorithm for mapping values between two temporal sequences to each other.

In the following, a brief explanation of the theory is given. First, the algorithm applies a distance between any two values of the signals using a weighting function, such as the euclidean distance for each parameter of each tuple. The output is referred to as a cost function. In the next step the algorithm seeks the lowest cost from the start to the end of both signals over the stretched matrix of pairwise current cost of all points of both signals. The actual path, referred to as a warping, is determined by backtracking the first pass of the algorithm. The backtracking allows a precise representation of each point of the shorter signal to one or more points of the longer signal. Thus the approximate time distortion is represented. Further information and a detailed review are presented by Senin [30].

Figure 2(a) illustrates two acceleration signals in x-direction of a boxing gesture. The signals differ in their amplitude. Signal 1 is defined as reference signal. Figure 2(b) presents the warping of signal 2 to the reference signal 1. The amplitudes are nearly the same and signal 2 is aligned.

In this work the standard DTW algorithm with a time complexity of $\mathcal{O}(N^2)$ is implemented. For a real-time capable modification Rakthanmanon et al. [26] propose a combination of four approaches to search and mine time series in a very efficient way.

After applying the DTW to each training and testing example a Random Forest is used to find discriminative (x, y, z)-acceleration values.

3.2 Random Forest

Random Forest was published by Leo Breiman in 2001 [6]. It is a substantial modification of bagging [5] with a random feature selection proposed by Ho [15, 16] and

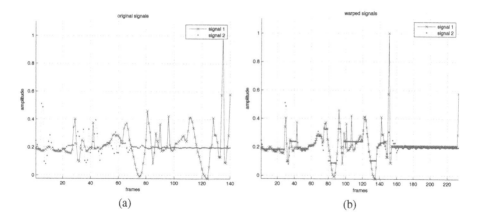

Fig. 2. (a) Original signals of the x-acceleration of a boxing action. The signals differ in their amplitude. (b) Acceleration signal in x-direction of a boxing action. Signal 2 is warped to signal 1. The amplitudes are nearly the same and outliers are compensated.

Amit [2]. A Random Forest consists of a collection of CART-like (Classification and Regression Tree) decision trees h_t, $1 \leq t \leq T$, [7]:

$$\{h(\boldsymbol{x}, \Theta_t)_{t=1,...T}\}$$

where $\{\Theta_t\}$ is a bootstrap sample from the training data. Each tree casts a vote on a class for the input $\boldsymbol{x}$. The class probabilities are estimated by majority voting and used to calculate the sample's label $y(\boldsymbol{x})$ with respect to a given feature vector $\boldsymbol{x}$:

$$y(\boldsymbol{x}) = \underset{c}{\operatorname{argmax}} \left(\frac{1}{T} \sum_{t=1}^{T} F_{h_t(\boldsymbol{x})=c} \right) \tag{1}$$

The decision function $h_t(\boldsymbol{x})$ returns the resulting class c of one tree with the indicator function F:

$$F_{h_t(\boldsymbol{x})=c} = \begin{cases} 1, & h_t(\boldsymbol{x}) = c, \\ 0, & \text{otherwise.} \end{cases} \tag{2}$$

Random Forest has a high classification accuracy and can deal with large data sets for multiple classes with outstanding time efficiency [6].

Classification. Time-series are classified by passing them down each tree until a leaf node is reached. The resulting class is defined by each leaf node and the final decision is determined by taking the class having the most votes (majority vote), see Equation (1).

3.3   Sensor Fusion

The sensor fusion part describes methods to combine decisions by different classifiers (or sensors) to the final decision. In this paper, the sensor fusion part has to handle the information of nine sensors. A feature is represented by a single DTW aligned acceleration value.

For all experiments, the input data for the Random Forest is composed of the concatenated acceleration values (a_x, a_y, a_z), each with m samples:

$$RF_{input} = [a_x(1), ..., a_x(m), a_y(1), ..., a_y(m), a_z(1), ..., a_z(m)], \tag{3}$$

RF_{input} is used for two approaches of determining the final decision:

1. Learning a Random Forest using all sensors (fusion is not required)
2. Learning a Random Forest for each sensor individually (fusion is required)

In the first experiment the input data for the Random Forest is composed by concatenating the acceleration values of n sensors:

$$RF_{input_{All}} = [RF_{input_1}, ..., RF_{input_n}]. \tag{4}$$

This approach leads to a huge pool of possible values. A feature vector consists of $n \times 3 \times m$ values. A sensor fusion is not necessary, because the Random Forest is learned with the input of all sensors. Usually the Random Forest algorithm is able to handle large dimensions of training data [6] but due to the random feature selection mechanism, we assume that this approach leads to poor results. The probability of selecting a discriminative feature is lower due to the number of chosen variables from the feature vector: For each tree $v = \sqrt{p}$ variables[1] with p = $n \times 3 \times m$ are selected to build the tree.

For the second approach, a Random Forest is learned from each sensor individually. Thus, n sensors require n classifiers. Similar to the first approach $v = \sqrt{p}$ variables with $p = 3 \times m$ are selected to build the tree leading to $n \times \sqrt{3 \times m}$ variables. In comparison to the first approach the number of variables to split is three times higher. We assume that this approach reaches higher and more robust accuracies. But an additional step of fusing n probability distributions to the final decision is required.

Fusing. By taking the probability distributions of $n = 9$ sensors into consideration the following combination strategies for finally determining the decision are proposed:

1. Choose class with highest probability
2. Choose class with majority voting
3. Fusion of probability distributions by product law
4. Fusion of probability distributions by summation rule

For the first case, we assume that the most reliable class gains the highest probability. For the second case the class which gains the most votes of all classifiers is chosen. This idea is inspired by the majority tree voting of a Random Forest. For the third case the probability distributions of all classifiers are taken into consideration and fused by the product law. The final decision is determined by combining the class probabilities $\Pr(A_i) \cdots \Pr(I_i)$ of one class i from each sensor $A_i \cdots I_i$ with the product law[2]. For the

---

[1] Random Forest is not restricted to use $v = \sqrt{p}$ variables. The number of variables can be freely chosen. Best results were obtained by taking $m = \sqrt{p}$ variables, as proposed by Breiman.

[2] With the assumption that sensors $A_i \cdots I_i$ are independent.

fourth case the class probabilities are fused using the summation rule. The class probabilities $\Pr(A_i) \cdots \Pr(I_i)$ are summed up and the final decision is determined using the class with the highest probability.

4 Experimental Results

This Section describes the selection and recording of acceleration data and the classification experiments. First, the dataset is defined and presented followed by the sensor fusion strategies. Finally a detailed discussion about the examined experiments is given.

4.1 Self-recorded Dataset

Inspired by the well-known KTH dataset for single human action recognition [29], six actions were defined: *walking, running, jogging, boxing, clapping and waving*. Each action was repeated three times by 20 subjects, leading to an overall dataset of 360 time series. The dataset is publicly available for download[3] in a Matlab file format.

The Xsens MTw Development Kit[4] was used for data recording. MTw stands for Motion Tracker wireless. It is a measuring instrument with built in 3D accelerometer, gyroscope, magnetometer (compass 3D) and a barometer (pressure sensor). The inertial sensors gather the acceleration values in the three-dimensional space. Each sensor determines the acceleration along (x, y, z)-axes. Figure 1 gives an overview of a subject equipped with nine sensors attached to the body.

4.2 Experiments

In this Section the proposed sensor fusion strategies are compared to each other. As mentioned in Section 3.3, we compare the strategy of learning a descriptor using all sensors to the strategy of learning a descriptor using each sensor individually. The optimal parameters for the Random Forest were determined by a cross validation mechanism and set to *maximum depth of a tree* = 64, *optimal number of trees* = 8 and *minimum number of leaves* = 2 for all experiments. The entropy was used as the splitting criterion. More information about different strategies are found in the literature [6]. As already discussed, using all sensors to learn a single Random Forest classifier results in poor accuracies. The classifier reached an averaged accuracy of 49.80%. The reason for these poor accuracies results from the lower number of variables to split each tree.

In the following experiments, the focus is on the evaluation of learning a classifier using each sensor individually. Results are reported for each fusion strategy individually:

Choose Class with Highest Probability. The final decision is determined by taking the class with the highest probability of all nine classifiers.

Figure 3a presents the confusion matrix. The accuracy of 26.50% is quite low. The results are not unusual, since only one decision by one sensor was taken into account. This leads to a higher sensitivity to noise and outliers.

---

[3] http://www.tnt.uni-hannover.de/staff/baumann/
[4] http://www.xsens.com

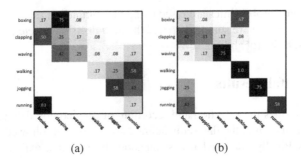

(a)   (b)

Fig. 3. (a) Take the class with the highest probability by using all nine classifiers with an averaged accuracy of 26.50%. (b) Choose class with majority voting by using all sensors, the averaged accuracy is 61.00%.

Choose Class by Majority Voting of All Classifiers. For this case, the final decision is determined by a majority voting of all sensors. Each Random Forest votes for one class while the majority class is chosen.

Figure 3b presents the confusion matrix for this experiment. The averaged accuracy is 61.00%. Since all decisions are fused by using a majority voting, the results are better leading to a more robust recognition. Walking is perfectly classified and waving and jogging reach 75.00% accuracy. Most confusions occur between boxing and clapping.

Fusion by Product Law. The probability distributions gained by all sensors are fused using the product law. For this experiment, three cases are compared:

1. Probabilities of 0% are taken into consideration
2. Probabilities of 0% are ignored
3. Introducing a threshold for taking only reliable probabilities

Figure 4a presents the results for the first case achieving an averaged accuracy of 42.00%. It is striking that most confusions occur between jogging and the other actions. Thus, taking all probabilities into account leads to low results.

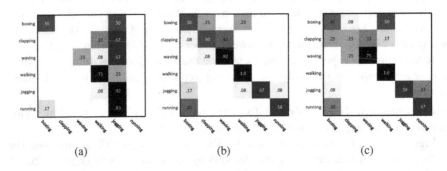

(a)   (b)   (c)

Fig. 4. Confusion matrices using the product law. (a) Taking all probabilities into consideration. Averaged accuracy is 42.00%. (b) Ignore poor decisions. Accuracy is 70.00%. (c) Thresholding the probabilities to take reliable decisions into consideration. The averaged accuracy is 61.00%.

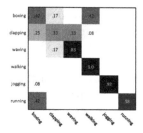

Fig. 5. Choose class using the summation rule. The averaged recognition rate is 68.00%.

Figure 4b presents a confusion matrix for the case of ignoring probabilities with 0% achieving the best accuracy of 70.00%. Walking is perfectly classified and waving reaches 92.00% accuracy. Boxing and clapping gain accuracies of 50% while most confusions occur between similar actions like boxing, waving and clapping.

Figure 4c presents the case of introducing a threshold. Only probabilities of more than 40.00% are taken into consideration leading to an averaged accuracy of 61.00%. The threshold was empirically chosen. Also, for this experiment walking is perfectly classified and most confusions occur between boxing and clapping.

Fusion by Summation Rule. The probability distributions gained by all sensors are fused using the summation rule.

Figure 5 presents the confusion matrix for this case. The averaged accuracy is 68.00%. Walking is perfectly classified and waving and jogging reach high accuracies too. Also, for this experiment most confusions occur between boxing and clapping.

4.3   Discussion

In this Section two sensor fusion strategies were proposed. The first experiment of learning a Random Forest using all sensors results in low accuracies. The second method describes several fusion methods. Best results were achieved by learning a Random Forest for each sensor individually. Fusing the decisions by the product law leads to an accuracy of 70.00% and by using the summation rule to 68.00%. Walking is perfectly classified for nearly all experiments while most confusions occur between boxing and clapping.

5   Conclusions and Future Work

In this paper, nine inertial sensors were used to recognize six typical human actions: *walking, running, jogging, boxing, clapping and waving*. In a pre-processing step a Dynamic Time Warping is applied to align the acceleration time series to each other. The aligned time series are directly used to learn a Random Forest classifier. Furthermore, two sensor fusion strategies are proposed. By applying the product law or summation rule for fusing the class probabilities, accuracies up to 70.00% were reached. The self-recorded dataset is publicly available for download at http://www.tnt.uni-hannover. de/staff/baumann/.

Future Work. Our plans for future work are to combine all decisions using the Dempster Shafer theory [31] or related works from the computer vision community basing on Dempster's theory of evidence, like [19,28,35]. Presumably, the results might be further improved.

Another idea is to realize a time series forest for classification and feature extraction [13] and to spend more attention on the type of feature instead of using the raw acceleration data. It should also be made some experiments whether it is more convenient to use the orientations (quaternions) of each sensor instead of using only the acceleration data.

References

1. Aggarwal, J., Ryoo, M.: Human activity analysis: A review. ACM Computing Surveys **43**(3), 16:1–16:43 (2011)
2. Amit, Y., Geman, D.: Shape quantization and recognition with randomized trees. Neural Computation **9**(7), 1545–1588 (1997)
3. Avci, A., Bosch, S., Marin-Perianu, M., Marin-Perianu, R., Havinga, P.: Activity recognition using inertial sensing for healthcare, wellbeing and sports applications: A survey. In: 2010 23rd International Conference on Architecture of Computing Systems (ARCS) (2010)
4. Bellman, R., Kalaba, R.: On adaptive control processes. IRE Transactions on Automatic Control **4**(2), 1–9 (1959)
5. Breiman, L.: Bagging predictors. Machine Learning **24**, 123–140 (1996)
6. Breiman, L.: Random forests. Machine Learning **45**(1), 5–32 (2001)
7. Breiman, L., Friedman, J.H., Olshen, R.A., Stone, C.J.: Classification and Regression Trees. Chapman & Hall, New York (1984)
8. Brock, H., Schmitz, G., Baumann, J., Effenberg, A.O.: If motion sounds: Movement sonification based on inertial sensor data. In: 9th Conference of the International Sports Engineering Association (ISEA). Elsevier (January 2012)
9. Brückner, H.P., Nowosielski, R., Kluge, H., Blume, H.: Mobile and wireless inertial sensor platform for motion capturing in stroke rehabilitation sessions. In: 2013 5th IEEE International Workshop on Advances in Sensors and Interfaces (IWASI), pp. 14–19 (2013)
10. Brückner, H.P., Wielage, M., Blume, H.: Intuitive and interactive movement sonification on a heterogeneous risc/dsp platform. In: The 18th Annual International Conference on Auditory Display (2012)
11. Chambers, G., Venkatesh, S., West, G., Bui, H.: Hierarchical recognition of intentional human gestures for sports video annotation. In: Proceedings of the 16th International Conference on Pattern Recognition (2002)
12. Cutti, A., Ferrari, A., Garofalo, P., Raggi, M., Cappello, A., Ferrari, A.: 'outwalk': a protocol for clinical gait analysis based on inertial and magnetic sensors. Medical and Biological Engineering and Computing **48**(1), 17–25 (2010)
13. Deng, H., Runger, G., Tuv, E., Martyanov, V.: A time series forest for classification and feature extraction. Information Sciences **239**, 142–153 (2013)
14. Ha, T.H., Saber-Sheikh, K., Moore, A.P., Jones, M.P.: Measurement of lumbar spine range of movement and coupled motion using inertial sensors-a protocol validity study. Manual Therapy **18**(1), 87–91 (2013)
15. Ho, T.K.: Random decision forests. In: Proceedings of the Third International Conference on Document Analysis and Recognition. IEEE (1995)
16. Ho, T.K.: The random subspace method for constructing decision forests. IEEE Transactions on Pattern Analysis and Machine Intelligence **20**(8), 832–844 (1998)

17. Karantonis, D., Narayanan, M., Mathie, M., Lovell, N., Celler, B.: Implementation of a real-time human movement classifier using a triaxial accelerometer for ambulatory monitoring. IEEE Transactions on Information Technology in Biomedicine **10**(1), 156–167 (2006)
18. Lebel, K., Boissy, P., Hamel, M., Duval, C.: Inertial measures of motion for clinical biomechanics: Comparative assessment of accuracy under controlled conditions - effect of velocity. PLoS ONE **8**(11) (2013)
19. Murphy, R.R.: Dempster-shafer theory for sensor fusion in autonomous mobile robots. IEEE Transactions on Robotics and Automation **14**(2), 197–206 (1998)
20. Myers, C., Rabiner, L., Rosenberg, A.: Performance tradeoffs in dynamic time warping algorithms for isolated word recognition. IEEE Transactions on Acoustics, Speech and Signal Processing **28**(6), 623–635 (1980)
21. van den Noort, J.C., Ferrari, A., Cutti, A.G., Becher, J.G., Harlaar, J.: Gait analysis in children with cerebral palsy via inertial and magnetic sensors. Medical & Biological Engineering & Computing, 1–10 (2013)
22. Olsen, E., Haubro Andersen, P., Pfau, T.: Accuracy and precision of equine gait event detection during walking with limb and trunk mounted inertial sensors. Sensors (2012)
23. Parel, I., Cutti, A., Fiumana, G., Porcellini, G., Verni, G., Accardo, A.: Ambulatory measurement of the scapulohumeral rhythm: Intra- and inter-operator agreement of a protocol based on inertial and magnetic sensors. Gait and Posture **35**(4), 636–640 (2012)
24. Pfau, T., Starke, S.D., Tröster, S., Roepstorff, L.: Estimation of vertical tuber coxae movement in the horse from a single inertial measurement unit. The Veterinary Journal (2013)
25. Poppe, R.: A survey on vision-based human action recognition. Image and Vision Computing **28**(6), 976–990 (2010)
26. Rakthanmanon, T., Campana, B., Mueen, A., Batista, G., Westover, B., Zhu, Q., Zakaria, J., Keogh, E.: Searching and mining trillions of time series subsequences under dynamic time warping. In: Proceedings of the 18th ACM SIGKDD International Conference on Knowledge Discovery and Data Mining, pp. 262–270. ACM (2012)
27. Sakoe, H., Chiba, S.: Dynamic programming algorithm optimization for spoken word recognition. IEEE Transactions on Acoustics, Speech and Signal Processing **26**(1), 43–49 (1978)
28. Scheuermann, B., Schlosser, M., Rosenhahn, B.: Efficient pixel-grouping based on dempster's theory of evidence for image segmentation. In: Lee, K.M., Matsushita, Y., Rehg, J.M., Hu, Z. (eds.) ACCV 2012, Part I. LNCS, vol. 7724, pp. 745–759. Springer, Heidelberg (2013)
29. Schuldt, C., Laptev, I., Caputo, B.: Recognizing human actions: a local svm approach. In: Proceedings of the 17th International Conference on Pattern Recognition (ICPR) (2004)
30. Senin, P.: Dynamic time warping algorithm review, Honolulu, USA (2008)
31. Shafer, G.: A mathematical theory of evidence, vol. 1. Princeton University Press, Princeton (1976)
32. Starrs, P., Chohan, A., Fewtrell, D., Richards, J., Selfe, J.: Biomechanical differences between experienced and inexperienced wheelchair users during sport. Prosthetics and Orthotics International **36**(3), 324–331 (2012)
33. Tautges, J., Krüger, B., Zinke, A., Weber, A.: Reconstruction of human motions using few sensors
34. Wang, S., Yang, J., Chen, N., Chen, X., Zhang, Q.: Human activity recognition with user-free accelerometers in the sensor networks. In: International Conference on Neural Networks and Brain, ICNN B (2005)
35. Wu, H., Siegel, M., Stiefelhagen, R., Yang, J.: Sensor fusion using dempster-shafer theory [for context-aware hci]. In: Proceedings of the 19th IEEE Instrumentation and Measurement Technology Conference, IMTC 2002, vol. 1, pp. 7–12. IEEE (2002)

Incremental Learning of Hand Gestures Based on Submovement Sharing

Ryo Kawahata[1]($\boxtimes$), Yanrung Wang[1], Atsushi Shimada[2],
Takayoshi Yamashita[3], and Rin-ichiro Taniguchi[4]

[1] Graduate School of Information Science and Electrical Engineering,
Kyushu University, Fukuoka, Japan
[2] Faculty of Arts and Science, Kyushu University, Fukuoka, Japan
[3] Department of Computer Science, College of Engineering,
Chubu University, Aichi, Japan
[4] Faculty of Information Science and Electrical Engineering,
Kyushu University, Fukuoka, Japan
{kawahata,kenyou,atsushi,rin}@limu.ait.kyushu-u.ac.jp,
yamashita@cs.chubu.ac.jp

Abstract. This paper presents an incremental learning method for hand gesture recognition that learns the individual movements in each gesture of a user. To recognize the movement, we use a subunit-based dynamic time warping method, which treats a hand movement as a sequence of ubmovements. In our method, each hand movement is decomposed into submovements and the arrangement of submovements is reflected in the training sample database. Experimental results from the lassification of ten gestures demonstrate that our method can improve the recognition rate compared with a method without incremental learning. In addition, the experimental results show that incremental learning of a single class of gestures can improve the recognition rate of multi-class gestures using our method.

Keywords: Incremental learning · Hand gestures · Subunit movement · Dynamic time warping · Gesture recognition

1 Introduction

As the use of computers becomes more widespread in society, natural human-computer interaction (HCI) becomes more important for ease of use. There has been considerable interest in HCI regarding intuitive approaches for operating devices. Vision based hand gesture recognition is a worthwhile research area in this field [1].

In hand gesture recognition, features such as appearance, shape, and movement are often important elements. In this paper, we focus on recognition of the movement trajectories among them.

© Springer International Publishing Switzerland 2014
A. Campilho and M. Kamel (Eds.): ICIAR 2014, Part II, LNCS 8815, pp. 58–65, 2014.
DOI: 10.1007/978-3-319-11755-3_7

Dynamic time warping (DTW) [2] and hidden Markov models [3] are widely used to recognize movement trajectories. DTW is a nonparametric method and measures the similarity between two temporal sequences, which may differ in time. DTW uses information about training samples and attempts to match them one by one. Therefore, the greater the number of training samples is, and hence the better the recognition rate is, the longer the time needed for recognition.

To address this issue, a subunit-based DTW method [4] has been proposed. Subunits have been extensively investigated in the field of sign language [5] [6]. The subunit method shares common submovements (subunits) across hand gestures to obtain a smaller training data set and then searches the space to improve recognition performance. As a result, subunit-based DTW can shorten recognition time yet still achieve a high recognition rate. However, there are still some remaining issues that need to be solved; for example, how to generalize the subunit-based method for any user and how to create a sufficiently large hand gesture database.

In this paper, we propose an incremental learning method for subunit-based hand gestures to address the above issues. Incremental learning is generally considered a good solution to improve the performance of a recognition system [7]. In terms of hand gesture recognition systems, it can tune the hand gesture database to fit the individual's gestures. Therefore, each user acquires his/her own hand gesture database through the proposed incremental learning system.

The rest of the paper is organized as follows. We introduce the subunit-based hand gesture recognition method in Section 2, while in Section 3 we present the proposed incremental learning approach. In Section 4, we present the experimental results followed by a discussion and our conclusions.

2   Subunit-Based Hand Gesture Recognition

This section gives an overview of the subunit-based DTW method, which forms the basis of our proposed method. This method shares a submovement (subunit) between gestures and interprets gestures as an arrangement of subunits. Compared with the conventional DTW method, subunit-based DTW is resistant to local variations and can shorten recognition time because it only relies on the similarity between subunits at the time of recognition.

The subunit-based DTW method treats each hand movement as a sequence of digits between 0 and 7 according to the orientation features as shown in Fig. 1. This codeword is divided into subsequences, called submovements, when the orientation changes suddenly and differs from the initial direction.

Fig. 2 depicts a flow chart of the subunit-based DTW method.

In the training phase, the subunit-based DTW method creates a database consisting of subunits and subunit sequences as shown in Fig. 2. Submovements are gathered from training samples and clustered based on the similarity measured by DTW. Representative submovements in the clusters are called subunits. Submovements can be replaced by subunits belonging to the same clusters and as a result, training samples are represented by subunit sequences.

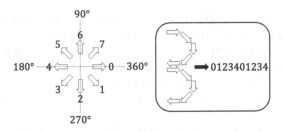

Fig. 1. Orientation codewords and an example of movement representation using these codewords

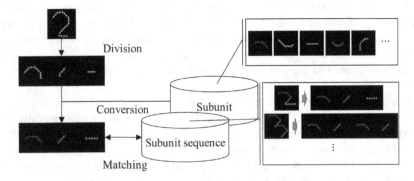

Fig. 2. Flow chart of the subunit-based DTW method

In the testing phase, a testing sample is decomposed and expressed as a subunit sequence in the same way as in the training phase. The obtained subunit sequence is then matched with the subunit sequences in the database. Recognition performance is thus, dependent on the number of subunit sequences in the database.

3   Incremental Learning of Subunit Sequences

In our proposed method, subunit sequences obtained from users are reflected in a database comprising training samples. Moreover, since our method uses continuous subsequences in subunit sequences, it is able to learn multiple motions from a single motion by identifying subunit subsequences that are shared by the motions.

3.1   Preliminary Experiment

Before explaining the proposed idea, we reiterate the research issues. A hand gesture database should be versatile in terms of changing environments, many different types of users, and so on. One of the ways of creating such a database is to collect as many training samples as possible under different conditions and from a variety of users. However, this increases the size of the database and results in greater computational cost of recognition, which is undesirable in real-time applications.

On the other hand, an incremental learning strategy is a principled way if a user can accept the initialization process before using the system. In the pre-training phase, the system learns a minimal sized training set. Then, the trained database is updated through the process of incremental learning to suit the current situation and user.

There are two possible strategies to update the database. One is to update both the subunits and subunit sequences, and the other is to update the subunit sequences only. From the viewpoint of computational cost, we have decided to employ the latter strategy in the proposed method. Before the main experiments, we have conducted a preliminary experiment to investigate whether the proposed strategy is reasonable or not.

The results of our preliminary investigation of incremental learning, shown in Fig. 3. In the investigation, we examined changes in the recognition rate while subunit sequences were continually added to the database. The horizontal axis denotes the number of subjects used to create the hand gesture database. As the number of subjects increased, so the recognition rate also increased. Note, however, that the size of the database also increases over time. The most important observation is that recognition accuracy improves using incremental learning even with a small database. This indicates not only the usefulness of incremental learning but also the configuration of incremental learning, where we do not have to pay considerable attention to subunits in the original database.

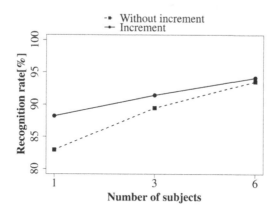

Fig. 3. Preliminary experimental results of incremental learning

3.2 Idea of Incremental Learning

The results of the preliminary investigation also confirmed that the alignment of subunits is an important aspect of incremental learning. Therefore, the proposed method uses subunit subsequences for incremental learning.

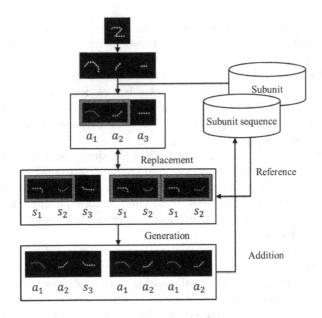

Fig. 4. Example of incremental learning

The proposed method substitutes subunit subsequences in test samples with those in the training samples. Let us consider the simple example shown in Fig. 4.

First, a subunit sequence (a_1, a_2, a_3) obtained from an input sample is decomposed into subsequences. Second, subunit sequences (s_1, s_2, s_3) and (s_1, s_2, s_1, s_2), which include the subsequence (s_1, s_2) similar to the obtained one (a_1, a_2), are selected as candidates for incremental learning from the database. Note that subsequence (s_1, s_2) is not always a member of a single class. It can also be shared by several gesture classes, in which case our incremental learning strategy propagates the new subsequence into several classes simultaneously. Third, occurrences of subsequence (s_1, s_2) in the candidate subunit sequences are replaced by (a_1, a_2) and finally, the new subunit sequences (a_1, a_2, s_3) and (a_1, a_2, a_1, a_2) are incrementally added to the database with class labels (s_1, s_2, s_3) and (s_1, s_2, s_1, s_2), respectively.

4   Experiments and Discussion

4.1   Dataset and Experimental Configuration

We performed several evaluations to investigate the effectiveness of the proposed method. First, we compared the proposed method with the original subunit-based hand gesture recognition, i.e., without the incremental learning strategy. The samples used contained ten different classes (see Fig. 5) of hand movement trajectories from a laboratory environment. Each of the ten classes of trajectories was repeated 25 times by each subject. We divided the subjects into two groups:

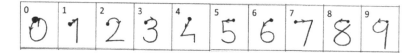

Fig. 5. Ten different hand gesture classes used in the experiments

three subjects for training and four subjects for incremental learning and testing. For each of the four subjects, 15 samples were used for incremental learning.

4.2   Class Dependence

In this evaluation, we investigated the positive and negative effects when using one gesture class for incremental learning. The proposed method uses subunit subsequences obtained from input samples. However, the subsequences vary according to the motion classes, and therefore, it seems that the effect of incremental learning also differs between motion classes.

Table 1. Recognition rates after incremental learning of each class independently

Incremental Class	Recognition rate						
	0	2	3	4	6	8	9
0	↑ 96.67%	95.00%	95.00%	↓ 95.00%	71.67%	↑ 98.33%	83.33%
1	93.33%	95.00%	95.00%	96.67%	71.67%	95.00%	83.33%
2	93.33%	95.00%	↑ 96.67%	96.67%	71.67%	↑ 96.67%	83.33%
3	93.33%	↑ 98.33%	↓ 93.33%	96.67%	71.67%	↑ 96.67%	83.33%
4	93.33%	95.00%	95.00%	96.67%	71.67%	95.00%	↑ 85.00%
5	93.33%	↑ 96.67%	95.00%	96.67%	↑ 73.33%	↑ 98.33%	83.33%
6	93.33%	95.00%	95.00%	96.67%	↓ 61.67%	95.00%	↓ 80.00%
7	93.33%	95.00%	95.00%	96.67%	71.67%	95.00%	83.33%
8	93.33%	↓ 93.33%	95.00%	96.67%	↑ 73.33%	↑ 96.67%	83.33%
9	↑ 96.67%	95.00%	95.00%	96.67%	↓ 68.33%	↑ 96.67%	83.33%
	93.33%	95.00%	95.00%	96.67%	71.67%	95.00%	83.33%

Table 1 shows the average recognition rates after incremental learning and the bottom of the table indicates the recognition rates without incremental learning. We report the results of classes 0, 2, 3, 4, 6, 8 and 9 only, since the recognition rates of the other classes were unchanged. The up- and down-arrows in the table denote that the recognition rate increased/decreased, respectively, after incremental learning. For example, when class 0 was used for incremental learning, the recognition rates of classes 0 and 8 improved. Improved results were also obtained from the incremental learning of classes 2, 4, and 5. Meanwhile, class 6 gave negative results for several classes. These results suggest that we should pay careful attention to the selection of gesture classes used for incremental learning.

We used samples from classes 2, 4, and 5 for incremental learning based on the results of the above experiment and investigated the recognition rate.

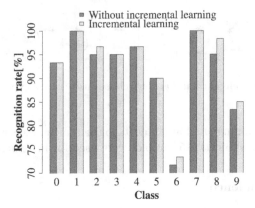

Fig. 6. Comprehensive recognition accuracy of the proposed incremental learning strategy

Fig. 6 shows the results of the investigation. Recognition performance improved markedly compared with using a single class of samples.

Next, we discuss the reason for a decrease in recognition rate. Our proposed method substitutes motions locally between classes; it changes one class into another depending on the similarity of the class, for instance, 0, 6, and 9 as shown Fig. 7. Fig. 8 illustrates an example of a change in class. The beginning of motion 0 is replaced and the motion appears similar to motion 6. As a result, the deformed motion is given a label 0 and causes false recognition of motion 6. To cope with this problem, subunit subsequence substitution should be done under high similarity.

Fig. 7. Example of motions 0, 6, and 9

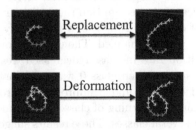

Fig. 8. Appearance of changing class

5 Conclusion

This paper proposed an incremental learning method for subunit-based hand gesture recognition. Our proposed method uses subunit subsequences for incremental learning and reflects the user's motion in a database. The investigation on the effectiveness of the proposed strategy showed that incremental learning of gestures of a single class can improve the recognition rate of multi-class gestures using our method. The investigation also showed that the proposed method is available only for subunit subsequences. In our future work, we intend applying the proposed idea to incremental learning independent of the class of input samples.

References

1. Rautaray, S.S., Agrawal, A.: Vision based hand gesture recognition for human computer interaction: survey. Springer Science+Business Media Dordrecht (2012)
2. Okada, S., Hasegawa, O.: Motion recognition based on dynamic-time warping method with self-organizing incremental neural network. In: The 19th International Conference on Pattern Recognition, pp. 1–4 (2008)
3. Elmezain, M., Al-Hamadi, A., Michaelis, B.: Real-time capable system for hand gesture recognition using hidden Markov models in stereo color image sequences. Journal of WSCG, 65–72 (2008)
4. Wang, Y., Shimada, A., Yamasita, T., Taniguchi, R.: A subunit-based dynamic time warping approach for hand movement recognition. In: Petrosino, A. (ed.) ICIAP 2013, Part I. LNCS, vol. 8156, pp. 672–681. Springer, Heidelberg (2013)
5. Roussos, A., Theodorakis, S., Pitsikalis, V., Maragos, P.: Hand tracking and affine shape-appearance handshape sub-units in continuous sign language recognition. In: Kutulakos, K.N. (ed.) ECCV 2010 Workshops, Part I. LNCS, vol. 6553, pp. 258–272. Springer, Heidelberg (2012)
6. Bauer, B., Kraiss, K.-F.: Towards an automatic sign language recognition system using subunits. In: Wachsmuth, I., Sowa, T. (eds.) GW 2001. LNCS (LNAI), vol. 2298, pp. 64–75. Springer, Heidelberg (2002)
7. Giraud-Carrier, C.: A note on the utility of incremental learning. AI Communications **13**(4), 215–223 (2000)

Gait Analysis from Video:
Camcorders vs. Kinect

Hoang Anh Nguyen[✉] and Jean Meunier

University of Montreal, Montréal, QC, Canada
{nguyenha,meunier}@iro.umontreal.ca
http://diro.umontreal.ca/

Abstract. Gait analysis is a domain of interest in clinical medical practice, both for neurological and non-neurological abnormal troubles. Marker-based systems are the most favored methods of human motion assessment and gait analysis, however, these systems require specific equipment and expertise and are cumbersome, costly and difficult to use. In this paper we compare two low-cost and marker-less systems that are: (1) A Kinect in front of a treadmill and (2) a set of two camcorders on the sides of the treadmill, used to reconstruct the skeleton of a subject during walk. We validated our method with ground truth data obtained with markers manually placed on the subject's body. Finally, we present an application for asymmetric gait recognition. Our results on different subjects showed that, compared to the Kinect, the two-camcorder approach was very efficient and provided accurate measurements for gait assessment.

1 Introduction

Current methods for precise measurement of human movement usually involve complex systems requiring a dedicated laboratory and trained specialist. These systems can be subdivided into two main classes: Marker-based and Marker-free systems.

Marker-based systems are still the most favoured methods of human motion assessment and gait analysis. Essentially, markers (acoustic, inertial, LED, magnetic or reflective) are placed on the body and tracked to measure the human motion. An example of such system is the popular motion capture system Vicon[1]. However, these systems require specific equipment and expertise and are cumbersome and difficult to use. Despite these drawbacks these systems are accurate and mature and remain the gold standard for human motion assessment and gait analysis and are available in the market.

Marker-free systems constitute an interesting alternative but are still in development within research groups. The structure of such system can be summarized as follows. Typically, an appropriate model of the subject must be established (skeleton, cylinders, ellipsoids etc.). Next the motion of the subject (model) is

---

[1] http://www.vicon.com/

© Springer International Publishing Switzerland 2014
A. Campilho and M. Kamel (Eds.): ICIAR 2014, Part II, LNCS 8815, pp. 66–73, 2014.
DOI: 10.1007/978-3-319-11755-3_8

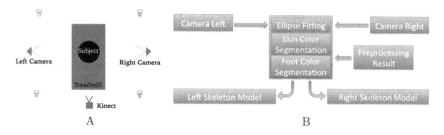

A   B

Fig. 1. (A) Our system consists of one treadmill and two camcorders on the left and right of the treadmill. Four light sources were placed at four corner to assure good light diffusion. (B) Work-flow of our system. The processing on each camera is treated independently resulting in left and right skeleton models, see [5] for more details.

tracked. This usually implies a way of segmenting the subject from the background and finding correspondences between segments in the following frames. Then the 3D pose of the subject's body needs to be estimated usually with a priori knowledge from a human model. With multi-camera systems, depth ambiguities are alleviated but at a higher computational cost. The final step analyzes the pose or other parameters for gait analysis, human identification or to recognize the actions performed by the subject. Generally these systems are not completely automated and require several measurements of the subject and/or manual intervention at various stages in order to work properly.

Another more recent direction of research has dealt with color-depth cameras (or RGB-D cameras). In a depth image each pixel indicates depth in the scene, rather than only a measure of intensity or color. This depth information can be obtained with different sensors: stereo camera, time-of-flight camera or structured light camera (e.g. Microsoft Kinect). However, to develop a low cost, reliable and easy-to-install system, the Kinect sensor is currently the best solution to obtain depth images. Moreover, the human pose method proposed by Shotton et al. [2,3] represents the state of the art for color-depth cameras and is implemented in the Microsoft Kinect system [4]. It computes the subject's pose using machine learning techniques with local 3D shape descriptors. The accuracy of the Kinect's calculations seems reasonable for gait analysis and was successfully used in [7,8,9] for instance. But the Kinect suffers problems due to hardware limitations: rather high price, very limited field of view (about $57.8°$), limited range (about from $0.2m$ to $4 - 5m$), low video resolution (640×480), noisy depth image, limited precision (e.g. 40mm at 2m from the sensor [6]), etc. causing not very consistent results, especially on the lower limbs. Furthermore, a disadvantage of the front view provided by the Kinect is the appearance of body part occlusion during a gait cycle that might lead to incorrect pose estimation results.

The two-camcorder system is an extension of the work from Courtney et al. [1], in which they estimate half body structure from side view. However, this system and other one-camera-based side-view systems suffer from one important limitation: they can only watch one side at a time, making it impossible to compute the symmetry of a gait. This is why we used a set of two camcorders on both sides of the treadmill as described in section 2. We show, compare and validate our reconstruction results in section 3 with comparisons to the Kinect sensor and a marker-based method used as ground truth, and finally conclude our work in section 4.

2   Methodology

2.1   Overview

For the best gait assessment, accuracy information of the pose and a sufficiently long time of evaluation are crucial. With that ultimate aim, we propose to use a treadmill and two monocular cameras placed on the left and right side of that treadmill as shown in Fig. 1(A) and compare the results with a Kinect placed in front. An advantage of letting the subject walk on a treadmill is to keep him/her relatively stationary to the camera point of view and thus help us to be almost immune to ambiguity issues which are a problem for systems in which the subject walks in a corridor back and forth. Each camcorder in our system is responsible for capturing the movement of its corresponding half body over time. In essence, we focus on estimating 2.5D pose information (two profile views but each view is 2D only) which will be used to calculate the left and right gait patterns. We are interested in criteria during a cycle of gait such as the angle variation of left body parts vs their counter parts (at elbow, knee and foot). To perform calculation on these characteristics, we find that placing the camera on the side of the subject can assure that we have a clear, occlusion-free view of each half body, and sufficient information to perform a thorough analysis. Furthermore, we argue that, if calculating the criteria above is the ultimate aim, there are little differences between a 2D pose and a 3D pose from the side point of view of a gait. This observation leads us to only reconstruct two (left and right) 2D human poses and thus much simplifies the process.

In the gait analysis domain, the correct location of leg and foot is on top priority. In the camcorder system, we propose a very simple way to quickly and efficiently detect and track each foot by requiring to wear left and right socks of different colors. This simple constraint guarantees the stable and high accuracy detection rate of foot. Another constraint is that the subject has to wear a short-sleeve T-shirt to expose the skin color as much as possible on which our arm reconstruction is based. Fig. 1(B) demonstrates the workflow of our system: in the preprocessing step, we calculate and store the global skin and each foot color models. Videos from each camcorder (left and right) are treated separately and similarly in order to construct the left and right skeleton model as follows: we use our own improved eclipse fitting technique [5] to estimate the head and torso orientation. The forehead, neck, shoulder and hip are deduced using anthropometry data [12]. The location of each foot is known based on its special color information, combining with the known hip joint and leg joint lengths gives us the correct location of the knee. In a similar manner, the skin

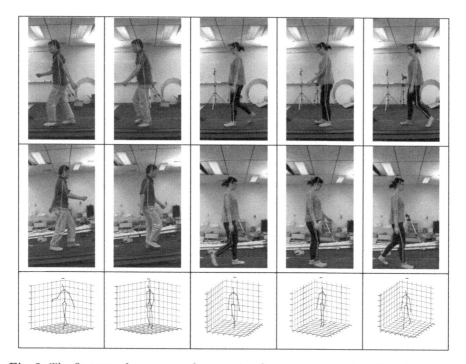

Fig. 2. The first row shows some of our testing frames captured from the left camera, the second row shows their corresponding frames from the right camera. Red lines indicated the ground-truth formed by red markers placed on the subject's body, our pose estimation produced the green lines and green ellipses. The third row shows the 3D skeleton from the Kinect SDK.

information helps us isolate the lower arm and small portion of the upper arm. We then sample points along the lower arm and apply line fitting to locate the hand and elbow. The upper arm orientation is finally estimated using a particle filter [5]. For evaluation, we aim to compare the gait characteristics calculated from our 2.5D skeleton models and the full 3D skeleton using the Kinect SDK, which we consider the marker-less state-of-the-art until now. For more details on the two-camera system, the reader can consult [5].

2.2 Asymmetry Index

Our ultimate aim is to clearly quantify the asymmetry between the left and right body parts in order to facilitate the gait assessment afterward. We experimentally observed that the curve which reflects the angle change at some interesting joints (such as knee, elbow, ankle, etc.) look similar (but out of phase) between the left side and their right counter part, in case of normal walk. But that is not the case if the subject walks abnormally in which either left or right joints produce different patterns. We hence propose a measure that allows quantifying this asymmetry value, we called it asymmetry index. This value will be updated

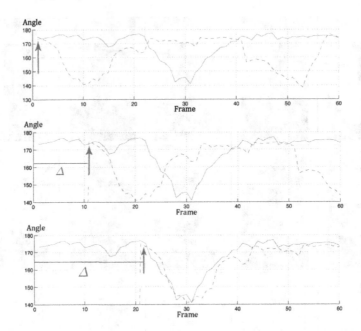

Fig. 3. From top to bottom, we shift the right knee angle curve (dash blue curve) while the left knee (red curve) remains stationary by increasing Δ. The bottom graphs gives the lowest error δ used as asymmetry index.

every some time T which is equivalent to one cycle of walk to constantly reflect abnormal changes of the index as they happens. Every T seconds ($T = 2$ seconds in our experiments), since the left and right steps are out of phase, we firstly need to align the left and right curves measured from left and right joints (knee, elbow, ankle, etc.) to minimize the error δ and obtain the asymmetry index δ as follows

$$\delta = \min_{0 \leq \Delta \leq T} \sum_{i=t_0}^{t_0+T} \frac{R(i+\Delta) - L(i)}{T} \tag{1}$$

where R represents the right curve, L represents the left curve and t_0 is the current time. Keeping L stationary, we start moving R along the timeline, using equation 1 to obtain the minimum error δ which is the asymmetric index of the gait for this period. Fig. 3 illustrates this minimization process for the knee joint.

3   Experimentation and Discussion

The ultimate aim of our test is to perform the asymmetry assessment on two different subjects using our system versus Kinect. We chose JVC camcorders (model GZ-HD6U) as our two monocular cameras. We also placed the Kinect in front of the treadmill (distance about 2 meters) to acquire the 3D pose, see Fig. 1(A). The frame synchronization of our cameras with Kinect was done by

Markers   Camcorders   Kinect

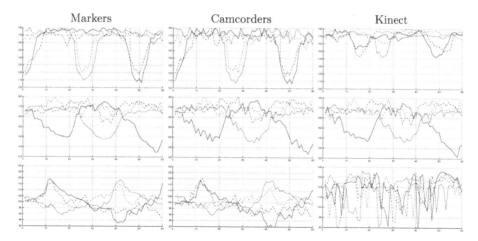

Fig. 4. Solid red and dash red lines represent the angle change at left joints for normal and abnormal cases respectively within a gait cycle. Solid blue and dash blue lines represent the angle change at right joints for normal and abnormal cases respectively during a gait cycle. The first, second and third rows show the angle changes at knee, elbow and ankle in that order. In case of abnormal walk, the dash lines demonstrate clearly the symmetry broken between left and right parts.

turning off and on again after one second the light to produce a sudden image brightness drop and rise. The videos from the Kinect (RGB data) and left/right cameras were then aligned temporally according to the image mean brightness changes. The ground truth was obtained by tracking red stickers put on subject's joints as shown in Fig. 2. Each subject was asked to walk in three different manners: normal walk, shorter-stride-length of the left leg and shorter-stride-length of the right leg. Once the pose was estimated from our system, from the Kinect SDK [6] and from markers, we started calculating the gait characteristics, explained in Section 2, on these three skeletons. In Fig. 4, we present the joint angle change curve at knee, elbow and ankle acquired from left and right parts of the three skeletons described above in both normal and abnormal cases. Our camcorder method outperformed Kinect at knee and ankle while was competitive with the Kinect at the elbow joint, see Fig. 4.

In our experimentation on both subjects, the asymmetry indexes on knee, elbow, ankle from normal cases were significantly smaller than that from the abnormal cases, see Table 1 (Camcorders). Our asymmetric quantization were consistently close to that from ground truth (shown in Table 1 (Markers)) at all three joints while the Kinect failed at knee and ankle (shown in Table 1 (Kinect)) since there were no obvious difference between normal and abnormal gait. This result leads us to an interesting asymmetry index, see Section 2.2, when classifying normal and abnormal gait. This index is deduced relatively to the gait characteristics of each individual, and thus allows an easy intra-subject assessment of gait at each time of a step.

Table 1. Asymmetry index (degrees) with the markers (ground truth), the camcorders and the Kinect on both subjects 1 and 2

Asymmetry Index (degrees) of subject 1								
	Markers			Camcorders			Kinect		
	Knee	Elbow	Ankle	Knee	Elbow	Ankle	Knee	Elbow	Ankle
Normal	7.64	6.29	5.29	8.97	7.95	7.33	10.58	7.43	26.76
Left Asymmetry	14.34	26.06	9.76	13.86	24.76	13.30	11.94	27.44	27.76
Right Asymmetry	12.51	28.99	11.05	13.48	29.50	12.62	13.61	27.70	22.76

Asymmetry Index (degrees) of subject 2								
	Markers			Camcorders			Kinect		
	Knee	Elbow	Ankle	Knee	Elbow	Ankle	Knee	Elbow	Ankle
Normal	5.99	4.31	5.32	6.63	7.38	5.04	11.12	5.94	22.45
Left Asymmetry	12.13	18.54	10.66	15.24	20.85	13.87	14.57	19.69	19.38
Right Asymmetry	10.72	32.03	9.93	12.04	23.26	14.07	15.68	23.82	24.03

We plan to further test our method on a sufficiently large number of subjects so that we can more precisely define which gait is normal with the help of appropriate angle thresholds at knee, elbow and ankle joints. In this study, a treadmill was used in order to have a relatively constant position of the subject relative to the camcorders/Kinect to facilitate measurements of several gait cycles. Thus, it restricts the use of the method to treadmill walking compared to other approaches based on a walkway. However a camcorder system could be easily developed for walkway gait analysis (with an appropriate perspective view rectification (e.g. [11]), which is not true for the Kinect that has a limited operating range.

Notice that a full 3D skeleton reconstruction could also be possible with the camcorder system at the cost of a more complex strategy based on known limb length, camera calibration and a pose estimation methodology such as [10].

4   Conclusion

In this paper we have presented a simple gait analysis system consisting of two cameras placed on the left and right sides of a treadmill with comparisons to the Kinect and a marker-based method used as ground truth. The results were very promising since the skeleton model was fully reconstructed with good accuracy and stability compared to the Kinect giving more exact information to experts for analyzing gait. We also have presented a simple method to quantify gait asymmetry with a simple index. The camcorder method only uses two camera on each side of a subject walking on a treadmill and does not need markers or sensors placed over the body. In addition to screening, this method could enable clinicians to make a follow-up of patients after a surgery or a treatment such as joint replacement or to measure recovery after stroke. The resulting system is low-cost and easy-to-use, which offers a promising tool for a wide range of applications in a clinical protocol.

Acknowledgments. The authors wish to thank Edouard Auvinet for helpful discussion on gait analysis and his assistance for the experimental setup. This work was supported by the Natural Sciences and Engineering Research Council of Canada (NSERC).

References

1. Courtney, J., de Paor, A.M.: A Monocular Marker-Free Gait Measurement System. IEEE Transactions on Neural systems and Rehabilitation Engineering **18**(4) (August 2010)
2. Shotton, J., Fitzgibbon, A., Cook, M., Sharp, T., Finocchio, M., Moore, R., Kipman, A., Blake, A.: Real-time human pose recognition in parts from a single depth image. In: Computer Vision and Pattern Recognition (CVPR) (2011)
3. Sun, M., Kohli, P., Shotton, J.: Conditional regression forests for human pose estimation. In: Computer Vision and Pattern Recognition (CVPR) (2012)
4. Kinect for Window software development kit, http://www.microsoft.com/en-us/kinectforwindowsdev
5. Nguyen, H.A., Meunier, J.: Video-based analysis of gait with side views. Image Processing Theory, Tools and Application, Paris (accepted 2014)
6. Windolf, M., Gtzen, N., Morlock, M.: Systematic accuracy and precision analysis of video motion capturing systems on the vicon-460 system. Journal of Biomechanics **41**(12) (2008)
7. Gabel, M., Gilad-Bachrach, R., Renshaw, E., Schuster, A.: Full Body Gait Analysis with Kinect. In: Int. Conf. IEEE Engineering in Medicine and Biology Society, San Diego (August 2012)
8. Stone, E., Skubic, M.: Evaluation of an Inexpensive Depth Camera for In-Home Gait Assessment. Journal of Ambient Intelligence and Smart Environments **3**(4), 349–361 (2011)
9. Stone, E., Skubic, M.: Unobtrusive, Continuous, In-HomeGait Measurement Using the Microsoft Kinect. IEEE Transactions on Biomedical Engineering **60**(10), 2925–2932 (2013)
10. Nguyen, H.A., Meunier, J.: Reconstructing 3D human poses from monocular image. In: International Conference on Information Science, Signal Processing and Their Applications, Canada (2012)
11. Jean, F., Bergevin, R., Branzan-Albu, A.: Human gait characteristics from unconstrained walks and viewpoints. In: Proceedings of the International Conference on Computer Vision Workshops, Barcelona, Spain, November 6–13, pp. 1883–1888 (2011)
12. Ceriez, E., Motmans, R.: Anthropometry table, Technical Report, Leuven, Belgium (2005)

Biometrics

Person Re-identification Using Region Covariance in a Multi-feature Approach

Volker Eiselein[(✉)], Gleb Sternharz, Tobias Senst, Ivo Keller,
and Thomas Sikora

Communication Systems Group, Technische Universität Berlin, Berlin, Germany
eiselein@nue.tu-berlin.de

Abstract. Person re-identification is an important requirement for
modern video surveillance systems and relevant for human tracking, especially over camera networks. Many different approaches have been proposed but a robust identification under real-life conditions still remains
hard. In this paper we investigate the fusion of multiple person descriptors in order to increase the performance using complementary feature
vectors. As an additional improvement to state-of-the-art region covariance descriptors, an extension of the comparison metric is proposed
which increases the robustness and performance of the system in cases
of rank deficiency. The proposed system is evaluated on the well-known
benchmarks CAVIAR4REID, VIPeR, ETHZ and PRID 2011 and shows
significant improvements over existing re-identification algorithms.

Keywords: Person re-identification · Region covariance · Surf ·
Information fusion · Color · Histogram · Covariance metric ·
Generalized · Eigenvalues

1 Introduction

Person re-identification is an important task in surveillance applications. Especially in multi-camera environments and for forensic search, a robust and accurate person description is a key aspect. For modern surveillance systems, semantic interpretation is also an often desired feature and the ability to identify if
an individual is perceived by the system for the first time or is re-appearing can
help to extract semantic information (e.g. for loitering detection etc.).

Person re-identification methods can be divided into methods based on point
feature descriptors (e.g. [1] [2]) and methods extracting appearance information
for an image patch within a region of interest. The first class uses local features
such as "Speeded Up Robust Features" (SURF) [3] in order to extract significant information from an object. Points and their respective features are then
compared with known matching candidates, and the final match is computed
by a majority vote over all points found. For quick comparisons and a fast ID
retrieval, the authors of [1] propose a k-d tree to store the feature vectors. In [2],

© Springer International Publishing Switzerland 2014
A. Campilho and M. Kamel (Eds.): ICIAR 2014, Part II, LNCS 8815, pp. 77–84, 2014.
DOI: 10.1007/978-3-319-11755-3_9

this method is refined with the least absolute shrinkage and selection operator (LASSO) performing a regression on the model and query feature vectors.

To extract information from an image patch, color histograms [4] are widely used since they have a low computational complexity, but they can perform poorly under low resolution and noise. Region covariance has been introduced in [5] as a way of compressing the spatial distribution of image features in a single descriptor and has since found much attention in the scientific community.

Choosing the right feature vector can be a difficult task among multiple datasets. In [6] the authors propose extracting a large number of features from the image and applying machine learning to find the metric maximizing the distance between known object models and a newly appearing ID.

In this paper we provide an evelution of region covariance for person re-identification and compare it to histogram- and SURF-based methods. In order to deal with rank-deficiency issues, we propose a new scheme for full-rank reduction of covariance matrices. Finally, we fuse these basic features in a system with increased re-identification performance. For the choice of suitable features and configurations for region covariance, we performed extensive tests and evaluate our system on four well-known datasets which cover different use cases and scenarios. An outlook to future work concludes the paper.

2   Multi-feature Person Re-identification Framework

Given a query image of a person, our goal is to find the best matching candidate from a list of known person models. Therefore, we propose to use three individual methods which exploit different image features ideally resulting in complementary information:

Color Histograms have been introduced in [4] and give an estimate of the color value distribution within a given patch. They are quickly computable and especially suited for scenarios with good contrast and lighting conditions. To extract the overall descriptor, we divide the region of interest into a set of areas and concatenate their histograms. The scores and the final person match are found by ranking the different models according to the L^1 distance.

Point feature descriptors according to [1] based on SURF [3] are extracted from the query image and, in contrast to color histograms, represent image gradients. For each descriptor, a nearest neighbour search in a k-d tree is performed and yields a set of candidate IDs. Candidate scores are then computed by a normalized vote for all feature points and known IDs. The ranking score is thus based on the maximal number of IDs assigned to the extracted feature.

The region covariance descriptor was firstly presented in [5] and incorporates color, spatial and gradient information in a given region of interest. It can be computed quickly using integral images. Similar as for the color histogram, scores and final person match are given by a ranking according to a non-euclidean distance based on the generalized eigenvalues of two covariance matrices [7].

As a result for a given query, three different matching scores are obtained for all person models known. The algorithms used are at least partially complementary and can thus be fused in order to increase the overall system performance.

For this purpose, a normalization of the scores and a fusion using weighted superposition are proposed.

Score normalization should be used in order to map the score ranges and distributions of all individual person descriptors onto a common space. This is especially important for region covariance because its feature vector lies on a nonlinear space and needs to be normalized. Score normalization in our approach is based on vector unity.

3   Region Covariance Descriptor with Full-Rank Reduction

As covariance matrices do not lie in Euclidean space, a special metric is necessary for feature comparison. Förstner *et al.* [7] proposed the following formula based on generalized eigenvalues to compute the distance between two covariance matrices C_1, C_2 of dimension d

$$d(C_1, C_2) = \sqrt{\sum_{i=1}^{d} ln^2(\lambda_i(C_1, C_2))} \tag{1}$$

where λ_i represents the $i - th$ generalized eigenvalue. Intuitively, this metric computes how the ellipsoid represented by C_1 must be shrinked or stretched in each dimension in order to be mapped onto the ellipsoid given by C_2.

However, there are problems when one of the matrices is not full-rank. Rank-deficiency is especially bad for evaluation when it occurs in a query matrix. In this case all known person models will be compared to a rank-deficient matrix resulting in at least one generalized eigenvalue being 0 or infinity. The distance in this case will be infinity for all models and it remains unclear which ID assignment would be better.

3.1   Rank Deficiency Issues

As shown above, rank deficiency is not desirable at it introduces randomness into the evaluation. Ideally there should be small differences in the assigned metric values between different model matrices, so in the evaluation a systematic assignment will be perceivable. But especially for larger matrices, rank deficiency is not seldom and has a negative impact on the system's performance. Tuzel *et al.* proposed in [8] to ignore these cases and just add a small identity matrix to the computed covariance matrix but this effectively changes the feature vectors and it has to be decided from case to case how small the weight for the identity matrix should be. We thus propose the algorithm in Listing 1 in order to reduce two covariance matrices to their rank and maintain the same features for comparison in both of them.

The idea behind the algorithm is to systematically build up a full-rank matrix by adding row after row and keeping track of the row indices which have been sorted out due to collinearity. Suppose, two matrices C_1 and C_2 of dimension 7×7 are to be compared, and the linearly independent rows of C_1 are $L_1 = \{1, 2, 3, 5, 6\}$ and $L_2 = \{1, 2, 3, 4, 6\}$ for C_2. The union of both sets $L_1 \cap L_2$ indicates which features will be present in the resulting matrices, and the missing rows in this set have to be removed from both matrices in order to keep the same features in both matrices. The resulting full-rank matrices will thus be composed by the rows and columns of indices $\{1, 2, 3, 6\}$.

Algorithm 1. Scheme for reduction to full-rank

```
 1: procedure REDUCE(C₁, C₂)
 2:     removedDims₁ ← {}, removedDims₂ ← {}, C₁reduced ← [], C₂reduced ← []
 3:     i ← 0
 4:     while (i < rows(C₁)) do
 5:         if hasFullRank([ C₁reduced / row(C₁,i) ]) then C₁reduced ← [ C₁reduced / row(C₁,i) ]
 6:         else
 7:             push_back(removedDims₁, i)
 8:         i ← i + 1
 9:     i ← 0
10:     while (i < rows(C₂)) do
11:         if hasFullRank([ C₂reduced / row(C₂,i) ]) then C₂reduced ← [ C₂reduced / row(C₂,i) ]
12:         else
13:             push_back(removedDims₂, i)
14:         i ← i + 1
15:     if removedDims₂ ≠ removedDims₁ then
16:         removeDims(C₁reduced, removedDims₂)
17:         removeDims(C₂reduced, removedDims₁)
```

It should be noted that apart from [7], there exists another metric to compare covariance matrices [9] but as it relies on matrix square root computation, the same issues apply in case of rank-deficient covariance matrices. Nonetheless, our proposed adaptation will also work for this metric.

3.2 Feature Configuration for Region Covariance

Region covariance as proposed in the baseline paper [5] uses a feature vector comprising x- and y-coordinate, RGB values and the magnitudes of first and second intensity derivatives in x- and y direction. In [10], the authors propose a 11-dimensional feature vector composed by point coordinates and intensity values, gradient magnitude and orientation in the R,G and B channel. Other publications propose even even more different feature configurations.

However, as many publications focus on specific datasets, it still remains unclear which combination is generally suitable for person re-identification. For this work, we evaluated a variety of feature configurations on four state-of-the-art datasets. The configurations are based on the following components:

Table 1. Study on color spaces for region covariance based on the ROC and CMC area under the curve (AUC). SURF and color histogram (HIST) are provided for reference.

	ETHZ ROC (CMC)	CAVIAR4REID ROC (CMC)	VIPeR ROC (CMC)	PRID2011 ROC (CMC)
RGB	**0.860 (0.865)**	0.622 (0.666)	**0.749** (0.734)	0.690 (0.684)
HSV	0.860 (0.861)	**0.719 (0.734)**	0.741 (**0.741**)	**0.750 (0.756)**
Lab	0.833 (0.835)	0.631 (0.651)	0.737 (0.726)	0.678 (0.664)
YCrCb	0.844 (0.843)	0.616 (0.642)	0.730 (0.720)	0.662 (0.649)
XYZ	0.839 (0.846)	0.625 (0.666)	0.752 (0.736)	0.696 (0.690)
HIST	0.900 (0.908)	0.744 (0.714)	0.467 (0.683)	0.522 (0.638)
SURF	0.949 (0.934)	0.824 (0.748)	0.625 (0.614)	0.792 (0.701)

$$X\ /Y \qquad \text{(x- and y-position of pixel)}$$
$$I^{gray}\ /I^c, \qquad \forall c \in \{1,2,3\} \text{ (channels' or grayscale intensity)}$$
$$\left|I^{gray}_{x/y}\right| / \left|I^c_{x/y}\right|, \qquad \forall c \in \{1,2,3\} \text{ (magnitude of image gradient)}$$
$$\theta^{gray}\ /\theta^c, \qquad \forall c \in \{1,2,3\} \text{ (gradient orientation)}$$
$$\left|I^{gray}_{xx/yy/xy}\right| / \left|I^c_{xx/yy/xy}\right|, \forall c \in \{1,2,3\} \text{ (magnitude of 2nd order derivatives).}$$

In our tests we found that the 14×14 feature vector

$$F = \left\{ I^c, Y, |I^c_x|, |I^c_y|, \theta^c, I^{gray}_{xy} \right\}, \ \forall c \in \{1,2,3\} \qquad (2)$$

performs best over all datasets. We also conducted experiments on segmentation and different color spaces (RGB, HSV, Lab, YCrCb, XYZ). Detailed results of them can be found in Section 4.

Tuzel et al. proposed in [5] a object representation using five covariance matrices in the region of interest: the full region and the upper, lower, left and right half of the region. This can have advantages in cases of occlusion. As in our datasets however, occlusion is seldom, we chose a different segmentation scheme based on a $n_x \times n_y$ grid of overlapping rectangles (with o as overlapping percentage). As the symmetry for a human is usually higher in x-direction than in y-direction, more segments in y-direction should be chosen than in x-direction.

4   Experimental Results

To evaluate the proposed method and configurations, we use public datasets from CAVIAR4REID[1], VIPeR[2], ETHZ [11] and PRID 2011 [12]. The datasets generally have different properties and are mostly challenging. While e.g. the VIPeR and the ETHZ dataset have been recorded from different viewpoints

---

[1] http://www.lorisbazzani.info/code-datasets/caviar4reid/
[2] http://vision.soe.ucsc.edu/?q=node/178

with better contrast and higher resolution, images from CAVIAR4REID show
a lot of noise, bad contrast and also changing lighting conditions in different
cameras. Persons in ETHZ dataset however are also subject to some occlusion.
PRID 2011 is especially interesting as it shows people on differently textured
background (e.g. a crosswalk). For none of the datasets, foreground masks were
used. Evaluation is done using the well-known cumulative matching characteristic (CMC) and receiver-operating characteristic (ROC) and is separated in two
parts. First, experiments for feature configuration for region covariance are provided, then an evaluation of the system using the fusion of all feature classes is
given.

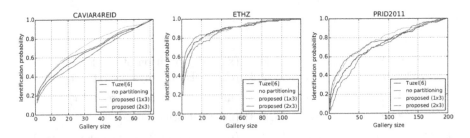

Fig. 1. Study of different partition schemes for region covariance with HSV color space
evaluated using CMC measure

Table 1 shows the results for different color spaces. For reference we also provide values for the color histogram- (HIST) and the SURF point-based method
[1]. For the HIST results, a set of histograms with 30 bins based on the HSV
color space are concatenated from 9×12 cells which overlap each other by 50%.
These configurations were found to be optimal in our experiments. The HSV
color space is a good choice since it gives the best results especially for the
PRID2011 and CAVIAR4REID datasets. None of the basic algorithms performs
best on all datasets which motivates the need to combine different features for
an overall performance improvement.

Figure 1 shows results for different partitioning configurations for region covariance. In our tests, an overlap of 25% gave best results. It is visible that the
partition from [5] gives better results than no partition at all, but both curves
can be outperformed using the proposed scheme. As we prefer higher recognition
values for small gallery sizes, we use a 2×3 grid for the following experiments
of our system. Table 2 shows the improvement of a score normalization step.

We finally evaluate the proposed multi-feature approach using feature scores
from each descriptor (SURF, HIST, region covariance). In order to obtain the
overall matching score, in our tests a weighted additive averaging gave best
results. As the descriptors were chosen to be at least partially complementary,
concepts excluding certain IDs (such as e.g. cascades, multiplicative averages,
maximum votes etc.) are error-prone and give worse results.

Table 2. Results of unity normalization on the test datasets based on ROC and CMC area under curve (AUC)

	ETHZ ROC (CMC)	CAVIAR4REID ROC (CMC)	VIPeR ROC (CMC)	PRID2011 ROC (CMC)
not normalized	**0.970 (0.936)**	0.843 (0.769)	0.797 (0.801)	0.873 (0.808)
normalized	0.968 (0.934)	**0.855 (0.776)**	**0.853 (0.807)**	**0.888 (0.814)**

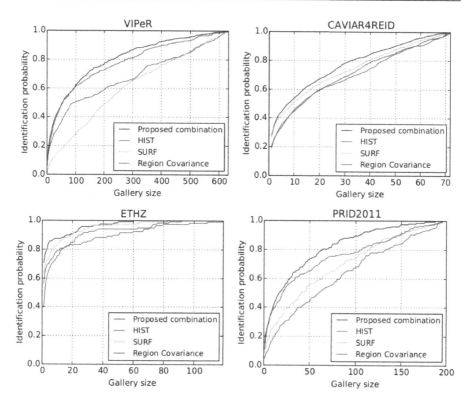

Fig. 2. Re-identification results of the proposed multi-feature system based on the CMC measure

Final results for our system can be seen in Figure 2. It performs better than the single-feature methods and improves their recognition rate considerably on all datasets and thus under very different conditions.

5 Conclusion

In this paper we proposed a multi-feature approach based on region covariance and a new partitioning scheme in order to increase the performance of a person re-identification system. A novel way of avoiding rank-deficiency which does not alter the covariance descriptor was introduced to reduce errors and cope with high-dimensional image data. The improvements have been extensively evaluated on four well-known datasets. Future work will enhance the system further in order to use it for forensic and real-time tracking applications. This will include fast feature retrieval on images and enhancements for processing speed as well as further work on self-adaptive data fusion.

References

1. Hamdoun, O., Moutarde, F., Stanciulescu, B., Steux, B.: Person re-identification in multi-camera system by signature based on interest point descriptors collected on short video sequences. In: 2nd ACM/IEEE International Conference on Distributed Smart Cameras (ICDSC 2008), p. 5 (2008), ISBN: 9781424426652
2. Khedher, M.I., El Yacoubi, M.A., Dorizzi, B.: Multi-shot SURF-based person re-identification via sparse representation. In: 2013 10th IEEE International Conference on Advanced Video and Signal Based Surveillance (AVSS), pp. 159–164 (2013)
3. Bay, H., Ess, A., Tuytelaars, T., van Gool, L.: Speeded-Up Robust Features (SURF). Computer Vision and Image Understanding **110**(3), 346–359 (2008), http://dx.doi.org/10.1016/j.cviu.2007.09.014, doi:10.1016/j.cviu.2007.09.014, ISSN: 10773142
4. Swain, M.J., Ballard, D.H.: Color indexing. International Journal of Computer Vision **7**, 11–32 (1991)
5. Tuzel, O., Porikli, F., Meer, P.: Region covariance: a fast descriptor for detection and classification. In: Leonardis, A., Bischof, H., Pinz, A. (eds.) ECCV 2006. LNCS, vol. 3952, pp. 589–600. Springer, Heidelberg (2006). http://link.springer.com/chapter/10.1007/11744047_45
6. Hirzer, M., Roth, P.M., Bischof, H.: Person Re-identification by Efficient Impostor-Based Metric Learning. In: 2012 IEEE Ninth International Conference on Advanced Video and Signal-Based Surveillance (AVSS), pp. 203–208 (2012)
7. Förstner, W., Moonen, B.: A Metric for Covariance Matrices (1999)
8. Tuzel, O., Porikli, F., Meer, P.: Human Detection via Classification on Riemannian Manifolds. In: 2007 IEEE Conference on Computer Vision and Pattern Recognition, CVPR 2007, pp. 1–8 (2007), ISSN: 1063–6919
9. Pennec, X., Fillard, P., Ayache, N.: A Riemannian Framework for Tensor Computing. International Journal of Computer Vision **66**, 41–66 (2006)
10. Bak, S., Corvee, E., Bremond, F., Thonnat, M.: Person Re-identification Using Spatial Covariance Regions of Human Body Parts. In: 7th IEEE International Conference on Advanced Video and Signal-Based Surveillance, AVSS 2010, Boston, USA (August 2010)
11. Schwartz, W.R., Davis, L.S.: Learning Discriminative Appearance-Based Models Using Partial Least Squares. In: 2009 XXII Brazilian Symposium on Computer Graphics and Image Processing, pp. 322–329 (Oktober 2009), http://dx.doi.org/10.1109/SIBGRAPI.2009.42
12. Hirzer, M., Beleznai, C., Roth, P.M., Bischof, H.: Person re-identification by descriptive and discriminative classification. In: Heyden, A., Kahl, F. (eds.) SCIA 2011. LNCS, vol. 6688, pp. 91–102. Springer, Heidelberg (2011). http://link.springer.com/chapter/10.1007/978-3-642-21227-7_9

Multi-biometric Score-Level Fusion and the Integration of the Neighbors Distance Ratio

Naser Damer and Alexander Opel[✉]

Fraunhofer Institute for Computer Graphics Research (IGD), Darmstadt, Germany
{naser.damer,alexander.opel}@igd.fraunhofer.de

Abstract. Multi-biometrics aims at building more accurate unified biometric decisions based on the information provided by multiple biometric sources. Information fusion is used to optimize the process of creating this unified decision. In previous works dealing with score-level multi-biometric fusion, the scores of different biometric sources belonging to the comparison of interest are used to create the fused score. The novelty of this work focuses on integrating the relation of the fused scores to other comparisons within a 1:N comparison. This is performed by considering the neighbors distance ratio in the ranked comparisons set within a classification-based fusion approach. The evaluation was performed on the Biometric Scores Set BSSR1 database and the enhanced performance induced by the integration of neighbors distance ratio was clearly presented.

Keywords: Multi-biometrics · Score-level fusion · Biometric verification

1 Introduction

Biometrics technology aims at identifying or verifying the identity of individuals based on their physical or behavior characteristics. Combining more than one biometric source is often performed to increase the accuracy, robustness and usability of biometrics [4]. The different biometric sources can be based on different characteristics, captures, algorithms, sensors, or instances. Putting together the information provided by those sources and creating a unified biometric decision is referred to as multi-biometric fusion.

The fusion process can be applied on different levels such as the data, feature, score, or rank level. Higher levels such as score and rank provide a more flexible and integrable solution. Data and feature fusion levels provide more information but affect the integrability and may be hard to achieve in certain multi-biometric combinations. In this work, the score-level fusion will be considered as it provides a fair trade-off between performance and integrability.

Score-level biometric fusion techniques can be categorized into two main groups, combination-based and classification-based fusion. Combination-based

© Springer International Publishing Switzerland 2014
A. Campilho and M. Kamel (Eds.): ICIAR 2014, Part II, LNCS 8815, pp. 85–93, 2014.
DOI: 10.1007/978-3-319-11755-3_10

fusion consists of simple operations performed on the normalized scores of different biometric sources. Those operations produce a combined score that is used to build a biometric decision. One of the most used combination rules is the weighted-sum rule, where each biometric source is assigned a relative weight that optimize the source effect on the final fused decision. The weights are related to the performance metrics of the biometric sources, a comparative study of biometric source weighting is presented by Chia et al. [3].

Classification-based fusion views the biometric scores of a certain comparison as a feature vector. A classifier is trained to classify those vectors optimally into genuine or imposter comparisons. Different types of classifiers where used to perform multi-biometric fusion, some of those are support vector machines (SVM) [9][5], neural networks [2], and likelihood ratio [8].

A biometric system usually operates under one of two scenarios, verification or identification. Verification is the authentication of a claimed identity based on the captured biometric characteristics. Identification is assigning an identity to an unknown individual based on their biometric characteristics. Identification can operate as a closed-set identification, where the user is known to be included in the biometric references set, or as an open-set identification with the user is not definitely included in the references set. In open-set identification, a verification final step is required to verify that the top ranked identification match is certainly the same captured subject and not an unenroled subject.

Keeping the open-set identification scenario in mind, this work tries to use the information provided by the ranked set of comparisons to perform more accurate verification of the top rank. The assumption here is that a genuine top rank comparison has a lower distance ratio to its rank neighbors than that of an imposter comparison. Those information are integrated into a classification-based fusion approach using SVM.

The proposed fusion technique is evaluated over the Biometric Scores Set BSSR1 - multimodal database [1]. A number of previously proposed base-line fusion approaches were evaluated including state-of-the-art combination rules and the use of SVM without consideration of the neighbor distance ratio. The proposed technique proved to outperform the base-line solution and the results are presented as Equal Error Rates (EER) and Receiver Operating Characteristics (ROC) curves.

In the next Section 2 the proposed solution is discussed along with a number of base-line solutions. The experiment setup and the achieved results are then presented in Section 3. Finally, in Section 4, a conclusion of the work is drawn.

2   Methodology

This section presents the proposed solution in more details. A number of baseline solutions used to benchmark the performance are also discussed.

2.1 Proposed Solution

The main assumption that builds the bases of the proposed solution in this work is anchored on the Neighbor Distance Ratio (NDR). Given a rank set of comparison scores that represents an $1 : N$ comparison, NDR is defined as the ratio between one score in this set and a score of a higher rank (neighbor distance). NDR was previously used in the literature to match interest key point descriptors in images [7].

Looking into the NDR from the biometric prospective, the inverse ratio between a genuine similarity score and the next highest score (within a ranked $1 : N$ comparison) is assumed to be lower than this ratio between an imposter score and the next highest score. In different words, a genuine score of a certain subject is relatively higher and distanced from the set of a clustered set of imposter scores produced by the same subject. This relative (to neighbor ranks) difference is not considered in conventional biometric verification where only the absolute value of the genuine or imposter comparison score is considered. A realistic genuine-impostor distributions of NDR values are show and discussed later on.

The proposed solution in this work aims at considering both, the scores absolute values and the relative distances to higher ranks in order to perform more accurate biometric verification. To achieve that, a classification-based fusion approach based on support vector machines (SVM) were used. In Classification-based multi-biometric fusion, the fusion process is viewed as a binary classification problem that aims to separate between two classes, genuine and impostor.

Support vector machines [11] is a statistical learning technique often used to learn binary classifiers, i.e. to learn how to separate two classes using information gained from known examples (training data). Classical learning techniques, such as Neural Networks (NN), focused on minimizing the empirical error (error on the training set). This approach is commonly referred to as Empirical Risk Minimization (ERM). However, the SVM follows the Structural Risk Minimization (SRM) instead of the ERM approach. The SRM insures a high generalization performance as it tries to minimize the upper bound of the generalization error. In simple words, SVM tries to build a class-separation surface in the feature space that is optimized in a manner which considers generalized unknown data.

In order to map the input data space into a feature space where the data is linearly separable, SVM uses kernel functions. In general, those functions help enhancing the discrimination power. In this work, the Radial Basis Function (RBF) is used as a kernel function as it proved to outperform linear kernels when dealing with low dimensional space [10], such as the problem dealt with in this work.

The feature vector considered for the SVM fusion process consisted of two concatenated parts. First is the set of comparison scores achieved by the N biometric sources, $\{S_1, \ldots, S_n\}$. The second part is a set of NDR values produced by the ranked list of the fused scores of the biometric sources. To produce those values, each biometric comparison (containing N scores) were fused using the simple sum rule. The resulted fused scores set is ranked and the NDR values are calculated. The considered NDR values were the 2nd-rank-to-1st-rank, 3rd-rank-to-1st-rank, and the 3rd-rank-to-2nd-rank values. The distribution of those values over imposter and genuine comparisons of the BSSR1 [1] fingerprint (Fli) and face (Fc) matchers (fused) are shown in Figure 1 where the high discrimination between impostor and genuine NDR values is clear. More details about the BSSR1 database are presented in Section 3.

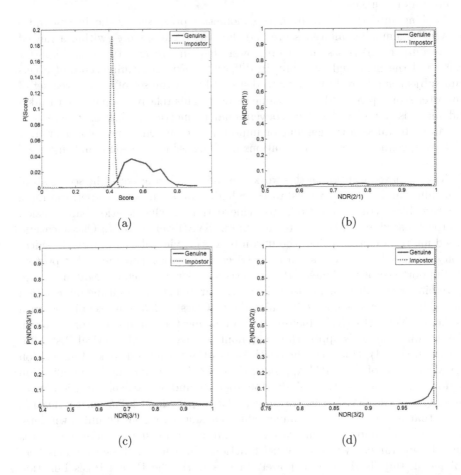

(a)

(b)

(c)

(d)

Fig. 1. BSSR1 [1] fingerprint (Fli) and face (Fc) matchers fused by sum-rule and the resulted NDR values (a) Fused score distribution. (b) 2nd-rank-to-1st-rank NDR distribution. (c) 3rd-rank-to-1nd-rank NDR distribution. (b) 3rd-rank-to-2nd-rank NDR distribution.

The NDR values were concatenated with the comparison score values of the comparison resulting in a feature vector of the size $N + 3$. The SVM classifies the input feature vector and the resulted decision function value (the signed distance to the margin) is considered as the final fused score. An overall look on the proposed method is presented in Figure 2.

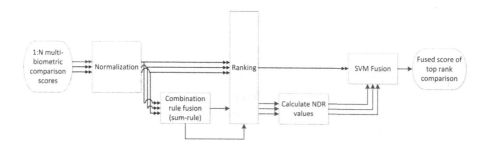

Fig. 2. An overview of the proposed solution. The input scores of an 1:N comparison is fused by simple sum combination rule and ranked based on the resulted scores. The NDR values based on this ranking is concatenated with the original scores of the comparison to be verified. The concatenated vector is fed into the SVM to create a final fused score.

2.2 Baseline Solution

A number of baseline solutions are presented here to build a reference for the performance evaluation presented in the next Section 3. The first baseline solution aims at direct comparison by using SVM-based approach for fusion without using NDR information. Two other solutions based on the widely used weighted-sum approach are also discussed, one utilizes the EER as a source performance measure while the second uses the Non-Confidence Width (NCW).

The conventional SVM baseline approach takes the biometric comparison scores of different sources $\{S_1, \ldots, S_n\}$ as a feature vector. The SVM is trained to classify this feature vector into genuine or impostor classes and reports the resulted decision function value as the fused score. The SVM used here also uses similar configuration to the proposed approach with RBF as a kernel function.

The two other baseline approaches are based on the weighted-sum combination rule that assigns each score value S_k with the weight of its source w_k to produce the fused score. The weights w_k are calculated from the training data of each biometric source. The fused score F by the weighted sum rule for N score sources is given as:

$$F = \sum_{k=1}^{N} w_k S_k, k = \{1, \ldots, N\} \tag{1}$$

The weights used here are based on either EER or NCW values. The EER weighting (EERW) is based on the EER value which is the common value of the false acceptance rate (FAR) and the false rejection rate (FRR) at the operational point where both FAR and FRR are equal. EER weighting was used to linearly combine biometric scores in the work of Jain et al. [6]. The EER is inverse proportional to the performance of the biometric source. Therefore, for a multi-biometric system that combines N biometric source, the EER weight for a biometric source k is given by:

$$w_k = \frac{\frac{1}{EER_k}}{\sum_{k=1}^{N} \frac{1}{EER_k}} \tag{2}$$

The Non-Confidence Width Weight (NCWW) was proposed by Chia et al. [3] to weight biometric sources for score-level multi-biometric fusion. NCW corresponds to the width of the overlap area between the genuine and imposter scores distributions. Given that Max_k^I is the maximum imposter score and Min_k^G is the minimum genuine score, NCW is given by:

$$NCW_k = Max_k^I - Min_k^G \tag{3}$$

as the NCW is inverse proportional to the biometric source performance, the weights based on the NCW is given as:

$$w_k = \frac{\frac{1}{NCW_k}}{\sum_{k=1}^{N} \frac{1}{NCW_k}} \tag{4}$$

3   Experiment and Results

The database used to develop and evaluate the proposed solution is the Biometric Scores Set BSSR1 - multimodal database [1]. The database contains comparison scores for left and right fingerprints (Fli and Fri) and two face matchers (Fc and Fg). BSSR1 - multimodal database contains 517 genuine and $266,772$ impostor scores. The experiments here considered all possible pairs between finger and face matchers as well as the fusion of all matchers. To evaluate the statistical performance of the proposed solutions, the database was splitted into three equal-sized partitions. Experiments were performed on all possible fold combinations were one partition is used as an evaluation set and the other two are used as a development set. All the reported results are the averaged results of the three evaluation/development combinations.

Min-max normalization was used to bring comparison scores produced by different biometric sources to a comparable range. Min-max normalized score is given as:

$$S' = \frac{S - min\{S_k\}}{max\{S_k\} - min\{S_k\}} \tag{5}$$

Where $min\{S_k\}$ and $max\{S_k\}$ are the minimum and maximum value of scores existing in the training data of the corresponding biometric source. And S' is the normalized score.

To train and test the proposed approach, every possible open-set identification scenario that can occur in the database was simulated. To do that, the comparisons in the database were splitted into separated 1:N comparison sets. Each comparison in those comparison sets were fused using the sum-rule fusion then ranked according to the resulted fused scores. The three considered NDR values were calculated for each entry in the ranked comparison sets, except the last two ranks, as the second and third rank to those entries does not exist and thus the NDR values cannot be calculated. The resulted NDR values of each comparison are concatenated with the original scores of the comparison to create the final feature vector for that comparison. The resulted feature vectors are passed along with their genuine/imposter labels to train the SVM classifier in the training mode.

For evaluation, similar concatenated feature vectors are created from the testing data. Those features are evaluated by the trained SVM classifier to produce a final fused score from each comparison. The performance achieved by the proposed solution and the base line approaches is presented as EER values in Table 1 and as ROC curves in Figure 3. Performance was presented for all possible bi-modal combinations as well as for the fusion of all available sources (two face and two fingerprint matchers).

Table 1. The EER values achieved by the proposed solution and the discussed baseline approaches on the different bi-modal biometric combinations, as well as the fusion of all four available sources. In the last two columns are the EER values of the single biometric sources involved in the fusion.

	SVM-NDR	SVM	EERW-Sum	NCWW-Sum	Face	Finger
Fc-Fli	**0.00582**	0.01133	0.01338	0.04069	0.04550	0.08669
Fc-Flr	**0.00397**	0.00406	0.00491	0.02015	0.04550	0.04674
Fg-Fli	**0.01148**	0.01156	0.02642	0.01194	0.05801	0.08669
Fg-Flr	0.00976	**0.00422**	0.01404	0.00425	0.05801	0.04674
All	**0.00012**	0.00167	0.00222	0.00371	X	X

The EER values stated in Table 1 shows the superiority of the proposed solution in most cases. The influence of the NDR integration in the fusion process is especially clear when dealing with the fusion of all four biometric sources. However, the main advantage of the proposed solution is providing high true acceptance rate (TAR) at very low false acceptance rate (FAR) values (below EER). This is clear in Figure 3e where all the ROC curves produced by different combinations of modalities shows the high performance of the proposed solution at very low FAR values.

4 Conclusion

This work presented a novel multi-biometric score-level fusion approach and evaluated it along with a set of baseline approaches. The novelty of the work focused

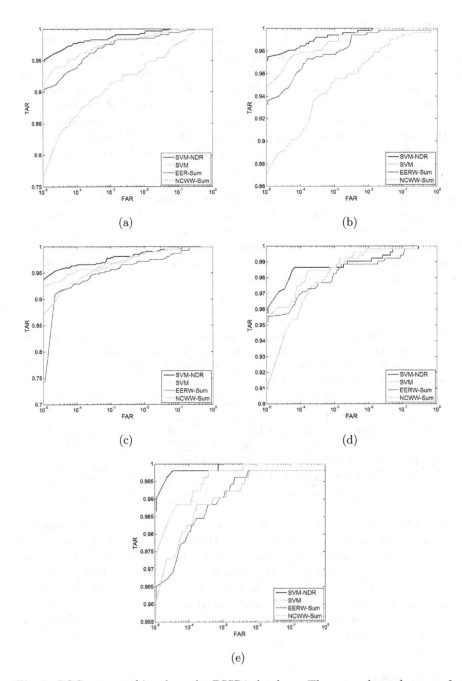

Fig. 3. ROC curves achieved on the BSSR1 database: The rates shown here are for all possible bi-modal combinations of face matchers (Fc and Fg) and finger matchers (Fli - Flr) in the BSSR1 database and the results achieved by the fusion of all four available sources. a) Fc and Fli, b) Fg and Fli, c) Fc and Flr. d) Fg and Flr, e) Fusion of all four sources (Fc, Fg, Fli, and Flr).

on the integration of neighbors distance ratio. Where the genuine/imposter decision does not only depend on the comparison scores from multi-biometric sources, but also on the relation to other comparisons within a 1:N biometric comparison. This integration was implemented in a classification-based fusion approach that utilized support vector machines. The evaluation was performed on the BSSR1 database and proved the superiority of the proposed solution compared to a number of baseline methods. The results clearly show the benefit of the neighbors distance ratio integration within the biometric decision making process.

Acknowledgments. This work is funded by the Federal Ministry of Education and Research (BMBF) of Germany in the context of the research program for public safety and security (GES-3D project under grant agreement $n°$ 13N12002).

References

1. National Institute of Standards and Technology: NIST Biometric Scores Set
2. Alsaade, F.: A study of neural network and its properties of training and adaptability in enhancing accuracy in a multimodal biometrics scenario. Information Technology Journal (2010)
3. Chia, C., Sherkat, N., Nolle, L.: Towards a best linear combination for multimodal biometric fusion. In: 2010 20th International Conference on Pattern Recognition (ICPR), pp. 1176–1179 (2010)
4. Damer, N., Opel, A., Shahverdyan, A.: An overview on multi-biometric score-level fusion - verification and identification. In: Marsico, M.D., Fred, A.L.N. (eds.) ICPRAM, pp. 647–653. SciTePress (2013)
5. Gutschoven, B., Verlinde, P.: Multi-modal identity verification using support vector machines (svm). In: Proceedings of the Third International Conference on Information Fusion, FUSION 2000, vol. 2, pp. THB3/3-THB3/8 (July 2000)
6. Jain, A., Nandakumar, K., Ross, A.: Score normalization in multimodal biometric systems. Pattern Recognition **38**(12), 2270–2285 (2005). http://www.sciencedirect.com/science/article/pii/S0031320305000592
7. Mikolajczyk, K., Schmid, C.: A performance evaluation of local descriptors. IEEE Trans. Pattern Anal. Mach. Intell. **27**(10), 1615–1630 (2005). http://dx.doi.org/10.1109/TPAMI.2005.188
8. Nandakumar, K., Chen, Y., Dass, S.C., Jain, A.: Likelihood ratio-based biometric score fusion. IEEE Trans. Pattern Anal. Mach. Intell. **30**(2), 342–347 (2008). http://dx.doi.org/10.1109/TPAMI.2007.70796
9. Singh, R., Vatsa, M., Noore, A.: Intelligent biometric information fusion using support vector machine. In: Nachtegael, M., Van der Weken, D., Kerre, E., Philips, W. (eds.) Soft Computing in Image Processing. STUDFUZZ, vol. 210, pp. 325–349. Springer, Heidelberg (2007)
10. Song, S., Zhan, Z., Long, Z., Zhang, J., Yao, L.: Comparative study of svm methods combined with voxel selection for object category classification on fmri data. PLoS ONE **6**(2), e17191 (2011)
11. Vapnik, V.N.: The Nature of Statistical Learning Theory. Springer-Verlag New York Inc., New York (1995)

Adaptive Haar-Like Features for Head Pose Estimation

Nam-Jun Pyun[1,2(✉)], Halima Sayah[1], and Nicole Vincent[1]

[1] LIPADE, Paris Descartes University, 45 rue des Saints-Pères, 75006, Paris, France
nicole.vincent@mi.parisdescartes.fr
[2] Konbini, 20 rue du Faubourg du Temple, 75011, Paris, France
namjun.pyun@konbini.com

Abstract. This paper presents a work on head pose estimation. Here, face images are tagged with head pose information. To achieve head pose estimation, anatomic regions (eyes, nose and mouth) are extracted using a facial descriptor. Candidates for these regions are extracted from an energy map based on Haar-like features. Then, a multi-threshold analysis is applied to find the position and the size of each region. Region projections on vertical and horizontal axis enable to define a set of rules in order to estimate head pose.

Keywords: Head pose estimation · Geometric information · Eye · Nose · Mouth · Haar feature · Energy map · Spatial relations · Multi-threshold analysis

1   Introduction

Head pose is an interesting information in many applications. It can also be a way to adapt a method for face recognition as the efficiency of recognition task is higher with frontal faces. Several works on head pose estimation have been implemented. They are divided generally into two main groups: appearance-based methods and model-based methods. [1] presents a survey of the head pose estimation methods.

Appearance-based methods decompose image into more simple elements and form a classifier from a large set of tagged images to obtain templates or statistical analysis [2]. In this group, appearance template methods try to match a head view to a set of examples labeled with a discrete pose in order to find the most similar one [3]. The major problem is the pairwise similarity operation which can be affected by the person identity.

Similar to appearance template methods, characteristic vectors are used to train a series of head detectors for each specific discrete pose and assign the discrete pose of the detector with the greatest support [4]. An early example used three SVMs for three discrete yaws [5]. With these methods, computational requirements increase linearly with the number of vectors.

Nonlinear regression methods develop a functional mapping from the image domain or feature space to a head pose label using nonlinear regression tools. Success has been demonstrated using Support Vector Regressors (SVRs) and principal component analysis (PCAs) to reduce dimensionality [6]. The multilayer perceptron (MLP) is the most widely used neural networks tool [7].

© Springer International Publishing Switzerland 2014
A. Campilho and M. Kamel (Eds.): ICIAR 2014, Part II, LNCS 8815, pp. 94–101, 2014.
DOI: 10.1007/978-3-319-11755-3_11

Image dimensionality is reduced in Manifold embedding methods, two of the most popular dimensionality reduction techniques, PCA and its nonlinear kernelized version, KPCA, discover the primary modes of variation from a set of data samples [8]. More recently, [9] the biologically inspired features combined with the local binary pattern achieves significant improvement in head pose estimation.

Model based methods can be divided into flexible models and geometric methods. Flexible models [10] fit a non-rigid model to the facial structure of each individual in the image plan; head pose can then be estimated from the feature-level comparison or from the instantiation of the model parameters. Flexible models include methods such as Active Shape Models [11] or Active Apperance Models [12]. These approaches are limited to pose in which eyes corners are visible.

On the other hand, geometric methods use facial feature such as the eyes, the mouth and the nose, and compute the head pose from the relative locations or fiducial points of these features. An approach of 3D head pose estimation is proposed using the vanishing points [13]. In [14] Haar-like features is used to detect facial features which are tracked in a given video sequence. Recently, a 3D face pose estimation method is proposed using a central profile and a nose model matching algorithm [15] to detect nose tip. These geometric methods are fast and simple. The main difficulty lies in detecting the features with high accuracy.

Our approach belongs to geometric methods and we want to show it is possible to estimate head pose when anatomic elements (AE) are positionned with a low precision. Section 2 describes the AE detector. Once eyes, nose and mouth are obtained, our head pose estimation method is described in section 3. In section 4 our approach is evaluated and section 5 concludes this paper. Fig. 1 shows the main steps of the proposed approach.

Fig. 1. Global scheme of our proposal

2   Facial Anatomic Salient Regions Detection

Here, salient regions are extracted using some basic knowledge of a human face. The starting materials are face images extracted in a rectangular window from a face detector (e.g. Viola and Jones [16] or LBP [17]). Assuming faces are detected in a suitable scale, a given face window size matches approximately with the scale of the current face window (Fig. 2a).To achieve extraction of salient regions, candidates are generated according to a binarization threshold of an energy map. Then a multi-threshold analysis is applied to choose the best regions.

2.1   Energy of Horizontal Lines

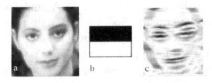

Fig. 2. a) Face window. b) Horizontal Haar feature. c) Horizontal energy map.

Lines in a face that match with salient regions of the face are almost horizontal. Many approaches can be used to extract horizontal lines. On the one hand, if the detector is too local, it gives noisy results. On the other hand, if it is not local enough, it gives results with lack of information. In other words, the horizontal line detector needs to find lines of a suitable length. Horizontal Haar-like features size can be fixed; they are adapted to a given length. Since face window gives the scale, a single horizontal adaptive Haar-like feature (Fig. 2b) depending only on H and W (the height and width of the face window) is used. Its height h and width w are given by (1).

$$\begin{cases} h = \max(2, 2 \cdot a) \text{ and } w = \max(2, 3 \cdot a) \\ \text{with } a = \min(H/40, W/40) \end{cases} \tag{1}$$

Equation (2) gives the energy E at the center (X, Y) of the Haar feature. p_w is the intensity of a pixel in the white area and p_b, the intensity of a pixel in black area.

$$E(X, Y) = \left| \sum_{white} p_w - \sum_{black} p_b \right| \tag{2}$$

Fig. 2c shows the energy map. The upper a value of the energy map is, the more confident we are on a presence of a horizontal contour in the neighborhood of the pixel.

2.2   Extracting Candidates for Eyes, Nose and Mouth

Since illumination may vary within the face, a suitable binarization threshold for an eye may differ from the one of the mouth. First, candidates of anatomic salient regions are extracted for different fixed thresholds (Fig. 3a). This part describes the extraction of candidates regions for a given threshold. Once energy map is binarized, connected components (CCs) and their bounding boxes are extracted. At this stage, CCs are either a part of a salient face region, or a noise (Fig. 3b). On the one hand, CCs have to be gathered together to define salient regions. On the other hand, CCs detected as noise must be deleted. The merging process is based on basic knowledge of a face appearance.

Extracting Eyes. CCs with a common projection on y-axis are merged to form a candidate anatomic region (CAR). Each CAR is represented by the bounding box including CCs, its left upper point is S and its right lower corner is T.

Since eyes are located in the upper part of a face, eyes are contained in the CAR of ordinate y_S^* which matches the criterion (3).

$$\begin{cases} y_S^* < 1/2 \cdot H \\ y_S^* = \min(|y_S - 1/2 \cdot H|) \end{cases} \qquad (3)$$

All CARs above the selected eyes region are removed. To separate left and right eyes, CCs with common vertical projection along the x-axis are merged into a CAR. Eyes region is now a list of eyes CARs. The two ones with highest area are selected.

When face window size is low or when the binarization threshold of the energy map is too high or when there are glasses, left and right eyes are not well separated. An upper level set at half the maximum value in the histogram of pixels along the vertical axis enables to separate the eye regions into left and right eyes. CARs are then updated, i.e. CCs bounding boxes are split, if necessary.

Fig. 3. a) Binarized energy map. b) Connected Components bounding boxes. c) CCs bounding boxes which belong to salient regions of the face. d) Results of the extraction.

Extracting Nose and Mouth. Nose tip and mouth are located with respect to eyes. All CCs which horizontal projection intersects the face symmetry axis are kept as they may belong to nose or mouth. The other CCs are removed (Fig. 3c). To separate those from nose from those from mouth, we use other basic knowledge about face. Mouth is larger than nose tip: mouth contains the widest CC (CCw) and all under. Nose is above the mouth: the upper CC (CCu) belongs to nose.

CCs between CCw and CCu are gathered into two clusters according to their width. Thus, two new CARs are obtained, the upper one is the nose and the other one represents the mouth (Fig. 3d).

2.3   Multi-threshold of the Energy Map

As illumination conditions may be inconstant, a binarization of energy map gives CARs that are not always optimum. As a solution we define a multi-threshold approach applied to CARs of a same salient anatomic region R. The best CAR position and size are assumed to be those that vary little according to a threshold variation. Thus, given (x_R, y_R), the coordinates of the left upper corner of CARs and w_R and h_R, the size of the CARs, a suitable threshold t^* is defined by (4).

The second line in (4) depends on α, the maximum ratio between a given anatomic region area and the CAR window area (e.g. for each eye α=0.1). ε_R is the D(t) mean value where D(t)≠0. Suitable thresholds for eyes, nose tip and mouth are computed separately and give anatomic regions (ARs) (Fig. 4).

$$D(t) = \left|\frac{\partial}{\partial t}x_R(t)\right| + \left|\frac{\partial}{\partial t}y_R(t)\right| + \left|\frac{\partial}{\partial t}w_R(t)\right| + \left|\frac{\partial}{\partial t}h_R(t)\right|$$

$$A(t) = \alpha \cdot W \cdot H - w_R \cdot h_R \tag{4}$$

$$t^* = \max_{A(t)>0 \text{ and } D(t)<\varepsilon_R} t$$

Fig. 4. Extraction of final eyes, nose and mouth regions: the central image shows final ARs. The other 4 images show CARs obtained with 4 different energy map binarization thresholds.

3   Head Pose Estimation

Our head pose estimation approach is based on ARs localization and uses the spatial distribution of the eyes, nose and mouth. Only the bounding boxes position and size of ARs are considered. In this article, yaw and pitch are estimated separately. Nine angles X_i with $i \in \{-4, ..., 4\}$ are considered for yaw (4 angles on the left and right sides and a front view). The pitch is characterized by 3 intervals (upper Y_{-1}, front Y_0 and lower view Y_1). The Fig. 5 shows five examples of ARs bounding boxes where yaw varies.

Once ARs are extracted, their bounding boxes are projected on the two axes. Yaw is determined by the vertical projection whereas pitch is computed using the horizontal projection. Then several criteria or rules are applied to determine yaw or pitch. In order to estimate the yaw, eyes widths and nose-mouth vertical projection relations are used, e.g. on frontal view eyes have almost the same widths and nose and mouth are located on face symmetry axis. Two intermediate decisions are defined. One involves only eye position (E) and the second involves nose and mouth positions (N). Then some combinations are performed. Given d_L and d_R, the respective width of left and right eyes ARs, the criterion E related to eye widths is computed by (5).

$$d = \left|d_L - d_R\right| \text{ and } s = \begin{cases} d/(d_L - d_R) \text{ for } d_L \neq d_R \\ 1 \text{ for } d_L = d_R \end{cases}$$

$$E = \begin{cases} E_1 \text{ if } d \in [0,\varepsilon], \\ E_{s\cdot 2} \text{ if } d \in]\varepsilon, C_{E1}], \\ E_{s\cdot 3} \text{ if } d \in]C_{E2}, +\infty[, \\ E_{s\cdot 4} \text{ if } d = +\infty \end{cases} \tag{5}$$

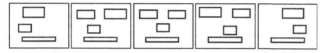

Fig. 5. ARs bounding boxes: left profile, left diagonal, front, right diagonal and right profile

Furthermore, given δ_L the abscissa difference of nose and mouth ARs left corners and δ_R the abscissa difference of nose and mouth ARs right corners, the criterion N related to nose position with regard to the mouth is computed by (6)

$$l = \left| \delta_L - \delta_R \right| \text{ and } s = \begin{cases} -1 \text{ if } \delta_L \leq \delta_R \\ 1 \text{ otherwise} \end{cases}$$

$$N = \begin{cases} N_{-3} \text{ if } \delta_L < 0 \\ N_3 \text{ if } \delta_R < 0 \\ N_{s \bullet 2} \text{ if } l \in [0, C_N] \\ N_{s \bullet 1} \text{ if } l \in \,]C_N, +\infty[\end{cases} \qquad (6)$$

The yaw orientation is finally defined by combining both of E and N criteria. Table. 1 shows the decision rules for the 4 left yaw orientations and the front view. Some intermediate decisions may be incoherent, e.g. eyes may indicate a side whereas nose and mouth may indicate the other or eyes and mouth may indicate the same side, but not the same poses. These cases yield to rejection (R).

Table 1. Yaw decisions for front view and 4 left yaw intervals combining E and N criterions

N & E	E_{-1}	E_{-2}	E_{-3}	E_{-4}
N_{-1}	X_0	X_0	R	R
N_{-2}	R	X_{-1}	X_{-3}	X_{-4}
N_{-3}	R	X_{-2}	X_{-3}	X_{-4}

Similar to the yaw estimation, some criteria about the eyes-nose distance and the nose-mouth one are used to determine pitch into 3 intervals.

4   Evaluation

ARs Extraction. The ARs are tested on the CMU Face database. Among labelled points of faces, eye, mouth and nose tip points are taken into account. We assume a region is correctly found if it contains the corresponding area constraints. Eyes must have an area less than 10% of the area of the face window, nose region area less than 5%, and mouth region less than 8%. Fig 6 shows some visual results.

Table 2 shows the extraction rates of two fixed threshold of the binarized energy map and the extraction rate of the multi-threshold approach. Notice that ARs extraction rates are better with the proposed multi-threshold method. This approach is based on the analysis of relative location of ARs. Mouth and nose are closer than eye with another part of the face. So, extraction rates of eyes are better than those of nose and mouth.

Fig. 6. Visual results of ARs extraction: eyes are well extracted whereas nose and mouth extraction are sometimes not accurate

Table 2. Detection percentage of CARs with our multi threshold method

Threshold	Left eye	Right eye	Nose	Mouth
175	**95.15**	**94.55**	69.70	**82.42**
195	87.27	84.84	**81.81**	76.97
Multi	*99.39*	*97.58*	*83.63*	*95.76*

Pose Estimation. To evaluate our head pose estimation approach, a custom database of 630 face images is built from a video sequence. For each of them, the yaw and the pitch are manually labeled. Table 3 shows the detection rate of ARs, as well as the results of head estimation for each left yaw and pitch orientations.

Table 3. ARs detection and head estimation percentages for left yaw and pitch. Only fully well detected ARs images are considered for pose estimation results.

Orientation	ARs detection (%)	Pose estimation (%)
X_0	100	**90.17**
X_{-1}	100	**85.30**
X_{-2}	100	53.85
X_{-3}	100	70.58
X_{-4}	77.78	**77.78**
Y_{-1}	62.83	66.11
Y_1	70.40	42.26

Pose estimation gives better results when ARs detection succeeds. Therefore, yaw estimations are more accurate than pitch ones. Better rates are obtained with frontal or almost frontal views, as well as profile views. Except for faces where all ARs are not found, rejected images where criteria E and N are incoherent seem rare, since they do not appear in our test face database. However, note that such a case can still happen, for example when eyes are occluded by hair or an object. ARs extraction runtime is less than 16 ms per face, whereas pose estimation process is almost immediate.

5   Conclusion

In this paper, we proposed a new method for head pose estimation using a single adaptive horizontal Haar feature to extract bounding boxes of left eye, right eye, nose and mouth. Experiments show that ARs relative positions can be enough to estimate approximately the face pose, especially for the yaw orientations. Our method does not depend on machine learning techniques nor requires human intervention. Pose estimation runtime is fast enough for real time process.

References

1. Murphy-Chutorian, E., Trivedi, M.M.: Head pose estimation in computer vision: A Survey. Pattern Analysis and Machine Intelligence 31 (2009)
2. Chen, C., Odobez, J.: We are not contortionists: coupled adaptive learning for head and body orientation estimation in surveillance video. In: CVPR, pp. 1544–1551 (2012)
3. Niyogi, S., Freeman, W.: Example-Based Head Tracking. In: Intern. Conf. on Automatic Face and Gesture Recognition, pp. 374–378 (1996)
4. Yan, Y., Ricci, E., Subramanian, R., Lanz, O., Sebe, N.: No matter where you are: Flexible graph-guided multi-task learning for multi-view head pose classification under target motion. In: ICCV, pp. 1177–1184 (2013)
5. Huang, J., Shao, X., Wechsler, H.: Face Pose Discrimination Using Support Vector Machines (SVM). In: Intern. Conf. on Pattern Recognition, pp. 154–156 (1998)
6. Li, Y., Gong, S., Liddell, H.: Support vector regression and classification based multi-view face detection and recognition. In: Intern. Conf. on Automatic Face and Gesture Recognition, pp. 300–305 (2000)
7. Seemann, E., Nickel, K., Stiefelhagen, R.: Head Pose Estimation Using Stereo Vision for Human-Robot Interaction. In: Intern. Conf. on Automatic Face and Gesture Recognition, pp. 626–631 (2004)
8. Wu, J., Trivedi, M.: A Two-Stage Head Pose Estimation Framework and Evaluation. Pattern Recognition 41(3), 1138–1158 (2008)
9. Bingpeng, M., Xiujuan, C., Tianjiang, W.: A novel feature descriptor based on biologically inspired feature for head pose estimation. Neurocomputing 115, 1–10 (2013)
10. Benfold, B., Reid, I.: Unsupervised learning of a scene-specific coarse gaze estimator. In: ICCV, pp. 2344–2351 (2011)
11. Lanitis, A., Taylor, C., Cootes, T.: Automatic Interpretation of Human Faces and Hand Gestures Using Flexible Models. In: Intern. Conf. on Automatic Face and Gesture Recognition, pp. 98–103 (1995)
12. Xiao, J., Baker, S., Matthews, I., Kanade, T.: Estimating face pose by facial asymmetry and geometry. In: CVPR, vol. 2, pp. 535–542 (2004)
13. Wang, J.-G., Sung, E.: EM Enhancement of 3D Head Pose Estimated by Point at Infinity. Image and Vision Computing 25(12), 1864–1874 (2007)
14. Khan, M.S.L., Réhman, S.U., Zhihan, L.V., Li, H.: Head Orientation Modeling: Geometric Head Pose Estimation using Monocular Camera. In: Intern. Conf. on Intelligent Systems and Image Processing, pp. 149–153 (2013)
15. Li, D., Pedrycz, W.: A central profile-based 3D face pose estimation. Pattern Recognition 47, 525–534 (2014)
16. Viola, P., Jones, M.: Rapid object detection using a boosted cascade of simple features. In: Intern. Conf. on Computer Vision and Pattern Recognition, vol. 1, pp. 511–518 (2001)
17. Ojala, T., Pietikainen, M., Maenpaa, T.: Multiresolution gray-scale and rotation invariant texture classification with local binary patterns. Pattern Analysis and Machine Intelligence 24(7), 971–987 (2002)

Face and Palmprint Recognition
Using Hierarchical Multiscale Adaptive LBP
with Directional Statistical Features

Ghada Shams[1(✉)], Mohamed Ismail[1], Sohier Bassiouny[2], and Nagia Ghanem[1]

Department of Computer and Systems Engineering,
Faculty of Engineering, University of Alexandria,
Alexandria, Egypt
{ghada.shams,drmaismail,nagia.mghanem}@gmail.com,
dr.soheir@yahoo.com

Abstract. In this paper, a new method for face and palmprint recognition has been proposed based on hierarchical multiscale local binary pattern (HMLBP) and adaptive LBP with directional statistical features (ALBPF) methods. It's build a hierarchical multiscale ALBPF histogram for an image. By using HMLBP, the representative features of "non-uniform" patterns are extracted at a smaller scale. On the other hand, using ALBPF improves the efficiency by incorporating mean and standard deviation statistical features in addition to minimizing the directional difference along different orientation .The results of experiments conducted on 2 public face databases and 2 public palmprint databases show that our proposed method has better recognition accuracy than LBP, ALBPF and HMLBP methods.

Keywords: Directional Statistical features · Face recognition · Local Binary Pattern · Palmprint recognition

1   Introduction

Reliable human identification and authentication in real time has become one of the most desirable tasks nowadays [1]. Biometrics refers to the automated process of identifying an individual based on his physical or behavioral characteristics. Physiological characteristics include fingerprints, face, palmprint, iris, DNA and hand geometry while behavioral characteristics are related to person behavior like gait and voice [2]. A major issue in biometric system is discriminative features extraction. Both face and palm provide robust, compact, efficient and discriminative features.

There are many approaches proposed for feature extraction such as Principal Component Analysis (PCA) [3], Linear Discriminate Analysis (LDA) [4], Gabor phase encoding [2], and local binary pattern (LBP) [5,6,7,8].LBP is an excellent and powerful texture operator. LBP has been applied successfully in numerous applications such as texture analysis, palmprint recognition [9], face recognition [3] and background modeling [10]. Hierarchical multiscale local binary pattern (HMLBP) approach is proposed by D. Zhang [11] to extract useful information from non-uniform patterns.

© Springer International Publishing Switzerland 2014
A. Campilho and M. Kamel (Eds.): ICIAR 2014, Part II, LNCS 8815, pp. 102–111, 2014.
DOI: 10.1007/978-3-319-11755-3_12

Guo et al. [12] has proposed adaptive LBP with Directional Statistical features (ALBPF) approach to minimize the directional difference along different orientation.

In this paper, an effective method for palmprint and face recognition has been proposed by combining HMLBP and ALBPF. The experimental results using palmprint datasets (PolyU, CASIA) and face datasets (JAFFE, ORL) demonstrate the performance and effectiveness of our proposed method.

The rest of the paper is organized as follows. Section 2 reviews LBP and HMLBP. Section 3 describes the proposed method Hierarchical Multiscale Adaptive LBP with Directional Statistical Features (HMALBPF). Section 4 demonstrates the experimental results and discussions. Finally, the conclusions are formulated in Section 5.

2   Local Binary Pattern

Local Binary Pattern (LBP) operator is a gray-scale texture operator proposed by Ojala et al. [10]. LBP transforms an image to an integer labels array. LBP encoding of pixels is evaluated by comparing a pixel with its neighbors. Comparison result is a binary number. LBP feature is the decimal value of the binary number. Fig.1 illustrates basic LBP encoding.

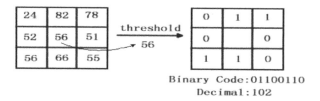

Fig. 1. Basic LBP Encoding

$LBP_{P,R}$ denotes the LBP feature where P is the total number of circular neighborhoods on a circle with radius R.

$$LBP_{P,R}(X_c, Y_c) = \sum_{p=0}^{P-1} S(g_p - g_c)2^P \qquad (1)$$

Where g_c is the gray value of the central pixel and g_p is the gray value of the neighborhood pixel.

The thresholding function S(z) can be computed by the following formula:

$$S(z) = \begin{Bmatrix} 1 & ,z \geq 0 \\ 0 & ,z < 0 \end{Bmatrix} \qquad (2)$$

A histogram of LBP labels is constructed to represent the whole texture image by the following formula:

$$H = \sum_{i,j}^{P-1} \{L(i,j) = l\}, l = 0, \dots, n-1 \qquad (3)$$

Where n is the maximal LBP pattern value. Uniform LBP patterns are LBP patterns with maximum number of bitwise 0/1 transitions is 2. Uniform LBP patterns have P*(P-1) +3 distinct output values. All "non-uniform" patterns are clustered into one cluster. LBP histogram dissimilarity is measured using the chi-square distance by the following formula:

$$D_{LBP}(X, Y) = \sum_{n=1}^{N} \frac{(X_n - Y_n)^2}{X_n + Y_n} \tag{4}$$

2.1   Hierarchical Multiscale LBP

As shown in LBP, $(2^P - P*(P-1)-2)$ patterns are grouped in one class label "non-uniform" patterns. Many discriminative non-uniform patterns fail to extract distinctive information. D. Zhang has proposed hierarchical multiscale LBP [11] by building multiscale LBP histogram from big radius to small radius, then that LBP map for each pixel in biggest radius, then pixels are divided into two types: uniform and Non-Uniform patterns ,A Sub histogram is built for uniform patterns while Non-uniform patterns are further processed at another smaller radius to extract uniform LBP patterns at smaller radius. HMLBP scheme is illustrated in Fig. 2. Multiscale could represent more image features than single LBP.

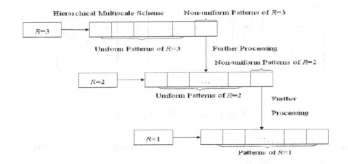

Fig. 2. Example of Hierarchical Multiscale LBP scheme

3   Combining Hierarchical Multiscale Scheme with Adaptive LBP and Directional Statistical Features

3.1   LBP with Directional Statistical Features

Local spatial structure isn't fully represented by single LBP. Given a central pixel g_c and its P circularly neighbors g_p, the distributions of the differences between g_c and g_p represents different orientations. As shown in Fig. 3 two texture images have the same LBP distribution but their local difference distribution $| g_c - g_p |$ is different.

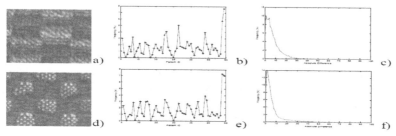

Fig. 3. a)-c) original image ,$LBP_{8,1}^{u2}$ distribution and $|g_c\text{-}g_p|$ distribution. d)-f) is another example [12].

Given a texture image with size N X M then its mean μ_p and standard deviation σ_p of the local difference $|\, g_c - g_p\,|$ can be computed by the following formula:

$$\mu_p = \sum_{i=1}^{N} \sum_{j=1}^{M} \frac{|g_c(i,j)-g_p(i,j)|}{M\,X\,N} \tag{5}$$

$$\sigma_p = \sqrt{\sum_{i=1}^{N} \sum_{j=1}^{M} \frac{(|g_c(i,j)-g_p(i,j)|-\mu_p)^2}{M\,X\,N}} \tag{6}$$

$\vec{\mu} = [\mu_0,\mu_1 , \ldots\ldots,\mu_{p-1}]$ represents the mean vector,$\vec{\sigma} = [\sigma_0,\sigma_1 , \ldots\ldots,\sigma_{p-1}]$ represents the standard deviation vector. $\vec{\mu}$ and $\vec{\sigma}$ represent the directional statistical features of the local difference $|g_c -g_p|$. Directional statistical features contain discriminative information can be used to weight the LBP dissimilarity.

Suppose that μ_s and σ_s represent the directional statistical features for a given test image S while μ_T and σ_T represent the directional statistical features for a model image T, then the normalized distances can be defined as:

$$d_\mu = \sum_{p=0}^{P-1} \frac{|\mu_S(p)- \mu_T(p)|}{P\,X\,k_\mu} \tag{7}$$

$$d_\sigma = \sum_{p=0}^{P-1} \frac{|\sigma_S(p)- \sigma_T(p)|}{P\,X\,k_\sigma} \tag{8}$$

Where k_μ and k_σ are the standard deviations of directional statistical features evaluated from training images [13].

Using (7) and (8) the weighted LBP dissimilarity with statistical features was calculated as:

$$D_{LBP}^{F}(S, T) = D_{LBP}(S, T) * \left(1 + C_1 - C_1 * e^{\frac{-d_\mu}{C_2}}\right) * \left(1 + C_1 - C_1 * e^{\frac{-d_\sigma}{C_2}}\right) \tag{9}$$

Where $D_{LBP}(S, T)$ is the LBP histogram dissimilarity, C_1 and C_2 are weights control parameters [12].

3.2   Adaptive LBP

To improve texture classification performance using directional statistical feature vectors, Guo et al. [12] has proposed Adaptive LBP (ALBP) to minimize the directional difference along different orientation of μ and σ vectors. Weight parameter (w_p) is introduced to minimize the overall directional difference $|g_c - w_p * g_p|$. The weight parameter w_p can be computed by using the following objective function:

$$J = \sum_{i=1}^{N} \sum_{j=1}^{M} (g_c(i,j) - w * g_p(i,j))^2 \tag{10}$$

Derive (10) then assign the derivation to zero [14] ,so we get

$$w_p = \frac{g_p^T\, g_c}{g_p^T\, g_p} \tag{11}$$

Weight parameter w_p is evaluated along one orientation $2\pi p/P$ for the whole texture image. The definition of the ALBP equation can be described by the following formula:

$$ALBP_{P,R} = \sum_{p=0}^{P-1} S(g_p * w_p - g_c)2^P \tag{12}$$

3.3   ALBP with Directional Statistical Features

Apply w_p weight to directional statistics features in equations (5) and (6), the directional statistics can be changed to [12]:

$$\mu_p = \sum_{i=1}^{N} \sum_{j=1}^{M} \frac{|g_c(i,j) - w_p * g_p(i,j)|}{M \times N} \tag{13}$$

$$\sigma_p = \sqrt{\sum_{i=1}^{N} \sum_{j=1}^{M} \frac{(|g_c(i,j) - w_p * g_p(i,j)| - \mu_p)^2}{M \times N}} \tag{14}$$

The normalized distance between W_s and W_T can be computed as:

$$d_w = \sum_{p=0}^{P-1} \frac{|w_S(p) - w_T(p)|}{P * k_w} \tag{15}$$

Where k_w is the standard deviation of w evaluated from training images.

Finally, the ALBP dissimilarity weighted by directional statistical features can be defined as:

$$D_{ALBP}^F(S,T) = D_{ALBP}(S,T) * \left(1 + C_1 - C_1 * e^{\frac{-d_\mu}{C_2}}\right) * \left(1 + C_1 - C_1 * e^{\frac{-d_\sigma}{C_2}}\right) *$$

$$\left(1 + C_1 - C_1 * e^{\frac{-d_w}{C_2}}\right) \tag{16}$$

Where $D_{ALBP}(S,T)$ is the ALBP histogram dissimilarity.

In our approach, hierarchical multi scale scheme is combined with ALBP and directional statistical features. Here, it's proposed to build a mutliscale ALBP histogram from big radius to small radius. First, ALBP map of the biggest radius for each pixel is built. The pixels are divided by two groups, "uniform" and "non-uniform" patterns. A sub histogram is built for those "uniform" patterns. Those pixels in Non-uniform pattern are further processed at another small radius to extract their ALBP patterns by smaller radius until the smallest radius. The histograms are concatenated into one multiscale histogram to form the final multiresolution for the whole texture image. Then calculate ALBP dissimilarity with statistical features defined in (16).

Finally, the hierarchical multiscale ALBP dissimilarity weighted by directional statistical features can be defined as:

$$D^F_{HMALBP}(S,T) = D_{HMALBP}(S,T) * \left(1 + C_1 - C_1 * e^{\frac{-d_\mu}{C_2}}\right) * \left(1 + C_1 - C_1 * e^{\frac{-d_\sigma}{C_2}}\right) *$$
$$\left(1 + C_1 - C_1 * e^{\frac{-d_w}{C_2}}\right) \tag{17}$$

Where $D_{HMALBP}(S,T)$ is the HMALBP histogram dissimilarity.

4   Experimental Results and Analysis

Our proposed method has been evaluated on PolyU palmprint dataset [15], CASIA palmprint dataset [16], JAFFE face dataset [17] and ORL face dataset [18].The performance of the proposed method is compared with the performance of LBP, ALBP, ALBPF and HMLBP methods. K-nearest neighbor classifier is used to classify the texture features extracted from the testing samples.

4.1   Results Analysis Using PolyU Dataset

PolyU dataset is the largest publicly available database that commonly used in palmprint recognition research. PolyU dataset contains 7752 grayscale palmprint images captured from 193 individuals. For each palm 20 samples are collected in two sessions. First session has 3889 palmprint images while second session has 3863 palmprint images. Some samples of one palm from PolyU Dataset are shown in Fig. 4.

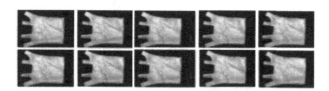

Fig. 4. Some PolyU Samples of One Palm

In this experiment five randomly selected images for each palm captured from the 386 palms are registered as the training samples, while the second session samples are registered as the testing samples. The number of test images is 3864. Fig. 5 displays the effectiveness of the proposed method on palmprint recognition using PolyU dataset. The proposed method could achieve better recognition accuracy than LBP, ALBP, ALBPF, HMLBP methods on PolyU palmprint dataset under different scales.

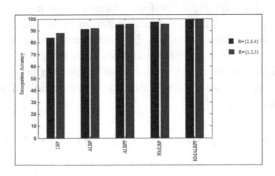

Fig. 5. Comparative Recognition Accuracy on PolyU Dataset

4.2　CASIA Palmprint Dataset

CASIA dataset has 5,502 grayscale palmprint images captured from 312 individuals. From each individual 8 images are collected from each hand. Fig.6 shows some samples of one palm from CASIA Database.

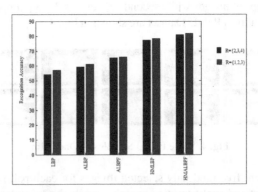

Fig. 6. Some CASIA Samples of one palm

In this experiment, eight randomly selected images captured from the 312 palms are registered as the testing samples. The number of test Images is 2496. Fig. 7

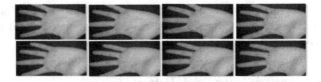

Fig.7. Comparative Recognition Accuracy on CASIA Dataset

displays the effectiveness of the proposed method on CASIA dataset. The proposed method could achieve better recognition accuracy than LBP, ALBP, ALBPF, HMLBP methods on CASIA palmprint dataset under different scales.

4.3   JAFFE Face Dataset

JAFFE (Japanese Female Facial Expression) dataset have 230 grayscale face images for ten Japanese females. Each female has expressed different facial expressions such as neutral, happy, angry, disgust, fear, sad and surprise. JAFFE dataset is commonly used in face recognition systems [19]. Fig. 7 shows different facial expressions for two females from the JAFFE dataset.

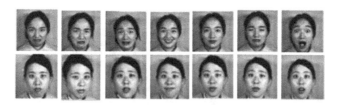

Fig. 8. Different seven face expressions for two females at JAFFE Dataset

In this experiment, ten images selected randomly from each class are registered as the training samples, while thirteen images are registered as the testing samples. The number of test Images is 130. Fig. 8 displays the effectiveness of the proposed method on face recognition using JAFFE database. The proposed method could achieve better recognition accuracy than LBP, ALBP, ALBPF methods but not better than HMLBP this is mainly because fewer training samples are provided for CASIA dataset.

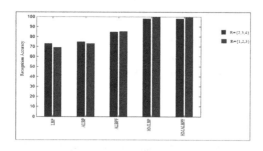

Fig. 9. Comparative Recognition Accuracy on JAFFE Dataset

4.4   ORL Face Dataset

ORL dataset has 400 grayscale face images for 40 distinct individuals. Face images are captured at different times, lighting conditions and face expressions. Some samples of one person captured from ORL Dataset are presented in Fig. 9.

Fig. 10. Some ORL Samples for one person

In this experiment, first five captured images from each class are registered as the training samples, while last five images are registered as the testing samples. Fig. 10 displays the effectiveness of the proposed method using ORL dataset. The proposed method could achieve better recognition accuracy than LBP, ALBP, ALBPF, HMLBP methods on ORL face database under different scales.

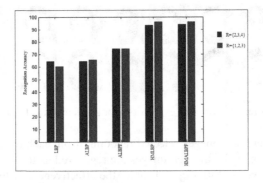

Fig. 11. Comparative Recognition Accuracy on ORL Database

Finally, from the above experiments we can find that using three scales R = {1, 2, 4} could achieve better result than using three scales R = {2, 3, 4} in HMLBP and HMALBPF methods. So, we can observe that increasing radius could decrease the recognition accuracy that's mainly because the percentage of non-uniform patterns increases, so much information is lost. The feature dimension of hierarchical multiscale scheme is a little higher than single LBP as features are extracted from different scales to obtain discriminative features.

5   Conclusion

LBP is simple and efficient in texture descriptor but single LBP may fail to describe some texture patterns. In this paper, to extract discriminative features from an image with full consideration of local spatial structure, a hierarchical multiscale adaptive local binary pattern with directional statistical features (HMALBPPF) method is proposed. The proposed method could extract ALBP features from non-uniform patterns to provide useful information for recognition. The effectiveness of the proposed method is demonstrated on PolyU, CASIA, ORL and JAFFE databases. Compared with LBP, ALBPF, and HMLBP methods, the proposed method could achieve better recognition accuracy.

References

1. Weaver, A.: Biometric authentication. Computer **39**(2), 96–97 (2006)
2. Belhumeur, V., Hespanha, J., Kriegman, D.: Eigenfaces vs. Fisherfaces: Recognition using Class Specific Linear Projection. IEEE Trans. PAMI **19**(7), 711–720 (1997)
3. Michael, G., Connie, T., Andrew, T.: Touch-less palm print biometrics: Novel design and implementation. Image and Vision Computing **26**(12), 1551–1560 (2008)
4. Turk, M., Pentland, A.: Face recognition using eigenfaces. In: IEEE Conf. on Computer Vision and Pattern Recognition, pp. 586–591 (June 1991)
5. Ahonen, T., Hadid, A., Pietikainen, M.: Face description with local binary patterns: application to face recognition. IEEE Trans. on Pattern Analysis and Machine Intelligence **28**, 2037–2040 (2006)
6. Raja, Y., Gong, S.: Sparse multiscale local binary patterns. In: Proceeding of 17th British Machine Vision Conference (2006)
7. Liao, S.C., Zhu, X.X., Lei, Z., Zhang, L., Li, S.Z.: Learning Multi-Scale Block Local Binary Patterns for Face Recognition. In: Proceedings of IAPR/IEEE International Conference on Biometrics, Seoul, Korea, pp. 828–837 (August 2007)
8. Wang, X., Gong, H., Zhang, H.: Palmprint Identification using Boosting Local Binary Pattern. In: 18th International Conference on Pattern Recognition, vol. 3, pp. 503–506 (2006)
9. Hanmandlu, M., Gureja, A., Jain, A.: Palm Print Recogntion using Local Binary Pattern Operator and Support Vector Machines. In: International Conference on Signal and Image Processing, pp. 158–162 (2010)
10. Ojala, T., Pietikainen, M., Maenpaa, T.: Multiresolution gray-scale and rotation invariant texture classification with local binary patterns. IEEE Transactions on Pattern Analysis and Machine Intelligence **24**(7), 971–987 (2002)
11. Guo, Z., Zhang, L., Zhang, D., Mou, X.: Hierarchical multiscale LBP for face and palmprint recognition. In: International Conference on Image Processing (ICIP), pp. 4521–4524 (2010)
12. Guo, Z., Zhang, L., Zhang, D., Zhang, S.: Rotation Invariant Texture Classification Using Adaptive LBP with Directional Statistical Features. In: 17th IEEE International Conference on Image Processing, Hong Kong, pp. 285–288 (2010)
13. Mohamed, A.A., Yampolskiy, R.V.: Wavelet-Based Multiscale Adaptive LBP with Directional Statistical Features for Recognizing Artificial Faces. ISRN Machine Vision 2012 (2012)
14. Wu, X., Wang, K., Zhang, D.: HMMs based palmprint identification. In: Zhang, D., Jain, A.K. (eds.) ICBA 2004. LNCS, vol. 3072, pp. 775–781. Springer, Heidelberg (2004)
15. PolyUPalmprint Database, http://www.comp.polyu.edu.hk/~biometrics
16. CASIA Palmprint Database, http://www.csbr.ia.ac.cn
17. JAFFE Facial expression database, http://www.kasrl.org/jaffe.html
18. ORL Face Database, http://www.cl.cam.ac.uk/research/dtg/attarchive/facedatabase.html
19. Shih, F.Y., Chuang, C.F., Wang, P.P.: Performance Comparison of Facial Expression Recongition in JAFFE Database. International Journal of Pattern Recognition and Artificial Intelligence **22**(3), 445–459 (2008)

Multispectral Iris Recognition
Using Patch Based Game Theory

Foysal Ahmad, Kaushik Roy[✉], and Khary Popplewell

Department of Computer Science, North Carolina A and T State University,
Greensboro, NC 27411, USA
{fahmad,ktpopple}@aggies.ncat.edu, kroy@ncat.edu

Abstract. Multispectral imaging offers potential to improve the recognition performance of an iris biometric system. The novelty of this research effort is that a Coalition Game Theory (CGT) is proposed to select only the important patches that are obtained using the modified Local Binary Pattern (mLBP) operator. The mLBP fuses both the sign and magnitude difference vector in an effort to extract feature from normalized iris images. The CGT selects patches based on the Shapely value that have better individual importance along with a strong interaction with other patches to improve the overall performance. Results show that CGT model maintains better recognition accuracy while reducing the overall surface area needed for recognition purpose.

Keywords: Multispectral iris recognition · Coalition game theory · Modified local binary pattern · Patch selection

1   Introduction

Iris recognition has been regarded as one of the most reliable and accurate biometric technologies in recent years [1]. However, commercial iris recognition systems operate predominately in the near-infrared (IR) range of the electromagnetic spectrum. While near-infrared imaging provides a very reasonable image of the iris texture, it only exploits a narrow band of spectral information. Due to the biological diversity of the composition of the iris, different portions of the electromagnetic spectrum may better represent certain physical characteristics of the epigenetic iris pattern. By incorporating other wavelength ranges (infrared, red, green, blue) in iris recognition systems, the reflectance and absorbance properties of the iris tissue can be exploited to enhance recognition performance and improve security and reliability of recognition systems [2, 3].

Feature extraction deals with the problem of finding the most compact and informative set of features to improve the efficiency of data storage and processing. Several feature extraction techniques such as Gabor wavelets, Daubechies wavelets, Discrete Cosine Transform (DCT), and Independent Component Analysis (ICA) are exploited in the area of iris recognition [4]. In this research effort, we deploy modified Local Binary Pattern (mLBP) to extract features from different patches of the normalized irises [5]. The mLBP technique fuses both the sign and magnitude features to

© Springer International Publishing Switzerland 2014
A. Campilho and M. Kamel (Eds.): ICIAR 2014, Part II, LNCS 8815, pp. 112–119, 2014.
DOI: 10.1007/978-3-319-11755-3_13

improve feature extraction where in regular LBP only the signed difference information is used [6]. Though the sign components preserve the most of the structural local information, mLBP provides additional information that increases the classification performance [5].

Feature selection is an important preprocessing step in machine learning and pattern recognition. In this research, a Coalition Game Theory (CGT) model is utilized to select only important patches over the entire image area instead of selecting only individual features. The CGT evaluates each patch according to its influence to the intricate and intrinsic interrelations among patches based on Shapley value [7]. Each patch performs as a player in this model and the patches with most contribution in the coalition's outcome are selected.

The rest of this paper is organized as follows. Section 2 briefly describes the preprocessing steps of multispectral iris images and patch based CGT. Section 3 reports the experimental results and Section 4 provides our conclusions.

2   Proposed Approach

2.1   Prepossessing

The traditional iris segmentation methods do not perform well on the multispectral iris images. In near infrared wavelength range, the darkest part of an iris image is the pupil. However, in visible spectrum images and channels beyond 1450nm, detecting the boundary between pupil and iris become a difficult task (see Fig. 1).

We first apply binary thresholding techniques to separate iris and pupil area. The Circular Hough Transform (CHT) [8, 9] approach is then utilized along with edge detection techniques to approximate the iris and pupil area. When the iris-sclera circle is defined, a similar circle with smaller radius is created with the same center point as

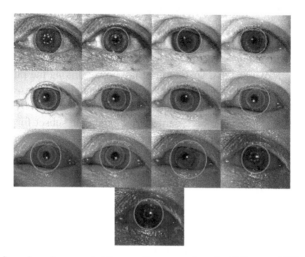

Fig. 1. Samples of segmented images from wavelengths 405nm to 1550nm [10]

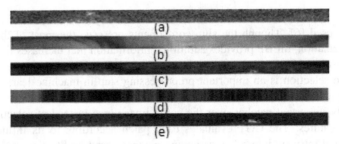

Fig. 2. Normalized iris samples at different wavelengths: (a) 405nm, (b) 505nm, (c) 700nm, (d) 1300nm, and (e) 1550nm [10]

the iris-sclera circle to represent the iris-pupil boundary (See Fig. 1). For spectral channels that do not clearly depict the iris-sclera boundary, only iris-pupil boundary is calculated using CHT. Daugman's Rubber Sheet model is used to normalize the iris images (see Fig. 2) [10].

2.2   Patch Based Coalition Game Theory (CGT)

CGT is concerned with situations in which the decision-makers interact with one another and the reward for each participant in the coalition depends not just on his own decisions but on the decisions made by everyone. Coalition games involve a set of players and a reward associated with different groups or coalitions of players. The reward of a certain coalition depends on individual contributions of players composing this coalition to the game. The larger the contribution of a player is, the higher the benefit of having this player in a coalition. Coalitions with high reward are naturally preferable over those with small reward. This perspective yields an iterative algorithm, contribution selection algorithm (CSA), for patch selection to optimize the performance of the classifier on unseen data [11]. In this approach, each patch obtained using mLBP extractor is regarded as player. The CSA algorithm ranks each patch on each step. The ranking is based on the Shapley value [7], a well-known concept from game theory, to estimate the importance of each patch considering the interactions between patches.

Shapley value measures the distribution of the power among the players in the voting game, which can be transformed into the arena of patch/feature selection attempting to estimate the importance of each patch. The idea is motivated by the observation that every subset of patches can be regarded as a candidate subset for the final selected optimal subset and the power of each patch can be measured by averaging the contributions that it makes to each of the subset which it belongs to.

The Shapley value is defined as follows [7]. Let the marginal importance of player i to a coalition S ($i \notin S$) be

$$\Delta_i = v(S \cup \{i\}) - v(S) \tag{1}$$

where $v(S)$ is the reward associated with coalition S. The reward can be negative, zero, or positive. The negative or zero reward implies no benefits of inclusion of player i into the current coalition. The Shapley value is then defined as

$$\phi_i(v) = \frac{1}{n!} \sum_{\pi \, \in \, \Pi} \Delta_i \left(S_i(\pi) \right) \tag{2}$$

where n is the total number of players, $S_i(\pi)$ is the set of players appearing before player i in permutation π, and Π is the set of permutations over n. Thus, the Shapley value of a given player is the mean of its marginal importance averaged over all possible coalitions of players.

The CSA iteratively selects patches through either forward selection or backward elimination. The forward selection variant iteratively adds a predefined number of patches with the highest contribution to the classification accuracy as long as there are patches with sufficiently large contribution values exceeding a preset contribution threshold. The backward elimination variant iteratively deletes a predefined number of patches with the lowest contribution to the classification accuracy as long as the contribution values of all candidate patches fall below a preset contribution threshold, i.e. such patches add insignificant contribution and therefore they can be safely eliminated. In this research effort, we apply the forward selection algorithm. This algorithm returns a contribution value for each patch according to its role in enhancing the classifier's performance considering its interaction with other patches. The Forward contribution selection algorithm is described below [11].

```
Forward Contribution Selection Algorithm(F,d, t, Δ,nsp)
     Selected: = ∅
     Remaining: = {1… D}
     While Remaining is not empty
          For each i ∈ Remaining
               If Selected is empty,
                    then cᵢ := Contribution (Remainingᵢ, ∅)
               Else {
                    s:= 0;
                    For j: =t
                         Selectedᵢᵢ = Random sample of d patches;
                         s:=s+Contribution(Remainingᵢ, Selected);
                    End For
                    Shapley value, cᵢ := s/t; }
          End For
     Find nsp patches based on highest values of c;
     Selected := Selected ∪ nsp;
     Remaining := Remaining \ nsp;
     End While
```

where F is the input set of patches, t is the number of permutations sample, d is the maximum permutation sample size, D is the number of total patches, Δ is the value threshold and nsp is the number of selected patches.

For this research experiment, we divide each normalized image into different number of patches (See Fig. 3a). These patches are given into to CGT model where each patch works as a player. The CGT model returns only important patches based

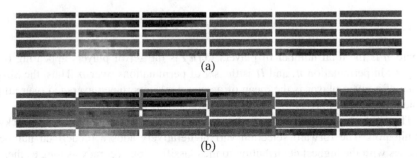

(a)

(b)

Fig. 3. Sample patch combination of iris images. (a) 56 patches given input to CGT model. (b) CGT model selects only 8 important patches.

on higher Shapley value (See Fig. 3b). These selected patches are then used for further calculations.

3   Experimental Results

We conduct this experiment on 3120 multispectral images spanning over 13 wavelengths for 40 subjects [12]. The Goodrich/Sensor digital camera was used to collect images at spectral channels ranging from 405 nm to 1550 nm. Images gathered at multiple wavelengths are normalized into grayscale images for each spectral channel. Each Subject has 78 sample iris images and 6 samples in each of the 13 wavelengths. We conduct our experiment in two ways. First, we separate 1 sample from each of the 13 wavelengths for 40 subjects randomly in test set and rest of the samples in train set. Then each sample of a subject in the test set is verified across its samples ranging over 13 wavelengths and samples from all other subjects of different wavelengths in the train set. Second, the experiment runs on each wavelength which consists of 240 samples for 40 subjects and each of the 40 subjects have 6 samples. We separate 1 sample from each subject randomly in test set and rest in train set. Samples in test set are verified across the samples in train set for each wavelength.

In the first approach, a test sample of a subject is compared with samples from its different wavelength as well as samples from different subjects. If the test sample of a subject matches with any of its different wavelength training sample, it is considered as a match. The result of this approach is included in Table 1. From Table 1, we see that the CGT based approach achieves the same accuracy with baseline but only exploring 50% of its surface area. The wavelength wise accuracies are enlisted in Table 2. In Table 2, the first column represents the different wavelength, second column includes the accuracies without CGT model and third column represents the

Table 1. Overall recognition accuracy

Approach	Accuracy	Percentage area used
mLBP	42.88	100 %
mLBP with CGT	42.88	50%

Table 2. Accuracy for different wavelengths

Wavelength	Accuracy without CGT	Accuracy with CGT (% area used)
405	17.5	17.5 (35 %)
505	52.5	52.5 (16%)
620	22.5	25 (35%)
700	55	65 (33%)
800	47.5	52.5 (41%)
910	45	50 (35%)
911	47.5	52.5 (33%)
970	50	50 (66 %)
1070	52.5	55 (35%)
1200	25	27.5 (62%)
1300	40	47.5 (41%)
1450	45	47.5 (33%)
1550	32.5	35 (60%)

Table 3. True positive rate (TPR) at False positive rate (FPR) approximately 1%

Wavelength(nm)	TPR (%)
405	1.5
505	0.0
620	6.5
700	6.0
800	8.5
910	3.0
911	1.5
970	5.5
1070	16.0
1200	2.0
1300	11.5
1450	6.0
1550	12.0

accuracies with CGT model including percentage of surface area explored in parenthesis. It is shown from Table 2, CGT model exceeds the base line accuracy using smaller surface area of the iris images. Further analysis is shown using the Cumulative Match Characteristics (CMC) curve and Receiver Operator Characteristics (ROC) curve only for important and selected patches using CGT model. Fig. 4(a) depicts the ROC chart for wavelengths up to 911 and Fig. 4(b) represents the ROC chart for wavelengths from 970 nm to 1550 nm. For spectral channels within this range, the

1070nm wavelength produces the best overall performance over all other available wavelengths. The 1070nm spectral channel provides the best True Positive Rate (TPR) of 16% for approximately 1% False Positive Rate (FPR). Table 3 enlists the TPRs for all available wavelengths when their FPRs are approximately 1%.

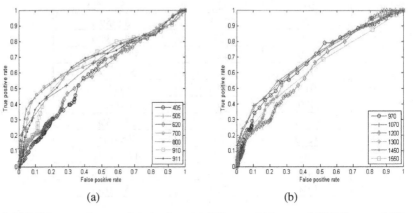

(a)   (b)

Fig. 4. (a) ROC curves for wavelengths from (a) 405 nm to 911 nm and (b) 970 nm to 1550 nm

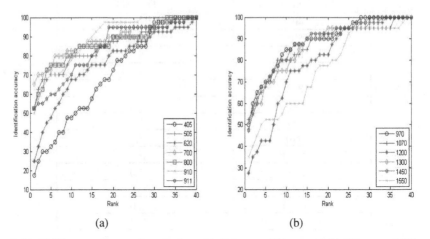

(a)   (b)

Fig. 5. (a) CMC curves for wavelengths from (a) 405 nm to 911 nm and (b) 970 nm to 1550 nm

The CMC curves for wavelengths from 405nm to 911nm are in displayed in Fig. 5(a) and wavelengths from 970nm to 1550nm are displayed in Fig. 5(b). It is shown from these figures that the 700nm spectral band has the highest rank-1 accuracy of 65% using only 33% of overall surface area. Although 700nm has the highest rank-1 accuracy, 910nm spectral band achieves 100% identification accuracy at rank 27 where 700nm band achieves 100% recognition accuracy at rank 35.

4   Conclusions

In this research approach, a CGT based feature/patch selection model is explored where each patch is considered as a player for multispectral iris recognition process. This selection model not only considers the individual importance of a patch but also considers its interactions with other patches based on Shapley value. Moreover, the multispectral iris images ranging from 405 nm to 1550 nm are segmented using circular Hough Transform, binary thresholding and edge detection algorithm. The CGT model not only maintains better accuracy but also it reduces the amount of surface area required for matching. Future work will be focused on the application of CGT model to more unique datasets on a larger scale.

Acknowledgments. This research was sponsored by the U.S. Government, including the Science and Technology Center: Bio/Computation Evolution in Action Consortium (BEACON). The authors would like to thank the NSF for their support of this research.

References

1. Daugman, J.: Biometric personal identification system based on iris analysis. United States Patent Patent Number: 5, 291, 560 (1994)
2. Boyce, C., Ross, A., Monaco, M., Hornak, L., Li, X.: Multispectral iris analysis: A preliminary study. In: Proc. IEEE Comput. Soc. Conf. Comput. Vision Pattern Recognition Workshop, pp. 51–59 (2006)
3. Chen, R., Lin, X., Ding, T.: Liveness detection for iris recognition using multispectral images. Pattern Recognition Letters **33**(12), 1513–1519 (2012)
4. Roy, K., Bhattacharya, P., Suen, C.Y.: Iris segmentation using variational level set method. Optics and Lasers in Engg. **49**(4), 578–588 (2011)
5. Ojala, T., Pietikäinen, M., Mäenpää, T.: Multiresolution gray-scale and rotation invariant texture classification with Local Binary Pattern. IEEE Trans. on Pattern Analysis and Machine Intelligence **24**(7), 971–987 (2002)
6. Guo, Z., Zhang, L., Zhang, D.: A Completed Modeling of Local Binary Pattern Operator for Texture Classification. IEEE Trans. on Image Processing **19**(6), 1657–1663 (2010)
7. Shapley, L.: A value for n-person games. In: Kuhn, H., Tucker, A. (eds.) Contributions to the Theory of Games. Annals of Mathematics Studies 28, vol. II, pp. 307–317. Princeton University Press, Princeton (1953)
8. Yuen, H.K., Princen, J., Illingworth, J., Kittler, J.: Comparative study of Hough transform methods for circle finding. Image and Vision Computing **8**(1), 71–77 (1990)
9. Masek, L. Kovesi, P.: MATLAB Source Code for a Biometric Identification System Based on Iris Patterns. The School of Computer Science and Software Engineering, The University of Western Australia (2003)
10. Popplewell, K., Roy, K., Ahmad, F., Shelton, J.: Multispectral Iris Recognition Utilizing Hough Transform and Modified LBP. In: IEEE SMC 2014, San Diego, CA (accepted 2014)
11. Cohen, S., Dror, G., Ruppin, E.: Feature selection via coalition game theory. Neural Computation **19**(7), 1939–1961 (2007). doi:10.1162/neco.2007.19.7.1939
12. Multispectral Iris Dataset: Portions of the research in this paper use the Consolidated Multispectral Iris Dataset of iris images collected under the Consolidated Multispectral Iris Dataset Program, sponsored by the US Government

Medical Image Processing
and Analysis

Periodic Background Pattern Detection and Removal for Cell Tracking

Tiago Esteves[1,3]([✉]), Ângela Carvalho[2,3], Fernando Jorge Monteiro[2,3], and Pedro Quelhas[1,3]

[1] Departamento de Engenharia Electrotécnica e de Computadores, Faculdade de Engenharia, Universidade do Porto, Rua Dr. Roberto Frias, 4200-465 Porto, Portugal
[2] Departamento de Engenharia Metalúrgica e de Materiais, Faculdade de Engenharia, Universidade do Porto, Rua Dr. Roberto Frias, 4200-465 Porto, Portugal
[3] INEB - Instituto de Engenharia Biomédica, Rua do Campo Algre, 823 4150-180 Porto, Portugal
dee11017@fe.up.pt

Abstract. The study of cell morphology and cell mobility variation when cells are grown on top of patterned substrates is becoming a very important factor in tissue regeneration.

In this paper we present a novel approach to automatically detect and remove periodic background patterns in brightfield microscopy images. This background removal process is fundamental for the analysis of cell mobility as the periodic background pattern would otherwise lead to erroneous cell analysis. The detection of the background is performed by searching for the periodic background pattern organization through the analysis of keypoints automatically obtained from images. Using this information we are able to both detect and reconstruct the periodic background and finally remove it from the original images.

We tested the proposed approach on microscopy images with different periodic background patterns. The effectiveness of the method was validated both by visual inspection and by the cell tracking results obtained.

1 Introduction

The analysis of cell behaviour when interacting with different micropatterned surfaces has gained increasing interest in the last years [1,2]. Biologist researchers started producing micropatterned surfaces on biomaterials to study the possibility to modulate cell behaviour only through topography stimulus of biomaterials [1]. Micropatterned surfaces can be developed with controlled chemistry, roughness, thickness and textures to study its influence on cells (figure 1). Those cell/surface interactions are analyzed in order to access cell metabolic activity, adhesion morphology, proliferation and lineage differentiation [2]. Measurements of cell alignment, elongation and guided mobility on the surface

© Springer International Publishing Switzerland 2014
A. Campilho and M. Kamel (Eds.): ICIAR 2014, Part II, LNCS 8815, pp. 123–131, 2014.
DOI: 10.1007/978-3-319-11755-3_14

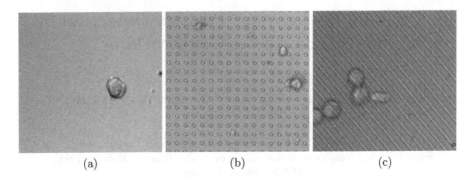

(a)   (b)   (c)

Fig. 1. Brightfield images with cells on top of different micropatterned surfaces: a) Flat surface; b) Pillar pattern surface; c) Line pattern surface

are essential to confirm these interactions [2]. Currently there is no automatic methodology to perform this measurements on patterned surfaces. Measurements are performed mainly by visual inspection alone [2].

The required cell mobility and morphology analysis is already performed on other studies where the background is flat [3–6]. Nevertheless it is known that there is an dependency between segmentation and interferences or changes in the image background like changes or distortions of image intensity or illuminance [7]. However, image background pre-processing steps are mainly concerned with intensity inhomogeneities and illumination [8–10].

Several other works tried to address similar problems with background pattern removal [11,12]. Andrew *et. al.* performed the removal of unwanted, nonperiodic patterns from forensic images by registering the image under analysis with a control background pattern image [11]. This is not possible in our case since we do not have an available control image from the background pattern and the existing pattern varies between images. Considering the case of periodic background patterns it is possible to perform image background removal by filtering in the Fourier domain [12]. However, this only works for periodic stripe patterns, which does not applies to our pillar patterned images (figure 1 (b)). If we consider the existence of background pattern as texture, there are also several methods that can be used to address this problem [13]. Such methods perform texture classification and segmentation. However, they do not provide a simple way to synthesize or remove the background image.

In order to facilitate cell detection and tracking for mobility and morphology analysis we propose a new approach to automatically detect the periodic background pattern, synthethize the full background, and remove it from the original image. The proposed approach consists of four steps: first we evaluate if there is a periodic background pattern or not; then, if it exists, we detect the background pattern based on its periodicity; after that we synthesize the full background image; finally we subtract the background from the original image obtaining only information related to the existing cells.

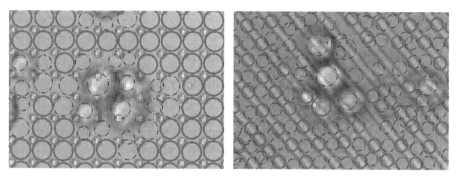

Fig. 2. Keypoint extraction from different background pattern brightfield images (colors represent different SIFT clusters).

2 Proposed Methodology

The first step of the proposed approach is to evaluate if there is a periodic background pattern in the image under analysis or if it has a flat background. We only perform the background pattern analysis if a periodic pattern exists.

2.1 Background Pattern versus Flat Background

In order to check if we have or not a periodic background pattern in the image under analysis we measure the image entropy:

$$E = -\sum_{i \in I} p_i . * \log_2(p_i),$$

(1)

where p is the histogram of image I and i is the pixel value. A high value indicates that we have high pixel values variation and we assume that it occurs in case of existing a periodic background pattern. Otherwise, a low value indicates that we are in presence of a flat background where pixel values do not differ to much from each other. We only consider the images for periodic background pattern detection that have entropy value over a defined threshold. Images in which the entropy value is low are assumed to have a flat background on which we only apply an illuminance and intensity inhomogeneities correction.

If a background pattern exists the first step for its detection is to extract keypoints from the image that will allow to infer the pattern periodicity.

2.2 Keypoints Extraction

In order to automatically obtain keypoints for periodic background pattern detection we use the Laplacian of Gaussian filter (LoG) [3,6]. This approach is based on the image scale-space representation and after applying this filter over several scales we search for local maxima of LoG response. We apply this approach to the images under analysis obtaining keypoints in positions that are related to both the background pattern and cell's position (figure 2). As we

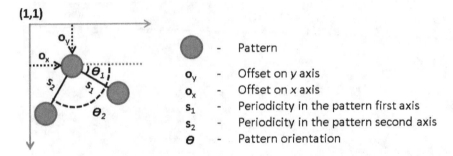

Fig. 3. Scheme used for detecting the pattern background periodicity. The background pattern is defined with a specific periodic interval s_1 and s_2, orientations θ_1 and θ_2, and image origin offset defined by (o_x, o_y).

observe in images from figure 2, as expected, the keypoints appear on locations with cells, however, they also appear in the regions of the background pattern. In the image from figure 2 (left) most keypoints are obtained with the same periodicity as the pillars from the background and in figure 2 (right) the same happens, in which most keypoints are obtained in the same orientation as the lines that compose the background.

After obtaining the keypoints we extract for each a SIFT descriptor [4]. We cluster the descriptors using k-means clustering ($k = 4$) and choose the largest cluster of descriptors that correspond to the keypoints obtained on the pattern repetition (figure 2 - red bold continuous circles). The selected keypoints will be used for the pattern periodicity analysis.

2.3 Background Pattern Periodicity Analysis

In order to detect the periodic background pattern we follow the scheme in figure 3. As we consider the periodic pattern to have two orthogonally independent periodicity spacings, we first search only over o_x, o_y, θ_1 and s_1 to find those that best fit our model. Given a set of values for o_x, o_y, θ_1 and s_1 we generate the predicted locations for our periodic pattern along the axis defined by θ_1. Given the selected LoG detection's coordinates in the image, we project each detection's location onto the axis defined by θ_1 along its normal. Each of those projections is then assigned to the nearest periodic pattern location, and the distance to the predicted periodic pattern is computed. As this distance calculation would favor smaller spacing in the periodic pattern it is normalized dividing by s_1. The set of parameters that lead to the lowest average distance are those assumed to represent the periodic pattern of the background in the image. Given o_x, o_y, θ_1 and s_1 we fix o_x, o_y and vary s_2 setting θ_2 to $\theta_2 = \theta_1 \pm 90$, but allowing for a 20 degree tolerance. If in this θ interval we find a second low average distance and the corresponding s_2 value is equal to s_1 value found previously, we assume that the background periodic pattern is pillar type (figure 2 (left)). We make this assumption because for both θ values (separated by ± 90 degrees) we have the same keypoints periodicity. Otherwise, we assume a line background periodic pattern.

The pseudocode that follows summarizes the algorithm used for finding the periodic background pattern:

Algorithm 1. Pseudocode of the proposed approach

Require: *KeyPoints* extraction
  for o_x, o_y, θ_1, s_1 **do**
    Generate periodic pattern locations
    distanceSum $\leftarrow$ 0
    for Each KeyPoint **do**
      Keypoint projection to obtain new coordinates in the axis defined by θ_1
      minDist $\leftarrow$ new coordinate distance to the closest pattern periodic location
      distanceSum $\leftarrow$ *distanceSum* + *minDist*/s_1
    end for
    distanceTotal$(o_x, o_y, \theta_1, s_1)$ $\leftarrow$ *distanceSum*
  end for
  Find θ_1, s_1 and o_x, o_y (pattern information) that minimizes *distanceTotal*
  Repeat the s_1 and o_x, o_y estimation cycle to find s_2 and θ_2 with $\theta_2 = \theta_1 \pm 90 \pm 10$

Given the information found we classify each region as being periodic background pattern or foreground using template matching.

2.4 Foreground Removal

To detect the foreground regions we measure the similarity of each region with their 8 neighbour regions (according to the pattern periodicity found) using cross correlation:

$$\gamma(u, v) = \frac{\sum_{x,y}[f(x, y) - \overline{f}_{u,v}][t(x - u, y - v) - \overline{t}]}{\sqrt{\sum_{x,y}[f(x, y) - \overline{f}_{u,v}]^2[t(x - u, y - v) - \overline{t}]^2}}, \tag{2}$$

where $\overline{t}$ is the mean of the template and $\overline{f}_{u,v}$ is the mean of the image $f(x, y)$ in the region under the template [14]. A higher cross correlation coefficient (γ) indicates similar image regions.

As we measure the similarity between regions according to the pattern periodicity we will obtain high γ in presence of background pattern regions, and low values for foreground regions (figure 4 - b). From this analysis we then assume a specific *threshold* that separates the background pattern (figure 4 - c) from the foreground regions (figure 4 - d). From the detected background we then synthesize the removed foreground regions as background to obtain the full background image.

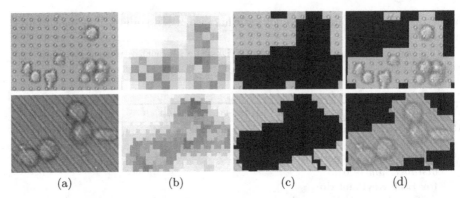

Fig. 4. Foreground and background separation: a) Original image; b) γ similarity map (white - high value); c) Background detection d) Foreground regions

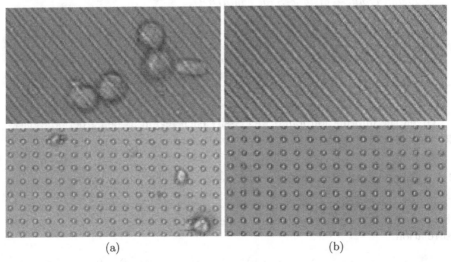

Fig. 5. Background reconstruction: a) Original image; b) Periodic background pattern detection and reconstruction

2.5   Background Reconstruction

The final step to obtain the entire background pattern image is to reconstruct the foreground regions based on the pattern's periodicity. We define a patch (9×9) and search the image. When the center pixel of the patch is located at a foreground location we synthesize the periodic background pattern and replace it in the image. To synthesize the background we use the similar background patches located according to the parameters (θ_1, θ_2, s_1, s_2, o_x, o_y) previously estimated. We average those similar patches to synthesise a valid background patch for that location and replace it in the background image. If pixels of that patch overlaps with already existing background, those pixels are combined

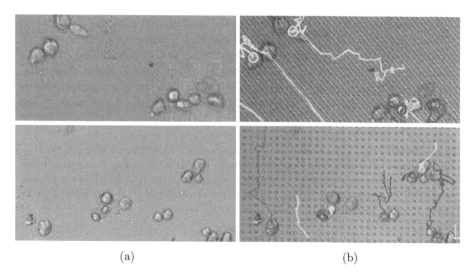

(a)   (b)

Fig. 6. Background removal and cell tracking results: a) Result from subtracting the reconstructed background pattern from the original image; b) Cell tracks on top of the original image

weighting the new pixels with 0.1 and the old pixels with 0.9. Examples of the final results are given in figure 5.

3   Results and Discussion

We applied our approach on several brightfield microscopy images with different periodic background patterns and cells on top. For each original image we obtained the periodic background pattern and then we subtracted it from the original image and observed the results (figure 6 - a). From the results we were able to visualize that the differences are given mainly due to the cell presence which is an indicator that the background reconstruction is performing well.

Given the removal of the periodic background pattern we use the LoG filter to detect cells and we obtain detections only on locations with cells with no background pattern interference. From the cell detection result the cell tracking is then possible (figure 6 - b).

4   Conclusion

In this paper we proposed a novel approach to detect and extract the existing periodic background pattern in cell brightfield images. The approach is based on the analysis of keypoints periodicity obtained from each image. Once we found the existing periodic background pattern, it enables its removal from the original image by image subtraction.

Using the images from which the periodic background pattern was removed it is possible to perform cell detection and tracking. Future work will be done on the analysis of cell morphology and mobility which is now possible based on the development methodology for periodic background pattern removal. The influence of different background pattern (resultant of different micropatterned surfaces) on cell mobility and morphology will be quantified and compared.

Acknowledgments. This work has been financed by FEDER funds through the Programa Operacional Factores de Competitividade - COMPETE and by Portuguese funds through FCT - Fundação para a Ciência e a Tecnologia in the framework of the project PEst-C/SAU/LA0002/2013. T. Esteves is recipient of SFRH /BD / 80508/ 2011 by FCT. P. Quelhas is a *Ciência2008* awardee.

References

1. Carvalho, A., Pelaez-Vargas, A., Gallego-Perez, D., Grenho, L., Fernandes, M.H., De Azaf, A.H., Ferraza, M.P., Hansford, D.J., Monteiro, F.J.: Micropatterned silica thin films with nanohydroxyapatite micro-aggregates for guided tissue regeneration. Dental Materials **28**(12), 11 (2012)
2. Pelaez-Vargas, A., Gallego-Perez, D., Carvalho, A., Fernandes, M.H., Hansford, D.J., Monteiro, F.J.: Effects of density of anisotropic microstamped silica thin films on guided bone tissue regeneration - in vitro study. Society for Biomaterials **101**(5), 762–769 (2013)
3. Esteves, T., Oliveira, M.J., Quelhas, P.: Cancer cell detection and morphology analysis based on local interest point detectors. In: Sanches, J.M., Micó, L., Cardoso, J.S. (eds.) IbPRIA 2013. LNCS, vol. 7887, pp. 624–631. Springer, Heidelberg (2013)
4. Esteves, T., Oliveira, M.J., Quelhas, P.: Cancer cell detection and tracking based on local interest point detectors. In: Kamel, M., Campilho, A. (eds.) ICIAR 2013. LNCS, vol. 7950, pp. 434–441. Springer, Heidelberg (2013)
5. Li, K., Kanade, T.: Cell population tracking and lineage construction using multiple-model dynamics filters and spatiotemporal optimization. Medical Image Analysis **12**(5), 546–566 (2008)
6. Esteves, T., Quelhas, P., Mendona, A.M., Campilho, A.: Gradient convergence filters for cell nuclei detection: a comparison study with a phase based approach. MVAP **23**(4), 623–638 (2012)
7. Vovk, U., Pernus, F., Likar, B.: A review of methods for correction of intensity inhomogeneity in MRI. IEEE Transactions on Medical Imaging **26**(3), 405–421 (2007)
8. Roy, S., Carass, A., Prince, J.L.: Compressed sensing based intensity non-uniformity correction. In: 2011 IEEE International Symposium on Biomedical Imaging: From Nano to Macro, pp. 101–104 (March 2011)
9. Madani, R., Bourquard, A., Unser, M.: Image segmentation with background correction using a multiplicative smoothing-spline model. In: 2012 9th IEEE International Symposium on Biomedical Imaging (ISBI), pp. 186–189 (May 2012)

10. Zheng, Y., Vanderbeek, B., Xiao, R., Daniel, E., Stambolian, D., Maguire, M., O'Brien, J., Gee, J.: Retrospective illumination correction of retinal fundus images from gradient distribution sparsity. In: 2012 9th IEEE International Symposium on Biomedical Imaging (ISBI), pp. 972–975 (May 2012)
11. Andrew, D.C., Zisserman, A., Bramble, S., Compton, D.: An automatic method for the removal of unwanted, non-periodic patterns from forensic images (1998)
12. Xie, Y., Chen, L., Hofmann, U.G.: Reduction of periodic noise in fourier domain optical coherence tomography images by frequency domain filtering (2012)
13. Tuceryan, M., Jain, A.K.: Texture analysis (1998)
14. Lewis, J.P.: Fast template matching. Vision Interface, 120–123 (1995)

Nerve Detection in Ultrasound Images Using Median Gabor Binary Pattern

Oussama Hadjerci[1]([⊠]), Adel Hafiane[1], Pascal Makris[2], Donatello Conte[2], Pierre Vieyres[3], and Alain Delbos[4]

[1] Laboratory PRISME EA 4229, INSA Centre Val de Loire, University of Orléans, 88 boulevard Lahitolle, 18020 Bourges, France
[2] Laboratory LI EA 6300, University of Francois Rabelais, 64 Avenue Jean Portalis, 37200 Tours, France
[3] Laboratory PRISME EA 4229, University of Orléans, 63 Avenue de Lattre de Tassigny, 18020 Bourges, France
[4] Clinique Medipole Garonne, 45 rue de Gironis CS 13624, 31036 Toulouse, France
oussama.hadjerci@univ-orleans.fr

Abstract. Ultrasound in regional anesthesia (RA) has increased in popularity over the last years. The nerve localization presents a key step for RA practice, it is therefore valuable to develop a tool able to facilitate this practice. The nerve detection in the ultrasound images is a challenging task, since the noise and other artifacts corrupt the visual properties of such kind of tissue. In this paper we propose a new method to address this problem. The proposed technique operates in two steps. As the median nerve belongs to a hyperechoic region, the first step consists in the segmentation of this type of region using the k-means algorithm. The second step is more critical; it deals with nerve structure detection in noisy data. For that purpose, a new descriptor is developed. It combines tow methods median binary pattern (MBP) and Gabor filter to obtain the median Gabor binary pattern (MGBP). The method was tested on 173 ultrasound images of the median nerve obtained from three patients. The results showed that the proposed approach achieves better accuracy than the original MBP, Gabor descriptor and other popular descriptors.

Keywords: Image segmentation · Feature extraction · Image texture analysis · Supervised learning · Nerve detection · Regional anesthesia

1 Introduction

Regional anesthesia (RA) is performed by injecting the anesthetic close to a nerve block to immobilize a part of human body. Ultrasound imaging is an essential way in the practice of RA, it allows the visualization of the anatomical tissues, and it facilitates the needle control [19]. However, RA is a complex technique that requires a long learning process and years of experience [10,19]. Hence, it

© Springer International Publishing Switzerland 2014
A. Campilho and M. Kamel (Eds.): ICIAR 2014, Part II, LNCS 8815, pp. 132–140, 2014.
DOI: 10.1007/978-3-319-11755-3_15

is important to provide anesthetists with a tool based on ultrasound images to improve the RA practice.

Segmentation and detection in ultrasound (US) images have been applied to several applications such as abdomen, breast, liver, kidney, etc [4, 7, 14, 17]. Very few works have studied the automatic nerve detection in the US images [16]. The nerve region is not a salient structure in the ultrasound images, due to the poor quality of the US imaging modality that generates many effects such as speckle noise, signal degradation, artifacts, etc [11]. Indeed, the segmentation and recognition in the US images are among the most challenging problems in the field of image processing and analysis. Numerous segmentation approaches, such as classification, active contour and graph cuts, have been used to tackle this issue [11]. According to the type of application, these methods require choosing relevant features to detect the regions of interest. Texture information is an important cue for many applications including the nerve blocks detection. However, texture analysis in US images is not an easy task. Nevertheless, several works have shown useful properties using texture to segment different tissues in US images. Features based on gray level correlation matrix (GLCM) [6], have been used for the detection of cardiac images [1], and the placenta [9]. In another work, GLCM has been utilized to guide the evolution of active contour for detecting the Thyroid Gland [15]. Recently the wavelet approach has been used with support vector machine (SVM) classifier to detect the prostate region [20], and also thresholding based wavelet has been used to remove the noise to detect the prostate [8]. In [13] Gabor filter bank has been combined with active contours for the prostate detection. Gabor filter is also utilized with expectation and maximization algorithm to detect liver and cystic kidney [7]. The local binary pattern (LBP) has been also utilized in the purpose of the prostate segmentation [4]. The performance of texture-based methods depends on the type of the tissue in the US images. Most of the state-of-the-art techniques have been applied to either hyperechoic or hypoechoic regions. The textural aspect of these regions is different each other, which requires different approaches. The nerve region presents a particular pattern that can be hypoechoic or hyperechoic structure, depending on the size of the nerve, the probe frequency and the angle of the ultrasound beam [10]. In this work, we address the problem of "median nerve" detection that presents a hyperechoic structure with a particular textural information. Due to the poor quality of the US images the nerve region is not easy to distinguish among others anatomical structures. The traditional texture features are not be sufficient to handle such a situation. In this paper, we propose a new method for detecting the median nerve. This method consists in two phases. The first one separates the foreground regions (hyperechoic tissues). The second phase extracts the nerve area in the foreground using support vector machine (SVM) and a new type of features that is a combination between Gabor filter and median binary patterns (MBP) [5]. Fig. 1 shows the flowchart of the proposed technique.

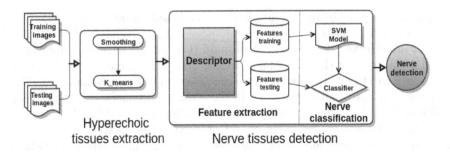

Fig. 1. Flowchart of the nerve detection in the ultrasound images

2   Nerve Detection

The median nerve appears brighter in the US images since it is a hyperechoic structure. Therefore, the first step requires the segmentation of the hyperechoic foreground tissues to reduce the non useful information. In the next stage, the nerve is extracted from the foreground using texture features, called Median Gabor Binary Pattern (MGBP).

2.1   Hyperechoic Tissues Segmentation

To extract the hyperechoic tissues, we used Gaussian filtering processing to reduce the image noise, then k-means algorithm is applied to classify each pixel into background and foreground regions. Fig. 2 shows an example of the segmentation result, where we can distinguish the hyperechoic tissues from the other ones.

Input image   Gaussian filter response   Clustering result

Fig. 2. Segmentation of hyperhecoic tissues using K-means

2.2   Feature Extraction

As we are dealing with noisy data, it is important for the descriptor not to be sensitive to the noise. The Gabor descriptor can help to reduce the noise effect, since it is based on band-pass filtering process [3]. However, frequency methods such as Gabor filter are not sufficient to characterize the nerve structure, it is more interesting to use additional information. The LBP based methods are among the best techniques for texture analysis and it can be combined with Gabor descriptors to achieve better performances as shown in [21]. This method called Local Gabor Binary Pattern (LGBP) has demonstrated some robustness with respect to the noise, while producing good performances for recognition task. LGBP can be suitable for ultrasound images, however it may fail to characterize the nerve texture due to the importance of the noise. Median Binary Pattern (MPB) has more interesting properties when it deals with noisy textures. MBP incorporates the median filtering processing which helps to reduce the noise. We propose to combine MBP with Gabor Filters producing the Median Gabor Binary Pattern (MGBP) descriptor, as shown in Fig. 3.

Input image   Gabor response   MGBP features

Fig. 3. The stage of MGBP feature extraction method

To compute the $MGBP$ at the position (x, y) on a given image I, first, I is convolved with Gabor kernel, expressed by the following equation,

$$g(x, y) = exp[-\frac{1}{2}(\frac{x'^2}{\sigma_x^2} + \frac{y'^2}{\sigma_y^2})]cos(2\pi f x') \qquad (1)$$

where $x' = xcos\phi + ysin\phi$, $y' = -xsin\phi + ycos\phi$, ϕ is the filter direction, σ is the standard deviation of Gaussian envelope, and f is the frequency of cosine wave. We use the magnitude of the Gabor filter response, that is $z(x, y) = |I(x, y) * g(x, y)|$. The MGBP is determined by mapping from the response $z(x, y)$ space to a localized binary pattern, thereby thresholding the neighborhood pixels against their median value. The MGBP at pixel (x, y) is defined as,

$$MGBP_{P,R} = \sum_{p=0}^{P-1} \delta(z_p - z_m)2^P \quad \delta = \begin{cases} 1, x \geqslant 0 \\ 0, x < 0 \end{cases} \qquad (2)$$

We adopted the same strategy as LBP and MBP [5,12] for the different parameters, where P is the number of neighbors and R is the radius of the circular neighborhood, z_p is the pixel value in R and z_m is the median value in this neighborhood. Rotational Invariance Uniform (RIU) is defined as,

$$MGBP_{P,R}^{riu2} = \begin{cases} \sum_{p=0}^{P-1} \delta(z_p - z_m) & if \ U(MGBP_{P,R}^U) \leq 2 \\ P+1 & otherwise \end{cases} \qquad (3)$$

where

$$(MGBP_{P,R}^U) = |\delta(z_{p-1} - z_m) - \delta(z_0 - z_m)| + \sum_{p=0}^{P-1} |\delta(z_p - z_m) - \delta(z_{p-1} - z_m)| \ (4)$$

After obtaining the local patterns in the processed image, we compute the MGBP hisotgram at each pixel within $N \times N$ centered patch. These histograms provide MGBP descriptors.

2.3   Nerve Classification

In the classification process, each pixel of the segmented foreground is labeled as belonging, or not, to a nerve tissues. For that purpose we use the SVM algorithm to identify the nerve pixels. SVM classifier [18] is based on intuitive geometric principles, aiming to define an optimal hyperplane in the training data so that minimum expected risk is achieved. SVM is widely used for image segmentation and classification showing very powerful discriminative properties. In this study, the linear kernel $K(x, x') = (< x, x' >)^n$ has shown the best performances compared to the non linear ones.

3   Experimentation

The experiments were conducted over 173 ultrasound images of the median nerve extracted from three US videos of patients. Data set was obtained in real conditions at Médipôle Garonne clinic (Toulouse, France). The ground truth was marked by regional anesthesia experts.

In the first stage the k-means segmentation was performed over all the images to segment the foreground (see section 2.1), then the classification process was applied over the foreground to extract the target region. For that purpose, the dataset were separated into three groups, each one containing a set of the US images of one patient; the images size is 633×418. We use one group for learning the model and the remaining ones for the tests. The cross validation procedure was used to generate the learning and testing sets (see Fig. 4). For each couple of learning/testing set, the SVM algorithm has been applied to classify the pixels. Specificity, sensitivity and accuracy were used to measure the performance of the tested methods,

$$Accuracy : Acc = \frac{Sn + Sp}{2}, Sensitivity : Sn = \frac{tp}{tp + fn}, Specificity : Sp = \frac{tn}{tn + fp} \quad (5)$$

where tp, tn, fp, fn are respectively true positives, true negatives, false positives and false negatives. In order to illustrate the effectiveness of the proposed approach for the nerve detection, we have conducted comparative experiments with most of the popular methods of texture analysis in ultrasound images, such as the Gabor descriptor, LBP, MBP, Wavelet, GLCM and LGBP with different parameters. The Gabor filters have been generated using different combination of parameters for the orientation $\theta = (0, \pi/4, \pi/2, 3\pi/4)$ and the scale $s = (1, 2, 3)$. The experiments of LBP and MBP have been generated using a several values for radius R and neighborhood P (i.e. $R = (1, 2, 3)$ and $P = (8, 16, 24)$). Different Wavelet families have been applied to our data, in this experiment we kept the best parameters of each family. The GLCM descriptor was also tested with different orientations, whereas the distance of one pixel showed better results. Finally, it is also important to study the influence of the patch size, for our experiments the size 35×35 produced the best classification scores.

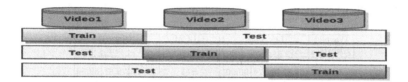

Fig. 4. Evaluation scheme

Table 1. Classification results for different parameters of Gabor

Params	Scale=1			Params	Scale=2			Params	Scale=3		
θ	Acc	Sn	Sp	θ	Acc	Sn	Sp	θ	Acc	Sn	Sp
0	66.13	52.36	79.90	0	65.37	50.58	80.15	0	63.91	46.96	80.86
$\pi/4$	64.88	49.30	80.46	$\pi/4$	67.64	52.68	82.59	$\pi/4$	70.17	58.03	82.31
$\pi/2$	**70.89**	58.47	83.32	$\pi/2$	68.04	53.97	82.10	$\pi/2$	66.22	45.32	87.12
$3\pi/4$	70.48	51.19	89.77	$3\pi/4$	68.91	49.70	88.12	$3\pi/4$	60.36	38.35	82.37

Table 2. Classification results for different parameters of LBP and MBP

Params			LBP			MBP		
Type	R	P	Acc	Sn	Sp	Acc	Sn	Sp
$u2$	1	8	65.24	86.90	43.59	37.78	23.44	52.12
ri	1	8	66.14	87.43	44.85	45.72	35.03	56.40
ri	2	16	66.15	87.43	44.86	46.65	24.12	69.19
$riu2$	1	8	66.14	87.43	44.85	58.77	47.11	70.42
$riu2$	2	16	66.12	87.41	44.83	56.65	33.33	79.98
$riu2$	3	24	**64.91**	86.39	43.42	53.59	32.61	74.57
$riu2$	1,2,3	8,16,24	64.42	52.21	76.63	**70.50**	65.87	75.14

3.1   Evaluation of the Texture Methods

In this section we measure the performance of several state-of-the-art methods, by varying the parameters of each method as shown in Tables 1, 2, 3, 4. From these tables, it can be seen that the best accuracy score for each method (bold type in the table) depends on the specific set of parameters. For the Gabor descriptor, scale=1, orientation ($\theta = \pi/2$) and frequency ($\lambda = 1$) yielded the highest value (70.89%). For the LBP and MBP, the best parameters are $LBP_{riu}^{3,24}$ and $MBP_{riu}^{8,16,24}$, respectively. For the Wavelet descriptor, the symlets wavelet, where the number of vanishing moments is five (sym5) [2] and level 3 produced 63.92%. GLCM yielded an accuracy of 62.45% for distance=1 and orientation=0. The best classification accuracy scores were obtained with Gabor and MBP descriptors produced the better accuracy (70.89% and 70.50%) compared to the traditional techniques. Best performance were obtained when these two methods were combined. Table 4 shows the MGBP and LGBP classification accuracies. It can be observed that MGBP achieves higher average accuracy (71.34%) than LGBP. The largest difference is about 8.79% when $R = 1$ and $P = 8$.

3.2   Overall Comparison

In this part, we compare the proposed method (MGBP) with the other techniques previously described, using only the best scores of each technique. Fig. 5

Table 3. Classification results for different Wavelet families and GLCM

Wavelet families	Level=3			GLCM Orientation	Dist=1		
	Acc	Sn	Sp		Acc	Sn	Sp
bior3.3	63.74	60.29	67.19	0	**62.45**	79.04	45.86
db6	63.82	60.74	66.90	$\pi/4$	59.58	79.61	39.56
sym5	**63.92**	61.18	66.66	$\pi/2$	60.35	79.46	41.25
coif1	63.92	61.15	66.33	$3\pi/4$	60.06	79.58	40.54

Table 4. Classification results for different parameters of LGBP and MGBP

Params(riu2)		LGBP			MGBP		
R	P	Acc	Sn	Sp	Acc	Sn	Sp
1	8	61,99	70.97	53.02	**71.34**	82.38	60.30
2	16	**62.55**	44.42	80.68	57.01	50.29	63.73
3	24	60.54	35.54	89.54	61,15	34.61	87.69
1_2	8_16	61.14	68.97	53.31	68,20	77.39	59.01
1_3	8_24	61.82	66.63	57.01	63,72	74.01	53.43
2_3	16_24	60.12	46.63	74.17	60,42	40.39	80.45
1_2_3	8_16_24	66.99	70.97	53.02	66.48	70.05	62.45

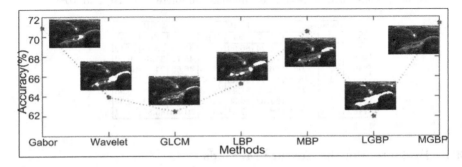

Fig. 5. Comparison of classification results of the proposed method and the best method of analysis texture

shows qualitative and quantitative experimental results. From this figure, we can see that MGBP reachs the highest correct classification rates (71.34%) among all the other approaches. The qualitative results demonstrate that MGBP provides better accuracy for nerve detection. In general, the combination of MBP and Gabor filter is more accurate than the original MBP or Gabor as a single feature. MGBP attains the best results and realizes a good tradeoff between the Sensitivity and Specificity, which enable an accurate nerve detection. However, the experimental results shows that the texture of nerve as hypoechoic tissues is hard to detect using mono model feature.

This demonstrates that MGBP is stable and robust for US images and proved to be a good descriptor for US images.

4   Conclusion

In this paper we have proposed a new technique for nerve detection in ultrasound images using two phases: the k-means clustering for foreground segmentation and the texture analysis to extract the nerve region amid the foreground hyperechoic tissues. The nerve identification presents the most critical part of this work. As the nerve presents some interesting textural properties, we focused on the texture analysis. A new method (MGBP) based on MBP and Gabor filter have been proposed as texture descriptor. The experimental evaluation on real data, showed that MGBP enables efficient detection of the nerve region compared to the tested state-of-the-art methods. This is due to the fact that MBP and Gabor enhance the texture profile in the noisy data, which increase the robustness of MGBP descriptor with respect to the speckle noise and other artifacts in the US images. In the future, we will explore the possibilities to extend the detection to others types of nerves.

References

1. Boukerroui, D., Basset, O., Baskurt, A., Gimenez, G.: A multiparametric and multiresolution segmentation algorithm of 3-d ultrasonic data(hrlk). IEEE Transactions on Ultrasonics, Ferroelectrics, and Frequency Control **48**(1), 64–67 (2001)
2. Daubechies, I.: Ten lectures on wavelets. In: SIAM, pp. 258–259 (1992)
3. Daugman, J.G.: Uncertainty relation for resolution in space, spatial frequency, and orientation optimized by two-dimensional visual cortical filters. Journal of the Optical Society of America **2**, 1160–1169 (1985)
4. Ghose, S., Oliver, A., Mart, R., Llad, X., Freixenet, J., Villanova, J., Meriaudeau, F.: Prostate segmentation with local binary patterns guided active appearance models. Medical Imaging: Image Processing (2011)
5. Hafiane, A., Seetharaman, G., Palaniappan, K., Zavidovique, B.: Rotationally invariant hashing of median binary patterns for texture classification. In: International Conference on Image Analysis and Recognition, pp. 619–629 (2008)
6. Haralick, R.M., Shanmugam, K., Dinstein, I.: Textural features for image classification. IEEE Trans. Syst. Man Cybern **3**, 610–621 (1973)
7. Khanna, A., Sood, M., Devi, S.: Us image segmentation based on expectation maximization and gabor filter. International Journal of Modeling and Optimization **2** (2012)
8. Knoll, C., Alcaniz, M., Monserrat, C., Grau, V., Juan, M.C.: Outlining of the prostate using snakes with shape restrictions based on the wavelet transform (doctoral thesis: Dissertation). Pattern Recognition **32**, 1767–1781 (1999)
9. Malathi, G., Shanthi, V.: Histogram based classification of ultrasound images of placenta, (hrlk). International Journal of Computer Applications (2001)
10. Marhofer, P., Vincent, W., Chan, S.: Ultrasound-guided regional anesthesia: Current concepts and future trends. Journal of Clinical Anesthesia **105** (2007)
11. Noble, A.: Ultrasound image segmentation: A survey. IEEE Transactions on Medical Imaging **25**, 28 (2006)
12. Ojala, T., Pietikinen, M., Menp, T.: Multiresolution grayscale and rotation invariant texture classification with local binary patterns. IEEE Trans. Pattern Analysis and Machine Intelligence **24**, 971–987 (2000)
13. Shen, D., Zhan, Y., Davatzikos, C.: Segmentation of prostate boundaries from ultrasound images using statistical shape model. IEEE Transactions on Pattern Analysis and Machine Intelligence (2003)

14. Stoitsis, J., Golemati, S., Tsiaparas, N., Nikita, K.S.: Texture characterization of carotid atherosclerotic plaque from b-mode ultrasound using gabor filters. In: Proc. IEEE Conf. Eng. Med. Biol. Soc., pp. 455–458 (2009)
15. Tesař, L., Smutek, D., Jiskra, J.: Genetic algorithms for thyroid gland ultrasound image feature reduction. In: Wang, L., Chen, K., S. Ong, Y. (eds.) ICNC 2005. LNCS, vol. 3612, pp. 841–844. Springer, Heidelberg (2005)
16. Thouin, E., Hafiane, A., Vieyres, P., Xylourgos, N., Triantafyllidis, G., Papadourakis, G.: Nerve region segmentation for ultrasound guided local regional anaesthesia (lra). In: Mediterranean Conference on Information Systems (2011)
17. Tsiaparas, N.N., Golemati, S., Andreadis, I., Stoitsis, J.S.: Comparison of multiresolution features for texture classification of carotid atherosclerosis from b-mode ultrasound. Transactions on Information Technology in Biomedicine 15(1) (2011)
18. Vapnik, V.: Statistical learning theory. Wiley-Interscience (1998)
19. Woodworth, G.E., Chen, E.M., Horn, J.-L.E., Aziz, M.F.: Efficacy of computer-based video and simulation in ultrasound-guided regional anesthesia training. Journal of Clinical Anesthesia (2014)
20. Zaim, A., Taeil, Y., Keck, R.: Feature based classification of prostate us images using multiwavelet and kernel svm. In: Proceedings of International Joint Conference on Neural Networks, pp. 278–281 (2007)
21. Zhang, W., Shan, S., Gao, W., Chen, X., Zhang, H.: Local gabor binary pattern histogram sequence (lgbphs): A novel non-statistical model for face representation and recognition. In: IEEE Intl. Conf. Computer Vision, pp. 786–791 (2005)

Automatic Localization of Skin Layers in Reflectance Confocal Microscopy

Eduardo Somoza, Gabriela Oana Cula$^{(\boxtimes)}$, Catherine Correa, and Julie B. Hirsch

Johnson and Johnson Consumer Companies, Inc.
Skillman, NJ, USA
{esomoza1,gcula,ccorrea1,jhirsch}@its.jnj.com

Abstract. Reflectance Confocal Microscopy (RCM) is a noninvasive imaging tool used in clinical dermatology and skin research, allowing real time visualization of skin structural features at different depths at a resolution comparable to that of conventional histology [1]. Currently, RCM is used to generate a rich skin image stack (about 60 to 100 images per scan) which is visually inspected by experts, a process that is tedious, time consuming and exclusively qualitative. Based on the observation that each of the skin images in the stack can be characterized as a texture, we propose a quantitative approach for automatically classifying the images in the RCM stack, as belonging to the different skin layers: stratum corneum, stratum granulosum, stratum spinosum, stratum basale, and the papillary dermis. A reduced set of images in the stack are used to generate a library of representative texture features named textons. This library is employed to characterize all the images in the stack with a corresponding texton histogram. The stack is ultimately separated into 5 different sets of images, each corresponding to different skin layers, exhibiting good correlation with expert grading. The performance of the method is tested against three RCM stacks and we generate promising classification results. The proposed method is especially valuable considering the currently scarce landscape of quantitative solutions for RCM imaging.

Keywords: Reflectance confocal microscopy · Image stacks · Skin texture · Textons · Clustering · Dimensionality reduction · Classification · Image recognition

1 Introduction

Reflectance Confocal Microscopy (RCM) is employed as a non-invasive imaging tool in clinical dermatology and skin research, as well in the evaluation of changes due to application of products in the cosmetics industry [1,2]. RCM allows for real time visualization of structural features at different skin depths at a resolution comparable to that of conventional histology [1].

The foundation of RCM imaging is based on the generation of endogenous contrast due to differences in the degree of light reflected from different structures [3]. In RCM, the surface of interest is illuminated by a laser light source and the reflected light is collected through a pinhole aperture where the photons of light encounter a photodetector [3]. Structures with highly reflective surfaces will have a high degree of

© Springer International Publishing Switzerland 2014
A. Campilho and M. Kamel (Eds.): ICIAR 2014, Part II, LNCS 8815, pp. 141–150, 2014.
DOI: 10.1007/978-3-319-11755-3_16

light dispersion and as a result, will produce a high intensity signal when illuminated by the laser light source; in contrast, structures that have poorly reflective surfaces will produce a low intensity signal. Some of the structures found in skin with high reflectance capabilities in comparison to surrounding structures are melanosomes, cytoplasmic granules, cellular organelles, and keratin-containing structures [1]. Different skin layers contain different reflective structures that can be used to distinguish each layer from one another during image acquisition with RCM.

RCM's depth of penetration allows for the visualization of all four layers of the epidermis (stratum corneum, stratum granulosum, stratum spinosum, stratum basale) and portions of the papillary dermis (uppermost layer of the dermis), depending on the thickness of the skin, as illustrated in Figure 1. In thinner regions of the skin, it is possible to reach the superficial reticular dermis (a lower level of the dermis) [4]. RCM is capable of providing a lateral resolution of approximately 1 μm, an axial resolution of 3-5 μm, and a penetration depth of 150-300 μm depending on the instrumentation and image acquisition parameters [3,4,5].

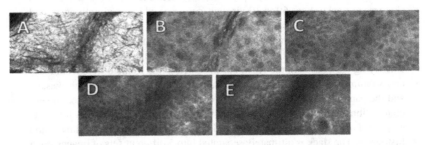

Fig. 1. Typical images within a normal skin RCM image stack. RCM's depth of penetration allows for the visualization of all four layers of the epidermis: stratum corneum (A), stratum granulosum (B), stratum spinosum (C), stratum basale (D) and portions of the papillary dermis, the uppermost layer of the dermis (E), depending on the thickness of the skin. Images in this figure were used as the training set for our method.

The penetration depth of RCM is highly dependent on the power of the laser component of the system: a higher power laser will allow for acquisition of images in the deeper layers of skin but at the same time, there will be a sacrifice in resolution and potential damage to skin structures [3]. Depending on the step size used for image acquisition, the resulting RCM image stack can contain anywhere from tens to hundreds of images. Once the RCM stack is acquired, typically, expert-based visual assessment of each image for characteristic structural and cellular features that distinguish adjacent skin layers needs to be performed to classify each image [5]. This visual assessment is time consuming when dealing with multiple RCM stacks with hundreds of images of different anatomical sites of skin. While visually investigating skin RCM stacks of images, we have observed a smooth change in the textural properties of the images as a function of depth. Therefore we propose a method based on texture characterization of different skin layers to classify RCM images into their respective layers as a function of depth.

1.1   Prior Work

Reflectance of light on the skin surface has been studied in relation to the appearance of skin texture. Different illumination parameters (e.g. direction and angle of light) lead to different visual perceptions of the appearance of skin texture due to differences in the reflectance of light. These changes in appearance are problematic for the identification and classification of different skin features: a single skin feature might be identified as a different skin feature depending on the illumination parameters. To gain independence from changes in appearance of texture due to illumination, texton-based classification systems have been employed [6,7,8]. Textons are texture representations of characteristic structural features found on a surface of interest.

By compiling an extensive vocabulary of textons for visually related surfaces of interest, classification and separation of images of these surfaces can be accomplished through texton-based texture representation. In the dermatological application of RCM, these closely related surfaces are different layers of the skin encountered during image acquisition. The RCM images of different layers of skin change smoothly from one acquisition step to the next, and in this work we generate texture representations for each layer based on a library of textons, which are texture representations for characteristic structural features of the inner layers of skin. Using this texton-based approach, we are automatically able to classify RCM images as one of the five skin layers encountered during RCM image acquisition. After the classification of individual images, we automatically separate adjacent skin layers. We then correlate the results from the automatic classification and separation of the RCM images to the classification and separation of images by expert visual assessment. To our knowledge, this is the first attempt in trying to classify RCM images of skin layers using a texton-based approach, while previous attempts utilized an intensity-based approach [9,10].

2   Methods

2.1   Acquisition of Representative RCM Image Stack

A representative image stack of normal skin was acquired with the Vivascope 1500 (Lucid Technologies, Rochester, NY, USA) using 785 nm laser illumination. The acquisition of the representative RCM stack was performed on the volar forearm region of a healthy adult male because of the ease of placement of the Vivascope 1500 confocal head on the skin surface, leading to a reduction in imaging artifacts due to movement. The image stack was collected at a step size of 1 μm, starting at the stratum corneum and ending at the uppermost layers of the papillary dermis. The dimensions of the images were 1000 by 1000 pixels. All pixels of the skin images in the representative stack were normalized to a normal distribution with parameters ($\mu=0$, $\sigma=1$). Images were classified into five layers of interest through visual assessment by an RCM expert: stratum corneum (SC), stratum granulosum (SG), stratum spinosum (SS), stratum basale (SB), and the papillary dermis (D).

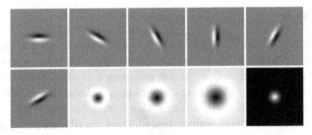

Fig. 2. The selection of 10 filters we employ in our method from the Leung-Malik filter bank [7]. The filters we select are six oriented derivative of Gaussians, three Laplacian of Gaussian derivative filter and one Gaussian filter.

2.2   Generation of Texton Filter Response Space

A representative image from each of the layers of interest is selected to create the training set, illustrated in Fig.1, needed to generate the texton filter response space. To ensure the training set consisted of images that exhibit characteristic structural features of each of the five skin layers, a 250 by 500 pixel subsection is chosen as part of the training set. To capture local orientation patterns of characteristic structural features, 10 filters from the Leung Malik (LM) filter bank are selected to create the filter set used to generate the texton filter response space [7]. The filters in the LM filter bank have been previously employed to generate texture representations of surfaces because of their ability to capture structural parameters, such as local orientation parameters, that contribute to texture representation for classification [6,7,8]. To decrease the likelihood of incorporating noise generated during image acquisition into the texton filter response space, the dimensions of the filters are matched to the dimensions of a keratinocyte (a predominant structural feature in skin), which are about 25 by 25 pixels [4] . The texton filter response space is generated by the convolution of the individual images in the training set with each of the filters in the filter set. The image windows of size 25x25 to which the filter set is applied to are normalized to a normal distribution with parameters (μ=0, σ=1).

2.3   Generation of Texton Library

The dimensionality of the filter response space generated was ten: each dimension corresponding to one of the filters. We use principal component analysis (PCA) to reduce the dimensionality of the filter response space. We find that 90% of the variability in the filter response space generated by filtering the representative images from each of the layers of interest could be accounted for by the first three principal components. The filter response space is re-projected onto these three principal components, reducing the dimensionality of the space from ten to three dimensions. To generate the texton library, K means clustering is performed on the reduced filter response space, resulting in 15 representative textons (cluster centers in the filter response space). K means clustering is also performed to generate a lower number of textons (10) and a higher number of textons (25), but we have determined empirically that 15 textons sufficiently characterize the structural features apparent in the RCM images.

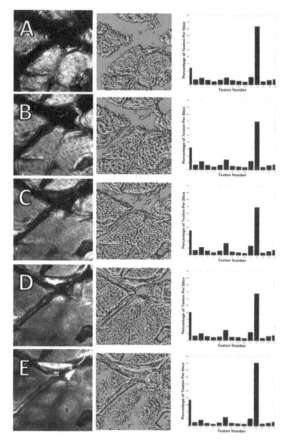

Fig. 3. Classification of representative images based on the texton library. A representative texton histogram was generated for each image showing the percentage of textons used in the classification. From Top to Bottom, Left to Right: (**A**) Stratum Corneum original image, classified image, and representative texton histogram. (**B**) Stratum Granulosum original image, classified image, and representative texton histogram. (**C**) Stratum Spinosum original image, classified image, and representative texton histogram. (**D**) Stratum Basale original image, classified image, and representative texton histogram. (**E**) Papillary Dermis original image, classified image, and representative texton histogram.

2.4   Classification of Images and Layer Separation

The same filter set is applied to all images within the RCM stack and the resulting filter response vectors are re-projected onto the same three principal components determined during the generation of the texton library. Each image pixel is classified as one of the 15 representative textons based on the shortest square Euclidean distance between the projected filter response and the textons in the library. The resulting classified image is the texture representation of the image based on the texton library. A representative 15-dimensional texton histogram is generated for each of the images and is employed to separate the RCM stack into the 5 representative skin layers.

To reduce the dimensionality of the collective texton histograms corresponding to the images within the RCM stack, PCA is performed one more time. It is determined that 90% of the variability in this universal eigenspace is accounted for by the first three principal components. The texton histograms are re-projected onto these three principal components, reducing the dimensionality of the histogram space from 15 to 3 dimensions. In this reduced 3D eigenspace, K-Means clustering with K=5 is performed to automatically separate the RCM stack into the five representative layers. Consequently, each texton histogram is classified to the closest center based on square Euclidean distance. The results of the automatic separation are compared to the separation of the RCM stack based on visual assessment by the RCM expert. To assess the consistency of the proposed method, this classification process is repeated with two other visually classified RCM image stacks of the volar forearm region from two different healthy adults with normal skin.

3   Results

3.1   Selection of Training Set and Filter Set

To generate the representative texton library, a training set of images and a filter set are selected. Five representative images of the SC, SG, SS, SB and D selected to be included in the training set. To ensure the training set captured the characteristic structural features of each layer as identified by RCM experts in the literature [5], a 250 by 500 pixel subsection is selected. The result was a training set (Figure 1) encompassing a majority of the characteristic structural features of the representative skin layers, but also excluding non characteristic structural features such as noisy patches.

The filters of the filter set are chosen from the LM filter bank: a filter bank that has been used in previous works concerning texture representations of textures [6,7,8]. Ten filters (Figure 2) from the LM filter bank are chosen for their ability to encode patterns of local orientations of characteristic structural features in the RCM images.

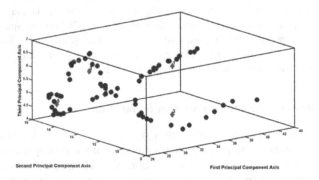

Fig. 4. K Means clustering of texton histogram space. The cluster centers (represented by a red diamond marker), as determined by K Means, correspond to a different skin layer classification within the imaging stack. The individual images in the stack are represented by blue circle markers.

3.2   Classification of RCM Images Using Texton Library

Each of the training images are filtered with the filters selected from the LM filter set, and a 10 dimensional filter response space is created. Each dimension corresponds to one of the filter responses obtained by convolving of the images with one of the filters in the filter set. Applying PCA on the texton response space, three principal components are identified and the space is re-projected onto these components. K Means clustering is performed on the reduced filter response space to generate the 15 textons in the library. The images in the representative RCM stack are labeled using the resulting library of 15 textons and each image is further represented by a texton histogram. Figure 3 shows the results from the texton classification of the five representative images of the original training set.

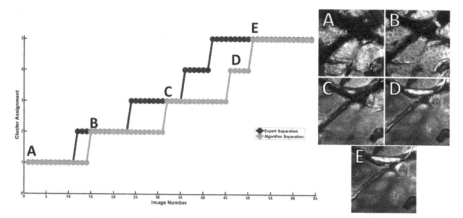

Fig. 5. Graphical representation of automatic separation of representative stack based on results from K-Means clustering of texton histogram space versus expert labeled images. Each cluster assignment, marked as 1 to 5 on the Y-axis corresponds to a different skin layer. From lowest to highest assignment, we find the following layers: Stratum Corneum, Stratum Granulosum, Stratum Spinosum, Stratum Basale, and Papillary Dermis. The images on the right (labeled A-E) are the training RCM images and they are found by the proposed method as belonging to the layer the expert grader assigns them to. The correlation coefficient corresponding to assessing the correlation between the automatic evaluation and that of the expert grader is 0.916.

3.3   Separation of Representative RCM Stack

The dimensionality of the texton histogram space is further reduced by applying PCA, and a three dimensional eigenspace is generated. Within this newly reduced texton histogram eigenspace, K Means clustering is performed to generate five representative centers corresponding to each of the five layers represented in the training set. The results of K Means clustering of the texton histogram space are shown in Figure 4, where a clear separation of the skin layers is evident.

Each of the five centers corresponds to a different layer of the skin. Each of the representative texton histograms of the images in the RCM stack are classified as one of these representative centers. The result of the classification leads to an automatic separation of the RCM stack into the five different representative skin layers. The resulting separation is a smooth transition between adjacent skin layers as a function of depth, indicating each layer is represented by a set of characteristic structural features (Figure 5). The results from the automatic separation were compared to the results from the separation based on the visual assessment of a RCM expert (Figure 5). Figure 5 shows some misalignment between the automatic classifications of the RCM stack versus the expert's visual assessment. This misalignment is addressed in more detail in Section 4.

To check the consistency of the algorithm in its ability to classify images and separate different layers of the skin within any RCM stack, the same texton library is used to classify and separate three additional RCM stacks. These RCM stacks are images of the volar forearm of three healthy adults, acquired and processed the same way as the representative RCM stack used to generate the texton library images. The results of the automatic classification and separation are compared to the visual assessment by an RCM expert (Figure 6). The results are very promising as the corresponding correlation coefficients vary between 0.84 and 0.95.

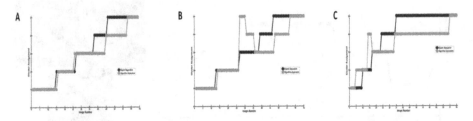

Fig. 6. We test the method on three extra RCM image stacks. Each graph corresponds to a different stack. The green line is the output from our method while the blue line corresponds to expert grading. We correlate the method based skin layer evaluation with that assessed by the expert and we obtain correlation coefficients 0.954, 0.844 and 0.865, respectively.

4   Discussion and Conclusions

We have identified the need for automatic image classification in normal skin RCM image stacks and we made the observation that skin RCM images at each step in the image stack have a repetitive nature and could be represented as textures. To capture the repetitive nature of the appearance in these images, we use the concept of texton, introduced in [11] as the up to second-order statistic of textural images that is relevant for texture discrimination at pre-attentive level of human perception. As in [6], we have generated a representative texton library for the characteristic structural features of the inner most layers of skin captured during image acquisition with RCM. With these textons, we have been able to create texture representations of each image in an RCM stack. With these texture representations, we classified each image into one of five skin layers: stratum corneum, stratum granulosum, stratum spinosum, stratum basale, and the papillary dermis. From the classification of each of the images, we automatically separate adjacent layers in the RCM stack.

The texton-based classification methodology proposed here is not only limited to being used for the classification and separation of RCM skin images of normal skin. This methodology can be used to study different diseased states of skin such as eczema, squameous cell carcinoma, and psoriasis by expanding our current texton library to include texture representations of characteristic structural features present in these diseases. With an expanded texton library, we can generate texture representations of the layers of the diseased skin and see if these representations change after medical treatment. This same approach could be used in the cosmetic industry when testing the efficacy of different moisturizing products. The texton library could further be expanded to include representations of structural skin features found in infant, adolescent, and elderly populations, hence studying the effects of developmental and aging processes on the skin.

We have compared the automatic classification and separation of three RCM skin image stacks with the results of visual assessments performed by an RCM expert. The results of these correlations are excellent with the correlation coefficients vary from 0.84 to 0.95. However, we observe a slight misalignment between the automatic and visual assessment results, which could be explained by the fact that the methodology proposed here relies only on texture characteristics of structural features in each layer to generate its classifications, while the RCM expert relies on high-level multiple factors for his assessment: the relative depth of the image within the RCM stack, the intensity of signal from low/high reflective surfaces, and cellular features (e.g. shape, size).

Currently, the textons are defined at pixel level and they encode local texture information that is a small part to what the expert perceives as different cells present in skin layers. Next steps include expanding the concept of textons to that of a more complex structural element that captures high level information relevant for the expert grader. Specifically, we plan to define the concept of "hierarchical texton" that will be able to go beyond representing the texture at pixel level, but to capture the relative positioning of textons up to the level of new textons being capable to represent features at cellular level. Moreover, next steps also include developing a supervised classification model capable of learning associations between expert-labeled skin features and computationally based texture features, ensuring that the expert information is encompassed in the computational model to maximize correlation between automatic classification and the expert grader outcome.

References

1. Gonzalez, S., Gilaberte-Clazada, Y.: In Vivo Reflectance-mode Confocal Microscopy in Clinical Dermatology and Cosmetology. International Journal of Cosmetic Science 30(1), 1–17 (2008)
2. Hofmann-Wellenhof, R., Pellacani, G., Malvehy, H., Soyer, P. (eds.) Reflectance Confocal Microscopy for Skin Diseases. Springer (2012)
3. Rajadhyaksha, M., Gonzalez, S., Zavislan, J.M., Anderson, R.R., Webb, R.H.: In Vivo Confocal Laser Microscopy of Human Skin II: Advances in Instrumentation and Comparison with Histology. Journal of Investigative Dermatology 113(3), 293–303 (1999)

4. Sanchez-Mateos, J.L.S., Rajadhyaksha, M.: Optical Fundamentals of Reflectance Confocal Microscopy. Monografias de Dermatologia **24**(2), 1–3 (2011)
5. Sanchez, V.P., Gonzalez, S.: Normal Skin. Monografias de Dermatologia **24**(2), 1–3 (2011)
6. Cula, O.G., Dana, K.J.: Skin Texture Modeling. International Journal of Computer Vision **62**(1/2), 97–119 (2005)
7. Leung, T., Malik, J.: Representing and Recognizing the Visual Appearance of Materials using Three-dimensional Textons. International Journal of Computer Vision **43**(1), 29–44 (2001)
8. Varma, M., Zisserman, A.: Classifying images of materials: achieving viewpoint and illumination independence. In: Heyden, A., Sparr, G., Nielsen, M., Johansen, P. (eds.) ECCV 2002, Part III. LNCS, vol. 2352, pp. 255–271. Springer, Heidelberg (2002)
9. Kurugol, S., Dy, J.G., Rajadhyaksha, M., Gossage, K.W., Weissmann, J., Brooks, B.H.: Semi-automated Algorithm for Localization of Dermal/Epidermal Junction in Reflectance Confocal Microscopy Images of Human Skin. In: Proceedings of SPIE 7904, Three-Dimensional and Multidimensional Microscopy: Image Acquisition and Processing XVIII, 79041A (2011)
10. Kurugol, S., Rajadhyaksha, M., Dy, J.G., Brooks, D.H. : Validation Study of Automated Dermal/Epidermal Junction Localization Algorithm in Reflectance Confocal Microscopy Images of Skin. In: Proceedings of SPIE 8207, Photonic Therapeutics and Diagnostics VIII, 820702 (2012)
11. Julesz, B.: Textons, the Elements of Texture Perception, and their Interactions. Nature **290**(1), 91–97 (1981)

Thermal Signature Using Non-Redundant Temporal Local Binary-Based Features

Adnan Al Alwani[1(✉)], Youssef Chahir[1(✉)], and Francois Jouen[2]

[1] GREYC CNRS (UMR 6072), University of Caen Basse-Normandie, Caen, France
[2] CHArt Laboratory, Practical School of High Studies (EPHE), Paris, France
{adnan.alalwani,youssef.chahir}@unicaen.fr,
francois.jouen@ephe.sorbonne.fr

Abstract. In this paper, we propose a method for event recognition from thermal signature based 1-D signal. We use the non-redundant temporal Local Binary Pattern NRTLBP as a descriptor of the Pattern Of Interest (POI) signal. The original signal is extracted directly from local patch in region of interest. We introduce the wavelet decomposition as a pre-processing stage in order to extract the approximation wave-components of the raw signal. Then, NRTLBP is applied on the wave-components which provide wavelet domain descriptor of the raw thermal signature. Finally, we provide an evaluation of our method on the real dataset (Preterm Pain in Infants "PPI") composed of thermal videos developed in the context of Infant pain project, a french project supported by the French National Research Agency Projects for science (ANR).

Keywords: Events recognition · Non-redundant temporal local binary pattern · Thermal signature · Support vector machine · Wavelet

1 Introduction

Feature extraction is an important challenge in pattern recognition, specifically if the pattern is represented by a temporal or spatial signal such as speech, acoustic signal or 2D signal. The temporal signals have finite durations and are sampled into digital format. In such case, it is more appropriate to represent a pattern as a finite time sequence $\{x[0], x[1], ..., x[N-1]\}$. Providing this sequence directly to a classifier is not typical due to the huge number of inputs and due to the randomness of the signal. Therefore, the sequence $x[n]$ must be encoded into a low-dimension feature vector $Y = (y_1, y_2, ..., y_D), D << N$, which better characterizes the pattern and provides a robust classifier training and classification. Feature extraction from One-Dimension (1D) signal is generally categorized into two approaches : temporal and spectral approach. Both approaches are deemed as nonparametric approaches. As well as parametric approaches, both approaches have been used in classification of many patterns examples. Spectral

© Springer International Publishing Switzerland 2014
A. Campilho and M. Kamel (Eds.): ICIAR 2014, Part II, LNCS 8815, pp. 151–158, 2014.
DOI: 10.1007/978-3-319-11755-3_17

approaches have gained a big popularity in the last two decades, which are out of scope of this paper. In the other hand, in temporal-based approach, the features are extracted directly from the temporal sequence. Moreover, use of multifunction allows to characterize the time sequence by the following quantities : mean value, slope absolute value, number of zero crossings, slope sign changes, and waveform length. Although there are techniques that claimed a successful discrimination in various applications, the above temporal characterizations didn't help much in the other applications. Techniques from the fields of machine learning and pattern recognition might be valuable for thermal pattern examination. Thermal pattern may have sufficient knowledge to understand the underlying characteristics of the patterns that we observe. However, reliable classification of thermal signature would help us to learn about an unknown physical aspects, discriminate the normal and abnormal states in the condition monitoring. The realization of such a tool can be difficult task in some cases.

This paper presents an approach for event recognition from temporal thermal signal. The recognition process is based on the Non-Redundant Temporal Local Binary Pattern-based features (NRTLBP) over the time series thermal sequences which are extracted from the thermal video sequences. A traditional way to characterize the properties of a time series sequence $x[n]$ is through its raw temperature value extracted from local patches that are defined over the objects face in image sequences. It has been shown that if a signal has band-limited characteristics, significant improvement in the performance of pattern recognition can be readily made by a relatively simple preprocessing of the signal in the time-frequency domain. The redundant representation of a 1D signal in a 2D time-frequency domain can provide an additional degree of freedom for signal analysis. Such pre-processing effectively separates the intertwined time domain features of the signal, allowing the important characteristics to be exposed in the time-frequency domain, resulting in more effective pattern matching. Hence, the signal being analyzed needs to be conducted only around in selected regions of interest in the time-frequency domain. For this, we use the wavelet transform to decompose the signal into pyramid structure in the form of approximation component and detail component. The approximation wave components are also known to be a robust and distortion tolerant feature space for many pattern recognition applications. Moreover, we consider the approximation component as the feature vector of raw signal, which is a necessary requirement for extracting NRTLBP-based features. As the temporal LBP produces efficient feature descriptor, we employ a Support Vector Machine SVM to evaluate our method on the real Preterm dataset.

Extracting features from one-dimensional signal based on thermal video monitoring methods, have been considered in a number of approaches. The body work of these approaches is based on measurement, quantifying and tracking of thermal signature. Many other approaches in the field of the thermal signature examination have been proposed in the literature. In [1] the authors examined the temperature changes around the neck and the nasal regions. These regions were identified manually in the recorded images, then the respiration rate signals were extracted from the thermal image by performing wavelet transform. Respiration signal rate monitoring is also explored in [2]. A tracking algorithm is developed to follow three facial features in order to produce the respiration signal rate. New non-contact respiration signal modality for neonatal was developed and investigated by [3], using infrared thermography imaging. This development includes subsequent image processing (region of interest (ROI) detection) and optimization based wavelet technique. In [4] F. AL-Khalidi et al. developed a technique to model the respiration signal from nasal region. A feature extracted from this region enabled a respiration signal to be produced. The ROI under the tip of the nose was segmented into eight parts. The pixel values within each segment were averaged to obtain a single value representing that segment. Additionally to the direction of vital signal examination. The approach in [5] used mid-wave IR sensors for the measurement of cardiac and breathing rates at a distance. They used the Fourier Transform to isolate the relevant frequency components from skin temperature in the vicinity of the major arteries. Furthermore, they showed that the frequency components from skin temperature is directly related to the pulse waveform related to the heart signal.

Our method differs from other approaches by taking the root of pattern recognition to recognize the event from thermal video. We investigate the discrimination power of NRTLBP in the field of the thermal pattern descriptor in Section 3, whereas Section 4 illustrates its performance using wavelet transform to decompose the raw statistical features and build new feature representation. In Section 5, the experimental protocol is recalled and we conduct comprehensive experiments to demonstrate the effectiveness of our approach in recognizing if an infant is in pain. Finally, conclusions are drawn in Section 6.

2   Event Recognition Framework

We propose a framework of using thermal attributes extracted from the video sequences. We assume that the layout of subjects is considered for all the cases in the front view, and ROI is defined over the subjects face. In addition, we build raw thermal signatures for all subjects samples. This is achieved first by defining local patch as shown in the Fig 1. Then the maximum Mx and the minimum Mn values are computed from the local patches along the video sequences. For more illustration, we compute the Mx and Mn temperature values and defined it as the raw thermal signals (we call it raw signals for abbreviation). Furthermore, we establish the raw signals for the three condition events, which characterize the monitoring state during daily care. For instance, normal event, disease event and post-disease event are three events adopted in our study. The time series of each event is shown in the Fig 2. As illustrated in this figure, the response nature of each event specify the discriminative features of that event.

Then, we apply the NRTLBP descriptor on the raw thermal signal in order to extract efficient feature vector. Another extension consists to approximate components, before using NRTLB, via wavelet decomposition of the temporal raw signal. A video sequence is then described by two descriptors which are directly applied into SVM for event recognition.

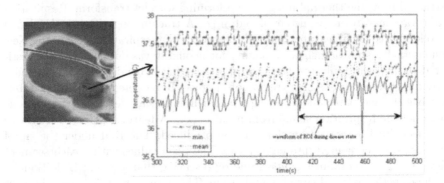

Fig. 1. Local temperature extracted from ROI defined over the object's face

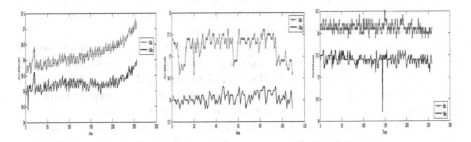

Fig. 2. Raw thermal signals of Mx and Min temperature values. From left to right, normal event, disease event and post-disease event signatures.

3   Non-Redundant Temporal Local Binary Pattern-Based Features

Once the thermal features are extracted, the video sequences is considered as a collection of raw signals. We denote by $X_i = T_1, T_2, \cdots, T_n$. $i = Mx$ or Mn, and T is the temperature value at each patch. In order to represent the raw signal in efficient manner we propose the Temporal Local Binary Pattern descriptor, which is an extension of original 2-D LBP operator into the temporal domain.

Normal LBP has originally been proposed for texture analysis and classification [6]. Recently, it has been applied on face recognition[7] and facial expression recognition[8]. The TLBP operator labels the samples of a signal by thresholding a center sample against neighborhood set within defined window. We denote by $x[n]$ the sampled signal, and w is the size of samples window. The TLBP operator on a sample kw in is given by:

$$TLBP_w(f[k]) = \sum_{q=0}^{\frac{w}{2}-1} (f[k] - f[k-j-q]2^q + f[\frac{w}{2}+q+1] - f[k]2^{q+\frac{w}{2}} \quad (1)$$

Where q is the number of sampled points (neighbor samples of k) whose the distances to k do not exceed the window w. For a M block, a TLBP histogram of 2^q bins is computed for feature representation. After the computation of the LBP for the whole signal, a histogram of the TLBP code is used as feature descriptor. It contains information about the distribution nature over the whole signal and characterizing a statistical description of signal. Another aspect of TLBP is called no-redundant TLBP. Intuitively, the NRTLBP considers a TLBP code and its complement as same. NRLBP is defined by:

$$NRTLBP(f[k]) = min(TLBP(f[k]), 2^q - 1 - TLBP(f[k])) \qquad (2)$$

This is motivated by the advantage of using dynamic shape of the signal at various instances and levels. Finally, the no-redundant local patterns formed from signal $f[k]$ are formed as a histogram distribution vector.

4   NRTLBP of Approximated Coefficients

We further extend the idea of LBP into a wavelet domain in order to perform the comparison results. The method is based on using multi-resolution wavelet transform to decompose the raw statistical features and build new feature representation [9].

The wavelet transform $C(j, k)$ of a finite-energy signal $f(t)$ is defined as its scalar product with the wavelet $\Psi_{jk}(t)$. In other words, the wavelet transform represents the correlation of the signal $f(t)$ and the wavelet $\Psi_{jk}(t)$ as:

$$a_{jk} = \sum_t f(t)\Psi_{jk}(t). \qquad (3)$$

Where $\Psi(t) = 2^j \Psi(2^j t - k)$ is the mother wavelet corresponds to scale $j = 1$, k is the translation factor, and j is the scale parameter. A wavelet representation of a function consists of, a coarse overall approximation a^j, and detail coefficients that influence the function at various scales. Therefore, the approximation coefficients are considered as raw feature vector in a wavelet-domain. Then using NRTLBP descriptor for feature description. The smooth change property of the approximation features is illustrated in the Fig 3. Where each sub-figure shows the feature in wavelet-domain for the corresponding event in the time domain explained in the Fig. 2.

5   Experiments

In this section, we evaluate the proposed method by experimenting with the real dataset from ANR preterm project. Due to non available of the benchmark related to our method, we did not attempt a comparison with other methods. Rather, we provide results only to show that our algorithm works well on a real data. The preterm data involves 20 neonates videos. Each includes the subject behaviors during daily condition monitoring (event and condition are used

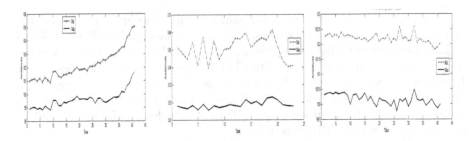

Fig. 3. Approximation component of raw features for three kinds of events. from left to right, normal event, disease event, and post-disease event signatures.

interchangeably). All events are performed for each subject and notated by the clinical during condition monitoring. From each video we select the set of events which includes normal health event (pre-disease), disease event, and post-disease event. A total of 60 clips were extracted ranging from N occurrences of normal event, to M occurrences of disease event and so on.

We divide the clips into three groups of 20 clips. For instance, each group divided into 2 subset of 10 clips each. In the training phase, we use half of the group and the rest was used for the test task. We consider a recognition task for three class problems including the normal event, disease event and post-disease event respectively. Furthermore, two features descriptors are used in the experiments. The first one is the descriptor of raw thermal signal, we denote it by NRTLBP and the second one is the descriptor based on the approximation components, and we denote it by WNRTLBP. The number of neighboring samples was set to 4 samples for NRTLBP codes, and the Daubechies wavelet with one level decomposition was used for approximation coefficients extraction. We performed the evaluation of our method using linear SVM.

In all experiments, first subset of each group was used for training and the second subset was used for testing. We started the experiment directly by providing the raw features (Mx, and Min raw features) into classifier. The recognition results are in the form of recognition rate, the results of the first experiment are reported in the table 1. We also run the test by using NRTLBP descriptor based on two types of raw features . The results are shown in table 2. In order to be able to do a full comparison of methods, WNRTLBP based experiments are performed in the same manner as above. Results from this experiment are presented in table 3. As we can see, the approach based on the wavelet achieves a good accuracy rate. From a comparison viewpoint, the results that are achieved based on feature descriptors reported that, NRTLBP and WNRTLBP perform best recognition rates when the maximum value of raw feature is used.

Table 1. Recognition rate results, from the Mx and Mn raw features that are directly applied into SVM

Events	Recognition rate% (Mx Temp.value)	Recognition rate% (Mn Temp. value)
Normal Response	50	60
Disease Response	90	60
Post-disease response	50	70
Overall	63.33%	63.33%

Table 2. Recognition rate results, using NRTLBP based raw feature descriptor

Events	Recognition rate% (Mx Temp.value)	Recognition rate% (Mn Temp. value)
Normal Response	80	50
Disease Response	90	90
Post-disease response	80	90
Overall	83.33%	76,67%

Table 3. Recognition rate results, using WNRTLBP based raw feature descriptor

Events	Recognition rate% (Mx Temp.value)	Recognition rate% (Mn Temp. value)
Normal Response	90	100
Disease Response	100	95
Post-disease response	85	93
Overall	91,667%	96%

6   Conclusion

In this paper, we have applied temporal NRLBP as a descriptor of thermal signature from thermal video based on local patch for events recognition. And shown NRTLBP to be suitable for the description of thermal signal containing information about dynamic characteristics of thermal signature. We have extended NRTLBP considering the wavelet transform of feature representation. We have also shown that the power of descriptors for one-dimensional thermal signature. The experimental results reveal that non redundant temporal LBP and its modifications tend to be good descriptor based approach for thermal features description.

References

1. Chekmenev, S.Y., Rara, H., Farag, A.A.: Non-contact, wavelet-based measurement of vital signs using thermal imaging. In: Graphics Vision Image Proc. (2005)
2. Ding, S., Zhu, X., Chen, W., Wei, D.: Derivation of respiratory signal from single-channel ECGs based on source statistics. Int. J. Bio. Electromagnetism **6**, 43–49 (2004)
3. Abbas, A.K., Heimann, K., Jergus, K., Orlikowsky, T., Leonhardt, S.: Neonatal non-contact respiratory monitoring based on real time infrared thermography. Biomedical Engineering Online (2011)
4. Al-Khalidi, F., Saatchi, R., Elphick, H., Burke, D.: An Evaluation of Thermal Imaging Based Respiration Rate Monitoring in Children. American Journal of Engineering and Applied Sciences **4**(4), 586–597 (2011)
5. Sun, N., Garbey, M., Merla, A., Pavlidis, I.: Imaging the cardiovascular pulse. In: Proceedings of the IEEE Computer Society Conference on Computer Vision and Pattern Recognition, pp. 20–25 (2005)
6. Ojala, T., Pietikinen, M., Menp, T.: Multiresolution gray-scale and rotation invariant texture classification with local binary patterns. PAMI **24**(7), 971–987 (2002)
7. Ahonen, T., Hadid, A., Pietikäinen, M.: Face recognition with local binary patterns. In: Pajdla, T., Matas, J.G. (eds.) ECCV 2004. LNCS, vol. 3021, pp. 469–481. Springer, Heidelberg (2004)
8. Ahonen, T., Hadid, A., Pietikinen, M.: Face Description with Local Binary Patterns: Application to Face Recognition. IEEE Transactions on Pattern Analysis and Machine Intelligence **28**(12), 2037–2041 (2006)
9. Mallat S.: A wavelet tour of signal processing, the sparse way, 2nd edn. (2001)
10. Doubechies, I.: Orthonormal Bases of Compactly Supported Wavelets. Comm. Pure Applied Math. **41** (1988)

Image Warping in Dermatological Image Hair Removal

Alexandra Nasonova[1], Andrey Nasonov[1]([✉]), Andrey Krylov[1], Ivan Pechenko[1],
Alexey Umnov[1], and Natalia Makhneva[2]

[1] Laboratory of Mathematical Methods of Image Processing,
Faculty of Computational Mathematics and Cybernetics,
Lomonosov Moscow State University, Moscow, Russia
nasonov@cs.msu.ru
[2] Moscow Scientific and Practical Center of Dermatology and Venereology
and Cosmetology of Moscow Healthcare Department, Moscow, Russia
kryl@cs.msu.ru

Abstract. The paper focuses on solving the problem of hair removal
in dermatology applications. The proposed hair removal algorithm is
based on Gabor filtering and PDE-based image reconstruction. It also
includes the edge sharpening stage using a new warping algorithm. The
idea of warping is to move pixels from the neighborhood of the blurred
edge closer to the edge. The proposed technique preserves the overall
luminosity and textures of the image, while making the edges sharper
and less noisy.

Keywords: Image warping · Edge sharpening · Hair detection · Inpainting · Dermatology

1 Introduction

One of the main problems of image processing in dermatology applications is
the presence of hair which should be removed before image analysis. The survey
of state of the art hair removal methods for dermoscopy images is presented
in [2]. All existing hair removal algorithms consist of two main stages: detection
of pixels covered by hair and restoration of pixels in hair regions with minimal
distortion. Hair-removal methods can be broadly classified as linear interpolation techniques, inpainting by non-linear-PDE based diffusion algorithms and
example based methods. An example of linear interpolation hair removal algorithm can be found in [18,21,23,24]. There are works which utilized the concept
of non-linear PDE based diffusion [5,9,13,26]. Also, an attention has been paid
to remove hair by example based inpainting technique [1,3,14,25].

The paper introduces a new method for the problem of hair removal which
adds the edge sharpening as the third main stage additional to hair pixel detection and restoration stages. The hair pixel detection stage of the proposed

A. Campilho and M. Kamel (Eds.): ICIAR 2014, Part II, LNCS 8815, pp. 159–166, 2014.
DOI: 10.1007/978-3-319-11755-3_18

method is based on the algorithm [4] and improves it using Gabor filters for line detection instead of difference of Gaussians. For the pixel restoration stage we use PDE-based algorithm [10].

In the case of large size of regions covered by hair, the reconstructed image is usually blurred so image sharpening algorithms are used to improve its quality. Image sharpening is generally viewed as the problem of image deconvolution [6]. In this case the blurred image is usually modeled as a convolution of the original image with some blur kernel [8,22]. This problem is ill-posed, and even the slightest error in the estimation of the blur kernel may introduce strong artifacts in the resulting image.

A new two-dimensional warping algorithms for solving the problem of image sharpening is used in this work. The idea of warping is to move pixels from the neighborhood of the blurred edge closer to the center of the edge. There is no need for an accurate estimation of the blur kernel. The input parameters of the proposed method are the edge map and the approximate blur level.

The warping approach for image enhancement was introduced in [7]. The warping of the grid is performed according to the solution of a differential equation that is derived from the warping process constraints. The solution of the equation is used to move the edge neighborhood closer to the edge, and the areas between edges are stretched. The method has several parameters, and the choice of optimal values for the best result is not easy. Due to the global nature of the method the resulting shapes of the edges are sometimes distorted.

In [16] the warping map is computed using simple local measures of the image. This approach does not introduce edge overshoot and does not amplify the noise. The measures are computed separately for rows and for columns of the image with restrictions that prevent two consecutive samples from interchanging their order in the 1D sequence, but it can introduce small local changes in the direction of edges.

In [15] an edge width estimation algorithm has been introduced. The method is based on the assumption that the blur of the image is close to Gaussian. The image is divided into blocks, and the blur kernel is supposed to be uniform inside the block. The estimation of the blurriness of the block is based on the maximum of difference ratio between an original image and its two re-blurred versions. In this work we use edge width estimation method [20] that works under the same assumption that the blur of the image is close to the Gaussian blur. We estimate the dispersion of the Gaussian kernel such that its convolution with the ideal step edge function gives the edge of interest.

2 Hair Detection

Hair pixel detection consists of initial detection of suspicious image fragments containing hair followed by connecting broken lines and removing possible mole contour which is often detected as hair region.

2.1 Initial Hair Pixel Detection

Initial hair pixel detection is usually performed by common line detectors [11]. In this work we use convolution with Gabor filters with different angles and scales to detect hair regions.

We use the Gabor filter kernel in the following form

$$g(x, y; \lambda; \theta; \psi; \sigma; \gamma) = \exp(-\frac{X^2 + \gamma^2 Y^2}{2\sigma^2}) \cos(\frac{2\pi X}{\lambda} + \psi),$$

where $X = x \cos\theta + y \sin\theta$, $Y = -x \sin\theta + y \cos\theta$.

To combine the results of the convolution with Gabor filters with different parameters, the maximum value is taken in every pixel. For the posed problem we use $\gamma = 1$, $\lambda = \frac{4}{\pi^2}$, $\psi = \frac{\pi}{2}$, $\theta = \frac{n\pi}{N}$, $n = 0, 1, \ldots, N-1$, $N = 8$, $\sigma = 2, 3, 4$. The initial hair region image is constructed by applying threshold to the combined Gabor filter response.

2.2 Accurate Hair Pixel Detection

We apply morphological closing to the initial hair pixel detection result to connect broken lines. Then we remove mole contour from the obtained mask using the algorithm that assumes that the mole is darker than outer skin. It consists of the following steps:

1. Calculate entire image histogram.
2. Take the part of the most dark pixels using the histogram — the set U.
3. Apply erosion to the set U with circular structure element with the radius n.
4. Apply dilation to the obtained set with the radius m and take only added pixels as pixels of the mole contour.

We use $n = m = 5$.

3 Hair Removal

The PDE-based method [10] was used to reconstruct the missing pixels after removing hair regions. It iteratively interpolates the pixels on the border of the reconstructed area until the area is completely filled. Local structures are smoothly inpainted from the outer part of the reconstructed area to the inner part. The pixels are interpolated using the method

$$u(x) = \frac{\sum_{y \in \varepsilon(x)} w(x, y) u(y)}{\sum_{y \in \varepsilon(x)} w(x, y)},$$

where

$$w(x, y) = \frac{1}{|x - y|} \exp\left(-\frac{1}{2\sigma^2} (c^{\perp}(x)(x - y))^2\right).$$

Here $\varepsilon(x)$ is the neighborhood of the reconstructed pixel with known pixel values, $c^{\perp}(x)$ is the direction tangential to the edge [10], σ is the parameter of the method. We use $\sigma = 1$.

4   Edge Sharpening by Image Warping

Finally the reconstructed image is sharpened using image warping.

4.1   One-Dimensional Edge Sharpening

Grid Warping. Compared to a sharp edge profile, the profile of a blurred edge is more gradual. So in order to make the edge sharper its transient width should be decreased (see Fig. 1).

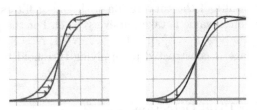

a. Proposed approach b. Unsharp masking approach

Fig. 1. One-dimensional edge sharpening

For any edge $g(x)$ centered at $x = 0$ its sharper version $h(x)$ can be obtained shifting the pixels from the neighborhood of the edge towards its center. The *displacement function* $d(x)$ describes the shift of a pixel with coordinate x to a new coordinate $x + d(x)$: $h(x + d(x)) = g(x)$.

The warped grid should remain monotonic (i.e. for any $x_1 < x_2$ new coordinates should be $x_1 + d(x_1) < x_2 + d(x_2)$), so the displacement function should match the following constraint:

$$d'(x) \geq -1. \tag{1}$$

Another constraint localizes the area of warping effect near the edge center:

$$d(x) \to 0, \qquad |x| \to \infty.$$

The displacement function $d(x)$ greatly influences the result of the edge warping. The displacement function should be chosen in a way that the slope of the edge becomes steeper yet the warping does not stretch the edge over some predefined limit. In the case of a discrete edge the rarefication is supposed to avoid wide gaps between adjacent pixels, and the values on the new warped grid are then interpolated to the old uniform grid.

Edge Model. The choice of the displacement function is based on the assumption that the blurred edge $E_\sigma(x)$ can be approximated by an ideal step edge $H(x)$ convolved with Gaussian filter with known parameter σ [12]:

$$H(x) = \begin{cases} 1, & x \geq 0, \\ 0, & x < 0, \end{cases} \qquad E_\sigma(x) = [H * G_\sigma](x),$$

where $G_\sigma(x) = \frac{1}{\sqrt{2\pi}\sigma} e^{-\frac{x^2}{2\sigma^2}}$.

Proximity Function. The displacement function $d(x)$ is connected with the *proximity* of image pixels $p(x)$:

$$p(x) = 1 + d'(x).$$

The proximity is the distance between adjacent pixels after image warping. This value is inverse to the density value. If the proximity function $p(x)$ is less than 1, then the area is densified at the point x. If the proximity is greater than 1, then the grid is rarefied. For an unwarped image $p(x) \equiv 1$.

The constraint (1) leads to non-negativity of the proximity function. Also high values of the proximity function should be avoided, because it will be hard to perform interpolation in rarefication areas if the rarefication is too strong.

We use the proximity function $p(x)$ to calculate the displacement function:

$$d(x) = \int\limits_{-\infty}^{x} (p(y) - 1)dy.$$

For the problem of edge sharpening, we use the difference of two Gaussian functions as the proximity function in order to control the areas of rarefication and densification independently:

$$p(x) = 1 + \kappa(G_{\sigma_1}(x) - G_{\sigma_2}(x)), \quad \sigma_2 > \sigma_1. \tag{2}$$

For the edge blurred with σ, we use $\sigma_1 = \sigma$. Parameter σ_2 is taken as $k\sigma_1 = k\sigma$. Good results are obtained with $1.5 \leq k \leq 2$. To achieve the strongest sharpening effect, we use the maximal values of κ that matches the constraint (1):

$$\kappa = 1/\left(G_{\sigma_1}(0) - G_{\sigma_2}(0)\right).$$

We use $\sigma_1 = \sigma, \sigma_2 = 2\sigma$.

4.2   Two-Dimensional Edge Sharpening

The 2D case is similar to 1D case with the following changes:

1. The displacement is a vector field $\boldsymbol{d}(x, y)$.

2. There cannot be any turbulence: rot $\boldsymbol{d} = 0$. Therefore, the displacement field is assumed to be gradient of some scalar function $u(x, y)$: $\boldsymbol{d}(x, y) = \nabla u(x, y)$.

3. The derivative of d is replaced by divergence so the condition (1) looks as div $\boldsymbol{d} \geq -1$ and the proximity function takes the form $p(x, y) = 1 + \text{div } \boldsymbol{d}(x, y)$.

Since $\text{div} \nabla \equiv \Delta$, where Δ is a Laplacian, the warping problem can be posed as follows

$$\begin{cases} \Delta u & = p(x, y) - 1, \\ \frac{\partial u}{\partial n} & = 0. \end{cases} \tag{3}$$

We solve the equation (3) by Gauss-Zeidel method.

Constructing the Warping Equation. In order to get the same results as in the 1D case and to keep the edge pixels unwarped, the proximity value should be equal to the 1D proximity function depending on the distance to the edge. To take into consideration multiple edge information, we suggest the following method for calculating the proximity function:

$$p(x_0, y_0) = \frac{\displaystyle\sum_{(x,y)\in E(x_0,y_0)} p(x_n)G_\sigma(x_t)|g(x,y)|}{\displaystyle\sum_{(x,y)\in E(x_0,y_0)} |g(x,y)|}$$

where $E(x_0, y_0)$ is the set of edge points in the neighborhood of (x_0, y_0).

The values x_n and x_t are projections of the vector $(x_0 - x, y_0 - y)$ on the edge gradient vector $g(x, y)$ and on the tangent to the edge respectively.

The function $p(x_n)$ is the 1D proximity function, $G_\sigma(x_t)$ is the weighting function with standard deviation equal to the edge's blur σ.

Interpolation. The idea of interpolation from the warped grid to the uniform grid is as follows: the intensity of the image at pixel (i, j) is computed as a weighted sum of intensities of all points on the warped grid in the neighborhood of that pixel: for a given radius r and all neighboring points $\{(x_k, y_k) : d_k = \sqrt{(i - x_k)^2 + (j - y_k)^2} \le r\}_{k=1}^K$ the intensity of a sharpened image I_s at (i, j) is computed as

$$I_s(i, j) = \sum_{k=1}^K \frac{1}{D_k} I(x_k, y_k), \text{ where } D_k = d_k / \sum_{l=1}^K d_l.$$

We use the interpolation radius $r = 1.5$.

5   Results and Discussion

The proposed hair removal algorithm was tested for a set of melanoma images and showed its effectiveness. Some results of hair removal and edge sharpening with comparison to other methods are illustrated in Fig. 2. It can be seen that the proposed method sharpens the mole border while keeping the other image part almost intact.

It is necessary to mention that the proposed warping algorithm corrupts the fractal structure of the mole border and should be taken into consideration in medical practice. The analysis of the fractal structure is to be performed before the hair removal method.

In this work we used $\sigma = 2$ for the warping algorithm. The future work will include an method to estimate the edge blur value σ basing on the number of inpainted mole boundary pixels.

The work was supported by Russian Science Foundation grant 14-11-00308.

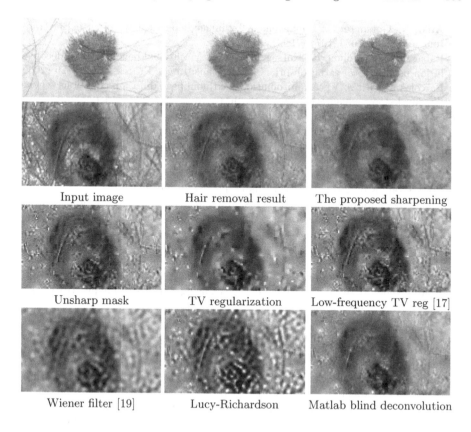

Input image	Hair removal result	The proposed sharpening
Unsharp mask	TV regularization	Low-frequency TV reg [17]
Wiener filter [19]	Lucy-Richardson	Matlab blind deconvolution

Fig. 2. The results of hair removal and sharpening using image warping

References

1. Feature-preserving artifact removal from dermoscopy images. In: Proc. SPIE Med. Imaging, pp. 1–9 (2008)
2. Abbas, Q., Celebi, M.E., Garcia, I.F.: Hair removal methods: a comparative study for dermoscopy images. Biomed Signal Process Control **6**, 395–404 (2011)
3. Abbas, Q., Fondon, I., Rashid, M.: Unsupervised skin lesions border detection via two-dimensional image analysis. Computer Methods and Programs in Biomedicine **27**(1), 65–78 (2010)
4. Abbas, Q., Garcia, I.F., Celebi, M.E., Ahmad, W.: A feature-preserving hair removal algorithm for dermoscopy images. Skin Research and Technology **19**(1), 27–36 (2013)
5. Abbas, Q., Garcia, I.F., Rashid, M.: Automatic skin tumor border detection for digital dermoscopy using a novel digital image analysis scheme. British Journal of Biomedical Science **67**, 177–183 (2010)
6. Almeida, M., Figueiredo, M.: Parameter estimation for blind and non-blind deblurring using residual whiteness measures. IEEE Trans. Image Processing **22**, 2751–2763 (2013)

7. Arad, N., Gotsman, C.: Enhancement by image-dependent warping. IEEE Trans. Image Proc. **8**, 1063–1074 (1999)
8. Babacan, S.D., Molina, R., Katsaggelos, A.K.: Variational bayesian blind deconvolution using a total variation prior. IEEE Trans. Image Process. **18**, 12–26 (2009)
9. Barcelos, C., Pires, V.: An automatic based nonlinear diffusion equations scheme for skin lesion segmentation. Appl. Math. Comput. **215**, 251–261 (2009)
10. Bornemann, F., Marz, T.: Fast image inpainting based on coherence transport. Journal of Mathematical Imaging and Vision **28**, 259–278 (2007)
11. Canny, J.: A computational approach to edge detection. IEEE Transactions on Pattern Analysis and Machine Intelligence **8**, 679–714 (1986)
12. Chernomorets, A.A., Nasonov, A.V.: Deblurring in fundus images. In: 22nd Int. Conf. GraphiCon 2012, Moscow, Russia, pp. 76–79 (2012)
13. Chung, D., Sapiro, G.: Segmentation skin lesions with partial-differentialequation-based image processing algorithms. IEEE Trans. Med. Imaging **19**, 763–767 (2000)
14. Criminisi, A., Perez, P., Toyama, K.: Region filling and object removal by exemplarbased image inpainting. IEEE Trans. Image Process. **13**, 1–13 (2004)
15. Hu, H., de Haan, G.: Low cost robust blur estimator. In: IEEE International Conference on Image Processing, pp. 617–620 (2006)
16. Prades-Nebot, J., et al.: Image enhancement using warping technique. IEEE Electronics Letters **39**, 32–33 (2003)
17. Krylov, A.S., Nasonov, A.V.: Adaptive image deblurring with ringing control. In: Fifth International Conference on Image and Graphics (ICIG 2009), pp. 72–75 (2009)
18. Lee, T., Ng, V., Gallagher, R., Coldman, A., McLean, D., Dullrazor, A.: Software approach to hair removal from images. J. Comput. Biol. Med. **27**, 533–543 (1997)
19. Nagy, J.G., Palmer, K., Perrone, L.: Iterative methods for image deblurring: A matlab object-oriented approach. Numerical Algorithms **36**(1), 73–93 (2004)
20. Nasonova, A.A., Krylov, A.S.: Determination of image edge width by unsharp masking. Computational Mathematics and Modelling **25**, 72–78 (2014)
21. Nguyen, N., Lee, T., Atkinsa, M.: Segmentation of light and dark hair in dermoscopic images: a hybrid approach using a universal kernel. In: Proc. SPIE Med. Imaging, pp. 1–8 (2010)
22. Oliveira, J., Bioucas-Dia, J.M., Figueiredo, M.: Adaptive total variation image deblurring: A majorization-minimization approach. Signal Process. **89**, 1683–1693 (2009)
23. Saugeona, P.S., Guillodb, J., Thiran, J.P.: Towards a computer-aided diagnosis system for pigmented skin lesions. Comput. Med. Imag. Grap. **27**, 65–78 (2003)
24. Schmid, P.: Segmentation of digitized dermatoscopic images by twodimensional color clustering. IEEE Trans. Med. Imaging **18**, 164–171 (1999)
25. Wighton, P., Lee, T., Atkinsa, M.: Dermoscopic hair disocclusion using inpainting. In: Proc. SPIE Med. Imaging, pp. 1–8 (2008)
26. Xie, F.Y., Qin, S.Y., Jiang, Z.G., Meng, R.S.: Pde-based unsupervised repair of hair-occluded information in dermoscopy images of melanoma. Comput. Med. Imag. Grap. **33**, 275–282 (2009)

3D Multimodal Visualization of Subdural Electrodes with Cerebellum Removal to Guide Epilepsy Resective Surgery Procedures

Nádia Moreira da Silva[1]([✉]), Ricardo Rego[2], and João Paulo Silva Cunha[1,3]

[1] INESC-TEC (Instituto de Engenharia de Sistemas e Computadores do Porto), University of Porto, Rua Dr. Roberto Frias, 4200-465 Porto, Portugal
nadiamoreirass@gmail.com
[2] Department of Neurophysiology, Hospital São João, Alameda Professor Hernâni Monteiro, 4200-319 Porto, Portugal
[3] Faculty of Engineeiring, University of Porto, Rua Dr. Roberto Frias, 4200-465 Porto, Portugal

Abstract. Patients with medically refractory epilepsy may benefit from surgical resection of the epileptic focus. Subdural electrodes are implanted to accurately locate the seizure onset and locate the eloquent areas to be spared. However, the visualization of the subdural electrodes may be limited by the current methods. The aim of this work was to assist physicians in the localization of subdural electrodes in relation to anatomical landmarks using co-registration methods and by removing the cerebellum from MRI images. Three patients with refractory epilepsy were studied, in whom subdural electrodes were implanted. All electrodes were correctly localized in a 3D view over the cortex and their visualization was improved by the removal of cerebellum. This method promises to be useful in the optimization of the surgical plan.

Keywords: 3D reconstruction · Co-registration · Subdural electrode · Epilepsy surgery · Cerebellum removal

1 Introduction

Up to 30% patients with epilepsy show resistance to antiepileptic drugs and continue to have seizures [1]. Ongoing uncontrolled seizures may cause brain injuries and diminish even more their quality of life. Epilepsy resective surgery is the most appropriate treatment for patients with refractory epilepsy [2]. The preneurosurgical evaluation is challenging and complex, requiring several expertises and multidisciplinary approaches [3,4].

In an initial phase, several non-invasive methods are required such as electroencephalography (EEG) recording and Video-EEG monitoring. However, when the results to identify epileptic onset are not conclusive, intracranial electrodes are implanted for a intracerebral electroencephalography recording (iEEG)

© Springer International Publishing Switzerland 2014
A. Campilho and M. Kamel (Eds.): ICIAR 2014, Part II, LNCS 8815, pp. 167–174, 2014.
DOI: 10.1007/978-3-319-11755-3_19

[5,6]. This approach is also recommended in cases in which the epileptogenic zone is adjacent to eloquent cortex. [7]

The positioning of iEEG electrodes and interpretation of the electric activity in the cortex is a mean to detect lesions and correlate it with the eloquent cortex in the vicinity [4]. As a result, eloquent areas are mapped and resection boundaries around epileptogenic zones are correctly planned [3,5].

The outcome of patients depend highly on the localization of the exact position of subdural electrodes for the interpretation of iEEG data, which will lead to a higher accurate identification of the epileptic lesions as well as the surrounding cortical areas [8]. Better symptom relief and low morbidity is seen in the patients whose electrodes were accurately detected [3].

Typically, the visualization of iEEG electrodes locations is performed in a 2D view. This approach can lead to uncertainties that can be solved only by intraoperative analysis [5]. Conversely, the main challenges for the physicians is to obtain reliable 3D images of the cortical surface and its relation with the implanted electrodes.

In current literature, the subdural electrodes location can be estimated in a 3D view by a number of techniques such as post-implant 3D MRI images, curvilinear reformatting of 3D MRI, surface reconstruction of CT scan and 3D CT/MRI co-registration. The 3D CT/MRI co-registration technique is commonly used since it allows the display of a 3D model with electrodes over the cortex. [8]

For some cases, the 3D visualization may not be sufficient after applying the co-registration technique. The most common type of epilepsy is temporal lobe epilepsy (TLE) [9]. In these cases, the removal of cerebellum can further enhance the visualization of subdural electrodes and, as a consequence, physicians can establish a more accurate relation of their positions with EEG recording and anatomic landmarks.

In this study, we describe a pipeline to obtain a 3D visualization of subdural electrodes over the cortex, as well as a method to remove cerebellum from the structural images. With our implementation, physicians can enhance their visualization of subdural electrodes and improve the delineation of resection borders for the surgery, in the pre-neurosurgical evaluation stage. The present pipeline has been used in 3 real cases. The first two cases were used for pipeline validation and in the third, our results were part of the surgery decision procedure.

2   Materials

2.1   Subjects

Three patients with medically intractable focal Epilepsy undergoing surgical implantation of subdural electrodes for epileptogenic zone localization were selected by Hospital São João for this study. All the data were anonymized to preserve the patient's personal information.

2.2   Clinical Process

All the patients underwent non-invasive methods (ictal/interictal EEG, normal conventional MRI, Video-EEG monitoring) and neurological examinations. In order to identify the region of the seizure onset and adjacent eloquent areas, intracranial EEG were implanted. The implantation of electrodes was based on the conjunct data resulted by the non-invasive methods. The number of the intracranial electrodes differed among patients. In patient 1 and 2, a 4x8 subdural electrode grid was implanted over the left temporal convexity and 2 subtemporal strips. Conversely, in patient 3, a 2x4 subdural electrode grid was implanted on basal surface of the interior temporal gyrus and an 8 contact strip was positioned aiming the hippocampal region.

Cortical mapping by electrical stimulation disclosed language functions for each patient.

2.3   Data Acquisition

A post-operative whole head T1-weighted images were acquired using a 1.5T MRI unit (SIEMENS, Magnetom Symphony Tim) with a voxel size of 0.875 x 0.875 x 0.88mm for patient 1 and 1.09 x 1.09 x 1.09 mm for patient 2. The electrodes position were confirmed by a CT unit (SIEMENS, Somatom Emotion Duo) with a voxel size of 0.547 x 0.547 x 1mm.

In the case of patient 3, two imaging studies were acquired, before and after the implantation. Structural pre-operative whole head T1-weighted images were gathered using a 3T MRI unit (SIEMENS, Magnetom Trio Tim) with a voxel size of 1.09 x 1.09 x 1.09mm. To confirm the electrodes position, a CT scan (PHILIPS, Brilliance 16) was acquired with a voxel size of 0.547 x 0.547 x 1mm.

3   Methods

3.1   Preprocessing

Data preprocessing was carried out using fMRIB software library (FSL version 5.0) tools. As it was intended to obtain a 3D cortical surface model, BET (Brain extraction tool) was used in all T1-weighted MRI images for skull removal, as depicted in Figure 1. BET uses a deformable model that fits to the brains surface, using locally adaptive model forces. Furthermore, the extraction depends highly on the fractional intensity threshold, which controls the distinction of brain from non-brain and, consequently the centre-of-gravity of the head in which the model surface is initialized. [10] The fractional intensity threshold was adjusted to preserve the visualization of electrodes implanted over the cortex in the post-operative MRI images. This adjustment allowed to confirm the accuracy of the co-registration of skull-stripping T1-MRI and electrodes masks given by CT data.

CT scans were linearly co-registered with T1-MRI images as reference using FLIRT tool (FMRIBs linear image registration tool). FLIRT performs a set of geometric transformations in the image, implying some constraints to preserve the image topology. A combination of local and global methods of optimization are applied in the search of the finest image orientation to minimize the cost function. [11]

For this study, a transformation space of 6 degrees of freedom was chosen, since the image modalities were of the same subject. Given the irrelevant motion between the images, it was used lower search values for the angular range over which the initial optimization search stage (local optimization) is performed. To measure the difference between the two images and minimizing it, it was used the normalized mutual information (NMI). NMI is an entropy based cost function commonly used for inter-modal alignment [12].

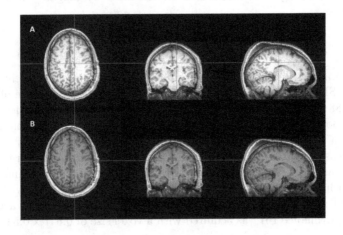

Fig. 1. A - Post-operative T1-MRI; **B** - Fusion of post-operative T1-MRI (**A**) and the extracted brain after applying BET (blue)

3.2   Processing

Electrodes Segmentation. For subdural electrodes segmentation, CT data previously co-registered with T1-MRI were thresholded and binarized, as shown in green in Figure 2. The threshold value was set to eliminate streak (beam hardening) artifact from the electrodes, brain and the skull.

Cerebellum Segmentation. The segmentation of cerebellum was carried out using FIRST (FMRIB's Integrated Registration and Segmentation tool), a recent tool available within FSL.

FIRST combines intensity and shape information of a training dataset of 336 subjects to develop a 3D mean model which is then adjusted to the target structure of the patient. The training dataset was aligned to the MNI-152 space using two-stage-affine registration [13]. In the first stage, an affine registration of the T1-MRI to the non-linear MNI-152 template was performed using 12 degrees of freedom. For the second stage, the previously aligned MRI was linearly transformed with a subcortical mask defined in the MNI space as a reference, in order to concentrate the registration only in the subcortical alignments. [13]

When using FIRST to segment cerebellum it is used the whole-head T1-MRI image of the patient and the transformation matrix resulted by the two-stage affine registration to the MNI space. However, the subcortical mask of the second stage is not yet available for cerebellum, so it was used a brain mask provided in FIRST preferences. Thus, this mask allows to exclude voxels outside of the brain and, as a consequence, cerebellum.

The resulted mask of cerebellum is binarized and multiplied by T1-MRI dataset to be subtracted to the MRI image.

In some cases the cerebellum mask does not cover the entire cerebellum and some of the bottom borders remain, after the subtraction step. This can be overcomed with an addition tool, fslroi, to extract the resulted brain without the bottom borders.

3.3   3D Multimodal Fusion

In order to obtain a 3D view of the datasets, a volume render approach available was used in MRIcron. (http://www.mccauslandcenter.sc.edu/mricro/) This software creates the 3D images directly from the volume data, allowing a combined display of different aspects such as opaque and semitransparent surfaces and cuts. For each voxel, a color and opacity is assigned. Opacity is the result of the product of an object-weighting function and a gradient-weighting function. The object-weighting function is often dependent on an intensity or a fuzzy segmentation algorithm. The gradient-weighting function is applied to enhance the surface smoothness.

For 3D visualization, T1 images without cerebellum and electrodes mask were added to MRIcron and rendered in a 3D view by a volume render approach.

In patient 3, some MRIcron options such as search depth and air/skin thresholding were studied more thoroughly for a better visualization of the electrodes.

4   Results and Discussion

As suggested in Figure 2, subdural electrodes were correctly segmented from the CT images for all patients. The threshold used was capable to remove streak (beam hardening) artifact from the electrodes, brain and skull. The beam hardening removal is specially confirmed in the sagital view of patient 3.

As previously mentioned, the cerebellum was not completely removed. Some parts of the bottom borders remain after the subtraction step and before applying fslroi.

There are many possibilities that may have interfered in the cerebellum segmentation. Considering that for this structure the corresponding subcortical mask was not available, the registration stage was incapable to concentrate only on the subcortical alignment. Therefore, the vertex positions of the 3D mean

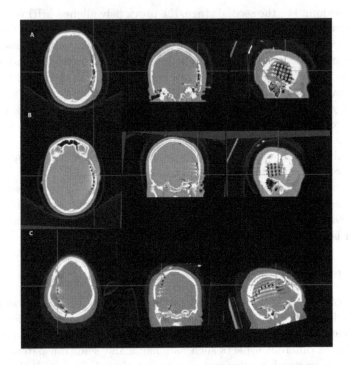

Fig. 2. Fusion of CT dataset with CT mask, for **(A)** patient 1, **(B)** patient 2 and **(C)** patient 3 data

model of cerebellum and the corresponding points in the MRI of the patient may have been misaligned. Since that each vertex of the shape is associated a statistical variation, the variation of the bottom misaligned vertices may have limit the model adjustment for this region and therefore the resulting masks. Furthermore, the performance of FIRST may be affected by several algorithm factors as described by Patenaude, B. et al [13].

As shown in Figure 3, MR and CT datasets resulted by the above processing were used to create a 3D combined data model in MRIcron. The results were reviewed and approved by an epileptologist (author Dr. Ricardo Rego).

In patient 3, the post-operative CT image showed a large swelling at the location where the electrodes were implanted. As seen in Figure 2 the brain was compressed by the swelling. Since T1-MRI image used was pre-operative and so no edema was present, the visualization of the electrodes position in the 3D model was limited. However, varying the search depth of the overlay, in MRIcron, made possible to the physicians to see the electrodes and therefore, do the anatomic relation of electrodes position with the surrounding tissues.

From all the data used in this study, our results were not used in the first two patients for the clinical decisions since they were used as test examples to

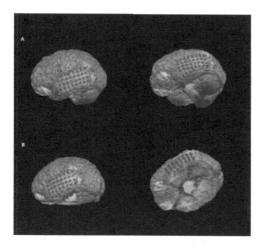

Fig. 3. A - 3D visualization, using MRIcron, of skull-stripped T1-MRI, from the patient 1, with the electrodes mask. **B** - 3D visualization of skull-stripped T1-MRI without cerebellum, from the patient 1, with the electrodes mask.

validate the pipeline. After the validation, our results were used for patient 3 in the pre-neurosurgical evaluation.

Patient 3 who had, on average, more than a seizure a week, was seizure-free. This outcome is an excellent result for the developed pipeline, since patient 3, when compared with the others patients results, was the one in which the 3D representation was more limited by the presence of the edema.

5   Conclusion

Visualization of subdural electrodes over the cortex is pivotal in the pre-neurosurgical evaluation to precisely define the cortical areas to be removed but also the ones that need to be preserved. In this study, we present a 3D model useful to relate the iEEG electric data with the anatomical position of the electrodes. This approach allowed us to delineate with higher precision the epileptic focus and the eloquent areas.

So far, several others methods to obtain a 3D multimodal view of subdural electrodes over the cortex have been used. However, with the removal of cerebellum proposed in this work, the visualization of strips and grids can be further improved, specially in the most common type of epilepsy, temporal lobe epilepsy.

This approach was already used for pre-neurosurgical evaluation by HSJ for one patient, who was seizure free.

In the future, other software can be used and compared with FSL-FIRST to determine which technique is most sensitive for cerebellum segmentation. Furthermore, to validate our methodology with higher accuracy, a larger number of patients will be included, as well as the validation of the proposed approach by at least two more neurologists, experts in this field.

Acknowledgments. This project is financed by the ERDF - European Regional Development Fund through the COMPETE Programme (operational programme for competitiveness) and by National Funds through the FCT - Fundação para a Ciência e a Tecnologia (Portuguese Foundation for Science and Technology) within project <<PEST_INESC   TEC/FCOMP-01-0124-FEDER-022701>>   and   <<ASD-MD/ PTDC/NEU-SCC/0767/2012(FCOMP-01-0124-FEDER-029673)>>.

References

1. Chen, Q., Lui, S., Li, C., Jiang, L., Ou-Yang, L., Tang, H., Shang, H., Huang, X., Gong, Q., Zhou, D.: MRI-negative refractory partial epilepsy: role for diffusion tensor imaging in high field MRI. Epilepsy Research **80**(1), 83–89 (2008)
2. Thivard, L., Adam, C., Hasboun, D., Clmenceau, S., Dezamis, E., Lehricy, S., Dormont, D., Chiras, J., Baulac, M., Dupont, S.: Interictal diffusion MRI in partial epilepsies explored with intracerebral electrodes. Brain **129**(2), 375–385 (2006)
3. Duncan, J.S.: Imaging in the surgical treatment of epilepsy, University College London Institute of Neurology. Nat. Rev. Neurology **6**(10), 537–550 (2010)
4. LaViolette, P.S., Rand, S.D., Ellingson, B.M., Raghavan, M., Lew, S.M., Schmainda, K.M., Mueller, W.: 3D visualization of subdural electrode shift as measured at craniotomy reopening. Epilepsy Research **94**(1–2), 102–109 (2011)
5. Winkler, P.A., Vollmar, C., Krishnan, G., Pfluger, T., Brckmann, H., Noachtar, S.: Usefulness of 3-D reconstructed images of the human cerebral cortex for localization of subdural electrodes in epilepsy surgery. Epilepsy Research **41**(2), 169–178 (2000)
6. So, E.L.: Integration of EEG, MRI and SPECT in localizing the seizure focus for epilepsy surgery Mayo Medical School. Epilepsia **41**(Suppl. 3), S48–S54 (2000)
7. Kamida, T., Anan, M., Shimotaka, K., Abe, T., Fujiki, M., Kobayashi, H.: Visualization of subdural electrodes with fusion CT/scan MRI during neuronavigation-guided epilepsy surgery. Journal of Clinical Neuroscience **17**(4), 511–513 (2010)
8. Tao, J.X., Hawes-Ebersole, S., Baldwin, M., Shah, S., Erickson, R.K., Ebersole, J.S.: The accuracy and reliability of 3D CT/MRI co-registration in planning epilepsy surgery. Clinical Neurophysiology **120**(4), 748–753 (2009)
9. Bernard, C., Anderson, A., Becker, A., Poolos, N.P., Beck, H., Johnston, D.: Acquired Dendritic Channelopathy in Temporal Lobe Epilepsy. Science **305**(5683), 532–535 (2004)
10. Smith, S.M.: Fast robust automated brain extraction. Human Brain Mapping **17**(3), 143–155 (2002)
11. Jenkinson, M., Bannister, P., Brady, J.M., Smith, S.M.: Improved Optimisation for the Robust and Accurate Linear Registration and Motion Correction of Brain Images. NeuroImage **17**(2), 825–841 (2002)
12. Cahill, N.D.: Normalized measures of mutual information with general definitions of entropy for multimodal image registration. In: Fischer, B., Dawant, B.M., Lorenz, C. (eds.) WBIR 2010. LNCS, vol. 6204, pp. 258–268. Springer, Heidelberg (2010)
13. Patenaude, B., Smith, S.M., Kennedy, D.N., Jenkinson, M.: A Bayesian model of shape and appearance for subcortical brain segmentation. Neuroimage **56**(3), 907–922 (2011)

Medical Image Segmentation

On the Automatic Normalization of Plaque Regions in Ultrasound Images of the Carotid

José Rouco[1]([⊠]), Jorge Novo[1], and Aurélio Campilho[1,2]

[1] INESC TEC - INESC Science and Technology, Porto, Portugal
jrouco@fe.up.pt
[2] FEUP - Faculdade de Engenharia da Universidade do Porto, Porto, Portugal

Abstract. In order to assess the atherosclerotic plaque disruption risk from B-mode ultrasound images of the carotid, an appropriate normalization of the plaque regions is required. This is usually achieved through the manual selection of two sample regions in the image containing blood and adventitia tissues, which are used as reference.

In this work, we propose a new plaque region normalization method that takes advantage of multiple blood and adventitia reference samples per image, and a method for the automatic selection of these reference samples. Several preliminary results are provided in order to demonstrate the possible capabilities of the proposed methods.

1 Introduction

Atherosclerosis is a vascular disease that is characterized by the thickening of the artery walls and the formation of atheromatous plaques. In its advanced stages, the plaque lesions can become vulnerable and eventually break, releasing clots and debris into the blood flow, which is one of the leading causes of serious cardiovascular accidents like myocardial infarction and stroke. The classical criterion to assess the risk of plaque rupture is the degree of stenosis (arterial lumen narrowing). However, more recently, additional markers that are related with the plaque tissue composition and morphology are being used to evaluate plaque vulnerability [6].

There are several imaging modalities allowing the measurement of such markers [18]. Among them, B-mode ultrasonography of the carotid is one of the most widely used in clinical practice, as it is a high-resolution, non-invasive, low cost and readily available medical imaging technology. These images allow the visualization of the anatomical layers of the vessel walls, being possible to measure the thickness of the vessel wall, the degree of stenosis or the identification and classification of plaques.

Several computer-aided plaque morphology markers, aiming to quantify the vulnerability of plaques from B-mode ultrasound images, have been proposed [10]. Most of them are based on the analysis of dark structures inside the plaque, corresponding to blood and lipids. The simplest and most widely used markers

© Springer International Publishing Switzerland 2014
A. Campilho and M. Kamel (Eds.): ICIAR 2014, Part II, LNCS 8815, pp. 177–184, 2014.
DOI: 10.1007/978-3-319-11755-3_20

of these are based on the measures of the overall Gray-Scale Median (GSM) [5,12,17], or the Percentage of Echolucent Pixels (PEP) [5]. Advanced markers based on pixel distribution analysis (PDA) of the plaque region [11], and on measures of the juxtaluminal black area (JBA) [7], have been also proposed. Other objective markers based on plaque texture and surface smoothness have been also studied in [1,8,13]. Computer-aided diagnosis (CAD) systems have been developed to ease a standardized and reproducible measurement of these markers, and to integrate them with other risk indicators [1,2].

However all these methods rely on the manual normalization of the plaque region intensities [5,14,17]. The normalization is required due to the coherent nature of the ultrasound (US) imaging process. The concrete echogenicity and contrast of the image regions depend on the changes in acoustic impedance between tissue the interfaces, on the direction of the US wave with respect to the interface orientation, and on the attenuation due to the absorption and scattering of the tissues in the path of the US waves. Additionally, interesting boundaries might be occluded (acoustic shadowing) under strong attenuators or reflectors. Fortunately, the recent advances in ultrasound imaging technology to improve the quality of B-mode ultrasonography and minimize the effects of some common artifacts are being included in the standard ultrasound equipment available in the medical centers [4]. Last, but not least, US images are highly dependent on the skill of the operator performing the examination, who is responsible for adjusting the insonation planes and the ultrasound parameters, according to his/her subjective judgment while following standard acquisition protocols and guidelines [3] This makes the ultrasound images, and derived markers, intrinsically difficult to reproduce in the absence of standardized acquisition protocols and appropriate contextual reference information.

In previous works, the plaque region normalization is performed using blood and adventitia (the outermost layer of the artery wall) regions as reference [5]. The normalization consists on a linear transformation of the image values that maps the median values of the regions to some values of reference for their tissues. In the existent CAD systems the regions are manually selected by the clinicians. The selected regions are required to be correctly imaged, so that their values can be safely assigned to the reference values. In addition, the reference regions should be near the plaque region, so they are likely to be subjected to similar imaging conditions.

However, manual selection methods may become tedious for some application scenarios in which several video frames or imaging planes are involved [9]. In addition, one reference region for each tissue may not be enough for normalizing large plaque, or sloping artery cases, for which the attenuation and other imaging conditions may locally vary along the plaque region. Finally, it would be desirable to incorporate objective mechanisms to allow the assessment of reference region imaging quality. All this motivate the research in advanced normalization strategies, which should be assisted by automatic procedures for reference region selection, which is the aim of this work. To that end, in section 2 we propose a new plaque region normalization method from multiple blood

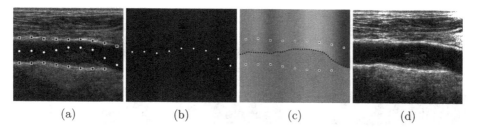

| (a) | (b) | (c) | (d) |

Fig. 1. Normalization method example. (a) Input image I with blood (white circles) and adventitia (black squares) reference points (b) Interpolated reference blood map B (c) Interpolated reference adventitia map A. (d) Normalized output image I_n.

and adventitia reference values. In section 3, an automatic method for reference region selection is proposed. Some preliminary results are shown and discussed in section 4. And, finally, the conclusions are summarized in section 5.

2   Normalization Method

We propose a plaque region normalization method that uses several lumen (blood) and adventitia image values along the whole image width, both for the near- and far-end artery walls. Each of these values is associated to a point in the image, corresponding to the reference region location from which they are estimated. These values are mapped, using a linear transformation, to the standard values for blood (v_b) and adventitia (v_a).

The transformation applied to the image follows the expression:

$$I_n = (v_a - v_b)\frac{I - B}{A - B} + v_b \tag{1}$$

where I denotes the input image, I_n the normalized output image, and A and B denote the local estimation maps of the nearby adventitia and blood values in the image, respectively.

The local maps are obtained by interpolation of the input reference value points. The blood map B is computed through horizontal linear interpolation of the blood reference points, followed by a Gaussian smoothing of scale σ_n. Using this same procedure, two additional maps are computed using the near- and far-end adventitia reference points. Then, the two maps are combined into an unique adventitia map A by vertically dividing the image into two halves, following an approximate lumen centerline. The approximate lumen centerline is obtained using the algorithm described in [16]. Figure 1 shows an example of these maps, and the resulting normalized image.

3   Automatic Reference Region Detection Method

The blood reference regions are taken from lumen region locations. The artery lumen is detected using dynamic programming over a local phase based

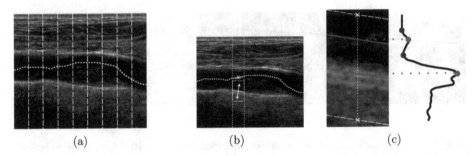

Fig. 2. Automatic reference region detection example. (a) Lumen detection and horizontal division. (b) Adventitia orientation estimation. (c) Offset selection based on the median image values.

symmetry measure, as described in [16]. This algorithm results in a path going through the lumen region, which is approximately located in its symmetry axis. The algorithm is robust to noise, to local contrast and intensity changes. In addition the resulting lumen path does not cross the plaque regions. Then the image is divided horizontally into N vertical bands of equal width, as shown in figure 2(a). For each of these vertical bands, a line segment approximating the lumen path is computed. Then, the median value of the image in band region of width w_b around each segment is computed as a reference blood value, and the center of the segment as its associated position.

The adventitia reference regions are detected on each of the previous vertical bands by searching in a range $[o_{min}, o_{max}]$ of vertical offsets from the lumen position. The algorithm for adventitia detection is divided in three steps, as described below. These steps are repeated with negative and positive offset ranges to detect the near- and far-end adventitias, respectively.

First, the adventitia orientation is estimated from the region defined by the offset range (depicted in figure 2(b)) as follows. The local gradient of the image is computed using Gaussian derivatives of scale σ_∇. Then, the gradient orientation is averaged over the offset region by using a double angle representation that is weighted by the squared gradient magnitude. In this way, all the gradients in the region contribute to the average orientation regardless of the polarity and depending on their strength. An alternative solution to the orientation estimation would be to consider the lumen path orientation instead. However this orientation may differ from the adventitia orientation near the plaque regions.

In the second step, the estimated orientation is used to compute a set of candidate adventitia line segments by that differ on the vertical offset from the lumen position. The median intensity in band region of width w_a around each segment is computed and arranged by the vertical distance from the lumen, as depicted in the profile of figure 2(c). The resulting profile is traversed, in increasing distance order, searching for local maxima with higher value than the previous local maxima found. These local maxima correspond to the adventitia segment candidates, for which their median values are reserved, for future use, as the reference adventitia value of the candidate. Additionally, the median value in the preceding local minima (the valley value) is also computed for each candidate. Then, the edge strength $S(x)$ of each candidate x is computed as the difference between its adventitia and valley values. Finally, the edge strengths are normalized dividing by the maximum candidate strength of each vertical band.

In the third step, the adventitia segment candidates are evaluated on the basis of a score combining their continuous connectivity and strength. In order to do this, it is required that the first two steps are completed for each of the vertical bands in the image.

For each transition between two adjacent vertical image bands (left and right), the continuity $C_0(L, R)$ of each candidate pair, with L a candidate of the left band, and R of the right band, is defined as:

$$C_0(L, R) = S(L)\ S(R)\ K\ (|L_r - R_l|) \tag{2}$$

where K denotes a kernel function, and R_l and L_r denote the left and right end points of a R and L candidates, respectively. For K, we use a Gaussian kernel function with scale σ_C, equivalent to two times the step between the vertical offsets in the second stage of the algorithm.

Then, for each candidate the maximum continuity among all its neighboring candidates on adjacent vertical bands is used as score. The candidate achieving maximum score for each band is selected if the score is above a quality threshold θ_q. The median value of the selected candidate is used as reference adventitia value, and the center of the adventitia segment as its associated position.

4   Results and Discussion

In order to perform a preliminary evaluation of the proposed method, a set of 11 longitudinal B-mode images of the common carotid artery is used. All of these images contain clearly identifiable plaque regions. The images were acquired with a Philips HDI 5000 ultrasound system, using a standardized acquisition protocol [3]. This is a subset of the dataset used in [15] and [16]. For each image, manual delineations of the intima-media regions by medical experts were available. These delineations included the existent plaque regions in the near- and far-end artery walls.

The image values are 8-bit gray-scale. The pixel size is different for each image, ranging from 0.05 mm/pixel to 0.09 mm/pixel. The method parameters are, thus, expressed in millimeters and converted accordingly for each image. The normalization parameters are set to: blood value $v_b = 0$, adventitia value $v_a = 190$ and smoothing scale to $\sigma_n = 0.75$ mm. For the detection algorithm the parameters are set as follows. The number of vertical bands N is estimated for each image to obtain 4 bands per cm, as a good balance between the density of reference points and the allowed lumen and adventitia curvature. The width of the blood and adventitia regions is set to $w_b = w_a = 0.5$ mm. The gradient scale is set to about the normal intima-media thickness $\sigma_\nabla = 0.75$ mm to capture

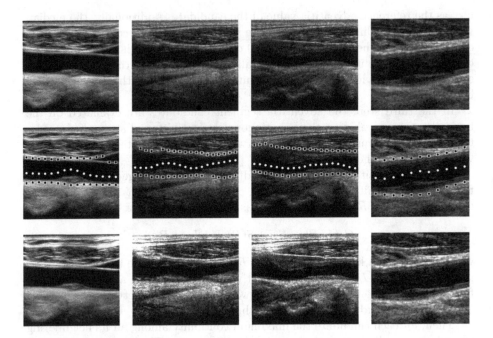

Fig. 3. Examples of automatic reference point and normalization results. First row, input images. Second row, detected reference blood (white circles) and adventitia (black squares) points. Third row, normalized output images.

the overall artery wall orientation, instead of the texture details. The range of vertical offsets $[o_{min}, o_{max}]$ is set to a wide range of $[1.5, 10]$ mm, to ensure that the adventitia lies within the offset region. The step between offsets is set to $o_{step} = \max(w_a/2, 1 \text{ pixel})$, and the scale of the continuity kernel is set accordingly to $\sigma_C = 2o_{step}$. Finally, the quality threshold is set to $\theta_q = 0.8$.

The lumen is correctly detected for all the images in the dataset. Good results are also obtained for adventitia detection. However some of the adventitia points are misdetected for some images. Nevertheless, these issues are limited to some few points in the near-end artery walls, which imaging quality is lower than for the far-walls. Some examples of the detected reference regions and the resulting normalization are shown in figure 3. Examples of misdetected near-wall adventitia points can be observed in the images of the first and fourth columns.

In order to test the resulting normalization the images are perturbed with random local contrast and intensity variations. To do this, ten control points are randomly placed in the image space with associated random transformations of dynamic range (from 0.75× to 1.5×), and gain (from -64 to +64). These control points are smoothly interpolated to locally transform the image. 100 different transformations are applied to each image. The resulting images are not perceptually different from the original image.

The automatic normalization algorithm is applied to all these images. Then, the GSM is measured for the near- and far-end intima-media regions, using the manual boundaries available, both before and after normalization. The standard deviations of the near- and far-wall GSMs along the 100 repetitions are computed for each image. The GSM of the near-wall resulted in an average standard deviations of 7.8 ± 1.3 and 3.0 ± 0.6, before and after normalization respectively. This is an image-wise reduction of $2.6 \pm 0.5\times$ the standard deviation. For the far-wall, the standard deviations are 7.9 ± 0.8 and 2.8 ± 1.5, before and after normalization, which is a reduction of $3.5 \pm 1.6\times$ the standard deviation.

5   Conclusions

In this work, we propose a new plaque region normalization method that takes advantage of multiple blood and adventitia reference samples per image, and a method for the automatic selection of these reference regions.

The results of the automatic adventitia detection method are good. However additional study and improvement is required to integrate new imaging quality criteria and features, and to integrate the method in a CAD system that allows human interaction for supervision. This should be accompanied by extended quantitative experimental evaluation on larger datasets.

The presented preliminary normalization results demonstrate the promising capabilities of the proposed method, which would require to be validated on risk prediction medical studies involving clinical data.

Acknowledgments. This work is supported by the European ERDF and ESF funds, and Portuguese funds through the COMPETE and POPH programs of the Fundação para a Ciência e a Tecnologia (FCT), in the framework of the PEst-C/EEI/LA0014/2013 project and the SFRH/BPD/79154/2011 grant contract.

References

1. Acharya, U.R., Faust, O., Sree, S.V., Alvin, A.P.C., Krishnamurthi, G., Seabra, J.C.R., Sanches, J., Suri, J.S.: Atheromatic: symptomatic vs. asymptomatic classification of carotid ultrasound plaque using a combination of HOS, DWT & texture. In: Annual Int. Conf. of the IEEE Engineering in Medicine and Biology Society, pp. 4489–4492 (2011)
2. Afonso, D., Seabra, J., Suri, J.S., Sanches, J.M.: A CAD system for atherosclerotic plaque assessment. In: Annual Int. Conf. of the IEEE Engineering in Medicine and Biology Society, pp. 1008–1011 (2012)
3. Trouboul, P.J., et al.: Mannheim Carotid Intima-Media Thickness Consensus (2004-2006-2011). An Update on Behalf of the Advisory Board of the 3rd, 4th and 5th Watching the Risk Symposium 13th, 15th and 20th European Stroke Conferences, Mannheim, Germany, 2004, Brussels, Belgium, 2006 and Hamburg, Germany 2011. Cerebrovascular Diseases 34, 290–296 (2012)
4. Contreras Ortiz, S.H., Chiu, T., Fox, M.D.: Ultrasound image enhancement: A review. Biomedical Signal Processing and Control 7(5), 419–428 (2012)

5. Elatrozy, T., Nicolaides, A., Tegos, T., Griffin, M.: The objective characterisation of ultrasonic carotid plaque features. European Journal of Vascular and Endovascular Surgery **16**(3), 223–230 (1998)
6. Fuster, V., Moreno, P.R., Fayad, Z.A., Corti, R., Badimon, J.J.: Atherothrombosis and high-risk plaque: part I: evolving concepts. Journal of the American College of Cardiology **46**(6), 937–954 (2005)
7. Griffin, M.B., Kyriacou, E., Pattichis, C., Bond, D., Kakkos, S.K., Sabetai, M., Geroulakos, G., Georgiou, N., Doré, C.J., Nicolaides, A.: Juxtaluminal hypoechoic area in ultrasonic images of carotid plaques and hemispheric symptoms. Journal of Vascular Surgery **52**(1), 69–76 (2010)
8. Kanber, B., Hartshorne, T.C., Horsfield, M.A., Naylor, A.R., Robinson, T.G., Ramnarine, K.V.: Quantitative assessment of carotid plaque surface irregularities and correlation to cerebrovascular symptoms. Cardiovascular Ultrasound **11**(1), 38 (2013)
9. Kanber, B., Hartshorne, T.C., Horsfield, M.A., Naylor, A.R., Robinson, T.G., Ramnarine, K.V.: Dynamic variations in the ultrasound greyscale median of carotid artery plaques. Cardiovascular Ultrasound **11**(1), 21 (2013)
10. Kyriacou, E.C., Pattichis, C., Pattichis, M., Loizou, C., Christodoulou, C., Kakkos, S.K., Nicolaides, A.N.: A review of noninvasive ultrasound image processing methods in the analysis of carotid plaque morphology for the assessment of stroke risk. IEEE Transactions on Information Technology in Biomedicine **14**(4), 1027–1038 (2010)
11. Lal, B.K., Hobson, R.W., Hameed, M., Pappas, P.J., Padberg, F.T., Jamil, Z., Durán, W.N.: Noninvasive identification of the unstable carotid plaque. Annals of Vascular Surgery **20**(2), 167–174 (2006)
12. Martínez-Sánchez, P., Fernández-Domínguez, J., Ruiz-Ares, G., Fuentes, B., Alexandrov, A.V., Díez-Tejedor, E.: Changes in carotid plaque echogenicity with time since the stroke onset: an early marker of plaque remodeling? Ultrasound in Medicine & Biology **38**(2), 231–237 (2012)
13. Niu, L., Qian, M., Yang, W., Meng, L., Xiao, Y., Wong, K.K.L., Abbott, D., Liu, X., Zheng, H.: Surface roughness detection of arteries via texture analysis of ultrasound images for early diagnosis of atherosclerosis. PloS One **8**(10), e76880 (2013)
14. Östling, G., Persson, M., Hedblad, B., Gonçalves, I.: Comparison of grey scale median (GSM) measurement in ultrasound images of human carotid plaques using two different softwares. Clinical Physiology and Functional Imaging **33**(6), 431–435 (2013)
15. Rocha, R., Silva, J., Campilho, A.: Automatic segmentation of carotid B-mode images using fuzzy classification. Medical & Biological Engineering & Computing **50**, 533–545 (2012)
16. Rouco, J., Campilho, A.: Robust Common Carotid Artery Lumen Detection in B-Mode Ultrasound Images using Local Phase Symmetry. In: 2013 IEEE Int. Conf. on Acoustics, Speech and Signal Processing (ICASSP), pp. 929–933 (May 2013)
17. Tegos, T.J., Sabetai, M.M., Nicolaides, A.N., Pare, G., Elatrozy, T.S., Dhanjil, S., Griffin, M.: Comparability of the ultrasonic tissue characteristics of carotid plaques. Journal of Ultrasound in Medicine **19**, 399–407 (2000)
18. de Vries, W., van Dam, G.M., Tio, R.A., Hillebrands, J.L., Slart, R.H.J.A., Zeebregts, C.J.: Current imaging modalities to visualize vulnerability within the atherosclerotic carotid plaque. Journal of Vascular Surgery **48**(6), 1620–1629 (2008)

Automatic Tear Film Segmentation Based on Texture Analysis and Region Growing

Beatriz Remeseiro[1]([✉]), Katherine M. Oliver[2], Eilidh Martin[2],
Alan Tomlinson[2], Daniel G. Villaverde[1], and Manuel G. Penedo[1]

[1] Departamento de Computación, Universidade da Coruña, A Coruña, Spain
{bremeseiro,daniel.garcia,mgpenedo}@udc.es

[2] Department of Life Sciences, Glasgow Caledonian University, Glasgow, UK
{k.oliver,eilidh.martin,a.tomlinson}@gcu.ac.uk

Abstract. Dry eye syndrome is a prevalent disease characterized by symptoms of discomfort and ocular surface damage. It can be identified by several types of diagnostic tests, one of which consists in capturing the appearance of the tear film by means of the Doane interferometer. Previous research has demonstrated that this manual test can be automated, with the benefits of saving time for experts and providing unbiased results. However, most images are made up of a combination of different patterns which makes their classification into one single category per eye not always possible. In this sense, this paper presents a first attempt to segment tear film images based on the interference patterns, and so to detect multiple categories in each individual subject. The adequacy of the proposed methodology was demonstrated since it provides reliable results in comparison with the practitioners' annotations.

Keywords: Dry eye syndrome · Tear film · Image segmentation · Texture analysis · Seeded region growing

1 Introduction

Vision would be impossible without an optically smooth anterior surface to the eye [1]. The cellular structure of the anterior cornea is, at a microscopic level, quite rough. Consequently we rely on a thin liquid layer, the tear film, to produce this essential smooth surface. The tear film is made up of three layers: an outer lipid layer, a relatively thick aqueous layer, and an inner mucous layer [2,3]. While each layer is important, in both the maintenance of a high quality optical surface and a healthy cornea, it is the lipid layer that is the subject of this paper.

The lipid layer retards the rate at which the aqueous layer evaporates [1,4]. When the lipid layer is absent or of poor quality, evaporation of the aqueous layer is relatively fast, resulting in blurring and discomfort. This induces blinking, and while this results in the reformation of a smooth optical surface, frequent blinking causes visual disturbance [5]. Additionally, excessive drying can cause damage to the corneal epithelium resulting in sterile ulceration of the cornea [6].

A. Campilho and M. Kamel (Eds.): ICIAR 2014, Part II, LNCS 8815, pp. 185–192, 2014.
DOI: 10.1007/978-3-319-11755-3_21

In an effort to categorize the quality of the lipid layer in a non-invasive, objective, manner the Doane interferometer was developed [7]. This instrument consists of an illumination and observation system linked to a PC-attached digital camera. With this system, multiple images of interference fringes produced by the lipid layer can be captured and stored for further analysis.

Initially these images were assessed and categorized by optometrists into a grading scale composed of five categories [8]: strong fringes, coalescing strong fringes, fine fringes, coalescing fine fringes, and debris. However, the variability of the fringes was such that even intra-observer gradings of the same image varied significantly. Consequently, an automated analysis system was deemed desirable and so previous studies have been carried out. It was demonstrated that the interference fringes can be characterized as a texture pattern [8]. Thus, the classification can be automated saving time for experts and eliminating the subjectivity of this manual task. By using the *co-occurrence features* method for texture extraction, and an ad-hoc feature selection process based on the INTERACT filter, it was also demonstrated [9] that the automatic classification can be achieved with maximum accuracy over 91% in less than 2 seconds.

Previous research classifies the input images obtained with the Doane interferometer into one of the five categories of the grading scale, i.e. a single image acquired from a patient's eye is classified in a single category. However, the heterogeneity of the tear film frequently makes classification into a single category impossible. Thus, it is highly desirable to perform local analysis and classification in order to detect multiple categories per patient. This paper presents a first attempt to perform tear film segmentation on the Doane images.

2   Research Methodology

The proposed methodology for tear film segmentation based on the interference patterns consists of six steps. The first one entails the acquisition of the image using the Doane interferometer. The second stage involves extracting the *region of interest* (ROI) which will be subsequently analyzed. Following, each window of the ROI is processed to extract its features and predict its class-membership probabilities. Finally, an adapted version of the seeded region growing algorithm and a post-processing step are applied in order to obtain the segmented image.

2.1   Image Acquisition

The input image acquisition was carried out with the Doane interferometer [7] and a digital PC-attached CMEX-1301 camera (Euromex Microscopen BV, NL). Its program ImageFocus was used for image capture, and images were stored at a spatial resolution of 1280×1024 pixels in the RGB color space. Due to the various artifacts associated with image capture, such as blinking and ocular movement, many images were unsuitable for analysis. Thus, it was necessary to select an image that was an appropriate representation of the tear film status during the image collection. The images were analyzed by an optometrist who selected those taken shortly after blinking, when the eye was fully open.

2.2   Location of the Region of Interest

Input images acquired with the Doane interferometer include an external area which does not contain relevant information for tear film segmentation (see Figure 1(a)). Previous research [8] located the *region of interest* (ROI) as a rectangle in the central part of the image. However, in this research the analysis is taken over the whole tear film and so a new process to locate the ROI is presented.

The acquisition procedure guarantees that the relevant part of the image is characterized by green or yellow tonalities. The input images are in the RGB color space and, taking into account these tonalities, the green channel was considered in [8]. Nonetheless, the green channel is noisier than the red one in which the tear film can also be perceived with a high contrast due to the yellow tonalities. Consequently, the red channel was considered when dismissing the background of the image from the tear film.

The background is determined by finding those pixels whose gray level is less, i.e. darker, than a threshold. This threshold is defined as $th = \mu - p \times \sigma$, where μ is the mean value of the gray levels of the image, σ is its standard deviation and p is a weight factor. The thresholded image may contain areas which do not correspond with the tear film, such as shadows or other artifacts. For this reason, all the detected areas are considered, and only the biggest one is selected as the preliminary ROI. As small holes inside it may appear, due to spots or dark fringes, the final ROI (see Figure 1(b)) is obtained by filling these holes.

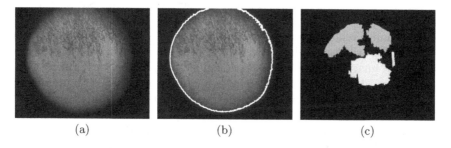

(a)   (b)   (c)

Fig. 1. (a) Input image acquired with the Doane interferometer. (b) Location of the region of interest. (c) Segmented image based on the interference patterns (cyan represents coalescing strong fringes, and yellow represents coalescing fine fringes).

2.3   Feature Extraction

Using a specified window size, the windows located in the ROI of the input image are processed and a descriptor per window is generated. This descriptor is composed of 16 features, and obtained according to next procedure:

1. Color analysis. The three channels of the input image in RGB are transformed into one gray channel to subsequently analyze its texture.

2. Texture analysis. The *co-occurrence features* technique [10] is used for texture extraction according to Remeseiro et al. [8]. The method generates a set of gray level co-occurrence matrices, and extracts a set of 14 statistical measures from their elements to finally obtain a texture descriptor.
3. Feature selection. The INTERACT algorithm [11] was used for feature selection to reduce the number of features, and so the computational requirements. An *ad-hoc* feature selection process based on this filter was used for dimensionality reduction, so the descriptor was reduced, from 476 to 16 features, with no degradation in performance [9].

2.4   Soft Classification

For each descriptor obtained from the windows located at the ROI, a *support vector machine* (SVM) [12] is used to compute its class-membership probabilities. Notice that partial class-memberships are used in soft classification to model uncertain labeling and mixtures of classes. Note also that the SVM was selected as the machine learning algorithm according to Remeseiro et al. [8].

2.5   Seeded Region Growing

Several methods for image segmentation can be found in the literature, one of which is the well-known *seeded region growing*. It segments an input image with respect to a set of initial points or seeds, which can be manually or automatically selected. The iterative process consists in analyzing each connected component of seeds, and performing the growing only if these components satisfy a homogeneity criterion.

Adams and Bischof proposed the original method [13] as applied to grayscale images. In this paper, an adapted version of this classic algorithm is presented as applied to images based on the class-membership probabilities provided by a soft classifier. The final target is to create a labeled image which represent the spatial distribution of the interference patterns over the tear film.

Firstly, the seeds are selected automatically by analyzing the windows of the ROI to calculate their feature vectors, and their corresponding class-membership probabilities. For each window, the maximum class-membership probability p_{max} is calculated and compared with the seed threshold α. If $p_{max} > \alpha$, then the center of the window becomes a seed and is added to the list of seeds L.

Following, the process of growing is carried out in order to obtain the final regions. The pixels corresponding to the seeds are labeled in the matrix of regions R, and their neighbors are added to a sorted list SSL. This list is sorted based on the homogeneity criterion, which represents the difference between the average class-membership probability of an existing region and the probability of the new pixel which is being analyzed. Therefore, the first element in the list will be the one with the minimum δ value defined as: $\delta = |CP[i] - mean[i]|$, where $CP[i]$ is the probability of the new element belongs to the class i, and $mean[i]$ is the average probability of belonging to the class i calculated over the pixels which are already labeled as i. Next, the sorted list SSL is processed until it does not contain any element, and so the process subsequently described is applied to each element of the list. The first element is removed from the list and its neighbors are analyzed. If all the neighbors which are already label have the same label, other than the boundary label, then its δ value previously calculated is obtained and compared with the growing threshold β. If $\delta < \beta$, then the element is labeled in R with the same label than its neighbors, the average probability of the region is updated, and all the neighbors of the element are added to the SSL list. Otherwise, if the neighbors already labeled do not have the same label, then the element is labeled in R as a boundary.

Finally, the output image (see Figure 1(c)) is created by processing the matrix of regions R: those elements which have a label different from the boundary label, are labeled as interference patterns in the output image whilst the rest of the elements are labeled as background pixels.

2.6 Post-processing

The labeled image obtained after applying the seeded region growing algorithm may contain regions with small holes due to the growing process. In order to homogenize these regions, each hole is "filled" in such a way that its pixels will belong to the region which encloses them. In addition, small regions may also appear in the labeled image, which can correspond to false positives or noisy areas. Thus, this post-processing step also includes their elimination. The process consists in finding the contour of each region and eliminating those whose perimeter is less than a minimum threshold m previously established.

3   Experimental Results

All the experimental results were obtained using a dataset composed of 100 images from patients with average age 55 ± 16. All the images have been annotated by two optometrists from the Department of Life Sciences, Glasgow Caledonian University. These two optometrists marked all the regions which appear in each image, so the dataset includes regions from the five categories considered.

3.1   Optimal Window Size

The optimal window size refers to the minimum window size which allows a precise segmentation and maintains the texture well-defined. In order to establish it, an experiment was carried out by analyzing squared windows with sizes from 64 to 240 pixels. Using the dataset annotated by the two optometrists, only the areas in which both of them marked the same category were considered. For this task, a SVM was trained and a 10-fold cross validation was performed. Figure 2 shows the different window sizes considered, and their accuracies. As can be seen, the accuracy for the bigger windows remains almost stable but for the smaller ones, the smaller the window the lower the accuracy. According to these results, the window size selected for tear film segmentation was 160×160 pixels.

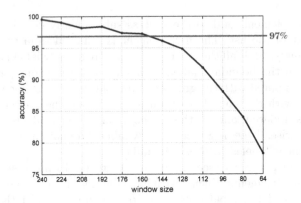

Fig. 2. Window size vs. accuracy

3.2 Image Segmentation

Using windows of 160×160 pixels, the results obtained with the dataset will be compared with the annotations made by two optometrists. Different parameter configurations were considered in the seeded region growing algorithm, but for reasons of simplicity only the best one is presented: $[\alpha = 0.9, \beta = 0.01]$. Regarding the threshold m used to eliminate the small regions, it was set to 295 pixels based on the minimum perimeter size of the regions marked by the optometrists.

Firstly, a SVM was trained with representative samples of the five categories, which correspond to areas in which the two optometrists marked the same category. Next, the proposed methodology was applied over the dataset composed of 100 images and so the segmentation process was performed on their ROIs. Before analyzing the results, the difficulty of the manual task and its subjectivity should be highlighted. Figure 3(a) depicts this difficulty and was obtained by analyzing all the annotations made by the two optometrists over the dataset. The graphic represents the probability of, given a random pixel classified in a given category by a random expert, the other expert (green) has classified this pixel in the same category. As can be seen, the level of disagreement is noticeable in all the patterns, and optometrists find more difficult to categorize the coalescing fine fringes pattern, closely followed by the strong fringes pattern, since the two optometrists only agree in about a 20% of the pixels marked. In contrast, they fully agree in almost the 50% of the pixels associated to the debris pattern.

The results obtained with the methodology were compared in a quantitative way, and so the regions marked by the system were compared with the annotations made by the two optometrists, pixel by pixel. Stacked histograms were used to represent this comparison, and show the percentage of pixels that the system agrees or disagrees with the optometrists. Figure 3(b) represents all the pixels classified by the system with three levels of agreement: the agreement with 0 experts means that only the system marked this area, the agreement with 1 expert means that the system and one expert marked this area, and the agreement with 2 experts means a total agreement between the system and the experts. Similarly, Figure 3(c) represents all the pixels not classified by the

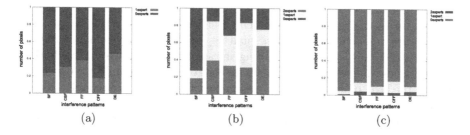

Fig. 3. Validation of the methodology: (a) reference graphic, (b) comparison between the system and the two optometrists using only the positive pixels, (c) comparison between the system and the two optometrists using only the negative pixels

system with three levels of disagreement: the disagreement with 2 experts means that the optometrists marked this area which was not classified by the system, the disagreement with 1 expert means that only one optometrist marked this area not classified by the system, and the disagreement with 0 experts means a total agreement between the system and the experts. This different levels of agreement/disagreement can be easily understood by using classical terminology: the *true positives* and the *true negatives* are represented by green/yellow in Figures 3(b) and 3(c), respectively; whilst the *false positives* and the *false negatives* are represented by red in Figures 3(b) and 3(c), respectively.

Using these basic concepts, some performance measures can be calculated from the histograms. For example, the accuracy of the system is around the 80% in four out of the five categories considered which demonstrates the feasibility of the problem despite the subjective data. However, it shows a noticeable difficulty in properly classifying the strong fringes category which is one of the most difficult patterns for the optometrists too. Regarding the sensitivity of the system, it surpasses the 80% in all the cases which means that the system does not misclassify too many pixels associated to an interference pattern. However, the specificity of the system is lower than the sensitivity, specially if the attention is focused on the strong fringes, which means that the system classifies as interference patterns pixels which are not categorized by at least 1 expert.

4   Conclusions and Future Work

The automatic grading system for human tear films previously developed provides, as a result, the interference pattern present at the central part of a Doane image. However, more than one pattern may appear per image and so a methodology for segmenting Doane images was proposed in this paper. This methodology includes the use of texture analysis, and an adapted version of the classic algorithm known as seeded region growing. Results obtained with this methodology provide information related to the different patterns which appear in an input image, and also their location and approximation size. Besides, it produces reliable results in comparison with the annotations done by the optometrists with maximum accuracy over 80%. In clinical terms, the manual process can be automated with the main benefit of being unaffected by subjective factors.

As future research, the authors plan to improve the system in order to increase its accuracy, specially regarding the strong fringes pattern. In addition, it would be desirable to include the annotations of a higher number of experts to minimize the level of disagreements, and make the system more reliable. Instead of processing only single images, it would be of great interest the investigation of dynamic changes seen in the tear film during the inter-blink time interval. This dynamic analysis could help in identifying subjects with poor tear film stability.

Acknowledgments. This research has been partially funded by the Secretaría de Estado de Investigación of the Spanish Government and FEDER funds of the European Union through the research project TIN2011-25476.

References

1. Rolando, M., Zierhut, M.: The Ocular Surface and Tear Film and Their Dysfunction in Dry Eye Disease. Survey of Ophthalmology **45**(2), S203–S210 (2001)
2. Korb, D., Craig, J., Doughty, M., Guillon, J., Smith, G., Tomlinson, A.: The Tear Film Structure, Function and Clinical Examination, ch. 2. Butterworth Heinemann (2002)
3. Bron, A.J., Tiffany, J.M., Gouveia, S.M., Yokoi, N., Voon, L.W.: Functional aspects of the tear film lipid layer. Experimental Eye Research **78**, 347–360 (2004)
4. Foulks, G.N.: The correlation between the tear film lipid layer and dry eye disease. Survey of Ophthalmology **52**(4), 369–374 (2007)
5. Dursun, D., Monroy, D., Knighton, R., Tervo, T., Vesaluoma, M., Carraway, K., Pflugfelder, S.C.: The effects of experimental tear film removal on corneal surface regularity and barrier function. Ophthalmology **107**(9), 1754–1760 (2000)
6. Lemp, M.A., Foulks, G.N.: The definition and classification of dry eye disease. The Ocular Surface **5**(2), 75–92 (2007)
7. Doane, M.G.: An instrument for in vivo tear film interferometry. Optometry and Vision Science **66**(6), 383–388 (1989)
8. Remeseiro, B., Oliver, K., Tomlinson, A., Martin, E., Barreira, N., Mosquera, A.: Automatic grading system for human tear films. Pattern Analysis and Applications (2014)
9. Villaverde, D.G., Remeseiro, B., Barreira, N., Penedo, M.G., Mosquera, A.: Feature selection applied to human tear film classification. In: 6th International Conference on Agents and Artificial Intelligence, Angers, France, pp. 395–402 (2014)
10. Haralick, R.M., Shanmugam, K., Dinstein, I.: Texture Features for Image Classification. IEEE Transactions on Systems, Man and Cybernetics **3**, 610–621 (1973)
11. Zhao, Z., Liu, H.: Searching for Interacting Features, pp. 1156–1161 (2007)
12. Burges, C.J.: A Tutorial on Support Vector Machines for Pattern Recognition. Data Mining and Knowledge Discovery **2**, 121–167 (1998)
13. Adams, R., Bischof, L.: Seeded Region Growing. IEEE Transactions on Pattern Analysis and Machine Intelligence **16**(6), 641–647 (1994)

An Improved Segmentation Method for Non-melanoma Skin Lesions Using Active Contour Model

Qaisar Abbas[1,2], Irene Fondón[3(✉)], Auxiliadora Sarmiento[3], and M. Emre Celebi[4]

[1] Department of Computer Science, COMSATS Institute of Information Technology,
Islamabad, Pakistan
[2] College of Computer and Information Sciences,
Al-Imam Muhammad ibn Saud Islamic University, Riyadh, Saudi Arabia
drqaisar@ntu.edu.pk
[3] Signal Theory Departament, University of Seville, Seville, Spain
irenef@us.es, sarmiento@us.es
[4] Department of Computer Science, Louisiana State University, Shreveport, LA, USA
pedromaria.alemany@uca.es

Abstract. Computer-Aided Diagnosis (CAD) systems are widely used to classify skin lesions in dermoscopic images. The segmentation of the lesion area is the initial and key step to automate this process using a CAD system. In this paper, an improved segmentation algorithm is developed based on the following steps: (1) color space transform to the perception-oriented CIECAM02 color model, (2) preprocessing step to correct specular reflection, (3) contrast enhancement using an homomorphic transform filter (HTF) and nonlinear sigmoidal function (NSF) and (4) segmentation with relative entropy (RE) and active contours model (ACM). To validate the proposed technique, comparisons with other three state-of-the-art segmentation algorithms were performed for 210 non-melanoma lesions. From these experiments, an average true detection rate of 91.01, false positive rate of 6.35 and an error probability of 7.8 were obtained. These experimental results indicate that the proposed technique is useful for CAD systems to detect non-melanoma skin lesions in dermoscopy images.

Keywords: Computer-Aided Diagnosis (CAD) · Dermoscopy · Non-melanoma skin lesions · Contrast enhancement · Segmentation · Active contour

1 Introduction

Computer-aided diagnosis (CAD) systems [1] have been rapidly being developed over the past decade for skin cancer classification. In fact, an important role of CAD systems is to provide a "second opinion" [2],[3] to the dermatologists in their decision making for effective diagnosis of patients. In dermatology, the major types of lesions for skin cancer are divided into malignant melanoma and non-melanoma. Compared to the existing melanoma CAD systems [6], the recognition rate of non-melanoma skin lesions is less than 75% maybe due to the existence of many lesions appearances. In previous studies, numerous methods try to distinguish between melanoma and non-melanoma lesions [6]. In all of them, the segmentation of the unhealthy skin is a key

© Springer International Publishing Switzerland 2014
A. Campilho and M. Kamel (Eds.): ICIAR 2014, Part II, LNCS 8815, pp. 193–200, 2014.
DOI: 10.1007/978-3-319-11755-3_22

step [7]. However, the segmentation of non-melanoma lesions detection is very difficult due to their fuzziness and irregularity. In the literature, thresholding, clustering, region growing and active contours (AC) [7]-[13] methods were commonly used to detect the area of melanoma skin lesions usually being the AC ones the algorithms with the best performance. These AC models [11]-[14] are semi-automatic because of the need a previous selection of regularization parameters. In all of these RAC techniques, the energy curve was controlled by an internal and external force without local influence method to control the applied force on the curve. In [15], the local histogram fitting energy technique is proposed to overcome this situation in a general way. In this paper we try to overcome these limitations by the use of an ACM technique and an effective image enhancement method, especially designed for low contrast non-melanoma skin lesions. In this ACM model, a CIECAM02 [16] (JCh) perceptually uniform color space is employed for the enhancement and J component is used for lesion segmentation. The homomorphic transform filter (HTF) [17] is mainly to reduce the specular reflection with a non-linear sigmoidal function (NSF) that improves contrast. Afterwards, the rough lesion area is detected using relative entropy (RE) (edge-based approach) and then refined using an ACM (edge-based & region-based) approaches. Experiments are performed on a total of 210 non-melanoma skin lesions, mainly collected from the EDRA Interactive Atlas of Dermoscopy [18]. A comparative study with three state-of-the-art techniques such as DTEA [9], RAC [14] and JSeg [19] have been also performed using the statistical measures of true positive rate (TPR), false positive rate (FPR), and error probability (EP).

The reminder of this paper is organized as follows. Section 2 describes the color space transform step, which converts the RGB image to CIECAM02 color model. In section 3, the preprocessing step is explained. Afterwards, the segmentation procedure is described in Section 4. In Section 5, the experimental results are presented and finally conclusions are given in Section 6.

2   Color Space Transform

To facilitate the segmentation step especially in case of non-melanoma skin lesions, the color space selection is critical having a significant influence on the result of image segmentation processes. In the literature, RGB, YUV, HSV, CIE $L^*a^*b^*$, and CIE $L^*u^*v^*$ color spaces have been utilized in the scope of dermoscopy images. Although RGB, YCbCr, and YUV color spaces are commonly used in raw data and coding standards, they do not correlate with human perception. In contrast, CIE color spaces are perceptually more uniform. However, CIECAM02 (JCh) color space can take into account more visual perception effects while showing better results [20]-[21] for image segmentation. Therefore, in the first step, the RGB dermoscopy color image is transformed into the perceptual-oriented JCh (lightness, chroma and hue) color space of CIECAM02 [16] appearance model. JCh dermoscopy image is normalized to the ranges h: [0, 360∘]/15∘, C: [0, 1]/0.43, and J: [0, 1]/0.43. The 15° and 0.43 values were empirically fixed to give the enough importance to hue while saving computational costs. The updated components of CIECAM02 (JCh) are denoted by $J^*C^*h^*$.

3   Preprocessing

Illumination correction and contrast enhancement facilitate the non-melanoma skin lesion segmentation process. For this purpose, an improved homomorphic transform filter (HTF) [17] in $J^*C^*h^*$ perceptual-oriented color space is used. Moreover, contrast is enhanced by a nonlinear sigmoid function (NSF) and finally we perform an smoothing by a 2-D Gaussian filtering. In the literature, the HTF is a technique for nonlinear image enhancement and correction use both RGB and grayscale images. However in this study, the normalized $J^*C^*h^*$ color space is selected.

Consider the J^* component of $J^*C^*h^*$ color space. It can be represented by

$$\log[k_{J^*}(x,y)] = (\log[i(x,y)] \times \log[r(x,y)]) + \alpha \tag{1}$$

where $i(x,y)$ is the intensity of illumination and $r(x,y)$ the spatial-distribution reflectance and α is added as a constant with a fixed value of 0.01. The transformed equation before and after performing 2-D Fast Fourier Transform (FFT) are in eq. (2):

$$S_{J^*}(x,y) = I(x,y) + R(x,y), F(u,v) = I(u,v) + R(u,v) \tag{2}$$

where the coordinate variables x and y become u and v, respectively. $F(u,v)$ is the Fourier transform of the logarithmic transformed image $S_{J^*}(x,y)$. Then, a Butterworth high pass filter is applied to amplify high frequencies and attenuate low frequencies. The HTF filter represented by $H(u,v)$ is calculated in Eq. (3):

$$H(u,v) = (H_H - H_L) \times \left(1 - \exp\left(-Bw\left(\frac{D_o}{D(u,v)}\right)\right)\right) + H_L \tag{3}$$

Bw is the Butterworth filter, $D(u,v)$ is the distance between point (u, v) and the origin point of frequency domain. The D_o is the normalized transition, H_L and H_H are chosen parameters of low and high frequencies respectively, with constant values $H_L = 0.5$ and $H_H = 1.0$. Bw parameter is calculated as follows:

$$Bw = (1 + ((u/2)^2 + (v/2)^{2^{0.5}}/c)^2 \times n)^{-1} \tag{4}$$

where c and n are the cut-off frequency and attenuation coefficient parameters, which are experimentally set to 0.25 and 1.4, respectively. After performing the Bw high pass filter, HTF transformed shown in Eq. (5) is applied on Eq. (4) as indicated below:

$$G(u,v) = F(u,v) + H(u,v)(u,v) = F(u,v) + H(u,v) \tag{5}$$

Then by taking the inverse Fourier transform and exponentiation on Eq. (7), an enhanced image is obtained as follows:

$$L(u,v) = \exp[FFT^{-1}G(u,v)] \tag{6}$$

Contrast enhancement by NSF is performed on h* plane. However in this paper, we perform the NSF procedure by calculating the minimum and maximum intensity values from h* plane denoted by $\min_{arg}\{(x,y)\}$ and $\max_{arg}\{(x,y)\}$, respectively. In fact, the NSF function i.e, $sgm_h(x,y)$ is a continuous non-linear function, which enhances the contrast of images by selecting appropriate values of gain and cut-off frequencies. We first calculate the estimated contrast image P(x,y) by using the eq. (9).

$$P(x,y) = (h * (x,y) - \min_{arg}\{(x,y)\}) / \max_{arg}\{(x,y)\} \qquad (7)$$

Next, the final NSF function $(sgm_h(x,y)))$ for h* plane is modified by Eq. (10) as:

$$sgm_h(x,y) = 1/(1 + \exp(gain \times (\beta - P(x,y)))) \qquad (8)$$

Where, the β parameter is the cut-off frequency. To get high-contrast image, we should just define the value in the range $((1 \leq \beta \leq 3)1 \leq \beta \leq 3)$. Finally, a 2-D Gaussian filter is applied in C* plane for image smoothing. After performing this enhancement step, the resultant illumination correction, contrast enhancement and smoothing dermoscopy images are shown in Fig. 2 (b) and (c), respectively.

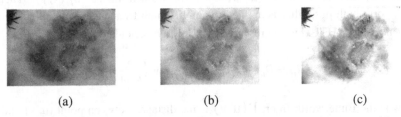

(a)   (b)   (c)

Fig. 1. An example of preprocessing enhancement step to enhance the contrast of a non-melanoma lesion (a). (b) specular reflection removed image, (c) contrast enhanced image.

4   Skin Lesion Segmentation

4.1   Rough Area Segmentation

A rough area segmentation step is used to help the subsequent AC model (ACM) by allowing the level set curves to be initialized close to lesion area. To this purpose the relative entropy (RE) threshold technique has been used as an edge-based approach [22]. The RE process produces a thresholded image which is very similar to the original one whenever they possess as similar co-occurrences as possible. It means that an optimal threshold (T) value is determined in such a manner that the gray level pixels transition has minimum RE concerning that of original image. Afterwards, by putting all the co-occurrence probabilities in the relative entropy expression, we are obtaining an optimum threshold value. However, the lesion boundary detected by this RE method is not smooth. An example of this rough segmentation step for non-melanoma is shown in Fig. 3. Rough regions are integrated using morphological area filling function.

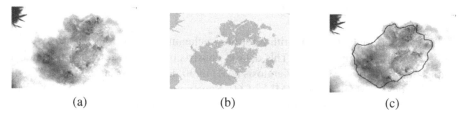

        (a)   (b)   (c)

Fig. 2. Rough lesion area extraction of the enhanced original image where figure (a) represents the preprocessed image, (b) is the thresholded image using the relative thresholding technique and (c) is the border detected using morphological functions

4.2 Segmentation Refinement

In this step, the rough region segmented by relative entropy is finally enhanced by a non parametric ACM [15] with local histogram fitting energy in J^* color plane . In this algorithm, the localize method employed is the Chan-Vese (CV) energy model. Compare to other level set based segmentation methods, the ACM with local energy fitting provides better results in terms of segmentation of fuzzy or irregular object areas. An example of this non-melanoma segmentation step is displayed in Fig. 4.

5   Experimental Results

The proposed segmentation algorithm for non-melanoma skin lesions was tested on a set of 210 dermoscopic images. This dataset consists of five common non-melanoma lesions of distributions: Actinic Keratosis (AK) of 30, Basal Cell Carcinoma (BCC) of 40, Melanocytic Nevus / Mole (ML) of 60, Squamous Cell Carcinoma (SCC) of 40 and Seborrhoeic Keratosis (SK) of 40. In all these images, the specular reflection and low contrast were generally presented. Therefore, the algorithm begins by enhancing the images using the proposed preprocessing steps. A ground truth for each of the images was drawn by an expert.

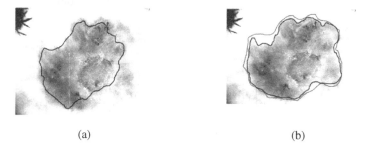

              (a)   (b)

Fig. 3. Refine lesion area extraction of the non-melanoma lesion. Image (a) represents rough the segmentation and (b) shows the refine border segmentation in which red contour represents the ground truth and black contour is the one obtained by the AC model (ACM).

6   Experimental Results

The proposed segmentation algorithm for non-melanoma skin lesions was tested on a set of 210 dermoscopic images. This dataset consists of five common non-melanoma lesions of distributions: Actinic Keratosis (AK) of 30, Basal Cell Carcinoma (BCC) of 40, Melanocytic Nevus / Mole (ML) of 60, Squamous Cell Carcinoma (SCC) of 40 and Seborrhoeic Keratosis (SK) of 40. A ground truth for each of the images was drawn by an expert. The results of the proposed segmentation method were compared to three state-of-the-art algorithms: JSeg (color and texture segmentation) [19], DTAE (dermatologist's tumor area extraction) [9], and traditional RAC (region-based AC) [14]. The iteration parameter for RAC is fixed with the value of 140 by empirical analysis on this dataset.

To objective evaluate the performance of the proposed technique, we have used the average values of true positive rate (TPR), false positive rate (FPR) and error probability (EP) measures that are calculated using Eqs (11) to (13), respectively.

$$\text{True Detection Rate (TDR)} = \left(\frac{TP}{TP+FN}\right) \times 100 \tag{9}$$

$$\text{False Positive Rate (FPR)} = \left(\frac{TN}{FP+TN}\right) \times 100 \tag{10}$$

$$\text{Error Probability (EP)} = \left(\frac{FP+FN}{TP+FN+FP+TN}\right) \times 100 \tag{11}$$

Where, TP, TN, FP and FN are True Positive, True Negative, False Positive and False Negative, respectively. An experimental result of the proposed segmentation algorithm for non-melanoma lesion is given in Fig. 3. The red contour is drawn manually from the ground truth, while the black one has been obtained with our segmentation technique. The proposed method obtains a significant improvement in true detection rate, which is very close to the ground truth. Furthermore, the average comparisons with other three (RAC, DTAE and JSeg) techniques are shown in Table 1 by using statistical measures of TDR, FPR and EP. From Table 1, it is clear that the proposed algorithm achieves a higher value of TDR of 91.01% and lower value of both FPR (6.35%) and error probability (7.8%). In adittion to these comparisons, we have

Table 1. Percentage of non-melanoma lesion-area-extraction error statistics

Methods	Numerical Results		
	TDR (%)	FPR (%)	EP (%)
JSeg	78.6	17.40	22
DTAE	81.09	15.50	17
RAC	83.06	12.22	14
Proposed	91.01	6.35	7.8

Table 2. Color spaces comparison

Color space Transform	Numerical Results			
	JSeg (%)	DTEA (%)	RAC (%)	Proposed (%)
RGB grascale	TDR:68.01 FPR:29.50	TDR:70.20 FPR:24.31	TDR:73.15 FPR:21.52	TDR:79.20 FPR:17.60
RGBCIE L*u*v*	TDR:70.50 FPR:23.30	TDR:74.22 FPR:19.50	TDR:76.11 FPR:18.19	TDR:81.45 FPR:15.63
RGB CIECAM02	TDR:78.60 FPR:17.40	TDR: 81.09 FPR: 15.50	TDR:83.06 FPR: 12.22	TDR: 91.01 FPR: 5.35

also performed experiments in terms of different color spaces such as RGB, HSV and CIECAM02 using TDR and FPR measures (Table 2). From this table, it should be noticed that the proposed algorithm in CIECAM02 color space obtains highest TDR and lowest FPR values compared to other two color spaces.

7   Conclusions

In this paper, an improved approach for non-melanoma skin lesion segmentation is presented. The algorithm uses a normalized and uniform color space ($J^*C^*h^*$) from CIECAM02 color model to increase the correlation to human perception. A preprocessing step has been added to enhance image contrast while reducing specular reflections. The segmentation step executes a non parametric ACM initialized by the RE technique. The experiments, based on the ground truth contributed by an expert, indicate that our method provides an effective solution for the segmentation of fuzzy lesions.

Acknowledgements. The completion of this research was made possible thanks to the project PM-IPFP/HRD/HEC/2011/3402.

References

1. Perednia, D.A., Gaines, J.A., Rossum, A.C.: Variability in physician assessment of lesions in cutaneous images and its implications for skin screening and computer-assisted diagnosis. Arch. Dermatol. **128**, 357–364 (1992)
2. Abbas, Q., Emre Celebi, M., Fondón, I., Ahmad, W.: Melanoma recognition framework based on expert definition of ABCD for dermoscopic images, skin research and technology (2012) (in press)
3. Argenziano, G., Soyer, H.P., Chimenti, S., Talamini, R., Corona, R., Sera, F., et al.: Dermoscopy of pigmented skin lesions: results of a consensus meeting via the Internet. J. Am. Acad. Dermatol. **48**(5), 679–693 (2003)

4. Ballerini, L., Fisher, R.B., Aldridge, B., Rees, J.: A color and texture based hierarchical k-nn approach to the classification of non-melanoma skin lesions. In: Color Medical Image Analysis. Springer (2012) (in press)
5. Ko, C.B., Walton, S., Keczkes, K., Bury, H.P.R., Nicholson, C.: The emerging epidemic of skin cancer. British Journal of Dermatology **130**, 269–272 (1994)
6. Celebi, M.E., Kingravi, H.A., Uddin, B., et al.: A methodological approach to the classification of dermoscopy images. Comput. Med. Imag. Grap. **31**(6), 362–373 (2007)
7. Celebi, M.E., Iyatomi, H., Schaefer, G., Stoecker, W.V.: Lesion border detection in dermoscopy images. Comput. Imag. Grap. **33**(3), 148–153 (2009)
8. Emre Celebi, M., Wen, Q., Hwang, S., Iyatomi, H., Schaefer, G.: Lesion Border Detection in Dermoscopy Images Using Ensembles of Thresholding Methods. Skin Res. Technol. (2012) (in press)
9. Iyatomi, H., Oka, H., Celebi, M.E., et al.: An improved Internet-based melanoma screening system with Dermatologist-like tumor area extraction algorithm. Comput. Med. Imag. Grap. **32**(7), 566–579 (2008)
10. Gomez, D.D., Butakoff, C., Ersboll, B.K., Stoecker, W.V.: Independent histogram pursuit for segmentation of skin lesions. IEEE T. Biomed. Eng. **55**(1), 157–161 (2008)
11. Tang, J.: A multi-direction GVF snake for the segmentation of skin cancer images. Pattern Recogn. **42**(6), 1172–1179 (2009)
12. Yuan, X., Situ, N., Zouridakis, G.: A narrow band graph partitioning method for skin lesion segmentation. Pattern Recogn. **42**(6), 1017–1028 (2009)
13. Abbas, Q., Fondón, I., Rashid, M.: Unsupervised skin lesions border detection via two-dimensional image analysis. Comput. Meth. Prog. Bio. (2010)
14. Lankton, S., Tannenbaum, A.: Localizing region-based active contours. IEEE T. Image Process. **17**(11), 2029–2039 (2008)
15. Liu, W., Shang, Y., Yang, X.: Active contour model driven by local histogram fitting energy. Pattern Recognition Letters **34**(6), 655–662 (2013)
16. Fairchild, M.D.: A revision of CIECAM97s for practical applications. Color Research & Applications **26**(6), 418–427 (2001)
17. Seow, M.J., Asari, V.K.: Ratio rule and homomorphic filter for enhancement of digital colour image. Neurocomputing **69**, 954–958 (2006)
18. Argenziano, G., Soyer, P.H., De, V.G., Carli, P., Delfino, M.: Interactive atlas of dermoscopy CD. EDRA medical publishing and New media, Milan (2002)
19. Celebi, M.E., Aslandogan, A., Stoecker, W.V.: Unsupervised Border Detection in Dermoscopy Images. Skin Research and Technology **13**(4), 454–462 (2007)
20. Smith, J.R.: Color for image retrieval. In: Image Databases, ch. 11, pp. 285–311. John Wiley & Sons, Inc. (2002)
21. Huang, Z.-K., Liu, D.-H.: Segmentation of color image using EM algorithm in HSV color space. In: Proceedings of IEEE International Conference on Information Acquisition, pp. 316–319 (July 2007)
22. Chang, C., Chen, K., Wang, J., Althouse, M.L.G.: A Relative Entropy Based Approach in Image Thresholding. Pattern Recognition **27**, 1275–1289 (1994)
23. Melanocytic Lesions. Medical Image Analysis **7**(1), 47–64 (2003)

Statistical-Based Segmentation of Bone Structures via Continuous Max-Flow Optimization

Jose-Antonio Pérez Carrasco[1]([⊠]), Carmen Serrano-Gotarredona[1],
Cristina Suárez-Mejías[2], and Begoña Acha-Piñero[1]

[1] Signal and Communications Department, University of Seville,
Camino de los Descubrimientos, s/n., 41092 Sevilla, Spain
{jperez2,cserrano,bacha}@us.es
[2] Virgen del Rocio Hospital, Seville, Spain
cristina.suarez.exts@juntadeandalucia.es

Abstract. In this paper an automatic algorithm for segmentation of bone structures in CT volumes has been developed. This is a complicated task because bones present intensities overlapping with those of surrounding tissues. This overlapping happens because of the presence of some diseases and the different densities present in the bones, providing values similar to those in other tissues like muscle, fat or some organs. In our implementation, gray information and statistical information have been combined to be used as input to a continuous max-flow algorithm to get accurate and fast bone segmentation. Twenty CT images have been automatically segmented and several coefficients such as DICE, Jaccard, Sensitivity and Positive Predictive Value (PPV) indexes have been computed. High sensitivity values above 0.97 were obtained, which shows that the results are promising. Besides, low computational times under 0.6s in the max-flow algorithm were obtained, implying lower times in comparison to many algorithms in the literature.

Keywords: Segmentation · Convex relaxation · Max-flow

1 Introduction

Accurate bone segmentation is very important in the diagnosis of several diseases (such as Osteoarthritis, Rheumatoid Arthritis , Osteoporosis), in analizing and locating many kinds of fractures and in plastic surgical planning. Bone segmentation is a difficult task because, in spite of bone structures presenting high values in CT modalities, the presence of such diseases provoke a reduction in bone density in different areas, making it difficult to get accurate segmentations. Besides, the different parts of the bones (mainly periosteum, compact (hard) bone, cancellous (spongy) bone and bone marrow) present wide differences in densities and thus, different Hounsfield values [1]. This implies that these values overlap with other tissue types such as muscle, fat or some organs. As a consequence,

© Springer International Publishing Switzerland 2014
A. Campilho and M. Kamel (Eds.): ICIAR 2014, Part II, LNCS 8815, pp. 201–208, 2014.
DOI: 10.1007/978-3-319-11755-3_23

some techniques that would be preferred as a first instance, such as thresholding techniques, are not useful in bone segmentation tasks. In Fig. 1 several bone structures can be seen. It is important to note that cortical bone and cancellous bone in these images presenting different Hounsfield values, due to their differences in density.

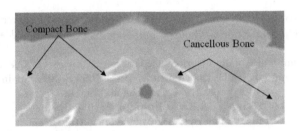

Fig. 1. Zoomed abdominal section of a ct volume. Note differences in compact bone with cancellous bone in the different bone structures.

Another important aspect to be considered in segmentation of bones is its 3D essence. Fast algorithms are required in order to segment bone structures in a considerably reduced computational time, in order to really help radiologists in the diagnosis and treatments of diseases and in surgical planning. Some algorithms have been presented addressing bone segmentation. Wang et al. [2] classifies the different segmentation techniques into four categories: intensity-based [3], edge-based [4], region-based [5], and model-based [4][6]. However, the lack of homogeneity in Intensity-based algorithms makes these methods invalid for bone segmentation. In edge-based implementations [4], the aim is to extract contour points and then reconstruct the boundaries of the bones connecting these points. Region-based algorithms [5] use global region information to divide the image according to some homogeneity conditions. Model-based methods [4][6] allow the incorporation of local features in edge-based algorithms and global features of region-based algorithms. In these algorithms the aim is to minimize a functional that takes into account these informations.

When considering bone segmentation, many works focus on just one or a reduced number of bone structures. For instance, in [7], Y. Cheng et al. seek the segmentation of the femoral head and proximal acetabulum in 3D data images based on intensity, neighbor and gradient information. In [8], T. Cervinka uses morphological operations and two fixed thresholds to get accurate cortical bone detections in pQCT images of distal tibia. In [9], Melih S. Aslan segment vertebral bones using graph cuts. In [9], the authors use a matched filter first to detect the vertebral body automatically and then they apply graph cuts to accurately segment the vertebral bones. As it can be seen, this lack of generalization is a problem, as radiologists do not want to consider different segmentation methods according to the regions to be analyzed. Thus, it would be desirable to have a more general method more suitable for a wide number of bone structures making the process more transparent to radiologists. When considering more general methods, level sets, active contours and graph cuts implementations are preferred [11] [12]. In [11] and [12] the authors employ level sets for bone segmentation. However, level set methods can drive to local optima of the minimization energy function and suffer from high sensitivity to initialization. Graph cut techniques consist in discrete minimization of the objective energy. They have the advantage that they guarantee the global optima (if bipartition is implemented and a Potts model is adopted) in nearly real time. Thus, this technique has been applied successfully in recent works [15][16].

The methodology applied in the approach here presented is based on continuous convex relaxation techniques[17][18], which share the advantages of both active curves and graph-cuts [18]. As shown in a recent study [18], in 3D grids, convex relaxation approaches outperform graph cuts in regard to speed and accuracy. Thus, in our implementation, gray level information, gradient values and statistical information computed using histogram distances have been combined and used as input to a convex relaxation algorithm in order to get accurate and fast segmentation of bones in 3D volumes.

2 Methodology

2.1 Preprocessing: Bone Enhancement

In our implementation 20 images extracted from 20 CT volumes have been used. Hounsfield values in CT volumes are usually between -2000 and 3000. Bones usually have values from 700 (cancellous bone) to 3000 (dense bone) approximately. In order not to consider values that do not correspond obviously to bones and to get a higher contrast, a thresholding operation has been applied to the different images. The threshold has been chosen taking the minimum value present in the bones within the segmented images provided by an expert. Secondly, the thresholded image is normalized and it is denoted as *Inorm*. To not lose generalization, the minimum and maximum values using during the normalization are common in all the volumes that have been used.

2.2 Computation of Histogram Distance Images

The CT volumes considered in this approach have been separated into two datasets. 10% of them have been used as training dataset. The rest has been used as test set. The images belonging to the training dataset are required to obtain a model histogram of the bone structures. On the other hand, for each pixel (i, j) within each image in the test dataset, a local histogram is computed considering a neighborhood of 21x21 pixels. Subsequently, for each local histogram, a distance measure to the histogram model is calculated and this distance is assigned to pixel (i, j) in a new Histogram Distance Image (*HDI*). χ^2 distance has been chosen to compare both histograms [21]. *HDI* will have values close to 0 in regions where bone tissue appears and close to 1 when no bones are encountered.

Finally, in order to combine this statistic information with the gray level information *Inorm*, we create a cost image term to be minimized (*CIT*) as:

$$CIT = ((1 - Inorm) + HDI)/2 \qquad (1)$$

Eq. 1 is the cost to be minimized using the continuous max-flow algorithm described in the next subsection. The first term of the right expression in Eq. 1 uses intensity information. Pixels corresponding to bone (mainly cortical bone) will have values close to '1'. On the contrary, pixels not corresponding to bones will have values close to '0'. Thus, we use 1-*Inorm* instead of *Inorm* directly because we want low values in bone structures. Something similar occurs with the second term in the right expression in Eq. 1. The distance to the model histogram in pixels corresponding to bones should be close to 0 whereas it should be close to '1' in pixels belonging to other kind of tissues. In Fig. 2 these computed images are shown for a CT slice. The first image (a) is the initial image without thresholding. The second image (b) corresponds to the thresholded and normalized image. The third image (c) corresponds to the distance image *HDI*. Finally, the last image (d) corresponds to *CIT* image which will be the input to the continuous max-flow algorithm. It can be seen that bone structures are darker in *CIT* image, which means that gray level information and distance between histograms information have been properly combined.

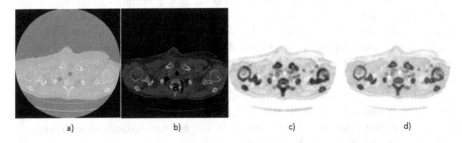

Fig. 2. Computed images used by the algorithm. The first image (a) is the initial image without thresholding. The second image (b) corresponds to the thresholded and normalized image. The third image (c) corresponds to the distance image *HDI*. Finally, the last image (d) shows the new computed image *CIT*.

2.3   Max-Flow Based Segmentation Stage

The algorithm proposed by J. Yuan et al. [17] has been employed. This algorithm solves the 3D multi-region image segmentation problem (Potts Model), based on the fast continuous max-flow method (CMF) proposed by J. Yuan et al [17]. Given the continuous image domain Ω (3D volume in our case), we assume that there are two terminals, the source s and the sink t. We assume that for each image position $x\epsilon\Omega$, there are three concerning flows: the source flow $p_s(x)\epsilon\Re$ directed from the source s to x, the sink flow $p_t(x)\epsilon\Re$ directed from x to the sink

t and the spatial flow passing x $p(x)\epsilon\Re^2$. The three flow fields are constrained by capacities:

$$p_s(x) \le C_s(x), p_t(x) \le C_t(x), |p(x)| \le C(x)\forall x\epsilon\Omega; \qquad (2)$$

where C_s is the source capacity, C_t is the sink capacity and $C(x)$ is the capacity at point x. In addition, for $\forall x\epsilon\Omega$, all flows are conserved, i.e.

$$p_t - p_s + divp = 0, \forall x\epsilon\Omega \qquad (3)$$

Therefore, the corresponding max-flow problem is formulated by maximizing the total flow from the source:

$$\max_{p_s,p_t,p} \int_\Omega p_s dx \qquad (4)$$

subject to flow constraints (2) and (3). Yuan et al [17] proved that such a continuous max-flow formulation is equivalent to the continuous s-t min-cut problem [19][20] as follows:

$$\min_{u(x)\epsilon[0,1]} \int_\Omega (u)C_s dx + \int_\Omega (1-u)C_t dx + \int_\Omega C(x)|\nabla u|dx \qquad (5)$$

Actually, (5) represents the dual model of (4). $u(x)$ is the labeling function and indicates if point x belongs to the region to be segmented. In (5) $u(x)$ operates as the multiplier to the flow conservation condition (3). If the minimization problem is well defined, the cost function C_s should take low values inside the bones and high values outside them. Similarly, C_t should take low values outside the bones and high values inside them. The most right term of Eq. (5) is the regularization term and $C(x)$ is a penalty function. $|\nabla u|$ is the absolute gradient of the labeling function $u(x)$, thus indicating the boundary of the segmented region. C_s and C_t are called regional terms. In the algorithm proposed here, the regional term C_s, provided as input to the continuous max-flow algorithm, is the CIT image computed through Eq. (1). Thus, in the algorithm proposed, the terms C_s and C_t (Eq. 5) are computed as follows:

$$C_s = CIT \qquad (6)$$

$$C_t = 1 - CIT \qquad (7)$$

Note that with Eq. (7) we force C_t to be low outside the bones and high inside them, as required by the minimization in (5). In addition, the algorithm penalizes an excessive area of the surface limiting the segmented volume. This penalization term is the most right term in Eq. (5). This penalization is modeled by a function $C(x)$ depending on the gradient of the CIT image along the surface, so that if the gradient is high along the surface, a large area of the surface is not penalized. The penalization function is computed as follows:

$$C(x) = \frac{b}{1 + a|\nabla CIT(x)|} \qquad (8)$$

where parameters a and b control the importance of the gradient in the penalization function. In our implementation a and b values have been obtained empirically and their values are 10 and 0.2, respectively. Note that at the surface, $|\nabla u|$ will have high values whereas $C(x)$ will have low values if the gradient of $CIT(x)$ is high. Thus, the most right term in Eq. 5 will not penalize a large area if a high border is encountered.

Finally, in order to smooth out the resulting segmented image, and to get a more accurate segmentation, a morphological operation of opening is performed.

It is important to note that the proposed algorithm uses the gradient information that is very high in the boundaries of cortical bone structures and histogram distance information, which is very useful mainly to segment cancellous bone structures, which present lower gray values and overlap with other tissue types such as muscle, fat or some organs.

3   Experimental Results

The CT volumes considered in this approach have been separated into two datasets. 10% of them have been used as training dataset. The rest has been used as test set. The images belonging to the training dataset are required to obtain a model histogram of the bone structures. To validate the proposed algorithm, twenty images in the test set corresponding to ten different patients have been used. Manual segmentations of all the slices were provided by an expert. Objective measures to analyze the performance were computed. These measures are the Jaccard, Dice, Sensitivity (S) and Positive Predictive Value (PPV) parameters. Both Jaccard and DICE coefficients measure the set agreement in terms of false positive, false negative, true negative and true positive counts. Values obtained for these parameters were those shown in Table 1. Note that values higher than 0.9 were obtained.

For comparison purspuses, in Table 1 the results when we use a technique based on thresholding is shown too. A common threshold was computed for all the images and the threshold providing the best results was 1200. As it has been stated before, the low results provided by this method are because bone structures do not have a pixel-wise constant object distribution, which means that they are composed by different structures with different Hounsfield values. Fig. 3 shows the results obtained for three different images using our algorithm. Right image in every set of images is a zoom of a region in the corresponding left image. The segmentation provided by our algorithm is shown in red. Blue contours correspond to ground truth segmentations. Note that the segmentations provided by our algorithm match quite well with the manual segmentations, being even better at some points, thus showing the effectiveness of the algorithm here described.

The segmentation step using the continuous max-flow algorithm offered an average computational cost of 0.5s per 512x512 slice. For a CT volume composed by 100 slices this time would imply only 50s to segment the whole volume, which is much smaller than values provided by other implementations.

Table 1. Assessment parameters for the segmentation algorithm

	Jaccard	Dice	Sensitivity	PPV
Proposed Method	0,8391	0,91	0,97	0,86
Thresholding	0,66	0,79	0,80	0,79

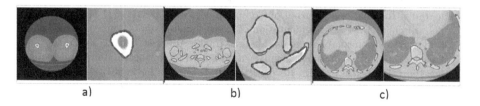

a)   b)   c)

Fig. 3. Results obtained for three different images. Right images are zooms of a region in left images. The segmentation provided by our algorithm is shown in red. Blue contours correspond to ground truth segmentations.

4 Conclusions

The segmentation of bone structures is a complicated task because they present intensities overlapping with those of surrounding tissues. A new automatic segmentation algorithm, which combines gray level information and statistical information extracted from histograms and based on continuous max-flow optimization, has been proposed to solve this problem. This algorithm has been validated using 20 CT images belonging to 10 different patients. The images were manually segmented, and several coefficients have been computed to measure its performance. Results obtained are over 0.9, which indicates neither the FP rate nor the FN rate are high. These results have to be analyzed under the assumption that exact segmentation of the bones is a difficult task even for an expert because of its diffuse borders (mainly when there is some bone disease). Thus, different experts should segment the bone structures for a better validation of the algorithm. Likewise, further validation, with a higher number cases would be desirable. Note that the segmentation stage using a continuous max-flow implementation is faster than the majority of algorithms in the literature. Future implementations will speed up the creation of the input image, which combines gray level information and statistical information.

Acknowledgments. This research has been supported by P11-TIC-7727.

References

1. Feeman, T.G.: The mathematics of medical imaging: a beginner's guide. Springer undergraduate texts in mathematics and technology. Springer (2010)
2. Wang, L.I., et al.: Validation of bone segmentation and improved 3-D registration using contour coherency in CT data. IEEE Transactions on Medical Imaging **25**(3), 324–334 (2006)

3. Kang, Y., et al.: A new accurate and precise 3-D segmentation method for skeletal structures in volumetric CT data. IEEE Transactions on Medical Imaging **22**(5), 586–598 (2003)
4. Pardo, X.M., et al.: A snake for CT image segmentation integrating region and edge information. Image and Vision Computing **19**(7), 461–475 (2001)
5. Beveridge, J.R., et al.: Segmenting images using localized histograms and region merging. International Journal of Computer Vision **2**(3), 311–347 (1989)
6. Sebastian, T.B., et al.: Segmentation of carpal bones from CT images using skeletally coupled deformable models. Medical Image Analysis **7**(1), 2–45 (2003)
7. Cheng, Y., et al.: Automatic segmentation technique for acetabulum and femoral head in CT images. Pattern Recognition **46**(11), 2969–2984 (2013)
8. Cervinka, T., Hyttinen, J., Sievänen, H.: Accurate cortical bone detection in peripheral quantitative computed tomography images. In: Roa Romero, L.M. (ed.) XIII Mediterranean Conference on Medical and Biological Engineering and Computing 2013. IFMBE Proceedings, vol. 41, pp. 289–292. Springer, Heidelberg (2014)
9. Aslan, M.S., Ali, A., Rara, H., Arnold, B., Farag, A.A., Fahmi, R., Xiang, P.: A novel 3D segmentation of vertebral bones from volumetric CT images using graph cuts. In: Bebis, G., et al. (eds.) ISVC 2009, Part II. LNCS, vol. 5876, pp. 519–528. Springer, Heidelberg (2009)
10. Shadid, W., Willis, A.: Bone fragment segmentation from 3D CT imagery using the Probabilistic Watershed Transform. In: Conference Proceedings - IEEE SOUTHEASTCON (2013)
11. Calder, J., et al.: A variational approach to bone segmentation in CT images. In: Progress in Biomedical Optics and Imaging - SPIE (2011)
12. Kratky, J., Kybic, J.: Three-dimensional segmentation of bones from CT and MRI using fast level sets. In: Progress in Biomedical Optics and Imaging - SPIE (2008)
13. Cervinka, T., Sievanen, H., Hannula, M., Hyttinen, J.: Statistical pre-processing method for peripheral quantitative computed tomography images. In: Bamidis, P.D., Pallikarakis, N. (eds.) XII Mediterranean Conference on Medical and Biological Engineering and Computing 2010. IFMBE Proceedings, vol. 29, pp. 212–215. Springer, Heidelberg (2010)
14. Schauerte, B., Fink, G.A.: Web-based learning of naturalized color models for human-machine interaction. In: Proceedings - 2010 Digital Image Computing: Techniques and Applications, DICTA 2010, pp. 498–503 (2010)
15. Boykov, Y., Funka-Lea, G.: Graph cuts and efficient N-D image segmentation. International Journal of Computer Vision **70**(2), 109–131 (2006)
16. Boykov, Y., Kolmogorov, V.: An experimental comparison of min-cut/max-flow algorithms for energy minimization in vision. IEEE Transactions on Pattern Analysis and Machine Intelligence **26**(9), 1124–1137 (2004)
17. Yuan, J., Bae, E., Tai, X.-C.: A study on continuous max-flow and min-cut approaches. In: Proceedings of CVPR, pp. 2217–2224 (2010)
18. Punithakumar, K., Yuan, J.: A Convex Max-Flow Approach to Distribution-Based Figure-Ground Separation. SIAM Journal of Imaging Sciences 5(4), 1333–1354
19. Chan, T.F., et al.: Algorithms for finding global minimizers of image segmentation and denoising models. SIAM Journal on Applied Mathematics **66**(5), 1632–1648 (2006)
20. Bresson, X., et al.: Fast global minimization of the active contour/snake model. Journal of Mathematical Imaging and Vision **28**(2), 151–167 (2007)
21. Rubner, Y., et al.: The Earth Mover's Distance as a Metric for Image Retrieval. International Journal of Computer Vision **40**(2), 99–121 (2000)

A Portable Multi-CPU/Multi-GPU Based Vertebra Localization in Sagittal MR Images

Mohamed Amine Larhmam[(⊠)], Sidi Ahmed Mahmoudi,
Mohammed Benjelloun, Saïd Mahmoudi, and Pierre Manneback

Faculty of Engineering, University of Mons, 20, Place du Parc., Mons, Belgium
{MohamedAmine.Larhmam,Sidi.Mahmoudi,Mohammed.Benjelloun,
Said.Mahmoudi,Pierre.Manneback}@umons.ac.be

Abstract. Accurate Vertebra localization presents an essential step for automating the diagnosis of many spinal disorders. In case of MR images of lumbar spine, this task becomes more challenging due to vertebra complex shape and high variation of soft tissue. In this paper, we propose an efficient framework for spine curve extraction and vertebra localization in T1-weighted MR images. Our method is a fast parametrized algorithm based on three steps: 1. Image enhancing 2. Meanshift clustering [5] 3. Pattern recognition techniques. We propose also an adapted and effective exploitation of new parallel and hybrid platforms, that consist of both central (CPU) and graphic (GPU) processing units, in order to accelerate our vertebra localization method. The latter can exploit both NVIDIA and ATI graphic cards since we propose CUDA and OpenCL implementations of our vertebra localization steps. Our experiments are conducted using 16 MR images of lumbar spine. The related results achieved a vertebra detection rate of 95% with an acceleration ranging from 4 to 173 × thanks to the exploitation of Multi-CPU/Multi-GPU platforms.

Keywords: Vertebra localization · MR images · Mean-shift · Heterogeneous computing · GPU · CUDA · OpenCL

1 Introduction

Medical image analysis presents a necessary tool for clinical purposes, especially for diagnosing many orthopedic conditions, such as osteoporosis, spinal fractures and spine metastasis. In order to obtain an efficient spine analysis, accurate vertebra localization provides a relevant information for disease recognition and surgical planning. However, automating vertebra detection remains a challenging task due to their complex shape, their various appearances between patients, and density variability in image modalities (MRI, CT, X-ray, etc.). Therefore, we propose a fast parameterized and accurate method of vertebra localization in MR images, based on clustering and features extraction techniques. On the other hand, a key variable that has to be taken into account in medical applications

© Springer International Publishing Switzerland 2014
A. Campilho and M. Kamel (Eds.): ICIAR 2014, Part II, LNCS 8815, pp. 209–218, 2014.
DOI: 10.1007/978-3-319-11755-3_24

is the computation time, which can be so elevated in case of processing large volumes of high definition images.

To overcome this constraint, one can imagine to exploit parallel-based architectures such as cluster, grid computing, Graphics Processing Units, etc. The GPUs present an efficient solution, which is seriously hampered by the high costs of data transfer between CPU and GPU memories. Therefore, we developed a version that exploits all the available computing units within computers (CPUs or/and GPUs). This implementation can exploit both NVIDIA and ATI graphic cards, based on CUDA[1] and OpenCL[2] respectively. The remainder of the paper is organized as follows: Section 2 presents the related works, while the third Section is devoted to describe our method of vertebra localization in MR images. In Section 4, we present the portable Multi-CPU/Multi-GPU implementation that we propose in order to reduce the computation time. Experimental results are presented and evaluated in the fifth section. Finally, conclusions and future works are described in the last section.

2   Related Work

In the literature, several segmentation techniques have been investigated on vertebra shape extraction. In this context, Kelm *et al.* [8] proposed a learning based method for automatic detection and labeling of 3D spinal geometry in MRI and CT-scan. Glocker *et al.* [7] presented a new method of localization and identification of vertebrae in arbitrary field of view CT-scan. Ma *et al.* [11] used learning based edge detection and deformable surface model in order to perform a hierarchical segmentation of thoracic vertebrae in 3D CT-scan. For X-ray images, Larhmam *et al.* [9] combined a template matching method with clustering techniques to analyze vertebra alignment. Dealing with MDCT images, Baum *et al.* [3] proposed an algorithm for osteoporotic vertebral fracture detection.

Otherwise, many image processing algorithms contain phases that consist of similar calculations between image pixels. As result, these algorithms fit naturally with parallel implementation on GPU. In this category, Yang *et al.* [19] implemented several classic image processing algorithms on GPU with CUDA. Reichenbach *et al.* [16] combined the advantages of multicore CPUs, GPUs, and FPGAs to build up a heterogeneous image processing pipeline for adaptive optical systems. Authors in [1] developed an OpenCL library of image processing primitives (OpenCLIPP) in order to simplify the exploitation of GPUs. Some GPU works were dedicated to medical imaging in [17] which presents a survey of GPU based medical applications, related to segmentation, registration and visualization methods. There are also some works related to the exploitation of heterogeneous architectures that dispose of both CPUs and GPUs such as OpenCL and StarPU [2]. Recently, we developed CPU [9], parallel [12] and heterogeneous [10] implementations for vertebra detection in X-ray images. Our main contributions can be summarized in two points:

---

[1] CUDA. www.nvidia.com/cuda

[2] OpenCL. www.khronos.org/opencl

1. Fast vertebra localization algorithm using T1-weighted MR images based on pre-processing, mean-shift clusetring and feature extraction algorithms. This method can localize abnormal vertebrae with irregular shapes since it require no prior models.
2. A portable and hybrid solution for vertebra segmentation which can exploit the full computing power of both ATI and NVIDIA GPUs and also Multi-CPU/Multi-GPU platforms. This solution offers an efficient scheduling and management of memories within heterogeneous platforms in order to improve our applications performance.

3   CPU Implementation

The proposed approach is an automated framework for spine extraction and vertebra localization in sagittal T1-weighted MR images. Indeed, our method is a fast parameterized approach based on image enhancing, mean-shift clustering and pattern recognition algorithms. As output, lumbar spine curve is extracted followed by a localization and segmentation of vertebrae. Our approach is based on the following steps:

3.1   Contrast-Limited Adaptive Histogram Equalization

In order to enhance contrast in the input MR images (Fig.1(a)), we apply a histogram based technique called CLAHE [15]. This filter first computes different local histograms corresponding to each part of the image, and uses them to change the contrast of distinct regions of the image. This method is well known for limiting noise amplification. The result of this step is shown in Fig.1(b)

3.2   Morphological Opening

In order to smooth shapes and remove morphological noises on the enhanced image, we apply a morphology opening operation. This step consists of a dilatation of erosion using an ellipse structuring element. Indeed, the use of ellipse allows to highlight the shape of vertebrae. Fig.1(c) shows the result of this step.

3.3   Mean-Shift Clustering

Mean-shift is a versatile nonparametric clustering method based on density estimation. The mean-shift procedure became widely used in computer vision and image processing after reintroduction in [4] and [5]. The mean-shift algorithm is based on an iterative mode, it initializes a window and data points before computing their center of gravity. Then, it shifts the search window to the mean and repeat until convergence. The mean-shift uses a Kernel Density Estimation to estimate the probability density function of a feature space. The segmentation using The mean-shift algorithm is performed in two stages, the smoothing process followed by the clustering step. The procedure can be summed as follows:

- Choose the spacial and range bandwidths (h_s, h_r) of the search window
- For each pixel x_i of the image,
    1. Compute the mean-shift term $m(x_i)$ and increment $x_{i,j}$ value.
    2. Repeat until convergence $x_{i,c}$.
    3. Assign $z_i = (x_i^s, x_{i,c}^r)$.
- $(z_i)_{i=1,...,n}$ are pixels of the output smoothed image.
- The clusters are constructed by grouping all the (z_i) which are closer by (h_s, h_r) in both spacial and rage domain
- Each pixel x_i of the image takes the same cluster label of its point of convergence z_i. These labels constitute the output segmented image.

where (x^s, x^r) are the spacial and range parts of a given data point.

the *mean shift* term defines the translation vector toward the direction of the maximum increase in the density function [5]. The choice of the bandwidths (h_s, h_r) has a significant influence in mean-shift procedure. In case of spine MR images, the value of the bandwidths that maximizes detection accuracy is determined during experimentation process. The result of this step is shown in Fig.1(d)

3.4   Contour Extraction

In this step, we use the algorithm of Suzuki *et al.* [18] to collect information on contours from the result of mean-shift clustering. This method extracts the different contours of the image and stores them into vectors. This generates a collection of external contours ready to by analyzed.

3.5   Vertebra Localization

Ellipse Fitting. For the high level contours analysis, the binary shape of the vertebra is approximated with a parametric elliptic curve. Fitzgibon *et al.* [6] proposed an ellipse fitting technique which is robust to noise. This algorithm uses a least square fitting to find the best ellipse that describes the extracted contour.

Given $(x_i, y_i)(i = 1, ..., n)$ an n points contour. The objective of the method is to minimize the error between an ellipse $Ax^2 + Bxy + Cy^2 + Dx + Ey + F = 0$ and the contour. The method uses a least square optimization with the algebraic criteria.

$$\begin{cases} \min \sum_{i=0}^n (Ax^2 + Bxy + Cy^2 + Dx + Ey + F)^2 \\ B^2 - 4AC = 1 \end{cases} \tag{1}$$

where the constraint $B^2 - 4AC = 1$ ensures that the problem is elliptical.

Indeed, solving the system (1) enables to link each stored contour to an ellipse. Finally, we eliminate ellipses which are out of the range of the accepted size and rotation depending on the size and the position of the vertebrae. As a result, vertebra candidate center points are detected and clustered in an accumulator.

Spine Curve Detection. The objective of this step is to compute the spine curve and eliminate false detection. Thus, we use a least square polynomial fitting as follows:

Let $(x_i, y_i)_{i=1...N}$ be the center points of the candidate vertebrae, detected by the ellipse fitting. We aim to fit a polynomial P of degree k with $k < N$ and coefficient $(a_j)_{j=0...k}$. A least square optimization method minimizes the error between the polynomial and the data point. The sum of squared residuals can be expressed (2).

$$S = \sum_{i=1}^{N}(y_i - P(x_i))^2 \tag{2}$$

The sum of squares S is a function of $(a_j)_{j=0...k}$. Then, its minimization is obtained by sitting the gradient to zero $\frac{\partial S}{\partial a_j} = 0, j = 0...k$

The problem can be expressed in matrix form $XA = Y$, where A is a column vector of the polynomial coefficient. Finally, the solution of the least squares problem is $A = X^{-1}Y$

After the extraction of a first curve, we calculate a mean error distance and we eliminate points which present a distance greater to this mean. We repeat this process until the convergence. Fig.1(e) shows the result of the final vertebra spine curve extraction and vertebra localization steps.

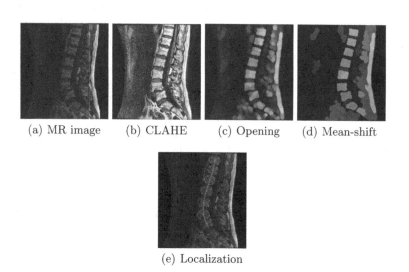

(a) MR image   (b) CLAHE   (c) Opening   (d) Mean-shift

(e) Localization

Fig. 1. Framework of vertebra localization in case of a lumbar MR image

4   Hybrid Implementation

Despite the high accuracy of the method presented above, its computing time becomes so significant in case of treating bigger sets of high definition images.

Thus, we developed a portable Multi-CPU/Multi-GPU method that exploits all the available computing units for improving our method's performance. For this aim, we use the executive support StarPU [2] that offers a runtime for launching tasks within heterogeneous platforms. Our method is well adapted for exploiting both NVIDIA and ATI graphic cards since we propose CUDA and OpenCL implementations of each method's step. Indeed, the steps of histogram equalization (CLAHE), morphological opening and MeanShift segmentation are implemented heterogeneously for improving the performance of our vertebra detection method. The proposed implementation consists of applying parallel functions with GPUs [12] and sequential functions with CPUs. These processings are launched simultaneously. Our heterogeneous version can be summarized with three steps: images loading, heterogeneous processing and output images saving.

1. **Images loading :** the first step consists of loading the input images in StarPU buffers.
2. **Hybrid Processing :** after loading the input images, we can apply (within StarPU) simultaneously the CPU and GPU functions on the high intensive steps. The CPU functions are described in Section 3, while the GPU functions are presented with two versions : the first one presents CUDA implementations of histogram equalization (CLAHE), morphological opening and MeanShift segmentation steps in order to exploit NVIDIA graphic cards. These implementations are developed with the CUDA module of OpenCV [3]. The second version presents OpenCL implementations of the same steps (histogram equalization (CLAHE), morphological opening and MeanShift segmentation) in order to exploit ATI graphic cards. The latter are developed with OpenCL module of OpenCV [4]. StarPU consists of two principal modules. The first one is the codelet that allows to specify the type of computing units (CPUs or/and GPU) and the related implementations (C/C++, CUDA or OpenCL). The second module is represented by tasks that apply the codelet on images. In our case, each image is processed within one task on CPU or GPU. Notice that the selection of the type of GPU (NVIDIA or ATI) is not required since our method selects automatically the available GPU with the corresponding implementations (CUDA or OpenCL).
3. **Results presentation :** the last step consists of copying the output images on buffers using StarPU, which provides a function for automatic data transfer from GPU to CPU memory.
   For a better exploitation of heterogeneous platforms, we employed an effective scheduling of tasks, and also CUDA streaming technique in order to overlap data transfers by kernels executions on GPU. The latter is used within multiple GPUs. More detail about the heterogeneous treatment are described in [10]. Fig. 2 summarizes our heterogeneous implementation. The steps of contours extraction and vertebra localization (Section 3.4 and 3.5) exploit multiple CPUs only since they are applied on images with reduced

---

[3] OpenCV CUDA. www.opencv.org/platforms/cuda.html
[4] OpenCV OpenCL. http://docs.opencv.org/modules/ocl/doc/introduction.html

informations (after applying the CLAHE, Opening and Meanshift steps). Moreover,these steps present a high computational dependecy which is not adapted for parallel calculation. These steps are grouped in one phase called "Vertebra localization" as shown in Table 2. Notice that the use of StarPU allowed to reduce our development time since it allows for automatic data transfer between CPU and GPU memories. Moreover, StarPU offers an automatic selection of computing units (CPUs or/and GPUs) within one line of code. In our case, the use of StarPU required no more than 25 lines of code compared to the CUDA implementation.

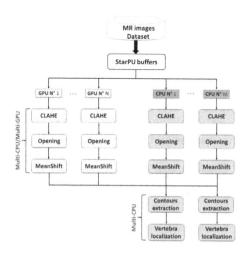

Fig. 2. Heterogeneous vertebra detection in MRI images

5 Experimental Results

Experimentations were conducted using 16 MRI data sets. The images were obtained from an online database proposed by SpineWeb[5]. All the images are T1-weighted MR data, and focus on the lumbar spine area. The data set contains some abnormal cases including degenerative diseases such as osteophyte and compression fractures. We extract the middle slice from each MR data set in order to get the maximum visible vertebrae. The image data set was inspected by an experienced radiologist, from our collaborative hospital, who annotated four landmarks on each visible vertebra. these landmarks are used to generate ground truth data for the detection validation step. Thus, a total of 106 vertebrae were annotated including the lumbar spine.

We set constant parameters for the automated process. Thereby, the band width (hs, hr) of the mean-shift algorithm, the size of the structuring element of

---

[5] http://spineweb.digitalimaginggroup.ca/

the morphological opening and the range of the accepted ellipses are experimental values determined according to the image data set and the size of vertebrae.

The validation of vertebra detection was performed by using our ground truth data. We focused on the detection of the five lumbar and the visible thoracic vertebrae. Therefore, candidate vertebra centers had to be located within the vertebra body. We compared the detection accuracy with the manual landmarks annotated by the expert radiologist. Indeed, we used the four landmarks that determined the corners to calculate a precise vertebra center. The method enabled a global vertebra detection rate of 95% on a total of 106 vertebrae and a RMS (root mean square) of 3.8 pixels. Intermediate results are shown in Fig 1.

Table 1 compares the detection rate and accuracy of the different lumbar (L1 to L5) and thoracic (Th12 to Th10) vertebrae. The final result showed a vertebra localization rate of 95%. Peng et al. [14] announced a mean detection rate of 95.5% of vertebra in MRI. Authors in [13] reported an average intervertebra disc localization rate of 95.4% based on MR images of the lumbar spine. Moreover, our automated method enabled a hight success rate and it is comparable to the state of the art. However, some vertebrae present a detection rate and accuracy lower than the mean. This is due to the presence of abnormal cases with degenerative diseases in the used data set. Therefore, some abnormal vertebrae showed irregular gray level which are difficult to segment. Also, the final accuracy of the detection can be decreased by the morphological opening that changes slightly the original shape of vertebrae.

Table 1. Detection rate and accuracy of vertebrae using 16 MR images

Vertebra type	Detection rate (%)	RMS distance error (px)
Th12-Th10	96	2.92
L1	100	2.74
L2	93	1.91
L3	100	4.43
L4	93	4.57
L5	87	4.68
Global mean	**95%**	**3.80**

The exploitation of heterogeneous architectures allowed to improve the performance of our method of vertebra localization in MR images. Table 2 compares the computing time between sequential (CPU), parallel (GPU) and hybrid version of the proposed method (Fig. 2). Notice that our performance scale up very well when exploiting multiple CPUs or/and GPUs. The experimentations have been applied on 200 MR images of 512 ×512 resolution. We note also that the NVIDIA GPUs offer better accelerations than the ATI ones. Thanks to CUDA which present actually the most performant GPU programming language. However, the use of OpenCL benefits from its compatibility with any type of GPU (NVIDIA or ATI). Notice that the tests were run on the following hardware:

Table 2. Vertebra localization using hybrid platforms (200 MR images of 512×512)

Steps	1CPU	1GPU		4GPU/8CPU			
				OpenCL (ATI)		CUDA (NVIDIA)	
	Time (T (s))	T (s)	Acc (x)	T (s)	Acc (x)	T (s)	Acc (x)
CLAHE	13.88 s	1.48 s	09.37 x	0.52 s	26.70 x	0.41 s	33.86 x
Opening	6.84 s	1.20 s	05.70 x	0.31 s	22.06 x	0.24 s	28.5 x
MeanShift	724 s	19.63 s	36.88 x	4.88 s	148.36 x	4.17 s	173.62 x
Vertebra localization	1.98 s	CPU only (1.98 s)		8CPU. T: 0.47 s Acc: 4.21 x			
Total Time	746.7 s	24.29 s	30.74 x	9.92 s	75.27 x	9.03 s	82.69 x

- CPU: 4 x Intel Core 2 Quad Q8200, 2.33GHz,
- GPU: 4 x NVIDIA GeForce GTX 580 with 1.5GB of RAM,

6 Conclusion and Future Works

In this paper, we presented an efficient method for spine extraction and vertebra localization in T1-weighted MR images. Our contribution is based on a pre-processing step, mean-shift clustering and pattern recognition techniques. This method is a fast parameterized processing with no prior learning. This work is a first step for a Computer Aided Diagnosis (CAD) system for spine abnormalities.

We proposed also a portable and heterogeneous implementation, which can exploit multiple CPUs and GPUs (from NVIDIA or ATI), of our method in order to improve its performance. This enabled to apply, in a fast way, the method on larger sets of MR images. Several techniques of optimizations were employed to achieve a full exploitation of the computing power of machines. As future work we plan to include a machine learning step in order to enhance vertebra detection and build a module for vertebra metastasis detection. We plan also to apply a complexity estimation of each step of our vertebra segmentation method in order to have a better distribution of tasks between the available computing units (CPUs or/and GPUs).

Acknowledgments. The authors would like to thank Dr. S. Drisis, radiologist from Jules Bordet Hospital, for the annotation process. The authors thank also the anonymous reviewers for their insightful comments.

References

1. Akhloufi, M., Campagna, A.: OpenCLIPP: OpenCL Integrated Performance Primitives library for computer vision applications. In: Proc. SPIE Electronic Imaging 2014, Intelligent Robots and Computer Vision XXXI: Algorithms and Techniques, pp. 25–31 (2014)

2. Augonnet, C., et al.: StarPU: a unified platform for task scheduling on heterogeneous multicore architectures. Concurrency and Computation: Practice and Experience **23**(2), 187–198 (2011)

3. Baum, T., et al.: Automatic detection of osteoporotic vertebral fractures in routine thoracic and abdominal MDCT. European Radiology, 1–9 (2014)

4. Cheng, Y.: Mean shift, mode seeking, and clustering. IEEE Trans. Pattern Anal. Mach. Intell. **17**, 790–799 (1995)

5. Comaniciu, D., et al.: Mean shift: A robust approach toward feature space analysis. IEEE Transactions on Pattern Analysis and Machine Intelligence **24**, 603–619 (2002)

6. Fitzgibbon, A., Fisher, R.B.: A buyer's guide to conic fitting. In: British Machine Vision Conference, pp. 513–522 (1995)

7. Glocker, B., Feulner, J., Criminisi, A., Haynor, D.R., Konukoglu, E.: Automatic localization and identification of vertebrae in arbitrary field-of-view CT scans. In: Ayache, N., Delingette, H., Golland, P., Mori, K. (eds.) MICCAI 2012, Part III. LNCS, vol. 7512, pp. 590–598. Springer, Heidelberg (2012)

8. Kelm, B.M., et al.: Spine detection in CT and MR using iterated marginal space learning. Medical Image Analysis **17**, 1283–1292 (2012)

9. Larhmam, M.A., et al.: Vertebra identification using template matching modelmp and k-means clustering. International Journal of Computer Assisted Radiology and Surgery, 1–11 (2013)

10. Lecron, F., et al.: Heterogeneous Computing for Vertebra Detection and Segmentation in X-Ray Images. Journal of Biomedical Imaging, 1–12 (2011)

11. Ma, J., Lu, L., Zhan, Y., Zhou, X., Salganicoff, M., Krishnan, A.: Hierarchical segmentation and identification of thoracic vertebra using learning-based edge detection and coarse-to-fine deformable model. In: Jiang, T., Navab, N., Pluim, J.P.W., Viergever, M.A. (eds.) MICCAI 2010, Part I. LNCS, vol. 6361, pp. 19–27. Springer, Heidelberg (2010)

12. Mahmoudi, S.A., et al.: GPU-Based Segmentation of Cervical Vertebra in X-Ray Images. In: International Conference on Cluster Computing, pp. 1–8 (2010)

13. Oktay, A.B., Akgul, Y.S.: Localization of the lumbar discs using machine learning and exact probabilistic inference. In: Fichtinger, G., Martel, A., Peters, T. (eds.) MICCAI 2011, Part III. LNCS, vol. 6893, pp. 158–165. Springer, Heidelberg (2011)

14. Peng, et al.: Automated vertebra detection and segmentation from the whole spine MR images. In: Proceedings of Medical Imaging Computing and Computer Assisted Intervention (2007)

15. Pizer, S.M., et al.: Adaptive histogram equalization and its variations. Comput. Vision Graph. Image Process. **39**(3), 355–368 (1987)

16. Reichenbach, M., Seidler, R., Fey, D.: Heterogeneous computer architectures: An image processing pipeline for optical metrology. In: International Conference on Reconfigurable Computing, pp. 1–8 (2012)

17. Shi, L., et al.: A survey of GPU-based medical image computing techniques. Quant. Imaging Med. Surg. **2**(3), 188–206 (2012)

18. Suzuki, et al.: Topological structural analysis of digitized binary images by border following. Computer Vision, Graphics, and Image Processing **30** (1985)

19. Yang, Z., et al.: Parallel Image Processing Based on CUDA. In: International Conference on Computer Science and Software Engineering, China, pp. 198–201 (2008)

An Automated Level-Set Approach for Identification of Aortic Valve Borders in Short Axis Windows of Transesophageal Echo Sequences (TEE)

César Veiga[1,2(✉)], Francisco Calvo[2], Emilio Paredes-Galán[2], Pablo Pazos[2], Carlos Peña[2], and Andrés Íñiguez[2]

[1] Instituto Biomédico de Vigo (IBIV), Vigo, Spain
[2] Cardioloxía, Complexo Hospitalario Universitario de Vigo Hospital Meixoeiro, 36214, Vigo, Spain
cesar.veiga.garcia@sergas.es

Abstract. The ability to identify and quantify two (2D) and three-dimensional (3D) morphological parameters of the aortic valve (AV) apparatus from transesophageal echocardiographic (TEE) imaging constitutes a valuable tool in diagnosis, treatment and follow-up of patients with aortic valve related diseases, as well as image-based morphological assessment for surgical interventions, so there is a considerable need to develop a standardized frameworks for 2D-3D valve segmentation and shape representation.

AV borders and leaflets quantification is still a challenging task, and commonly based on intensive user interaction that limits its applicability. We propose a fast and accurate model free, automated method for segmenting and extracting morphological parameters. This work integrates level-set techniques to automatically delineate and quantitatively describe aortic geometry in echocardiographic images, a challenging task that has been explored only to a limited extent. The algorithm accuracy was tested on 5 patients compared to "gold standard" manual analysis, showing strong agreement between both. The proposed technique appears promising for clinical application.

Keywords: Computer Aided Diagnostic · CAD · Calcified Aortic Valve Disease (CAVD) · echocardiographic sequences · level sets framework · Geodesic Active Contours

1 Introduction

The topic of automatic interpretation of cardiological images is an extremely interesting and important discipline due to the number of population affected by heart related diseases in the world [1], and the need to provide portable, accurate and real-time evaluation techniques [2] for heart function diagnosis. In fact, cardiovascular diseases are among the most important public health concerns today in the industrialized countries. More specifically, heart and cerebrovascular diseases were identified respectively as the first and third cause of death in 2010 in the world [1]. Among them, the primary cause of cardiovascular morbidity and mortality in Europe is Cardiovascular

© Springer International Publishing Switzerland 2014
A. Campilho and M. Kamel (Eds.): ICIAR 2014, Part II, LNCS 8815, pp. 219–226, 2014.
DOI: 10.1007/978-3-319-11755-3_25

Arterial Disease (CAD) [2], a process in which calcium deposition takes place in the cardiac structures as coronary arteries or several valves including the aortic valve, which is the subject of our study. Therefore, due to their public health relevance in western countries there are strong interests in deploying new technologies that strengthen research and diagnostic techniques for cardiovascular diseases [3,4].

Calcific Aortic Valve Disease (CAVD) is a slow and continuous progressive disease ranging from mild thickening of the valve without obstruction of blood flow, known as aortic sclerosis, to severe calcification with impaired mobility of veils, or aortic stenosis [5, 6]. The coincidence in the clinical factors associated with calcified valve disease and atherosclerosis and the correlation between the severity of coronary artery and aortic valve calcification provide more support for a process of common disease [6, 7, 8]. Calcification of the aortic valve can be an early sign of heart disease, even in a situation of absence of any other heart disease related symptoms [2,6]. Several studies have shown consistently that a high index of calcium levels increase the risk of coronary artery disease events and, consequently, the possibilities of suffering a heart attack [9]. The detection and quantification of calcification levels can help to determine the level of the severity. In this framework, detecting AV borders is the initial step to more sophisticated processes of AV parameterization.

Besides all the recent advances in cardiological imaging and the quality achieved by many modalities such as Cardiac Magnetic Resonance (MRC), new multi-detector CT (MDCT), Optical Coherence Tomography (OCT) or Near Infra Red Spectroscopy (NIRS), the long standing echocardiographic techniques remain at center stage of effective cardiovascular diagnostic tests. Ultrasound offer the advantage of being ubiquitous in almost all clinical departments of hospitals and outpatient [8] compared to most part of new imaging techniques, which show drawbacks in terms of radiation safeness, time generation or unavailability for widespread use by the population due to its costs. This ubiquity, versatility and portability have made echocardiography since its introduction about 70 years ago [8], the most cost-effective noninvasive imaging approach to detect the presence of significant cardiac disease. Therefore, cardiologists are still exploiting new interesting aspects in ultrasound techniques especially its diagnostic accuracy, speed and availability.

For this reason, pattern recognition techniques and computer vision tools applied to automated ultrasound analysis, as reported in several works [9, 10], allows the implementation of computer aided diagnosis (CAD) systems for cardiology.

In this scenario, the development of computer vision techniques and CAD systems to improve usefulness of echocardiographic sequences, are of great interest. And so, there are many interests in deploy new techniques and schemes for automatic image processing and analysis for those images.

2   Methods

2.1   EchoCardiographic Problem

The aortic valve is the anatomical structure that lies between the left ventricular outflow tract and aortic root, and has three cusps, which open widely during systole. It is possible to see such valve in different windows in a echocardiographic study [8]. The most clear views of the valve appear in long and short axis, where the aortic valve appears as bright regions with very characteristic shape. In diastole, the valve closes and, in the short axis view (aortic valve level), it shows a clear Y-shaped appearance (sometimes referred to as resembling a "Mercedes-Benz badge"; Fig. 1.b) which allows to be identified with pattern recognition techniques (described in detail in next section).

Transesophageal echocardiograms, or TEE, is an alternative way to perform an echocardiogram [8], it comprises a specialized probe containing an ultrasound transducer at its tip which is passed into the patient's esophagus, see Fig 1.a, Due to its superior image quality, the TEE probe is indicated in situations where conventional transthoracic study is unable to deliver the image quality required to make a correct diagnosis, as assessment of aortic diseases (e.g. aortic dissection/trauma), regurgitant heart valves, judgment of suitability for surgical repair prosthetic valves, etc. With this technique, due to the proximity to the aortic valve the Y-pattern (rotated Mercedes-Benz badge) can be more clearly distinguished as shown in Fig.1 b. On those sequences the valve evolution can be seen as shown in sequence Fig.2.

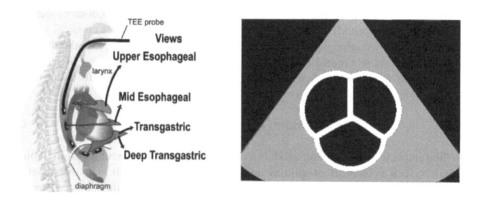

Fig. 1. a) Schema of Trans-esophageal echocardiographic study. b) Typical view of aortic valve in transesophageal short-axis window.

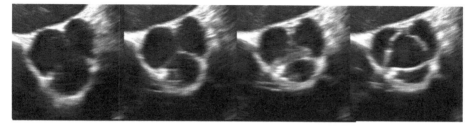

Fig. 2. Several Region of Interest (ROIs) capturing the aortic valve through time evolution from systole to diastole, in a short axis cardiographic TEE window

2.2   Framework, Geodesic Level-Sets

Level-set were introduced [15], in order to mitigate the drawbacks of explicit parameterization of object boundaries in active contour models like snakes. The formulation is based on solving a convection equation, using implicit representation, φ the zero level set, by the field I through the next Partial Differential Equation (PDE).

$$\frac{\partial \Phi}{\partial t} + F|\nabla \Phi| = 0 \text{ with } \Phi(x, y, 0) = \Phi_0(x, y) \tag{1}$$

where F (speed function) depends on the image data I as well as φ.

Within this framework the segmentation problem is reduced to finding curve(s) to enclose regions of interest based on a level-sets approach. So C(t)=(x , y),/ φ (x, y, t) =0 , also called level-set function.

In this work, the geodesic active contour model, introduced as a geometric alternative for snakes, is considered. Geodesic Active Contour approach is an improvement of previous models of geometric PDEs active contours, allowing stable boundary detection when their gradients suffer from large variations, including gaps, as echocardiographic sequences. Such technique [16], based on actives contours evolving in time according to intrinsic geometric measures of the image, is based on the relation between active contours and the computation of geodesics (minimal distance curves). This geodesic approach for object segmentation allows to connect classical snakes, based on energy minimization, with geometric active contours based on the theory of curve evolution, in a model that theoretically combines explicit Active Contour Models (snakes) with Implicit Active Contour Models (Level Sets), and fits better to our problem. So, previous equation (1) can be converted into:

$$\frac{\partial \Phi}{\partial t} = |\nabla \Phi| div \left(g(I) \frac{\nabla \Phi}{|\nabla \Phi|} \right) + cg(i)|\nabla \Phi| \tag{2}$$

While implicit active contour models avoid several known difficulties from explicit models, such as inability of splitting and merging of objects, their main disadvantage is an increased computational complexity. The solution to the object detection problem is then given by the zero level-set of the steady state (u_t=0) of this flow. As described in the experimental results, it is possible to choose $c = 0$ (no constant velocity), and the model still converges (in a slower motion). Above geodesic flow includes a new component in the curve velocity that improves those models. The new velocity component allows to accurately tracking boundaries with high variation in their gradient, including small gaps, a task that was difficult to accomplish with the previous curve evolution models.

This work is based on the formulation proposed in [18], which incorporates shape priors,

$$\frac{\partial \Phi}{\partial t} = f(i)(\alpha c + \beta k)|\nabla \Phi| + \gamma \nabla f \nabla \Phi + \delta(\Phi^a - \Phi) \tag{3}$$

Where φ is the level-set function and the zero level-set corresponds to the segmentation curve/surface. The firs term include the propagation, curvature and advection terms. The parameters as α, β, and γ   are user-defined setting for the relative scaling of the three speeds α propagation scaling, β smoothness and γ boundary attraction term, all ranging in [0,1].

2.3   Algorithm

In order to automate the identification of aortic valve borders, an imaging pipeline was developed, following the schema shown in Fig. 3.a. An algorithm that requires minimal user interaction for segmentation was developed in C++ (VTK and ITK libraries). Such algorithm has the following steps:

1. Denoise images using anisotropic diffusion.
2. Identifying heart cycle time positions (systolic and diastolic occurrence which means opened and closed valve) by analyzing the histogram in a ROI. Using the Kolmogorov-Smirnov test to match the ROI with a black image. So, to detect systole's occurrence by analyzing the lowest value in cumulative histograms (*greyness*) through the whole sequence. See fig 3.b as an example of time evolution of the cumulative histogram in the ROI.
3. Identifying the aortic valve border using geodesic level-sets in a systolic occurrence. For initialization, a seed in the center of the geometric moments of the black region, corresponding to the valve Centroid: $\{x, y\} = \{\ \overline{x},\ \overline{y}\}$ is used. The black region is chosen by thresholding pixels with grey levels lower than 50 in the ROI.
4. Propagating the result through the whole sequence, using the final result of the previous step as the initial position for the level-set identification.

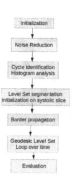
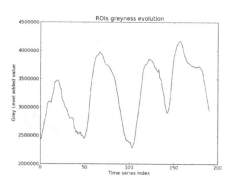

Fig. 3. a) Flowchart of the essential steps in the identification of Aortic Valve border. b) Time Evolution of ROI greyness thorough a weighted cumulative histogram.

For implementing the subroutines the well-known ITK library [11] has been used. ITK is currently one of the most powerful toolkit for medical image processing all over the world, which includes the great majority of the most important and well-known algorithms for image processing nowadays, and those more relevant to the scientific community, published in prestigious journals[15].

3   Experiments and Results

3.1   Image Protocol

Data from 5 patients, enrolled at the University of Vigo Meixoeiro Hospitals (Vigo, ES), undergoing clinically indicated TEE imaging for assessment of valvulopathies, were considered. The protocol was approved by the local Institutional Review Board (Comité Ético de Galicia), and informed consent was obtained from all participants. Studies were performed using the iE33 system (Philips Medical Systems, Andover, MA) equipped with a fully sampled matrix-array TEE transducer. The probe was positioned at the midesophageal level with a 30-45° tilt (optimal search) and images were acquired using narrow-angled acquisition mode, in which wedge-shaped sub-volumes were obtained over several consecutive cardiac cycles. Each acquired sequence included the aortic valve and the proximal ascending aorta together with 2D views, which is the subject of this study.

3.2   Performance Evaluation

The evaluation of the performance and accuracy of a segmentation algorithm in medical imaging is still a challenging problem [14]. In order to evaluate the method, an algorithm was implemented, and tested. The results of the proposed method were compared with manually segmented images by experts with slice-by-slice delineation of contours. Fig. 4 shows the result of AV border segmentation, with a level-set approach, through the TEE time evolution.

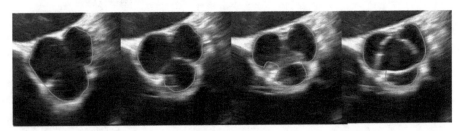

Fig. 4. Results of the segmentation process on several images of the cardiographic sequence

The performance of the method was evaluated by comparison with manual segmentation. For each point in the contour, the difference with the manual traced border was computed in both x,y axis. Differences (mean and standard deviation) are summarized in Tab.1, clearly indicating that the method achieves an acceptable accuracy.

Evaluation of the method in a larger set of data, comparison with more complex methodologies and comparison between 2D and 3D data is still pending and will be carried out in a future work.

Table 1. Differences in x,y coordinates between the proposed method and the manual segmentation results

	short axis			
	X		y	
	mean	std	mean	std
pixel	1.9	1.8	1.8	1.2

4   Conclusions

The inherent characteristics of ultrasound images as noise, movement blur and the large quantity of data in echocardiographic sequences increase the difficulty to segment efficiently structures as the aortic valve, with the associated inconveniences to shift shape and size derived methodologies into clinical application. In this paper a new approach to perform automatic valve border identification, based on level sets, was presented. This work provides an effective tool for automatic detection of AV borders in TEE image sequences that could support further aortic valve segmentation, modeling and parameterization. The actual application on echocardiographic sequences shows that the algorithm accurately segments the valve structure and reduces the manual procedure greatly. The results must be evaluated in a larger dataset (from both transthoracic and transesophagic sources), as well as in different echocardiographic window as the long-axis. The algorithm should be analyzed in a 2D/3D comparison, but this task falls out of the scope of this work.

Acknowledgements. This work has been partially supported by European Commission under the 7th Framework Programme, FP-7-REGPOT 2012-2013-1 through BIOCAPS (Biomedical Capacities Support Program) grant agreement no. FP7- 316265.

References

1. Lozano, R., Naghavi, M., Foreman, K., et al.: Global and regional mortality from 235 causes of death for 20 age groups in 1990 and 2010: a systematic analysis for the Global Burden of Disease Study 2010. Lancet **380**, 2095–2128 (2010)
2. Villines, et al.: Prevalence and severity of coronary artery disease and adverse events among symptomatic patients with coronary artery calcification scores of zero undergoing coronary computed tomography angiography: results from the CONFIRM (Coronary CT Angiography Evaluation for Clinical Outcomes: an International Multicenter) registry. J. Am. Coll. Cardiol. **58**, 2533–2540 (2011)
3. Freeman, R.V., Otto, C.M.: Spectrum of Calcific Aortic Valve Disease Pathogenesis, Disease Progression, and Treatment Strategies. Circulation **111**, 3316–3326 (2005). doi:10.1161/CIRCULATIONAHA.104.486738
4. Budoff, M.J.: Interpreting the Coronary-Artery Calcium Score. N. Engl. J. Med. **366**, 1550–1551 (2012)
5. Otto, C.M., Lind, B.K., Kitzman, D.W., et al.: Association of aortic-valve sclerosis with cardiovascular mortality and morbidity in the elderly. N. Engl. J. Med. **341**, 142 (1999)

6. Stewart, B.F., Siscovick, D., Lind, B.K., et al.: Clinical factors associated with calcific aortic valve disease. Cardiovascular Health Study. J. Am. Coll. Cardiol. **29**, 630 (1997)

7. Gharacholou, S.M., Karon, B.L., Shub, C., Pellikka, P.A.: Aortic valve sclerosis and clinical outcomes: moving toward a definition. Am. J. Med. **124**, 103 (2011)

8. Weyman, A.E.: Principles and Practice of ECHOCARDIOGRAPHY, 2nd edn.

9. Zhou, X.S., Georgescu, B.: Intelligent Computer Aided Interpretation in Echocardiography: Clinical Needs and recent Advances. In: Principles and Advanced Methods in Medical Imaging and Image Analysis, ch. 29, pp. 725–743

10. Alison Noble, J., Boukerroui, D.: Ultrasound Image Segmentation: A Survey. IEEE Transactions on Medical Imaging **25**(8), 987–1010 (2006)

11. Ibánez, L., Schroeder, W., Ng, L., Cates, J.: The ITK Software Guide, 2nd edn. Kitware, Inc. (2005), http://www.itk.org/ItkSoftwareGuide.pdf, ISBN 1-930934-15-7

12. Schroeder, W., Martin, K., Lorensen, W.: The Visualization Toolkit: An Object Oriented Approach to Computer Graphics, 3rd edn. Kitware, Inc. (2004) http://www.vtk.org

13. Platz, E., Solomon, S.D.: Point-of-Care Echocardiography in the Accountable Care Organization Era. Advances in Cardiovascular Imaging

14. Bland, J.M., Altman, D.G.: Statistical methods for assessing agreement between two methods of clinical measurement. Lancet **327**(8476), 307–310 (1986)

15. Osher, S., Sethian, J.A.: Fronts propagating with curvature-dependent speed: Algorithms based on Hamilton-Jacobi formulations. J. Comput. Phys. **79**, 12–49 (1988)

16. Kimmel, R., Caselles, V., Sapiro, G.: Geodesic active contours. International Journal on Computer Vision **22**(1), 61–97 (1997)

17. Lin, N., Yu, W., Duncan, J.S.: Combinative multi-scale level set framework for echocardiographic image segmentation. Med. Image Anal. **7**(4), 529–537 (2003)

18. Leventon, M., Grimson, W., Faugeras, O.: Statistical shape influence in geodesic active contours. In: Proc. IEEE Conference on Computer Vision and Pattern Recognition (CVPR), vol. 1, pp. 316–323 (2000)

Reliable Lung Segmentation Methodology by Including Juxtapleural Nodules

J. Novo[1](✉), J. Rouco[1], A. Mendonça[2], and Aurélio Campilho[1]

[1] INESC TEC - INESC Technology and Science, Porto, Portugal
[2] INEB - Instituto de Engenharia Biomédica, Porto, Portugal
{jnovo,jrouco,amendon,campilho}@fe.up.pt

Abstract. In a lung nodule detection task, parenchyma segmentation is crucial to obtain the region of interest containing all the nodules. Thus, the challenge is to devise a methodology that includes all the lung nodules, particularly those close to the walls, as the juxtapleural nodules. In this paper, different region growing approaches are proposed for the automatic segmentation of the lung parenchyma. The methodology is organized in five different steps: first, the image intensity is corrected to improve the contrast of the lungs. With that, the fat area is obtained, automatically deriving the interior of the lung region. Then, the traquea is extracted by a 3D region growing, being subtracted from the lung region results. The next step is the division of the two lungs to guarantee that both are separated. And finally, the lung contours are refined to provide appropriate final results.

The methodology was tested in 50 images taken from the LIDC image database, with a large variability and, specially, including different types of lung nodules. In particular, this dataset contains 158 nodules, from which 40 are juxtapleural nodules. Experimental results demonstrate that the method provides accurate lung regions, specially including the centers of 36 of the juxtapleural nodules. For the other 4, although the centers are not included, parts of their areas are retained in the segmentation, which is useful for lung nodule detection.

Keywords: Computer-aided diagnosis · Thoracic CT imaging · Lung parenchyma · Region growing · Segmentation

1 Introduction and Previous Work

Among all the different pathologies, lung cancer is one of the most dangerous cancers in the world. For instance, in the United States, the total number of deaths regarding lung cancer is higher than the sum of colon, breast and prostate cancers all together [1]. For that reason, an early diagnosis becomes crucial in order to maximize the effectiveness of the treatments and, therefore, maximize the chances of survival.

A. Campilho and M. Kamel (Eds.): ICIAR 2014, Part II, LNCS 8815, pp. 227–235, 2014.
DOI: 10.1007/978-3-319-11755-3_26

The Computed Tomography (CT) of the thorax, among other implemented modalities, is widely used for the analysis of numerous lung diseases, which is the most common imaging modality for detecting and diagnosing lung nodules. These scans imply a large amount of data that has to be analyzed.

Regarding the detection of lung nodules, the very first step is the lung parenchyma segmentation, in order to obtain the region of interest (ROI) where the nodules are included. Over the years, several different approaches have appeared. They can be categorized under three main different strategies: thresholding methods, deformable models and region growing techniques. In thresholding methods, Wei et al. [2] proposed an optimal iterative threshold. Moreover, lung separation and contour repairment are included in the approach. Armato and Sensakovic [3] also uses a grey-level thresholding to segment the lungs in two iterative steps, the thorax from the background firstly and the lungs from the thorax secondly. Ye et al. [4] employed an 3D adaptive fuzzy thresholding to obtain the lung parenchyma using Gaussian smoothing. Regarding deformable models, Sun et al. [5] presented a method that extract the lungs in two different steps, where a 3D active shape model is used for obtaining a general initial contour and then a global optimal surface finding method is used for refining the final results. In [6] the authors proposed an active shape model to extract the lung region, model that was posteriorly optimized by Ginneken et al. [7]. Finally, region growing techniques [8] were less applied. Some approaches have appeared [9][3] that mainly used region growing for iteratively removing the different parts of the thorax until reaching the lung regions. For instance, Hedlund et al. [9] define a method that begins in a starting point within the lungs and use the steepest gradient descent heuristic to grow the lung parenchyma region.

Region growing techniques have as main advantage the robustness and fidelity, but they need an initial position as seed to grow, as well as they show some difficulties in separating the lungs. Both drawbacks have to be handled with care. Trying to take advantage of the robustness of the paradigm, we propose different region growing approaches to perform the different segmentation tasks, specially handling juxtapleural nodules. The proposal includes full removal of the traquea and bronqui, lung division and an appropriate final contour refinement.

2   Methodology

The entire lung segmentation methodology implies a set of image processing procedures. Firstly, intensity modifications are applied to the input image in order to increase the contrast of the lung region in comparison with the surrounding fat area. Then, an appropriate and accurate seed point is obtained to run a region growing technique that is applied in the fat region. Thus, the soft tissue included inside the results conform the initial lung region candidate. After that, another region growing technique is performed to extract the traquea region in order to be removed from the final results. Then, when the two lungs are connected they are separated. Finally, a circular closing is applied to the final contours with the aim of smoothing the final results. We proceed to detail further each step.

Image Enhancement. The methodology base its accuracy in the differentiation between intensities of the fat and intensities of the lung background. As the lung parenchyma is filled with air, it has a low density and, therefore, its intensities are lower than the surrounding fat region. Thus, having the highest possible contrast among both groups of intensities will facilitate the region growing proposals. Moreover, we normalize the intensities to standardize the input data.

The typical histogram of a CT thorax image shows that there are two main regions: the region corresponding to fat and bones (bright intensities) and the region corresponding to the background and lung tissue (dark intensities). Since the bright areas do not provide useful information, for this specific lung segmentation problem, we compress the histogram from the fat peak intensity, obtaining a larger range of intensities for lower intensities, that is, the lung tissue. Finally, intensities are normalized to homogenize the input data. Figures 1 1st row (a) and (b) show an example of the image enhancement phase.

Initial Segmentation of Lung Parenchyma. As mentioned before, the lung parenchyma is a region filled with air, having a lower density tissue with respect to the surrounding fat area and, therefore, consisting of lower image intensities. Based on this property, a region growing technique was employed to obtain the initial candidate region. The method uses an initial seed point to iteratively grow. It uses, as intensity reference, the mean of all the points that belong to the segmented area, which adapted in the progressive inclusion of new pixels in the segmentation results.

Other approaches use region growing techniques to iteratively extract the different parts from the background until the lung region is reached, having to apply the region growing strategy several times for the different parts. Others identify a seed point in the lungs and apply the region growing from the inside. This approach implies a higher complexity in the correct localization of acceptable seed points for both lungs and needs to refine the results to include all the bronqui as part of the lung region results.

In our case, we propose a more simplified approach. We firstly identify a seed point in the fat area because it is easy to be localized. Thus, a region growing technique is run from this point obtaining the entire fat area. The initial lung parenchyma region is directly calculated as the holes that are contained in the fat segmentation result. Region growing is applied for each 2D slice as the following:

Selection of a seed point: on the assumption that the fat region occupies de entire central part of the image, we trace a diagonal and select the peak point of intensity as the seed point for the fat extraction. As there is always fat in the image, this approximation always find an appropriate seed point.

Region growing criteria: region growing defines threshold of tolerance t where higher or lower values are not included. In our case, we only define this criteria with respect to lower values because we want to distinguish the region with respect to the dark areas. Brighter ones (bones or any other bright artifact) are automatically included in the extracted fat region.

Stopping criteria: in the iterative process of growing the fat area, when the
new area is equal to the previous one, the process is stopped.

We tested region growing in two different ways: growing for the entire 3D
images and growing for each 2D slice that compose each image. Finally, we
decided to apply it to each 2D slice because in the 3D application the extracted
region grows deeply from the fat into the bronqui, significantly disturbing the
extracted lung parenchyma. In the 2D case, the region grows less deeply in each
slice making the results more accurate. In Figure 1 an example of initial lung
region segmentation can be seen.

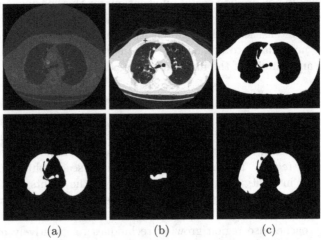

      (a)   (b)   (c)

Fig. 1. Initial lung parenchyma segmentation and traquea and bronqui removing. 1st
row, (a) input image, (b) enhanced image and initial seed point, (c) extracted fat
region. 2nd row, (a) First lung parenchyma candidate, (b) segmented traquea and
bronqui dilated, (c) Final lung without traquea and bronqui.

Traquea and Main Bronqui Removal. The initial lung parenchyma region,
as it is based on intensity, always contains the traquea and main bronqui, because
they are also structures filled with air that present similar intensities as the lung
parenchyma. The main purpose of the lung parenchyma segmentation is the
delimitation of the area where the lung nodules are present. Despite the fact that
traquea and bronqui do not interfere in the objective (even included, they never
contain structures that could be confuse with lung nodules), we remove them to
obtain a more clear results, with the following 3D region growing approach:

Selection of seed point: the first step for obtaining the traquea and the bronqui is the identification of an appropriate seed point. As the traquea always
appears as the first dark structure in the upper part of the body, firstly,
we need to find the orientation of the scan given that it can be presented
from the top (shoulders) or the bottom (abdomen) of the body. As the body
presents a more circular shape at the level of the body with respect to the

shoulders, we calculate their circularity coeficient in each limit of the scan in order to identify which border contains the shoulders, that is, where to locate the beginning of the traquea. Thus, the seed point is selected in the first slice with a dark structure in the first slices at the level of the shoulders.

Region growing criteria: we define a threshold value t and a short level of tolerance with respect to the pixels included. The goal of the selection of a short tolerance is to extract the traquea and main bronqui only, as if we provide a large tolerance we take the risk that the region growing includes parts of the lungs in the removing results.

Stopping criteria: once again, when the new area is equal to the previous area, the growing stops.

As we define a conservative region growing threshold, the final results were dilated to guarantee that the entire traquea and main bronqui are successfully removed. Figure 1, 2nd row, shows an example of this removal procedure.

Lung Division. One of the main drawbacks of using region growing is the possible touching between both lungs. Therefore, we include the analysis and division of the lungs. Thus, after removing small tiny artifacts that can perturb the results, we analyze if we have only one object left, meaning that both lungs are connected (two different lungs should be presented). Normally, the overlapping area is not relevant so we try to break the structure and recompose the objects with the following:

Eroding step: Firstly, we erode the object, iteratively until the structure breaks into two different objects. These are the core structures for both lungs.

Reconstruction step: We implemented an intermediate 2D region growing that uses as seed entire regions instead of a simple point. Thus, using each lung core, the intermediate region growing, that uses a more conservative threshold, continues with the growth of each lung, recovering portions of lung that were lost in the eroding step.

In Figure 2 two different examples of the lung division procedure are shown.

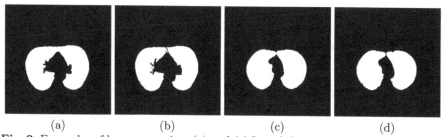

(a)   (b)   (c)   (d)

Fig. 2. Examples of lung separation. (a) and (c) Initial slices with the lungs connected. (b) and (d) Results after erode and reconstruction steps.

Contour Refinement. Finally, once we extracted both lungs, the last step is the contour inspection to include missing parts. Normally the lung contours are being disturbed by different bronqui and bright artifacts generating an irregular contour that needs to be corrected, as Figures 3 (a) and (c) show.

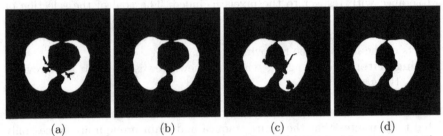

(a)	(b)	(c)	(d)

Fig. 3. Examples of lung contour refinement. (a) and (c) Original lung segmentation. (b) and (d) Results after circular closing operation.

Therefore, we added a final step of contour refinement that tries to include all these excluded parts in the final lung parenchyma results. Thus, following the idea of the rolling ball method [3], we applied a circular morphological operation of closing in each slice to refine all the contours (Figure 3 (b) and (d)). In particular, the filtering is applied to the binarized lung segmentation, inspecting the contour to include all the missing parts of the lungs.

3   Results

To test the methodology we selected 50 3D scans from the LIDC-IDRI image database [10]. These images contain a variable number of DICOM slices between 113 and 305 in a total amount of 8697 images, being the slice resolution of 512×512. These images include different levels of complexity: complicated traquea and bronqui, touching lungs and have 158 nodules, from which 40 are juxtapleural nodules, as we said the most difficult to be retained in the results.

Regarding the region growing approaches, in the experiments, the thresholds of tolerance were set to those values that provided the most adequate results. The values employed were 35% for the fat extraction (a large tolerance to guarantee that the method extract most parts of the fat as possible), 4% for the traquea and main bronqui subtraction (restricted tolerance to avoid the growing on the lungs) and 10% for the lung reconstruction after dividing (a normal tolerance to reconstruct the lungs and avoid possible touching once again).

As the final goal is the detection and classification of lung nodules, we particularly evaluated if all the nodules are included in this lung segmentation phase. For that reason, as an appropriate evaluation measure, we analyze if the center of the nodules are included in the segmented lungs. Please note that LIDC dataset provides ground truth information regarding the nodule centers. Particular attention is given to the juxtapleural nodules, that are the most likely lost in the segmentation process.

For this purpose, we selected a set of images that include a total number of 158 nodules, 40 of them juxtapleural. From all the 118 inner nodules, 117 were included. The only nodule that has problems to appear in the results was the one in Figure 4(a). In this case, the nodule is almost embedded in a large pathological area, so the region surrounding the nodule is really bright, being included as part of the fat, excluding the nodule. Normally, most of the problems that appear in the results are due to pathological structures that are included in the lung parenchyma, as the examples of Figure 4(b) and (c) show. As described before, this methodology is based on the intensity only, which may result in some local segmentation errors.

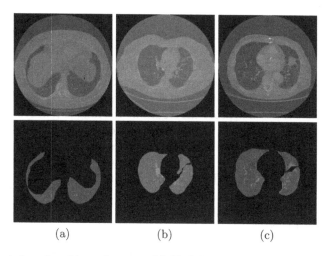

(a)   (b)   (c)

Fig. 4. Examples of problematic cases. (a) Nodule not included. (b) and (c) Results with pathological lung parenchyma.

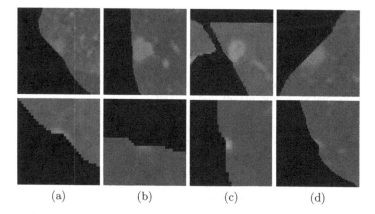

(a)   (b)   (c)   (d)

Fig. 5. Examples of results with juxtapleural nodules. 1st row, juxtapleural nodules entirely included. 2nd row, juxtapleural nodules partially included.

From the 40 total amount of juxtapleural nodules, 36 have their centers included in the final results. The other 4 cases, only a part of the nodule is included in the segmented lung area. This is a consequence of the fact that the juxtapleural nodules do not have a circular structure and are stuck along the wall. In such cases, a circular refinement, as the proposed, is not capable to recover the entire nodule region, being included only part of it. In figure 5 we can see some examples well segmented of juxtapleural nodules and the 4 problematic cases. Even in these cases, as the nodule is partly represented it can ease its entire segmentation in a more focused detection phase.

4   Conclusions

In this paper, we propose a complete methodology for lung parenchyma segmentation. The main purpose is the extraction of the region of interest for lung nodule detection. The method includes intensity correction, lung parenchyma identification, traquea and main bronqui removal, lung separation, in case they were touching, and boundary correction, performing a complete set of approaches that handles all the possible problems regarding the lung parenchyma segmentation. The method takes special care in the inclusion of the juxtapleural nodules in order to guarantee that all kind of lung nodules are included.

The approach was tested in 50 images taken from the LIDC image database, presenting 158 nodules with 40 juxtapleural. The method shows accurate results, with the great majority of the centers inside the segmented region, including most of the juxtapleural nodules, where at least some significant area of the nodule was included in the segmented lungs.

Acknowledgments. This work is supported by the European ERDF and ESF funds, and Portuguese funds through the COMPETE and POPH programs of the Fundação para a Ciência e a Tecnologia (FCT), with the PEst-C/EEI/LA0014/2013 project and the SFRH/BPD/85663/2012 grant contract.

References

1. Greenlee, R.T., Murray, T., Bolden, S., Wingo, P.A.: Cancer statistics. CA: A Cancer Journal for Clinicians **50**, 7–33 (2000)
2. Wei, Y., Shen, G., Li, J.: A Fully Automatic Method for Lung Parenchyma Segmentation and Repairing. J. Digit Imaging **26**, 483–495 (2013)
3. Armato, S.G., Sensakovic, W.F.: Automated lung segmentation for thoracic CT : Impact on computer-aided diagnosis. Academic Radiology **11**, 1011–1021 (2004)
4. Ye, X., Lin, X., et al.: Shape-Based Computer-Aided Detection of Lung Nodules in Thoracic CT Images. IEEE Trans. Biomed. Eng. **56**, 1810–1820 (2009)
5. Sun, S., Bauer, C., Beichel, R.: Automated 3-D segmentation of lungs with lung cancer in CT data using a novel robust active shape model approach. IEEE Trans. Med. Imaging **31**, 449–460 (2012)
6. Tsai, A., Yezzi, A., Wells, W., et al.: A shape-based approach to the segmentation of medical imagery using level sets. IEEE Trans. Med. Imaging **22**, 137–154 (2003)

7. van Ginneken, B., Stegmann, M.B., Loog, M.: Segmentation of anatomical structures in chest radiographs using supervised methods: a comparative study on a public database. Medical Image Analysis **10**, 19–40 (2006)
8. Adams, R., Bischof, L.: Seeded region growing. IEEE Transactions on Pattern Analysis and Machine Intelligence **16**, 641–647 (1994)
9. Hedlund, L.W., Anderson, R.F., Goulding, P.L., et al.: Two methods for isolating the lung area of a CT scan for density information. Radiology **144** (1982)
10. Armato, S.G., McLennan, G., Bidaut, L., et al.: The lung image database consortium (LIDC) and image database resource initiative (IDRI): a completed reference database of lung nodules on CT scans. Medical Physics **38**, 915–931 (2011)

Computer-Aided Diagnosis

Fully Automatic 3D Glioma Extraction in Multi-contrast MRI

Pavel Dvorak[1,2](✉) and Karel Bartusek[2]

[1] Department of Telecommunications, Faculty of Electrical Engineering
and Communication, Brno University of Technology, Technicka 12,
612 00 Brno, Czech Republic
[2] Institute of Scientific Instruments of the ASCR, v.v.i., Kralovopolska 147,
612 64 Brno, Czech Republic
{pdvorak,bar}@isibrno.cz
http://www.splab.cz,
http://www.isibrno.cz

Abstract. This work deals with the fully automatic extraction of a
glioma, the most common type of brain tumor, in multi-contrast 3D magnetic resonance volumes. The detection is based on the locating the area
that breaks the left-right symmetry of the brain. The proposed method
uses multi-contrast MRI, where FLAIR and T2-weighted volumes are
employed. The algorithm was designed to extract the whole pathology
as one region.

The created algorithm was tested on 80 volumes from publicly available BRATS databases containing multi-contrast 3D brain volumes affli-
cted by a brain tumor. These pathological structures had various sizes
and shapes and were located in various parts of the brain. The extraction
process was evaluated by Dice Coefficient(0.75). The proposed algorithm
detected and extracted multifocal tumors as separated regions as well.

Keywords: Brain tumor · Image segmentation · MRI · Multi-resolution
analysis · Symmetry analysis

1 Introduction

This work focuses on the first step in automatic brain tumor segmentation in
Magnetic Resonance Images (MRI), the extraction of the whole pathological
area. Nowadays, the brain tumor segmentation is a frequent research topic. Most
methods are still semi-automatic, such as the Support Vector Machines (SVM)
based method used in [14], and the proposed method could help to eliminate the
need for human work, which could improve the efficiency of medical's work. The
results from the proposed analysis could also help to detect the presence of this

This work was supported by SIX CZ.1.05/2.1.00/03.0072, GACR 102/12/1104 and
COST CZ LD14091.

A. Campilho and M. Kamel (Eds.): ICIAR 2014, Part II, LNCS 8815, pp. 239–246, 2014.
DOI: 10.1007/978-3-319-11755-3_27

kind of pathological area in brain volume and automatically display the regions of interest to medicals.

Pattern recognition algorithms usually rely on the shape of the required objects. But the tumor shape varies in each case so other properties have to be used. The general properties of healthy brain are widely used as a prior-knowledge. One of them is the probability of tissues locations using probability brain atlas, which is used e.g. in [5] and [17]. Another widely used knowledge, which is used in this paper, is the sagittal symmetry of healthy brain. This approach is also used e.g. in [2], [16], [19] or [10]. Areas that break this symmetry are most likely parts of a tumor or any other type of pathological tissue.

Current methods usually also rely on T1-weighted contrast enhanced images [3]. This is the image that we are trying to avoid, since it requires contrast enhanced agent (usually gadolinium) to be injected into the patient blood, which breaks the non-invasivity of magnetic resonance.

The first part of the proposed method, the preliminary locating of this kind of pathological area, can be used as the first step in the automatic tumor segmentation process using whichever MR contrast or combination of more MR contrasts. More information about the suitability of particular MR contrasts and their comparison can be found in [7]. The subsequent extraction is performed using Otsu's thresholding technique [15].

2   Proposed Method

The main idea behind this work is to detect and locate anomalies in 3D brain volumes using symmetry analysis. The sagittal symmetry of healthy brain is a frequent knowledge used for pathological area detection.

The input of the whole process is a 3D magnetic resonance volume containing a tumor. The tumor detection process consists of several steps. The first step is the extraction of the brain followed by cutting the image. Since all images in testing BRATS database are skull stripped, this step was skipped during testing. However, there are several methods used for brain extraction from 3D volumes and could be used here, e.g. method described in [20].

From this new cut volume, the mid-sagittal plane should be detected, using e.g. [12] or [18], to correctly align the head. In the aligned volume, the asymmetric parts are located. Since the detection process is region-based rather than pixel-based, the method does not need a perfectly aligned volume.

2.1   Tumor Locating

At first, the input volume is divided into left and right halves. Assuming that the head has been aligned and the skull is approximately symmetric, the symmetry plane is parallel to y-z plane and divides the volume of detected brain into two parts of the same size. The algorithm goes through both halves symmetrically by a cubic block. The size of the block is computed from the size of the image. The step size is smaller than the block size to ensure the overlapping of particular areas. These areas are compared with its opposite regions. Normalized histograms with the same range are computed for both cubic regions, left and right, and they are compared by Bhattacharya coefficient (BC) [1], which expresses the similarity of two sets. BC is computed as follows:

$$BC = \sum_{i=1}^{N} \sqrt{l(i) \cdot r(i)}, \tag{1}$$

where N denotes the number of bins in the histogram, l and r denote histograms of blocks in left and right half, respectively. The range of values of Bhattacharya coefficient is $[0, 1]$, where the smaller value means the bigger difference between histograms. For the next computation, the asymmetry is computed as $A = 1 - BC$.

This asymmetry is computed for all blocks. Since the regions overlap during the computation, the average asymmetry is computed for each pixel. The whole cycle is repeated three times but for different resolution of the volume. The resolution of each axis is iteratively reduced to the half of the previous value. This approach corresponds to the multi resolution image analysis described in [11]. The output of each cycle is an asymmetry map. The product of values corresponding to a particular pixel creates new multi-resolution asymmetry map. This computation is performed for each contrast volume separately. The example of the asymmetry map for multifocal tumor is shown in Figure 1.

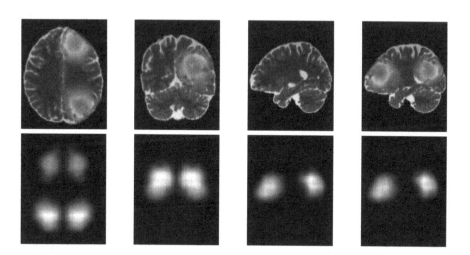

Fig. 1. Example of asymmetry map. The top row shows the T2 slices with the highest asymmetry. The bottom row shows the asymmetry maps of the T2-weighted volume of the corresponding slices.

For the pathology extraction purpose, the thresholding of the multi-resolution 3D asymmetry map is performed. The threshold is computed from the particular asymmetry map as 30% of the maximal assymetry. This was set experimentally and ensures that at least small region is extracted. The results of the both-sided mask that contains both the tumor on one side and the healthy tissue on the other side.

Since multifocal tumor can appear, the detection process is not limited to only one region. All regions created by thresholding are considered. As a result, multifocal tumors located in both halves asymmetrically can be correctly detected.

2.2   Tumor Extraction

For the extraction of the tumor area, the both-sided mask computed in previous step is used, which means the decision which parts contain tumor is not made here. The extraction process is based on the method proposed in [8]. Gliomas and edemas can be well separated from white and gray matter using T2-weighted volume, since they appear hyperintense in this MR contrast. The automatic thresholding is performed to extract these pathological areas.

The threshold is determined from the points inside the resulting mask of asymmetry detection using the technique proposed by Otsu in 1979 [15]. Since the pathological area could extend beyond the asymmetry area border, the thresholding process is applied to the whole volume. Morphological erosion and dilation are performed with the resulting mask of the thresholding process to smooth the region borders and separate regions connected by a thin area. Those regions situated mostly outside the asymmetry mask are eliminated.

Since Cerebrospinal fluid (CSF) appears hyperintense in T2-weighted images as well, the FLAIR volume is employed, because in this MR contrast, the CSF produces much weaker signal than the white matter and the tumor itself. Hence, the areas with the lower intensity than the median intensity (which is most likely the white matter intensity) in FLAIR volume are eliminated.

3   Testing

The method is not composed of a training and a testing phase as most current method are, therefore no division into training and testing data is performed and all the available volumes are considered to be testing.

3.1   Dataset

Brain tumor image data used in this work were obtained from the MICCAI 2012 Challenge on Multimodal Brain Tumor Segmentation organized by B. Menze, A. Jakab, S. Bauer, M. Reyes, M. Prastawa, and K. Van Leemput. The challenge database contains fully anonymized images from the following institutions: ETH Zurich, University of Bern, University of Debrecen, and University of Utah. (http://www.imm.dtu.dk/projects/BRATS2012)

The data contains real volumes of 20 high-grade and 10 low-grade glioma subjects and simulated volumes of 25 high-grade and 25 low-grade glioma subjects. All the simulated images are in BrainWeb space [4]. The information about the simulation method can be found in [17].

No attempt was made to put the individual patients in a common reference space and no modifications were needed for the testing dataset.

3.2 Evaluation Criteria

The extraction process is evaluated by the Dice Coefficient (DC) [6], which is computed according to the equation:

$$DC = \frac{2\,|A \cap B|}{|A| + |B|}, \tag{2}$$

where A and B denote the ground truth and the result masks of the extraction, respectively. The range of the DC values is [0;1], where the 1 expresses the perfect segmentation.

4 Results

The results of extraction process are evaluated by Dice Coefficient are summarized in Table 1. Even though the maximum of the FLAIR and T2 asymmetry map was situated outside the ground truth in 3 of 80 cases, there was no intersection between ground truth and automatic extraction result only in 1 of them. In other words, even though the maximum was located outside the tumor, the extracted regions contained this pathological area.

Table 1. The Dice coefficient (DC) for pathological area extraction in particular sets

		Real Data		Simulated Data		
		High Gr.	Low Gr.	High Gr.	Low Gr.	Overall
DC	Mean	0.67 ± 0.22	0.78 ± 0.10	0.80 ± 0.10	0.72 ± 0.05	0.74 ± 0.14
	Median	0.75	0.78	0.82	0.71	0.75

It has to be stated that these results are for non-aligned volumes. The method would not work for highly rotated volumes, nevertheless since it is region-based rather than pixel-based, the perfect alignment is not necessary. According to [21], the DC>0,7 indicates an excellent similarity. This statement was met for both high and low grade gliomas in both real and simulated data.

The examples of extraction results on the real data of the low grade glioma and the simulated data of the high grade multifocal glioma are shown in Figures 2 and 3, respectively. Slices with maximum asymmetry are shown in both figures. As can be seen in Figure 2, the precise vertical alignment of the head is not necessary.

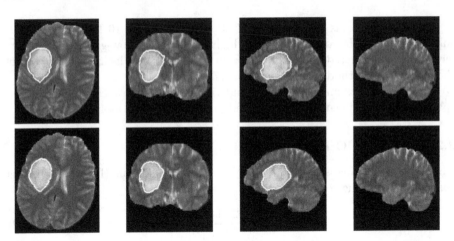

Fig. 2. Example of brain tumor extraction on volumes from real data of the low grade glioma with the DC = 0.93. The top and bottom rows show the ground truth and the automatic segmentation result, respectively.

Even though the proposed method was tested on publicly available BRATS 2012 database, the comparison with other methods is not straightforward. The MICCAI 2012 Challenge was focused on segmentation of tumor and edema separately. Hence, the described results in this paper cannot be compared to those described in the proceedings of MICCAI-BRATS 2012 [13]. On the other hand, our work is fully automated and does not require training phase as all methods proposed in the proceedings. Training phase requires normalized intensities in all involved images, which brings another inaccuracy into the segmentation process and cannot be always reached accurately. An alternative to intensity normalization is patient specific training dataset that requires manual selection of several points in foreground and background tissues.

5   Conclusion

The purpose of this work was to show an automatic brain tumor extraction technique for multi-contrast MRI. The proposed method reached promising results, but there are still areas for improving the extraction performance. The proposed algorithm automatically detected and extracted multifocal tumors as separated regions as well.

To improve the performance, the combination with the brain tissue probabilistic atlas or more sophisticated image segmentation algotihms such as Active Contour or Graph Cut will be considered. The attention of future work will also be paid on the automatic probabilistic determination of pathological area presence based on our previous method for 2D axial images [9] and separation of particular parts of pathology.

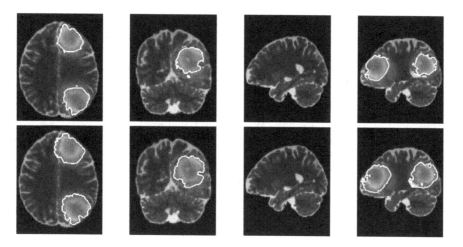

Fig. 3. Example of brain tumor detection on volumes from simulated data of high grade glioma with DC = 0.80. The top and bottom rows show the ground truth and the automatic segmentation result, respectively.

References

1. Bhattacharyya, A.: On a measure of divergence between two statistical populations defined by their probability distribution. Bulletin of the Calcutta Mathematical Society **35**, 99–110 (1943)
2. Cap, M., Gescheidtova, E., Marcon, P., Bartusek, K.: Automatic detection and segmentation of the tumor tissue. In: Progress in Electromagnetics Research Symposium, pp. 53–56 (2013)
3. Capelle, A.S., Colot, O., Fernandez-Maloigne, C.: Evidential segmentation scheme of multi-echo MR images for the detection of brain tumors using neighborhood information. Information Fusion **5**(3), 203–216 (2004). http://www.sciencedirect.com/science/article/pii/S1566253503000848
4. Cocosco, C.A., Kollokian, V., Kwan, R.K.S., Pike, G.B., Evans, A.C.: Brainweb: Online interface to a 3d mri simulated brain database. NeuroImage **5**, 425 (1997)
5. Cuadra, M.B., Pollo, C., Bardera, A., Cuisenaire, O., Villemure, J.G., Thiran, J.P.: Atlas-based segmentation of pathological mr brain images using a model of lesion growth. IEEE Trans. Med. Imaging **23**(1), 1301–1314 (2004)
6. Dice, L.R.: Measures of the amount of ecologic association between species. Ecology **26**(3), 297–302 (1945)
7. Dvorak, P., Bartusek, K.: Brain tumor locating in 3d mr volume using symmetry. In: Proc. SPIE 9034, Medical Imaging 2014: Image Processing, 903432 (2014)
8. Dvorak, P., Bartusek, K., Kropatsch, W.G.: Automated segmentation of brain tumor edema in flair mri using symmetry and thresholding. In: Progress in Electromagnetics Research Symposium, pp. 936–939 (2013)
9. Dvorak, P., Kropatsch, W.G., Bartusek, K.: Automatic brain tumor detection in t2- weighted magnetic resonance images. Measurement Science Review **13**(5), 223–230 (2013)

10. Khotanlou, H., Colliot, O., Bloch, I.: Automatic brain tumor segmentation using symmetry analysis and deformable models. In: Conf. on Advances in Pattern Recognition ICAPR, Kolkata, India (January 2007)
11. Kropatsch, W.G., Haxhimusa, Y., Ion, A.: Multiresolution image segmentations in graph pyramids. In: Kandel, A., Bunke, H., Last, M. (eds.) Applied Graph Theory in Computer Vision and Pattern Recognition. SCI, vol. 52, pp. 3–41. Springer, Heidelberg (2007)
12. Liu, Y., Collins, R.T., Rothfus, W.E.: Robust midsagittal plane extraction from normal and pathological 3-d neuroradiology image. IEEE Transactions on Medical Imaging **20**(3), 175–192 (2003)
13. Menze, B., Jakab, A., Bauer, S., Kalpathy-Cramer, J., Farahani, K., Kirby, J., Burren, Y., Porz, N., Slotboom, J., Wiest, R., Lanczi, L., Gerstner, E., Weber, M.A., Arbel, T., Avants, B., Ayache, N., Buendia, P., Collins, L., Cordier, N., Corso, J., Criminisi, A., Das, T., Delingette, H., Demiralp, C., Durst, C., Dojat, M., Doyle, S., Festa, J., Forbes, F., Geremia, E., Glocker, B., Golland, P., Guo, X., Hamamci, A., Iftekharuddin, K., Jena, R., John, N., Konukoglu, E., Lashkari, D., Antonio Mariz, J., Meier, R., Pereira, S., Precup, D., Price, S.J., Riklin-Raviv, T., Reza, S., Ryan, M., Schwartz, L., Shin, H.C., Shotton, J., Silva, C., Sousa, N., Subbanna, N., Szekely, G., Taylor, T., Thomas, O., Tustison, N., Unal, G., Vasseur, F., Wintermark, M., Hye Ye, D., Zhao, L., Zhao, B., Zikic, D., Prastawa, M., Reyes, M., Van Leemput, K.: The Multimodal Brain Tumor Image Segmentation Benchmark (BRATS), http://hal.inria.fr/hal-00935640
14. Mikulka, J., Gescheidtova, E.: An improved segmentation of brain tumor, edema and necrosis. In: Progress in Electromagnetics Research Symposium, pp. 25–28 (2013)
15. Otsu, N.: A Threshold Selection Method from Gray-level Histograms. IEEE Transactions on Systems, Man and Cybernetics **9**(1), 62–66 (1979). http://dx.doi.org/10.1109/TSMC.1979.4310076
16. Pedoia, V., Binaghi, E., Balbi, S., De Benedictis, A., Monti, E., Minotto, R.: Glial brain tumor detection by using symmetry analysis. In: Proc. SPIE. vol. 8314, pp. 831445-1–831445-8 (2012), http://dx.doi.org/10.1117/12.910172
17. Prastawa, M., Bullitt, E., Moon, N., Van Leemput, K., Gerig, G.: Automatic brain tumor segmentation by subject specific modification of atlas priors. Academic Radiology **10**(12), 1341–1348 (2003)
18. Ruppert, G.C.S., Teverovskiy, L., Yu, C., Falcao, A.X., Liu, Y.: A new symmetry-based method for mid-sagittal plane extraction in neuroimages. In: International Symposium on Biomedical Imaging: From Macro to Nano (2011)
19. Saha, B.N., Ray, N., Greiner, R., Murtha, A., Zhang, H.: Quick detection of brain tumors and edemas: A bounding box method using symmetry. Computerized Medical Imaging and Graphics **36**(2), 95–107 (2012). http://www.sciencedirect.com/science/article/pii/S0895611111000796
20. Uher, V., Burget, R., Masek, J., Dutta, M.: 3d brain tissue selection and segmentation from mri. In: 2013 36th International Conference on Telecommunications and Signal Processing (TSP), pp. 839–842 (2013)
21. Zijdenbos, A., Dawant, B.: Brain segmentation and white matter lesion detection in mr images. Critical Reviews in Biomedical Engineering **22**, 401–465 (1994)

Grading Cancer from Liver Histology Images Using Inter and Intra Region Spatial Relations

Mickaël Garnier[1]([✉]), Maya Alsheh Ali[1], Johanne Seguin[2], Nathalie Mignet[2], Thomas Hurtut[3], and Laurent Wendling[1]

[1] LIPADE, Université Paris Descartes, Paris, France
garnier.mickael@gmail.com
[2] UPCGI, Université Paris Descartes, Paris, France
[3] École Polytechnique de Montréal, Montréal, Canada

Abstract. Histology image analysis is widely used in cancer studies since it preserves the tissue structure. In this paper, we propose a framework to grade metastatic liver histology images based on the spatial organization inter and intra regions. After detecting the presence of metastases, we first decompose the image into regions corresponding to the tissue types (sane, cancerous, vessels and gaps). A sample of each type is further decomposed into the contained biological objects (nuclei, stroma, gaps). The spatial relations between all the pairs of regions and objects are measured using a Force Histogram Decomposition. A specimen is described using a Bag of Words model aggregating the features measured on all its randomly acquired images. The grading is made using a Naive Bayes Classifier. Experiments on a 23 mice dataset with CT26 intrasplenic tumors highlight the relevance of the spatial relations with a correct grading rate of 78.95 %.

1 Introduction

Histology images are becoming more and more used in computer science. This particular modality of imaging preserves the underlying tissue architecture through its preparation process, making the use of histology images the *gold standard* in diagnosing a considerable number of diseases, especially cancers [5]. The automated quantitative analysis of histology images can help to understand the reasons behind a diagnosis, as well as to reduce the inter and intra expert variations and to bring a better understanding of the growth of a disease.

Depending on the objects of interest, histology images are acquired on specimens stained by one or several dyes that highlight their particular features and give contrast to the tissue. The best solution for histopathologists is to analyze whole slide images, however it is very costly thus limiting their introduction and diffusion in research. Alternative solutions are used, either relying on analyzing regions of interest [13], or using images taken randomly over all the slide [7].

Biologists, using histology images in cancer studies, are interested in analyzing both primary tumors and secondary metastases. In this paper, we propose a framework to grade cancer development in metastatic liver histology images. This work investigates

© Springer International Publishing Switzerland 2014
A. Campilho and M. Kamel (Eds.): ICIAR 2014, Part II, LNCS 8815, pp. 247–254, 2014.
DOI: 10.1007/978-3-319-11755-3_28

the relevance of the spatial relations to recognize the advancement of cancer. The spatial relations are measured at two scales, between tissue types and between biological objects inside each type of tissue.

The most common framework for automatic analysis of multi-stained histology images follows three steps. First a segmentation of biological objects is performed, then these objects can be quantified, usually based on first-order measures [7], and biological object-based features can be extracted [17]. These methods are usually used for detection rather than grading, the latter being a more complex issue. Other methods focusing on texture analysis are applied to grade histology images for several cancers, such as lymphoma [15] and carcinoma [6].

Our description focuses on the encoding of the pairwise spatial relations which are already used in histology images analysis, usually between pairs of elements after a segmentation process. The spatial information is extracted using second order statistics, the most common being Ripley's K function, the Pair Correlation Function and Besag's L function, see [8]. They are used in various biomedical applications such as the description of tumors in breast [12] or brain [9]. These functions aims at representing the distribution of distances between pairs of point objects but are not able to handle regions as we need.

Other methods of spatial relations measurement are proposed in computer vision. They can be split into quantitative and qualitative approaches. Qualitative approaches correspond to symbolic relations such as positioning [2]. Since we are interested in a measure between possibly unconnected subset of pixels, we cannot use a symbolic representation. Fuzzy quantitative approaches are commonly used in multiple application domains, such as medical imaging [1]. In this study, we use and extend the Force Histogram Decomposition (FHD) method [4] to accurately describe the spatial organization of objects.

2   Materials

CT26 tumor intrasplenic implantation. CT26 is an undifferentiated murine colon adenocarcinoma cell line syngeneic to the BALB/c mice strain. CT26 tumor was very tumorigenic in vivo and often produces pulmonary and hepatic metastases in mice. To develop a reproducible model of hepatic metastasis, tumor cells have been implanted into the spleens of mice. From this site of injection, tumor cells access to the liver via the blood vessels and proliferate to form secondary tumor. Using the model described by Wai [19], Female BALB/c mice, 6 to 7 weeks old were acclimated for 1 week while separated in groups of five. All animal studies were carried out according to the Institutional Animal Care and Use Committee of Paris Descartes. Splenectomy were performed 5 min after intrasplenic injection of $5x10^4$ cells in culture media.

Histological analyses. At 7, 11, 13 and 17 days after implantation, liver were removed, frozen, cut and stained with the same protocol for all animals. Each slice of liver was counterstained with Hematoxylin and Eosin. From this biological material, 246 histology images were digitized (Leica DM6000B) into 90 images from healthy liver and 156 from metastatic tumor model: day 7 (5 mice) and days 11, 13, and 17 (3 mice each).

The mean number of images per mouse is 10, these images were taken randomly from all over a single slide. The resolution of the images is 2592 × 1944 pixels.

Mice cancer grading. The liver slices were analyzed by an expert and graded according to three criteria. First, the number of metastases, which was done with a macroscopic observation. The second criterion is the number of metastases per square millimeters and finally the area of metastases per square millimeters. The final grade of the mice is defined accordingly to these three criteria. The dataset is composed of 9 sane mice, 3 of grade 1, 7 of grade 2 and 4 of grade 3.

3   Methods

We use texture analysis and spatial relation measures in order to describe histology images. The analysis of texture is performed to detect the presence of metastases inside the tissue section while the final description only relies on the spatial relations. The different measures of every images are then aggregated to accurately describe each mouse.

3.1   Metastases Detection

Our aim is to detect if there is metastases in each image. As shown in Figure 1, the textures of sane tissue and metastases are quite different, both stains have different hues and the shapes of the nuclei are more random in tumorous tissue. Thus, a texture analysis method is carried out to detect these variations.

We use a multiresolution texture analysis method introduced in [3]. The multiresolution is achieved using a wavelet filter-bank which also gives us access to high frequency information. All the information resulting from this decomposition is then described using the completed model of Local Binary Patterns (cLBP). A Linear Discriminant Analysis is conducted and used for classification. This detection serves as a preprocessing to induce a semantic information into the spatial relations measurement step.

3.2   Spatial Relations Measurement

We seek to describe the spatial organization of the tissue at two scales: between types of tissue and between biological objects inside each tissue type. All the spatial relations are here represented using FHD.

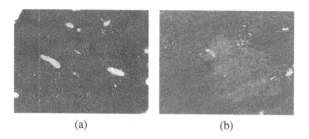

(a)   (b)

Fig. 1. Images showing the variations in texture between sane tissue and metastases. (a) without metastases despite being of grade 1 while (b) with metastases and of grade 3.

Force Histogram Decomposition. The FHD is an object recognition method where the description relies on both the shapes and the spatial relations underlying the object structure. These two information are acquired using histograms of forces [11]. The histogram of forces computed between two objects A and B with a force φ along a direction θ is defined as:

$$\mathcal{F}^{AB}(\theta) = \sum_{C_\theta} \int_{c_A} \int_{c_B} \varphi(\|\mathbf{ab}\|) \, db \, da \tag{1}$$

where C_θ is a set of θ−oriented lines spanning the image and, c_A and c_B are respectively a single line from C_θ cutting through the objects A and B, see Figure 2.

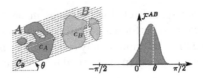

Fig. 2. Principle of computation of histograms of forces

In order to access the object structure, the FHD first requires to decompose the object into several layers. Histograms of forces are then computed between every pairs of layers for the spatial relation information, and on every layer with itself to get a shape description. The FHD is defined as the set of all these histograms of forces. This method presents the advantage of being invariant to both scale and position, and can easily achieves rotation invariant using a circular dissimilarity measure. The FHD requires the definition of a force, we choose to set a constant force in all our measures, i.e. $\varphi = 1$. Thus our description does not take the distance between objects into consideration but allows for objects overlapping. This description is also robust to the accuracy of the decomposition method.

In this study, we are interested in reducing the amount of information contained in each histogram of forces. Thus, we use a signature based on the Fourier series. The final description retains only the S first amplitude values which are not considered as noise. This signature was introduced and its efficiency was assessed in [18]. This signature also has the advantage of ensuring that our description is rotation invariant.

Inter Regions Spatial Relations. An adaptive multi-channel wavelet representation [10] is applied to separate the different tissue types. This method aims at separating the image into meaningful texture sets based on a wavelet packet transform using Lemarié's wavelet. Each pixel of the image is classified into a layer according to both its high and low frequencies wavelet coefficients envelopes. The Figure 3 shows the outcome of this decomposition on a representative image of our dataset.

This method is used to separate the image into three layers: sane tissue, metastastic tissue and the remaining image content. In the case of an image without metastases, we only decompose two layers, the metastases layer being forced to a blank image. The shapes of these three regions and their spatial relations are measured using the FHD.

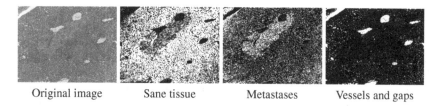

| Original image | Sane tissue | Metastases | Vessels and gaps |

Fig. 3. Representative image from our dataset decomposed into three layers

Intra Regions Spatial Relations. We aim at describing the biological objects organization inside each type of tissue. In order to keep this measure relevant and as disjoint as possible from the shape of the region, we define a circular patch inside the most attractive set of connected components of this region. This set of connected component has to be wider than the size of the patch and possess both the highest solidity and the largest area possible. If no group of connected components fits these criteria, the one with the largest area is chosen. The resulting three patches are shown in the first row of figure 4.

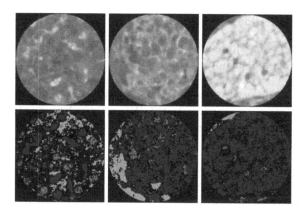

Fig. 4. Three patches extracted on a representative image and their decomposition into biological objects. RGB channels respectively represent the nuclei, the stroma and the remaining tissue.

Once the patches are defined, we apply a color deconvolution [14] to separate the hematoxylin from the eosin. This operation allows access to the cells' nuclei, the stroma and the remaining objects. The outcome of the color deconvolution is rather noisy and the FHD requires binary layers, therefore, every stain channel is thresholded using the Otsu method with three classes, the background, the noise and the dye. The resulting layers for the three previous patches are displayed in the second row of Figure 4. As for the inter regions spatial relations, we apply the FHD to describe the shapes of each object and the spatial relations between them.

3.3 Mice Signature and Classification

Since each mouse is represented by several images, we have to aggregate their descriptors in the classification process. Thus we use a Bag of Words model [16] with a coding-pooling scheme. This method requires the computation of a visual codebook composed of prototype descriptors, called visual words. A mouse is then described by counting the occurrences of each visual words within its images. The visual codebook is generated using a k-means algorithm on the training data to group the descriptors. The description computed on a single image correspond to a single word.

The coding-pooling scheme consists in dividing the mapping in two steps. Each descriptor is first mapped to the closest one in the visual codebook, a binary signature, where a 1 corresponds to the closest visual word, is then obtained. The second step aggregates these signatures into a single description by adding up all the mapped visual words. This method is more complicated to implement than the simple Bag of Words but allows to keep a small signature size. The final classification is made using a Naive Bayes Classifier on the outcome of the coding pooling scheme.

4 Experimental Results

4.1 Metastases Detection

This step requires to set both the base parameters of the cLBP and the depth of the wavelet decomposition. We chose a LBP radius of 1 with a number of neighbors of 8 and a depth of 4. This step provides good results, see Table 1, especially in terms of false positive with using only one mouse per grade as training data. Almost all the images presenting metastases are correctly detected. We prefer to have a very good sensitivity rather than a good specificity so that the grading method does not miss metastases related spatial relations.

Table 1. Confusion matrix obtained on our dataset. It shows a specificity of 76.2%, a sensitivity of 98.3% and a recognition rate of 87.1%.

Output	Healthy	93	2		Specificity	Sensitivity	Recognition Rate
	Metastases	29	116		76.2%	98.3%	87.1%
		Healthy	Metastases				
			Target				

4.2 Grading of Cancer

In this step, we have to set several parameters. The first parameter is the number of directions of the computed histograms of forces. We chose to use 180 directions, thus giving an angular resolution of one degree. The Fourier series signature length (S) is set to several values (4, 8, 16 and 32) in order to measure the influence of this parameter. The next parameter is the size of the patch (r), its effects are also studied by using four different values (50, 100, 200 and 400 pixels). Our last parameter is the size of the visual codebook (C), we conducted our experiments using 8, 16 and 32 different visual words in our codebook.

The results of our grading method, with the same training data as the metastases detection, for the different sets of parameters are summarized in Table 2. It achieves good results and is rather robust to the choice of the parameters with the exception of the patch radius. This shows that the intra-regions spatial relations hold useful information for the cancer grading but they require enough materials in order to accurately describe the tissue. The size of the visual codebook seems to have little influence on the grade recognition. However, the length of the Fourier series signature has to be chosen wisely since a length of 8 appears to bring a loss of more than 20% in recognition.

Table 2. Tables showing the cancer grade recognition rates (%) of our method according to the size of the intra-region patch (r), the length of the Fourier series signature (S) and the size of the visual codebook (C)

S	32				S	4	8	16	32	S		32	
C	8				C		8			C	8	16	32
r	50	100	200	400	r		400			r		400	
%	52.6	57.9	63.2	**79.0**	%	**79.0**	57.9	**79.0**	**79.0**	%	**79.0**	73.7	73.7

5 Conclusion

In this paper, we proposed a framework to grade cancerous histology images. After a metastases detection using texture features, the method aims at describing the spatial relations between and inside the different types of tissue. We first decompose each image into several layers corresponding to the three types of tissue: sane, metastatic, and others such as blood vessels and gaps. Then, to access the biological organization inside each type of tissue, we further decompose a representative circular patch per tissue into its three types of biological objects: nuclei, stroma and gaps. The spatial organization at both scales are then described using an extended Force Histograms Decomposition.

Our work shows correct grading recognition of 79.0% despite our dataset being composed of random images taken from a single whole slide per mice. Thus, it could provides a better description in the case of whole slide images. This work does not take into consideration a description of the pairwise spatial relations between biological objects which seems to hold additional information. In the future, we aim at integrating this statistical information. We are also interested in studying the relevance of this method for grading other types of cancer.

Acknowledgments. This work was supported by the ANR SPIRIT #11-JCJC-008-01.

References

1. Bloch, I.: Fuzzy spatial relationships for image processing and interpretation: a review. Image and Vision Computing **23**(2), 89–110 (2005)
2. Freeman, J.: The modelling of spatial relations. Computer Graphics and Image Processing **4**(2), 156–171 (1975)
3. Garnier, M., Hurtut, T., Ben Tahar, H., Cheriet, F.: Automatic multiresolution age-related macular degeneration detection from fundus images. In: SPIE Medical Imaging, p. 903532. International Society for Optics and Photonics (2014)
4. Garnier, M., Hurtut, T., Wendling, L.: Object description based on spatial relations between level-sets. In: Proc. DICTA, pp. 1–7 (2012)
5. Gurcan, M.N., Boucheron, L.E., Can, A., Madabhushi, A., Rajpoot, N.M., Yener, B.: Histopathological image analysis: a review. IEEE Reviews in Biomedical Engineering **2**, 147–171 (2009)
6. He, L., Long, L.R., Antani, S., Thoma, G.R.: Histology image analysis for carcinoma detection and grading. Computer Methods and Programs in Biomedicine **107**(3), 538–556 (2012)
7. Heldmuth, L.O.: In vivo monitoring of elastic changes during cancer development and therapeutic treatment. PhD thesis, Université Paris Diderot (2012)
8. Illian, J., Penttinen, P.A., Stoyan, H., Stoyan, P.D.: Statistical Analysis and Modelling of Spatial Point Patterns. Statistics in Practice. John Wiley and Sons (2008)
9. Jiao, Y., Berman, H., Kiehl, T.R., Torquato, S.: Spatial organization and correlations of cell nuclei in brain tumors. PLoS One **6**(11), e27323 (2011)
10. Lee, N., Laine, A.F., Smith, T.R.: Learning non-homogenous textures and the unlearning problem with application to drusen detection in retinal images. In: Proc. ISBI, pp. 1215–1218 (2008)
11. Matsakis, P., Wendling, L.: A new way to represent the relative position between areal objects. In: Proc. PAMI, vol. 21(7), pp. 634–643 (1999)
12. Mattfeldt, T., Eckel, S., Fleischer, F., Schmidt, V.: Statistical analysis of labelling patterns of mammary carcinoma cell nuclei on histological sections. Journal of Microscopy **235**(1), 106–118 (2009)
13. Mikalsen, L.T.G., Dhakal, H.P., Bruland, Ø.S., Nesland, J.M., Olsen, D.R.: Quantification of angiogenesis in breast cancer by automated vessel identification in cd34 immunohistochemical sections. Anticancer Research **31**(12), 4053–4060 (2011)
14. Ruifrok, A.C., Johnston, D.A.: Quantification of histochemical staining by color deconvolution. Analytical and Quantitative Cytology and Histology **23**(4), 291–299 (2001)
15. Sertel, O., Kong, J., Catalyurek, U.V., Lozanski, G., Saltz, J.H., Gurcan, M.N.: Histopathological image analysis using model-based intermediate representations and color texture: Follicular lymphoma grading. Journal of Signal Processing Systems **55**(1–3), 169–183 (2009)
16. Sivic, J., Zisserman, A.: Video google: A text retrieval approach to object matching in videos. In: Proc. ICCV, pp. 1470–1477. IEEE (2003)
17. Swamidoss, I.N., Kårsnäs, A., Uhlmann, V., Ponnusamy, P., Kampf, C., Simonsson, M., Wählby, C., Strand, R.: Automated classification of immunostaining patterns in breast tissue from the human protein atlas. Journal of Pathology Informatics **4**(Suppl.) (2013)
18. Tabbone, S., Wendling, L., Tombre, K.: Matching of graphical symbols in line-drawing images using angular signature information. Document Analysis and Recognition **6**(2), 115–125 (2003)
19. Wai, P.Y., Mi, Z., Guo, H., Sarraf-Yazdi, S., Gao, C., Wei, J., Marroquin, C.E., Clary, B., Kuo, P.C.: Osteopontin silencing by small interfering rna suppresses in vitro and in vivo ct26 murine colon adenocarcinoma metastasis. Carcinogenesis **26**(4), 741–751 (2005)

eFis: A Fuzzy Inference Method for Predicting Malignancy of Small Pulmonary Nodules

Aydın Kaya$^{(\boxtimes)}$ and Ahmet Burak Can

Hacettepe University, Computer Engineering Department, Ankara, Turkey
{aydinkaya,abc}@cs.hacettepe.edu.tr

Abstract. Predicting malignancy of small pulmonary nodules from computer tomography scans is a difficult and important problem to diagnose lung cancer. This paper presents a rule based fuzzy inference method for predicting malignancy rating of small pulmonary nodules. We use the nodule characteristics provided by Lung Image Database Consortium dataset to determine malignancy rating. The proposed fuzzy inference method uses outputs of ensemble classifiers and rules from radiologist agreements on the nodules. The results are evaluated over classification accuracy performance and compared with single classifier methods. We observed that the preliminary results are very promising and system is open to development.

Keywords: Small pulmonary nodules · Nodule characteristics · Fuzzy inference · Ensemble classifiers

1 Introduction

In lung cancer, detection of small pulmonary nodules is a challenging process for radiologists. A small pulmonary nodule is a lung lesion with diameter around 2-30 mm and indistinct boundaries. These nodules are generally found fortuitously on tomography scans [1]. The diagnostic challenge for evaluation of patient's nodule is to determine whether it's benign or malignant. Diagnosis made by radiologists is highly subjective and results can be significantly different according to expertise of the radiologist.

Publicly available Lung Image Database Consortium (LIDC) database [2] provides researchers nodule characteristics as radiographic descriptors. In this database, all cases are evaluated by four radiologists. Each radiologist gives her/his estimations for boundaries and ratings for nodule characteristics. As Zinovev et al. [10] stated, lack of ground truth and radiologist anonymity over database is a challenging situation; however it gives opportunity to build different computer aided diagnosis methods.

In this study, we present an approach based on Ensemble classifiers and a rule-based Fuzzy Inference System (*eFis*) to estimate malignancy rating of nodules from nodule characteristics. Since most of our datasets are highly unbalanced, our method applies dataset balancing methods on the datasets. Ensemble classifiers and a convex hull method are used to classify nodule characteristics. Outputs of these classification

© Springer International Publishing Switzerland 2014
A. Campilho and M. Kamel (Eds.): ICIAR 2014, Part II, LNCS 8815, pp. 255–262, 2014.
DOI: 10.1007/978-3-319-11755-3_29

steps provide a base for finding a malignancy rating in the fuzzy inference step. Experiments showed that classification of malignancy rating using nodule characteristics produces promising results. General schema of the proposed work is shown on Figure 1.

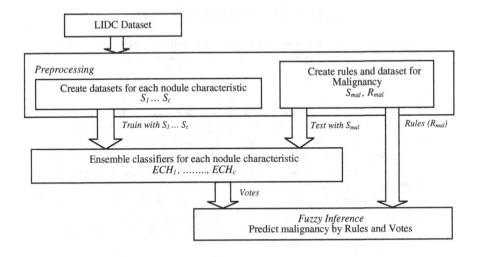

Fig. 1. General schema for eFis

Studies on pulmonary nodules are usually focused on classification of nodules as benign or malignant. In recent years, information retrieval and nodule characterization studies have developed by virtue of public databases like NELSON and Lung Image Database Consortium [2].

Xu et al. [3] classified nodules based on size, shape and margin characteristics that included by NELSON screening trial. Li et al. [4] used feature-based, a pixel-value-difference based, a cross-correlation-based and neural-network-based techniques for determination of similarity measure among radiologist's evaluation over nodule types. Horsthemke et al. [5] used probabilistic region of interest selection and predicted radiologist opinions by image features. Giuca et al. [6] developed a content based image retrieval method to annotate large unlabeled data with small amount of labeled data. Zinovev et al. [7] proposed an ensemble classifier and active learning method (active-DECORATE) to predict nodule characteristics. Li et al. [8] proposed a method for predicting malignancy using nodule characteristics in neural network classifiers.

Dasovich et al. [9] proposed a model for semantic and content based image retrieval to determine relation between nodule characteristics and image features. This model finds correlated images by using linear regression on semantic features of nodules and similarity measure (e.g. Euclidean distance) on low level image features. Zinovev et al. [10] proposed a system for predict nodule characteristics by ensemble of probabilistic classifiers based on belief decision trees and ADABoost learning.

2   Method

2.1   Data

National Cancer Institute has formed a demand in 2001 for a lung CT image database, which can be accessed via the Internet under the heading of "Lung Image Database Resource for Imaging Research". For this purpose, a consensus achieved image database named Lung Image Database Consortium (LIDC) has been developed. For the evaluation of images, radiologists are assigned from four different institutions. Evaluation phase is divided into two steps "blinded" (first evaluation of case) and "unblinded" (evaluation after taking consideration of other readers) reads. Same process occur in both steps: a radiologist should detect all possible nodules in a CT scan and provide information about the structure of nodules. A suspicious region that has size smaller than 3mm is also marked as suspicious but not evaluated. After "blinded" reading session is finished, all information of different institutions are gathered and distributed again. Thus, each radiologist considered the evaluation of other radiologists and then updated his/her decisions. Only the unblinded reading phase results are added to the database. Each case folder contains DICOM images of the related CT scans and an XML file contains nodule characteristics and marked nodule areas of each reading session. Nodule characteristics are calcification, lobulation, subtlety, sphericity, internal structure, spiculation, margin, texture, and malignancy. Each of them were rated 1 to 5(or 6) by radiologists. Final LIDC database contains 1010 cases and information about all nodule matches of different radiologists that are available at wiki site [17]. All cases in LIDC dataset are used in this study.

2.2   Feature Set

We calculate a set of 155 features for each nodule sample. There are shape, size, and texture features by type and; some features are extracted from largest nodule slice, some from all nodule slices and nodules surrounding structures (found by dilating nodule area by six pixel diameter disk structure element). High and low degree Zernike moments are obtained from the largest nodule area. Eccentricity, solidity, circularity, aspect ratio, area of bounding box, standard deviation, and Haralick features are extracted from the largest area of a nodule, average of all nodule slices, and nodule surrounding areas.

2.3   Preprocessing

Individual datasets, which at least three radiologists agreed on ratings, are created for each nodule characteristic. All agreed samples are included without modification. This provides us separate datasets for each nodule characteristic with different amount of nodules. Let S_{chr} be such a set where chr is a nodule characteristic. General description of LIDC nodule dataset S can be given as in (1). In the equation, m is the extracted features(x) and y is the rating for c characteristic.

$$S_{chr} \subset (S = \{x_1, ..., x_m, y_1, ... y_c\}^{1..n} \in \mathbb{R}^m) \tag{1}$$

In characteristic datasets, some samples have missing values in consequence of small nodule size. Sometimes values could not be obtained because of the assumptions in feature extraction methods. We use k-nearest neighbor imputation [14] method to complete missing values.

Most nodule characteristic datasets are highly unbalanced. For example, more than 70% of all nodules are marked 5 in subtlety dataset. Similar situation is also observed in the other nodule characteristic datasets. To get rid of inadequate expression of small sample class problem, balancing methods are applied before each training step.

Data are oversampled with Synthetic Minority Over-sampling Technique (SMOTE) [13], if a rating value is below 10% of dataset size. SMOTE method artificially generates synthetic samples, rather than by over-sampling with replacement. Depending on the amount of over-sampling required, minority class is over-sampled by taking each minority class sample of k-nearest neighbors.

Similarly, if a rating is above thirty percent of dataset size, data are under sampled by class-specific feature space convex hull points approach. Barber et al. [18] have described convex hull as "a set of points is the smallest convex set that contains the points". These points are n dimensional feature values for characteristic datasets. Nodules that have feature values on the convex hull are chosen for under sampling dataset, others are discarded. Qhull algorithm is used for finding convex hull points [18]. We also benefited from convex hull points in ensemble classifier voting phase.

2.4   Ensemble Classifier

For each rating of each nodule characteristic, a separate classifier is trained. Thus, training datasets are built for each rating of each nodule characteristic. For example, five training datasets are created for rating values of subtlety characteristic. In each classifier, each rating value and other rating values (all remaining classes) are considered as two separate classes. In this way, we built 5 classifiers corresponding to 5 rating values of subtlety characteristic.

We applied a feature selection procedure for each class of nodule characteristics. Relieff [11] method is applied for feature selection and the most important six features are selected. Number of selected features can be changed arbitrarily, or defined according to performance requirements. Selected features are intended to facilitate class discrimination especially on underexpressed classes. Furthermore, this procedure decreases computational cost of ensemble classifiers and the convex hull algorithm used in the second step of classification.

After feature selection, 2-class Support Vector Machine [12] classifiers are trained with rebalanced datasets for each rating. When a test sample is given to these separate classifiers, relevant rating vote is increased by one if the sample belongs to a class. In this study, all classifiers are assumed to be having the same weight.

Kodell et al. [15] and Nalbantov et al. [16] showed that using convex hull points can contribute classification performance. After classification with SVM classifiers, convex hull points are determined for each rating of each nodule characteristic. If a rating is undersampled in the preprocessing step, the convex hull is not calculated again. Training samples are checked if they fall in the convex hull area. If a sample is in this area, rating vote is increased by one. After applying ensemble classifiers, a final vote matrix for each nodule sample is obtained as in Table 1.

Table 1. A vote matrix for a nodule sample with votes for each characteristic

Ratings (1-6)	(1)	(2)	(3)	(4)	(5)	(6)
Subtlety	1	1	0	0	2	-
Calcification	0	0	1	0	1	2
Sphericity	0	1	1	0	0	-
Margin	1	1	1	1	0	-
Lobulation	1	1	1	1	1	-
Spiculation	0	1	1	1	1	-
Texture	1	2	1	1	2	-

2.5 Fuzzy Inference

Subsequent to voting phase, a rule based fuzzy inference system is built to predict malignancy rating of nodules. Fuzzy inference is defined as "process of formulating the mapping from a given input to an output using fuzzy logic". Our fuzzy inference system uses a rule set and a malignancy dataset as inputs. Using the rating values of radiologists on nodule characteristics, a rule set for malignancy is generated. A sample rule set is shown in Table 2. In the rule set, the nodules that at least three radiologists agreed on malignancy values are included.

Table 2. Sample rule table for malignancy with nodule characteristics

Sub.	Cal.	Sph.	Mar.	Lob.	Spi.	Tex.	Mal.
5	3	4	5	2	1	5	1
5	3	5	5	1	1	5	1
5	6	4	2	4	5	5	5
....							
4	6	4	5	1	1	5	3
4	6	5	5	1	1	5	3
4	6	4	4	2	2	5	4

Additionally, for the nodules in the malignancy dataset, image features are calculated and stored. In the testing experiments, these features are used as input to the ensemble classifiers. Then, using votes produced by ensemble classifiers, the fuzzy inference system calculates a value for each rule in the rule set according to Eq. 2.

$$P(j) = \{\Sigma_{i=1}^{7} V(i, R(j, i)), mr(j)\} \tag{2}$$

In Eq. 2, V is a 7x6 voting matrix, where each row represents a vote vector for a nodule characteristic as given Table 1. R is the r x 7 rule table, where j is the rule number in R. Thus, $R(j, i)$ represents the value of ith characteristic in j^{th} rule. $P(j)$ holds the value calculated as in Eq. 2 and the malignancy rating (mr) of jth rule. After calculating $P(j)$ values for all rules, P vector is sorted in descending order and the malignancy value that mostly occurs in the first N rule is considered correct. N is an arbitrary number, which is set to 50 in our system.

3   Results

3.1   Ensemble Classifier Results

Single classifiers on highly unbalanced datasets usually produce poor results on underexpressed classes. Exemplarily, subtlety characteristic's confusion matrix of single SVM classifier is shown in Table 3. For rating 1 and 2, sample sizes are lower than 1% of all data. For the dominant rating 5, this ratio is over 70%. As it can be observed from Table 3, misclassification ratios of underexpressed classes by single classifier are eminent.

Therefore, ensemble classifiers are used for voting mechanism of *eFis*. Ensemble classifiers produce a vector result instead of a single classification result for each nodule characteristic. This vector voting mechanism increases representation of underexpressed ratings. In Table 4, the highest votes for subtlety characteristics are shown. Bold values on the diagonal are the highest votes achieved by the related rating. Other values on the table represent the votes that are different from the true rating. We call this situation an ambiguity. For example, in Table 1, subtlety ensemble produces 2 votes for rating 5, which is the highest vote. However, lobulation ensemble gives 1 for all ratings. This is a highly ambiguous result for a classification phase. Thus lobulation characteristic has no distinctive effect for predicting malignancy, but subtlety, calcification, and texture have more distinctive values for the sample in Table 1.

Table 3. Confusion matrix of subtlety for a 5-class SVM

	1	2	3	4	5	Sample Size	Sample Ratio
1	**0**	0	9	1	5	15	<0,01
2	0	**0**	5	4	0	9	<0,01
3	0	0	**60**	64	7	131	~0,09
4	1	0	32	**146**	92	271	~0,19
5	1	0	9	75	**945**	1030	~0,71

Table 4. The highest votes for subtlety ratings for ensemble classifier

	1	2	3	4	5	Sample Size	Sample Ratio
1	**14**	10	2	5	0	15	<0,01
2	6	**9**	1	1	0	9	<0,01
3	42	38	**53**	46	1	131	~0,09
4	111	115	87	**179**	22	271	~0,19
5	395	383	16	125	**793**	1030	~0,71

3.2   Fuzzy Inference System Results

We use leave-one-out procedure for method evaluation. A single sample is chosen from the original malignancy dataset as the validation data and its corresponding rule is removed from the rule set. The rules of remaining samples are used as the training data for the fuzzy inference system. Each sample has a case id and nodule id. Selected sample is also discarded from nodule characteristics datasets, if datasets have a nodule with the same id. The testing procedure is repeated until each sample in the dataset is used once as the validation data.

To find the optimum rule size N in Eq. 2, we tried different rule sizes in experiments. Due to variety in class sample amounts, scale from 10 to 100 is tested. Optimal rule size value in our experiments was around 50-60.

The performance of *eFIS* and other single classifiers are evaluated based on classification accuracy (*CA*) metric. Single classifiers are trained using image features from the malignancy dataset with leave-one-out cross validation method. Malignancy characteristic has 5 ratings: Highly unlikely (1), moderately unlikely (2), indeterminate (3), moderately suspicious (4), and highly suspicious (5). Classification accuracy results using 5 class malignancy rule set are shown in Table 5. We also set up another experiment with grouping malignancy ratings (1,2) as unlikely, 3 as indeterminate and (4,5) as suspicious. As seen in Table 5, classification accuracies of all methods are improved after grouping ratings. Linear discriminant analysis showed the highest performance improvement among single classifiers. However, our method still has the best classification accuracy.

Table 5. Classification accuracy of methods for 5 and 3 ratings

	5 ratings	3 ratings (grouped)
Method	**CA**	**CA**
LDA	0.6610	0.8200
Adaboost	0.7254	0.8135
Naive Bayes	0.7250	0.8100
kNN	0.7665	0.7959
SVM	0.7828	0.8005
eFIS	0.8044	0.8328

4   Conclusion

In this paper we presented eFis, a rule based fuzzy inference method for malignancy prediction on pulmonary nodules. Ensemble classifiers with SVM and convex hull points are built for each nodule characteristics; and used as one of the input for the fuzzy system. Additionally, the fuzzy system takes a rule set extracted from radiologists' annotations on LIDC database as another input. Separate datasets are defined for each nodule characteristic. Since most datasets have imbalanced data, we used dataset balancing and class specific feature selection methods. We have observed that ensemble classifiers and rule based fuzzy inference method is performing better than single classifiers. Grouping malignancy ratings have also improved classification performance. For the future work, we plan to extract new features, use various classification methods, and compare with different performance metrics. Additionally, using feature weights with boosting may improve results and helps us to develop a content based retrieval system based on nodule characteristics.

References

1. Austin, J.H., et al.: Glossary of terms for CT of the lungs: recommendations of the Nomenclature Committee of the Fleischner Society. Radiology **200** (1996)
2. Armato, S.G., et al.: Lung image database consortium: Developing a resource for the medical imaging research community. Radiology **232**, 739–748 (2004)
3. Xu, D.M., et al.: Limited value of shape, margin and CT density in the discrimination between benign and malignant screen detected solid pulmonary nodules of the NELSON trial. European Journal of Radiology **68**(2), 347–352 (2008)
4. Li, Q., Li, F., Shiraishi, J., Katsuragawa, S., Sone, S., Doi, K.: Investigation of new psychophysical measures for evaluation of similar images on thoracic computed tomography for distinction between benign and malignant nodules. Medical Physics **30**(10), 2584–2593 (2003)
5. Horsthemke, W.H., et al.: Predicting LIDC diagnostic characteristics by combining spatial and diagnostic opinions. In: SPIE Medical Imaging. International Society for Optics and Photonics (2010)
6. Giuca, A.M., Seitz, K.A., Furst, J., Raicu, D.: Expanding diagnostically labeled datasets using content-based image retrieval. In: 2012 19th IEEE International Conference on Image Processing (ICIP), pp. 2397–2400. IEEE (2012)
7. Zinovev, D., Raicu, D., Furst, J., Armato, S.G.: Predicting radiological panel opinions using a panel of machine learning classifiers. Algorithms **2**(4), 1473–1502 (2009)
8. Li, G., et al.: Semantic characteristics prediction of pulmonary nodule using Artificial Neural Networks. In: 35th Annual International Conference of the IEEE Engineering in Medicine and Biology Society (EMBC) (2013)
9. Dasovich, G.M., Kim, R., Raicu, D.S., Furst, J.D.: A model for the relationship between semantic and content based similarity using LIDC. In: SPIE Medical Imaging, pp. 762431–762431. International Society for Optics and Photonics (March 2010)
10. Zinovev, D., Furst, J., Raicu, D.: Building an Ensemble of Probabilistic Classifiers for Lung Nodule Interpretation. In: 10th International Conference on Machine Learning and Applications and Workshops (ICMLA), vol. 2, pp. 155–161. IEEE (2011)
11. Sun, Y., Li, J.: Iterative RELIEF for feature weighting. In: Proceedings of the 23rd International Conference on Machine Learning, pp. 913–920. ACM (2006)
12. Cortes, C., Vapnik, V.: Support-vector networks. Machine Learning **20**(3), 273–297 (1995)
13. Chawla, N.V., Bowyer, K.W., Hall, L.O., Kegelmeyer, W.P.: SMOTE: synthetic minority over-sampling technique. arXiv preprint arXiv:1106.1813 (2011)
14. Troyanskaya, O., et al.: Missing value estimation methods for DNA microarrays. Bioinformatics **17**(6), 520–525 (2001)
15. Kodell, R.L., Zhang, C., Siegel, E.R., Nagarajan, R.: Selective voting in convex-hull ensembles improves classification accuracy. Artificial Intelligence in Medicine **54**(3), 171–179 (2012)
16. Nalbantov, G.I., Groenen, P.J., Bioch, J.C.: Nearest convex hull classification (No. EI 2006-50). Erasmus School of Economics (ESE) (2006)
17. The Cancer Imaging Archive Wiki Site: https://wiki.cancerimagingarchive.net/display/Public/Wiki (last access: December 20, 2013)
18. Barber, C.B., Dobkin, D.P., Huhdanpaa, H.: The quickhull algorithm for convex hulls. ACM Transactions on Mathematical Software (TOMS) **22**(4), 469–483 (1996)

Degradation Adaptive Texture Classification: A Case Study in Celiac Disease Diagnosis Brings New Insight

Michael Gadermayr[1]($\boxtimes$), Andreas Uhl[1], and Andreas Vécsei[2]

[1] Department of Computer Sciences, University of Salzburg, Salzburg, Austria
[2] Department of Pediatrics, St. Anna Children's Hospital, Medical University Vienna, Vienna, Austria
mgadermayr@cosy.sbg.ac.at

Abstract. Degradation adaptive texture classification has been claimed to be a powerful instrument for classifying images suffering from degradations of dissimilar extent. The main goal of this framework is to separate the image databases into smaller sets, each showing a high degree of similarity with reference to degradations. Up to now, only scenarios with different types of synthetic degradations have been investigated. In this work we generalize the adaptive classification framework and introduce new degradation measures to extensively analyze the effects of the approach on real world data for the first time. Especially computer aided celiac disease diagnosis based on endoscopic images, which has become a major field of research, is investigated. Due to the weak illuminations and the downsized sensors, the images often suffer from various distortions and the type as well as the strength of these degradations significantly varies over the image data. In a large experimental setup, we show that the average classification accuracies can be improved significantly.

Keywords: Adaptive classification · Endoscopic images · Celiac disease

1 Introduction

The degradation adaptive classification framework [1] has been investigated with reference to "idealistic" degradations. For this purpose, based on the Kylberg texture database [2], the three types of degradations isotropic Gaussian blur, Gaussian white noise and isotropic scale variations have been simulated separately. The authors showed that the approach is able to improve the classification rates (overall classification accuracies), with most configurations. While it is highly interesting that the method works in case of the respective simulated scenarios, the impact in case of real world image degradations is not clear yet.

In this work, a real world classification scenario is investigated with endoscopic images, suffering from various distortions. The final task is to discriminate between images of a healthy person and a person suffering from celiac disease [3–6]. The database shows the following divergences from the previous scenario [1] based on synthetic distortions:

© Springer International Publishing Switzerland 2014
A. Campilho and M. Kamel (Eds.): ICIAR 2014, Part II, LNCS 8815, pp. 263–273, 2014.
DOI: 10.1007/978-3-319-11755-3_30

- The real world image degradations differ from the simulated ones. For example, in the previous work [1] only isotropic scale variations are simulated, but in endoscopy, due to varying viewing angles, anisotropic scale variations, perspective distortions and even non-linear deformations [7] are omnipresent.
- The distortions on average are less significant and furthermore the distribution of the distortion strengths differs (in the preceding paper [1], a uniform distribution is generated).
- In this database, not just one single distortion, but even combinations of distortions are prevalent. In the previous paper [1], three scenarios (one for each degradation type) are considered separately.
- The available training set is significantly smaller (about 300 instead of 10,000 images) which potentially induces very small training subsets in case of adaptive classification.

In previous work [8], the impact of various degradations such as blur and noise on computer aided celiac disease diagnosis has been investigated. The authors showed that especially noise and blur have a major impact on the classification accuracy. Furthermore, the impact of lens distortions as well as distortion correction has been prospected in a large experimental setting [7]. In another study [9], the authors investigate the impact of varying scales with respect to computer aided celiac disease diagnosis.

A concept related to degradation adaptive classification is given by domain adaption [10]. Although the nomenclature suggests a high similarity, in opposite to the approach investigated in our paper, this method has been developed to allow domain shifts between the training and the evaluation dataset. Consequently, domain adaption would be applicable if the type or the extent of the prevalent degradations significantly differs between the training and the evaluation set, which is not the case in our scenario. Due to collisions in nomenclature, we have to mention that the term adaptive classification in the following always refers to degradation adaptive classification.

In this paper, we investigate the impact of adaptive classification on real world image data, which has not been done before. Therefore, seven different similarity (or degradation) measures are deployed. Three of them have already been investigated [1] and have been deployed to capture the three simulated degradations. Four more measures which do not directly address specific degradations are introduced and investigated with respect to the final classification rates. These new measures are implemented as degradation adaptive classification turned out to be advantageous even if no (simulated) degradations are prevalent [1]. Consequently, we suspect that metrics which do not directly measure degradations, but other image properties, could be powerful as well. Furthermore, we extend the adaptive classification framework, to additionally investigate multi-dimensional similarity measures. This potentially is useful as we have to cope with multiple degradations in one database. Finally, the results are extensively analyzed in order to understand, how the adaptive classification works.

This paper is structured as follows: In Sect. 2, the distortion adaptive classification framework is explained and extended to a multidimensional adaptive classification framework and the degradation measures are described. In Sect. 3, the experimental results are presented and discussed. Section 4 finally concludes this paper.

2   Degradation Adaptive Classification

In recent work [1], we showed that an absolutely robust feature is harder to achieve than a relatively robust one. Relative robustness in this context means that the classification accuracy does not decrease strongly if all images in a database (i.e. all images in the training and the evaluation set) similarly suffer from a degradation. In opposite, absolute robustness (or invariance) means that the accuracy can even be maintained if the images in the training and the evaluation set suffer from the same degradation, but with a dissimilar extent. Degradation adaptive classification [1] exploits this knowledge by dividing a dataset into several smaller datasets with similar properties with respect to degradation type and severity. Thereby absolute robustness becomes less decisive.

Based on a normalized degradation measure $D : \Omega \rightarrow [0,1)$ (Ω is the image domain) the original training set $T \subset \Omega$, is divided into the subsets

$$T_i = \{I \in T : d \leq D(I) \cdot C - i < d + 1\}. \tag{1}$$

where $i \in \{0, 1, ..., C - 1\}$, C denotes the cardinality of the set of generated subsets and d defines the overlap.

In a similar manner, the evaluation set $E \subset \Omega$ is partitioned into the subsets

$$E_i = \{I \in E : 0 \leq D'(I) \cdot C - i < 1\}, \tag{2}$$

where $D'(I) = \max(\min(D(I), 1 - \epsilon), 0)$ and ϵ is a small constant, to ensure that each sample belongs to exactly one evaluation subset. Finally for each i, the evaluation set E_i is classified by the discriminant generated by T_i.

This methodology could also be interpreted in terms of a classifier selection system [11]. Classifier selection is done by means of a degradation measure, based on all images in the training set. The decision of this selection defines one specific classifier (which is based on a specific training set) to compute the final decision.

A subdivision using soft-assignment clustering (e.g. kmeans) instead of the linear intervals which has been also considered, did not lead to improved results.

2.1   Multidimensional Adaptive Classification

The degradation adaptive classification framework allows the use of one-dimensional degradation measures ($D : \Omega \rightarrow [0,1)$). In order allow the usage of measures of an arbitrary dimensionality n ($D : \Omega \rightarrow [0,1)^n$), the definition has to be slightly adapted. The training set has to be divided into the subsets

$$T_{i_1,...,i_n} = \{I \in T : \bigwedge_{j=1}^{n} d_j \leq \pi_j(D(I)) \cdot C_j - i_j < d_j + 1\}. \tag{3}$$

where $i_j \in \{0, 1, ..., C_j - 1\}$, C_j denotes the cardinality of the set of generated subsets for each dimension and d_j defines the overlap for each dimension separately. The projection π_j selects the jth element of an n-tupel. In the experiments, for each j, C_j is set to the same value (C) and the same is done for d_j, in order to limit the search space.

In a similar manner, the evaluation set E is partitioned into the subsets

$$E_{i_1,...,i_n} = \{I \in E : \bigwedge_{j=1}^{n} 0 \leq \pi_j(D'(I)) \cdot C_j - i_j < 1\}. \tag{4}$$

Finally for each n-tupel $(i_1, ..., i_n)$, the evaluation set $E_{i_1,...,i_n}$ is classified by the discriminant generated by $T_{i_1,...,i_n}$.

2.2 Similarity Measures

In order to divide a dataset into several smaller ones with higher similarities (and/or similar degradations), a normalized metric D to capture this similarity or degradation is required. In this work we focus on the following metrics which are furthermore min-max normalized to the interval $[0, 1)$:

- Noise Metric (D_n): Noise being prevalent in images can be measured by computing the total pixelwise sum of the absolute difference between an image and the Gaussian filtered $(\sigma = 1)$ version of this image.
- Blur Metric (D_b): In oder to measure blur, the metric which has been introduced in [12] is deployed. After identifying the edges in the horizontal direction by extracting all local minima and maxima for each row, the ratio between the overall lengths and the magnitudes of these edges are computed indicating the blur level.
- Scale Metric (D_s): For estimation the texture scale, the scale-space method introduced in [13] is utilized. The global scale of an image is estimated by first constructing a scale space by convolving an image with Laplacian-of-Gaussians (LoG) in varying scales. As proposed in [13], for the LoGs, the scales $\sigma = \hat{c}\sqrt{2}^k, k \in \{-4, -3.75, ..., 7.75, 8\}$ are chosen with $\hat{c} = 2.1214$. The scales for each pixel are obtained by using the index of the highest filter responses. The final global scale of an image is estimated by computing the histogram of this scale values over all pixels, followed by a Gauss-fitting.
- Mean Metric (D_m): This measure captures the average overall gray value. The intention is to separate properly illuminated images from weakly illuminated ones which usually show more noise in combination with a lack of contrast.
- Contrast Metric (D_{c_*}): Contrast is not only able to measure degradations, but it is already able to discriminate between healthy and diseased patients. Although it seems to work in a different way, we would like to investigate the effect of such a discriminating metric on the adaptive classification framework. For that, the three contrast neighborhood sizes of two (D_{cS}), four (D_{cM}) and six pixels (D_{cL}) are utilized.
- Two-dimensional Metric Combinations: Finally we combine the most appropriate measure D_{cL} (i.e. the measure corresponding to the highest accuracies on average in Sect. 3), with the second $(D_{cM:cL})$, the third $(D_{cS:cL})$ and the

fourth placed measure ($D_{b:c_L}$) utilizing the multidimensional adaptive classification framework.

3 Experiments

3.1 Experimental Setup

The image testsets utilized for the experiments contain images of the duodenal bulb and the pars descendens taken during duodenoscopies at the St. Anna Children's Hospital using pediatric gastroscopes (Olympus GIF N180 and Q165). In a preprocessing step, texture patches with a fixed size of 128×128 pixels have been manually extracted. The size turned out to be suitable in earlier experiments [5]. Prior to feature extraction, all patches are converted to gray scale images. In Fig. 1 example texture patches are shown.

To get the ground truth for the texture patches, the condition of the mucosal areas covered by the images has been determined by histological examination of biopsies from corresponding regions. The severity of the villous atrophy has been classified according to the modified Marsh classification [14]. Although it is possible to distinguish between different stages of the disease, we aim in distinguishing between images of patients with (Marsh-3) and without the disease (Marsh-0), as this two classes case is most relevant in practice. Our experiments are based on a training and an evaluation dataset containing 300 (151 Marsh-0 and 149 Marsh-3) and 312 (155 Marsh-0 and 157 Marsh-3) images, respectively.

After defining nine sensible subset counts ($C \in \{1, 5, 9, 13, 17, 21, 25, 29, 33\}$) as well as six sensible overlaps ($d \in \{0, 2, 4, 6, 8, 10\} \cdot 10^{-2}$), training and evaluation sets for all combinations (C, d) are generated, the classifiers are trained and the decisions for each evaluation set are processed. Finally, the most appropriate configuration is predicted in a leave-one-patient-out cross validation. The experiment is repeated with reversed training and evaluation set and the mean rates, featuring a higher reliability, are finally utilized.

To extensively study the effect of the proposed approach on the overall classification accuracy, eight different feature extraction techniques which turned out to be appropriate for celiac disease classification are investigated. The chosen parameters turned out to be optimally suited in earlier experiments.

- Graylevel Contrast (CON) [15]: This feature vector consists of the Haralick feature contrast [15] computed from the gray level co-occurrence matrices with different offset vectors $(0, c)^T$, $(c, 0)^T$ and $(c, c)^T$. For the experiments c is fixed to four pixels.

Fig. 1. Example image patches of healthy patients (left) clearly showing the villi structure and patches of diseased patients (right) suffering from villous atrophy. It can be seen that the discrimination in some cases is quite difficult.

- Edge Co-occurrence Matrix (ECM) [16]: After applying eight differently orientated directional filters, the orientation is determined individually for each pixel, followed by masking out pixels with a low gradient magnitude (75% below the maximum response). Then the methodology of the gray-level co-occurrence matrix is applied to obtain the ECM for one specific displacement (two pixels in our experiments).
- Local Binary Patterns (LBP) [17]: LBP describes a texture by computing the joint distribution of binarized pixel intensity differences represented by binary patterns. We deploy the uniform LBP version, capturing only patterns with at most two bitwise transitions, in combination with eight circular samples and a radius of two pixels.
- Extended Local Binary Patterns (ELBP) [18]: ELBP is an edge based derivative of Local Binary Patterns. As LBP it is used with eight neighbors and a radius of two pixels.
- Fourier Power Spectrum Features (FF) [19]: To get this descriptor, first the Fourier power spectra of the patches are computed in a way that the low frequencies are located in the center. After that, rings with a fixed inner and outer radius are extracted and the medians of these values are calculated. For our experiments we use one single ring with an inner radius of seven and an outer radius of eight pixels.
- Shape Curvature Histogram (SCH) [20]: SCH is a shape feature especially developed for computer aided celiac disease diagnosis. A histogram collects the occurrences of the contour curvature magnitudes. The proposed histogram bin count of eight is used in our experiments.
- Histogram of Gradients (HOG) [21]: Similar to SCH, this well known feature computes the distribution of gradient orientations to describe a texture. The standard bin count of nine is used, which corresponds to an angular resolution of 20 degrees.
- Random Feature (RDF): Finally we investigate a random feature, which returns a random value between zero and one, independently from the input signal. Although this feature is not useful in practical scenarios, it helps us to understand the behavior of adaptive classification.

As it could have been shown [1] that the classifier has a significant impact on the effectiveness of the adaptive classification approach, we deploy three very different classifiers consisting of the (highly non-linear) nearest neighbor classifier (NNC), a linear (Bayes normal) classifier (LDC) [22] as well as a support vector classifier (SVC) [22] which is based on a polynomial kernel. To evaluate if an improvement is significant, McNemar's test [23] ($\alpha = 0.01$) is deployed.

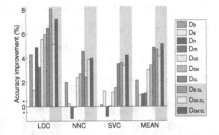

Fig. 2. Average classification accuracies achieved with the three classifiers. Improvements or aggravations exceeding the asterisk symbol (*) are significant.

3.2   Experimental Results

First of all, in order to identify the most appropriate similarity measure, in Fig. 2 the accuracy increases (and decreases) for all features are averaged separately for each mode and each classifier. Additionally the mean over the three classifiers is given which shows that the most appropriate measures on average are given by D_{c_L} (followed by D_{c_M}, D_{c_S} and D_b considering one dimensional measures) and $D_{c_M:c_L}$ (which is the overall best measure). The scale based D_s and the noise based D_n correspond to the lowest average improvements. Obviously scale and noise differences do not deeply affect the traditional classification, compared to the simulated scenario [1] which showed significant accuracy increases using these measures. For this experiment, the random RDF feature is not considered, as it is not relevant in practice. It can be observed that the two-dimensional features which are highlighted by the gray background, do not significantly outperform the one-dimensional D_{c_L}. This behavior is supposed to be due to the limited dataset sizes as especially a large C in case of two dimensions causes extremely small training sets.

Furthermore, it can be seen that the LDC classifier on average profits more significantly than the NNC and the SVC classifiers from the new framework. Such a behavior has already been reported and discussed in recent work [1]. In another study [13] which investigates the impact of classifying images of varying scales the nearest neighbor classifier is analyzed extensively. Considering for each subject in the evaluation set only the corresponding training subject with the smallest distance, the NNC classifier induces a highly non-linear decision boundary. The authors have shown, that this classifier is able to most likely ("implicitly") choose a similarly degraded corresponding subject as nearest neighbor. The achieved accuracy benefit with this classifier on average is supposed to be smaller as adaptive classification also aims in grouping similarly degraded data. In opposite to the NNC classifier, the LDC classifier has to cope with a linear decision boundary and is not able to simply "ignore" subjects with a larger distance. The SVC classifier is investigated as it is widely used in practice and furthermore represents an intermediate method. Finally we notice that, although

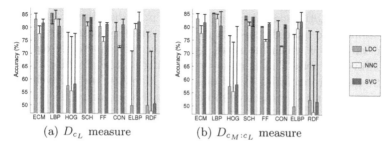

(a) D_{c_L} measure   (b) $D_{c_M:c_L}$ measure

Fig. 3. This figure shows the obtained performances in combination with the two similarity measures. The bars indicate the rates achieved with traditional and the horizontal lines indicate the accuracies obtained with adaptive classification.

the LDC classifier corresponds to the highest average improvements, consistent improvements are also achieved with the classifers NNC and SVC in our experiments. These two methods seem to profit similarly from adaptive classification.

In the following we only consider the measures corresponding to the lowest error rates D_{c_L} (as best one-dimensional measure) and $D_{c_L:c_M}$ (as best overall measure). In Fig. 3, the accuracies are given separately for each feature and each classifier.

Using the D_{c_L} measure, with all features the highest overall accuracies are achieved utilizing the adaptive classification framework. Using the two-dimensional measure $D_{c_M:c_L}$, with all features but SCH the best accuracies are obtained. Altogether, 39 improvements face eight aggravations. The two-dimensional measure corresponds to the highest average improvement, however, the higher continuity (i.e. the number of improvements) is achieved with the one-dimensional measure.

3.3   Discussion

A quite interesting behavior is seen with HOG and the random feature RDF. Although in case of traditional classification with all classifiers the accuracies are very low with HOG and as expected around 50 % with RDF, with the adaptive classification framework, with both features, rates above 75 % can be achieved. Considering the increased accuracies of HOG with adaptive classification, the reader could think that the feature benefits because it is not absolutely robust but quite relatively robust to the distortions prevalent in the database. However, we observe a similar behavior with RDF which does not provide any discriminative power and therefore absolute and relative robustness of this feature do not play any role.

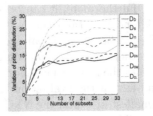

Fig. 4. Variations of prior probabilities

Inspired by these results, we identified another effect of the adaptive classification framework on the database. Whereas in the original dataset the classes are distributed approximately equally, by grouping the training and evaluation set images using adaptive classification this equal prior distribution is not necessarily maintained. To quantify this behavior, in a small experiment we compute an average variance v which measures the distance to a perfectly equal prior distribution over all sets. This is done by summing up the absolute differences between the prior probabilities P_{T_i} of one class (Marsh-0) and 0.5 weighted by the ratio of images in the respective subset, for each training set T_i:

$$v(C) = \sum_{i=0}^{C-1} |P_{T_i}(X = \text{Marsh-0}) - 0.5| \cdot \frac{\#T_i}{\#T} . \tag{5}$$

For the introduced one-dimensional similarity measures and varying numbers of subsets C (horizontal axis), these values are presented in Fig 4. We notice that the prior distribution definitely varies in case of adaptive classification and as expected the variation raises with an increasing number of subsets. Moreover, we observe that the most effective measures (D_{c_L} and D_{c_M}) as far as the accuracy improvement is concerned correspond with the highest variations. This analysis shows that adaptive classification not only divides a database into smaller sets with similar properties, but furthermore changes the prior distributions considerably. This definitely has a positive impact in case of the RDF feature. However, this mechanism is supposed to potentially increase the classification performances in case of all features, especially in combination with the D_{c_*} similarity measures which do not directly capture any degradation but rater act as discriminative features.

4 Conclusion

We have investigated the effect of degradation adaptive classification on a real world classification problem. To additionally analyze two-dimensional degradation measures, the framework has been generalized. Finally the best improvements on average are achieved with the contrast based one-dimensional D_{c_L} and the two-dimensional $D_{c_M:c_L}$ measure. Except for one feature (SCH), the accuracies can be continuously (i.e. in case of both measures) improved. The average increase of the accuracy is 5.2 % ($D_{c_M:c_L}$) and 4.9 % (D_{c_L}), respectively. However, in the studied scenario the introduction of multidimensional measures did not lead to significant improvement compared to one-dimensional ones. In previous work, the authors found out that the framework improves accuracies especially in case of a large range of degradation strengths by separating the original dataset in similarly degraded smaller datasets. We have shown that adaptive classification furthermore improves the classification performance, especially in case of features with low discriminative powers, by changing the prior distributions within the datasets.

References

1. Gadermayr, M., Uhl, A.: Degradation adaptive texture classification. In: IEEE International Conference on Image Processing 2014 (ICIP 2014) (October 2014) (accepted)
2. Kylberg, G.: The kylberg texture dataset v. 1.0. Technical Report 35, Centre for Image Analysis, Swedish University of Agricultural Sciences and Uppsala University, Sweden (2011)
3. Ciaccio, E.J., Tennyson, C.A., Lewis, S.K., Krishnareddy, S., Bhagat, G., Green, P.: Distinguishing patients with celiac disease by quantitative analysis of videocapsule endoscopy images. Comp. Methods and Prog. in Biomedicine **100**(1), 39–48 (2010)
4. Ciaccio, E.J., Tennyson, C.A., Bhagat, G., Lewis, S.K., Green, P.H.R.: Classification of videocapsule endoscopy image patterns: comparative analysis between patients with celiac disease and normal individuals. BioMedical Engineering Online **9**(1), 1–12 (2010)

5. Vécsei, A., Amann, G., Hegenbart, S., Liedlgruber, M., Uhl, A.: Automated marsh-like classification of celiac disease in children using an optimized local texture operator. Computers in Biology and Medicine **41**(6), 313–325 (2011)
6. Hegenbart, S., Uhl, A., Vécsei, A., Wimmer, G.: Scale invariant texture descriptors for classifying celiac disease. Medical Image Analysis **17**(4), 458–474 (2013)
7. Gadermayr, M., Liedlgruber, M., Uhl, A., Vécsei, A.: Evaluation of different distortion correction methods and interpolation techniques for an automated classification of celiac disease. Computer Methods and Programs in Biomedicine **112**(3), 694–712 (2013)
8. Hegenbart, S., Uhl, A., Vécsei, A.: Impact of endoscopic image degradations on lbp based features using one-class svm for classification of celiac disease. In: Proceedings of the 7th International Symposium on Image and Signal Processing and Analysis (ISPA 2011), pp. 715–720 (2011)
9. Hegenbart, S., Uhl, A., Vécsei, A.: On the implicit handling of varying distances and gastrointestinal regions in endoscopic video sequences with indication for celiac disease. In: Proceedings of the IEEE International Symposium on Computer-Based Medical Systems (CBMS 2012), pp. 1–6 (2012)
10. Saenko, K., Kulis, B., Fritz, M., Darrell, T.: Adapting visual category models to new domains. In: Daniilidis, K., Maragos, P., Paragios, N. (eds.) ECCV 2010, Part IV. LNCS, vol. 6314, pp. 213–226. Springer, Heidelberg (2010)
11. Giacinto, G., Roli, F.: Methods for dynamic classifier selection. In: Proceedings of the Intern. Conf. on Image Analysis and Processing (ICIAP 1999), pp. 659–664 (1999)
12. Marziliano, P., Dufaux, F., Winkler, S., Ebrahimi, T., Sa, G.: A no-reference perceptual blur metric. In: IEEE International Conference on Image Processing (ICIP 2002), pp. 57–60 (2002)
13. Gadermayr, M., Hegenbart, S., Uhl, A.: Scale-adaptive texture classification. In: Proceedings of 22nd International Conference on Pattern Recognition (ICPR 2014) (August 2014) (accepted)
14. Oberhuber, G., Granditsch, G., Vogelsang, H.: The histopathology of coeliac disease: time for a standardized report scheme for pathologists. European Journal of Gastroenterology and Hepatology **11**, 1185–1194 (1999)
15. Haralick, R.M., Dinstein, I., Shanmugam, K.: Textural features for image classification. IEEE Transactions on Systems, Man, and Cybernetics **3**, 610–621 (1973)
16. Rautkorpi, R., Iivarinen, J.: A novel shape feature for image classification and retrieval. In: Campilho, A.C., Kamel, M.S. (eds.) ICIAR 2004. LNCS, vol. 3211, pp. 753–760. Springer, Heidelberg (2004)
17. Ojala, T., Pietikäinen, M., Harwood, D.: A comparative study of texture measures with classification based on feature distributions. Pattern Recognition **29**(1), 51–59 (1996)
18. Liao, S.C., Zhu, X.X., Lei, Z., Zhang, L., Li, S.Z.: Learning multi-scale block local binary patterns for face recognition. In: Lee, S.-W., Li, S.Z. (eds.) ICB 2007. LNCS, vol. 4642, pp. 828–837. Springer, Heidelberg (2007)
19. Gadermayr, M., Uhl, A., Vécsei, A.: Barrel-type distortion compensated fourier feature extraction. In: Bebis, G., Boyle, R., Parvin, B., Koracin, D., Li, B., Porikli, F., Zordan, V., Klosowski, J., Coquillart, S., Luo, X., Chen, M., Gotz, D. (eds.) ISVC 2013, Part I. LNCS, vol. 8033, pp. 50–59. Springer, Heidelberg (2013)
20. Gadermayr, M., Liedlgruber, M., Uhl, A., Vécsei, A.: Shape curvature histogram: A shape feature for celiac disease diagnosis. In: Menze, B., Langs, G., Montillo, A., Kelm, M., Müller, H., Tu, Z. (eds.) MCV 2013. LNCS, vol. 8331, pp. 175–184. Springer, Heidelberg (2014)

21. Dalal, N., Triggs, B.: Histograms of oriented gradients for human detection. In: Proceedings of the IEEE Conference on Computer Vision and Pattern Recognition (CVPR 2005), pp. 886–893 (2005)
22. Duin, R., Juszczak, P., Paclík, P., Pekalska, E., de Ridder, D., Tax, D., Verzakov, S.: PR-Tools4.1, a matlab toolbox for pattern recognition (2007)
23. McNemar, Q.: Note on the sampling error of the difference between correlated proportions of percentages. Psychometrika $12(2)$, 153–157 (1947)

Retinal Image Analysis

Optic Disk Localization for Gray-Scale Retinal Images Based on Patch Filtering

F. Sattar[1]([⊠]), Aurélio Campilho[2], and M. Kamel[3]

[1] Toronto Rehabilitation Institute, University of Toronto, Toronto, ON, Canada
fsattar@uwaterloo.ca
[2] INESC Technology and Science and the Faculdade de Engenharia,
Universidade do Porto, Porto, Portugal
[3] Department of Electrical and Computer Engineering, University of Waterloo,
Waterloo, ON, Canada

Abstract. In this paper, an optic disk (OD) localization method is proposed for the retinal images based on a novel patch filtering approach. The patch filtering has been performed sequentially based on clustering in two stages. In the first stage, the patches are selected exploiting an 'isotropic' measure based on the ratio of maximum and minimum eigenvalues of the moment matrix representing the structure tensor. In the second stage, the patch filtering is based on the saliency measure. Finally, the optic disk is located from the centroids of the selected patches. Promising results are obtained for the low-contrast pathological retinal images using STARE database providing high localization accuracy.

Keywords: Optic disk localization · Patch filtering · Retinal image

1 Introduction

The localization of optic disc (OD) is necessary to analyse the OD, such as in glaucoma characterization as well as finding a reference location for other measures, such as AVR (arteriolar-to-venular diameter ratio). OD usually looks like bright, yellowish with circular/slightly oval shaped for a normal retinal image [1,2]. The symptom of various retinopathies particularly for glaucoma causes the changes in the structure of OD [3], [4]; that is why, the shape of OD is often used to qualify the abnormal retinal features [5]. According to the geometric relationships between the location of OD and the vascular structure, the fovea (central macula) can be roughly located [6]. Moreover, as the retinal blood vessels radiate from the OD, the location of OD can also be used as a beginning point for vessels tracking [7]. It is evident that precise OD localization improves the segmentation of the exudates regions [8].

Diabetic retinopathy is a chronic disease which is the primary cause of blindness [9],[10],[11],[12]. For the computer assisted-diagnosis of several diabetic retinopathies, it is necessary to evaluate several eye fundus image features.

© Springer International Publishing Switzerland 2014
A. Campilho and M. Kamel (Eds.): ICIAR 2014, Part II, LNCS 8815, pp. 277–284, 2014.
DOI: 10.1007/978-3-319-11755-3_31

Among these features, the location of the optic disk is very important because it is indirectly used to quantify retina lesions (i.e., the levels of severity of the retina lesion), and to help detecting other retinal structures, like the fovea (i.e. the macula center).

In [13], the proposed OD localization method separates first a circular ROI (region of interest) with the brightest area of the image by morphological operations, followed by detecting the main circular feature (corresponding to the OD) using Hough transform within the ROI and assumes the circular-shaped OD relating to the normal retinal image. The recent work proposed in [14] on OD localization is based on color (RGB) retinal images, by combining information extracted from the vascular network using the intensity data from the red (R) and green (G) channels. The OD is located based on the distribution and variability of vessels around each image point which are estimated based on the entropy along vascular directions.

In this paper, we present an automated method for locating the OD in the gray-scale pathological retinal image. We propose a new patch filtering approach based on two-stage clustering by exploiting the isotropic and saliency measures of the patch images. Promising performance has been achieved in relying solely on the information of the gray-scale image and outperforms the results obtained by the baseline method [15], where the image is processed first by an averaging mask of size (31 × 31) followed by detecting the maximum gray values of the image histogram based on the assumption that the gray values of OD are brighter than the background values.

2   The Proposed Method

The proposed OD localization method is based on a new idea of patch filtering on retinal image. The main concept is to extract the local structural/spectral information followed by locating the object (i.e., OD) by filtering out the patches based on saliency measures. To extract the structural information, a sequence of isotropic measures is formed which is then mapped into a functional data representing a distribution of spectral energies over the patches. Then the OD is located by further separating the patches based on the saliency measures. The flow diagram of the proposed OD localization scheme and the corresponding inputs/outputs for illustration, are shown in Fig. 1. First, an input gray-scale retinal image is divided into N small spatial regions, called patches. Each patch is then described by the proposed isotropic measure followed by saliency measure for patch filtering in the following two stages (stage 1 and stage 2) to locate the optic disk as follows.

2.1   Stage 1: Patch Filtering Based on the Isotropic Measure

Step 1: The input patch image $I_p(x,y), p = 1, \cdots, N$ is first convolved with the log-Gabor wavelets $\psi_{j,k}(x,y)$ along $K(k = 1, \cdots, K)$ directions and $S(s = 1, \cdots, S)$ number of scales, i.e.,

$$W_{j,k}(x,y) = I_p(x,y) * \psi_{j,k}(x,y) \tag{1}$$

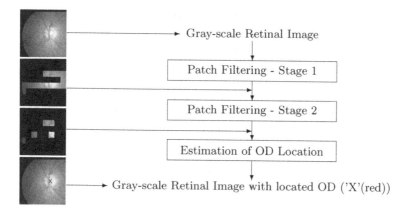

Fig. 1. The overall flow diagram of the proposed optic disk (OD) localization scheme (right panel) and the illustrative inputs/outputs (left panel)

where '*' denotes the 2D-convolution and $W_{j,k}(x,y)$ represents the log-Gabor WT(wavelet transform) coefficients at scale j and orientation k.

Step 2: The second-order moment matrix at each point (x, y) is calculated as follows (we ignore the position (x, y) for simplicity):

$$M = \begin{bmatrix} J_{11} & J_{12} \\ J_{21} & J_{22} \end{bmatrix} \tag{2}$$

where

$$J_{11} = \sum_j \sum_k (W_{j,k} \cos(\theta_k))^2$$
$$J_{12} = J_{21} = \sum_j \sum_k |W_{j,k}| \cos(\theta_k) W_{j,k} \sin(\theta_k)$$
$$J_{22} = \sum_j \sum_k (W_{j,k} \sin(\theta_k))^2$$

and θ_k is the angle of the orientation k.
Step 3: The eigenvalues of the moment matrix are

$$\lambda_{1,2} = \frac{1}{2} \left(J_{11} + J_{22} \pm \sqrt{(J_{11} - J_{22})^2 + 4J_{12}^2} \right) \tag{3}$$

Step 4: The ratio of the eigenvalues, i.e., $R = \frac{\lambda_1}{\lambda_2}$ is calculated. From the geometrical point of view, the moment matrix relates to the structure tensor representing an ellipse whose radii are λ_1, λ_2. In practice, the R value determines the shape of the structure tensor (isotropic or anisotropic) in the principal direction with respect to the horizontal axis. The corresponding mean value $\bar{R}$ is then used for patch filtering.

Then the $\bar{R}$ values of all patches are mapped into a functional data (or descriptor) that is characterized by a distribution of spectral energies across the patches. This is done by the STFT (short-time Fourier transform) analysis followed by integration across the frequency as presented below:

$$X(p,k) = \sum_{m=0}^{N-1} w(m)\bar{R}(p-m)e^{-\frac{2\pi}{N}kp} \tag{4}$$

where $X(p,k)$ and $w(m)$ are the STFT and the analysis window, respectively. In Eq.(4), N are the FFT points whereas p $(1 \leq p \leq N)$ is the patch index and k $(0 \leq p \leq N-1)$ is the frequency index.

$$C(p) = \sum_{k=0}^{N-1} X(p,k) \tag{5}$$

where $C(p)$ is a descriptor representing probabilistic approximation of the spectral energies along the patches. The $C(p)$ is normalized to 1, i.e. 0 dB defined as $C_n(p)(\text{dB}) = 20\log(C(p)/\max(C(p)))$ where $C_n(p)$ is the normalized $C(p)$ with $\max(\cdot)$ denoting the maximum value. The patches with dominating spectral energies are then selected corresponding to the $C_n(p) \in [0,-2]$ dB.

2.2 Stage 2: Patch Filtering Based on the Saliency Measure

In stage 2, the patch filtering has been done by saliency measures, S based on SVD (singular-value-decomposition) approach. Each selected patch image $\mathbf{I}_{sp}$ in stage 1 is firstly decomposed by SVD according to [17].

$$\mathbf{I}_{sp} = \mathbf{U}_{sp}\mathbf{D}_{sp}\mathbf{V}_{sp}^T \tag{6}$$

In Eq. (6), the matrices $\mathbf{U}_{sp}$ and $\mathbf{V}_{sp}$ are unitary, and $\mathbf{D}_{sp}=diag(\sigma_1,\sigma_2,\cdots,\sigma_d)$, is a diagonal matrix containing the singular values $\sigma_1,\sigma_2,\cdots,\sigma_d$ and T denotes the transposition. The saliency measure S is then obtained as:

$$S = \frac{1}{N_p \times M_p} \sum_{i=1}^{N_p}\sum_{j=1}^{M_p}(\mathbf{I}_{sp} - \mu_{sp})\mathbf{D}_{sp}^{-1}(\mathbf{I}_{sp} - \mu_{sp})^T \tag{7}$$

where μ_{sp} is the mean-value of the patch image $\mathbf{I}_{sp}$ with image size $(N_p \times M_p)$. Lastly, P patches are further selected based on the highest saliency values. Note that the saliency measure, which is based on subspace technique, is used here to identify the salient region (e.g. region with OD) from the non-salient region (e.g. region without OD).

2.3 Estimating the OD Location

Here, the (x,y) co-ordinates of the P selected patches are determined based on the maximum intensity. Finally, the centroid of the determined (x,y) co-ordinates gives the estimated location of the optic disk (OD).

3   Experimental Results

The proposed method for OD localization has been evaluated using the images for the publicly available database STARE [16]. This dataset consists of 31 images of normal retinas, and 50 images showing some pathology. Here, we have considered the difficult pathological images for our evaluation and considered the image size of (512 × 512) for simplicity. The input gray-scale retinal images are presented in Fig. 2 showing the examples of swollen optic disk, where the circular shape and size are distorted as well as sometime bright circular lesion that appears similar to OD, are present. In Fig. 2, the results of patch filtering in stage 1 are demonstrated in terms of the selected patches as marked in green boundaries (on screen). Here, the size of the non-overlapping rectangular patches is (64 × 64) which is set empirically. The results of patch selection in stage 2 are displayed in Fig. 3. Here, the five patch images with the highest saliency values are selected. The results of the OD localization are depicted in Fig. 4, where mark 'X'(red) indicates the correctly detected OD location and mark 'X'(blue) indicates the location of OD with false detection. The high localization accuracy is obtained by the proposed method in comparison to the baseline method [15] as demonstrated in Fig. 5. Here, we have chosen the baseline method for comparison because it is based on the gray-scale information without having any assumption that the OD has circular-shape. The performance of the OD localization is tabulated in Table 1 showing high localization accuracy by the proposed method in comparison to the baseline method.

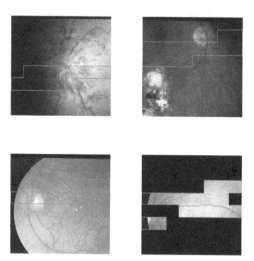

Fig. 2. The illustrative input gray-scale retinal images with pathology and the corresponding outputs of the gray-scale retinal images after patch filtering in stage 1

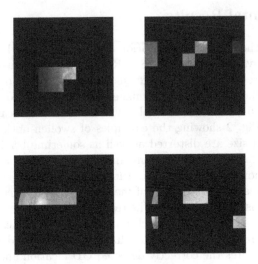

Fig. 3. The corresponding outputs of the gray-scale retinal images after patch filtering in stage 2

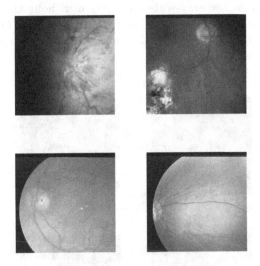

Fig. 4. The illustrative results of the optic disk localization for the gray-scale retinal images by the proposed method ('X'(red): correctly detected OD location

Table 1. Performance results for the OD localization

Method	Total images	Successful locations	False locations	Accuracy(%)
Proposed	50	49	1	98
Baseline	50	20	30	40

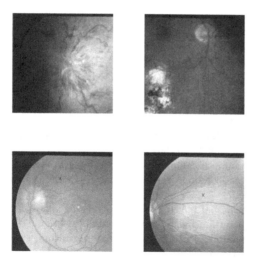

Fig. 5. The illustrative results of the optic disk localization for the gray-scale retinal images using the baseline method ('X'(red): correctly detected OD location; 'X'(blue): falsely detected OD location)

3.1   Discussion

The patch size is chosen is a way such that it would be larger than the size of OD. In stage 1, the threshold parameter is the range of the highest normalized spectral energies, which is chosen to be $[0-2]$ dB considering the fact that prominent spectral energies lie within this range. Also, it is found in stage 2 that the dominant saliency values lie within 4-5 patches. So, we set our threshold to 5 patches in stage 2. Most interestingly, we have achieved promising results by solely exploiting the gray-scale image and its local structural/spectral information without requiring the knowledge of color channel as well as intensity.

4   Conclusion

In this paper, we have proposed an automated OD localization method based on the new idea of patch filtering using isotropic and saliency measures. Unlike other methods, the presented method has only exploited the information of the gray-scale image, while achieved promising performance for the difficult pathological retinal images and outperformed the baseline method. Future work includes more detail evaluation of the proposed method using different types of database under various noisy conditions.

References

1. Hoover, A., Goldbaum, M.: Locating the optic nerve in a retinal image using the fuzzy convergence of the blood vessels. IEEE Trans. on Medical Imaging **22**, 951–958 (2003)

2. Hsiao, H.-K., Liu, C.-C., Yu, C.-Y., Kuo, S.-W., Yu, S.-S.: A novel optic disc detection scheme on retinal images. Expert Systems with Applications **39**(12), 10600–10606 (2012)
3. Li, H., Chutatape, O.: Automated feature extraction in color retinal images by a model based approach. IEEE Trans. on Biomedical Engineering **51**, 246–254 (2004)
4. Welfer, D., Scharcanski, J., Marinho, D.R.: A coarse-to-fine strategy for automatically detecting exudates in color eye fundus images. Comput. Med. Imaging Graphics **34**(3), 228–235 (2010)
5. Xu, C., Prince, J.L.: Snakes, shapes, and gradient vector flow. IEEE Trans. on Image Processing **7**, 359–369 (2007)
6. Tobin, K.W., Chaum, E., Govindasamy, V.P., Karnowski, T.P.: Detection of anatomic structures in human retinal imagery. IEEE Trans. on Medical Imaging **26**, 1729–1739 (2007)
7. Tolias, Y.A., Panas, S.M.: A fuzzy vessel tracking algorithm for retinal images based on fuzzy clustering. IEEE Trans. on Medical Imaging **17**, 263–273 (1998)
8. Osareh, A.: Automated identification of diabetic retinal exudates and the optic disc, Dissertation, University of Bristol (2004)
9. Akita, K., Kuga, H.: A computer method of understanding ocular fundus images. Pattern Recognition **15**, 431–443 (1982)
10. Aquino, A., Gegúndez-Arias, M.E., Marín, D.: Detecting the optic disc boundary in digital fundus images using morphological, edge detection, and feature extraction techniques. IEEE Trans. on Medical Imaging **29**, 1860–1869 (2010)
11. Manivannan, A., Sharp, P.F., Phillips, R.P., Forrester, J.V.: Digital fundus imaging using a scanning laser ophthalmoscope. Physiological Measurement **14**, 43–56 (1993)
12. Taylor, H.R., Keeffe, J.E.: World blindness: A 21st century perspective. British Journal of Ophthalmology **85**, 261–266
13. Sekhar, S., Nuaimy, W.A., Nandi, A.K.: Automated localisation of retinal optic disk using Hough transform. In: IEEE Int. Conf. Medical Imaging (2008)
14. Mendonça, A.M., Sousa, A., Mendonç, L., Campilho, A.: Automatic localization of the optic disc by combining vascular and intensity information. Computerized Medical Imaging and Graphics **37**, 409–417 (2013)
15. Usman Akram, M., Khan, A., Iqbal, K., Butt, W.H.: Retinal images: Optic disk localization and detection. In: Campilho, A., Kamel, M. (eds.) ICIAR 2010, Part II. LNCS, vol. 6112, pp. 40–49. Springer, Heidelberg (2010)
16. The STARE project, http://www.ces.clemson.edu/~ahoover/stare
17. Scharf, L.L.: Statistical signal processing: Detection, estimation, and time series analysis. Addison-Wesley, Reading (1991)

Automatic Optic Disc Detection in Retinal Fundus Images Based on Geometric Features

Isabel N. Figueiredo and Sunil Kumar[✉]

CMUC, Department of Mathematics, University of Coimbra, Coimbra, Portugal
{isabelf,skumar}@mat.uc.pt

Abstract. Regular eye examinations are the key to limiting the vision loss caused by glaucoma and diabetic retinopathy. Optic disc (OD) detection is of vital importance in developing automated diagnosis systems for these diseases. In this work we present a method for automatic localization and boundary detection of the optic disc in retinal fundus images. In the first step, we rely on the OD geometric feature and utilize gaussian and mean curvatures for the localization of the OD. In the second step, we extract a region of interest based on the OD localization. Then, to the edges of this extracted region a circular Hough transform is applied to segment the OD boundary. The experimental results on three public datasets show the efficacy of the proposed method.

Keywords: Optic disc detection · Fundus images · Diabetic retinopathy · Computer-aided techniques

1 Introduction

Fundus images are visual records which document the current ophthalmoscopic appearance of a patient's retina, the retinal vasculature, and the optic nerve head (optic disc) from which the retinal vessels enter the eye. Fundus images are routinely ordered in a wide variety of ophthalmic conditions, such as glaucoma (increased pressure in the eye), diabetic retinopathy (damage to the retina from diabetes), and so on. The optic disc (OD) is considered one of the main component of a retinal fundus image. It often serves as a landmark for other anatomical retinal structures, such as macula [1,2] and retinal blood vessels [2,3]. The OD detection is a very important step in many computer-aided algorithms for finding lesions in retinal fundus images [4,5]. A quantitative understanding of the shape deformation within OD is used for evaluating the progression of glaucoma [6]. Due to these reasons there has been a great interest in automatic detection of the OD in retinal fundus images.

This work was partially supported by the project PTDC/MATNAN/0593/2012, and also by CMUC and FCT (Portugal), through European program COMPETE/FEDER and project PEst-C/MAT/UI0324/2011.

A. Campilho and M. Kamel (Eds.): ICIAR 2014, Part II, LNCS 8815, pp. 285–292, 2014.
DOI: 10.1007/978-3-319-11755-3_32

In normal fundus images the OD corresponds to the brightest region where blood vessels converge. The OD is considered close to a circular or vertically slightly oval shape. Measured relatively to the retinal fundus image, its size may vary significantly and different estimations have been proposed in the literature. According to [1], it occupies about one seventh of the entire image; whereas in [7] it was mentioned that the OD size varies from one person to another, occupying about one tenth to one fifth of the image.

The automatic detection/localization of the OD aims to find the centroid (center point) of the OD. On the other hand, the OD boundary detection aims to segment the OD by detecting the boundary between the retina and the optic nerve head. Recent years have witnessed some OD detection and segmentation techniques in retinal fundus [1,8–12]. A survey of various automatic methods related to diabetic retinopathy can be found in [8]. Sinthanayothin et al. [1] presented a method to locate the OD by detecting the area in the image which has the highest variation in brightness. As the optic disk often appears as a bright disc covered with dark vessels the variance in pixel brightness is the highest there. Hoover et al. [10] described a method based on a fuzzy voting mechanism to find the optic disc location. In this method the vasculature was segmented and the vessel centerlines were obtained through thinning. After removal of the vessel branches each vessel segment was extended at both ends by a fuzzy element. The location in the image where most elements overlap was considered to be the OD. Youssif et al. [9] presented an OD location method based on a vessels direction matched filter. As a first step a binary mask was generated followed by image brightness and contrast equalization. Finally, the retinal vasculature was segmented, and the directions of the vessels were matched to the proposed filter representing the expected vessels directions in the vicinity of the OD. Foracchia et al. [11] used the idea of the convergence of the vessels to detect the OD center. Lalonde et al. [12] detected optic disc edge using the Canny edge detector, and the optic disc region was determined by matching the edge map with a circular template.

The purpose of this paper is to present a method for automatic localization and boundary detection of the OD in retinal fundus images, using a different approach based on some geometric features. Firstly, based on the particular OD geometric feature, we use gaussian and mean curvatures for identifying the location of the OD. We note that in [13–15] a similar technique was used (with success) in the analysis of wireless capsule endoscopy images, for detecting colonic polyps (which are round-shaped objects). Secondly, to detect the OD boundary we extract the region of interest based on our OD localization. Then, to the edges of this region a circular Hough transform is applied to segment the OD boundary. The results given in the paper show the efficacy of the proposed method.

After this introduction, the outline of the paper is as follows. The details of the proposed method are described in Section 2. Experimental results are shown and discussed in Section 3. Finally, some conclusions are given in Section 4.

2   The Method

2.1   Optic Disc Localization

Let Ω be an open subset of R^2, (x, y) an arbitrary point of Ω, and $f : \Omega \to R$ a twice continuously differentiable and scalar function. Then the Gaussian curvature $\mathcal{K}$ and the mean curvature $\mathcal{H}$ of the surface $S = \{(x, y, f(x, y)) | (x, y) \in \Omega\}$ are defined by

$$\mathcal{K} = \frac{f_{xx} f_{yy} - f_{xy}^2}{(1 + f_x^2 + f_y^2)} \tag{1}$$

$$\mathcal{H} = \frac{(1 + f_{xx})^2 f_{yy} - 2 f_x f_y f_{xy} + (1 + f_{yy})^2 f_{xx}}{2(1 + f_x^2 + f_y^2)^{3/2}}, \tag{2}$$

where f_x, f_y and f_{xx}, f_{xy}, f_{yy} are first and second order partial derivatives of f with respect to x and y.

It is observed that the OD appears most contrasted in the green channel compared to red and blue channels in the RGB image [8]. Moreover, it appears as a concave region (protrusion) in the green channel. The idea is to use the protrusion measure of an optic disc computed from curvatures of the input image (more specifically of the input green channel) to develop an efficient method for the localization of the OD. Therefore, we use only the green channel image, herein identified with a scalar function f, for computing the function, herein called $\mathcal{OD}_{loc}$, that gives the location of the OD. We expect that the Gaussian curvature of the OD surface to be relative higher than those of other regions, which may be either flat or ridge-like. However, the Gaussian curvature does not distinguish concavity of the graph of f (protrusion) from convexity (depression), so we need additional information for such distinction. For this purpose, we decide to rely also on the mean curvature of the graph of f, and from it we create a cut-off function which filters out the convex part of the graph. So we define

$$\mathcal{OD}_{loc} := -\mathcal{K} \min(\mathcal{H}, 0),$$

to identify the potential OD in the given images.

Since we have only a discrete representation of S, we must estimate the partial derivatives in (1)-(2). Let now $(x_i, y_j) = (ih, jh)$, with $1 \leq i, j \leq M$ for some $h > 0$, be a Cartesian grid, defined in Ω. The function $f(x, y)$ corresponds to the given green channel at continuum, and each pixel in the given image corresponds to a point $(x_i, y_j) = (ih, jh)$ on the grid. Then $f_{i,j}$ is the image intensity of f at (x_i, y_j). We use the following standard centered difference formulae to approximate the partial derivatives that appear in the formulas for $\mathcal{K}$ and $\mathcal{H}$. We remark that the green color channel is smoothed using Gaussian smoothing operator before computing the $\mathcal{OD}_{loc}$ function.

Some examples of $\mathcal{OD}_{loc}$ are shown in Figure 1 (third row). Mathematically, the value of the $\mathcal{OD}_{loc}$ function is closely related to the size of the protrusions in the images. Therefore, the optic disc location in the frame can be inferred by identifying the locations where $\mathcal{OD}_{loc}$ is higher. Hence, applying a threshold we

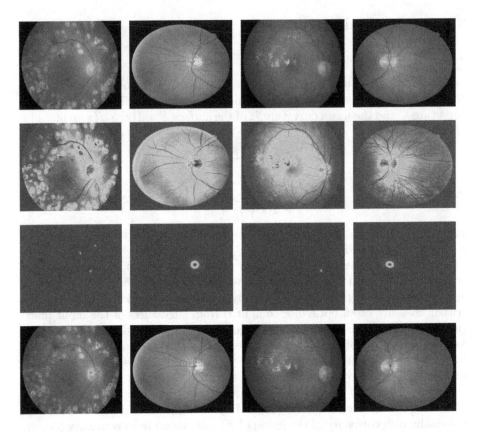

Fig. 1. First row: Original retinal fundus images from various publicly available datasets. Second row: The second component of the RGB color space. Third row: $\mathcal{OD}_{loc}$ function in the second component of the RGB color space. Fourth row: Results of the proposed method (black cross represents the estimated OD center.)

can separate the candidate region(s) for the location of the optic disc. We extract the highest 15% of pixels of $\mathcal{OD}_{loc}$. The entire thresholded image is scanned to count the number of connected components. For each connected component, in the thresholded image, we compute the area and the $\mathcal{OD}_{loc}$ mean intensity. The component corresponding to the maximum of the product between the area and the $\mathcal{OD}_{loc}$ mean intensity is considered to be the location of the OD. We then compute the centroid of this same component to get the estimated OD center and consequently the OD location.

2.2 Optic Disc Boundary Detection

The Hough transform [16], used to detect geometrical features that can be defined through parametric equations like straight lines and circles, is a widely considered technique in Computer Vision and Pattern Recognition. In our case, since the OD has circular/round boundary shape, we are looking for circular patterns within an image [17]. The circular Hough transform (CHT) relies on equations for circles. The parametric representation of the equation of the a circle is

$$x = a + r * cos(\theta) \quad y = b + r * sin(\theta),$$

where a and b represent the coordinates for the center, $\theta \in [0, 2\pi]$, and r is the radius of the circle. We consider the radius r between r_{min} and r_{max} which are one-tenth and one-fifth of the image (as these measurements are estimated to be the OD diameter) divided by two. The minimum value makes sure that the OD cup (an internal circular object in the OD) is not considered, while the maximum value is such that too wide areas are eliminated. The CHT transforms a set of feature points in the image space into a set of accumulated votes in a parameter space. Then, for each feature point, votes are accumulated in an accumulator array for all parameter combinations. The array elements that contain the highest number of votes indicate the presence of the desired shape, i.e. the OD, in the retinal image, in this case.

Based on our optic disc localization (described in the previous subsection) we define a region of interest (ROI), containing the OD location, of size $m \times n$, where m and n are one-ninth of the respective dimensions of the image multiplied by two. So finally, for segmenting the OD boundary from the retinal image we apply the CHT to the edges of the ROI, which are computed using Canny edge detector [18].

2.3   Main Steps

For each retinal image the method consists of the following four steps:

1. We consider the green channel of the RGB color space for the input image.
2. We then compute the function $\mathcal{OD}_{loc}$ to localize the OD.
3. With the OD locus, a region of interest (ROI) is defined as a preprocess to detect the OD boundary.
4. The CHT is applied to the edge points of the ROI, obtained using Canny edge detector, for identifying the OD boundary.

3   Results and Discussion

We evaluate the performance of our proposed method on three public datasets. The first two datasets are DIARETDB0 [19] and DIARETDB1 [20] with 130 and 89 retinal images of different qualities, respectively, that are created for benchmarking diabetic retinopathy detection from digital retinal images. The third dataset is the DRIVE dataset [21] that consists of 40 retinal images and is created for benchmarking blood vessel extraction from retinal images.

The estimated localization of the OD center for some of the images from the three datasets is shown in Figure 1. The third row represents the computation

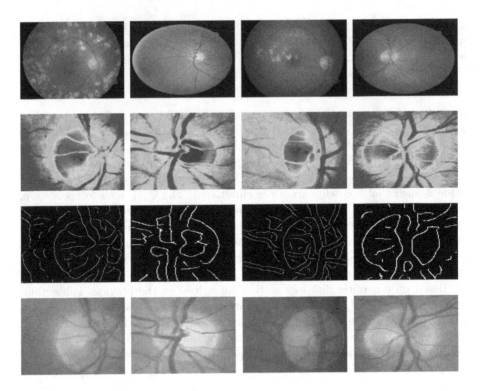

Fig. 2. First row: Original retinal fundus images from various publicly available datasets. Second row: The region of interest for boundary detection (the green channel image). Third row: The input to the circular Hough transform. Fourth row: The OD boundary determined by the Circular Hough transform.

of $\mathcal{OD}_{loc}$ function in the green channel of the RGB color space. The fourth row shows the estimated OD center, which is labeled by " $+$ " sign. The proposed method achieves an average accuracy of 96.5% (we recall that the accuracy is by definition the number of correct predictions divided by the sum of the number of positives and negatives). In particular, the accuracy of the proposed method is 96.9%, 96.6%, and 95% for DIARETDB0, DIARETDB1, and DRIVE datasets, respectively. Most of the failed outcomes resulted from poor image quality or very blurred and unclassifiable OD. From Figure 1 one can also see that the proposed method is tolerant to various types of retinal lesion and imaging artifacts.

Figure 2 illustrates the detection of the OD boundary for a number of retinal images from the three public datasets. In particular, the second row shows the region of interest; the third row represents the computation of the edges by using Canny edge detector. The fourth row displays the detected OD boundary using the CHT.

We notice that the proposed method has a limitation that is related to the fact that it localizes the OD based on the observations that the optic disc is usually a protrusion in the green color channel of the images. As a result, it cannot handle some special retinal images, as for example: i) when the OD is not protruding enough from the surrounding region, ii) or if there are other bright concave regions (e.g. bright lesions), in the green color channel of the image, that protrude more than the OD. However several strategies can be devised for correcting this drawback or for transforming it into an advantage. For example, the region where most vessels with vertical orientation are present is in the vicinity of the optic disc [22], so this region should coincide with, or be very close to, the OD location, given by $\mathcal{OD}_{loc}$.

4   Conclusions

We have presented a method for automatic localization and boundary detection of the OD in retinal fundus images. The location of the OD is done by utilizing the particular OD geometric shape and based on gaussian and mean curvatures of the images. After setting the OD localization, a region of interest, containing this location, is defined to detect the OD boundary. A circular Hough transform is then applied to the edges of this defined region in order to segment the OD boundary from the images. The method is tested on three public datasets (with normal and abnormal images) and resulted an average accuracy of 96.5%. In the future, complementary strategies, as those described in the previous section, can be also incorporated in this approach in order to improve its performance.

References

1. Sinthanayothin, C., Boyce, J., Cook, H., Williamson, T.: Automated localisation of the optic disc, fovea, and retinal blood vessels from digital colour fundus images. Br. J. Ophthalmol. **83**, 902–910 (1999)
2. Gagnon, L., Lalonde, M., Beaulieu, M., Boucher, M.C.: Procedure to detect anatomical structures in optical fundus images. In: Proc. Conf. Med. Imag. 2001: Image Process, San Diego, CA, pp. 1218–1225 (2001)
3. Tobin, K.W., Chaum, E., Govindasamy, V., Karnowski, T.: Detection of anatomic structures in human retinal imagery. IEEE Transactions on Medical Imaging **26**(12), 1729–1739 (2007)
4. Walter, T., Klein, J.C., Massin, P., Erginay, A.: A contribution of image processing to the diagnosis of diabetic retinopathy-detection of exudates in color fundus images of the human retina. IEEE Transactions on Medical Imaging **21**, 1236–1243 (2002)
5. Ben Sbeh, Z., Cohen, L., Mimoun, G., Coscas, G.: A new approach of geodesic reconstruction for drusen segmentation in eye fundus images. IEEE Transactions on Medical Imaging **20**(12), 1321–1333 (2001)
6. Chrstek, R., Wolf, M., Donath, K., Niemann, H., Paulus, D., Hothorn, T., Lausen, B., Lmmer, R., Mardin, C., Michelson, G.: Automated segmentation of the optic nerve head for diagnosis of glaucoma. Medical Image Analysis **9**, 297–314 (2005)
7. Li, H., Chutatape, O.: Automatic location of optic disc in retinal images. In: IEEE Int. Conf. Image Process, pp. 837–840 (2001)

8. Winder, R., Morrow, P., McRitchie, I., Bailie, J., Hart, P.: Algorithms for digital image processing in diabetic retinopathy. Computerized Medical Imaging and Graphics **33**, 608–622 (2009)
9. Abdel-Razik Youssif, A.H., Ghalwash, A., Abdel-Rahman Ghoneim, A.: Optic disc detection from normalized digital fundus images by means of a vessels direction matched filter. IEEE Transactions on Medical Imaging **27**, 11–18 (2008)
10. Hoover, A., Goldbaum, M.: Locating the optic nerve in a retinal image using the fuzzy convergence of the blood vessels. IEEE Transactions on Medical Imaging **22**, 951–958 (2003)
11. Foracchia, M., Grisan, E., Ruggeri, A.: Detection of optic disc in retinal images by means of a geometrical model of vessel structure. IEEE Transactions on Medical Imaging **23**, 1189–1195 (2004)
12. Lalonde, M., Beaulieu, M., Gagnon, L.: Fast and robust optic disc detection using pyramidal decomposition and hausdorff-based template matching. IEEE Transactions on Medical Imaging **20**, 1193–1200 (2001)
13. Figueiredo, I.N., Prasath, S., Tsai, Y.H.R., Figueiredo, P.N.: Automatic detection and segmentation of colonic polyps in wireless capsule images, UCLA-CAM Report 10–65 (2010), http://www.math.ucla.edu/applied/cam/
14. Figueiredo, P.N., Figueiredo, I.N., Prasath, S., Tsai, R.: Automatic polyp detection in pillcam colon 2 capsule images and videos: preliminary feasibility report. Diagnostic and Therapeutic Endoscopy, 1–7 (2011)
15. Figueiredo, I.N., Kumar, S., Figueiredo, P.N.: An intelligent system for polyp detection in wireless capsule endoscopy images. In: Computational Vision and Medical Image Processing, VIPIMAGE, pp. 229–235 (2013)
16. Hough, P.V.C.: Methods and means for recognizing complex patterns. (U.S. Patent 3 069 654, December 1962)
17. Kimme, C., Ballard, D., Sklansky, J.: Finding circles by an array of accumulators. Commun. ACM **18**, 120–122 (1975)
18. Canny, J.: A computational approach to edge detection. IEEE Transactions on PAMI **8**, 679–698 (1986)
19. Kauppi, T., Kalesnykiene, V., Kamarainen, J.K., Lensu, L., Sorri, I., Uusitalo, H., Kalviainen, H., Pietila, J.: DIARETDB0: Evaluation database and methodology for diabetic retinopathy algorithms, Tech. Rep., Lappeenranta Univ. Technol., Lappeenranta, Finland (2006)
20. Kauppi, T., Kalesnykiene, V., Kamarainen, J.K., Lensu, L., Sorri, I., Uusitalo, H., Kalviainen, H., Pietila, J.: DIARETDB1 diabetic retinopathy database and evaluation protocol, Tech. Rep., Lappeenranta Univ. Technol., Lappeenranta, Finland (2007)
21. Staal, J., Abramoff, M., Niemeijer, M., Viergever, M., van Ginneken, B.: Ridge-based vessel segmentation in color images of the retina. IEEE Transactions on Medical Imaging **23**, 501–509 (2004)
22. Pinão, J., Oliveira, C.M.: Fovea and optic disc detection in retinal images with visible lesions. In: Camarinha-Matos, L.M., Shahamatnia, E., Nunes, G. (eds.) DoCEIS 2012. IFIP AICT, vol. 372, pp. 543–552. Springer, Heidelberg (2012)

Optic Nerve Head Detection via Group Correlations in Multi-orientation Transforms

Erik Bekkers[✉], Remco Duits, and Bart ter Haar Romeny

Department of Biomedical Engineering and Department of Mathematics and Computer Science, Eindhoven University of Technology, Eindhoven, The Netherlands
{E.J.Bekkers,R.Duits,B.M.TerHaarRomeny}@tue.nl

Abstract. Optic nerve head detection is a fundamental step in automated retinal image analysis algorithms. In this paper, we propose a new optic nerve head detection algorithm that is based on the efficient analysis of multi-orientation patterns. To this end, we make use of invertible orientation scores, which are functions on the Euclidean motion group. We apply the classical and fast approach of template matching via cross-correlation, however, we do this in the domain of an orientation score rather than the usual image domain. As such, this approach makes it possible to efficiently detect multi-orientation patterns. The method is extensively tested on public and private databases and we show that the method is generically applicable to images originating from traditional fundus cameras as well as from scanning laser ophthalmoscopes.

Keywords: Optic nerve head · Optic disk · Retina · Multi-orientation · Orientation scores · Template matching · SLO

1 Introduction

Retinal imaging is a standard procedure in ophthalmology and plays a central role in screening for diabetic retinopathy. To allow for large scale screening and population studies, effort has been made to automate the process of retinal image analysis. The foundation of these analyses consists of the identification of the key anatomical landmarks: 1) the *optic nerve head* (ONH), the place where the blood vessels and nerves leave the eye; 2) the *fovea*, the central spot of the retina that contains the highest concentration of photoreceptors; and 3) the *retinal vasculature*. Correct identification of these landmarks (see Fig. 1) is crucial as they are either part of the analysis itself (classification of glaucoma [1]), or are used as reference points in measurement protocols [2]. The focus of this paper is on automated, robust, and efficient localization of the ONH.

Automated detection of the optic nerve head is a challenging task and has therefore been the subject of many previous studies [3–9][10, and references therein]. On conventional fundus (CF) images the ONH appears as a bright disk-like feature, whereas it appears generally dark on images taken with scanning laser ophthalmoscopy (SLO) cameras. Traditionally, ONH detection methods

© Springer International Publishing Switzerland 2014
A. Campilho and M. Kamel (Eds.): ICIAR 2014, Part II, LNCS 8815, pp. 293–302, 2014.
DOI: 10.1007/978-3-319-11755-3_33

Fig. 1. Two central fundus images of the same eye. A conventional color fundus image (left) and an artificial color image constructed from a near infrared and green laser image (right).

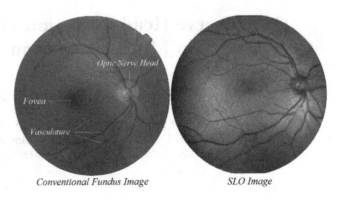

Conventional Fundus Image   *SLO Image*

are developed for use with CF images. Conventional ONH detection algorithms are based on the analysis of pixel intensities [3,4]. These approaches are fast and effective, however, the performance typically decreases in the presence of pathologies. As an alternative, methods have been developed that include more contextual information and consider the typical pattern of blood vessels that emerge from the ONH [5–10]. These methods generally perform better than traditional methods; however, they are computationally more expensive and often difficult to implement. Though these methods would perform well on any retinal image showing typical vessel patterns, the authors of [3–10] have not validated their methods on SLO images. To our knowledge, validation of optic nerve head detection methods on SLO images has until now not been reported in literature.

We present an effective, direct and fast approach to ONH detection and show that it works on both CF and SLO images. The proposed ONH detection method is closest to the method by Youssif et al. [10]. Their method is based on vessel segmentation and the construction of a vessel orientation map via directional matched filters. Subsequently, the ONH location is found by searching the orientation map for a pattern that is similar to a predefined template. However, to reduce the computational burden they only apply template matching on a set of candidate ONH locations. Our method is also based on matching orientation templates, however, we do this via correlations in the domain $\mathbb{R}^2 \rtimes S^1$ of complex valued functions called invertible orientation scores [11]. In invertible orientation scores we obtain a comprehensive overview of how an image is decomposed into local orientations without losing information (Fig. 2). As we will show, this allows us to effectively detect orientation patterns in an intuitive and direct way. As such our fast ONH detection algorithm has the advantage that we do not rely on the explicit identification of vessels, nor do we need to define a set of candidate locations to reduce computational costs.

2   Theory

As the method proposed in this paper is based on template matching in the domain of an orientation score, we start with an introduction to orientation scores. Next, template matching via cross correlation in the image domain $\mathbb{R}^2$

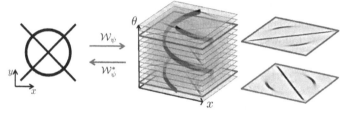

Fig. 2.
Orientation score
of an exemplary
image

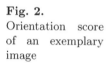

is explained, and we extend this concept to the domain $SE(2) = \mathbb{R}^2 \rtimes S^1$ of an orientation score. This section ends with details on the implementation of the algorithm.

2.1   Orientation Scores

Orientation Score Transform. An orientation score, constructed from image $f : \mathbb{R}^2 \to \mathbb{R}$, is defined as a function $U_f : \mathbb{R}^2 \times S^1 \to \mathbb{C}$ and depends on two variables $(\mathbf{x}, \theta)$, where $\mathbf{x} = \{x, y\} \in \mathbb{R}^2$ denotes position and $\theta \in [0, 2\pi]$ denotes the orientation variable. An orientation score U_f of image f can be constructed by means of correlation with some anisotropic wavelet ψ via

$$U_f(\mathbf{x}, \theta) = (\mathcal{W}_\psi f)(\mathbf{x}, \theta) = (\overline{\psi}_\theta \star f)(\mathbf{x}) = \int_{\mathbb{R}^2} \overline{\psi(\mathbf{R}_\theta^{-1}(\mathbf{y} - \mathbf{x}))} f(\mathbf{y}) d\mathbf{y}, \quad (1)$$

where $\psi \in \mathbb{L}_2(\mathbb{R}^2)$ is the correlation kernel with orientation $\theta = 0$, where $\mathcal{W}_\psi$ denotes the transformation between image f and orientation score U_f, and $\star$ denotes the correlation operator. The overline denotes complex conjugate, $\psi_\theta(\mathbf{x}) = \psi(\mathbf{R}_\theta^{-1}\mathbf{x})$ and the rotation matrix $\mathbf{R}_\theta$ gives a counter clockwise rotation over angle θ. The domain of an orientation score is essentially the classical Euclidean motion group $SE(2)$ of planar translations and rotations, equipped with product $g \cdot g' = (\mathbf{x}, \theta) \cdot (\mathbf{x}', \theta') = (\mathbf{R}_\theta \mathbf{x}' + \mathbf{x}, \theta + \theta')$.

Oriented Wavelets. In principle, the choice for wavelet ψ is free and depends on the application. If one wants to detect oriented structures at a certain scale, the Gabor wavelet is a suitable choice. On the other hand, if one wants to detect all scales with the same wavelet and does not want to tamper with the data evidence, cake wavelets are a better choice [11]. A comparison between Gabor and cake wavelets, with the application to retinal vessel detection, is given in [12]. Here we use cake wavelets as we want to maintain data evidence in the new representation.

2.2   Template Matching in $\mathbb{R}^2$

Template Matching via Cross Correlation. Let us consider two 2D functions $t, f : \mathbb{R}^2 \to \mathbb{R}$, e.g., a template and an image. We will denote translation by $\mathbf{b}$ and rotation by α of template t using the representation

$(\mathcal{U}_g t)(\mathbf{x}) = t(\mathbf{R}_\alpha^{-1}(\mathbf{x}-\mathbf{b}))$ and write $g = (\mathbf{b},\alpha) \in SE(2)$. We then define the cross correlation coefficient as a function of translation and rotation of the template by g as follows:

$$c_{t,f}(g) = (\mathcal{U}_g t, f)_{\mathbb{L}_2(\mathbb{R}^2)} = \int_{\mathbb{R}^2} \overline{t(\mathbf{R}_\alpha^{-1}(\mathbf{x}-\mathbf{b}))} f(\mathbf{x}) d\mathbf{x} = (\bar{t}_\alpha \star f)(\mathbf{b}), \qquad (2)$$

where $(\cdot,\cdot)_{\mathbb{L}_2(\mathbb{R}^2)}$ denotes the $\mathbb{L}_2$ inner product.

Normalized Template Matching. While Eq. (2) can be seen as a scalar projection of image f onto the template t, its value is meaningless if the norm of the patch does not equal the norm of the template, i.e., a high value of this projection does not mean the two vectors are close per se. This problem is solved by normalizing the template and image to a zero mean and unit standard deviation, resulting in the normalized cross correlation coefficient. To be able to normalize the image locally we make use of an additional mass function $m : \mathbb{R}^2 \to \mathbb{R}^+$ with $\int m(\mathbf{x}) d\mathbf{x} = 1$, that indicates the relevant region of the template, and define the $\mathbb{L}_2(\mathbb{R}^2)$ inner product using probability measure $m(\mathbf{x}) d\mathbf{x}$ as follows:

$$(t, f)_{\mathbb{L}_2(\mathbb{R}^2, m\, d\mathbf{x})} = \int_{\mathbb{R}^2} \overline{t(\mathbf{x})} f(\mathbf{x}) m(\mathbf{x}) d\mathbf{x}. \qquad (3)$$

The normalized cross correlation coefficient $\hat{c}_{t,f}(g)$ is then defined as follows:

$$\hat{c}_{t,f}(g) = (\mathcal{U}_g \hat{t}, \hat{f}_g)_{\mathbb{L}_2(\mathbb{R}^2, \mathcal{U}_g m\, d\mathbf{x})}, \qquad (4a)$$

$$\hat{t}(\mathbf{x}) = \frac{t(\mathbf{x}) - \langle t \rangle_m}{\|t - \langle t \rangle_m\|_{\mathbb{L}_2(\mathbb{R}^2, m\, d\mathbf{x})}}, \qquad (4b)$$

$$\hat{f}_g(\mathbf{x}) = \frac{f(\mathbf{x}) - \langle f \rangle_{\mathcal{U}_g m}}{\|f - \langle f \rangle_{\mathcal{U}_g m}\|_{\mathbb{L}_2(\mathbb{R}^2, \mathcal{U}_g m\, d\mathbf{x})}}, \qquad (4c)$$

with $\langle t \rangle_m = (1, t)_{\mathbb{L}_2(\mathbb{R}^2, m\, d\mathbf{x})}$ the local average with respect to the area covered by m, and with $\|\cdot\|_{\mathbb{L}_2(\mathbb{R}^2, m\, d\mathbf{x})} = \sqrt{(\cdot,\cdot)_{\mathbb{L}_2(\mathbb{R}^2, m\, d\mathbf{x})}}$. We always take the convention that the mass m rotates and translates with the template.

Approximation of $\hat{f}_g$. Since the normalized image $\hat{f}_g$ depends on g it needs to be calculated for every translation of the template, making this approach a rather computationally expensive one. Instead, we will approximate (4c) by assuming that the local average is approximately constant in the area covered by m and that the mass is rotation invariant (i.e., $m(\mathbf{R}_\alpha^{-1}\mathbf{x}) = m(\mathbf{x})$). That is, assuming $\langle f \rangle_{\mathcal{U}_{(\mathbf{b},\alpha)} m}(\mathbf{x}) \approx \langle f \rangle_{\mathcal{U}_{(\mathbf{x},\alpha)} m}(\mathbf{x})$ for $\|\mathbf{b} - \mathbf{x}\|_{\mathbb{L}_2(\mathbb{R}^2)} < r$, with r the radius that determines the extent of m, we approximate (4c) as follows:

$$\hat{f}_g(\mathbf{x}) \approx \frac{f(\mathbf{x}) - (m \star f)(\mathbf{x})}{\|f - (m \star f)(\mathbf{x})\|_{\mathbb{L}_2(\mathbb{R}^2, (\mathcal{U}_{(\mathbf{x},\alpha)} m)(\mathbf{x}) d\mathbf{x})}} = \frac{f(\mathbf{x}) - (m \star f)(\mathbf{x})}{\sqrt{(m \star (f - (m \star f))^2)(\mathbf{x})}}. \qquad (5)$$

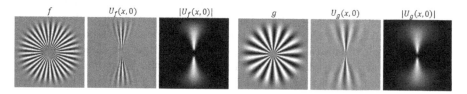

Fig. 3. Two patterns f and g and their respective orientation scores U_f and U_g at $\theta = 0$. While the local intensities are different, the orientation pattern is approximately equal.

2.3 Template Matching in $SE(2)$

Analogue to the $\mathbb{R}^2$ case, for two normalized orientation scores $\hat{T}, \hat{U}_f \in \mathbb{L}_2(SE(2))$ the normalized correlation is given by

$$\hat{C}_{T,U_f}(g) = \left(\mathcal{L}_g \hat{T}, \hat{U}_f \right)_{\mathbb{L}_2(SE(2)), \mathcal{L}_g M \, dxd\theta}. \tag{6}$$

There we take the $SE(2)$ inner product with probability measure $M(\mathbf{x}, \theta) dxd\theta$:

$$\left(\hat{T}, \hat{U}_f \right)_{\mathbb{L}_2(SE(2), M \, dxd\theta)} = \int_{\mathbb{R}^2} \int_0^\pi \overline{\hat{T}(\mathbf{x}, \theta)} \hat{U}_f(\mathbf{x}, \theta) M(\mathbf{x}, \theta) d\theta dx, \tag{7}$$

and the shift-twist operator $(\mathcal{L}_g T)(\mathbf{x}, \theta) = T(\mathbf{R}_\alpha^{-1}(\mathbf{x} - \mathbf{b}), \theta - \alpha)$. Rotations and translations are done using the shift-twist operator as we have $(\mathcal{W}_\psi \mathcal{U}_g f)(\mathbf{x}, \alpha) = (\mathcal{L}_g \mathcal{W}_\psi f)(\mathbf{x}, \alpha)$. The normalized template $\hat{T}$ and orientation score $\hat{U}_f$ are calculated in a similar fashion as described in Eq. (4b) and (5), where one can replace all inner products $(\cdot, \cdot)_{\mathbb{L}_2(\mathbb{R}^2, m \, dx)}$ by $(\cdot, \cdot)_{\mathbb{L}_2(SE(2), M \, dxd\theta)}$ and where the correlation operator $\star$ can be replaced by its $SE(2)$ equivalent:

$$(T \star_{SE(2)} U_f)(\mathbf{x}, \theta) = \left(\mathcal{L}_{(\mathbf{x}, \theta)} T, U_f \right)_{\mathbb{L}_2(SE(2))} \tag{8}$$

Non-linear Template Matching. Since both the orientation score transform (1) and template matching schemes, (4a) and (6), rely on a series of linear operators (correlations), it is possible to show that both Eq. (4a) and (6) produce the same results if the orientation score objects originate from their image equivalents, i.e., $\underset{g \in SE(2)}{\operatorname{argmax}} \hat{c}_{t,f}(g) = \underset{g \in SE(2)}{\operatorname{argmax}} \hat{C}_{T,U_f}(g)$, if $U_f = \mathcal{W}_\psi f$, $T = \mathcal{W}_\psi t$. However, the orientation score approach only becomes effective after we implement a non-linear step in the framework. Therefore, we find the ONH location g^* via

$$g^* = \underset{g \in SE(2)}{\operatorname{argmax}} \left(\mathcal{L}_g |\hat{T}|, |\hat{U}_f| \right)_{\mathbb{L}_2(SE(2))}, \tag{9}$$

where template matching in $SE(2)$ is done via the modulus of the orientation scores. This adaptation makes that the *appearance* (encoded in the phase) of structures is not measured, it is rather the *presence* of structures that is being detected, consider to this end Fig. 3. The rationale behind this adaptation is that in every image of the eye the location and appearance of blood vessels may be different, their orientations however follow more or less the same orientation pattern as the structures depicted in Fig. 3. In case the input image is locally normalized to zero mean (background is set to zero and structures have either positive or negative values), taking the modulus of the score is an appropriate basic form of line/vessel detection. We therefore normalize the image via the method in [13] as pre-processing. While in practice this choice appears to be adequate, more advanced filters, such as differential invariants like vesselness [14], could be used as well.

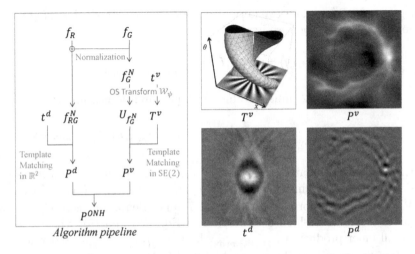

Fig. 4. Optic nerve head detection pipeline. In this figure, the displayed template t^d is the trained template for SLO images. Probability maps P^v and P^d are exemplary results of template matching, obtained by taking the SLO image from Fig. 1 as input

2.4 Optic Disk Detection

Our optic disk detection routine is based on template matching with templates $t^d : \mathbb{R}^2 \to \mathbb{R}$ and $T^v : SE(2) \to \mathbb{C}$. These are based on detection of the typical disk shape and vessel pattern near the ONH, and which are respectively applied in the image and orientation score domain. Template $t^d = \frac{1}{N} \sum_{i=1}^{N} f_i$ is calculated as the average of a set of $N = 100$ image patches, where f_i is centered around the ONH in the i-th image of a training dataset. For all CF images used in our experiments, we used the first N images of the publicly available MES-SIDOR database (http://messidor.crihan.fr/index-en.php), for SLO images we used our private database (see Section 3). To detect the typical pattern of blood vessels emerging from the ONH we use a multi-orientation model template T^v:

$$T^v(\mathbf{x}, \theta) = (\mathcal{W}_\psi \, t^v)(\mathbf{x}, \theta), \quad \text{with} \quad t^v(\mathbf{x}) = \mathcal{M}_n(r) \sin \omega \, \phi, \qquad (10)$$

with $\mathbf{x} = (r\cos\phi, r\sin\phi)$, and with ω the angular frequency. Here the function $\mathcal{M}_n(r) = e^{-\left(\frac{r}{s}\right)^2} \sum_{i=0}^{n} \frac{(r/s)^{2i}}{i!}$ smoothly approximates the indicator function $1_{[0,\sqrt{s(n+\frac{1}{2})}]}(r)$, see [12, section 2.1].

The entire processing pipeline is shown in Fig. 4. While, in principle, the ONH is best detected on the red channel of the fundus image, we notice that this channel is quite often over-saturated in CF images. Instead, we work with the average of the red and green channel f_{RG}. For the detection of the orientation pattern we use the green channel f_G as it contains best contrast for blood vessels. The images are normalized via the scheme proposed by Foracchia et al. [13]. The resulting image f_{RG}^N together with t^d, and the orientation score $U_{f_{RG}^N}$ together with T^v, are used as input for template matching [cf. Eq. (4a) and Eq. (9)]. The resulting probability maps $P^d = \hat{c}_{t^d,f}$ and $P^v = \hat{C}_{|T^v|,|U_{f_{RG}^N}|}$ are rescaled to a range of [0,1]. Their sum gives the final ONH probability map P^{ONH}.

Practical Considerations and Parameters. Since template T^d is rotation invariant, and since the optic disk generally appears under the same orientation in every fundus image, we restrict our search for the ONH to translations only and assume $\alpha = 0$. In this case calculating P^v boils down to a standard $\mathbb{R}^3$-correlation. To further reduce computation time the images are downsized to a width of 256 pixels. For each image, template t^d is resized such that the ONH radius of the template corresponds to an estimated radius r_{est}. For T^v we set $\omega = 16$, $s = (5\,r_{est})^2/(\frac{1}{2} + n)$ and $n = 8$. The mass functions are given by $m(\mathbf{x}) = M(\mathbf{x}, \theta) = \mathcal{M}_n(\|\mathbf{x}\|)$ with the same settings for s and n. For the normalization step [13] we used a window size of $\frac{1}{2}r_{est}$ and for the orientation score transformation we used cake wavelets [11] at a resolution of $s_\theta = \frac{\pi}{12}$.

Table 1. Optic nerve head detection results and the number of fails (in parentheses)

	ES	TC	MESSIDOR	DRIVE	STARE	All Images
P^{ONH}	95.7% (9)	100.0% (0)	99.5% (6)	100.0% (0)	93.8% (5)	98.8% (20)
P^v	78.8% (44)	81.7% (38)	86.8% (158)	72.5% (11)	67.9% (26)	84.1% (277)
P^d	92.7% (15)	91.3% (18)	96.9% (37)	97.5% (1)	71.6% (23)	94.6% (94)

3   Results and Discussion

For validation, we made use of a private database consisting of 208 SLO images taken with an EasyScan (i-Optics B.V., the Netherlands) and 208 CF images taken with a Topcon NW200 (Topcon Corp., Japan). The two sets of images are labeled as "ES" and "TC" respectively. The ES-TC database consist of images taken from both eyes of 52 patients, where for each eye both a fovea and an optic nerve head centered image were taken. Our method is also tested

Table 2. Comparison to state of the art: Optic nerve head detection results and the number of fails (in parentheses)

	MESSIDOR	DRIVE	STARE
Aquino et al. [4]	98.8% (14)		
Yu et al. [8]	99.1% (11)		
Lu et al. [6]		97.5% (1)	96.3% (3)
Sekhar et al. [7]		100.0% (0)	100% (0)[a]
Foracchia et al. [5]			97.5% (2)
Proposed method	99.5% (6)	100.0% (0)	93.8% (5)

[a] *The authors used 80 (of 81) images from the dataset.*

on a set of widely used public databases: MESSIDOR, DRIVE (http://www.isi.
uu.nl/Research/Databases/DRIVE) and STARE (http://www.ces.clemson.edu/
~ahoover/stare), consisting of 1200, 40 and 81 images respectively. For each
image, the detected ONH position was marked as correct if it was located within
the circumference of the actual ONH. To this end we used the annotations kindly
provided by the authors of [4] (http://www.uhu.es/retinopathy), and manually
outlined the ONH border for the other databases.

The results are reported in Tables 1 and 2 and illustrated by examples in
Fig. 5. From Table 1 we can see that the proposed method is applicable to both
conventional and SLO images. Compared to the 100% success rate for the CF
image database (TC) we notice a mild decrease in performance for the corresponding SLO images (ES). This suggests that ONH detection on SLO images
is slightly more challenging. It is therefore reasonable to expect a decrease in
performance of the methods described in [3–10], or adaptations hereof, when
applied to SLO images. Finally, Table 1 demonstrates the significant contribution of template matching in the orientation score domain (P^v) in addition to
basic template matching in the image (P^d). This becomes especially apparent
when working with severely pathological images, as is the case in the STARE
database.

In Table 2 our results are compared to state of the art methods that have
been validated using the public databases. For a more complete comparison with
literature we would like to refer to [10, Table 1]. Though our method is rather
basic in nature, i.e. it exploits merely a sequence of correlations, it competes well
with the state of the art. On the MESSIDOR and DRIVE database our method
scores well above average. With respect to the challenging STARE database; our
method scores slightly lower than the state of the art, but outperforms most the
conventional methods reported in [10, Table 1]. The wide variety of pathologies
and image artifacts (Fig. 5) could simply not be captured by the templates used
in our algorithm. As part of future work we therefore aim to improve our method
by optimization of templates using variational methods [15].

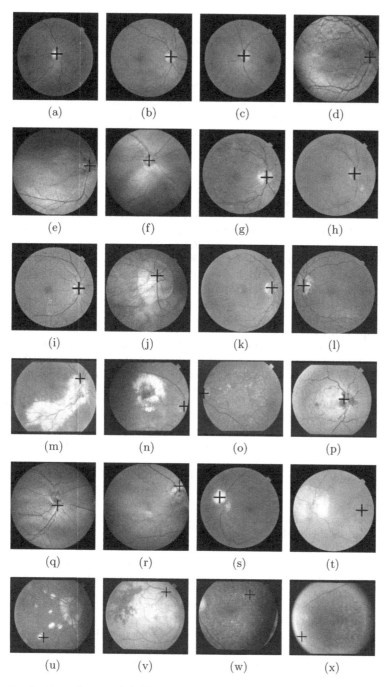

Fig. 5. A selection of successful ONH detections from the databases TC (a-c), ES (d-f), MESSIDOR (g-i), DRIVE (j-l) and STARE (m-p); And a selection of unsuccessful ONH detections from the databases ES (q-r), MESSIDOR (s-t) and STARE (u-x)

4　Conclusion

In this paper we have proposed a new approach to optic disk detection based on the efficient identifying of orientation patterns. Our method purely relies on a series of correlations and is therefore fast and highly parallelizable. The method was tested on conventional fundus photographs as well as on data from SLO cameras. We have shown that the method performs excellent on both modalities with a total success rate of 98.8% on a set of 1737 images.

References

1. Jonas, J.B., Budde, W.M., Panda-Jonas, S.: Ophthalmoscopic evaluation of the optic nerve head. Survey of Ophthalmology **43**(4), 293–320 (1999)
2. Hubbard, L.D., et al.: Methods for evaluation of retinal microvascular abnormalities associated with hypertension/sclerosis in the Atherosclerosis Risk in Communities Study. Ophthalmology **106**(12), 2269–2280 (1999)
3. Sinthanayothin, C., Boyce, J.F., Cook, H.L., Williamson, T.H.: Automated localisation of the optic disc, fovea, and retinal blood vessels from digital colour fundus images. The British Journal of Ophthalmology **83**(8), 902–910 (1999)
4. Aquino, A., Gegundez-Arias, M.E., Marin, D.: Detecting the optic disc boundary in digital fundus images using morphological, edge detection, and feature extraction techniques. IEEE TMI **29**(11), 1860–1869 (2010)
5. Foracchia, M., et al.: Detection of optic disc in retinal images by means of a geometrical model of vessel structure. IEEE TMI **23**(10), 1189–1195 (2004)
6. Lu, S., Lim, J.: Automatic optic disc detection from retinal images by a line operator. IEEE TBME Biomedical Engineering **58**(1), 88–94 (2011)
7. Sekhar, S., Abd El-Samie, F.E., Yu, P., Al-Nuaimy, W.: Automated localization of retinal features. Applied Optics **50**(19), 3064–3075 (2011)
8. Yu, H., et al.: Fast localization and segmentation of optic disk in retinal images using directional matched filtering and level sets. IEEE TITB **16**(4), 644–657 (2012)
9. Niemeijer, M., Abràmoff, M.D., van Ginneken, B.: Fast detection of the optic disc and fovea in color fundus photographs. MEDIA **13**(6), 859–970 (2009)
10. Youssif, A., et al.: Optic disc detection from normalized digital fundus images by means of a vessels' direction matched filter. IEEE TMI **27**(1), 11–18 (2008)
11. Duits, R., Felsberg, M., Granlund, G.H., ter Haar Romeny, B.M.: Image analysis and reconstruction using a wavelet transform constructed from a reducible representation of the euclidean motion group. IJCV **72**(1), 79–102 (2007)
12. Bekkers, E., Duits, R., Berendschot, T., ter Haar Romeny, B.: A Multi-Orientation Analysis Approach to Retinal Vessel Tracking. JMIV **49**(3), 583–610 (2014)
13. Foracchia, M., Grisan, E., Ruggeri, A.: Luminosity and contrast normalization in retinal images. MEDIA **9**(3), 179–190 (2005)
14. Hannink, J., Duits, R., Bekkers, E.: Crossing-Preserving Multi-scale Vesselness. In: Barillot, C., Golland, P., Hata, N., Hornegger, J., Howe, R. (eds.) MICCAI 2014, Part II. LNCS, vol. 8674, pp. 603–610. Springer, Heidelberg (2014)
15. Janssen, B., Duits, R., Florack, L.: Coarse-to-fine image reconstruction based on weighted differential features and background gauge fields. In: Tai, X.-C., Mørken, K., Lysaker, M., Lie, K.-A. (eds.) SSVM 2009. LNCS, vol. 5567, pp. 377–388. Springer, Heidelberg (2009)

A Robust Algorithm for Optic Disc Segmentation from Colored Fundus Images

Anam Usman[1], Sarmad Abbas Khitran[2], M. Usman Akram[2(✉)],
and Yasser Nadeem[3]

[1] Center for Advanced Studies in Engineering, Islamabad, Pakistan
[2] College of Electrical and Mechanical Engineering, National University of Sciences
and Technology, Islamabad, Pakistan
[3] Armed Forces Institute of Ophthalmology, Rawalpindi, Pakistan
{anam.tariq86,sarmadkhitran,usmakram}@gmail.com

Abstract. Efficient and accurate optic disc (OD) segmentation is an essential task in automated diagnosis of different retinal diseases from digital fundus images. Due to presence of non-uniform illumination, noise, vessels and other lesions in the fundus images, it is challenging to come up with an algorithm which can accurately segment the OD from the fundus images. It is even more difficult to detect OD accurately for real time patient data in which the images are not captured in the very control environment. This paper presents a novel approach for efficient and robust OD segmentation even in presence of high retinal pathologies and noise. The proposed system consists of four modules i.e. preprocessing, candidate OD regions detection, vessel segmentation and OD detection based on vessel density in candidate regions. The proposed system is tested and validated on publicly available fundus image databases and images gathered locally for real patients. The experimental results show the validation of proposed system.

1 Introduction

Fundus image analysis is used to diagnose various eye diseases. An automated fundus image analysis system can be used as a tool to diagnose eye abnormality in its early stage which is a major help for ophthalmologists to treat the disease [1]. Optic Disc is a key component of retina. The information about the optic disc is used to detect severity of retinal diseases like glaucoma, diabetic retinopathy and papilloedema. Changes in the optic disc indicate the mildness or severity of the disease. So, automatic extraction of optic disc is very vital for computerized fundus image analysis systems [1]. Optic disc (OD) is one of the main features in digital fundus images. OD is a bright yellowish circular spot in the retinal image The brightest circle inside the optic disc is known as optic cup. It can also be used to detect other landmark features such as macula and fovea. All blood vessels of the retina emerge from optic disc.

© Springer International Publishing Switzerland 2014
A. Campilho and M. Kamel (Eds.): ICIAR 2014, Part II, LNCS 8815, pp. 303–310, 2014.
DOI: 10.1007/978-3-319-11755-3_34

There are many methods presented in the literature for the automatic extraction of optic disc. Youssif et al. [2] detected OD from normalized fundus images using Gaussian matched filter. The directional vascular pattern is also considered in finding OD using this approach. The method is tested on publicly available DRIVE and STARE databases which showed 100% and 98.7% accuracy respectively. Sekhar et al. [3] proposed a method for OD localization by using morphological operations and Hough transform. The proposed method is tested on DRIVE and STARE databases showing 94.4% and 82.3% accuracy respectively. Statistical techniques are proposed by C. Kose et al. [4] for the automated detection of optic disc. A characteristic image is taken in this approach and statistical properties like intensity distribution, standard deviation, maximum and minimum intensity values and texture properties are taken into account for OD detection. The method is tested on STARE dataset and achieved 97% accuracy. H. Ying et al. [5] proposed a fractal based method for automatic OD localization. OD is segmented from fundus image using local histogram analysis. The approach is tested on DRIVE dataset and it showed 97.5% accuracy. R.J. Qureshi et al. [6] proposed an automatic OD segmentation method based on pyramidal decomposition, edge detection, entropy filter and hough transformation. The method showed 96.7%, 94.02% and 100% accuracies on Diaretdb0, Diaretdb1 and DRIVE databases respectively. A method based on vessel distribution and OD appearance characteristics is presented by D. Zhang et al. [7]. Horizontal and vertical projection appearance is used to extract OD using this method. This method is tested on publicly available four databases which are DRIVE, STARE, Diaretdb0 and Diaretdb1. The method showed 100%, 91.4%, 95.5% and 92.1% accuracies on these databases respectively. Lupascu et al. [8] proposed a method based on Hough transform for the segmentation of Optic Disc. The method is tested on DRIVE database giving 95% accuracy.

The exiting methods tends to fail to detect OD properly when fundus images contain a large number of lesions especially bright lesions (exudates) and some acquisition artifacts. In this paper, we present an automated system for detection of Optic Disc in colored fundus images. The proposed methodology consists of preprocessing stage in which background estimation is done and the noise is eliminated from the fundus image. The next stage is to detect candidate OD regions followed by extraction of blood vessels from the preprocessed image. Finally, OD is detected by measuring vessel density in candidate OD regions.

This paper comprises of four sections. Section 2 contains proposed methodology followed by experimental results in section 3. Section 4 contains conclusion.

2   Proposed Methodology

Optic Disc is the bright circular region of the human retina. It is the location on the human retina from where the optic nerve and blood vessels enter the eye [9]. Automatic Optic Disc detection is an important step while designing automated systems for screening of diabetic retinopathy, glaucoma or papilloedema. Localization of OD is also essential for checking the severity of these retinal diseases [10].

OD detection is challenging in the presence of other bright lesions in the retina or if the images are not captured in a very controlled environment. So there is need for an accurate algorithm which can locate the OD correctly. Keeping in mind the above issues, we propose a system which segments the OD in efficient and accurate manner. The main steps involved in the detection of the OD in the proposed algorithm are; Preprocessing, Segmentation of candidate OD regions, Vessel detection and finally OD detection. First of all preprocessing is applied on the fundus image followed by segmentation of candidate OD regions. After the segmentation, the number of regions which are greater than one are checked. If there are, then vessel segmentation is done on the image otherwise vessel segmentation is skipped to improve the efficiency of the system. Finally, vessel density with in a bounding box is checked in each candidate region and a region with highest vessel density is called as "OD". The flow diagram in figure 1 shows the sequence of the steps as used in our proposed method.

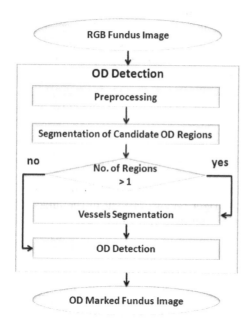

Fig. 1. Flow diagram of proposed system

2.1   Preprocessing

The initial step of our system is preprocessing and its goal is to segment a background (BG) mask. There are two stages of our proposed preprocessing algorithm. The steps for first stage of preprocessing are as follows;

- An initial threshold is applied on the red plane of fundus image and morphological operations are used to remove holes and false regions.

- Labeling of the objects that are present in the binary image is done using connected component labeling algorithm [11].
- Select the object having the largest area [12] as the fundus region. Figure 2(b) shows the result of background segmentation.

The steps for the second stage of preprocessing are listed below;

- Convert the colored fundus image to grayscale either by selecting red channel from original colored image or by converting colored image in gray scaled using equation 1 [13]. This selection depends on the saturation level of red channel.

$$F = 0.2989 \times R + 0.5870 \times G + 0.1140 \times B \qquad (1)$$

where F, R, G and B are the grayscale image, the Red plane, Green plane and the Blue plane of RGB fundus image.
- Apply padding technique to increase the fundus region of the gray scaled image. The main reason for this step is that the edge detection filter has highest response near the boundary of fundus region due to a sharp change which causes error in OD detection if it is present near the boundary.
- Resize the gray scaled image by using bilinear interpolation, crop it and then apply masking on it with the negative of the BG mask in order to obtain a ring, that we add with the grayscale image (fig-2(c)).
- Apply adaptive histogram equalization to enhance the bright regions of the image (fig-2(d)).

2.2   Candidate OD Region Segmentation

For candidate OD region segmentation, Laplacian of Gaussian (LoG) kernel is applied to enhance the bright regions present in the image [13]. Equations 2 and 3 represent mathematical expression for LoG [13]

$$h_g(n_1, n_2) = e^{\frac{-(n_1^2 + n_2^2)}{2\sigma^2}} \qquad (2)$$

$$h(n_1, n_2) = \frac{-(n_1^2 + n_2^2 - 2\sigma^2)h_g(n_1, n_2)}{2\pi\sigma^6 \sum_{n_1} \sum_{n_2} h_g} \qquad (3)$$

Where σ, n_1 and n_2 are standard deviation of the LoG kernel, the n_1^{th} row and n_2^{th} column respectively.

Due to the presence of non-uniform illumination, it is not efficient to detect the bright regions by only applying global thresholding. So, LoG kernel is used in frequency domain to increase the efficiency of the system. As OD is the circular shaped bright spot, so an inverted log kernel is used which is a circular shaped template having bright peak at its center to enhance the location of OD. Figure-2(e) shows the enhanced image from inverted Gaussian Kernel.

A threshold value is calculated using $T = 0.6 * Gkmx$, where T and Gkmx are calculated Threshold Value and the maximum value in Gaussian Kernel-Processed Image respectively. This selects pixels having top 40% response from

Gaussian kernel. Morphological opening is applied to remove noisy regions from thresholded image. Connected component labeling algorithm [11] is applied for labeling on the binary image and small objects present in the image are removed having area [12] less than a certain threshold which is variable for different databases. This gives some segmented regions which may or may not be candidate OD regions particularly when there is more than one region present in the image. Figure-2(f) shows the candidate OD regions.

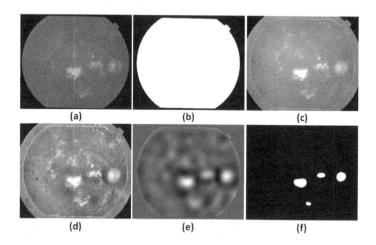

Fig. 2. Preprocessing and candidate od region segmentation. a) Original retinal image; b) Background mask; c) Padded gray scaled image; d) Contrast enhanced image; e)Enhanced image using inverted Gaussian kernel; f) Binary image containing candidate regions.

2.3   Vessel Segmentation

The next step is extraction of blood vessels to measure vessel density in each candidate OD region. In proposed system, vascular pattern is enhanced by using 2-D Gabor wavelet for their better visibility. Gabor wavelets have directional selectiveness capability and since the vessels have directional pattern so Gabor wavelets enhance the vessels very well. The second step which is used in vascular extraction is the segmentation. In order to increase the accuracy of vessel segmentation, the proposed system uses multilayered thresholding approach to make sure the extraction of small vessel along with large ones [18]. Figure 3(a) and 3(b) show the result of blood vessels enhancement and segmentation.

2.4   OD Detection

The final step of this system is optic disc detection. If there is only one candidate OD region, the proposed system considers it as OD. In case of multiple regions,

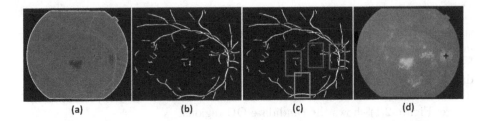

Fig. 3. a) Enhanced vessel using Gabor wavelet; b) Binary blood vessels; c) Segmented Candidate Regions Marked on the Vessels Mask; d) Region with highest vessel density marked as OD

vessel density is checked with in each candidate region and considers a region as OD that has maximum vessel density. The figure 3 (c) and 3 (d) shows the results of OD detection.

3   Results

The quantitative assessment of the proposed system of OD detection is done by using publicly available databases such as DRIVE, STARE and DiaretDB. We have also tested our system on some locally collected data with large number of pathologies and variety of noise. DRIVE database has 40 retinal fundus images of size 768 × 584 [19]. The images were captured using Canon CR5 Non-Mydriatic

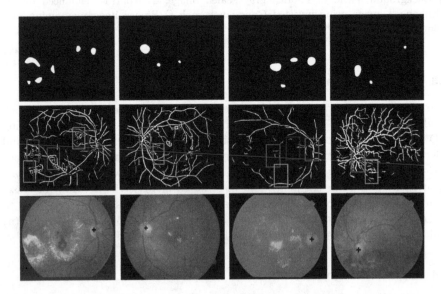

Fig. 4. Row1: Candidate regions, Row2: Bounding box marked on segmented vessels showing vessel density calculation, Row3: OD Detection and marked with cross on it

retinal camera with a 45 degree Field of View (FOV). STARE database has 400 retinal images which are acquired using TopCon TRV-50 retinal camera with 35 degree FOV having size of 700×605 [20]. DIARETDB (DIAbetic RETinopathy DataBase) is a database which is designed to evaluate automated lesion detection algorithms [21]. It contains 89 retinal images with different retinal abnormalities. The images are captured with a 50 degree FOV and a resolution of 1500×1152. Furthermore, we have used some locally collected images i.e. 462 images with a resolution of 1504×1000 and 100 images with a resolution of 1936×1296. Figure 4 shows results on different retinal images using proposed methodology.

A MATLAB based annotation tool is designed and OD centers are marked for all images with help of an ophthalmologist. These OD centers are considered as ground truths and the distance of automatically detected OD centers are calculated from these ground truths. OD is considered as correctly detected if the difference between automated and ground truths centers is less than 10 pixels.

4   Conclusion

Optic disc is a major landmark in digital fundus images and its automated detection helps in segmentation of other retinal landmarks. A novel and robust optic disc detection algorithm is presented in this paper. The proposed system consisted of four phases i.e. preprocessing, candidate regions for OD segmentation, retinal vessel segmentation and finally OD detection. The main contribution is that the proposed system is robust even in the presence of noise and large number of retinal abnormalities. The accuracy of the proposed system is 100%, 97.50%, 100% and 95.85% on DRIVE, STARE, DiaretDB and local images respectively. This algorithm can be used for automated detection of OD for grading of diseases like diabetic retinopathy, glaucoma and papilloedema.

Acknowledgments. This research is funded by National ICT Fund, Pakistan.

References

1. Ronald, P.C., Peng, T.K.: A textbook of clinical ophthalmology: a practical guide to disorders of the eyes and their management, 3rd edn. World Scientific Publishing Company, Singapore (2003)
2. Youssif, A.R., Ghalwash, A.Z., Ghoneim, A.R.: Optic Disc Detection From Normalized Digital Fundus Images by Means of a Vessels' Direction Matched Filter. IEEE Transactions on Medical Imaging **27**(1) (2008)
3. Sekhar, S., Nuaimy, W.A., Nandi, A.K.: Automated Localisation of Optic Disc and Fovea in retinal Fundus Images. In: 16th European Signal Processing Conference (EUSIPCO 2008), Lausanne, Switzerland, August 25-29 (2008)
4. Kose, C., Ikibas, C.: Statistical Techniques for Detection of Optic Disc and Macula and Parameters Measurement in Retinal Fundus Images. Journal of Medical and Biological Engineering **31**(6), 395–404 (2010)
5. Ying, H., Zhang, M., Liu, J.C.: Fractal-based Automatic Localization and Segmentation of Optic Disc in Retinal Images. In: 29th Annual International Conference of the IEEE EMBS, pp. 4139–4141 (2007)

6. Qureshi, R.J., Kovacs, L., Harangi, B., Nagy, B., Peto, T., Hajdu, A.: Combining algorithms for automatic detection of optic disc and macula in fundus image. Computer Vision and Image Understanding **116**(1), 138–145 (2012)

7. Zhang, D., Yi, Y., Shang, X., Peng, Y.: Optic Disc Localization by Projection with Vessel Distribution and Appearance Characteristics. In: 21st International Conference on Pattern Recognition (ICPR 2012), pp. 3176–3179 (2012)

8. Lupascu, C.A., Tegolo, D., Rosa, L.D.: Automated Detection of Optic Disc Location in Retinal Images. In: 21st IEEE International Symposium Computer based Medical Systems (CBMS), pp. 17–22 (2008)

9. Godse, D.A., Bormane, D.S.: Automated Localization of Optic Disc in Retinal Images. International Journal of Advanced Computer Science and Applications (IJACSA) **4**(2) (2013)

10. Kaur, J., Sinha, H.P.: Automated localization of optic disc and macula from fundus images. International Journal of Advanced Research in Computer Science and Software Engineering **2**(4), 242–249 (2012)

11. Haralick, R.M., Shapiro, L.G.: Computer and Robot Vision, vol. I, pp. 28–48. Addison-Wesley (1992)

12. Pratt, W.K.: Digital Image Processing, p. 634. John Wiley & Sons Inc., New York (1991)

13. Gonzalez, R.C., Woods, R.E.: Digital Image Processing, 3rd edn. Prentice Hall (2008)

14. Kharghanian, R., Ahmadyfard, A.: Retinal Blood Vessel Segmentation Using Gabor Wavelet and Line Operator. International Journal of Machine Learning and Computing **2**(5) (October 2012)

15. Sinthanayothin, C., Boyce, J.F., Cook, H.L., Williamson, T.H.: Automated location of the optic disk, fovea, and retinal blood vessels from digital color fundus images. Br. J. Ophthalmol. **83**, 902–910 (1999)

16. Mahfouz, A.E., Fahmy, A.S.: Fast localization of the optic disc using projection of image features. IEEE Trans. Image Process. **19**, 3285–3289 (2010)

17. Usman Akram, M., Khan, A., Iqbal, K., Butt, W.H.: Retinal Images: Optic Disk Localization and Detection. In: Campilho, A., Kamel, M. (eds.) ICIAR 2010, Part II. LNCS, vol. 6112, pp. 40–49. Springer, Heidelberg (2010)

18. Akram, M.U., Khan, S.A.: Multilayered thresholding-based blood vessel segmentation for screening of diabetic retinopathy. Engineering with computers (EWCO) **29**(2), 165–173 (2013)

19. Lalonde, M., Gagnon, L., Boucher, M.C.: Non-recursive paired tracking for vessel extraction from retinal images. In: Vision Interface, pp. 61–68 (2000)

20. Hoover, A., Goldbaum, M.: Locating the optic nerve in a retinal image using the fuzzy convergence of the blood vessels. IEEE Transactions on Medical Imaging **22**(8), 951–958 (2003)

21. Kauppi, T., Kalesnykiene, V., Kamarainen, J.K., Lensu, L., Sorri, I., Raninen, A., Voutilainen, R., Uusitalo, H., Klviinen, H., Pietil, J.: DIARETDB1 diabetic retinopathy database and evaluation protocol. Technical report (2006)

Coupled Parallel Snakes for Segmenting Healthy and Pathological Retinal Arteries in Adaptive Optics Images

Nicolas Lermé[1,2]([✉]), Florence Rossant[2], Isabelle Bloch[1],
Michel Paques[3], and Edouard Koch[3]

[1] Institut Mines-Télécom, Télécom ParisTech, CNRS LTCI, Paris, France
[2] LISITE, Institut Supérieur d'Électronique de Paris, Paris, France
[3] CIC 503, Centre Hospitalier National des Quinze-Vingts, Paris, France
nicolas.lerme@isep.fr

Abstract. In this paper, we propose two important improvements of an existing approach for automatically segmenting the walls of retinal arteries of healthy/pathological subjects in adaptive optics images. We illustrate the limits of the previous approach and propose to (i) modify the pre-segmentation step, and (ii) embed additional information through coupling energy terms in the parallel active contour model. The interest of these new elements as well as the pre-segmentation step is then evaluated against manual segmentations. They improve the robustness against low contrasted walls and morphological deformations that occur along vessels in case of pathologies. Noticeably, this strategy permits to obtain a mean error of 13.4 % compared to an inter-physicians error of 17 %, for the wall thickness which is the most sensitive measure used. Additionally, this mean error is in the same range than for healthy subjects.

Keywords: Active contour model · Adaptive optics · Retina imaging

1 Introduction

Arterial hypertension and diabetes mainly and precociously affect the physiology and the structure of retinal blood vessels of small diameter (i.e. less than $150\mu m$). According to the Public Health Agency of Canada, these chronic diseases affected 15 to 20% of the world's adult population in 2009. Hypertensive retinopathy (HR) and diabetic retinopathy (DR) are common ocular complications of the above diseases. The lesions caused by these complications include diffuse or focal narrowing, or dilation of the vessel and of the wall. Although HR and DR do not present early warning signs, they are predictive of end-organ damage such as stroke or visual loss [1,4]. In [8], the authors estimate that 98% of visual damages could be avoided if DR was treated in time. Accurate measurements of walls are therefore necessary to better prevent the DR

This work is funded by the ANR project ANR-12-TECS-0015-03 (2013–2015).

A. Campilho and M. Kamel (Eds.): ICIAR 2014, Part II, LNCS 8815, pp. 311–320, 2014.
DOI: 10.1007/978-3-319-11755-3_35

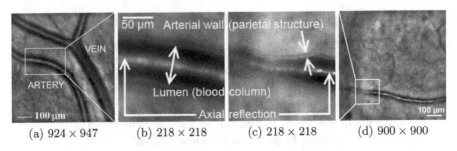

(a) 924 × 947   (b) 218 × 218   (c) 218 × 218   (d) 900 × 900

Fig. 1. Examples of images acquired by the AO camera [9] and a detailed view of them for an healthy subject (a),(b) and a pathological one (c),(d). The sizes below each image are expressed in pixels.

and the complications of the HR. Fundus photographs and Doppler-based measurements cannot however resolve the vessel walls due to their limited spatial resolution. Adaptive Optics (AO) is a recent opto-electronic technology that improves the resolution of fundus photographs. AO-based cameras permit to visualize microstructures such as vascular walls [2], noninvasively. In the present study, the rtx1 camera [9] is used to acquire 2D images by flood illumination at 10Hz using a 850nm LED light source with a pixel-resolution of 0.8μm. These images are registered and averaged to increase the signal-to-noise ratio [6]. In the resulting images, blood vessels appear as dark elongated structures with a bright linear axial reflection, over a textured background. Outer borders of walls are however only visible along arteries and the present study will focus on them. Parietal structures (arterial walls) appear as a gray line along both sides of the lumen (blood column), with a thickness of about 15% of it [5] (see Figure 1).

Segmenting the artery walls in these images is a challenging problem. For both pathological and healthy subjects, (i) the background of the related images is highly textured, (ii) significant intensity changes can occur along axial reflections, (iii) the outer borders of walls are low contrasted, and (iv) some vessel segments can be locally blurred due to the geometry of the retina. This problem is by far more challenging for images from pathological cases since a large variability of morphological deformations can locally occur along arteries, which generally present a poor contrast on walls. Since AO-based fundus cameras remain uncommon yet, only few papers have addressed this issue. Recently, an automatic procedure was proposed where the walls are modeled as four curves approximately parallel to a common reference line located near axial reflections [7]. Once the line is detected, the artery walls are pre-segmented using a tracking procedure to cope with morphological deformations. Then, they are segmented using an active contour model embedding a parallelism constraint to both control their distance to the reference line and improve the robustness against the noise and lack of contrast. The accuracy of this approach on pathological cases has however not been assessed.

In this paper, we propose two important improvements to this approach: (i) a piecewise constant estimation of the vessel diameter in the first stage of the pre-segmentation, and (ii) coupled energy terms in the active contours model. The purpose of these new elements is to improve the robustness against noise, low contrasted walls and morphological deformations in case of pathologies, while keeping a computational cost similar to the one of [7].

The rest of this paper is organized as follows. In Section 2, we briefly remind the approach in [7] for segmenting arterial walls on healthy subjects. Afterwards, we illustrate the limits of this approach and present the above new elements, in Section 3. Finally, we evaluate in Section 4 the relevance of the pre-segmentation step as well as these new elements, against manual segmentations.

2   An Approach for Segmenting Arterial Walls and Its Limits

2.1   Description

In this section, we remind the strategy presented in [7] for segmenting walls of retinal arteries. Let us consider one artery branch represented by a fixed curve located on the axial reflection, resulting of an automatic segmentation process [7]. We denote this branch as the reference line $V(s) = (x(s), y(s))^T$, parameterized by s. The artery walls are modeled by V_1, V_2 (inner) and V_3, V_4 (outer), four curves approximately parallel to the reference line V, defined by:

$$\begin{cases} V_1(s) = V(s) + b_1(s)n(s) \\ V_2(s) = V(s) - b_2(s)n(s) \\ V_3(s) = V(s) + b_3(s)n(s) \\ V_4(s) = V(s) - b_4(s)n(s), \end{cases} \quad \text{such that} \quad \begin{cases} b_1(s) < b_3(s) \\ b_2(s) < b_4(s), \end{cases} \quad \forall s, \quad (1)$$

where $n(s)$ is the normal vector to V and $b_k(s)$ is the local distance (or half-diameter) of any curve V_k to V. In the above model, notice the direct correspondence between the points of any curve V_k to those of the reference line V. The segmentation procedure amounts to compute the half-diameters $\{b_k\}_{k=1,\ldots,4}$.

The artery walls are first pre-segmented. This is achieved by simultaneously positioning the curves using a tracking procedure to cope with morphological deformations. All along this pre-segmentation, it is assumed that the opposite curves lie at the same distance from the reference line V (i.e. $b_1(s) = b_2(s) = b^{int}(s)$ and $b_3(s) = b_4(s) = b^{ext}(s)$, $\forall s$) and that the wall thickness is constant (i.e. $b^{ext}(s) - b^{int}(s) = cst$, $\forall s$). The reference line V and all the elements that refer to it are discretized into m equally spaced points. The pre-segmentation is based on a criterion to be maximized, defined for every $i \in \{1, \ldots, m\}$ by:

$$G(b^i, b^e, i) = \frac{\bar{D}^{int}(b^i, i, r)}{\bar{I}^{int}(b^i, i, r)} + \bar{D}^{ext}(b^e, i, r), \quad (2)$$

where $\bar{D}^{int}$ and $\bar{I}^{int}$ respectively denote the mean local gradient and the mean local intensity along inner curves while $\bar{D}^{ext}$ denote the mean local gradient along outer curves. $\bar{D}^{int}$, $\bar{I}^{int}$ and $\bar{D}^{ext}$ are averaged over a small window of size $(2r + 1)$. The function G encourages inner and outer curves to be located near large image gradients. Dividing by the mean intensity also favors inner curves to be located in dark areas. The pre-segmentation aims at estimating inner and outer half-diameters $b^{int}(s)$, $b^{ext}(s)$ and consists of the following steps:

1. Constant half-diameters b^{int_0} and b^{ext_0} along the artery, are estimated. This is achieved by maximizing the mean of $G(b^i, b^e, i)$ over $(b^i, b^e) \in (\mathbb{R}^+ \times \mathbb{R}^+)$ along the curves defined by the half-diameters b^i and b^e. We then denote by $\bar{e} = (b^{ext_0} - b^{int_0})$ the wall thickness estimated from the resulting curves.
2. The position i^* maximizing (2) along the curves from Step 1 is determined.
3. Variable half-diameters $b^{int}(s)$ and $b^{ext}(s) = b^{int}(s) + \bar{e} + e$ are estimated using tracking by maximizing for any $i \in \{i^* + 1, \ldots, m\}$ and for $j = i - 1$:

$$\alpha G(b^{int}(i), b^{int}(i) + \bar{e} + e, i) - (1 - \alpha)(b^{int}(i) - b^{int}(j))^2, \quad \alpha \in [0, 1], \quad (3)$$

where α is a regularization parameter. The closer α is to zero, the more the right term in (3) penalizes large local deviations of b^{int}. The above scheme is also applied to any $i \in \{i^* - 1, \ldots, 1\}$ and for $j = i + 1$. Once b^{int} has been fixed for any error e, the optimal error e^* is taken as the one that maximizes the sum of (3) over any $i \in \{2, \ldots, m\}$ and for $j = i - 1$ (see [7] for details).

Then, an active contour model (parallel snakes) is applied to accurately position the curves found by the pre-segmentation. This model is an extension of [3] for extracting four curves approximately parallel to a fixed reference line V. This is achieved by minimizing

$$E(V_1, \ldots, V_4, b_1, \ldots, b_4) = \sum_{k=1}^{4} \left(\underbrace{\int_0^1 P(V_k(s))\, ds}_{E_{Image}(V_k)} + \underbrace{\int_0^1 \varphi_k(s)(b_k'(s))^2\, ds}_{R(V_k, b_k)} \right), \quad (4)$$

where E_{Image} is designed to attract the curves towards large image gradients while R controls the variation of the half-diameter $b_k(s)$, thus imposing a local parallelism. The strength of this parallelism is controlled by the parameters $\{\varphi_k\}_{k=1,\ldots,4}$: the larger these parameters are, the more strict the parallelism to the reference line V is. It is worth noting that the assumptions made for the pre-segmentation are fully relaxed, i.e. the four curves can now evolve independently of each other. They are implicitly linked by the parallelism constraint but no symmetry property w.r.t. the reference line V is imposed. The minimization of (4) is obtained by solving the Euler-Lagrange equations w.r.t. the half-diameters b_k. The resulting algorithm uses standard numerical approximation of derivatives and converges until some accuracy ε is reached.

2.2   Limits

The approach detailed in [7] has two important limitations. For some cases, the pre-segmentation can fail to accurately position the curves close to artery walls. This situation is illustrated in the top row of Figure 2. The inner and outer half-diameters are underestimated at Step 1 due to the local narrowing of the artery. These poor estimations therefore prevent to perform the tracking procedure from a good initial position found at Step 2. The tracking procedure therefore fails to follow correctly morphological deformations. This suggests a more robust way to estimate the half-diameters at Step 1.

For some cases, the parallel snake model can also fail to accurately position the curves close to artery walls. This situation is illustrated in the bottom row of Figure 2. Although the solution provided by the pre-segmentation is correct, the positioning of the curves is inconsistent on an artery segment. Such a behavior is due to a poor contrast on the outer borders of walls. This suggests to enforce the regularity of the wall thickness along the arteries and also symmetry properties w.r.t. the reference line, as wall thicknesses are generally similar on both sides. Last but not least: the model (4) does not ensure that the constraints expressed in (1) hold. This point must also be addressed to ensure the anatomical consistency of the solution.

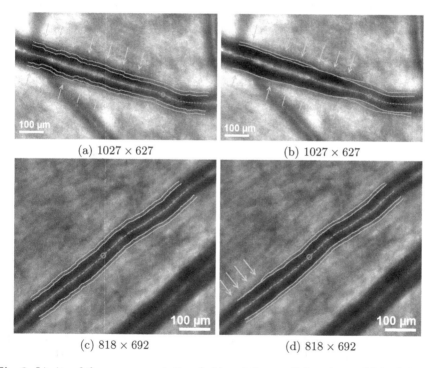

(a) 1027×627 (b) 1027×627

(c) 818×692 (d) 818×692

Fig. 2. Limits of the pre-segmentation (a,b) and the parallel snake model (c,d) for two distinct pathological subjects. Pre-segmentations and segmentations are respectively given in (a,c) and (b,d) columns, superimposed on the original image. Yellow arrows point misplacements of curves. The green dashed line corresponds to the reference line while the circle denotes the position from which the tracking procedure operates (see Step 2). The size of the images are expressed in pixels.

3 Improvements

3.1 Pre-segmentation

We propose a simple modification to overcome the difficulties outlined in Section 2.2. Instead of estimating inner and outer half-diameters as constant along vessels in Step 1, we propose to estimate them as piecewise constant. Then, the initial estimates of the inner and outer half-diameters are those found at the position maximizing (2) along the resulting piecewise constant curves (Step 2). In such a manner, these new half-diameters estimates are less prone to morphological deformations while keeping a good robustness against intensity changes along the artery walls. The robustness of the tracking process (Step 3) is therefore improved. In accordance to morphometric features, the piecewise constant estimations are performed on vessel segments whose length is 50 pixels ($\simeq 40\mu$m).

3.2 Coupled Parallel Snakes Model

To overcome the difficulties of the parallel snake model highlighted in Section 2.2, we propose to modify the energy (4) (see Section 2.1) as follows

$$E(V_1, \ldots, V_4, b_1, \ldots, b_4) = \sum_{k=1}^{4} \Big(E_{Image}(V_k) + R(V, V_k) \Big) + S(V_1, V_3, b_1, b_3)$$
$$+ S(V_2, V_4, b_2, b_4) + T(V_1, \ldots, V_4, b_1, \ldots, b_4), \quad (5)$$

where

$$S(V_i, V_j, b_i, b_j) = \int_0^1 \psi_{i,j}(s)(b_j(s) - b_i(s) - \beta_{i,j}^0)(b_j(s) - b_i(s) - \beta_{i,j}^1)ds,$$

$$T(V_1, \ldots, V_4, b_1, \ldots, b_4) = \int_0^1 \lambda(s)(b_3(s) - b_1(s) - b_4(s) + b_2(s))^2 ds,$$

and λ, $\psi_{1,3}$, $\psi_{2,4}$ are weighting parameters (independent of s in our application). Notice that E_{Image} and R in (5) are the same as in (4). The term T controls the wall thickness difference between $b_3(s) - b_1(s)$ and $b_4(s) - b_2(s)$, $\forall s$. It reaches a minimum for $b_3(s) - b_1(s) = b_4(s) - b_2(s)$, $\forall s$. The larger the parameter λ is, the more identical the wall thickness on both sides of the reference line $V(s)$ is. The main role of S is to control the variation of the wall thicknesses $b_3(s) - b_1(s)$ and $b_4(s) - b_2(s)$, with respect to the initial estimate $(b^{ext}(s) - b^{int}(s))$ found in the pre-segmentation step. This term reaches a minimum when the wall thickness is between $\beta_{i,j}^0$ and $\beta_{i,j}^1$, for $(i, j) = (1, 3)$ or $(i, j) = (2, 4)$. The larger the weighting parameters $\psi_{1,3}$ and $\psi_{2,4}$ are, the closer the wall thicknesses $b_3(s) - b_1(s)$ and $b_4(s) - b_2(s)$ are to $(b^{ext}(s) - b^{int}(s))$. Here, we set for any s

$$\beta_{1,3}^0 = \beta_{2,4}^0 = (1 - \gamma)(b^{ext}(s) - b^{int}(s)), \quad \beta_{1,3}^1 = \beta_{2,4}^1 = (1 + \gamma)(b^{ext}(s) - b^{int}(s)),$$
$$(6)$$

where $\gamma \in [0, 1]$. Since the resulting curves found by the pre-segmentation lie at the same distance from the reference line V, S also controls both the amount of symmetry of the curves V_1 / V_2 and V_3 / V_4 w.r.t the reference line V. The larger the parameters $\psi_{1,3}$ and $\psi_{2,4}$ are, the more strict the symmetry is. Unlike (4), (5) ensures that the constraints (1) hold as the parameters $\psi_{1,3}$ and $\psi_{2,4}$ tend to $+\infty$. Notice that when the weighting parameters λ, $\psi_{1,3}$ and $\psi_{2,4}$ are null, the energy (5) becomes the same as (4). Finally, the energy (5) is minimized in the same way as for (4).

4   Experimental Results

4.1   Data and Experimental Protocol

17 images from pathological subjects were manually segmented by 3 physicians. These physicians have several years of experience in AO image interpretation. Each physician segmented the images[1] two times, separated by several weeks to diminish the memory effect between both segmentations. The images were selected by the medical experts to ensure the representativeness of the quality of the images and the vessel deformations encountered during clinical routine.

Let us denote by S_1 and S_2 two distinct segmentations. To evaluate the accuracy of the segmentation S_1 w.r.t. the segmentation S_2, we choose to use the same measures as the ones described in [7], i.e. the absolute relative difference on the inner diameter δ_{int}, the outer diameter δ_{ext} and the total walls thickness δ_{wt} (i.e. the difference between outer and inner diameters). For each image, notice that these measures are expressed in percentages and are performed on the intersection of all manual segmentations from medical experts for that image. Then, we first estimate the intra-physician variability by computing the mean and standard deviation of the above measures between the segmentations of the same image, delineated by the same physician (see Table 1). Table 1 provides the same statistics but for a unit displacement of one pixel all along a curve.

As shown in Table 1, the physician $Phys_3$ has the smallest intra-physician variability for two measures out of three. Because this physician produced the most stable segmentations, we choose him as a reference and denote him as $Phys_{Ref}$. Next, we pre-segment all images with either variable (VHDI) or constant (CHDI) half-diameter estimations and using $r = 10$ (see Section 2.1). For both pre-segmentations, half-diameters are estimated in a piecewise constant manner, as proposed in Section 3.1. VHDI is for $\alpha = 0.95$ while CHDI is for $\alpha = 0$. From these pre-segmentations, parallel snakes (PS) and the coupled parallel snakes (CPS) models are applied (see Section 3.2). For both, we set $\varepsilon = 0.05$ and $\varphi_k = 100$, $\forall k \in \{1, \ldots, 4\}$. CPS is for $\gamma = 0.5$ while PS is for $\psi_{1,3} = 0$, $\psi_{2,4} = 0$ and $\lambda = 0$. The weighting parameters $\psi_{1,3}$, $\psi_{2,4}$ and λ involved in the CPS model have been optimized experimentally on a training set[2], consisting of eight images extracted from the database. The optimized values are the ones

---

[1] Each segmentation consists of a single artery branch.
[2] By convenience, we make the weighting parameters $\psi_{1,3}$ and $\psi_{2,4}$ equal.

Table 1. Overall intra-physician variability for inner diameter (ID), outer diameter (OD) and wall thickness (WT). All measures are in percentages. The numbers in parentheses correspond to a unit displacement all along a curve.

	$Phys_1$ / $Phys_1$	$Phys_2$ / $Phys_2$	$Phys_3$ / $Phys_3$
ID	4.0 ± 3.1 (1.0 ± 0.3)	4.7 ± 3.8 (1.0 ± 0.3)	4.3 ± 3.8 (1.1 ± 0.3)
OD	3.3 ± 2.8 (0.8 ± 2.2)	4.1 ± 3.5 (0.8 ± 0.2)	2.6 ± 2.1 (0.8 ± 0.2)
WT	16.5 ± 15.6 (2.9 ± 0.9)	23.8 ± 26.4 (3.4 ± 1.3)	15.2 ± 12.3 (2.9 ± 0.8)

Table 2. Accuracy of pre-segmentations with variable (VHDI) and constant (CHDI) half-diameters, parallel snakes (PS) and coupled parallel snakes (CPS), against manual segmentations from $Phys_{Ref}$ for inner diameter (ID), outer diameter (OD) and walls thickness (WT). The three first and last rows are respectively for training and test sets. Mean and standard deviations are given in percentages. The mean error produced by a unit displacement of a curve for δ_{int}, δ_{ext} and δ_{wt} over the whole database is respectively 1.01%, 0.74% and 3.1%.

	CHDI	CHDI+PS	CHDI+CPS	VHDI	VHDI+PS	VHDI+CPS	Inter-physicians.
ID	8.8 ± 7.3	6.6 ± 6.8	6.7 ± 6.8	6.0 ± 4.8	5.8 ± 4.3	5.8 ± 4.5	4.5 ± 3.7
OD	8.2 ± 6.9	8.2 ± 8.1	7.6 ± 7.7	4.6 ± 4.3	3.4 ± 3.1	3.3 ± 3.0	3.7 ± 2.9
WT	19.5 ± 16.2	32.3 ± 33.7	26.2 ± 27.7	16.3 ± 13.9	15.5 ± 12.7	13.8 ± 10.5	18.1 ± 14.1
ID	11.2 ± 12.6	12.5 ± 17.3	11.0 ± 13.6	5.7 ± 4.8	6.3 ± 6.4	5.7 ± 5.2	4.9 ± 2.2
OD	9.1 ± 9.5	8.1 ± 9.2	8.4 ± 9.3	4.2 ± 3.2	3.8 ± 2.8	3.9 ± 2.8	3.8 ± 3.1
WT	18.6 ± 17.0	30.8 ± 41.2	21.2 ± 20.7	16.6 ± 14.5	14.6 ± 12.9	13.4 ± 10.6	17.0 ± 13.1

that minimize the mean of the overall errors δ_{int} and δ_{ext}. A test set is composed of the nine remaining images. The optimized values are also applied in all configurations that involve the CPS, in both training and test sets. This leads to six distinct configurations: CHDI, VHDI, CHDI+PS, CHDI+CPS, VHDI+PS and VHDI+CPS. The accuracy of all of them is evaluated by computing the mean and the standard deviation of δ_{int}, δ_{ext} and δ_{wt} w.r.t. the manual segmentations from the physician $Phys_{Ref}$. The results are summarized in Table 2 and illustrated in Figure 3. The inter-physicians error is also given in Table 2: it is estimated between the segmentations from the physicians $Phys_1$ and $Phys_2$ w.r.t. those from the physician $Phys_{Ref}$.

4.2   Discussion

First, the overall mean error on δ_{wt} is much larger than the overall mean errors on δ_{int} and δ_{ext}. Due to the size of the parietal structures, the measure δ_{wt} is indeed very sensitive to curves displacements. In Table 2, the accuracy for the CPS model is almost the same between the training and test databases, meaning a good generalization of the parameters $\psi_{1,3}$, $\psi_{2,4}$ and λ.

The accuracy of CHDI is poor w.r.t. the inter-physician error, significantly worse that the one obtained with VHDI. Although this accuracy is globally improved when applying the PS or CPS models (CHDI+PS or CHDI+CPS), the final results are always worse than when relying on variable half-diameters (VHDI), showing the importance of the tracking in the pre-segmentation.

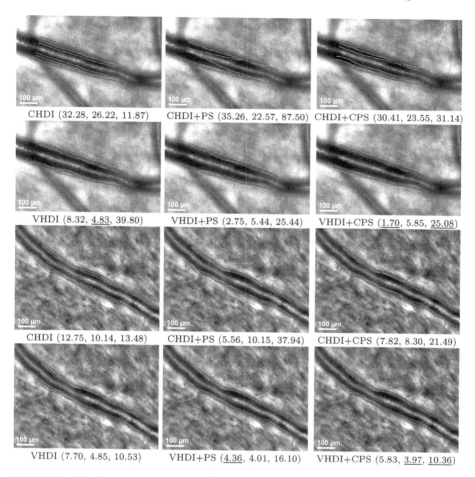

CHDI (32.28, 26.22, 11.87)   CHDI+PS (35.26, 22.57, 87.50)   CHDI+CPS (30.41, 23.55, 31.14)

VHDI (8.32, <u>4.83</u>, 39.80)   VHDI+PS (2.75, 5.44, 25.44)   VHDI+CPS (<u>1.70</u>, 5.85, <u>25.08</u>)

CHDI (12.75, 10.14, 13.48)   CHDI+PS (5.56, 10.15, 37.94)   CHDI+CPS (7.82, 8.30, 21.49)

VHDI (7.70, 4.85, 10.53)   VHDI+PS (<u>4.36</u>, 4.01, 16.10)   VHDI+CPS (5.83, <u>3.97</u>, <u>10.36</u>)

Fig. 3. Results for Subject 9 (half-top) and 7 (half-down) against manual segmentations from the physician $Phys_{Ref}$. Automatic and manual segmentations are respectively drawn in cyan and red. The green dashed line is the reference line. The green circles denote the position from which the tracking operates. The numbers below each image are respectively for δ_{int}, δ_{ext} and δ_{wt} (in percentages). For each subject and each measure, the underlined numbers represent the configuration having the better accuracy among all the other ones.

As mentioned previously, the accuracy provided by VHDI is much closer to the inter-physician error than with CHDI. It is still improved with the application of the PS model, except for δ_{int} on the test database, and, in average, it is always improved after the application of the CPS model. The final mean errors (VHDI+PS or VHDI+CPS) are close to the inter-physician errors for the internal and external diameters and lower for the wall thickness measures, the most sensitive ones. Overall, the VHDI+CPS flow reaches the best accuracy.

These observations are confirmed by the results depicted in Figure 3. For both subjects, VHDI+CPS reaches globally a better accuracy for two measures out of three. The interest of using variable half-diameters against constant ones in the pre-segmentation step is clear. However, it is less obvious when comparing CPS against PS. For Subject 9, VHDI+CPS shows a better accuracy than VHDI+PS for δ_{int} and δ_{wt}. The coupling permitted indeed to correct the position of the top inner curve. For Subject 7, the segmentation for VHDI+CPS is however a little worse than for VHDI+PS. This reduced performance is due to a local asymmetry w.r.t. the axial reflection. However, such asymmetries are very uncommon in practice (including on the presented images). Also, when we evaluate the interest of using either the energy terms S or T (see (5)), we found that the latter has a stronger impact on the accuracy than the former. Finally, we applied the VHDI+CPS flow on the database of healthy subjects (the one used in the study presented in [7]) and found an accuracy very close to the presented results, for all measures. Finally, for a typical 600μm long vessel branch, the processing time for the pre-segmentation and the CPS model is respectively about 120 and 30 secs. Future work will focus on a methodology for optimizing the parameterization of the CPS model (i.e. the weighting parameters $\psi_{1,3}$, $\psi_{2,4}$ and λ), according to the type of image to be segmented, in order to better manage the uncommon cases.

References

1. Buus, N.H., Mathiassen, O.N., Fenger-Grøn, M., Præstholm, M.N., Sihm, I., Thybo, N.K., Schroeder, A.P., Thygesen, K., Aalkjær, C., Pedersen, O.L., Mulvany, M.J., Christensen, K.L.: Small artery structure during antihypertensive therapy is an independent predictor of cardiovascular events in essential hypertension. Journal of Hypertension **31**(4), 791–797 (2013)
2. Chan, T.Y., Vannasdale, D.A., Burns, S.A.: The use of forward scatter to improve retinal vascular imaging with an adaptive optics scanning laser ophthalmoscope. Biomedical Optics Express **3**(10), 2537–2549 (2012)
3. Ghorbel, I., Rossant, F., Bloch, I., Paques, M.: Modeling a parallelism constraint in active contours. Application to the segmentation of eye vessels and retinal layers. In: International Conference on Image Processing (ICIP), pp. 445–448 (2011)
4. Heagerty, A.M., Aalkjær, C., Bund, S.J., Korsgaard, N., Mulvany, M.J.: Small artery structure in hypertension: Dual processes of remodeling and growth. Journal of Hypertension **21**, 391–397 (1993)
5. Koch, E.: Morphometric study of human retina arteriolars in high resolution imaging. Master's thesis, Universite Pierre et Marie Curie (2012)
6. Kulcsár, C., Le Besnerais, G., Ödlund, E., Levecq, X.: Robust processing of images sequences produced by an adaptive optics retinal camera. In: Optical Society of America, Adaptive Optics: Methods, Analysis and Applications, p. OW3A.3 (2013)
7. Lerme, N., Rossant, F., Bloch, I., Paques, M., Koch, E.: Segmentation of retinal arteries in adaptive optics images. In: International Conference on Pattern Recognition (2014)
8. Taylor, H., Keeffe, J.: World blindness: A 21st century perspective. British Journal of Ophtalmology **85**(3), 261–266 (2001)
9. Viard, C., Nakashima, K., Lamory, B., Paques, M., Levecq, X., Chateau, N.: Imaging microscopic structures in pathological retinas using a flood-illumination adaptive optics retinal camera. In: Photonics West: Biomedical Optics (BiOS), vol. 7885, pp. 788 509+ (2011)

Automatic Arteriovenous Nicking Identification by Color Fundus Images Analysis

Carla Pereira[1]($\boxtimes$), Diana Veiga[1,2], Luís Gonçalves[3], and Manuel Ferreira[1,2]

[1] Enermeter, Parque Industrial Celeirós, Lugar de Gaião, 4705-025 Braga, Portugal
cpereira@enermeter.pt
[2] Centro Algoritmi, Campus Azurém, 4800-058 Guimarães, Portugal
[3] Oftalmocenter, Azurém, 4800-045 Guimarães, Portugal

Abstract. Retinal arteriovenous nicking (AVN) assessment has been considered a very important indicator of cardiovascular and cerebrovascular diseases. A computerized method to infer the AVN presence in retinal images could increase the reproducibility and accuracy of this analysis that for now has been done by ophthalmologists in a subjective and qualitative manner. Therefore, a new approach is proposed for the AVN assessment in color fundus images. First the algorithm segments the blood vessels by means of a multi-scale line detector. The arteriovenous cross points are then detected and classified as AVN presence or absence with an SVM. The proposed approach is clearly efficient in separating normal cases from the evident or severe AVN cases.

Keywords: Arteriovenous nicking · Fundus images · Image processing

1 Introduction

The retinal arteriovenous nicking (AVN) is the phenomenon where a stiff artery crosses and compresses a vein (Fig. 1). The stiffness of the artery seems to be a persistent and long-term marker of hypertension and thus the assessment of AVN has been considered a very important indicator of cumulative vascular damage due to hypertension, ageing and other processes. For now, the assessment of AVN has been done by the ophthalmologists in a subjective and qualitative manner, being a very time consuming process, with low accuracy and reproducibility since it is heavily human expertise dependent. In this way, a computerized method to infer the AVN presence in retinal images could be very useful as a second opinion for the physiologists and to be used for large-scale clinical applications. In this study we propose an automatic method for the arteriovenous cross point (CP) detection in retinal images and for determining the AVN presence in each of them. As far as known,there is only one method in literature for the automatic AVN assessment [4].

This paper is organized as follows: section 2 describes the proposed approach constituted by several steps. The results are shown and discussed in section 3. Section 4 presents conclusions and some proposals for future research.

© Springer International Publishing Switzerland 2014
A. Campilho and M. Kamel (Eds.): ICIAR 2014, Part II, LNCS 8815, pp. 321–328, 2014.
DOI: 10.1007/978-3-319-11755-3_36

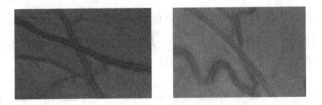

Fig. 1. Arteriovenous normal cross point (left) and arteriovenous nicking cross point (right)

2 Methodology

The algorithm initialized with the blood vessel segmentation followed by the vessel skeleton (centerline) extraction and the diameters measurement for the entire image. Then, the arteriovenous CP were detected, vein and artery were identified and the AVN presence was determined.

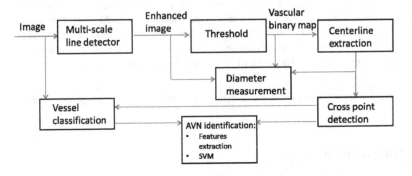

Fig. 2. Proposed approach schematic

2.1 Blood Vessel Segmentation

The multi-scale line detection technique developed by Nguyen et al. [5] for the blood vessel segmentation was chosen to be used in this study. This method consists of applying several line detectors at varying scales to produce an enhanced retinal image which is thresholded to obtain the final segmentation. This method revealed good results dealing well with the vessel central reflex and the noise presence while giving accurate vessel boundary detection.

2.2 Centerline Extraction

The vessel skeleton identification was very important for the next steps of the algorithm. Its extraction was performed by means of an iterative morphological thinning. The final result was a new binary image with connected lines of "on" pixels running along the vessel centers (centerlines). For each pixel P of the skeleton, the number of "on" neighbors was calculated and in that way, end pixels ($<$ 2 neighbors) and branch pixels ($>$ 2 neighbors) were identified. After removing the branching points, the vascular tree was divided into individual segments. Short segments ($<$ L pixels) including an end point were then removed, because they were considered spur segments.

2.3   Diameter Measurement

For the calculation of the vessel diameter for each pixel of the centerline, the algorithm developed by Bankhead et al. [1] was used with some differences. Firstly, a coarse vessel diameter estimation was calculated using the distance transform of the inverted binary vessel segmented image. With this coarse diameter, profiles for each vessel segment were generated and then used to obtain the edges points by means of local gradient. Actually, vessel profiles in fundus images resemble Gaussian functions and thus edges can be identified using the zero-crossing of the second derivative. The problem of that method is the "central light reflex", commonly present in wider vessels, and which is like a "hill" in the center of the vessel profile. In the present work, vessel profiles were taken from the enhanced image resulting from the multi-scale line detector to reduce this "central reflex" effect (Fig. 3). Finally, the diameter corresponded to the Euclidean distance between the determined edges points.

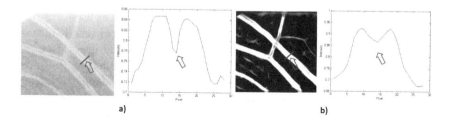

Fig. 3. Images and examples of cross section profile of a vessel: a) inverted green channel; b) enhanced image resulting from the multi-scale detector

2.4   Cross Point Detection

The detection of the CP position was inspired in the Nguyen et al. [4] work. From the skeleton image, pixels with more than 3 "on" neighbors were considered CP. Moreover, the branch candidates determined in the previous step distanced less than T pixels from each other were grouped and considered CP candidates. This phase permits to detect CPs that were represented by two branch points in the skeleton image when two vessels intersect at an acute angle (Fig. 4). The segment that connects the two branch points was identified and its middle point was determined for being the location of the CP. Then an analysis of the four segments connected to the two branch points was performed to distinguish true CP from spurious points resulting from locations that have the same configuration. By analyzing the intersection angles formed by the two vessels at the crossing (θ_1 and θ_2 in Fig. 4) and the angles representing the curvature of each vessel at the crossing (β1 and β2 in Fig. 4) it was possible to distinguish true CP from the falsely ones. Angles θ_1, θ_2, β1 and β2 were calculated using the vessel orientations determined in the previous step. In that way, a CP candidate was considered as a true CP if it satisfies condition (1).

$$max(\theta_1, \theta_2) < \theta_{max} \; and \; min(\beta_1, \beta_2) > \beta_{min} \qquad (1)$$

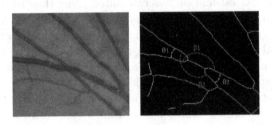

Fig. 4. Green channel image (left) and vessel skeleton image centered on a cross point (right)

2.5 Vessel Classification

For distinguishing vein from artery some color information was used. Nguyen et al. [4] studied the accuracy in distinguishing these two kinds of vessels in several channels of the RGB and HSV color spaces as well as the gray level. They demonstrated best results with the green channel by calculating the median intensity value of each vessel. Therefore, in this study the same metric was used to identify the veins. As the segments were pairwise, the use of the mean of the median values of both segments showed an improvement of the results. Actually, due to illumination variation present in this kind of images, one segment that corresponds to a vein can have a little higher median value than the arteries segments in the same CP.

2.6 Arterio-Venous Nicking Measurement

A supervised approach for the AVN assessment was used in the proposed approach. Three features for each vein of the CP under consideration were extracted. The chosen features are determined by equations (2)-(4), where D, Dc, A and $A_{missing}$ are represented in Fig. 5. D represents the normal vessel diameter obtained by the median value of the diameters of the segment that are situated in a minimum distance N from the CP. Dc is the vessel diameter at the region close to the CP and it is determined by the minimum value of the first N vessels diameters of the segment. A is the total number of pixels inside the vessel at region close to the CP if there is no decrease in vessel diameter (absence of AVN) and it is calculated by $N \times D$. $A_{missing}$ is determined by $A_1 + A_2 = N \times D - \sum_{i=1}^{N} d_i$ and corresponds to the number of pixels that is missing due to the presence of AVN.

$$M_A = \frac{A_{missing}}{A} \tag{2}$$

$$M_R = 1 - \frac{Dc}{D} \tag{3}$$

$$M_S = D - Dc \tag{4}$$

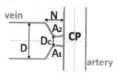

Fig. 5. Representation of a arteriovenous nicking cross point and respective measurements used as features for the supervised classification

In that way for each venular segment of a CP there were three different measures that should be bigger in the presence of AVN than in normal CP. For each feature, the maximum value of the two venular segments was then determined and the so obtained three measures for each CP were used as input to a support vector machine (SVM) [2]. The SVM classifies each CP relative to the presence or absence of AVN.

3   Results and Discussion

The algorithm performance was evaluated on a set of images online available (http://people.eng.unimelb.edu.au/thivun/projects/AV_nicking_quantification/). This dataset consists of 90 high resolution cropped images centered on arteriovenous CPs that were manually graded using a 3-scale grading system, in which 0 corresponds to a normal CP and 3 to the most severe AVN level. The dataset was divided in training and testing sets, each containing 45 images and the same number of images with AVN presence. To train the SVM two classes were defined: presence and absence of AVN.

There are several parameters referred along the proposed approach. They were empirically chosen by trial and error and their values are described in Table 1. It should be noticed that the parameters values are dependent on the camera resolution and magnification of the optical system, and they should be adapted to each retinal camera and the used setting.

Figure 6 illustrates a cropped image and the results obtained with the proposed approach. From left to right, it is possible to observe the green plane image

Table 1. Parameters values used in the proposed approach

Parameter	Threshold	Area	Eccentricity	L	T	θ_{max}	β_{min}	N
Value	0.56	600	0.8	20	40	115	135	10

with the detected arteriovenous CP and the determined centerlines and edges, the selected vessel segments that belong to a detected CP and the differentiation between veins, in blue, and arteries, in red.

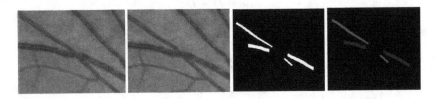

Fig. 6. From left to right: green channel image centered in a arteriovenous cross point with detected cross points; detected edges and centerlines superimposed in the green channel image; vessel segments belonging to the CP; representation of veins in blue and arteries in red

Quantitative results were obtained in terms of receive operating characteristic (ROC) curve where sensitivity values were plotted against the false negative rate values (1-Specificity). Moreover, the area under the curve and sensitivity and specificity values for the maximum accuracy [3] were calculated. Since there were three levels of AVN available and an SVM was used to classify the arteriovenous CP as AVN presence or absence, the original CP manual classification had to be divided in two classes. The SVM was trained by considered 0-level as normal CP and the other levels as CP with AVN. To verify the proposed approach performance in separate low and severe AVN presence, the following divisions were evaluated: 0 versus 1, 2, 3; 0, 1 versus 2, 3; 0, 1, 2 versus 3. Figure 8 and Table 2 show the results for all images of the dataset considered these three groups. Despite having good performance (over 80%) for all the groups, the algorithm is more efficient in the division 0, 1 versus 2, 3. In that way, the SVM was trained again, but considered 0 and 1–levels as normal CP and the other levels as CP with AVN, and the results for all images (0, 1 versus 2, 3 (new)) were very good with an AUC of 0.96.

From Table 2, it can be noticed that the specificity decreases from first to third group affecting also the accuracy. However, these values are more affected by the number of cases considered as CP with severe AVN which is very low comparing to the other class cases number (12 against 78).

Hereupon, the algorithm is very efficient to separate normal CP from CP with evident AVN. The 0 and 1 levels are very difficult to separate by the algorithm and even by human experts. Figure 8 illustrates two AVN grading: one provided with the dataset and another made by the retinal specialist of our research group,

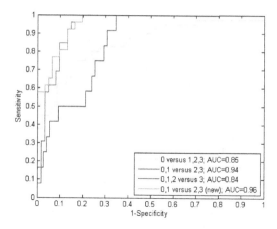

Fig. 7. ROC curves obtained for the several groups of classes

Table 2. Quantitative results in terms of accuracy, sensitivity and specificity

	Accuracy	Sensitivity	Specificity	AUC	AUC (Nguyen et al.)
0 versus 1,2,3	0,808989	0,738095	0,87234	0.85	0.86
0,1 versus 2,3	0,853933	0,961538	0,809524	0.94	0.92
0,1,2 versus 3	0,696629	0,916667	0,662338	0.84	0.91
0,1 versus 2,3 (new)	0,88764	0,846154	0,904762	0.96	-

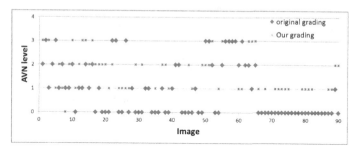

Fig. 8. Arteriovenous nicking level graded by different retinal specialists

who did not know the original classification. The difficulty and subjectivity of classifying a CP with an AVN level is evident in this figure. Actually, there are a few number of images classified with the same level of AVN.

The comparison with literature can be possible by comparing the AUC values from Fig. 7 with the equivalent values of Nguyen et al. [4] work (Table 2). The proposed approach performs as good or better than Nguyen et al. work for the two first groups of classes and for the third group (0,1,2 versus 3) a worse value was obtained.

4   Conclusion

This paper presents a new method for the AVN assessment. First the algorithm detects the arteriovenous CPs and then an SVM is used to classify the AVN presence or absence. Our approach is clearly efficient in separating normal cases from the evident or severe (over 1 level) AVN cases. It has some difficulties in separating between similar levels such as between 0 and 1 and between 2 and 3. However, these difficulties are common with human graders because this classification is very subjective.

As future work it would be important to add a first step of image quality evaluation to attribute a degree of confidence to the AVN level obtained. Moreover, other features should be integrated to improve the separation between the low level AVN CP and the normal CP, such as the arteriolar narrowing and the relationship between the arteriolar and venular calibers that are parameters considered by the retinal specialists to infer the possibility of presence of cardiovascular diseases.

References

1. Bankhead, P., Scholfield, C.N., McGeown, J.G., Curtis, T.M.: Fast retinal vessel detection and measurement using wavelets and edge location refinement. PloS One 7(3), e32435 (2012)
2. Gunn, S.R.: Support vector machines for classification and regression. ISIS Technical report 14 (1998)
3. Lalkhen, A.G., McCluskey, A.: Clinical tests: sensitivity and specificity. Continuing Education in Anaesthesia, Critical Care and Pain 8(6), 221–223 (2008)
4. Nguyen, U.T., Bhuiyan, A., Park, L.A., Kawasaki, R., Wong, T.Y., Wang, J.J., Mitchell, P., Ramamohanarao, K.: An automated method for retinal arteriovenous nicking quantification from color fundus images. IEEE Transactions on Biomedical Engineering 60(11), 3194–3203 (2013)
5. Nguyen, U.T., Bhuiyan, A., Park, L.A., Ramamohanarao, K.: An effective retinal blood vessel segmentation method using multi-scale line detection. Pattern Recognition 46(3), 703–715 (2013)

Detection of Hemorrhages in Colored Fundus Images Using Non Uniform Illumination Estimation

M. Usman Akram[1,2(✉)], Sarmad Abbas Khitran[1,2], Anam Usman[1,2], and Ubaid ullah Yasin[3]

[1] College of Electrical and Mechanical Engineering, National University of Sciences and Technology, Islamabad, Pakistan
[2] Center for Advanced Studies in Engineering, Islamabad, Pakistan
[3] Armed Forces Institute of Ophthalmology, Rawalpindi, Pakistan
{usmakram,sarmadkhitran,anam.tariq86}@gmail.com

Abstract. Hemorrhages are retinal lesions caused because of different eye diseases such as diabetic retinopathy, hypertensive retinopathy and macular oedema. This paper presents a novel method for detection of hemorrhages form digital fundus images. The proposed system consists of preprocessing, candidate hemorrhage detection, removing of false regions and hemorrhage detection. The proposed system also consists of illumination estimation using non uniform circular points grid for proper detection of hemorrhages. The evaluation of proposed system is done using publicly available fundus image databases along with some locally collected images. The analysis has been done at image level and results are compared with existing techniques for hemorrhage detection.

1 Introduction

Automatic fundus image analysis system proved to be quite helpful for ophthalmologists and an important area of medical imaging. These systems help in early diagnosis of the eye disease and treatment planning hence saving patients' vision. One of the common eye abnormality caused due to diabetes is Diabetic Retinopathy [1]. It damages the retina due to high glucose in blood resulting in total vision loss. Hence this disease should be detected at an early stage in order to save the vision. Hemorrhage is a major sign of Diabetic retinopathy.

Hemorrhages are caused due to bleeding of blood vessels in the retina. This retinal bleeding can be seen as dot and flame hemorrhages in retinal images. Hence the detection of hemorrhages is an important task for the early diagnosis of diabetic retinopathy. The shape and size of the hemorrhages is determined by the retinal layers that are affected [1]. There are two types of retinal hemorrhages which are common in diabetic retinopathy i.e. 'dot hemorrhages' and 'flame hemorrhages'.

© Springer International Publishing Switzerland 2014
A. Campilho and M. Kamel (Eds.): ICIAR 2014, Part II, LNCS 8815, pp. 329–336, 2014.
DOI: 10.1007/978-3-319-11755-3_37

Several state of the art techniques are presented in literature for the detection of hemorrhages [2]-[9]. Hatanaka et al. [2] proposed an automated lesion detection system which detects hemorrhages also. Hemorrhages are detected using double-ring filter and machine learning method using 64 textural features. This method was tested on DRIVE dataset yielding 83% and 67% sensitivity and specificity respectively. Kande et al. [4] also proposed a system for automatic detection of Hemorrhages in digital fundus images. The method involved mathematical morphology, matched filter and support vector machine (SVM) classification. This method was tested on STARE, Diaretdb0 and Diaretdb1 databases having overall sensitivity and specificity values of 100% and 91% respectively. Hatanaka et al. [5] proposed another method for retinal hemorrhages detection using brightness correction. After that, hemorrhage feature set is formulated using density analysis and classification is done using rule based method. The technique was examined on 125 fundus images having sensitivity and specificity of 80% and 88% respectively. Another retinal hemorrhage detection method using morphological top hat and rule based classification was proposed by Kleawsirikul et al. [6]. The proposed method was tested on Diaretdb1 database achieving sensitivity of 80.37%, specificity of 99.53% and accuracy of 99.12%. Tang et al. [8] and R. V. Athira et al [9] proposed a splat feature classification approach for the detection of hemorrhages. MESSIDOR dataset is used to evaluate the algorithm and area under the curve (AUC) of 0.87 was obtained.

This paper comprises of four sections. Section 2 contains proposed methodology followed by experimental results in section 3. Section 4 contains conclusion.

2   Proposed Method

Hemorrhages are retinal lesions which appear as a sign of different eye diseases. Computer aided eye diagnostic systems should be able to detect hemorrhages from digital fundus images if present. The proposed system takes colored fundus image is as input and applies preprocessing on this image which results in padded green channel and Back Ground Mask (BG Mask). Then it applies illumination estimation with in non-uniform circular shaped gird and segments out candidate dark lesions. The blood vessels are extracted from preprocessed image and then false candidate regions are removed to give final hemorrhages. Figure 1 shows the flow diagram of proposed system for hemorrhage detection.

2.1   Preprocessing

Preprocessing of the image involves the segmentation of the background and extraction of the green channel because it has the most contrast [10]. After that a padding of fundus region on green channel is applied to reduce occurrence of error near border, as due to the sharp change of gray levels a strong response is produced by the filters near border. This process involves the series of steps which are:

1. First the green channel is extracted from the RGB Fundus image.

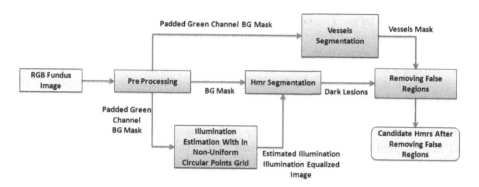

Fig. 1. Flow diagram of proposed system

2. For background mask (BG mask) estimation, an optimal threshold value is selected and with this an initial thresholding operation is applied on the green channel and then morphological operations i.e opening and closing are applied to remove small false objects present in the BG mask.
3. To pad the fundus region a resize of the image using bilinear interpolation is applied and then a sub-image (same size as the actual image) is selected at the center.
4. Multiply cropped image with compliment of the BG mask to get a ring of image which is added with the actual green channel to get the final padded green channel image.

2.2 Illumination Estimation with in Non-uniform Circular Shaped Grid

This phase takes a segmented BG mask and Green channel as inputs and performs illumination estimation with in non-uniform circular shaped gird. Due to issues during acquisition, retinal images contain non-uniform illumination contrast in intra/inter image [11].

In the retinal imaging scenario, the degradation functions have to be estimated from a given image. According to the image formation model presented in [12], the image $f(x, y)$ can be formed by product of two components

$$f(x, y) = i(x, y)r(x, y) \tag{1}$$

where $i(x, y)$ is the illumination component which causes degradation in fundus image and $r(x, y)$ is the reflectance component. In order to remove the effect of non uniform illumination, the estimation of illumination component is required so that the reflectance component can be calculated by using equation 1.

Illumination Estimation with Non-uniform Circular Points Grid. Retina is a round surface illuminated by a source of light located very close to eye, a few centimeters away. The camera close to eye captures the reflected illumination from the retina. Due to this geometry, the peripheral part of retina gets less illumination and appears dark than the central region of the retinal image [13]. So with the above setup in mind, we work on a non-uniform circular shaped grid to approximate the perimeters for the estimation of degradation component of retinal surface. Furthermore the fundus background, without any other fundus components, can be modeled statistically using Gaussian distribution $N(\mu_b, \delta_b)$ where μ_b represents uniform luminosity and δ_b means natural variability of retinal fundus pigmentation. For each pixel (x, y), the Mahalanobis distance [14] from μ_b, i.e. $DM(x, y)$, is defined as

$$DM(x, y) = |\frac{I_c(x, y) - \mu_b(x, y)}{\delta_b(x, y)}| \tag{2}$$

Now if $DM(x, y)$ is less than appropriate threshold th, then pixel (x, y) belongs to background, otherwise it belongs to foreground (including all kind of anatomies and lesions) [14]. In order to calculate $DM(x, y)$, we need to estimate μ_b and δ_b. The sequence of steps involve computing these parameters are:

1. Initialize a non-uniform circular shaped gird. The proposed system uses a grid of scale 6 times less than the actual image in order to increase the efficiency of the system (fig-2 (a)).
2. Calculate grid of Local Mean (*Lmean*) $lg(x, y)$, and standard deviation (STD) $sg(x, y)$ with in window of size $w_x \times w_y$ (fig-2 (b) and (c)).
3. Filter the empty regions present in the grid image of $sg(x, y)$ and $lg(x, y)$ to estimate $\mu_b(x, y)$ and $\delta_b(x, y)$ using equations 3 and 4 respectively.

$$\mu_b(x, y) = (lg(x, y) * mask)/g(x, y) * mask \tag{3}$$

$$\delta_b(x, y) = (sg(x, y) * mask)/g(x, y) * mask \tag{4}$$

where $mask(n_1, n_2) = \frac{-(n_1^2 + n_2^2 - 2\sigma^2)h_g(n_1, n_2)}{2\pi\sigma^6 \sum_{n_1} \sum_{n_2} h_g}$ is Gaussian kernel, with the standardize parameters $h_g(n_1, n_2) = e^{\frac{-(n_1^2 + n_2^2)}{2\sigma^2}}$.

4. Up sample $\mu_b(x, y)$ and $\delta_b(x, y)$ by using bilinear interpolation to bring it back to actual scale of the image (fig-2 (d), (e)).
5. Calculate absolute Mahalonobis (MHB) Distance $DM(x, y)$ given in equation 2.
6. Select background pixels by choosing all those pixels which have $DM(x, y) \leq t$ where t is a fixed threshold (fig-2 (f)).
7. Apply 2-D order-statistic filter to fill foreground holes present in the selected background image to estimate the illumination (fig-2 (g)).
8. Perform illumination equalization of the green channel by using equation 5 (fig-2 (h))

$$R(x, y) = f(x, y)/i(x, y) \tag{5}$$

Figure-2 shows the results of each step for illumination estimation.

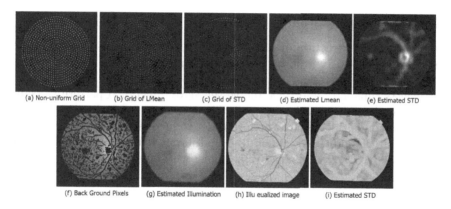

(a) Non-uniform Grid   (b) Grid of LMean   (c) Grid of STD   (d) Estimated Lmean   (e) Estimated STD

(f) Back Ground Pixels   (g) Estimated Illumination   (h) Illu eualized image   (i) Estimated STD

Fig. 2. Illumination estimation with in non-uniform circular shaped gird

2.3   Hemorrhage Segmentation

A two stage approach is proposed to eliminate the disturbance of other anatomy and lesions while detection of hemorrhages. First $\mu_b(x, y)$ and $\delta_b(x, y)$ are estimated from original image and $DM(x, y)$ is thresholded with a threshold t which separates foreground and background. Then after illumination equalization, corresponding $\delta_b(x, y)$ is estimated again (fig-2 (i)) and $\mu_b(x, y)$ is used form the previous calculation. Hmr appers as dark lesions so proposed system should consider only dark foreground containing vessels, macula and dark lesions. This is done using equation 6

$$DM_d(x, y) = DM(x, y) < t \tag{6}$$

It is not efficient to find a fixed threshold value to implement a best separation, due to the large variability of illumination and contrast in intra/inter image. Therefore, an adaptive approach to control suitable threshold Th_{df} is required to attain well segmentation results. Excluding dark lesions, vessels and fovea regions we assume that at least 50% of the pixels are background pixels, the neighborhood N with larger hemorrhages has larger standard deviation but smaller mean intensity, while in a neighborhood N with less vasculature or MAs, it appears smaller standard deviation but larger mean intensity. So an adaptive threshold selection method is taken using equation 7

$$Th_{df}(x, y) = thl - k_d * \frac{\mu_b(x, y)/\delta_b(x, y) - min(\mu_b(x, y)/\delta_b(x, y))}{max(\mu_b(x, y)/\delta_b(x, y)) - min(\mu_b(x, y)/\delta_b(x, y))} \tag{7}$$

where $max(\mu_b(x, y)/\delta_b(x, y))$ and $min(\mu_b(x, y)/\delta_b(x, y))$ are the maximum and minimum values of ratio of μ_b and δ_b for each and every pixel respectively. k_d is a gain parameter and in our experiments it is set to 2.5. thl is a base threshold, which can be specified to different values during detection of hemorrhages ($thl = -1 or - 1.25$). Figure-3 (a) shows the results of segmentation of candidate dark lesions.

2.4   Vessel Segmentation

The next step is extraction of blood vessels to measure vessel density in each candidate OD region. In proposed system, vascular pattern is enhanced by using 2-D Gabor wavelet for their better visibility. Gabor wavelets have directional selectiveness capability and since the vessels have directional pattern so Gabor wavelets enhance the vessels very well. The second step which is used in vascular extraction is the segmentation. In order to increase the accuracy of vessel segmentation, the proposed system uses multilayered thresholding approach to make sure the extraction of small vessel along with large ones [15].

2.5   Removing False Candidate Regions

In order to remove false candidate regions, some shaped based features and a gradient based feature are calculated for each candidate region. The sequences of steps on processing of shape based feature are:

1. Subtraction of thinned vessels mask from the $DM_d(x, y)$ to make the vessels weaker near the branches points.
2. Mark all dark pixels as candidate hemorrhage or non-hemorrhage using following steps
   (a) Morphologically open the original dark region mask with the structuring element.
   (b) Remove small objects from the mask by morphological erosion.
   (c) Remove pixels that have already been marked from the mask.
   (d) For all separate objects left in the mask, calculate properties of the object such are compactness and ratio of major to minor axis.
   (e) If compactness of the object is higher than a preset threshold and the ratio of the object is higher than a preset threshold then mark this object as hemorrhage otherwise mark this object as non-hemorrhage object.

The other feature that is calculated is gradient near the boundary of each object and all the object having feature value greater than t_{gd} are kept as dark lesions. t_{gd} is calculated using equation 8

$$t_{gd} = 0.16 * std(f(x, y)^4 \qquad (8)$$

Figure-3 (c) shows the results after removing false candidates by applying features and figure-3 (d) shows the masked final results of hemorrhages detection.

3   Results

The quantitative assessment of the proposed system of hemorrhage detection is done by using two publicly available databases i.e. DiaretDB [16] and MESSI-DOR [17]. We have also tested our system on some locally collected data with large number of pathologies and variety of noise. Local database consists of 462 images with a resolution of 1504 × 1000 and 100 images with a resolution of 1936

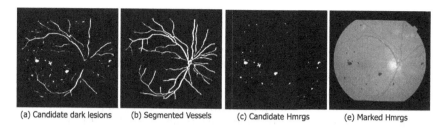

(a) Candidate dark lesions   (b) Segmented Vessels   (c) Candidate Hmrgs   (e) Marked Hmrgs

Fig. 3. Candidate dark lesions and Hemorrhages after removing false regions

Table 1. Comparative analysis of proposed system with existing techniques

Author	Accuracy (%)	Sensitivity (%)	Specificity (%)	AUC
Hatanaka et al. [2]	-	83	67	-
Kande et al. [4]	-	100	91	-
Kleawsirikul et al. [6]	99.1	80.37	99.5	-
Tang et al. [8]	-	-	-	0.87
Proposed System	**97.3**	**94.7**	**95.5**	**0.92**

× 1296. The quantitative analysis of proposed system is done using performance measures i.e. sensitivity, specificity, accuracy and area under the curve (AUC) at image level. The comparative analysis of proposed system with existing methods have been done in table-1.

4   Conclusion

This paper presented a novel method for detection of hemorrhages form digital fundus images. The proposed system estimated background from input retinal image using preprocessing step and used non-uniform illumination estimation using circular points grid. The proposed system removed all false regions before deciding for final hemorrhage regions. The vascular pattern is extracted and removed to cater for any false region because of blood vessels. The proposed system consists of preprocessing, candidate hemorrhage detection, removing of false regions and hemorrhage detection. The proposed system also consists of illumination estimation using non uniform circular points grid for proper detection of hemorrhages. The evaluation of proposed system is done using publicly available fundus image databases along with some locally collected images. The analysis has been done at image level and results are compared with existing techniques for hemorrhage detection.

Acknowledgments. This research is funded by National ICT Fund, Pakistan.

References

1. Ronald, P.C., Peng, T.K.: A textbook of clinical ophthalmology: a practical guide to disorders of the eyes and their management, 3rd edn. World Scientific Publishing Company, Singapore (2003)
2. Hatanaka, Y., Mizukami, A., Muramatsu, C., Hara, T., Fujita, H.: Automated lesion detection in retinal images. In: 4th International Symposium on Applied Sciences in Biomedical and Communication Technologies (ISABEL) (2011)
3. Akram, M.U., Khalid, S., Tariq, A., Khan, S.A., Azam, F.: Detection and Classification of Retinal Lesions for Grading of Diabetic Retinopathy. Elsevier Journal of Computers in Biology and Medicine **45**, 161–171 (2014)
4. Kande, G.B., Savithri, T.S., Subbaiah, P.V.: Automatic Detection of Microaneurysms and Hemorrhages in Digital Fundus Images. Journal of Digital Imaging **23**(4), 430–437 (2010)
5. Hatanaka, Y., Nakagawa, T., Hayashi, Y., Kakogawa, M., Sawada, A., Kawase, K., Hara, T., Fujita, H.: Improvement of Automatic Hemorrhages Detection Methods using Brightness Correction on Fundus Images. In: Proc. of SPIE, Medical Imaging, Computer Aided Diagnosis (2008)
6. Kleawsirikul, N., Gulati, S., Uyyanonvara, B.: Automated Retinal Hemorrhage Detection Using Morphological Top Hat and Rule-based Classification. In: 3rd International Conference on Intelligent Computational Systems (ICICS 2013), pp. 39–43 (2013)
7. Akram, M.U., Khalid, S., Khan, S.A.: Identification and Classification of Microaneurysms for Early Detection of Diabetic Retinopathy. Pattern Recognition **46**(1), 107–116 (2013)
8. Tang, L., Niemeijer, M., Reinhardt, J.M., Garvin, M.K., Abrmoff, M.D.: Splat Feature Classification With Application to Retinal Hemorrhage Detection in Fundus Images. IEEE Transactions on Medical Imaging 32(2) (2013)
9. Athira, R.V., Shahila, F.D.: Detection of Retinal Hemorrhage Using Splat Feature Classification Technique. Int. Journal of Engineering Research and Applications **4**(1), 327–330 (2014)
10. Tariq, A., Akram, M.U.: An Automated System for Colored Retinal Image Background and Noise Segmentation. In: IEEE Symposium on Industrial Electronics and Applications (ISIEA 2010), October 3-6, Penang, Malaysia, pp. 405–409 (2010)
11. Foracchia, M., Grisan, E., Ruggeri, A.: Luminosity and contrast normalization in retinal images. Medical Image Analysis **3**(9), 179–190 (2005)
12. Gonzalez, C., Woods, R.E.: Digital Image Processing, 3rd edn. Prentice Hall (2008)
13. Joshi, G.D., Sivaswamy, J.: Colour Retinal Image Enhancement based on Domain Knowledge. In: Sixth Indian Conference on Computer Vision, Graphics & Image Processing
14. Zhang, D., Li, X., Shang, X., Yi, Y., Wang, Y.: Robust Hemorrhage Detection in Diabetic Retinopathy image
15. Akram, M.U., Khan, S.A.: Multilayered thresholding-based blood vessel segmentation for screening of diabetic retinopathy. Engineering with computers (EWCO) **29**(2), 165–173 (2013)
16. Kauppi, T., Kalesnykiene, V., Kamarainen, J.K., Lensu, L., Sorri, I., Raninen, A., Voutilainen, R., Uusitalo, H., Klviinen, H., Pietil, J.: DIARETDB1 diabetic retinopathy database and evaluation protocol. Technical report (2006)
17. MESSIDOR: http://messidor.crihan.fr/index-en.php

Automatic Robust Segmentation of Retinal Layers in OCT Images with Refinement Stages

Ana González-López[1][(✉)], Marcos Ortega[1],
Manuel G. Penedo[1], and Pablo Charlón[2]

[1] Departamento de Computación, Universidade da Coruña, A Coruña, Spain
[2] Sociedad Gallega de Optometría Clínica, Santiago de Compostela, Spain
{ana.gonzalez,mortega,mgpenedo}@udc.es,
pcharlon@sgoc.es

Abstract. At the present, Optical Coherence Tomography (OCT) is a very promising imaging technique used by ophthalmologists for diagnosing because it provides more information than other classical modalities. Retinal structures can be studied on these images, so image processing-based methods are emerging to extract their information. Previously to any automatic feature extraction process, delimitation of retinal layers must be automated. With that purpose, this paper presents an active contour-based method to segment retinal layer boundaries. Regarding previous work, it is remarkable that this proposal includes processes of refinement for segmented layers. Thus, validation done by an opthalmologic expert shows that the method obtains accurate results even when some of these layers present alterations or low definition, making it robust, which is a very important feat.

1 Introduction

Optical Coherence Tomography (OCT) retinal images are useful for ophthalmologists to diagnose disease, since they provide a cross sectional image of the retina in a non-invasive, real time fashion[1]. Retinal morphology can be identified effectively with this technique, allowing explaining disease pathogenesis and progression. Several diseases can be diagnosed with an OCT retinal analysis, such as diabetic retinopathy[2]. Therefore, a precise segmentation of retinal layers is essential for opthalmologic experts.

The aim of this paper is presenting an automatic method for retinal layer segmentation in OCT images. Internal Limiting Membrane (ILM) and Myoid/Ellipsoid are considered, as well as limits of Retinal Pigment Epithelium-Bruch's Complex (RPE-BC) with the Interdigitation and Choroid. They will be referenced as ILM, M/E, I/RPE and RPE/C in this work. ILM and RPE/C correspond to limits of the retinal surface, whereas M/E and I/RPE bound the

---

This paper has been partly funded by the Secretaría de Estado de Investigación, Desarrollo e Innovación of the Spanish Government (A. González-López acknowledges its support under *FPI* Grant Program).

A. Campilho and M. Kamel (Eds.): ICIAR 2014, Part II, LNCS 8815, pp. 337–345, 2014.
DOI: 10.1007/978-3-319-11755-3_38

External Zone of Photoreceptors (marked in Fig. 1 as EZFR). Bounding this zone is interesting because it is the focus of several opthalmologic studies, since its layers are strongly correlated with retinal sensitivity[3] or visual recovery after surgery[4].

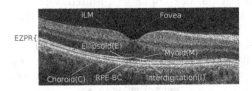

Fig. 1. Sample OCT image marked with the retinal layers considered in this work

Different approaches have been studied to segment retinal layers. Although graph-based[5] and shortest path-based[6] techniques obtain promising results, other methods can be used, such as active contours-based methods[7,8], which also provide appropriate segmentation. Not many methods offer a quantitative analysis of results and, from these ones, most of them are very restricted and do not seem be valid in a general case. Therefore, the aim of this work is proposing a method for retinal layer segmentation which provides appropriate segmentation not only when layers are appreciable, but also when vessel shades are present, altered layers and fusion or absence of some of them in certain parts of the retina. This method is based on active contours and includes a phase to correct the possible mistakes made in the segmentation task, derived from these situations.

This paper is organized as follows: in Sec. 2, general methodology for automatic layer boundary segmentation is exposed. Section 3 shows results obtained with this technique and in Sec. 4 conclusions and future work are presented.

2   Methodology

This work proposes an active contour-based method to segment retinal layer boundaries. Global methodology (Fig. 2) is composed by four stages of segmentation (ILM, M/E, I/RPE and RPE/C) and two later stages of refinement of these boundaries. Firstly, ILM is segmented. Using that information, foveal area can be located roughly using several frames (it corresponds to a hollow in the layer). After that, segmentation of RPE/C and then, M/E and I/RPE is done.

Segmentation stages provide appropriate results. However, due to alterations in the retina caused by some pathologies, M/E segmentation can be wrong and a refinement process is needed. In the same way, I/RPE and RPE/C are also refined combining information of their location to achieve a better adjustment.

Regarding the method to segment layer boundaries, it is described in the next section.

Fig. 2. Global method: segmentation of layer boundaries with refinement stages

2.1 Segmentation of Layer Boundaries

Layer boundary segmentation requires two phases, shown in Fig. 3: region of interest (ROI) is bounded and a first approach for the boundary is obtained, using it as initialization of the active contour used in the second stage. The configuration of the active contour depends on each layer boundary, given that they present different features. Finally, positions of contour nodes are interpolated to determine the entire boundary. This method is applied for all boundaries considered in this work: ILM, M/E, I/RPE and RPE/C.

Fig. 3. Steps to segment a layer boundary

Preprocessing. Firstly, ROI where the searching will be done is bounded. After image enhancement and binarization, morphological operators are applied. First approach for layer boundary is determined based on the pixels that remains at each column. This boundary is fitted to a curve to initialize the active contour in next phase. ROI is bounded with n_a and n_b pixels above and below the initial boundary.

Active Contour Model-Based Segmentation. Segmentation is based on active contours. An active contour[9] is an energy-minimizing spline guided by external and internal forces that pull it towards features in the image. Internal forces govern model behaviour (curvature, continuity), whereas external forces attract the contour to the desired features in the image, following:

$$E_{\text{total}} = \int E_{\text{int}}(v(s)) + E_{\text{ext}}(v(s))ds \qquad (1)$$

Topology used in this problem is a lineal sequence of equidistant n_{ac} nodes. Each node corresponds to one pixel in the image and has two neighbors, except for the first and the last ones. Experiments are done using a greedy approach.

Regarding internal forces, first and second-order terms are included to reflect curve behaviour, represented by $v_s(s)$ and $v_{ss}(s)$, but also $v_{ss_{nhb}}(s)$, defined as the second-order term over a neighborhood n_{nhb}, to encourage curve continuity:

$$E_{\text{int}} = \alpha(s)|v_s(s)|^2 + \beta(s)|v_{ss}(s)|^2 + \gamma(s)|v_{ss_{nhb}}(s)|^2 \qquad (2)$$

With regards to external forces, it is necessary to introduce that the proposed model works over two images at once: first one is the original image after smoothing and augmenting contrast, while the second one is resulting of a more aggressive preprocessing, based on a median filter. That allows considering different level of information at once during the process. External energy terms are extracted from both preprocessed images. Intensity of the current pixel, as well as intensity of the area above (or below) it are considered. Also, edge functional, extracted using Sobel algorithm with Non-maximum suppression, and gradient distance (edges corresponding to light-to-dark or dark-to-light transitions, depending on the boundary). A new term is included to represent distance between a node and the strongest edge in the area of searching.

Obviously, active contour configuration depends on the boundary of interest. Internal energy terms, as well as information of edges, are used to segment all boundaries. Edges considered for ILM, M/E and I/RPE correspond to dark-to-light transitions, while RPE/C is identified with light-to-dark ones. Term encouraging light intensities below is used to segment RPE/C and M/E, whereas only M/E requires term encouraging dark intensity above. An additional term encouraging areas located at the top of image regarding those located at bottom is used in ILM model.

Segmentation is obtained through n_s steps of adjustment of the active contour, depending on the boundary. These steps allows to adjust parameters dynamically, in function of the information that must be considered (in general, external energy is more predominant in the first steps to attract the contour to the desired features, whereas the internal typically increases in the final steps). For ILM, $n_s = 3$: firstly, external energy governs the process; then, internal energy increases and finally, more nodes are added in the center of the image to segment the fovea accurately.

For RPE/C, $n_s = 2$: a coarse detection and then, a more refined adjustment, are done. Regarding M/E, it requires $n_s = 4$ steps: external energy governs the process; then, internal energy is increased; after a step with more nodes in the area of fovea, final adjustment is done. For I/RPE, only a step is applied, since the contour, initialized based on M/E and RPE/C, is near its real position.

Once the active contour-based process ends, node points are interpolated to obtain the entire boundary. Figure 4 shows all process over a sample image, with some of the external energy terms considered (in this case, RPE/C is segmented).

2.2   Refinement of M/E

Although segmentation obtained for M/E is appropriate, when the EZPR is altered, information is misleading and the active contour tends to segment I/RPE instead of M/E, as Fig. 5 shows, where (a) shows successful result and (b) unsuitable segmentation of M/E. Therefore, a new process to refine M/E is done.

Refinement is done through a new energy-minimization process. Active contour is initialized considering that a minimal distance should exist between current M/E and I/RPE boundaries. Thus, distance between points in both boundaries is computed and when it is lower than a threshold t_{thick}, point in

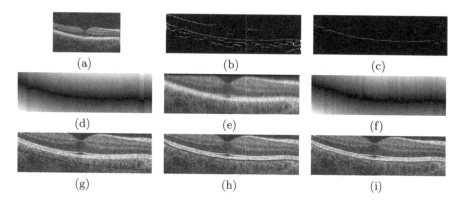

Fig. 4. Segmentation of RPE/C: (a) original image where the rectangle identifies the ROI after the preprocessing; some energy terms: (b) edges; (c) best edge per column; (d) gradient distance over (b); (e) accumulated intensities above; (f) gradient distance over best pixel per column in (e); (g) initial active contour; (h) final configuration; (i) boundary after interpolating nodes

M/E boundary is translated n_t pixels above. The energy minimization process is now composed of two steps: firstly, the contour is attracted to the boundary and then, more nodes are added in the area of fovea to obtain a refined segmentation. Figure 5 (c) shows result of this process over (b).

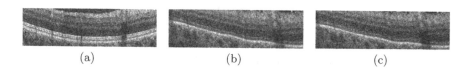

Fig. 5. Segmentation of M/E and I/RPE: (a) successful segmentation; (b) wrong result for M/E, caused by the altered EZPR; (c) refinement applied over (b)

2.3   Refinement of I/RPE and RPE/C

Once I/RPE and RPE/C have been both segmented, a simultaneous refinement can be done for them by taking advantage relationship between them. Considering that both boundaries can be assumed as parallel (they are the limits of the same layer). Therefore, the purpose of this step is finding a 3-degree parametric polynomial that fits both layer boundaries. To do that, a set C of curves is built, defined by all combinations of nc_{min} points corresponding to nodes in the active contour used to segment I/RPE. Each curve is evaluated as follows: distance between each node from I/RPE and point in the curve in the same column is computed. Then, the curve is displaced to overlap RPE/C boundary, studying all the possible rows around RPE/C (covering range m_{ci}), as Fig. 6 shows.

Fig. 6. Displacement of the curve obtained for nodes in M/E boundary to overlap RPE/C: Curve (red dot-line) fitted to nodes in M/E (red points) is displaced to each node in RPE/C (in green), covering row range m_{ci} defined by this boundary

Fitness measure (number of nodes falling in the curve) is defined as the distance d_{cn_i} between the curve c and a node n_i, considering its 8-connected neighborhood M_i. Therefore, distance between a curve $c \in C$ and a layer boundary l_j is defined as the accumulated distance to each of its nodes (with N the number of nodes):

$$d_{cl_j} = \frac{1}{N} \sum_{i=0}^{N} d_{cn_i}, \quad d_{cn_i} = \begin{cases} 0 \text{ if } \exists \, m \, \in M_i \mid m \in c \\ 1 \, otherwise \end{cases} \quad (3)$$

Since c is built based on I/RPE, it should be displaced to obtain its projection c' over RPE/C. Considering $l_{\text{I/RPE}}$ and $l_{\text{RPE/C}}$ representing I/RPE and RPE/C boundaries and that c' can be on different rows covering range m_{ci} (shown in Fig. 6), global measure dg of distance for both boundaries is defined as:

$$dg = d_{cl_{\text{I/RPE}}} + min(d_{c'_r l_{\text{RPE/C}}}), r = 0..m_{ci} \quad (4)$$

Thus, the searched curve $c \in C$ is that which minimizes the distance to both boundaries, following (5). Once the curve c is obtained, it replaces M/E and RPE/C, taking into account the appropriate displacement for each of these boundaries.

$$argmin_k \; dg_k, \quad k = 1..|C| \quad (5)$$

Figure 7 shows results for a sample image (with zoomed area of interest) applying this refinement method to the obtained previously, which nodes at the end of the segmentation are marked with small circles. Segmentation done for I/RPE presents mistakes in some regions, where it tends to M/E or RPE/C. After exploring all the curves generated with nodes of I/RPE boundary, the best one is given by the control points represented as big yellow circles. Results show an evident improvement.

Fig. 7. Refinement for I/RPE and RPE/C: Zoom applied to the region of interest to show final nodes (red circles) in the segmentation process; big circles represent control points generating the best curve, which replaces each boundary after the refinement

3 Results and Discussion

This methodology has been tested in a set of 40 OCT retinal sequences (128 images per sequence). Therefore, 5120 images have been validated. In this set, 36 sequences are from healthy patients and 4 from pathological patients (Diabetic Retinopathy). Resolution of images is 501x478 pixels. Axial resolution is 4.18 μm/pixel. Image sides are not considered in the validation[10] (10% of the image width was excluded from either side of each image to avoid including regions with low signal). In these experiments, images have been analyzed individually, without considering information of adjacent frames in the sequence. This is a possibility to be tackled in the future, after frames alignment.

Parameters have been extracted empirically. Table 1 shows those used in the configuration of active contours for each boundary. In refinement stages, value for t_{thick} is set to 10, $n_t = 5$ and $nc_{\min} = 4$. Although parameters have been computed over this dataset, they represent information of physical properties of the retinal layers. Therefore, when images with different properties are considered, they can be easily adjusted to maintain method robustness.

Table 1. Parametrization of the active contour-based model for all boundaries

Boundary	n_a	n_b	n_{ac}	n_s	n_{nhb}
ILM	10	20	40	3	5
M/E	20	10	26	4	5
I/RPE	−5	5	25	1	5
RPE/C	70	0	21	2	5
M/E Refinement	−	−	31	2	5

Two experiments have been designed to evaluate the method. Firstly, the set of 5120 images is checked by an opthalmologic expert to indicate if each boundary has been segmented successfully or has not. Thus, a qualitative measure of the segmentation obtained with the method is obtained. In the second experiment, results provided by this method are compared with those marked manually by the expert. As the set of images is too large to be segmented, this experiment considers a subset of 56 images. Figure 8 shows samples of the segmented images presented to the expert in these experiments.

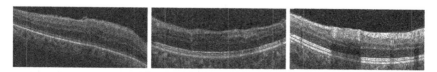

Fig. 8. Segmentation obtained over sample images, with segmented boundaries in red. Green vertical lines indicate zones on the image sides excluded from the validation.

Results obtained in the first experiment (segmented boundaries marked as successful/non-successful) are presented in Table 2. Best rates are obtained for ILM and M/E, being results for RPE/C mildly lower. Most of mistakes were made in I/RPE segmentation, which was expected, since it is the less evident boundary and its presence is not always immediate, even for an expert.

Though first experiment shows that the method works appropriately, it is essential to tackle a quantitative study. With that purpose, second experiment is

Table 2. Success rates obtained by the proposed method over a set of 5120 images. First row shows number of images segmented success and not successfully (S/NS). Second row shows correspondent success rate (percent of images with successful segmentation).

	ILM	M/E	I/RPE	RPE/C
S/NS	5118/2	4979/141	4581/539	4738/382
Success rate(%)	99.96	97.24	89.47	92.54

presented. Since the original set is too large to be segmented manually, 56 images are extracted and differences between segmentation provided by the automatic method and those marked by the expert are computed. Thus, comparison with other methods can be done. As not all existing methods provide quantitative measures, comparison is made taking as baseline the work presented in [6], which is one of the best methods considering the same context that in this work.

Baseline method was tested over 88 images composed of 512 A-scans, with axial resolution of $3.5\mu m$/pixels. In that work, M/E and RPE/C correspond to IS/OS and BM/Choroid, respectively, while I/RPE is not considered (they consider OS/RPE). Besides that, that method allows M/E overlapping OS/RPE, while in the proposed method it is not. Experiments for that method, as well as for other previous works, were done in restricted conditions, such as excluding boundaries considered as not visible by the expert from the validation. Method proposed here was validated considering entire boundaries (when information is not enough, it can provide good approach for the boundaries), what really makes the method salient. Table 3 shows results for both methods.

Table 3. Results obtained by proposed and baseline methods: boundary unsigned errors (mean ± std in pixels) are shown

	ILM	M/E	I/RPE	RPE/C
Proposed	1.10 ± 1.35	0.98 ± 1.26	1.19 ± 1.50	1.13 ± 1.32
Baseline[6]	1.02 ± 0.71	1.12 ± 0.33	–	1.32 ± 0.65

Although a precise comparison is difficult, because considered settings are different, results at pixel level obtained by this method follow the same line that previous work, being even improved in some cases. Mean errors obtained for both methods are similar, despite the fact that images considered in this work (as images size and axial resolution show) present lower quality. Besides that, approach designed for M/E is different here (in case overlapping, a more exhaustive process is done to obtain an accurate detection). Therefore, obtaining such similar accuracy to the baseline method is remarkable. Regarding RPC/C, error is lower in the proposed method. That leads to assume that refinement process is useful to obtain higher accuracy for this boundary.

In spite of considering entire boundaries without excluding any part (even when they are not evident), the proposed method obtain results that do not vary significantly regarding baseline method. This is the most salient aspect because it suggests the method provides accurate results in a less controlled environment, what makes the method feasible for ophthalmologists daily clinical practice.

4   Conclusions and Future Work

This work presents an automatic method to segment retinal layer boundaries in OCT images. Four boundaries are segmented. The lack of information and the low definition in these boundaries involves an important challenge. Refinement processes are proposed to correct mistakes in the segmentation. Although there is previous work in this area, designing a method that provides accurate segmentation in the EZPR, valid not only for healthy but also for layers presenting alterations and low visible boundaries, involves a novelty. Comparison with other method shows potential of this proposal. As future work, information between frames in the sequence could be considered in the segmentation (after a process of alignment) to improve accuracy in results.

References

1. Puzyeyeva, O., Lam, W.C., Flanagan, J., et al.: High-resolution optical coherence tomography retinal imaging: A case series illustrating potential and limitations. J. Ophthalmology, 764183–764186 (2011)
2. Sanchez-Tocino, H., Alvarez-Vidal, A., Maldonado, M.J., Moreno-Montañes, J., Garcia-Layana, A.: Retinal thickness study with optical coherence tomography in patients with diabetes. Investigative Ophthalmology & Visual Science **43**(5), 1588–1594 (2002)
3. Yohannan, J., Bittencourt, M., Sepah, Y.J., Hatef, E., Sophie, R., Moradi, A., Liu, H., Ibrahim, M., Do, D.V., Coulantuoni, E., Nguyen, Q.D.: Association of retinal sensitivity to integrity of photoreceptor inner/outer segment junction in patients with diabetic macular edema. Ophthalmology **120**(6), 1254–1261 (2013)
4. Itoh, Y., Inoue, M., Rii, T., Hirota, K., Hirakata, A.: Correlation between foveal cone outer segment tips line and visual recovery after epiretinal membrane surgery. Investigative Ophthalmololgy & Visual Science **54**(12), 7302–7308 (2013)
5. Garvin, M.K., Abràmoff, M.D., Wu, X., Russell, S.R., Burns, T.L., Sonka, M.: Automated 3-d intraretinal layer segmentation of macular spectral-domain optical coherence tomography images. IEEE Trans. Med. Imaging **28**(9), 1436–1447 (2009)
6. Yang, Q., Reisman, C.A., Chan, K., Ramachandran, R., Raza, A., Hood, D.C.: Automated segmentation of outer retinal layers in macular oct images of patients with retinitis pigmentosa. Biomed. Opt. Express **2**(9), 2493–2503 (2011)
7. Yazdanpanah, A., Hamarneh, G., Smith, B., Sarunic, M.: Intra-retinal layer segmentation in optical coherence tomography using an active contour approach. In: Yang, G.-Z., Hawkes, D., Rueckert, D., Noble, A., Taylor, C. (eds.) MICCAI 2009, Part II. LNCS, vol. 5762, pp. 649–656. Springer, Heidelberg (2009)
8. Mishra, A., Wong, A., Bizheva, K., Clausi, D.A.: Intra-retinal layer segmentation in optical coherence tomography images. Opt. Express **17**(26), 23719–23728 (2009)
9. Kass, M., Witkin, A., Terzopoulos, D.: Snakes: Active contour models. International Journal of Computer Vision **1**(4), 321–331 (1988)
10. Chiu, S.J., Li, X.T., Nicholas, P., Toth, C.A., Izatt, J.A., Farsiu, S.: Automatic segmentation of seven retinal layers in sdoct images congruent with expert manual segmentation. Optics Express **18**(18), 19413–19428 (2010)

3D Imaging

Accurate Multi-View Stereo 3D Reconstruction for Cost-Effective Plant Phenotyping

Lu Lou[1]([✉]), Yonghuai Liu[1], Jiwan Han[2], and John H. Doonan[2]

[1] Department of Computer Science, Aberystwyth University, Aberystwyth, UK
[2] NPPC, IBERS, Aberystwyth University, Aberystwyth, UK
lul1@aber.ac.uk

Abstract. Phenotyping, which underpins much of plant biology and breeding, involves the measurement of characteristics or traits. Traditionally, this has been often destructive and/or subjective but the dynamic objective measurement of traits as they change in response to genetic mutation or environmental influences is an important goal. 3-D imaging technologies are increasingly incorporated into mass produced consumer goods (3D laser scanning, structured light and digital photography) and may represent a cost-effective alternative to current commercial phenotyping platforms. We evaluate their performance, cost and practicability for plant phenotyping and present a 3D reconstruction method for plants from multi-view images acquired with domestic quality cameras. We exploit an efficient Structure-From-Motion followed by stereo matching and depth-map merging processes. Experimental results show that the proposed method is flexible, adaptable and inexpensive, and promising as an generalized groundwork for phenotyping various plant species.

Keywords: Plant phenotyping · Multi-view images · Structure from motion · Stereovision · 3D reconstruction

1 Introduction

The phenotype of an organism emerges from the interaction of its genotype with its developmental history and its environment. The range of phenotypes, therefore can be large, even from a single genotype. The measurement of phenotypes, as they change in response to genetic mutation and environmental influences, is a laborious and expensive process. Phenotyping is a major bottleneck that limits the exploitation of genomics in plant science, as well as animal biology and medicine. Important requirements include improving the accuracy (how close the measurement is to the absolute ground truth), precision (the repeatability or variance of the measurement process) and throughput of phenotyping at all levels of biological organization while reducing costs and minimizing human labor by means of automation, integrated techniques and experimental design [2].

© Springer International Publishing Switzerland 2014
A. Campilho and M. Kamel (Eds.): ICIAR 2014, Part II, LNCS 8815, pp. 349–356, 2014.
DOI: 10.1007/978-3-319-11755-3_39

In recent years, various automatic high-throughput plant growth and phenotyping platforms have been developed, PHENOPSIS [4] is used by French National Institute for Agricultural Research (INRA) for Arabidopsis. TraitMillTM [15], developed by the company CropDesign, was used to evaluate transgenic rice (Oryza sativa). Commercial high-throughput phenotyping platforms, with automated plant handling and imaging systems that capture morphological and physiological data using a variety of sensors, are aimed at reducing the need for manual acquisition of phenotypic data but do so at considerable cost. Their functionality remains, to a greater or lesser extent, limited by the dynamic morphological complexity of plants.

Although commencing as a relatively simple structure, the plant body plan rapidly becomes more complex due to a variety of processes – re-iterative organ formation, changes in organ spacing and identity, branching – that lead to overlapping and variable 3-D organization. Recording and measuring this complexity in a dynamic (non destructive) manner remains a serious challenge in biology.

The extent of this challenge is illustrated by the diversity of proposed methods that include laser scanning, digital camera photography, and structured light ranging. Stereo vision was used to reconstruct the 3D surface of maize for measurement and analysis [7]. Kaminumaet et al., [9] applied a laser range finder to reconstruct 3D models that represented the leaves and petioles as polygonal meshes and then quantified morphological traits from these models. Biskup designed a stereo vision system with two cameras to build 3D models of soybean plants foliage and analyzed the angle of inclination of the leaves and its movement over time [1]. Quan proposed a method to interactively create a 3D model of the foliage by combining clustering, image segmentation and polygonal models [14]. 3D plant analysis based on mesh processing technique was presented in [13], where the authors created a 3D model of cotton from high-resolution images using a commercial 3D digitization product named 3DSOM. Thiago developed an image-based 3D digitizing method for plant architecture analysis and phenotyping [17], and showed that the state-of-the-art SFM and multi-view stereovision are able to produce accurate 3D models with a few limitations. Li et al. [10] presented a framework to track and detect plant growth by a forward-backward 3D point cloud analysis, where the 3D point cloud was produced based on a structured light scanner over time. Yamazaki et al. presented a practical shape-from-silhouettes approach to acquire 3D models of intricate objects with severe self-occlusions, repeated thin structures, and surface discontinuities, including tree branches, bicycles and insects [18].

In this paper, we describe an accurate multi-view stereo (MVS) 3D reconstruction method of plants using multi-view images, which takes both accuracy and efficiency into account. The key of our method is efficient Structure-From-Motion followed by a stereo matching and depth-map merging process. Compared to the state-of-art MVS methods, the proposed method has three main advantages: i) It uses structure-from-motion to estimate the camera's parameters from an sequence of images; ii) It can reconstruct accurate and dense point clouds; iii) It is computationally efficient and therefore much faster than other state-of-the-art methods.

2   The Proposed Method

3D sensors being developed for non-destructive plant phenotyping are based, variously, on laser scanning , structured light, multi-view stereovision, visual hull, etc., and each has its own merits and limitations. Unfortunately, there does not exist a widely accepted benchmark that can be used to compare those different methods. Therefore, we have investigated the existing methods of 3D reconstruction and conclude that the 3D laser/lidar scanner (we did not consider the hand-held laser scanner due to its low efficiency) or the structured-light scanner (including Kinect sensor) do not work well on plants, especially on complex or even marginally occluded specimens or tiny plants. Consequently, we sought to build an efficient and accurate image-based 3D reconstruction system that could cope with a diversity of plant form and size, while using equipment available to most biology labs. Fig.1 illustrates the system framework. Briefly, the system can be divided into three main modules: SFM, stereo matching and depth optimization and merging. Unlike other SFM methods that consider input images as an unordered set, we organize the input images into a sequence of images. We directly select the starting pair of images to begin an incremental SFM to estimate the camera parameters as described in our previous work [11], and then rectify the stereo pairs by depth-map computation and optimization. Finally, all the refined depth-maps are merged together into a 3D point cloud to provide a final reconstruction. We elaborate on each of the steps as follows:

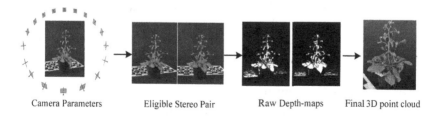

Camera Parameters   Eligible Stereo Pair   Raw Depth-maps   Final 3D point cloud

Fig. 1. 3D reconstruction framework

2.1   Structure from Motion

Given a short baseline image/video sequence I with n frames taken by a turntable or freely moving camera, we denote $I = \{I_t | t = 1, 2, ...n\}$, where I_t represents the color image captured at the frame t. The set of camera parameters for frame t in an image sequence is denoted as $C_t = \{K_t, R_t, T_t\}$, where K_t is the intrinsic matrix, R_t is the rotation matrix, and T_t is the translation vector. The parameters can be estimated reliably by the SFM techniques [5] [16]. Our system employs the SFM method of Snavely et al. [16] via the open source software *Bundler*. We improve the *Bundler* at two important steps: i) We sort the images as an ordered sequence according to incremental image name, and thereby reduce the computational cost from $O(n^2)$ to $O(n)$ in feature matching procedure ; ii) We speed up the SIFT features detection based on GPU hardware, which is around 10 times faster than CPU. In addition, as alternative methods, we have also tried to use ASIFT(Affine-SIFT) [12] feature detection and matching in SFM. Although more features can be detected and matched, the ASIFT does not significantly improve the experimental results.

2.2   Stereo Pair Selection

Not all image pairs are eligible for stereo matching. The selection of stereo image pairs is important not only for the accuracy of the final MVS result but also for the time performance of the system. A good candidate neighboring image pairs should have sufficient ray intersection angles with the reference images, and have a suitable baseline neither too short to degrade the reconstruction accuracy nor too long to have less common coverage of the scene. Hence, the pair selection is based on two statistics from i-th possible image pair: the angle between principal view directions and the distance between camera optical centers.

To select eligible stereo pairs, we supposed to have n frames, and for the i-th one, we computed θ_{ij} ($j = 1, 2, ...n$) which is the angle between principal view directions of cameras i and j, and d_{ij} ($j = 1, 2, ...n$) which is the distance between optical centers of cameras i and j. In our system, eligible stereo pairs are determined by the following rules:

i) Firstly, θ_{ij} satisfies $3° < \theta_{ij} < 15°$.

ii) Secondly, we compute the median $\bar{d}$ of d_{ij}, and remove the stereo pair whose $d_{ij} > 2\bar{d}$ or $d_{ij} < 0.05\bar{d}$.

iii) Finally, each remaining image view i has at most two stereo pairs with its neighbours j according to the metric d_{ij}.

Suppose the number of images is n, the number of eligible stereo pair is less than $2n$.

2.3   Depth Maps Computation

Let I_b and I_m be a eligible image pair, our objective is to estimate a set of depth maps. The classic SGM algorithm [6] aims to recover disparities across stereo pairs by minimizing the following global cost function:

$$E(\mathbf{D}) = \sum_{\mathbf{x}_b}(C(\mathbf{x}_b, \mathbf{D}(\mathbf{x}_b)) + \sum_{\mathbf{x}_N} P_1 T[\|\mathbf{D}(\mathbf{x}_b) - \mathbf{D}(\mathbf{x}_N)\| = 1] + \sum_{\mathbf{x}_N} P_2 T[\|\mathbf{D}(\mathbf{x}_b) - \mathbf{D}(\mathbf{x}_N)\| > 1])$$

Where $\mathbf{D}(\mathbf{x}_b)$ represents the disparity estimations of all base image pixels $\mathbf{x}_b$ of I_b, $\mathbf{x}_N$ denotes base image pixels in the neighborhood of $\mathbf{x}_b$, P_1 and P_2 are penalty constants to control the gain of a little or a larger disparity changes respectively, T is an operator evaluating to one if the subsequent condition is true and evaluate to zero else. $C(\mathbf{x}_b, \mathbf{D}(\mathbf{x}_b))$ computes the pixel-wise similarity measures. Our method is based on the OpenCV API which implements a memory and time efficient modification of SGM, where a hierarchical approach was proposed to initialize and refine the Mutual Information (MI) matching cost, and initial disparity images were computed by matching high level (low resolution) image pyramids. The resulting disparities were then used to refine the MI matching cost for processing the subsequent pyramid level.

2.4   3D Reconstruction

Since the raw depth maps may not completely agree with each other due to depth errors, a refinement process is necessary to enforce consistency over neighboring views. For each point p in image I_t, we back projected it to 3D using its depth value and the camera parameters. Therefore erroneous disparities were filtered additionally by checking for geometric consistency in object space. After refinement, all the depth-maps could be integrated into a 3D point cloud to represent the object scene. While the depth-maps may contain lots of redundancies, because different depth-maps may have common coverage of the object scene in neighboring images, we do not consider removing the redundancies for the sake of cost-effectiveness at the moment.

3   Experimental Results

Plant images were mainly captured using Canon digital cameras (Canon 600D) with $18 - 55mm$ lens, and Nikon digital cameras (D60 and D700) with $28 - 105mm$ lens and network camera with 50mm lens. The images were stored in JPG format with 3184×2120 or 3696×2448 high-resolution. Video were captured at 1920×1024 with AVI format. In order to keep even illumination and uniform background, two diffuse lighting rigs and a black backdrop were used. The method was run on an Intel i7 laptop (Dell Precision M6700 with 16G ram and Nvidia graphics card).

Fig.2 shows the 3D reconstruction of the plants produced by the proposed method. Fig.3 shows the 3D reconstruction of an Arabidopsis from 66 images , produced by the existing state of the art methods [3], [8] and our method respectively. Generally, the running time of our method was 10-30 minutes depending on the number of images. In the case of Fig.3, Our method ran 15 minutes to produce the final 3D point cloud from 66 input images. The CMPMVS software from [8] was very slow and ran around 182 minutes. The PMVS software from [3] was faster than our method and only ran 3 minutes but quality was poor. The proposed method is able to produce more dense and complete 3D point cloud of plants than previously reported methods.

In order to evaluate the quality of 3D reconstruction, we have extracted the plant height, stem width, leaf area, branch angle from resulting 3D point cloud of plant in case study, and compared results with limited ground truth that came from the manual measurement or commercial 2D image measuring software. Fig.4 shows an Arabidopsis and the produced 3D point cloud, and Table.1 shows the comparison errors of some leaves and main stem.

Experimental results show that the accuracy of the proposed method is high enough to distinguish different genotypes plant and precision is stable enough to adapt slightly deviated experimental conditions.

With the proposed method, no extra camera calibration or other strict environmental conditions is required, and data acquisition times are in the range 1-2 minutes per specimen, depending on plant complexity. The camera parameters, such as focus length, depth of field and time of exposure, etc., can be adapted

Fig. 2. Raw image (top) and 3D reconstruction (bottom) of diverse plants. (a)-(d) Arabidopsis strains and mutants. (e) wheat. (f) Brachypodium. (g) maize. (h) clover.

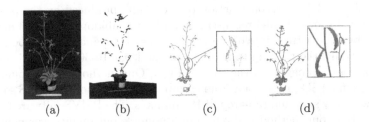

Fig. 3. 3D reconstruction of an Arabidopsis. (a) raw image (one of 66 images). (b)(c)(d) 3D results by CMPMVS [8], PMVS [3] and the proposed method respectively.

Fig. 4. (a) Raw image of an Arabidopsis (one of 62 images) (b)(c)(d) 3D reconstruction by the proposed method, CMPMVS [8], PMVS [3] respectively. (e) Measurement of the leaves and stem using WinDas scanner and software.

Table 1. Errors in different parameters of an Arabidopsis using different methods

Item	Ground truth (mm)	Proposed method (mm)	Ref [3] (mm)	Ref [8] (mm)
Length of leaf1	21.5	-1.2	N/A	N/A
Width of leaf1	10.7	0.9	N/A	N/A
Length of leaf2	19.5	-0.1	N/A	N/A
Width of leaf2	7.6	0.6	N/A	N/A
Length of leaf14	41.7	-0.5	N/A	2.2
Width of leaf14	21.1	1.0	N/A	3.5
Length of leaf16	36.7	-1.7	N/A	2.6
Width of leaf16	19.3	-0.9	N/A	3.1
Length of main stem	84.8	-2.1	-3.4	N/A
width of main stem	1.4	-0.1	NA	N/A
Root mean square error (RMSE)		1.1		
Mean absolute percentage error (MAPE)		4.7%		

widely to obtain high quality and clear images with an optimal resolution from a diverse set of plants. Only basic photography skills are required for effective capture and storage of data.

4   Conclusion

In this paper, we demonstrated that 3D reconstruction based multi-view images can be employed as a low-cost, powerful alternative for non-destructive plant phenotyping. The proposed dense 3D reconstruction method excelled in producing accurate 3D point cloud of various plants while retaining colors, textures, shapes as compared to other current methods [3][8]. It is flexible and efficient. Abundant useful phenotypic data as plant height, plant topology, stem width and length, numbers of leaves, leaf area and leaf angle, etc. can be extracted.

The main limitations of the proposed method are (i) the final 3D model of plants was only pure point clouds without meshes so that it cannot be directly processed in the common commercial CAD/3D software (ii) there are still some gaps or holes in the final 3D model of the plants due to occlusions, texture-less regions and blurred images. In addition, the proposed method is still relatively slow, especially when processing hundreds of images. Therefore, future work will aim at improving computational performance and accuracy.

Acknowledgments. We acknowledge funding from the European Union FP7 Capacities Programme (Grant Agreement No. 284443: European Plant Phenotyping Network, an Integrating Activity Research Infrastructure project) and BBSRC NCG Grant Ref: BB/J004464/1.

References

1. Biskup, B., Scharr, H., Rascher, U.S.: A stereo imaging system for measuring structural parameters of plant canopies. Plant, Cell & Environment **30** (2007)
2. Cobb, J.N., et al.: Next-generation phenotyping: requirements and strategies for enhancing our understanding of genotype-phenotype relationships and its relevance to crop improvement. Theoretical and Applied Genetics **126**, 867–887 (2013)
3. Furukawa, Y., Ponce, J.: Accurate, dense, and robust multiview stereopsis. IEEE Tran. PAMI **32**, 1362–1376 (2010)
4. Granier, C., et al.: Phenopsis, an automated platform for reproducible phenotyping of plant responses to soil water defficit in arabidopsis thaliana permitted the identification of an accession with low sensitivity to soil water deffcit. New Phytologist **169**, 623–635 (2006)
5. Hartley, R.I., Zisserman, A.: Multiple View Geometry in Computer Vision. Cambridge University Press (2004)
6. Hirschmuller, H.: Stereo processing by semiglobal matching and mutual information. IEEE Trans. PAMI **30**(2), 328–341 (2008)
7. Ivanov, N., et al.: Computer stereo plotting for 3-d reconstruction of a maize canopy. Agricultural and Forest Meteorology **75**, 85–102 (1995)
8. Jancosek, M., Pajdla, T.: Multi-view reconstruction preserving weakly-supported surfaces. In: Proc. CVPR, pp. 3121–3128 (2011)
9. Kaminuma, E., Heida, N., et al.: Automatic quantification of morphological traits via three-dimensional measurement of arabidopsis. Plant **38**, 358–365 (2004)
10. Li, Y.Y., Fan, X.C., Mitra, N.J., Chamovitz, D., Cohen-Or, D., Chen, B.Q.: Analyzing growing plants from 4d point cloud data. ACM Trans. Graphics **32** (2013)
11. Lu, L., Yonghuai, L., Minglan, S., Jiwan, H., John, H.D.: A cost-effective automatic 3D reconstruction pipeline for plants using multi-view images. In: Proc. 15th Towards Autonomous Robotic Systems (2014)
12. Morel, J.M., Yu, G.: Asift: A new framework for fully affine invariant image comparison. SIAM J. Img. Sci. **2**(2), 438–469 (2009)
13. Paproki, A., Sirault, X., Berry, S., Furbank, R., Fripp, J.: A novel mesh processing based technique for 3d plant analysis. BMC Plant Biology **12** (2012)
14. Quan, L., Tan, P., Zeng, G., Yuan, L., Wang, J.D., Kang, S.B.: Image-based plant modeling. ACM Trans. Graphics **25**, 599–604 (2006)
15. Reuzeau, C.: Traitmill (tm): A high throughput functional genomics platform for the phenotypic analysis of cereals. Vitro Cellular & Developmental Biology-Animal **43**, S4–S4 (2007)
16. Snavely, N., Seitz, S.M., Szeliski, R.: Photo tourism: Exploring photo collections in 3d. In: Proc. SIGGRAPH, pp. 835–846 (2006)
17. Santos, T., Oliveira, A.: Image-based 3d digitizing for plant architecture analysis and phenotyping. In: Proc. Workshop on Industry Applications in SIB-GRAPI (2012)
18. Yamazaki, S., et al.: The theory and practice of coplanar shadowgram imaging for acquiring visual hulls of intricate objects. IJCV **81**, 259–280 (2009)

Truncated Signed Distance Function:
Experiments on Voxel Size

Diana Werner$^{(\boxtimes)}$, Ayoub Al-Hamadi, and Philipp Werner

University of Magdeburg, Magdeburg, Germany
{Diana.Werner,Ayoub.Al-Hamadi}@ovgu.de

Abstract. Real-time 3D reconstruction is a hot topic in current research. Several popular approaches are based on the truncated signed distance function (TSDF), a volumetric scene representation that allows for integration of multiple depth images taken from different viewpoints. Aiming at a deeper understanding of TSDF we discuss its parameters, conduct experiments on the influence of voxel size on reconstruction accuracy and derive practical recommendations.

Keywords: TSDF · KinectFusion · 3D reconstruction

1 Introduction

Accurate 3D reconstruction in real-time has a lot of applications in entertainment, virtual reality, augmented reality and robotics. The introduction of Microsoft's low-cost RGB-D camera Kinect [5] has made 3D sensing available to everyone. So it also has boosted research and commercial activities in 3D reconstruction and its applications. Several popular and widely used approaches such as KinectFusion [4,6], Kintinious [10,11], the open source implementation of KinectFusion in the point cloud library (PCL) [12] or KinFu Large Scale [1] are based on the truncated signed distance function (TSDF).

TSDF is a volumetric representation of a scene for integrating depth images that has several benefits, e. g. time and space efficiency, representation of uncertainty or incremental updating [2]. It further is well-suited for data-parallel algorithms, i. e. for implementation on GPUs. The attained speed-up facilitates real time processing at high frame rate.

There has been some investigations on hole filling to generate more natural looking reconstructions, which is partly done automatic using the TSDF method [2], and can be done in an energy conservation way [7]. However, to our knowledge there has been no closer look at scenarios with multiple objects and other important questions on object size and resolution. For instance: Up to which point is a true hole reconstructed as a hole? In comparison with camera position and direction: Is the reconstruction influenced by distance or angle? Are there problems at the very left or right border of an object seen from an specific direction? In which way is the reconstruction influenced by the voxel size used in the world grid?

© Springer International Publishing Switzerland 2014
A. Campilho and M. Kamel (Eds.): ICIAR 2014, Part II, LNCS 8815, pp. 357–364, 2014.
DOI: 10.1007/978-3-319-11755-3_40

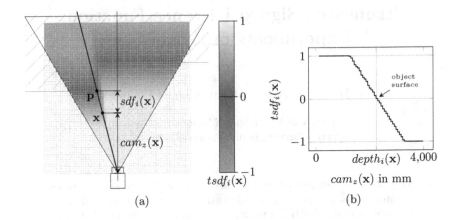

Fig. 1. 2D TSDF example. (a) Solid object (green), camera with field of view, optical axis and ray (blue), and TSDF grid (unseen voxels are white, for others see color bar). The signed distance value of voxel $\mathbf{x}$ is determined by the depth of the corresponding surface point $\mathbf{p}$ and the voxel's camera distance $cam_z(\mathbf{x})$. b) 1D TSDF sampled along the ray through $\mathbf{p}$ with $t = 1000$ mm. Object surface is at zero crossing.

In this paper we analyze the influence of distance, object size and angle to camera viewing direction. We will have a look at this with combination of several world grid voxel sizes.

This paper is structured as follows. Section 2 describes the TSDF in detail. It is shown how this function is generated from a depth map after sensing the environment and how one can compute the 3D reconstruction given the TSDF. Section 3 describes parameters and algorithmic options to consider for improving results. In section 4 we describe our experiments and discuss our results. Section 5 concludes this paper.

2   TSDF

The signed distance function (SDF) was proposed to reconstruct a 3D model from multiple range images [2]. A d-dimensional environment is represented in a d-dimensional grid of equally sized voxels. The position of a voxel $\mathbf{x}$ is defined by its center. For each voxel there are two relevant values. First, $sdf_i(\mathbf{x})$ which is the signed distance in between voxel center and nearest object surface in direction of current measurement. In front of an object (in free space) the values are defined to be positive. Behind the surface (inside the object) distances are negative. Second, there is a weight $w_i(\mathbf{x})$ for each voxel to assess uncertainty of the corresponding $sdf_i(\mathbf{x})$. The subscript i denotes the i'th observation. Fig. 1a and the following equation define $sdf_i(\mathbf{x})$ precisely.

$$sdf_i(\mathbf{x}) = depth_i(pic(\mathbf{x})) - cam_z(\mathbf{x}) \tag{1}$$

$pic(\mathbf{x})$ is the projection of the voxel center $\mathbf{x}$ onto the depth image. So $depth_i(pic(\mathbf{x}))$ is the measured depth in between the camera and the nearest object surface point $\mathbf{p}$ on the viewing ray crossing $\mathbf{x}$. Accordingly, $cam_z(\mathbf{x})$ is the distance in between the voxel and the camera along the optical axis. Consequently, $sdf_i(\mathbf{x})$ is a distance along the optical axis as well.

In [4,6] the SDF has been truncated at $\pm t$. This is beneficial, because large distances are not relevant for surface reconstruction and a restriction of the value range can be utilized to memory footprint. The truncated variant of $sdf_i(\mathbf{x})$ is denoted by $tsdf_i(\mathbf{x})$.

$$tsdf_i(\mathbf{x}) = \max(-1, \min(1, \frac{sdf_i(\mathbf{x})}{t})) \tag{2}$$

In Fig. 1a $tsdf_i(\mathbf{x})$ of the voxel grid is encoded by color. Fig. 1b shows the TSDF sampled along a viewing ray.

As mentioned above, multiple observations can be combined in one TSDF to integrate information from different viewpoints to improve accuracy or to add missing patches of the surface. This is done by weighted summation, usually through iterative updates of the TSDF. $TSDF_i(\mathbf{x})$ denotes the integration of all observations $tsdf_j(\mathbf{x})$ with $1 \leq j \leq i$. $W_i(\mathbf{x})$ assesses the uncertainty of $TSDF_i(\mathbf{x})$. A new observation is integrated by applying the following update step for all voxels $\mathbf{x}$ in the grid. The grid is initialized with $TSDF_0(\mathbf{x}) = 0$ and $W_0(\mathbf{x}) = 0$.

$$TSDF_i(\mathbf{x}) = \frac{W_{i-1}(\mathbf{x})TSDF_{i-1}(\mathbf{x}) + w_i(\mathbf{x})tsdf_i(\mathbf{x})}{W_{i-1}(\mathbf{x}) + w_i(\mathbf{x})} \tag{3}$$

$$W_i(\mathbf{x}) = W_{i-1}(\mathbf{x}) + w_i(\mathbf{x}) \tag{4}$$

Most approaches set the uncertainty weight to $w_i(\mathbf{x}) = 1$ for all updated voxels and to $w_i(\mathbf{x}) = 0$ for all voxels outside the camera's field of view [4,6,9,12]. This simply averages the measured TSDF observations over time.

For surface reconstruction one can think of the TSDF like a level set. To find the object surface you look for the zero level. This is usually done by ray casting from a given camera viewpoint. For each considered ray the TSDF is read step by step until there is a switch in sign. The information of surrounding TSDF values is then interpolated to estimate the refined point of zero crossing along the ray. This point is returned as an object surface point.

3 Parameters and Algorithmic Options

The TSDF representation requires to select several parameters.

Grid volume size determines the dimensions of the TSDF grid, i. e. the maximum dimensions of the scene to reconstruct in a physical unit like mm. In practice it is bounded by the available Random Access Memory on the GPU. However, several previous works suggested to overcome this limitation by shifting the TSDF grid when the camera's field of view leaves the grid [1,8,10,11]. The grid dimensions increase with voxel size in constant memory footprint, however at cost of reconstruction accuracy.

Voxel size v is a crucial parameter as it influences memory requirements and surface reconstruction accuracy. If dimensions of a 3D grid are fixed, doubling the voxel size means to reduce the number of voxels to one-eighths. This is associated with the same reduction in memory footprint. Further, it reduces computational cost for updating the TSDF and for ray tracing. The other way around, an increased voxel size facilitates to increase the scene volume without needing more memory or increasing computational cost. However, an increase in voxel size comes along with a decrease in the level of representable details resp. with lowered reconstruction accuracy. So it is worth thinking about the optimal voxel size for a particular application. In Sect. 4 we conduct experiments to assess the influence of this parameter on the accuracy.

Distance representation and truncation distance t i. e. the coding of distance values $TSDF_i(\mathbf{x})$ is crucial for the reconstruction accuracy. Intuitively, there should be as many quantization steps as possible to minimize information loss caused by rounding and maintain the accuracy of $TSDF_i(\mathbf{x})$. Especially, this is important near zero level, as those values of $TSDF_i(\mathbf{x})$ are used for surface estimation. So floating point is appropriate. In terms of memory footprint it is beneficial use two byte integer per voxel as in the implementation of PCL [12]. However, here the selection of t influences reconstruction accuracy. Two byte integer has 65,536 quantization steps to represent a distance, i. e. integer values between $-32,768$ and $32,767$. With a fixed point number coding and a given truncation distance t, signed distances in range $\pm t$ are mapped to $\pm 32,767$. So signed distances are quantized in steps of $\frac{t}{32,767}$, i. e. the quantization error is proportional to t and a lower t should be better. E. g. with $t = 1,000$ mm the coding will round the each distance to multiples of 0.03 mm whereas with $t = 10$ mm it will round to multiples of 0.0003 mm. On the other hand, t should be larger than length of voxel diagonal $\sqrt{d} \cdot v$ and the level of noise. A detailed analysis of this parameter is out of scope, but will be addressed in future work.

Next to the parameters there are some algorithmic options for variation.

TSDF update i. e. the integration of multiple observations in one TSDF can be accomplished in different ways. Above, we introduced the classical equally weighted sum update. Recently, [3] proposed to select $w_i(\mathbf{x})$ individually for each voxel based on the uncertainty of the measurement. The authors model $w_i(\mathbf{x})$ dependent on the corresponding depth value, as the depth estimation provided by the used Kinect sensor is more accurate in close range. They further propose two modified update methods and evaluate their benefit for the model reconstruction accuracy. Their variants of the TSDF update, which consider characteristics of the sensing hardware, outperform the classical update step in the presented experiments.

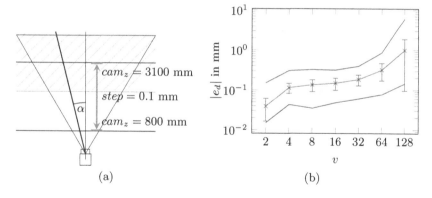

(a)   (b)

Fig. 2. Depth experiment. (a) Planar object and its variation. (b) Absolute depth error for different voxel sizes: mean with standard deviation (red), maximum and minimum (blue), $t = 255$ mm.

Surface reconstruction is done via ray tracing. You start at a point on the ray as near as possible to camera but in TSDF volume. From this you are going with a **individually chosen step size** to the next ray point and so on. You have to decide whether to look at the value $tsdf_i(x)$ for the voxel x related to a ray point or to interpolate a TSDF value from surrounding voxels. You also have to decide for an **interpolation** method. In PCL [12] and in other works like [4] the trilinear interpolation is used. After a zero crossing is detected between two ray points from positiv to negative you are able to compute a surface point via the chosen interpolation. You also can decide whether to stop the ray tracing after computing one surface point to reconstruct only surface points seen from camera or not.

4   Experiments and Discussion

In this section we conduct several experiments aiming at a deeper understanding of TSDF, i. e. at effects of spacial discretization in a grid on the reconstruction accuracy. To focus on these effects, we created synthetic depth maps which do not suffer from noise or other measurement errors. Another advantage of synthetic data is the availability of perfect ground truth. On purpose of simple illustration experiments are conducted with a 2D TSDF grid, i. e. we have a 1D depth map and a 2D surface. All the experiments demonstrate the result after a single depth measurement. Integration of multiple depth maps is out of scope and will be addressed in future work. We decompose the reconstruction accuracy in two components and investigate each in a dedicated experiment.

4.1   Depth Error

In this experiment we calculate the depth error e_d for each pixel of a synthetic depth map and the according depth reconstructed from the TSDF. The synthetic

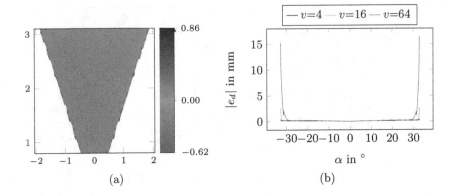

Fig. 3. Angular depth error. (a) Map of e_d across TSDF volume for voxel size v of 64 mm. (b) Mean error along rays for different voxel sizes v.

depth maps contain a planar object surface which is perpendicular to the optical axis (see Fig. 2a). We placed the object 800 mm in front of camera position and move it from this position in steps of 0.1 mm till a distance of 3100 mm. The camera is placed as in Fig. 1a with optical axis passing through the middle of the TSDF grid and aligned with one of its axes. The size of the world grid is fixed to 4096 mm width and height in all experiments.

Fig. 2b shows the mean, standard deviation, minimum and maximum of the absolute depth error across tested field of view for several voxel sizes v. It is apparent that the absolute depth error increases with voxel size. However, the mean error increases slower than voxel size. Whereas the mean error is 0.04 mm for $v = 2$ mm (1.9 %), it is 0.97 mm for $v = 128$ mm (0.7 %). There is a similar effect for the maximum and minimum error.

Further, looking at the spacial distribution of the error one can observe that the most severe errors occur on the border of the field of view (see Fig. 3a) whereas the object distance seems to have no influence on reconstruction accuracy. To investigate the influence of the angle in between grid axis and ray we calculate the mean of absolute error along each viewing ray. The results are given in Fig. 3b. Here it is apparent that the error is at least two orders of magnitude larger on the borders of the field of view, and even more the higher v gets. The high error at the borders are artefacts caused by the trilinear interpolation. The PCL implementation of KinectFusion that we used for our experiments [12] does not pay attention to the fact that some TSDF voxels $\mathbf{x}$ involved in the interpolation may be unseen. For these voxels $tsdf_i(x) = 0$ from initialization. There has been no sensing for these voxels and therefore you can not expect to have a surface there, which would be true for seen voxles x with a TSDF value of 0. With increasing voxel size this error gets apparent, as more reconstructed 3D points are affected by this problem because the influence of the interpolation is one voxel size.

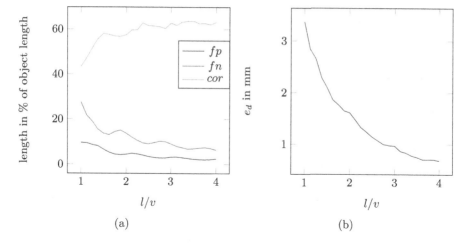

Fig. 4. Lateral depth error. (a) Average length of wrongly reconstructed (*fp*), wrongly not reconstructed (*fn*) and correctly reconstructed (*cor*) object in percent of true object length. (b) Average depth error in connection to ratio of true object length *l* and voxel soze *v*. Voxel size *v* is 64 mm.

4.2   Lateral Error

With this experiment we investigate how the ratio of voxel size *v* and the length *l* of an planar object, located perpendicular to the optical camera axis, influence the reconstruction accuracy. The objects were moved in a camera distance from 1280 mm to 1536 mm, wich are 4 voxels with 64 mm size. We chosed step sizes 8 mm in vetical and horizontal direction. The object bounds laid inside the viewing area with an distance of 128 mm from border. For all objects of same length generated for this experiment we calculated mean values and looked at depth error d_e and at the length *fp*, *fn* and *cor* which are the length of the reconstructed object wich are wrongly reconstructed, wrongly not reconstructed and correctly reconstructed in % of the true object length.

In Fig. 4 you can assert that all of these length together with e_d are clearly influenced by the ratio of *l* and *v*. It is also obvious that the objects are reconstructed too small in average.

5   Conclusion

In this paper we gave a detailed look at TSDF and the parametric and algorithmic options. We showed that for PCL's implementation depth errors are in same magnitude for voxel sizes 4 to 64 mm. The errors are 2 magnitudes larger at the border of viewing field due to interpolation effects. For lateral errors there is a strong relation between ratio of object length and voxel size and the reconstruction accuracy whith the object being too small in average. The negative impact of increase in voxel size is lower for depth error than for lateral error.

Acknowledgments. This work was supported by Transregional Collaborative Research Centre SFB/TRR 62 ("Companion-Technology for Cognitive Technical Systems") funded by the German Research Foundation (DFG).

References

1. Bondarev, E., Heredia, F., Favier, R., Ma, L., de With, P.H.: On photo-realistic 3D reconstruction of large-scale and arbitrary-shaped environments. In: 2013 IEEE Consumer Communications and Networking Conference (CCNC), pp. 621–624. IEEE (2013)
2. Curless, B., Levoy, M.: A volumetric method for building complex models from range images. In: Proceedings of the 23rd Annual Conference on Computer Graphics and Interactive Techniques, SIGGRAPH 1996, pp. 303–312. ACM, New York (1996)
3. Hemmat, H.J., Bondarev, E., de With, P.H.N.: Exploring distance-aware weighting strategies for accurate reconstruction of voxel-based 3D synthetic models. In: Gurrin, C., Hopfgartner, F., Hurst, W., Johansen, H., Lee, H., O'Connor, N. (eds.) MMM 2014, Part I. LNCS, vol. 8325, pp. 412–423. Springer, Heidelberg (2014)
4. Izadi, S., Kim, D., Hilliges, O., Molyneaux, D., Newcombe, R., Kohli, P., Shotton, J., Hodges, S., Freeman, D., Davison, A.: KinectFusion: real-time 3D reconstruction and interaction using a moving depth camera. In: Proceedings of the 24th Annual ACM Symposium on User Interface Software and Technology, pp. 559–568. ACM (2011)
5. Microsoft: Kinect (2014), http://www.xbox.com/en-us/kinect/
6. Newcombe, R.A., Izadi, S., Hilliges, O., Molyneaux, D., Kim, D., Davison, A.J., Kohli, P., Shotton, J., Hodges, S., Fitzgibbon, A.: KinectFusion: real-time dense surface mapping and tracking. In: Proceedings of the 2011 10th IEEE International Symposium on Mixed and Augmented Reality, ISMAR 2011, pp. 127–136. IEEE Computer Society, Washington, DC (2011)
7. Paulsen, R.R., Bærentzen, J.A., Larsen, R.: Regularisation of 3D signed distance fields. In: Salberg, A.-B., Hardeberg, J.Y., Jenssen, R. (eds.) SCIA 2009. LNCS, vol. 5575, pp. 513–519. Springer, Heidelberg (2009)
8. Roth, H., Vona, M.: Moving volume KinectFusion. In: Proceedings of the British Machine Vision Conference, pp. 1–11. BMVA Press (2012)
9. Whelan, T., Johannsson, H., Kaess, M., Leonard, J.J., McDonald, J.: Robust tracking for real-time dense RGB-D mapping with kintinuous. Technical Report 031. MIT-CSAIL (2012), http://hdl.handle.net/1721.1/73167
10. Whelan, T., Johannsson, H., Kaess, M., Leonard, J.J., McDonald, J.: Robust real-time visual odometry for dense RGB-D mapping. In: 2013 IEEE International Conference on Robotics and Automation (ICRA), pp. 5724–5731. IEEE (2013)
11. Whelan, T., Kaess, M., Fallon, M., Johannsson, H., Leonard, J., McDonald, J.: Kintinuous: Spatially extended KinectFusion. Technical Report 020. MIT-CSAIL (2012), http://hdl.handle.net/1721.1/71756
12. Willow Garage and other contributors: Open source implementation of KinectFusion in PCL 1.7.1 (2014), http://www.pointclouds.org/downloads/

Human Activity Analysis in a 3D Bird's-Eye View

Gang Hu$^{(\boxtimes)}$, Derek Reilly, Ben Swinden, and Qigang Gao

Faculty of Computer Science, Dalhousie University, Halifax, NS, Canada
{ghu,reilly,swinden,qggao}@cs.dal.ca

Abstract. Efficient and reliable human tracking in arbitrary environments is challenging, as there is currently no single solution that can successfully handle all scenarios. In this paper we present a novel approach that uses a top view 3D camera, which employs a simplified yet expressive human body model for effective multi-target detection and tracking. Both bottom-up and high level processes are involved to construct a saliency map with selective visual information. We handle the tracking task in a hierarchical data association framework, and a novel salience occupancy pattern (SOP) descriptor is proposed as the motion representation for action recognition. Our real-time bird's-eye multi-person tracking and recognition approach is being applied in a human-computer interaction (HCI) research prototype, and has a wide range of applications.

Keywords: Human body detection · People tracking · 3D bird's-eye view · Saliency map · HCI

1 Introduction

Efficient and reliable tracking of multiple people in arbitrary environments has been a goal of broad interest in computer vision, and finding robust solutions is at the foundation of a wide range of demanding human activity analysis systems, in areas such as HCI, surveillance, health care and some augmented reality applications. Although much progress has been made in recent years [1-8], it remains a very challenging problem due to numerous performance factors such as articulated body structure, illumination variation, occlusion, as well as background clutter, and there exists no single tracking approach that can successfully handle all scenarios. Recently, the tracking-by-detection method has become popular in object tracking systems. Such an approach involves continuous object detection in each individual frame and the association of detections across frames. The main challenge of the tracking-by-detection method is the accuracy of the detections. With the development of low-cost 3D cameras and advancements in human skeleton joint detection techniques [9], the task of human body detection has been significantly simplified, and good performance has been achieved for 3D video games in living rooms. However, occlusion still occurs when the camera is placed horizontally, and cannot be well handled without applying several operational constraints (a clear and wide open area, a front facing camera position, enough spatial distance among users, limited number of concurrent tracking targets). Occlusion

© Springer International Publishing Switzerland 2014
A. Campilho and M. Kamel (Eds.): ICIAR 2014, Part II, LNCS 8815, pp. 365–373, 2014.
DOI: 10.1007/978-3-319-11755-3_41

disappears in many cases if we have a bird's-eye view on the world. Despite losing facial appearance, color and frontal body shape, many human movements and actions are still distinguishable from a   bird's-eye view, and some even more so. For instance, broad limb movements (punch, throw, push, kick, etc) can be well perceived, as can a person's movement trajectory. Human motion detection methods using bird's-eye views have been explored in prior research [11-13]. However, due to the limitations of 2D images, a body from a bird's-eye view was usually represented as a generic blob, and could not be distinguished from other objects, raising the probability of false positives.

In this work, we address the human detection, tracking and action recognition problems via a top view 3D camera that captures human activities. The advantages of setting a 3D camera above a tracking area are 3-fold: 1) avoiding occlusion between multiple people and between people and objects; 2) providing a simple yet expressive human shape appearance; and 3) making background filtering trivial. We follow the tracking-by-detection strategy for multi-person tracking. The proposed human activity analysis method is based on the principle of saliency maps [10], a hierarchical association-based tracking framework, and a 4D salient occupancy pattern (SOP) action descriptor. Experimental results show that our approach has robust performance.

The rest of the paper is organized as follows: related work is discussed in Section 2; the proposed top-down human activity analysis approach is explained in Section 3; experiments, discussion and conclusion are reported in Section 4 and 5.

2   Related Work

Many recent methods for multi-person tracking follow the tracking-by-detection strategy [3-4] in which the output of a human detection algorithm is the initial state space for tracking. Such an approach involves continuous object detection and the association of detections across frames. Those methods typically require robust human detection algorithms. Human detection has been an active research topic for decades. The approach of using Histograms of Oriented Gradients (HOG) descriptor and SVM as a linear classifier for pedestrian detection was proposed in [1], and its robust performance has been well acknowledged. Some later approaches for pedestrian detection also achieved comparable results. A more complete report can be found in [14]. Shotton et al. [9] presented a robust solution to detecting human skeleton joints with a depth sensor. Its accurate skeleton output opens up a wide range of gesture-based applications. These detection approaches mainly rely on the visibility of full bodies, i.e. that people can be seen mostly from frontal views. Various approaches have been proposed in the literature to handle the occlusion that inevitably occurs in crowded scenes. Such methods often rely on additional information, such as stereo disparity [15], or 3D scene context [16]. Although good progress has been made, the issue of handling of multiple occlusions remains difficult. Occlusion becomes trivial in many cases if we have bird's view on the world. Human detection methods using bird's-eye views have been explored in prior research and applied in industrial applications. A commercial human detection system [11] achieves high-accuracy real-time performance using a top view camera and a shape-based representation. The Censys3D People Tracking System [12] from Point Grey Research also uses a top view stereo camera to detect the human heads based on the depth data only. A human detection method in [13] uses real-time depth images and applies Haar-like filtering based on a human model to extract the convex shape of shoulder-head-shoulder. Our approach for top view people tracking also looks for the distinctive shoulder-head-shoulder shape, but with a more reliable model based on the saliency map principles. Multiple-target tracking can be treated as a MAP data association problem: long optimal object trajectories are found by linking a series of detections or short tracklets. A variety of methods can be found in the literature, such as Viterbi algorithm [3], Hungarian algorithm [4], continuous-discrete optimization [6] and higher-order motion models [7]. In this work, we adopt the framework of a hierarchical association-based approach for multi-person tracking, scene knowledge from specific applications are modeled into the system as well.

3   Our Approach

Fig. 1 illustrates the application environment and the overall flowchart of our approach. The depth images are captured from a top view camera as the input data to the system. Based on the extracted 3D perceptual shape saliency entities, a novel saliency-based human body detection method is applied to find human targets within each frame. Our tracking approach links the detected targets into stable trajectories by a hierarchical data association process. Finally, a 4D salient occupancy pattern (SOP) action descriptor is proposed for top view action recognition. We describe our approach below.

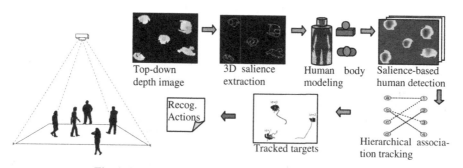

Fig. 1. System environment (left) and the process flowchart

3.1   3D Shape-Based Bottom-Up Salient Objects

Contour-based shape features exploit object boundary information and are able to provide more detailed descriptions about object shapes. In our approach, the preprocessed grayscale depth image is first processed by an edge extractor and a perceptual curve partitioning and group (PCPG) model [18], which partitions 2D image curves into minimum sets of Generic Edge Token (GET) types as illustrated in Fig. 2(a) which are connected at Curve Partitioning Points (CPP) illustrated in Fig. 2(b). Since XYZ coordinates are available from depth images, 3D GET/CPPs provide bottom-up salient entities, and can be further clustered into several groups according to their spatial distribution. A salience score is assigned to each group as the salience confidence including two factors: spatial area and texture density. Spatial area A is the ratio of the salience object size to the whole image. Texture density D is the ratio of GET pixels of the saliency object. Then we model the bottom-up (BU) salience score in (1):

$$S_{BU} = A \cdot \exp\{ D \}. \tag{1}$$

While the assumption that a region with bigger D is related to a salience object always holds in our system, the saliency degree of an area could be degraded when its size over certain value, because if something is almost everywhere, it is not salience anymore. To this end, we give the texture density D higher significance and discriminative power than A. An exponential function is used in order to emphasize D. This salience score indicates the likelihood of the detected region being the bottom-up salience. It only contains low-level visual features, without being updated by high-level prior knowledge about the target.

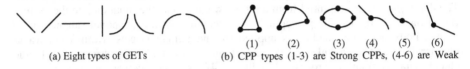

| | | (1) | (2) | (3) | (4) | (5) | (6) |
(a) Eight types of GETs   (b) CPP types (1-3) are Strong CPPs, (4-6) are Weak

Fig. 2. GET and CPP types

3.2   Higher-Level Prior Knowledge Integration

According to visual attention theory [10], high-level domain knowledge can help the visual system select effective features in a scene. Here we model feature representation by constructing saliency maps weighted by high-level prior knowledge. To detect a person's head and shoulders, we segment the salient object into 2 regions according to the depth data using the K-means algorithm (k=2). Since GETs are the object shape salience, GET pixels are the data input for efficient segmentation. The output is 2 groups of GETs: the top (closest to the camera) and bottom (further away) parts of the target. Then, we explore several effective features to detect human bodies.

Depth Convex Feature (DCF). *DCF* describes the depth gradient in the saliency area. It is defined by comparing the depth distribution of the top part (T) and the bottom part (B) of the target as:

$$P_{DCF} = \exp\{ -(N_t + N_b)^{-1}\}, \tag{2}$$

where, N_t is the ratio of pixels lower than the depth threshold d_{th} in the top part T, and N_b means the ratio of pixels higher than d_{th} in part B. The threshold d_{th} is equal to the sum of the minimum depth in T and a constant fluctuation δ. Depth changes around the shoulder-head-shoulder area are significant. As a result, *DCF* can be taken as reliable evidence for shoulder-head-shoulder detection, and can be taken as one of the indicators of a target being a human body.

Projected Size Difference (PSD). The size difference between the bottom and top parts of the target is still a stable discriminative property of this salient area. *PSD* is defined to describe the difference as:

$$P_{PSD} = \exp\{ -D_{size}^{-1} \},\qquad(3)$$

where *PSD* is the ratio of the 2D top part size to the size of the bottom part. A bigger *PSD* means the bottom part of a saliency region is larger than top one, which reflects the size difference between the shoulder and head.

Relative Position Feature (RPF). The human head is set in between the shoulders. *RPF* describes the position relationship between the top and bottom parts of the object. The distance D_{bt} between centers of bottom and top parts reflects the relative position of both parts. The prior probability of RPF is defined as:

$$P_{RPF} = \exp\{ -D_{bt}^{-1} \}.\qquad(4)$$

The final salience score for a salience area is updated as:

$$S_{Final} = S_{BU} \cdot P_{DCF} \cdot P_{PSD} \cdot P_{RPF},\qquad(5)$$

which integrates both bottom-up salience and high-level domain knowledge. The detected human body is the region in the final saliency map with a high score.

3.3   Hierarchical Association Tracking

Multi-person tracking is carried out within a hierarchical association tracking framework similar to [4], where the final global level association is refined based on the affinity measure from the local level Figure 4 shows the overall tracking approach.

Local-Level. Individual people detected in each frame have location information, height, and a salience score. At this local stage,   multiple short target traces (*tracklets*), are extracted within a short time period (less than 0.1s) as the intermediate data, they likely link to a person if their locations, heights and salience weights are similar.

Global-Level. Local-level association will leave some targets unmatched due to noise or errors, and global-level tracking refinement is needed for reliable results. Two tracklets are believed to be one target if their motions and spatiotemporal gap are highly coherent. I.e. the speeds and directions of 2 tracklets should be similar, and their spatial distance and temporal interval shouldn't be significant within a connected time period. To support various application domains, scene constraints are also considered at the global stage. For example, in the basic setting, we impose entering and leaving constraints into the tracking system, the region surrounding 4 edge lines of the FOV is defined as the EE-zone (entry/exit). We assume that people cannot enter/exit the tracking area without passing through the EE-zone. Likelihoods of enter/exit object events are determined using spatial and temporal factors:

- the direction and distance to the closest boundary edge,
- the direction and distance to the area center,
- the duration of its *tracklet's* head within the EE-zone;

If the head of a long trajectory stays longer in the EE-zone and gets closer to its closest edge, it is more likely to be a leaving target, and if the head of a *tracklet* in the EE-zone gets closer to the region center it is most likely to be an entering target.

Fig. 3. Top-down body shape modeling

In general, the global-level tracking process is a MAP association problem with priors of scene constraints. The inverse values of the likelihoods are the cost of *tracklet* association, and can be arranged into a cost matrix C. The optimal association is obtained via the Hungarian algorithm [4]. and the refined multi-target trajectories yield more robust tracking results.

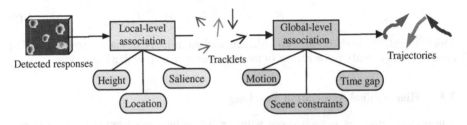

Fig. 4. Online hierarchical association tracking

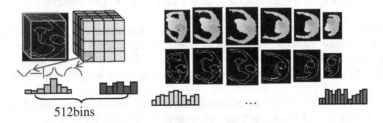

Fig. 5. Salience Occupancy Patterns for action representation

3.4   Salience Occupancy Action Descriptor

Tracking is a fundamental step towards human activity analysis. Based on the tracked results, recognizing gestures and actions of tracked targets is the next step. The action of the human subject in a 3D bird's-eye view is characterized by the 4D *Salience Occupancy Patterns* (*SOP*). In each frame, a *SOP* feature computes the occupancy information based on 8 types of bottom-up 3D GETs of each tracked target, so that the temporal dynamics of such occupancy patterns within a time window can discriminate different actions. Specifically, we have 3D GETs for each tracked target at frame t, and its 3D boundary is divided into $w \times h \times z$ (4×4×4) spatial cells, each of which has 8 GET type bins (see Figure 5). Thus we have 512 bins for each tracked target on one frame. The pixel number of a certain GET type within each cell is counted, and L2-norm is computed. We take a 6-frame window size to detect gestures. The final action descriptor is a concatenation of the *SOPs* obtained from all the cells, and taken as the input to a SVM classifier for recognition.

4   Experiments

The speed of the tracking system is about 10-15fps, including processes of edge extraction, human detection, tracking and action recognition. The test machine is an Intel Core 2 CPU with 2G RAM and the program is coded in C++ without any parallel procedures. We validate our approach by evaluating a HCI research interactive application, titled *the future kitchen*, and by testing on recorded datasets.

The bird's-eye view *Future Kitchen* displays a virtual environment from a top-down perspective. Users are able to interact with the virtual appliances, moving/placing within the space. Our system serves as the backbone that needs to not only track a normal walking posture but also be able to recognize the users' specific movements and gestures with a wider range of body movements and shapes. Fig. 6(a-b) shows screen-shots of this application, where a yellow box follows the visitor tracked by our tracking system.

We validate our approach by evaluating the detection, tracking and recognition performance on recorded datasets consisting of 40-minute depth videos with the resolution of 320×240 taken in an indoor environment. The height of the camera is set 4.5 meters high, and the total tracking area is around 2×2.5 meters. 6 users of varying builds and of both genders participated in the data collection. They randomly walked in the area and performed 4 actions including pick-up (PU), put-down (PD), holding(HD), raise an arm (RA), each of which is performed 4 or 5 times by each subject. Roughly 10 samples per action were collected.

We use the detection rate (recall) to evaluate detection performance and compare with 2 other methods for top view human detection: mean-shift method [19], Haar-like Filtering method [13]. Our detection method has a detection rate of 95.5%, verse 88.3% and 86.5% for Mean-shift and Haar-like filtering respectively (Table 1). We adopt common metrics to evaluate the tracking performance:

- **GT**: The number of trajectories in ground truth;
- **MT**: Mostly Tracked trajectories (≥80%);
- **ML**: Mostly Lost trajectories (<20%);
- **PT**: Partially tracked trajectories (btw   20%,   80%);
- **FRAG**: Fragmentation, interrupted ground true;
- **IDS**: ID Switches, two trajectories switch their IDs.

We compared the performance of our low-level tracking method with the hierarchical tracking approach. This comparison data demonstrates the progressive improvement achieved by the global-level tracking association (Table 2).

Table 1. Detection accuracies on our dataset

Method	Detection Rate
Mean-shift[19]	88.3%
Haar-like filtering[13]	86.5%
Our approach	95.5%

Table 2. Results of local and global level tacking

Method	Recall	Precision	GT	MT	ML	PT	FRAG	IDS
Local tracking	76.90%	90.9	52	40	7	5	11	5
Global tracking	86.50%	91.80%	52	45	4	3	8	4

SVM classifiers are trained for SOP action representation, with χ^2-RBF-kernel using Leave-One-Out (LOO) cross validation. Since it is the multi-class classification case, one-against-rest approach is applied to select the gesture class with the highest score as the recognized one. Fig. 6(c) shows the confusion matrix for the classification. Majority gestures are well classified. The worst performance is "holding", which requires both hands are raised up in front of the body, and keep steady. It looks similar to pick up, and is easy to be confused with each other.

(a) A virtual kitchen   (b) Tracking on the virtual space   (c) Confusion matrix

Fig. 6. Future Kitchen Project

5   Conclusion

Tracking multiple people in arbitrary environments is a challenging problem due to numerous performance affecting factors, and there exists no single tracking approach that can successfully handle all scenarios. In this paper, we tackle the human detection, tracking and action recognition problem by using a top view 3D camera. Under the top-down setting, the human body and motions still present descriptive shape appearance, and the occlusion issue becomes trivial. Inspired by visual attention theories, saliency map-based feature representation for 3D human body shape is modeled for detection. The tracking task is handled in the hierarchical association framework, where local and global affinities, motion patterns and scene constraints are modeled to obtain optimal trajectories of multi-targets. Finally, based on the tracking results, salience occupancy pattern features is computed for action recognition. This complete top-down human tracking solution is being applied into several HCI applications, and has opened up several interesting research directions for future work.

References

1. Dalal, N., Triggs, B.: Histograms of oriented gradients for human detection. In: CVPR, vol. 2, pp. 886–893 (June 2005)
2. Li, Y., Huang, C., Nevatia, R.: Learning to associate: Hybridboosted multi-target tracker for crowded scene. In: CVPR (2009)
3. Andriluka, M., Roth, S., Schiele, B.: People-tracking-bydetection and people-detection-by-tracking. In: Proc. IEEE CVPR 2008, pp. 1–8 (2008)
4. Huang, C., Wu, B., Nevatia, R.: Robust object tracking by hierarchical association of detection responses. In: Forsyth, D., Torr, P., Zisserman, A. (eds.) ECCV 2008, Part II. LNCS, vol. 5303, pp. 788–801. Springer, Heidelberg (2008)
5. Zhang, L., Li, Y., Nevatia, R.: Global data association for multi-object tracking using network flows. In: CVPR (2008)
6. Andriyenko, A., Schindler, K., Roth, S.: Discretecontinuous optimization for multi-target tracking. In: CVPR (2012)
7. Collins, R.: Multi-target data association with higher-order motion models. In: CVPR (2012)
8. Yang, B., Nevatia, R.: Online learned discriminative part-based appearance models for multi-human tracking. In: Fitzgibbon, A., Lazebnik, S., Perona, P., Sato, Y., Schmid, C. (eds.) ECCV 2012, Part I. LNCS, vol. 7572, pp. 484–498. Springer, Heidelberg (2012)
9. Shotton, J., et al.: Real-time human pose recognition in parts from single depth images. In: IEEE Conference on Computer Vision and Pattern Recognition (2011)
10. Itti, L., Koch, C., Niebur, E.: A model of saliency-based visual attention for rapid scene analysis. IEEE Trans. Pattern Anal. Mach. Intell. **20**(11), 1254–1259 (1998)
11. http://www.trastem.co.jp/eng/palossie_01.html (retreaved April 30, 2014)
12. http://ptgrey.com/products/censys3d/samples.asp (retreaved April 30, 2014)
13. Ikemura, S., Fujiyoshi, H.: Human detection by haarlike filtering using depth information. In: 2012 21st International Conference on Pattern Recognition (ICPR), pp. 813–816. IEEE (2012)
14. Dollar, P., Wojek, C., Schiele, B., Perona, P.: Pedestrian detection: An evaluation of the state of the art. IEEE Transactions on Pattern Analysis and Machine Intelligence **34**(4), 743–761 (2012)
15. Enzweiler, M., Eigenstetter, A., Schiele, B., Gavrila, D.M.: Multi-cue pedestrian classification with partial occlusion handling. In: CVPR (2010)
16. Wojek, C., Walk, S., Roth, S., Schiele, B: Monocular 3D scene understanding with explicit occlusion reasoning. In: CVPR (2011)
17. Gao, Q., Wong, A.K.C.: Curve detection based organization. Pattern Recognition **26**(1), 1039–1046 (1993)
18. Hu, G., Gao, Q.: A non-parametric statistics based method for generic curve partition and classification. In: Proc. of IEEE 17th ICIP, Hong Kong, pp. 3041–3044 (September 2010)
19. Comaniciu, D., Meer, P.: Mean Shift : A Robust approach towards feature space analysis. IEEE Transactions on Pattern Analysis and Machine Intelligence **24**(5) (May 2002)

3D Spatial Layout Propagation
in a Video Sequence

Alejandro Rituerto[1]([⊠]), Roberto Manduchi[2], Ana C. Murillo[1],
and J.J. Guerrero[1]

[1] Instituto de Investigación en Ingeniería de Aragón, University of Zaragoza,
Zaragoza, Spain
[2] Computer Vision Lab at University of California, Santa Cruz, USA
{arituerto,acm,josechu.guerrero}@unizar.es,
manduchi@soe.ucsc.edu

Abstract. Intelligent autonomous systems need detailed models of their
environment to achieve sophisticated tasks. Vision sensors provide rich
information and are broadly used to obtain these models, particularly,
indoor scene understanding has been widely studied. A common initial step to solve this problem is the estimation of the 3D layout of
the scene. This work addresses the problem of scene layout propagation
along a video sequence. We use a Particle Filter framework to propagate the scene layout obtained using a state-of-the-art technique on
the initial frame and propose how to generate, evaluate and sample new
layout hypotheses on each frame. Our intuition is that we can obtain better layout estimation at each frame through propagation than running
separately at each image. The experimental validation shows promising
results for the presented approach.

1 Introduction

This paper investigates the construction of indoor scene models given an image
sequence. The models contain essential information about the environment structure that may allow us to better understand the image. Prior approaches demonstrate the fact that obtaining information about the 3D structure of the scene
is a powerful tool to improve the accuracy of other tasks [11].

Previous approaches on layout estimation use to assume certain constrains,
like the Manhattan World assumption, and try to solve this problem for single images [3,8,9,13]. Other papers use sequential information to model the
environment from a mobile camera. These approaches use to rely on SLAM or
Structure-from-Motion [4,5,19].

The goal of this work is to provide semantic information about the scene
layout traversed during the sequence (Fig. 1). Our approach propagates the
estimated scene by taking advantage of restrictions in the sequential data and

This work was supported by the Spanish FPI grant BES-2010-030299 and Spanish
projects DPI2012-31781, DGA-T04-FSE and TAMA.

© Springer International Publishing Switzerland 2014
A. Campilho and M. Kamel (Eds.): ICIAR 2014, Part II, LNCS 8815, pp. 374–382, 2014.
DOI: 10.1007/978-3-319-11755-3_42

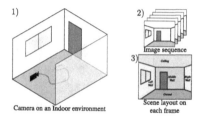

Fig. 1. 3D layout estimation along a sequence. 1) We have a mobile camera recording indoors, and we want to process the acquired sequence 2) to estimate the scene layout describing the 3D information of the environment at each frame 3).

prior knowledge of the projection of man made environments in images. We show how to achieve this task without the need to compute accurate camera motion or 3D maps.

Related Work. Recognizing the 3D structure of an environment captured in an image is a widely studied problem. To solve the scene structure in general scenes, study in [10] proposes to learn appearance-based models of the scene parts and describe the scene geometry using these labels. Similarly, Markov Random Fields are used to infer plane parameters for homogeneous patches extracted from the image [18].

For indoor environments, additional assumptions can be made, such as the Manhattan World assumption [2]. Using this constrain, a Bayesian network model is proposed in [3] to find the "floor-wall" boundary in the images. The work in [13] generate interpretations of a scene from a set of line segments extracted from an indoor image. Similarly, the approach in [7] models the scene as a parametric 3D box. The spatial layout in omnidirectional images was solved in [14]. Extending similar ideas to outdoors, the work in [6] proposes to create physical representations where objects have volume and mass.

If we consider images of a video sequence we can propagate the scene information and get better and robust results. This is the idea exploited in this work. Acquiring sequential information is the usual scenario in mobile platforms, and the spatio-temporal restrictions between frames can provide both efficiency and accuracy advantages.

Most of the papers using sequential data to obtain scene models, are based on SLAM or structure-from-motion techniques. In. [4] geometric and photometric cues are combined to obtain the scene model from a moving camera. Similarly, structure-from-motion is used in [5]. The work in [19] describes a method to model the environment using images from a mobile robot.

Attending how to propagate semantic information in video sequences using probabilistic frameworks. We find the work in [1], that uses pixel-wise correspondences, image patch similarities and semantical consistent hierarchical regions in a probabilistic graphical model. The approach in [16] focus on label propagation indoors for mobile robots. Similarly, the work in [15] estimates the 3D structure of outdoor scenes by computing appearance, location and motion features.

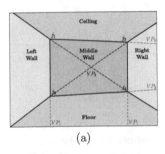 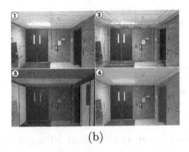

(a)   (b)

Fig. 2. Scene model used to create the scene structure hypotheses, (a), and steps of the base method [13], (b): **1**, lines and vanishing points are detected, many structure hypotheses are proposed, **2**, and the orientation map is computed, **3**. Hypotheses are compared against the orientation map and the best is chosen as solution, **4**.

Our work proposes a probabilistic framework to propagate information in sequences. We aim to propagate the 3D layout of the environment traversed by the camera. The initial frame layout is obtained using a single image technique [13], and we then propagate this information in each consecutive frame.

2   Single Image 3D Layout

Our method uses the single image algorithm proposed by Lee et al. [13] to create layout hypotheses on the first frame. Their approach proposes several physically valid scene structures and validate them against an orientation map to find the best fitting model (Fig. 2(b)). Authors adopt the Indoor World model that combines the Manhattan World assumption [2] and a single-floor-single-ceiling model. Layout hypotheses are generated randomly from the lines detected in the image and then compared with an orientation map. The orientation map expresses the local belief of region orientations computed from the line segments.

To extract the image lines Canny edge detector (Kovesi [12] Matlab toolbox) is run and the vanishing points are detected following the method presented by Rother [17]. The generation of hypotheses is made based on the model showed in Fig. 2(a).

3   Propagating the 3D Layout in a Video Sequence

The objective of this work is to compute the 3D layout at every frame of a video sequence. We exploit the fact that consecutive frames in a video have certain spatio-temporal restrictions that constrain the possible variations in the scene acquired. By propagating the possible layouts, we improve the results and obtain a more robust estimation of the layout on each frame. We adopt a particle filter based strategy to track the posterior probability of the layout given all the observations up to the current frame.

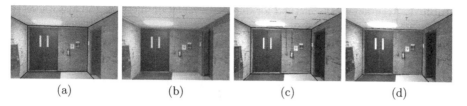

(a)   (b)   (c)   (d)

Fig. 3. Layout and correspondent plane orientation, (a), and the orientation map computed from the observed lines, (b). Both orientations maps are compared to compute S_{omap}. Lines supporting the model, S_{lines}, (c), and evaluated hypothesis (black) and closest observed layout (red), used to compute S_{model}, (d). Best seen in color.

The process followed by our approach is the following: For the first frame, hypotheses are created using the base algorithm (Section 2). These hypotheses are evaluated and ranked and the best one is selected as the solution for that frame. For next frames, new hypotheses (particles) are randomly generated depending on previous hypotheses and their evaluation score.

Layout Parametrization. We parametrized the scene layout model (Fig. 2(a)) by the image coordinates of the junctions defining the middle wall, j_k, and the directions of the scene vanishing points, VP_l: $x_i = \{j_1, j_2, j_3, j_4, VP_1, VP_2, VP_3\}$.

Hypotheses Evaluation. The evaluation of the hypotheses is performed on every frame. For all the images, lines and vanishing points are computed and used to evaluate the compatibility of the layout hypotheses. We define three evaluation measurements computed for each layout hypothesis x_i:

Orientation Map. The orientation map [13] expresses the local belief of region orientations computed from line segments (Fig. 3(b)). This observed orientation map, $omap(\mathsf{l}_i)$, is compared with the orientation map defined by the hypothesis being evaluated, $omap(x_i)$ (Fig. 3(a)). The evaluation score is computed as the number of pixels where the orientation of both maps is the same divided by the total number of image pixels, $nPix = width \times height$

$$S_{omap\ i} = \frac{\sum_{k=0}^{nPix} omap(\mathsf{l}_i)_k = omap(x_i)_k}{nPix} \qquad (k = 1 \ldots nPix) \qquad (1)$$

Lines Supporting the Model. This evaluation measures how many of the observed lines support the hypothesis being evaluated (Fig. 3(c)). To evaluate how a hypothesis fits the new observation, we look for lines parallel and close to the model lines. The score is computed as the number of lines supporting the model divided by the total number of lines detected.

$$S_{lines\ i} = \left(\frac{\#\ supporting\ lines}{\#\ total\ lines} \right)_i \qquad (2)$$

Table 1. Accuracy of the method for different evaluation methods (50 hypotheses)

	mean	Max
S_{omap} [13]	70.58	95.12
S_{lines}	75.47	93.78
S_{model}	59.38	93.78
$mean(S_{omap}, S_{lines})$	78.70	93.78
$mean(S_{omap}, S_{model})$	84.05	95.57
$mean(S_{lines}, S_{model})$	75.14	93.78
S_{total}	86.86	95.93

Distance to the Closest Layout Obtained with New Observed Lines. This last evaluation scores a propagated layout hypothesis, x_i, by computing the closest lines to this layout in the current image and determining a layout based on these lines, x_{obs} (Fig. 3(d)). The distance between layouts, $d(x_i, x_{obs})$, is computed as the mean distance between the junctions, j_k, of both layouts:

$$S_{model\ i} = \frac{1}{1 + d(x_i, x_{obs})} \quad \text{where} \quad d(x_i, x_{obs}) = \underset{k=1...4}{mean}(\|j_k, j_{k\ obs}\|) \quad (3)$$

The mean of the three scores, $S_{total\ i}$, is used as evaluation.

Sampling New Hypotheses. A new set of hypotheses is created by sampling from the hypotheses of the previous frame. The probability of generating a new hypothesis, x'_i, from previous hypothesis x_i is $p_i = S_{total\ i}$.

Given the camera motion, a homography relates the projection of the coplanar junctions between frames and the vanishing points are related by the rotation matrix. To create a new hypothesis from a previous one, we assume a random motion of the camera, with zero velocity and random noise in camera translation and rotation. From hypothesis x_i, sampled hypothesis x'_i will be related by the random rotation, R, and translation, t. The junctions are related by a homography, H, and the vanishing points are related by the rotation matrix:

$$j'_k = H \cdot j_k = (R - \frac{t\ n^T}{d})j_k \text{ and } VP'_l = R \cdot VP_l \quad (k = 1...4, l = 1...3) \quad (4)$$

where n is the normal of the plane where the junction points lie and d the distance between the camera and the plane. We assume d distance as unitary so the scale of the random translation t is defined by the real distance to the plane.

4   Experiments

Experimental Settings. We have tested our method on the 10 sequences included in the dataset presented in [5]. These sequences have been acquired indoors with two different mobile cameras and include between 203 and 965 images. For all the sequences, the ground-truth has been manually annotated in one of each ten images. Fig. 4 shows example frames of the dataset sequences and the layout computed.

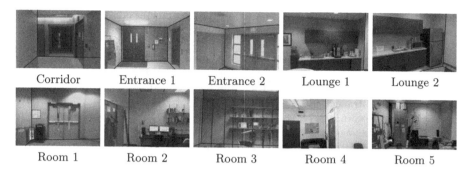

| Corridor | Entrance 1 | Entrance 2 | Lounge 1 | Lounge 2 |

| Room 1 | Room 2 | Room 3 | Room 4 | Room 5 |

Fig. 4. Examples of the resulting layout in some frames of all the dataset sequences. Best seen in color.

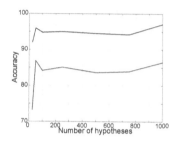

Fig. 5. Accuracy of our method for different number of hypotheses. Mean (red) and maximum accuracy (blue) of the layout solution along the sequence.

The accuracy of the solution is computed as the number of pixels where the orientation defined by the ground-truth and the orientation computed from the layout hypothesis is the same divided by the total number of pixels of the image.

Analysis of the Proposed Method Parameters. The accuracy of our method varies with two important choices: a) the evaluation measurements used and b) the number of particles used.

Influence of the Evaluation Measurement. Table 1 shows the mean and maximum value of the accuracy of the solution hypothesis on all the frames of the sequence Entrance 1. Results show that combining the different evaluation measurements we get to choose always a better solution. Therefore, all the evaluation measurements are used together in the remaining experiments.

Influence of the Number of Particles. Fig. 5 shows the accuracy of the algorithm presented depending on the number of particles. Results show poor accuracy when few hypotheses are considered (25 particles), and how the accuracy grows rapidly with the number of particles. For more than 50 particles, augmenting the number of hypotheses do not represent a big change in the method accuracy.

Table 2. Mean and standard deviation (σ) of the accuracy of our algorithm and the base algorithm for all the dataset sequences (50 hypotheses)

	Our Algorithm		Lee et al. Algorithm [13]	
	mean	σ	*mean*	σ
Corridor	42.93	**11.99**	**56.84**	30.78
Entrance 1	**86.80**	**9.90**	80.13	11.47
Entrance 2	71.34	15.49	**74.27**	15.76
Lounge 1	**56.52**	**17.47**	47.40	30.68
Lounge 2	31.78	31.17	**36.38**	**28.20**
Room 1	**60.69**	**14.52**	50.73	25.97
Room 2	**75.91**	**10.20**	66.79	25.11
Room 3	**63.42**	**16.83**	36.82	35.82
Room 4	20.64	**13.41**	**25.93**	24.24
Room 5	**69.27**	**16.07**	64.70	22.63
Average	**57.93**	**15.71**	54.00	25.07

Method Evaluation. Table 2 shows results of our method run on all the dataset and compared with the base method [13]. The base method is intended to work on single images so we run this algorithm over all the frames of the sequence independently. For each sequence, the mean and the deviation of the accuracy obtained for the solution hypothesis in all frames are shown. Our method performs better for the majority of sequences and the average accuracy value is higher. At the same time, our solutions are more stable across all frames, since the standard deviation is smaller.

Fig. 4 shows examples of the layout solution obtained for some frames of the dataset. The results for Entrances 1 and 2 are good (mean accuracies of 83.63 and 72.70, respectively). In sequences Lounge 1 and 2, Room 2, 3 and 5 the layout fits the environment, but the method fails in adjusting hypotheses lines to the structure. Finally, our method shows lower performance for sequences Corridor, and Room 4 where more than 3 walls appear, and Room 1 that violates the Manhattan World assumption.

5   Conclusions

In this paper we presented an approach to obtain the 3D spatial layout of all the frames of a video sequence. The method is designed to work indoors, makes use of the Manhattan World assumption and it is based in the previous work from Lee et al. [13]. This technique, is integrated with a Particle Filter to take advantage of the sequential information of video sequences. We have presented different evaluation methods to measure how well a spatial layout fits to an image. Experiments showed how our approach presents better accuracy than the state-of-the-art base algorithm.

References

1. Badrinarayanan, V., Galasso, F., Cipolla, R.: Label propagation in video sequences. In: IEEE Conference on Computer Vision and Pattern Recognition (CVPR), pp. 3265–3272 (2010)
2. Coughlan, J.M., Yuille, A.L.: Manhattan world: Compass direction from a single image by bayesian inference. In: IEEE International Conference on Computer Vision (ICCV), pp. 941–947 (1999)
3. Delage, E., Lee, H., Ng, A.Y.: A dynamic bayesian network model for autonomous 3d reconstruction from a single indoor image. In: IEEE Conference on Computer Vision and Pattern Recognition (CVPR), pp. 2418–2428 (2006)
4. Flint, A., Murray, D., Reid, I.: Manhattan scene understanding using monocular, stereo, and 3d features. In: IEEE International Conference on Computer Vision (ICCV), pp. 2228–2235 (2011)
5. Furlan, A., Miller, S., Sorrenti, D.G., Fei-Fei, L., Savarese, S.: Free your camera: 3d indoor scene understanding from arbitrary camera motion. In: British Machine Vision Conference (BMVC) (2013)
6. Gupta, A., Efros, A.A., Hebert, M.: Blocks world revisited: image understanding using qualitative geometry and mechanics. In: Daniilidis, K., Maragos, P., Paragios, N. (eds.) ECCV 2010, Part IV. LNCS, vol. 6314, pp. 482–496. Springer, Heidelberg (2010)
7. Hedau, V., Hoiem, D., Forsyth, D.: Recovering the spatial layout of cluttered rooms. In: IEEE International Conference on Computer Vision (ICCV), pp. 1849–1856 (2009)
8. Hedau, V., Hoiem, D., Forsyth, D.: Thinking inside the box: using appearance models and context based on room geometry. In: Daniilidis, K., Maragos, P., Paragios, N. (eds.) ECCV 2010, Part VI. LNCS, vol. 6316, pp. 224–237. Springer, Heidelberg (2010)
9. Hoiem, D., Efros, A.A., Hebert, M.: Geometric context from a single image. In: IEEE International Conference onComputer Vision (ICCV), pp. 654–661 (2005)
10. Hoiem, D., Efros, A.A., Hebert, M.: Recovering surface layout from an image. International Journal of Computer Vision 75(1), 151–172 (2007)
11. Hoiem, D., Efros, A.A., Hebert, M.: Putting objects in perspective. International Journal of Computer Vision 80(1), 3–15 (2008)
12. Kovesi, P.D.: MATLAB and Octave functions for computer vision and image processing
13. Lee, D.C., Hebert, M., Kanade, T.: Geometric reasoning for single image structure recovery. In: IEEE Conference on Computer Vision and Pattern Recognition (CVPR), pp. 2136–2143 (2009)
14. López-Nicolás, G., Omedes, J., Guerrero, J.: Spatial layout recovery from a single omnidirectional image and its matching-free sequential propagation. Robotics and Autonomous Systems (2014)
15. Raza, S.H., Grundmann, M., Essa, I.: Geometric context from video. In: IEEE Conference on Computer Vision and Pattern Recognition (CVPR) (2013)
16. Rituerto, J., Murillo, A., Kosecka, J.: Label propagation in videos indoors with an incremental non-parametric model update. In: IEEE/RSJ International Conference on Intelligent Robots and Systems (IROS), pp. 2383–2389 (2011)
17. Rother, C.: A new approach to vanishing point detection in architectural environments. Image and Vision Computing 20(9), 647–655 (2002)

18. Saxena, A., Sun, M., Ng, A.Y.: Make3d: Learning 3d scene structure from a single still image. IEEE Transactions on Pattern Analysis and Machine Intelligence **31**(5), 824–840 (2009)
19. Tsai, G., Kuipers, B.: Dynamic visual understanding of the local environment for an indoor navigating robot. In: IEEE/RSJ International Conference on Intelligent Robots and Systems (IROS), pp. 4695–4701 (2012)

SASCr3: A Real Time Hardware Coprocessor for Stereo Correspondence

Luca Puglia, Mario Vigliar, and Giancarlo Raiconi(⊠)

Dipartimento di Informatica, Universitá degli Studi di Salerno, Fisciano, Italy
{lpuglia,mvigliar,gianni}@unisa.it
http://neuronelab.unisa.it

Abstract. Main focus of this paper is to show the relevant improvements for a real time hardware co-processor for Stereo-Matching. The approach follows the well-known scheme for strings alignment proposed by Needleman&Wunsch, commonly used in bio-informatics. The principal improvement concerns the algorithm parallelization in FPGA design, in an hardware architecture many resources can work at the same time avoiding the reduction of system performance. The architecture, highly modular, was designed by using Bluespec SystemVerilog development tool and is described in detail. For many parallelism degrees the synthesis and performance results are shown, for this purpose a Lattice ECP3-70 is set as target device. The aim of this project is to build stereo vision system for embedded application, charaterized by low power usage and device cost. The actual circuit is an updated version of SASCr2 design. Performance is benchmarked against the former implementation.

1 Introduction

The stereo vision techniques permit to reconstruct the scene model starting from multiple images taken from different point of views. The target is to match the pixels between the images. The relative span between matched pixels is called disparity, the more two matched pixels are spanned, the greater the disparity. Less generically is possible to perform this techniques using only two images, so once that each pixel of one image is matched with the relative pixel of the other image the computation ends, the result of this procedure is a new image built according the disparity information, the so called disparity map. Problems may occur when some objects are visible in one image but hidden in the other, this may occur due to scene perspective, in this case the visible object pixels in the first image are said occluded in the first one, thus hidden from the view.

During the last years many techniques were proposed to solve the stereo-matching problem, that is the problem of finding match between pixels of two stereo-images. The great majority of this method consist of alignment algorithms, this alignment is performed locally or globally according the target performances, in fact a local alignment is faster than a global, but the result is less

© Springer International Publishing Switzerland 2014
A. Campilho and M. Kamel (Eds.): ICIAR 2014, Part II, LNCS 8815, pp. 383–391, 2014.
DOI: 10.1007/978-3-319-11755-3_43

reliable. In literature is possible to find both approaches, as an example of local methods there are [1,2], while as an example of global methods there are [3–5]. For a complete discussion about the problem and principal solutions there is [6].

These techniques are of particular interest in the ASIC/FPGA field due to the characteristic role played in the artificial vision field. A fast Hardware implementation can be used for multiple purposes, e.g. automatic drive, object recognition and so on. So in the past few years many architectures have been proposed to achieve the real time performance, this achievement is mandatory for critical application requiring low power usage and minimum device cost, as an example [7–9]. For a complete discussion about the problem is possible to reference [10]. Concerning our project we use the works done in [5], so we use the Dynamic Programming (DP) to global align the pixels string of two image pairs, the approach is based upon the well known bio-informatics algorithm of Needleman&Wunsh (N&W) [11].

2   Algorithm Overview and Parallelization

The dynamic programming approach allows to build optimal alignment by superimposing optimal sub-alignment, and keeping the intermediate "scoring" results in a table of integer values (Score Matrix - "SM" from now on). To adapt this technique to pixels alignment we define the score as absolute difference of the pixels values. To this starting value a penalty term is added according to the direction along which the next optimal sub-alignment can extend the actual one. Gap, Egap and Match weights are defined in the original algorithm as constant integer values, in ascending order by value. In this implementation the Match score value is inversely proportional to the local pixels difference, while the other two are kept constant. An SM example is shown in Fig. 1, a direction is stored with each score. After the scoring procedure ends a backtrack phase begins. Strating from the cell storing the highest score in the table, we follow in backward order the directions stored. The path founded (highlighted number in Fig. 1) is converted into an alignment, which is used as proportional indicator of local disparities in the left/right images pair.

-	-	E	D	E	C	E
-	0	-1	-2	-3	-4	-5
A	-1	0	-1	-2	-3	-4
D	-2	-1	2	1	0	-1
C	-3	-2	1	2	3	2
E	-4	-1	0	3	2	5

Fig. 1. Scoring and directions matrix example

This algorithm is not easily parallelizable, this is due to the strict dependency between the matrix cells. There is only one way to parallelize the matrix filling procedure and it is based upon the cells dependency, looking closer at the *SM* of Fig. 1 is possible to see that the cells are anti-diagonal independent, the anti-diagonal dotted lines represent the cells sets that can be computed at the same time.

This observation can be used to parallelize the matrix filling process building a system able to fill multiple cells at once. This particular idea has been exploited for the well known and similar algorithm of Smith&Waterman [12] in [13].

3   Architecture

The implementation consists of various modules. The *Top Module* (Fig. 2) instantiate multiple copies of *Processor Module* ("*PM*" from now on). *PM* implements an enhanced parallel architecture that improve the work done in [14] and [15]. Other sub-modules are instantiate by each *PM* in the architecture.

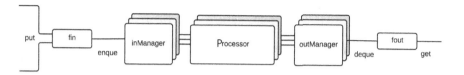

Fig. 2. *Top Module* diagram

3.1   Processor Module

A *PM* is an atomic working unit, its input are two images row (one for each stereoscopic image) and its output is the correspondent disparity row. Iterating on the whole image the obtained output is the complete disparity map.

Each *PM* includes a modules chain composed by *Raster, Scoring, Tracking* and *Disparity Modules*. Total processing time depends only on pixels processing time, and in this specific application even the backtrack procedure timing can be upper-bounded in advance.

In the previous version we focus on the memory requirements reduction preserving the needed accuracy, in this update we focus on the parallelization of the filling matrix process. The parallelization procedure is based upon [13], in which the cells of the matrix are filled in anti-diagonal order. Actually this is the only way to fill two or more cells in the same clock tick due to the *DP* computation constraints. The *PM* splits the computing session into four stages, each one associated to specific features. In detail:

1. Read and store input pixels coming from left and right image queues (*RasterL* and *RasterR Modules*)
2. Compare pixels and populate the scoring matrix (*Scoring Modules*)
3. Evaluate alignment (*Tracking Modules*)

4. Evaluare disparity according to the precedent scoring values (*Disparity Modules*)

PM schedules the activities of the stages. Once the session is finished the disparity row is complete. This row is available as output and a new pair of lines can be transmitted to the rasters for a new computation. In the next the parameter p denote the Parallelism Degree (*PD*).

3.2   Raster Module

Populating the *SM* implies storing the image pixels lines into a raster module, one for each image line (*RasterL* and *RasterR*). For each (i, j)-th *SM* cell (with $1 < i, j < n$) a pixel couple is sent from the Rasters. Setting $p = 1$ is possible to define the sequence of pixels submitted from the *RasterL/R* to the *Scoring Module* as follows:

$$(1,1), (1,2), ..., (i-1, j-1), (i-1, j), (i-1, j+1), ...,$$
$$(i, j-1), (i, j), (i, j+1), ..., (i+1, j-1), (i+1, j), \tag{1}$$
$$(i+1, j+1), ..., (n, n-1), (n, n)$$

This specific requirement affects the size of *RasterL/R* local memory, that needs to be capable to store two whole input lines. In this release the raster output port size is proportional to p since at each clock tick the *Scoring Module* can fill at most p cells. So we have p couples of pixels moving from the rasters at each clock tick. The glue logic needed to produce such pixels stream is quite simple:

- *RasterR* sends the j-th pixel with the following $p-1$ pixels, at the next clock tick it sends the $j+1$-th pixel plus the following $p-1$ pixels. When the line ends *RasterR* stops and restarts the cycle.
- *RasterL* sends the i-th pixel with the following $p-1$ pixels until *RasterR* stops, after *RasterR* restarts, *RasterL* send the $(i+p-1)$-th pixel with the following $p-1$ pixels until *RasterR* stops and so on.

Let i and j be respectively the indexes for *RasterL* and *RasterR*, k and l generic offsets and p the fixed *PD*, is possible to define $s(i, k, j, l) = [(i+k, j+l), (i+k+1, j+l+1), (i+k+2, j+l+2), ..., (i+k+p-2, j+l+p-2), (i+k+p-1, j+l+p-1)]$ as the sequence of pixels couple sent in a single clock tick, thus the stream of sequences traveling from *RasterL/R* to *Scoring Module* is:

$$s(1,0,1,0), s(1,0,1,1), s(1,0,1,2), ...s(1,0,1,n-p-1), s(1,0,1,n-p),$$
$$s(1,1,1,0), s(1,1,1,1), s(1,1,1,2), ...s(1,1,1,n-p-1), s(1,1,1,n-p),$$
$$...,$$
$$s(1,u,1,0), s(1,u,1,1), s(1,u,1,2)...s(1,u,1,n-p-1), s(1,u,1,n-p),$$
$$...,$$
$$s(1,n-p,1,0), s(1,n-p,1,1), ...s(1,n-p,1,n-p-1), s(1,-n-p,1,n-p)$$

Setting $p = 1$ is trivial to show that is possible to get back the (1) expression.

3.3   Scoring Module

The Scoring module directly applies the "N&W" algorithm. It stores the direction used in the late backtrack phase. Since there are 3 possible directions each cell is 2 bits wide.

In input there are $2p$ pixels (or p pixels couples), at each clock tick these are used to fill p cells. The module input is unpacked and sent to the relative pipeline. These pipelines are called *fillers*, in fact each one fills a matrix cell per clock tick. A *filler* use the body part of the N&W Algorithm to compute the value of a cell. So it uses the neighbor value increased by the matching score and set the cell direction. The core of internal parallelism can be found in this module, 2 pixels are used to compute 1 direction at each clock tick, this happens for p fillers, in output there are p directions that must be written in the *SM*, these directions are packed in group of 16 to store 32 bit word.

As you can see in Fig. 3 the parallelism degree affects positively the number of clock ticks needed by the computation.

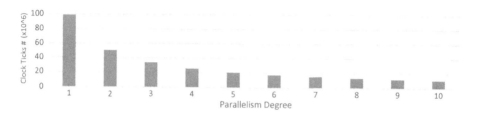

Fig. 3. Clock ticks needed by the computation of 640×480 image depending on the Parallelism Degree

3.4   Tracking and Disparity Modules

Once the scoring procedure is complete the BackTrack (BT) phase starts. While the Scoring procedure can be parallelized in some way, the BT phase is not.

Nothing can be done to predict the next directions, and so nothing can be done to reduce the computation time needed by this phase. By the way this is not a big problem because the real computation complexity is host by the Scoring phase. In fact the worst case of BT phase can take $2n$ clock ticks where n is the image width, while the complexity for the Scoring procedure is fixed to the dimension of the matrix. So the Tracking Module follows the path made by directions in the SM and compute the alignment.

So the *Tracking Module* send a stream of $n \leq x \leq 2n$ values to the *Disparity Module*. This module computes the disparity row. The output is a 8 bit gray scale pixels stream expressing the estimated distance between the observer and the homologous points in the neighborhood. The closer is the object, the brighter are the pixels.

4   Error Evaluation

To avoid the possibilities of multiple optimal alignment we chose to store only the first alignment evaluated. This heuristic does not significantly lower disparity map quality as shown in [14]. We tested the accuracy of the new version of the algorithm with the verilog simulation, in Fig. 4 are shown the disparity map relative to the standard images present in the Middlebury stereo vision dataset (http://vision.middlebury.edu/).

Fig. 4. Disparity map computed from Middlebury dataset, respectively: Cones (450 × 375), Teddy (450 × 375), Venus (434 × 383), Tsukuba (384 × 288)

With these results we run the Middlebury test obtaining the report shown in Table 1, the upper row label indicates the error index measured in various image areas, NO: error evaluated in the Non Occlusion zone, ALL: error evaluated in all pixels of the image, DISC: error evaluated in the discontinuity zone, AVG: average error.

Table 1. Error Evaluation

Rank 134.4	Tsukuba			Venus			Teddy			Cones			AVG 14.0%
	NO	ALL	DISC	NO	ALL	DISC	NO	ALL	DISC	NO	ALL	DISC	
	5.10	7.19	14.8	7.98	9.54	26.7	11.9	21.0	20.1	7.61	17.8	17.8	

5   Synthesis and Performance

The modules have been designed from scratch in Bluespec SystemVerilog language (BSV). Verilog files have been generated by using Bluespec Compiler. For our synthesis we used Lattice's Diamond 2.2 targeted to ECP3-70 devices (LFE3-70EAFPBGA484).

In the reference version [15] we had instantiated 6 *PMs* on the device, this had leads to the performance of 6 fps, with 97 Mhz closure frequency. In that case the device memory usage was very high, but the design area had minimum usage, this situation has been solved using the internal parallelism, that use more area depending on the *PD*. In Fig. 5 is possible to see the resulting frame rate varying the *PD* parameter for a single *PM*.

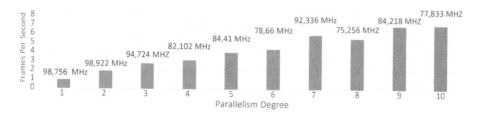

Fig. 5. Obtained frame rate for a single *PM* in function of different value of *PD* for 640 × 480 images, the labels in MHz represents the relative Fmax of each systhesis

So with a single *PM* we had outperformed the results obtained in the reference. More information are given by the comparison made in Table 2.

Table 2. SASCr2 execution time - *versus* - SASCr3 execution time (1 PM)

	Tsukuba	Venus	Teddy	Cones
Matlab	23.22 s	38.74 s	40.92 s	40.07 s
C	2.57 s	3.65 s	4.58 s	3.39 s
1 PM	0.19 s	0.33 s	0.35 s	0.35 s
4 PM	0.064 s	0.11 s	0.1 s	0.1 s

	Tsukuba	Venus	Teddy	Cones
$PD=1$	0.27 s	0.46 s	0.48 s	0.48 s
$PD=5$	0.03 s	0.09 s	0.1 s	0.1 s
$PD=10$	0.008 s	0.05 s	0.05 s	0.05 s

In order to obtain the maximum frame rate we tried many combinations of external and internal parallelism, so we have tuned the number of processors and the *PD* parameter. Obviously is not possible to instantiate an arbitrary number of *PMs*, furthermore the higher the *PD* the more are the LUTs used for a single *PM*. So we had to find the best trade off. We start increasing the *PD* parameter with only one *PM*, so we have increased the filled cells rate till to 20 at clock tick, obtaining optimal result of 16 fps. Then we tried to instantiate 2 *PMs* setting *PD* to 15, this configuration had leads to 20 fps. The best result is shown in Fig. 6, with the particular combination of 3 *PMs*, *PD* setted to 13, and a closure frequency of 78.852 Mhz, we obtained 27 fps with 640 × 480 images.

Our result is not easily comparable with other stereoscopic/string alignment approaches, actually there exist applications which are better in speed performance and/or disparity map quality. For example in [16] an FPGA architecture reaches 12.75 GCUPS (Giga Cell Update Per Second), in our implementation the

```
basicstyle={\scriptsize}]
Number of registers: 15123 PFU registers: 15102 PIO registers: 21
Number of SLICEs: 32128 out of 33264 (97%)
    SLICEs(logic/ROM): 26356 out of 26460 (100%)
    SLICEs(logic/ROM/RAM): 5772 out of 6804 (85%)
        As RAM: 5772 out of 6804 (85%)
        As Logic/ROM: 0 out of 6804 (0%)
Number of logic LUT4s: 33917 Number of distributed RAM: 5772
(11544 LUT4s) Number of ripple logic: 8138 (16276 LUT4s) Total
number of LUT4s: 61737 ...
Number of block RAMs: 102 out of 240 (43%)
```

Fig. 6. Synthesis result

speed is stuck at 5.6 GCUPS, but the results shown in that study are obtained removing the *BT* phase and *SM* storing, this is not an available option for stereo vision problems. Other studies [17,18] show Desktop GPU reaching really high frame rate and disparity map quality, but again is not possible to make a direct comparison, in fact an embedded application cannot use such power expensive device, so Desktop GPU are not suitable for our aim.

6   Conclusion and Future Works

This work shows a new hardware architecture to solve the stereo-matching problem, this architecture has proven to reach real time performances. Furthermore, the choice of a small target FPGA device obliged us to figure out innovative techniques to keep the area consumption as smallest as possible, resulting in a low thermal and energetic impact. Thanks to these results, it is possible to project the usage of the resulting component in low-power, low-cost embedded devices, like cell-phones, consumer cameras and automotive devices. The next step will concern the further enhancement of the frame rate using systolic architecture or more deep pipeline to increase the device maximum frequency.

References

1. Baha, N., Larabi, S.: Accurate real time disparity map computation based on variable support window. Computer Vision and Image Understanding **2**(3) (2010)
2. Stefano, L.D., Marchionni, M., Mattoccia, S.: A fast area-based stereo matching algorithm. Image and Vision Computing **22**(12), 983–1005 (2004)
3. Kim, J.C., Lee, K.M., Choi, B.T., Lee, S.U.: A dense stereo matching using two-pass dynamic programming with generalized ground control points. In: 2005 IEEE Computer Society Conference on Computer Vision and Pattern Recognition (CVPR 2005), vol. 2, pp. 1075–1082 (2005)
4. Veksler, O.: Extracting dense features for visual correspondence with graph cuts. In: Computer Vision and Pattern Recognition 2003 (2003)
5. Dieny, R., Thévenon, J., del Rincón, J.M., Nebel, J.-C.: Bioinformatics inspired algorithm for stereo correspondence. In: VISAPP 2011, Vilamoura, Algarve, Portugal, March 5–7, pp. 465–473 (2011)

6. Scharstein, D., Szeliski, R., Zabih, R.: International Journal of Computer Vision
7. Murphy, C., Lindquist, D., Rynning, A.M., Cecil, T., Leavitt, S., Chang, M.L.: Low-cost stereo vision on an fpga. In: 15th Annual IEEE Symposium on Field-Programmable Custom Computing Machines (FCCM 2007), pp. 333–334 (April 2007)
8. Masrani, D., MacLean, W.: Expanding disparity range in an fpga stereo system while keeping resource utilization low. In: 2005 IEEE Computer Society Conference on Computer Vision and Pattern Recognition (CVPR 2005) - Workshops, vol. 3, pp. 132–132 (2005)
9. Wong, S., Vassiliadis, S., Cotofana, S., Ce, S., Tudelft, E.T.: A sum of absolute differences implementation in fpga hardware, p. 5 (2002)
10. Nalpantidis, L., Sirakoulis, G.C., Gasteratos, A.: Review of stereo vision algorithms: from software to hardware. International Journal of Optomechatronics 2(4), 435–462 (2008)
11. Needleman, S.B., Wunsch, C.D.: A general method applicable to the search for similarities in the amino acid sequence of two proteins. Journal of Molecular Biology 48(3), 443–453 (1970)
12. Smith, T.F., Waterman, M.S.: Identification of common molecular subsequences. Journal of Molecular Biology 147(1), 195–197 (1981)
13. Nawaz, Z., Nadeem, M., van Someren, H., Bertels, K.: A parallel fpga design of the smith-waterman traceback. In: 2010 International Conference on Field-Programmable Technology, pp. 454–459 (December 2010)
14. Vigliar, M., Fratello, M., Puglia, L., Raiconi, G.: SASC: A hardware string alignment coprocessor for stereo correspondence. In: 2012 IEEE International Conference on Electronics Design, Systems and Applications (ICEDSA), pp. 56–62. IEEE (November 2012)
15. Vigliar, M., Puglia, L., Fratello, M., Raiconi, G.: SASCr2: Enhanced hardware string alignment coprocessor for stereo correspondence. In: Mediterranean Embedded Computing Resources (MECO) (2014)
16. Benkrid, K., Member, S., Liu, Y., Member, S., Benkrid, A.: A highly parameterized and efficient fpga-based skeleton for pairwise biological sequence alignment 17(4), 561–570 (2009)
17. Mei, X., Sun, X., Zhou, M., Jiao, S., Wang, H., Zhang, X.: On building an accurate stereo matching system on graphics hardware. In: 2011 IEEE International Conference on Computer Vision Workshops (ICCV Workshops), pp. 467–474 (2011)
18. Wang, L., Liao, M., Gong, M., Yang, R., Nister, D.: High-quality real-time stereo using adaptive cost aggregation and dynamic programming. In: Third International Symposium on 3D Data Processing, Visualization, and Transmission (3DPVT 2006), pp. 798–805 (June 2006)

Motion Analysis and Tracking

Adaptive Feature Selection for Object Tracking with Particle Filter

Darshan Venkatrayappa[1(✉)], Désiré Sidibé[2],
Fabrice Meriaudeau[2], and Philippe Montesinos[1]

[1] Ecole des Mines d'Ales, LGI2P, Parc Scientifique Georges Besses,
30035 Nimes, France
{darshan.venkatrayappa,philippe.montesinos}@mines-ales.fr
[2] Laboratoire Le2i, 12 rue de la Fonderie, 71200 Le Creusot, France
{dro-desire.sidibe,fabrice.meriaudeau}@u-bourgogne.fr

Abstract. Object tracking is an important topic in the field of computer vision. Commonly used color-based trackers are based on a fixed set of color features such as RGB or HSV and, as a result, fail to adapt to changing illumination conditions and background clutter. These drawbacks can be overcome to an extent by using an adaptive framework which selects for each frame of a sequence the features that best discriminate the object from the background. In this paper, we use such an adaptive feature selection method embedded into a particle filter mechanism and show that our tracking method is robust to lighting changes and background distractions. Different experiments also show that the proposed method outperform other approaches.

Keywords: Tracking · Particle filter · Mean-shift filter · Feature selection

1 Introduction

Object tracking is a basic requirement in many applications related to video surveillance, robotics and interactive video games. Object trackers can be used to improve our understanding of large video sequences from medical and security applications. Tracking algorithms should be able to cope with the variation of the size of the target, orientation and pose of the target, reflectance of the target, illumination changes and background clutter. The success or failure of a tracking algorithm depends on how distinguishable an object is from the background. If the object is distinguishable from its background, then mean shift[1] or particle filters[10] can track the object successfully. On the other hand, if object and background are not distinguishable, then the tracker needs to handle the targets appearance changes as well as illumination changes and background clutter.

Many researchers have proposed different approaches to cope up with appearance change, illumination change and background clutter. In [2] visual appearance variations at a short time scale are represented as linear subspace of the

© Springer International Publishing Switzerland 2014
A. Campilho and M. Kamel (Eds.): ICIAR 2014, Part II, LNCS 8815, pp. 395–402, 2014.
DOI: 10.1007/978-3-319-11755-3_44

image space. Tracking algorithm updates this subspace on-line by finding a linear subspace that best approximates the observation made in the previous frames. Some methods use fixed features which are determined a priori depending on the application. A good example is the case of head tracking using skin color. Different color spaces are first evaluated and the one for which pixels values of skin clusters the most is used for tracking [3]. The authors of [13] use a new approach for face detection. This approach adaptively switches between a number of color space models as a function of the state of the environment, as well as, dynamically updates the corresponding color distribution model. In [8] the authors assemble multiple heterogeneous features then likelihood images are constructed for the various subspaces of the combined feature space, then the most discriminative feature is extracted by Principal Component Analysis (PCA) based on those likelihood images. They embed this feature selection mechanism in an mean shift tracker. In [9] the authors come up with an approach for evaluating multiple color histograms during object tracking. The method adaptively selects histograms that well distinguish foreground from background. The variance ratio is utilized to measure the separability of object and background and to extract top-ranked discriminative histograms. In [4], feature values from background patches and object observations are sampled during tracking and Fisher discriminant is used to rank the features based on sampled values. [5] combine saliency information with color features to make tracking more robust to changing illumination. [6] use mutual information to track multi-view objects in real time. They use the variance of mutual information to acquire reliable features for tracking by making use of the images of the tracked object in previous frames to refine the target model.

We address the problem of adaptive feature selection for real time tracking. As shown by Collins and Liu [7], the best features for tracking are those able to distinguish the object to be tracked from the background. The authors propose a framework for the on-line selection of the best combination of color values in each frame of a sequence. Following the same approach, we propose a particle filter based tracking algorithm which can cope with difficult conditions such as lighting variations and background distractions.

This paper is organised as follows. A brief overview of particle filtering based tracking is given in Section 2. In Section 3, the proposed method is described, explaining the adaptive feature selection method. Experimental results and discussion are shown in Section 4. Eventually, section 5 concludes this paper.

2   Particle Filter Based Tracking

A particle filter is a sequential Bayesian estimation technique, which recursively approximates the a posteriori distribution using a finite set of weighted samples $\{x_t^i, w_t^i\}_{i=1,\dots N}$. Each sample x_t^i represents a hypothetical state of the target with a corresponding importance weight w_t^i. For tracking purpose, the state is defined as $\mathbf{x} = [x, y, s_x, s_y]^T$, where (x, y) is the center of the target and s_x and s_y are the scale of target window in the x and y directions. The particles, or samples, $\{x_t^i\}_{i=1,...N}$ are propagated from frame t to frame $t+1$ using a dynamic model:

$$\mathbf{x}_{t+1} = A\mathbf{x}_t + \mathbf{v}_t, \tag{1}$$

where $\mathbf{v}_t$ is a multivariate Gaussian random noise and A defines the deterministic system model. A constant velocity model is usually used for the dynamic model.

The weights are computed based on the similarity between each particle and a reference model. Finally, $E[x]$ the estimated state of the target in frame $t+1$ is obtained as the mean state of the system:

$$E[x] = \sum_{(i=1)}^{N} w_t^i x_t^i, \tag{2}$$

where x_t^i is the state of the ith particle and w_t^i its weight.

3   Adaptive Feature Selection

The good performance of particle filter based tracking mainly depends on the features used to describe the target, i.e. the features used to compute the similarity measure and, hence, the weights of the particles. The basic color-based particle filter tracking algorithm [10] uses color information to represent the appearance of the target. This tracking method makes use of fixed color space such as RGB or HSV to represent the color histogram. The features used to construct the appearance model are fixed regardless of the tracking conditions. The lack of adaptation in color models leads to performance degradation when handling situations such as illumination changes or background distraction. This can be seen in the top row of figure 1 where the tracker fails to adapt to the changing illumination conditions in the sequence.

Fig. 1. Tracking results with the sequence David. Top Row: particle filter using a fixed RGB color model fails due to varying lighting conditions. Bottom Row: a particle filter with adaptive feature selection can accurately track the face over the entire sequence. Please note that this figure is best viewed in color.

Fig. 2. Tracking results with the Winter sequence. Row 1: tracking failure with PF. Row 2: Enlarged version of the tracker window from Row 1. Row 3: tracking with PFFS. Row 4: Enlarged version of the tracker window from Row 3. Please note that this figure is best viewed in color.

3.1   Selecting the Best Features

The limitation of using fixed color features is the main motivation for an adaptive feature selection mechanism. The main idea of feature selection is to select for each frame of a sequence, the set of features that best discriminates the background and the object [7].

Different features can be used for tracking including color, shape or texture. Color distribution [10] is robust against noise and partial occlusions, but becomes ineffective in the presence of illumination changes, or when the background and the target have similar colors. Edges or contour features [11] are more robust to illumination variations, but are sensitive to clutter and are computationally expensive.

In this work, we focus on color features and use RGB color space, HSV color space and the transformed RGB space. The latter color space is based on the normalization of each channel independently [12]:

$$\left(R'\ G'\ B' \right) = \left(\frac{R - \mu_R}{\sigma_R}\ \frac{G - \mu_G}{\sigma_G}\ \frac{B - \mu_B}{\sigma_B} \right) \tag{3}$$

where σ is the standard deviation of the color channel and μ is its mean value.

Given the targets position in the frame, we generate two color distributions p_f and q_f for the object and the background, respectively, for each color feature f. The background area can be defined as the region surrounding the target location. The separability between the background and the foreground for feature f is given by the log-likelihood ratio computed as $L_f = \log(p_f/q_f)$. The log-likelihood ratio provides natural separability between the object and the background. Thus, thresholding L_f at zero is equivalent to classifying the object and the background using maximum likelihood rule.

In order to rank the different features, Collins and Liu [7] suggest the use of the two-class variance ratio of the likelihood function:

$$var(L; p, q) \equiv \frac{var(L; (p+q)/2)}{var(L; p) + var(L; q)}, \qquad (4)$$

The variance ratio in equation 4 is large for the features f which clearly separate the object from the background. We can then use this measure to rank all our features and use to one with highest variance ratio value to track the object in the next frame. The main advantage here is that, depending on the conditions, different features will be selected in different frames of the sequence.

4   Experiments and Discussion

In this section, we evaluate the performance of the proposed tracking method using four video sequences acquired in different conditions. The conditions include indoor and outdoor scenes, moving objects and persons, difficult illumination changes, occlusion and background distraction (background similar in color with the target).

For a quantitative evaluation, we have manually generated the ground truth for all sequences and use the distance between the centres of the ground-truth window and the output of the tracker as a measure of performance. In all experiments the target is manually initialized in the first frame. We compare the performance of the proposed particle filter with feature selection method (PFFS) against the conventional particle filter (PF) and mean-shift (MS) using a fixed set of color features, and a mean-shift with feature selection method (MSFS).

All the 4 filters MS, MSFS, PF and PFFS are our own implementation. Both PF and PFFS use variable size windows. The number of particles used in both the type of particle filters is 250. Increasing the number of particles reduces the frame rate producing almost the same performance. We have experimented with correlation of histograms, intersection of histograms , χ^2 and Bhattacharyya coefficient as the similarity measure. In our experiments Bhattacharyya coefficient performed best for most of the sequences. All the implementation were carried out on Matlab platform.

The first sequence under consideration is the 'David' [14]. In this video sequence, we see a person slowly emerging out of a dark room to a brightly illuminated room with varying scale and out-of-plane pose changes. As he emerges out, he performs certain actions with his hand which partially occludes his face. The results obtained with the David sequence are shown in figure 1. As can be seen in Top row of figure 1, a simple particle filter (PF) using a fixed set of color features, in this case fixed RGB features, fail to correctly track the face when the illumination conditions are varying. This is the same in the case of mean shift filter (MS). On the other hand, the proposed method using an adaptive feature selection technique with particle filter (PFFS) performs extremely well in this difficult situation. The same observations apply for the results with the Winter sequence presented in figure 2.

A comparison of the different tracking algorithms for the David sequence is shown in figure 3. Both the particle filter (PF) and the mean-shift (MS) trackers lose the target before the end of the sequence. On the contrary, an adaptive feature selection approach makes the trackers to robustly follow the target despite illumination variations. We can also observe that the particle filter with feature selection (PFFS) performs better than mean-shift with feature selection (MSFS) as shown by the error in figure 3. Note that the target is said to be lost by a tracker if the error, i.e. the distance between the centres of the ground-truth window and the output of the tracker, is greater or equal to the size of the ground-truth window.

In the Browse While Waiting sequence from CAVIAR test data set, the object of interest is a person. In this sequence a person standing in the sunlight gradually moves towards a shadowed area and again moves back to the region with sunlight. For this sequence the three filters MS, PF and MSFS fail as the person moves from sunlight to the shadowed area. Where as the PFFS overcomes all the difficulties. The results are shown in figure 4.

The Fog sequence is a challenging one even for a human observer due to the foggy condition. For this sequence, the target car is hardly distinguishable from the background and all tracking algorithms fail since none of the color features used can discriminate the car from the background. This is illustrated in figure 5. The results for four sequences are summarized in table 1. For three

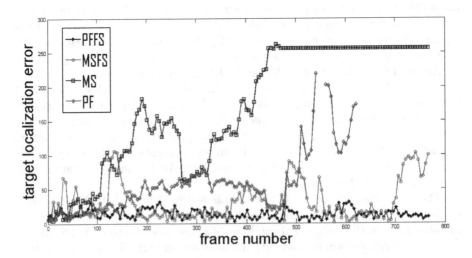

Fig. 3. Performances comparison for the sequence David

Table 1. Mean Error in pixels for different sequences using all the four filters. PF = particle filter; MS = mean-shift; MSFS = mean-shift with feature selection; PFFS = particle filter with feature selection; TF = tracking failure.

Sequence	MS	PF	MSFS	PFFS
David	TF	TF	31.41	13.46
Browse While Waiting	TF	TF	TF	14.48
Winter	TF	TF	16.64	6.78
Fog	TF	TF	TF	TF

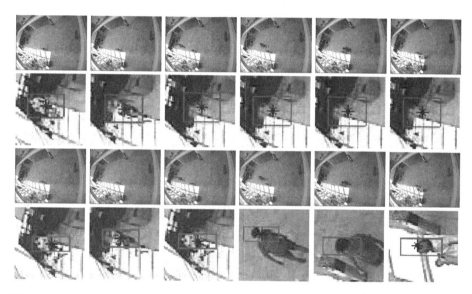

Fig. 4. Tracking results with the Browse While Waiting sequence. Row 1: tracking failure with PF. Row 2: Enlarged version of the tracker window from Row 1. Row 3: tracking with PFFS. Row 4: Enlarged version of the tracker window from Row 3. Please note that this figure is best viewed in color.

Fig. 5. 1st Row : Tracking results for the FOG sequence using PFFS. 2nd Row: Enlarged version of the tracker window. Note that this figure is best viewed in color.

of the four sequences, the PFFS algorithm outperforms other methods resulting in less average tracking error.

5   Conclusion

In this paper a robust tracking method is proposed. It is based on an adaptive feature selection mechanism which makes the tracker robust against occlusion, confusing background color and large illumination variation. Experiments with different sequences show that a particle filter based tracker with adaptive feature selection outperforms other established color based tracker in difficult tracking environments. A direction of future work would be the integration of shape and texture features and an extension for multi-objects tracking.

References

1. Comaniciu, D., Ramesh, V., Meer, P.: Real-Time Tracking of Non-Rigid Objects using Mean Shift. In: Computer Vision and Pattern Recognition (CVPR), pp. 142–149. IEEE Computer Society (2000)
2. Ho, J., Lee, K.C., Yang, M.H., Kriegman, D.J.: Visual Tracking Using Learned Linear Subspaces. In: Computer Vision and Pattern Recognition (CVPR), pp. 782–789. IEEE Computer Society (2004)
3. Zarit, B.D., Super, B.J., Quek, F.K.H.: Comparison of Five Colour Models in Skin Pixel Classification. In: International Conference in Computer Vision (ICCV), pp. 58–63 (1999)
4. Grabner, H., Grabner, M., Bischof, H.: Realtime Tracking via On-line Boosting. In: British Machine Vision Conference (BMVC), pp. 47–56 (2006)
5. Sidibe, D., Fofi, D., Meriaudeau, F.: Using Visual Saliency For Object Tracking with Particle Filter. In: European Signal Processing Conference (EUSIPCO), pp. 1776–1780 (2010)
6. Leung, A.P., Gong, S.: Online Feature Selection using Mutual Information for Real-time Multi-view Object Tracking. In: Zhao, W., Gong, S., Tang, X. (eds.) AMFG 2005. LNCS, vol. 3723, pp. 184–197. Springer, Heidelberg (2005)
7. Collins, R.T., Liu, Y.: On-line Selection of Discriminative Tracking Features. In: International Conference in Computer Vision (ICCV), pp. 346–352 (2003)
8. Han. B., Davis. L: Object Tracking by Adaptive Feature Extraction. In: International Conference in Computer Vision (ICCV), pp. 1501–1504 (2004)
9. Kwolek, B.: Object Tracking using Discriminative Feature Selection. In: Blanc-Talon, J., Philips, W., Popescu, D., Scheunders, P. (eds.) ACIVS 2006. LNCS, vol. 4179, pp. 287–298. Springer, Heidelberg (2006)
10. Nummiaro, K., Koller-Meier, E., Van Gool, L.J.: An Adaptive Color-based Particle Filter. In: Image and Vision Computing, pp. 99–110 (2003)
11. Isard, M., Blake, A.: Condensation - Conditional Density Propagation for Visual Tracking. Int. Journal of Computer Vision (IJCV) 28, 99–110 (1998)
12. Van de Sande, K.E.A., Gevers, T., Snoek, C.G.M.: Evaluating Color Descriptors for Object and Scene Recognition. IEEE Transactions on Pattern Analysis and Machine Intelligence (PAMI) 32, 1582–1596 (2010)
13. Stern, H., Efros, B.: Adaptive Color Space Switching for Tracking under Varying Illumination. Image and Vision Computing 23, 3–346 (2005)
14. Ross, D., Lim, J., Lin, R.S., Yang, M.H.: Incremental Learning for Robust Visual Tracking. Int. Journal of Computer Vision (IJCV) 77, 125–141 (2008)

Exploiting Color Constancy for Robust Tracking Under Non-uniform Illumination

Sinan Mutlu[1,2]([✉]), Samuel Rota Bulò[1], and Oswald Lanz[1]

[1] FBK Fondazione Bruno Kessler, Povo (TN), Italy
[2] ICT Doctoral School, University of Trento, Povo (TN), Italy
{mutlu,rotabulo,lanz}@fbk.eu

Abstract. Tracking objects in environments under non-uniform illumination condition is particularly challenging as the observed appearance may change in space and time. Adapting the appearance model increases the risk of drifts, while iltering out the illumination information through built-in invariance reduces the discriminative capabilities. In this work we adhere to color constancy principles to learn the appearance variation induced by non-uniform illumination and we use this information to perform location-dependent color corrections to boost tracking performance. The training procedure is carried out in an unsupervised manner by exploiting walking people as illumination probes and an online, non-parametric regression method is developed to densely predict the location-specific color transformations.

Keywords: Object tracking · Color constancy · Illumination

1 Introduction

Image processing and computer vision applications predominantly assume color imaging as the capturing modality. Colors sensed by the imaging device are hereby determined through a digitalized measurement of incident light that depends on intrinsic properties of objects within the scene and on the different illumination sources. For many vision tasks, it is thus desired to filter out the variability induced by the light sources to render subsequent representations of image objects and features invariant to the illumination conditions under which they were captured. A large body of work addressing this problem is available in computational color constancy research [6,10,14].

In this paper, we are interested in exploring principles of color constancy for robust object tracking under non-uniform illumination conditions. Despite the enormous progress, dealing with the variable and non-uniform illumination conditions of real-world scenarios is still a major research challenge in this context. We claim that object tracking under such assumption is well related to color constancy research: object appearance can most effectively be described if the influence of the light source can be isolated from the intrinsic properties of objects, upon which robust appearance descriptors can then be built. Alternatively, one has to resort to illuminant-invariant features such as edges, motion, SIFT, LBP,

© Springer International Publishing Switzerland 2014
A. Campilho and M. Kamel (Eds.): ICIAR 2014, Part II, LNCS 8815, pp. 403–410, 2014.
DOI: 10.1007/978-3-319-11755-3_45

HOG, or to apply a color space transformation that allows to roughly eliminate the illumination component from the data. Built-in invariance, however,
suppresses information present in the data, resulting in sub-optimal solutions
in terms of discriminative capability. Moreover, ambiguity is increased in the
invariant feature-space, thus rendering the tracking more challenging.

Most recent works have been focused on integrating adaptive background
and/or appearance models [1,4,7,8,11] in challenging scenes to deal with major
burdens: occlusions and non-uniform illumination as well. While the proposed
methods give a solution to these problems on a single camera, only a few
approaches combined information from multiple cameras [5,16]. In this end, considering the illumination of a scene can change drastically in 3D which cannot
be estimated from image plane due to the lack of depth information, authors
of [2] propose to explicitly model light sources and to track their positions
in outdoor enviroments. In our opinion modeling the light sources in complex
indoor/outdoor enviroments will bring more burden to the tracking system, particularly if indoor enviroment is not totally isolated from outdoor. Unlike to
these methods, to cope with spatial variability of target appearance in non-
uniformly illuminated scenes, illumination maps are first introduced in [17] for
multi-camera 3D tracking. This method has more recently been extended for
dynamic environments where the illumination maps are updated over time using
a 1D color correction model per each camera[15]. As this algorithm was performing reasonably in our experiments, it suffers from curse of dimensions when
extended to multiple channels. In this paper, we come up with a new algorithm
which scales linearly with the dimension of the color correction model. Beside
this in [15] a sum-product message passing inference on a hybrid cyclic-graph was
adapted, which converges after a certain number of iterations. However integrating k-nearest neigbour way of solution to compute the illuminant transformation
keeps the complexity of our new method in linear time with the given number
of neighbours.

To make it clear, Fig.1 sketches the use of our unsupervised location-
dependent color correction method, that can be used for tracking, to transform
the target's appearance in a form that yields a good match with its reference
model. The second image in Fig.1, shows the color-based likelihood (detailed in
Sec.2 and used for our experiments in Sec.5) of the reference model in a different
frame at different locations. As we can see, the confidence is not well peaked
around the true target's position.

2   Overview

In this work, a color based multi-target particle filter is used to estimate the
2D ground positions of people as they move around in an environment moni-
tored by multiple calibrated cameras [12]. In the particle filter, a coarse 3D shape
model is used to validate ground location hypotheses (particles) on image projections obtained using camera calibration information. The color-based likelihood
is defined by the Bhattacharyya distance between extracted color histogram and

a reference model of the target acquired during detection [13]. To render the likelihood more reliable we apply for each particle a color correction following a full-diagonal *von Kries* model [9] to the image pixels identified by the shape projection, before the histogram extraction. The parameters of the *von Kries* correction are hereby determined for each particle from illumination probes collected from the environment and properly integrated via the methods detailed in Sec.3 and Sec.4.

In a static environment, such illumination probes can be collected off-line by using a calibration target (e.g., a color plate). This requires on-site manual intervention, and must be repeated each time the illumination condition changes. Instead, We collect appearance patterns of people, associated with their ground positions as illumination probes using the people detector [13], which is motion based and illumination invariant, and then *von Kries* correction parameters for each such probe are computed with the method in Sec.3. An illuminant map representing the *von Kries* correction parameters for each position on the ground is produced automatically for each camera using the non-parametric regression technique in Sec.4.

Fig. 1. Left-to-right: 1) frame with the person used as reference pattern; 2) color likelihood over ground locations on a new image; 3) color likelihood on the same frame by using the learned location-dependent illuminant transformations; 4) effect of the application of the illuminant transformation on the target pattern

3 Illuminant Transformation Estimation

Let $\mathcal{R} = \{r_1, \ldots, r_n\}$ be a reference image pattern consisting of n RGB pixels $r_i \in \mathbb{R}^3$, and let $\mathcal{T} = \{t_1, \ldots, t_m\}$ be a target image pattern with m pixels. The aim of this section is the estimation of an illuminant transformation $\Lambda : \mathbb{R}^3 \to \mathbb{R}^3$ that modifies the observations comprising $\mathcal{R}$ in a way to best match the observations in $\mathcal{T}$. The transformation is assumed to follow the von Kries model [9], *i.e.* we consider a linear, invertible transformation Λ of the form $\Lambda(r) = \Lambda r$, where Λ is a diagonal transformation matrix with positive diagonal elements $\boldsymbol{\lambda} = (\lambda_1, \lambda_2, \lambda_3)^\top$.

We begin by introducing a random variable (r.v.) $X \in \mathbb{R}^3$ describing the *i.i.d.* observations in $\mathcal{R}$, and a random variable $Y = \Lambda(X)$ describing the *i.i.d.* observations in $\mathcal{T}$. According to our premises, we assume Y to be distributed as

X, modulo the transformation Λ. We denote by f_X and f_Y the density functions related to r.v. X and Y, respectively.

For the sake of simplicity and efficiency, we assume X to be a Gaussian variate with mean $\mu_{\mathcal{R}}$ and covariance $\Sigma_{\mathcal{R}}$, i.e. $f_X(x) = f_{\text{gauss}}(x|\mu_{\mathcal{R}}, \Sigma_{\mathcal{R}})$. The Gaussian parameters are estimated from the observations in $\mathcal{R}$ in terms of the sample mean and the sample covariance matrix of the observations in $\mathcal{R}$ (a.k.a. maximum likelihood estimates for the Gaussian distribution): $\mu_{\mathcal{R}} = \sum_{i=1}^{n} r_i/n$ and $\Sigma_{\mathcal{R}} = \sum_{i=1}^{n} r_i r_i^{\top}/n - \mu_{\mathcal{R}}\mu_{\mathcal{R}}^{\top}$. Since X is a Gaussian variate and Λ is an affine transformation, also Y is Gaussian distributed with mean and covariance parametrized by Λ: $f_Y(y|\Lambda) = f_{\text{gauss}}(y|\Lambda\mu_{\mathcal{R}}, \Lambda\Sigma_{\mathcal{R}}\Lambda)$. Finally, the transformation Λ can be estimated from the observations in $\mathcal{T}$ by taking a maximum likelihood approach. The likelihood of Λ given the i.i.d. observations of r.v. Y in $\mathcal{T}$ is

$$L(\Lambda) = f_Y(\mathcal{T}|\Lambda) = \prod_{j=1}^{m} f_Y(t_j|\Lambda). \tag{1}$$

Instead of maximizing the likelihood directly, it is more convenient to work with the log-likelihood $\log L(\Lambda)$. By performing this shift, maximizers are preserved and the optimization problem becomes strictly concave in the inverse transformation Λ^{-1}. As a consequence, there is a unique local, and thus global, solution. Since concavity holds for the inverse transformation we define $w_h = \lambda_h^{-1}$ for $1 \leq h \leq 3$ and consider the maximum log-likelihood estimate of $w = (w_1, \ldots, w_3)^{\top}$. After some algebraic manipulations of the log-likelihood objective, and by neglecting additive and multiplicative terms that do affect the maximizers, we end up with the following optimization problem in the new variables:

$$w_{\text{MLE}} \in \arg\max_{w} \sum_{h=1}^{3} \log(w_h) - \frac{1}{2}w^{\top}(Aw + 2b). \tag{2}$$

Here, matrix A and vector b are defined as $A = (\mu_{\mathcal{T}}\mu_{\mathcal{T}}^{\top} + \Sigma_{\mathcal{T}}) \circ \Sigma_{\mathcal{R}}^{-1}$ and $b = -\mu_{\mathcal{T}} \circ \Sigma_{\mathcal{R}}^{-1}\mu_{\mathcal{R}}$, where $\circ$ denotes the entry-wise matrix product (a.k.a. Hadamard product).

The optimization algorithm that we propose to solve (2) is a coordinate ascent with exact line search. Due to the concavity of the optimization problem, we are guaranteed that a global solution will be reached. By setting the first-order partial derivative of the objective to zero, we obtain the following set of equations for $1 \leq h \leq 3$:

$$w_h^{-1} - A_{hh}w_h - \Delta_h = 0, \tag{3}$$

where $\Delta_h = b_h + \sum_{k \neq h} A_{hk}w_k$. By multiplying both sides of this equation by w_h, which is assumed to be positive, we obtain a quadratic equation in w_h, from which the following update rule can be derived:

$$w_h \leftarrow \frac{-\Delta_h + \sqrt{\Delta_h^2 + 4A_{hh}}}{2A_{hh}}. \tag{4}$$

By initializing to the null vector $w = 0$ and by iteratively updating each component of w, we converge to the global solution of (2) in few steps. Once the optimal w has been found, we can recover the optimal illuminant parameters as $\lambda = (w_1^{-1}, w_2^{-1}, w_3^{-1})^\top$.

4 Learning the Scene Illumination

Assume we have a process that generates over time measurements about the illuminant transformation in the environment. Each measurement comprises the ground position of the observation, the illuminant transformation estimated according to Sec.3 from the detected pattern and the reference pattern, the timestamp of the measurement, and optionally a confidence weight. Given this stream of measurements, we pursue the goal to maintain over time a *dense* illuminant transformation map that allows the tracker to query about the transformation to be applied to a pattern in a given ground position. Clearly, we have to rule out the option of maintaining the whole set of measurements collected up to a given moment, which might soon become extremely large. Hence, we assume to have a *limited memory budget* to work with. On the other hand, we cannot simply maintain the most recent observations because this might prevent our map from providing a *good covering* of the environment. Indeed, if this strategy was adopted, portions of the environment that are rarely crossed would be quickly discarded. Finally, the map updates should be *efficient* to compute to be suitable for a real-time tracking system, and the map should *promptly counteract* to changes in the environment's illumination conditions.

To accommodate all the aforementioned requirements, we propose a non-parametric regression approach that maintains over time a restricted set of measurements that fits the limited memory budget, guarantees a good coverage of the environment, and can be efficiently and promptly updated.

Let $\mathcal{M}$ be the set of all possible measurements and $\mathcal{M}^t \subset \mathcal{M}$ be the set of measurements collected up to time $t > 0$, where time is assumed discrete. Clearly, $\mathcal{M}^t \subseteq \mathcal{M}^{t+1}$ for all $t > 0$. To guarantee the good covering property, we fix a set $\mathcal{V} \subseteq \mathbb{R}^2$ of ground positions spanning approximately the environment, *e.g.* the nodes of a 2D grid. Moreover, assume we are given a nonnegative function $\phi : \mathbb{R}^2 \times \mathcal{M} \to \mathbb{R}_+$ such that $\phi(v, m)$ scores the relevance of the measurement $m \in \mathcal{M}$ for the ground position $v \in \mathbb{R}^2$. To take into account the limited memory budget, we allot to each node $v \in \mathcal{V}$ a buffer to index the best k measurements according to the score function with respect to the whole history of measurements. This buffer, denoted by $\mathcal{B}_v^t$ at time t, can be tracked over time without holding the whole history of measurements. In fact, the set of the k best measurements can be derived from local quantities such as the latest state of the buffer $\mathcal{B}_v^{t-1}$ and the new observations at time t. In other terms, if we set $\Delta_v^t = (\mathcal{M}^t \setminus \mathcal{M}^{t-1}) \cup \mathcal{B}_v^{t-1}$, we have that

$$\mathcal{B}_v^t \in \underset{\mathcal{Q} \subseteq \Delta_v^t, \, |\mathcal{Q}| \leq k}{\arg\max} \left\{ \sum_{m \in \mathcal{Q}} \phi(v, m) \right\}. \tag{5}$$

This boils down to finding the k best scoring measurements in the small set Δ_v^t. Once the buffer of each node has been updated, the set of measurements that will be actively used at time t for subsequent queries is given by $\mathcal{B}^t = \bigcup_{v \in \mathcal{V}} \mathcal{B}_v^t$. Obviously, by construction, this set has a number of elements upper bounded by $k|\mathcal{V}|$, thus representing the maximum allotted memory budget required to store the measurements.

To compute an illuminant transformation for an arbitrary ground position, we use a nearest-neighbor approach. Given a query position $v \in \mathbb{R}^2$ at time t, we recover the ℓ best ϕ-scoring measurements for that position from the set $\mathcal{B}^t$. Finally, we use the recovered measurements to compute a ϕ-weighted mean of the corresponding illuminant parameters.

5 Experiments

To evaluate the proposed approach, we report quantitative tracking performance on publicly available video recordings with manually annotated ground truth[1]. The recorded scene exhibits highly non-uniform illumination conditions generated using two Balcar Fluxlite illuminators as sources of *directional* light. The first illuminator is located outside of the room at a window, while the second one is mounted on the ceiling. This setting creates a sharp illumination transition all across the room. We use the first part of the recording (two people entering in sequence and moving around the room) to automatically compute the illuminant transformation maps, and report MOTA/MOTP (Multiple Object Tracking Accuracy/Precision) metrics [3], false positive rate (fp), ratio of misses (miss) and ratio of mismatches (mme) for real time tracking on the second part (about 3mins). The second part used for evaluation shows four people moving under very challenging illumination with frequent occlusion – see Fig.2. The subjects used for map creation are different from those present in the evaluation sequence – see, the two right-most images in Fig.2.

The scoring function $\phi(v, m)$ we adopt for the experiments penalizes with exponential decay measurements m that are either far from the ground position v or outdated. For real time tracking we reduce image resolution to 320x240 and use 200 particles for each target. All parameters are the same for the different experiments.

In Table 1 we compare the performance of the tracker in the following cases: (no-map) no illuminant transformation map is used ; (1D-map) illuminant map with 1-dimensional von Kries model [2]; and (3D-map) illuminant map with full-diagonal von Kries model. We report for each tested setting the average scores (and standard deviation) obtained over 10 runs.

When no color correction is applied (no-map), many false-positive (fp) are obtained, meaning that the tracker very often drifts. Indeed, when persons move

---

[1] http://tev.fbk.eu/DATABASES/VIPT.html

[2] By imposing $\lambda_{1,2,3} = \alpha$ as in [15], the solution of the parameter estimation according to our method has closed-form solution $\alpha = 2\sum_{hk} \mathsf{A}_{hk}/(-\sum_h b_h + \sqrt{(\sum_h b_h)^2 + 12\sum_{hk} \mathsf{A}_{hk}})$.

Fig. 2. Frames with tracking results for 3D-map experiments in Tab.1. Note the similar appearance of the targets. Bottom-right: the full-diagonal *von Kries* transformation estimated from a video of two different people (the two on the right).

Table 1. Experimental result obtained on the test video sequence (see text for details)

	MOTP (mm)	miss (%)	fp (%)	mme (%)	MOTA (%)
no-map	110.5±17.3	4.9±1.5	38.6±11.1	4.5±1.5	56.5±12.0
1D-map	78.7±7.5	7.7±1.7	11.3±9.6	3.6±3.2	81.0±11.0
3D-map	70.9±8.2	0.8±0.3	6.3±7.9	0.2±0.2	92.9±8.0

away from the location where their appearance model was acquired, the change in illumination produces poor cluttered likelihood as shown in Fig.1 (central image). With the full-diagonal *von Kries* correction (3D-map) fp drops down to 6.3 resulting in a MOTA score of about 93%, meaning that we achieve persistent tracking in spite of challenging illumination, similar target appearance and significant occlusions. The precision hereby reached (7cm MOTP) is in the range of the inaccuracy of manually labeling the groundtruth from the images. For comparison, we report also the scores for the 1D von Kries model, which accounts only for intensity and does not discriminate the color of the illuminant. The results obtained in this setting are clearly better than the no-map case, but still significantly worse than the full-diagonal setting. This highlights the necessity to account for the color of the illuminant, not only its intensity.

6   Discussion and Future Work

In this work we have shown that tracking can be significantly boosted by learning and exploiting the appearance variations induced by non-uniform illumination. We have achieved our goal by adopting principles from color constancy to effectively estimate the color transformations within an intriguing unsupervised learning setting that uses walking people as illumination probes. Experiments conducted on challenging scenarios have proved the effectiveness of our findings. Future works are devoted to both improve the expressiveness of the color transformations and their estimation with the inclusion of spatio-spectral statistics (*e.g.* as done in [6]) and by taking into account more general illuminant transformations, going beyond the simple von Kries model.

References

1. Babenko, B., Yang, M.H., Belongie, S.: Visual tracking with online multiple instance learning. IEEE Trans. on PAMI (August 2011)
2. Bardet, F., Chateau, T., Ramadasan, D.: Illumination aware mcmc particle filter for long-term outdoor multi-object simultaneous tracking and classification. In: ICCV (2009)
3. Bernardin, K., Stiefelhagen, R.: Evaluating multiple object tracking performance: The clear mot metrics. J. Image Video Process (2008)
4. Vezzani, R., Grana, C., Cucchiara, R.: Probabilistic people tracking with appearance models and occlusion classification. Pattern Recogn. Lett. 32(6) (2011)
5. Camplani, M., Salgado, L.: Adaptive background modeling in multicamera system for real-time object detection. SPIE Optical Eng. 50(12) (2011)
6. Chakrabarti, A., Hirakawa, K., Zickler, T.: Color constancy with spatio-spectral statistics. IEEE Trans. on PAMI (2012)
7. Cristani, M., Farenzena, M., Bloisi, D., Murino, V.: Background subtraction for automated multisensor surveillance: A comprehensive review. EURASIP Journal on Advances in Signal Processing 2010(1), 343057 (2010)
8. Ellis, L., Dowson, N., Matas, J., Bowden, R.: Linear regression and adaptive appearance models for fast simultaneous modelling and tracking. Int. J. Comput. Vision 95(2), 154–179 (2011)
9. Finlayson, G., Drew, M., Funt, B.: Diagonal transforms suffice for color constancy. In: ICCV (1993)
10. Gijsenij, A., Gevers, T., van de Weijer, J.: Computational color constancy: Survey and experiments. IEEE Trans. on Image Processing 20(9), 2475–2489 (2011)
11. Jepson, A., Fleet, D., El-Maraghi, T.: Robust online appearance models for visual tracking. IEEE Transactions on PAMI 25(10), 1296–1311 (2003)
12. Lanz, O.: Approximate bayesian multi-body tracking. IEEE Trans. on Pattern Analysis and Machine Intelligence (2006)
13. Lanz, O., Messelodi, S.: A sampling algorithm for occlusion robust multi-target detection. In: AVSS (2009)
14. Lecca, M., Messelodi, S.: Linking the von Kries Model to Wien's Law for the estimation of an Illuminant Invariant Image. Pattern Recognition Letters 32(15), 2086–2096 (2011)
15. Mutlu, S., Hu, T., Lanz, O.: Learning the scene illumination for color-based people tracking in dynamic environment. In: Petrosino, A. (ed.) ICIAP 2013, Part II. LNCS, vol. 8157, pp. 683–692. Springer, Heidelberg (2013)
16. Tsai, Y., Ko, C., Hung, Y., Shih, Z.: Background removal of multiview images by learning shape priors. IEEE Trans. on Image Processing (2007)
17. Zen, G., Lanz, O., Messelodi, S., Ricci, E.: Tracking multiple people with illumination maps. In: ICPR (2010)

Wavelet Subspace Analysis of Intraoperative Thermal Imaging for Motion Filtering

Nico Hoffmann[1]([⊠]), Julia Hollmach[1], Christian Schnabel[1], Yordan Radev[2],
Matthias Kirsch[2], Uwe Petersohn[3], Edmund Koch[1],
and Gerald Steiner[1]

[1] Department of Anesthesiology and Intensive Care Medicine, Clinical Sensoring
and Monitoring, Technische Universität Dresden, 01307 Dresden, Germany
`nico.hoffmann@tu-dresden.de`
[2] Department of Neurosurgery, Technische Universität Dresden, 01307
Dresden, Germany
[3] Applied Knowledge Representation and Reasoning, Technische Universität
Dresden, 01062 Dresden, Germany

Abstract. Intraoperative thermography allows fast capturing of small temperature variations during neurosurgical operations. External influences induce periodic vibrational motion to the whole camera system superimposing signals of high-frequent neuronal activity, heart rate activity and injected perfusion tracers by motion artifacts. In this work, we propose a robust method to eliminate the effects induced by the vibrational motion allowing further inference of clinical information. For this purpose, an efficient wavelet shrinkage scheme is developed based on subspace analysis in 1D wavelet domain to recognize and remove motion related patterns. The approach does not require any specific motion modeling or image warping, making it fast and preventing image deformations. Promising results of a simulation study and by intraoperative measurements make this method a reliable and efficient method improving subsequent perfusion and neuronal activity analysis.

1 Introduction

Thermal imaging is a contact-less, marker-free, white light independent and non-invasive method for online measurement of temperature variations up to 30 mK. Since thermography records the emitted heat of bodies, local dynamic behavior due to heat flow and convection effects are likely, leading to highly variate images even of static scenes. In neurosurgery, small temperature gradients are caused by perfusion or neuronal activity related heat transfers and respiratory and pulse motion of the exposed cortex. The neurosurgical application of thermography covers, among others, the detection of functional areas and brain tumors [1]. In a previous work, we have shown the direct link between temperature gradients and an injected ice-cold saline solution to investigate the cerebral blood flow[2]. Because of its temporal resolution, thermography might also allow inference about triggers of focal epilepsies.

© Springer International Publishing Switzerland 2014
A. Campilho and M. Kamel (Eds.): ICIAR 2014, Part II, LNCS 8815, pp. 411–420, 2014.
DOI: 10.1007/978-3-319-11755-3_46

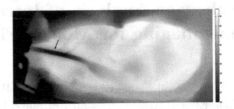

Fig. 1. During Neurosurgery, the exposed human cortex can be easily identified by its warm and smooth temperature profile ($\geq 30°C$) in thermographic recordings. Yet, near cortical electrodes (arrow) or perfused blood vessels strong gradients are visible. Especially at these sites, vibrations of the camera system lead to a superposition of the time course of the affected pixels with time and neighborhood-dependent patterns, hampering subsequent data analysis.

The thermal imaging system is mounted at the operating table by an adjustable mount and a supporting arm. This supporting arm has three freely orientable spheroidal joints enabling the surgeon to align the camera just before the recording. This setup makes intraoperative recordings at low object distances – typically 20 to 30 cm – feasible consequently minimizing the influence of background heat sources and allows spatial resolutions between 170 to 250 μm. This setup is prone to vibrations originating, among others, from the patient's respiratory motion and the surgeon's initial alignment of the camera. Such short-time periodic displacement of the whole thermographic camera leads to changing point-to-point mappings of consecutive thermographic images what introduces characteristic patterns into the data. This not only hampers the analysis of high-frequent neuronal activity or heart rate patterns in the same frequency band. Also thermographic signals of injected ice-cold saline solutions are overlain by these motion artifacts, especially in parenchyma near well perfused cortical arteries with strong temperature gradients, hampering their detection and hereby the analysis of cortical blood flow for medical decision support.

2   Related Work

Digital video stabilization algorithms aim to eliminate unwanted motion artifacts from video streams, for example caused by hand-held cameras. Common approaches can be divided into intensity-based (direct) and feature matching algorithms. Latter match robust features of adjacent images to align the images [3] [4]. Intensity-based approaches in general minimize a cost function on the pixel's intensity to align the images or rather smooth the between-frame motion trajectory [5][6]. Further subsequent analysis then allows the differentiation between local and global motion. A comprehensive review of image alignment methods can be found in [7].

Most of these approaches originate from whitelight imaging, which is an orthogonal modality to thermal imaging. Thermographic sequences inherit a non-stationary spatially varying heteroscedastic behavior, leading to local non-linear temperature shifts between adjacent frames, which is not necessarily related to any motion. Pixels with strong temperature gradients can be super-imposed by air flow or heat transfers, which is easily misinterpreted as motion of the affected areas. For robust and time-efficient correction of camera vibration artifacts, we therefore propose a signal based method. This multivariate post-processing approach is not affected by local motion artifacts, between-frame temperature dynamics or long term drifts and prevents unwanted image defor-mations. The analysis is carried into a sparse frequency domain and exploits the spatial characteristics of motion artifacts to identify respective frequency components.

3   Motion Filtering in Wavelet Subspace

Temperature series contain non-linear trends and time varying frequency com-ponents at differing amplitude and frequency, for example at pulse or respiration frequency. Therefore, the time-resolved multi-resolution analysis is a desirable approach for the detection of dynamic frequency components. One such compo-nent originates from vibrations of the camera system, hereby inducing charac-teristic artifacts into the data. In what follows, the spatial distribution of the motion induced frequency pattern is exploited by pixel-wise change of basis into frequency domain by means of the 1D real-valued discrete wavelet transform (DWT) [8][1] and following subspace analysis using the Karhunen-Loève trans-form (KLT).

3.1   Feature Description

Vibrations of the camera system lead to periodic translations of the whole image. The trajectory of these shifts is the same for all pixels of a single frame, whereas the amplitude of the artifact depends on the neighborhood of a pixel. To quan-tify this effect, the gradient image is examined. Let ∇I_c denote the gradient magnitude of the recordings first frame I at discrete pixel coordinate c. The set $\mathcal{X}^+$ contains the coordinates of a pre-specified amount of k pixels of maximum gradient, for example those indicated by the arrow in figure 1,

$$\mathcal{X}^+ = \arg\max_{\{c_1,\dots,c_k\}} \sum_i |\nabla I(c_i)|$$

while the counterpart $\mathcal{X}^-$ contains pixels of minimal gradient while being in a smooth neighborhood[2]

---

[1] There are complex valued extensions to the wavelet transform, for example CWT and dual-tree WT, yet these double the space requirements and are therefore not further considered here.

[2] $B_p(y)$ denote the n-dimensional p-ball of a space $\mathbb{M}$: $B_p(y) := \{x \in \mathbb{M} \mid ||x-y|| < p\}$. $B_p(\mathcal{Y})$ extends this definition to a set of p-Balls: $B_p(\mathcal{Y}) := \cup_{y \in \mathcal{Y}} B_p(y)$.

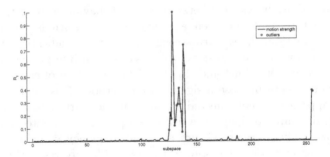

Fig. 2. The normalized motion impact R_n contains some strongly deviating values. These outliers indicate that the affected subspace inherits significant activity at locations with strong gradients caused by camera motion.

$$\mathcal{X}^- = \arg\min_{\{c_1,\dots,c_k\}} \sum_i |\nabla I(c_i)| \quad \text{subject to} \quad c_i \notin B_p(\mathcal{X}^+)$$

Smooth regions are described by low spatial gradients, thus if the spatial position of a single pixel is periodical changing in this neighborhood, only weak motion artifacts are induced into the time course.

3.2   Motion Analysis

The time course of n pixels $X \in \mathbb{R}^{n \times m}$ with $m = 2^{j_{max}+1}$ frames contains various components with some being related to camera movement. In order to isolate time-varying motion artifacts, the data is pixel-wise projected into the sparse frequency domain by the DWT. Following, the KLT is used to identify global frequency patterns and quantify their local weight. The wavelet coefficients $X_F^j \in \mathbb{R}^{n \times 2^j}$ at scales $1 \leq j \leq j_{max}$ are projected into 2^j n-dimensional subspaces $W^j = [w_1^j \cdots w_{2^j}^j]$. The number of subspaces is determined by j and the KLT, since latter decomposes X_F^j into a linear combination of all 2^j eigenvectors, that are stored as columns of $\Phi \in \mathbb{R}^{2^j \times 2^j}$, of its empirical covariance matrix $\Sigma_{X_F^j}$. This change of basis into $W^j \in \mathbb{R}^{n \times 2^j}$ is done by $W^j = X_F^j \Phi$. Subspace w_i^j along with eigenvector $v_i^j \in \mathbb{R}^{2^j}$ describe the distribution of a frequency pattern, that contributes to the global variance of the respective wavelet coefficients at scale j weighted by its eigenvalue $\lambda_i \in \Lambda$. Hereby we are able to identify global patterns, that contribute to all pixels at varying extent. The local weight of pixel c in subspace i is denoted by $w_i(c)$. The mean contribution $w_i(\mathcal{Y})$ of specific pixels $y \in \mathcal{Y}$ to subspace i is given by

$$w_i(\mathcal{Y}) = \frac{1}{|\mathcal{Y}|} \sum_{y \in \mathcal{Y}} |w_i(y)|$$

For the identification of motion related subspaces, it is necessary to take the spatial characteristics of motion artifacts into account. For this purpose, the subspace contribution ratio r_i

$$r_i = w_i(\mathcal{X}^+) \; / \; w_i(\mathcal{X}^-)$$

is used to quantify the effect of motion artifacts at areas with strong gradients, like electrodes, cortical arteries or the boundary of the trepanation. Subspaces i related to camera motion artifacts show significant contributions $w_i(c)$ at pixels c in distinct neighborhoods, compared to pixels in smooth neighborhoods. This behavior leads to deviating r_i in the across subspace motion impact $R = (r_1, r_2, ..., r_{2^j})$ (see figure 2), which are subject to the subsequent detection scheme.

3.3 Outlier Detection for Subspace Filtering

As discussed, frequency patterns related to motion artifacts have a characteristic spatial footprint, inducing outliers into R. For their identification, the motion impact $R = (r_1, r_2, ..., r_m)$ is modeled as a linear Gaussian random variable $R \sim N(aX + b, \sigma)$. Robust estimation schemes (e.g. iteratively reweighted least squares (IRLS)) are further needed, since R is expected to contain outliers making its variance heteroscedasticity. These outliers are found by applying a t-Test on the model residuals with respect to Bonferroni corrected significance level $\alpha = 0.05/m$.

This outlier detection scheme yields a set $\mathcal{K}$ of motion related subspace indices, that are now filtered by zeroing the weights of the respective subspaces $w_k = \mathbf{0}$ for all $k \in \mathcal{K}$. Lastly, the corrected data is recovered by backprojection from KLT space and inverse wavelet transformation. In order to halve the required maximum amount of memory, the algorithm is separately applied to each wavelet scale. The proposed motion correction scheme is sketched in algorithm 1. It assumes a periodized and orthogonal wavelet transform with symmlet4 basis, which is denoted by (I)DWT_PO_SYMM4.

4   Results

We will simulate deterministic motion conditions without heat flow and convection for performance comparison under optimal conditions. Afterwards, the proposed method is evaluated on two representative intraoperative cases, whereas case 1 inherits fast motion of large spatial extent and case 2 contains weak gradients leading to low amplitude motion artifacts while also having strong thermic dynamics. In order to compare the wavelet subspace analysis (WSA) with a common approach of whitelight imaging, matching of SURF features[3] is

---

[3] SURF feature matching was done using the *matchFeatures* routine of Matlab implementing the nearest neighbor distance ratio method described by Mikolajczyk et al. [9].

Algorithm 1. Wavelet domain subspace motion correction algorithm

---

input: data set, $X \in \mathbb{R}^{n \times m}$

input: number of gradient points, $k \in \mathbb{N}^+$

output: motion stabilized data set, $X^* \in \mathbb{R}^{n \times m}$

estimate pixel coordinate sets $\mathcal{X}^+, \mathcal{X}^-$ *with* $|\mathcal{X}^+| = |\mathcal{X}^-| = k$;

$X_F = [X_F^1 \cdots X_F^{j_{Max}}] = DWT\_PO\_SYMM4(X)$;

for $j \leftarrow 1$ **to** j_{max} **do**

    solve $\Sigma_{X_F^j} \Phi = \Lambda \Phi^T$;

    $W^j = [w_1^j \; ... \; w_{2^j}^j] = X_F^j \Phi$;

    $\forall i \in [1, 2^j] \; : \; r_i^j = w_i^j(\mathcal{X}^+) \, / \, w_i^j(\mathcal{X}^-)$;

    $R^j = [r_1^j \cdots r_{2^j}^j]$;

    $\mathcal{K} = outlierDetection(R^j)$;

    $\forall k \in \mathcal{K} \; : \; w_k^j = 0$;

    $X_F^{j^*} = W^j \Phi^{-1}$;

$X_F^* = [X_F^{1^*} \cdots X_F^{j_{max}^*}]$;

$X^* = IDWT\_PO\_SYMM4(X_F^*)$;

---

employed. Hereby, SURF features of a frame with respect to a reference frame or its motion corrected predecessor are matched[4] and an affine transformation matrix is computed to correct the motion artifacts. In order to further quantify the effect of the proposed outlier detection scheme, a one-class Support Vector Machine [10] (RBF kernel) is employed to infer unlikely values of R. Latter is denoted as *WSA-1SVM*, whereas the outlier detection approach of section 3.3 is denoted as *WSA-GT* and employs IRLS with a bisquare weighting function as robust estimation scheme.

For performance evaluation, an intensity-based as well as an frequency-based metric is employed. The root mean squared error (RMSE) quantifies to deviation of the estimated video $\widetilde{I}$ to the ground truth image sequence I. The average spectral density (SD) of all pixels $c \in \widetilde{I}$ describes the global energy content

$$SD = \frac{1}{|I| \times |fc|} \int \int_{2Hz}^{10Hz} \left| \int_{-\infty}^{\infty} |\widetilde{I}_c(t)| exp(-i\omega t)dt \right|^2 d\omega dc$$

of pixel intensities $I_c(t)$ at coordinate c, frame t and number of frequency coefficients $|fc|$ between 2 and $10Hz$. For reasons of comparison, the image sequences are cropped after the application of the motion correction schemes, since several rows and columns are lost after the application of SURF feature matching.

---

[4] Best results are chosen.

4.1 Simulation Study

The expected camera motion is modeled as a sinusoidal coordinate displacement over time. Let $A(t) = I_3 = [a_1(t)^T a_2(t)^T a_3(t)^T] \in \mathbb{R}^{3 \times 3}$ be an affine transformation operator to simulate periodic displacement of $3D$ homogeneous coordinates as a function of time t. Let further be $a_3(t) = (a_3(t)^1, a_3(t)^2, a_3(t)^3)$ the last column vector of A. Now define the periodic sinusoidal coordinate displacement at time t and displacement period p_d as

$$a_3^1(t) = a_3^2(t) = \gamma \sin(2\pi t/p_d)$$

This model is applied to a static thermographic image to simulate the expected behavior. The parameter γ allows for modeling the spatial extent[5] of the camera motion and is chosen from $[1; 10]$, whereas the frequency p_d is fixed to 20 since its influence is negligible.

Table 1. Evaluation of mean-squared error and integrated frequency band of the proposed simulation study. For this a static thermographic frame of case 1 was continously shifted by the discussed periodic motion model.

	$\gamma = 1$		$\gamma = 2$		$\gamma = 3$		$\gamma = 4$		$\gamma = 10$	
	RMSE	SD	RMSE	SD	RMSE	SD	RMSE	SD	RMSE	SD
SURF	0.03	26.71	0.06	10.74	0.08	143.31	0.1	56.6	0.21	36.17
WSA-GT	0.03	0.28	0.04	4.35	0.06	4.1	0.07	19.43	0.16	13.48
WSA-1SVM	0.03	0.33	0.04	4.23	0.06	12.94	0.07	19.53	0.16	13.48

The results indicate the applicability of motion correction approaches from whitelight imaging to thermographic image sequences of the simulation model when no heat transfers or convection are prevalent. Real data typically show non-stationary and highly dynamic development, for what reason the feature-based approach will lose performance. Since the subspace analysis exploits more information about the motion pattern, its better performance is not surprising.

4.2 Intraoperative Data

The algorithms are applied to raw recordings of two intraoperative cases and the average spectral density is compared. The evaluation of the RMSE is discarded, since the ground truth is a dynamic time-varying unknown. The first case was recorded during an intraoperative ECoG measurement of a patient with suspicion of frontal lobe epilepsy, wherein high-frequent vibrations of the camera system at a spatial extent of 5 pixels ($\sim$ 1cm) are recognizable. After application of the methods the motion visually disappeared, yet the SURF corrected dataset contains some deformed frames caused by mismatched features. Case 2 denotes a tumor case whereas less motion but strong spatial varying thermic

---

[5] Intraoperative, $\gamma = 10$ depicts a maximum displacement of 5cm.

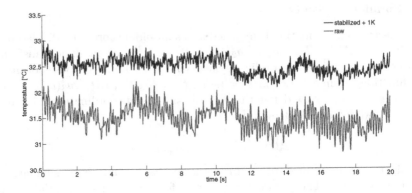

Fig. 3. Example of a single pixel time course of case 1 before (lower curve) and after motion correction (upper curve, increased by 1 K for visual reasons)

background activity is dominating the data. This leads to a mean temperature drift of 0.45K in 41s at an average activity of $\sigma = 0.2435K$. An increase of the SURF point detection threshold several times was necessary, since no feature matching between adjacent frames was possible. Hereby, enough corresponding features were found, yet the estimated transformation matrix was prone to errors yielding skewed frames. In contrary, in both datasets, the wavelet subspace analysis was not affected by respiratory, heart rate and other local motion artifacts or thermic background activity. This results in a higher reduction of energy content in the relevant frequency band as shown in table 2 and a visual disappearance of global motion.

The average spectral density in the high-frequency band of case 1 and case 2 was significantly lowered after the application of the wavelet subspace analysis approach, yet some activity was preserved suggesting local activity independent of camera motion artifacts. Further contrast analysis of the video sequences of case 1 shows, that wavelet subspace analysis lowers the mean contrast[6] of the raw video $\bar{c} = 0.0741$ ($\sigma = 0.0012$) to $\bar{c}_{wsa} = 0.0732$ ($\sigma_{wsa} = 0.0012$) while the SURF approach resulted in $\bar{c}_{SURF} = 0.0694$ ($\sigma_{SURF} = 0.004$). This indicates, that some smoothing was introduced, yet since thermographic images do not show sharp edges, the visual effect is considerably small and the gain in data quality dominates. In case of SURF feature matching, the high variance and low mean contrast is expected to be caused by mismatched features resulting in non-perfect geometric transforms and therefore wrongly interpolated pixel values. A retrospective global optimization over the matched SURF features might improve the quality of the estimated transform and yield better results. Furthermore, the accuracy of wsa strongly depends on features that introduce gradients into the thermal images, thus if no such features are detectable, the

---

[6] The mean contrast is computed by $\bar{c} = \frac{1}{|T| \cdot |C|} \sum_{t \in T} \sum_{c \in C} \nabla I_c(t)$ over all pixels $c \in C$ and frames $t \in T$.

Table 2. Evaluation of average spectral density of the algorithms with respect to two intraoperative cases

spectral density	uncorrected	SURF	WSA-GT	WSA-1SVM
Case 1	7541.724	1952.466	1285.724	1279.722
Case 2	1951.909	116347.54	927.683	937.244

algorithm will not work efficiently. Yet, since the boundary of the trepanation of the cortex is always visible, this situation is negligible.

The mean per-frame computation time was 0.08s (SURF), 0.04s (WSA-1SVM) and 0.06s (WSA-GT), whereas it is important to notice that the wavelet subspace analysis requires a dyadic length sequence of frames as input, while SURF feature matching allows registration of subsequent frames. Yet, a global optimization to improve SURF feature matching will affect this advantage. Since the fast wavelet transform has linear complexity, the KLT primary contributes to the time-complexity of WSA by the eigenvalue decomposition of the covariance matrix at each wavelet scale:

$$\Theta(n \sum_{j=1}^{j_{max}} 2^{2j}) \approx \Theta(2n2^{2j_{max}})$$

with n pixels and highest wavelet scale j_{max}. The performance of WSA-GT and WSA-1SVM is comparable, whereas the time-complexity of IRLS significantly affects the runtime making the one-class SVM the better outlier detection scheme.

The mounting of the camera at the operating table decreases the degrees of freedom of the camera movement trajectory. This constrains the motion artifacts to short-term quasi-periodic behavior (see figure 3), which affects all pixels and can be identified and removed by exploiting its multi-resolution- and spatial characteristics. In general, the results on intraoperative as well as on synthetic data demonstrate the advantages of the wavelet subspace analysis. The proposed posterior removal of global camera movement artifacts in frequency domain is therefore a reliable and fast method for compensation of this kind of artifacts. This makes the proposed approach a valuable tool for intraoperative decision support systems.

5   Conclusion

Vibrational motion of the whole camera system leads to a degradation of signal to noise ratio. Common image stabilization algorithms cannot be employed directly to thermal imaging since the data originates from the emitted mid to long-wavelength infrared radiation of the captured objects making it highly dynamic. Heat flow, convection, perfusion as well as neuronal activity are typical causes of temperature variations causing image gradient changes that do not relate to any change of the observed scene. We therefore propose a robust and fast framework for the identification of global frequency patterns by analyzing their spatial distribution. One application of this approach is the estimation and removal of camera motion artifacts. This roots on the assumption, that motion artifacts can be described in sparse time-frequency domain of all pixels at varying power depending on their local neighborhood. A simulation study was done in order to compare the approach with a well known method from white-light imaging for video stabilization under deterministic conditions. The results of this study as well as intraoperative data clearly suggest the application of the wavelet-subspace analysis framework for posterior global motion correction. Since the general framework is expendable by adapting the feature selection step to domain specific needs, its applications for the compensation or extraction of other kinds of spatially characteristic patterns are possible.

Acknowledgments. This work was supported by the European Social Fund and the Free State of Saxony. The authors would additionally like to thank all other organizations and individuals that supported this research project.

References

1. Gorbach, A.M., Heiss, J.D., Kopylev, L., Oldfield, E.H.: Intraoperative infrared imaging of brain tumors. Journal of Neurosurgery **101**(6), 960–969 (2004). pMID: 15599965
2. Steiner, G., Sobottka, S.B., Koch, E., Schackert, G., Kirsch, M.: Intraoperative imaging of cortical cerebral perfusion by time-resolved thermography and multivariate data analysis. Journal of Biomedical Optics **16**(1), 016001-1–016001-6 (2011)
3. Battiato, S., Gallo, G., Puglisi, G., Scellato, S.: Sift features tracking for video stabilization. In: 14th International Conference on Image Analysis and Processing, ICIAP 2007, pp. 825–830 (2007)
4. Hu, R., Shi, R., fan Shen, I., Chen, W.: Video stabilization using scale-invariant features. In: 11th International Conference on Information Visualization, IV 2007, pp. 871–877 (July 2007)
5. Litvin, A., Konrad, J., Karl, W.C.: Probabilistic video stabilization using kalman filtering and mosaicking. In: Proceedings of SPIE Conference on Electronic Imaging (2003)
6. Matsushita, Y., Ofek, E., Ge, W., Tang, X., Shum, H.-Y.: Full-frame video stabilization with motion inpainting. IEEE Transactions on Pattern Analysis and Machine Intelligence **28** (2006)
7. Szeliski, R.: Image alignment and stitching: A tutorial. Microsoft Research Tech. Rep. (2006)
8. Mallat, S.: A Wavelet Tour of Signal Processing, 3rd edn. Academic Press (2008)
9. Mikolajczyk, K., Schmid, C.: A performance evaluation of local descriptors. IEEE Transactions on Pattern Analysis and Machine Intelligence **27**(10), 1615–1630 (2005)
10. Schölkopf, B., Platt, J.C., Shawe-Taylor, J.C., Smola, A.J., Williamson, R.C.: Estimating the support of a high-dimensional distribution. Neural Comput. **13**(7), 1443–1471 (2001)

A Spatio-temporal Approach for Multiple Object Detection in Videos Using Graphs and Probability Maps

Henrique Morimitsu[1]([⊠]), Roberto M. Cesar Jr.[1], and Isabelle Bloch[2]

[1] University of São Paulo, São Paulo, Brazil
[2] Institut Mines Télécom, Télécom ParisTech, CNRS LTCI, Paris, France
henriquem87@gmail.com

Abstract. This paper presents a novel framework for object detection in videos that considers both structural and temporal information. Detection is performed by first applying low-level feature extraction techniques in each frame of the video. Then, additional robustness is obtained by considering the temporal stability of videos, using particle filters and probability maps, which encode information about the expected location of each object. Lastly, structural information of the scene is described using graphs, which allows us to further improve the results. As a practical application, we evaluate our approach on table tennis sport videos databases: the UCF101 table tennis shots and an in-house one. The observed results indicate that the proposed approach is robust, showing a high hit rate on the two databases.

Keywords: Object detection · Structural information · Graph · Tracking · Video

1 Introduction

Several works address the detection of each object as an individual task, i.e. do not consider the possible relationships between objects. This approach is appropriate for certain tasks, such as image retrieval [12] or detecting everything that belongs to a given class [5]. It has also been applied for videos, in which case the most common approach is the use of background subtraction methods combined with a blob descriptor for people detection. Almajai *et al.* [1], for example, use such a method to extract player blobs from tennis videos. The blobs are then filtered by classifying 3DHOG descriptors.

However, individual detection is a difficult task, and often produces undesirable results that could be avoided by considering more information, such as the spatial relations. This approach has been explored lately for scene understanding in static images. The work of Choi *et al.* [4] shows that by detecting multiple objects and considering their relationships it is possible to improve the detection of each object as a whole. The idea of considering the global scene

© Springer International Publishing Switzerland 2014
A. Campilho and M. Kamel (Eds.): ICIAR 2014, Part II, LNCS 8815, pp. 421–428, 2014.
DOI: 10.1007/978-3-319-11755-3_47

configuration has been receiving great attention in the field of more complex activity recognition as well [7]. Wang *et al.* [14] encoded structural relations using Markov Random Fields in order to perform player action detection in tennis matches. Even though widely studied for action and activity recognition tasks, this approach has not been well explored for the task of object detection in videos. Perhaps the most similar field is that of multi-object tracking, where the inclusion of structural information has been showing some very interesting results [15].

In this work we present a framework for multiple object detection and tracking in videos using graphs and temporal information obtained from probability maps to improve the tracker performance. The process starts by performing detection in each frame of the video using classic low-level features, such as color and motion data. Videos in general present several challenges, such as arbitrary view-points, possibly moving camera, unstable, low-quality image (e.g., obtained by a cell phone camera). Therefore, the results obtained from this step are usually very noisy. In order to face these challenges, the temporal properties of the video are used to filter undesired detections. This step is accomplished by obtaining information from what is referred to as probability maps and also from trackers implemented using particle filters. A structural approach is also employed, where a graph is built using the detected objects. This allows the scene to be described using higher-level information considering the relationships between the objects.

The contributions of this paper are twofold. First, we present a framework that encodes structural and temporal information about the objects in videos using graphs and trackers. Secondly, we explore the collected information to improve object detection in videos that share a common structure.

In Sec. 2 we show how low-level features are used to obtain detection candidates. In Sec. 3 the use of temporal information is explored to remove inconsistent candidates. In Sec. 4 structural information is used to improve the detection. Then, the results of the methods applied on table tennis videos are presented in Sec. 5.

2   Low-Level Object Detection

The low-level detection is highly dependent on the type of video being analyzed. However, in the proposed framework, the only requirement is that the chosen detector produces several candidate detections, that must include the correct ones. Note that different detectors can be used for the same task in order to produce more candidates, if necessary. Examples of possible detectors include, but are not limited to: background subtraction methods for moving objects, HOG [5] for people, keypoints methods like SIFT [9] or keygraphs [11] for rigid objects, parts-based detector [6] for multiview scenarios.

3   Temporal Consistency

Videos, as opposed to static images, provide a very important information in the form of temporal consistency. In other words, it is expected that two consecutive frames do not present very large differences. This information can be used to improve current results by relying on past information. In this work, temporal consistency is considered by means of two approaches: probability maps and object trackers.

3.1 Probability Maps

Probability maps encode the regions of the images where each object is more likely to appear, assuming that videos are acquired from a single camera and without cuts.

The maps are built online, while the video is being analyzed. For that reason, the maps improve as longer video periods are considered. In order to build the maps, it is assumed that, even though the detectors produce some errors, they usually produce correct results. For each frame, detected object regions are accumulated in a voting map, causing more frequent regions to receive higher values. The probability map M^t at instant t is obtained by:

$$M^t = M^{t-1}\gamma + I_B^t(1 - \gamma) \tag{1}$$

where $\gamma \in [0, 1]$ is a given temporal weighting factor and I_B^t is a binary image whose non-zero pixels represent regions where an object was detected. This updating method decreases the influence of older frames over time, thus coping with camera and object movements.

This approach is more suited for videos captured with a static camera. However, it may also be used on video that present not too abrupt movement by first applying a camera stabilization method, such as in [10].

3.2 Object Tracking

This work employs particle filters with the ConDensation algorithm that is implemented in OpenCV[1]. ConDensation uses factored sampling [8] on particle filters models in order to track objects. The particle filter tracking consists in estimating the posterior distribution $p(\mathbf{x}_t|\mathbf{z}_{1:t})$ of a set of weighted particles $\{(\mathbf{x}_t^i, w_t^i)\}$, where $\mathbf{x}_t^i$ is the state of particle i and w_t^i its weight, computed from the observed measurements $\mathbf{z}_{1:t}$ until the instant t. The ConDensation approach computes this distribution by generating a new set of n particles by sampling them, with repositions, from the old ones. By assuming $\sum_{j=1}^{n} w_t^j = 1$, the probability of each particle i being chosen in this step is w_t^i. Hence, more likely particles can be sampled several times, while others may not be chosen at all. Then, for each particle, a new state is predicted. The prediction phase involves two steps: drift and diffusion. Drift is a deterministic step, which consists in applying the motion dynamics for each particle. Diffusion, on the other hand, is random and it is used to include noise in the model. The new state of a particle i can be expressed as:

$$\mathbf{x}_{t+1}^i = A\mathbf{x}_t^i + B\mathbf{u} \tag{2}$$

where A is the motion dynamics matrix and $B\mathbf{u}$ is the noise term.

---

[1] http://opencv.org/

Finally, for each particle i, its weight is computed by:

$$w_{t+1}^i = \frac{p(\mathbf{x}_{t+1}^i|\mathbf{z}_{t+1})}{\sum_{j=1}^n p(\mathbf{x}_{t+1}^j|\mathbf{z}_{t+1})} \tag{3}$$

In this work, the state of each particle is a 4-tuple (x, y, h, w) consisting of the centroid (x, y) of the object bounding box as well as its height and width. As it is assumed that the initial states of the objects are unknown, a set of trackers $TR = \{tr_i\}$ is kept, one for each object detected in image I^t at instant t. The set TR is updated at each instant using a two-step approach. First, let $b(.)$ be the bounding box of an object and $A(b(.))$ be the area of $b(.)$. For each object-tracker pair (o_k^t, tr_i^{t-1}), the intersection ratio is computed:

$$r(o_k^t, tr_i^{t-1}) = \frac{A(b(o_k^t) \cap b(tr_i^{t-1}))}{\max\{A(b(o_k^t)), A(b(tr_i^{t-1}))\}} \tag{4}$$

After that, every pair such that $r(o_k^t, tr_i^{t-1}) < \tau_{area}$ is removed and all the remaining pairs are matched using a greedy approach. In order to match pairs in which the bounding box size incorrectly changed abruptly, a second step is performed by computing the distance $d(o_m^t, tr_n^{t-1})$ between every non-matched object o_m^t and tracker tr_n^{t-1}. Pairs are again filtered the same way as before. Finally, a new tracker is created and associated to each object that was not matched. In order to avoid that the number of trackers grow indefinitely, trackers that are not matched on τ_{window} consecutive frames are deleted.

4   Structural Properties

Let $\mathcal{O}_l = (o_1^l, o_2^l, ...o_m^l)$ be the set of detected objects using low-level features and temporal consistency. The goal is to consider high-level information in order to correct $\mathcal{O}_l$. It is assumed that the low-level detector produces an over-detection, i.e. all the desired objects are detected along with some possible misdetections. Therefore, the correction aims at removing inconsistent objects, yielding the new set $\mathcal{O}_h = (o_1^h, o_2^h, ...o_n^h)$ where $n \leq m$. Each object o_i^h is assigned to a class $c_i \in \Omega$ where $\Omega = \{\omega_1, \omega_2, ..., \omega_k\}$ represents the set of classes, e.g. "person" or "car".

It is assumed that there is a correlation between the behaviors of the objects. Such information is encoded using attributed relational graphs (ARGs). In this work, an ARG is a tuple $\mathcal{G} = (\mathcal{V}, \mathcal{E}, \Sigma_\mathcal{V}, \Sigma_\mathcal{E}, C)$ where $v \in \mathcal{V}$ represents one object, and an edge $e_{ij} = (v_i, v_j) \in \mathcal{E}$ encodes the relationships between v_i and v_j. $\Sigma_\mathcal{V}$ and $\Sigma_\mathcal{E}$ are the attributes of $\mathcal{V}$ and $\mathcal{E}$, respectively. C is a $k \times k$ matrix which specifies whether there is a relationship between classes ω_i and ω_j or not. In other words, C is used to generate the set of edges $\mathcal{E} = \{(v_i, v_j) \mid c(v_i) = l, c(v_j) = m, C_{lm} = 1\}$, where $c(v)$ represents the class of vertex v.

By considering that the scenes always present a common set of objects with a common spatial structure, the problem of improving object detection can be reduced to a subgraph matching between the scene and model graphs.

More precisely, let $\mathcal{H}_s$ be a subgraph of the scene graph $\mathcal{G}_s$. The best $\mathcal{H}_s$ is computed as:

$$\arg\max_{\mathcal{H}_s} s(\mathcal{H}_s, \mathcal{G}_m) \tag{5}$$

where $s(\mathcal{H}_s, \mathcal{G}_m)$ is a score function between both graphs, comparing attributes of the two vertex sets and the two edge sets.

5   Results

5.1   Sample Application: Table Tennis Videos

We have chosen to work with table tennis videos, as an example where structural information may be used mainly because of the presence of the table. This object is very important to the game, as everything is organized around it. In that sense, it can be used as a reference to obtain a better global understanding of the scene.

5.2   Object Detection

For this application, the selected objects to detect were the table and the players. The table was detected by backprojection histogram matching [3] in HSV color space. The color model for the table was learned by evaluating several samples of tables. The players, on the other hand, were detected using a background subtraction approach. However, instead of building a background model, motion was detected by the absolute difference between every two consecutive frames. Afterwards, player blobs were obtained by applying a morphological closing with a large structuring element.

5.3   Graph Description

In this example, we set $\Omega = \{player, table\}$ and $C = \begin{bmatrix} 0 & 1 \\ 1 & 0 \end{bmatrix}$, indicating that only the relation between table and player is considered. The videos represent singles matches (one player on each side of the table), hence the model graph $\mathcal{G}_m$ is a path of 3 vertices. From the rules of the game, it is known the ball trajectory must include the table. It is also known that from a top view of the game, the ball follows a nearly linear path from one player to another. Therefore, if the players are represented by the points p_1 and p_2 and the table by t, it is expected that the internal angle of the vectors $\overrightarrow{tp_1}$ and $\overrightarrow{tp_2}$ is as close to π as possible.

One common misdetection is to consider other moving objects or people as players. Therefore, the player probability map M_P is used in order to take into account if the player candidate is in a player zone. By taking everything into consideration, the score function is defined as:

$$s(\mathcal{H}_s, \mathcal{G}_m) = i(\mathcal{H}_s, \mathcal{G}_m) \left[\frac{\theta(\overrightarrow{tp_1}, \overrightarrow{tp_2})}{\pi} + \alpha \sum_{j=1}^{n} \mu(b_j, M_P) \right] \tag{6}$$

Table 1. Detection statistics on both databases. The first two rows represent the sum of detected objects along the whole video, while the third one is the ground truth.

	Local		UCF101	
	Table	Players	Table	Players
Detected	378	749	706	541
Hit	374	661	208	346
Expected	378	756	394	394
Hit / Expected	0.99	0.87	0.53	0.88
Hit / Detected	0.99	0.88	0.29	0.64

where

- $i(\mathcal{H}_s, \mathcal{G}_m) = 1$ if the graphs are isomorph, 0 otherwise;
- $\theta(\overrightarrow{tp_1}, \overrightarrow{tp_2})$ is the internal angle function between the two vectors;
- $\mu(b_j, M_P)$ is a relevance function, weighted by a given α, of bounding box b_j belonging to a player zone in player probability map M_P. This function is defined as: $\sum_{x,y \in b_j} \frac{M_P(x,y)}{w(b_j)h(b_j)}$, where $w(b_j)$ and $h(b_j)$ are the width and height of b_j. In this work α is experimentally chosen as 2.

5.4 Databases

The results were obtained from tests performed on two databases: one local database created for this research featuring two videos of amateur table tennis matches under different points of view and another with some videos from the UCF101 [13] table tennis shots. The results were evaluated by considering the hit rate of the detection given by the proposed method. As the videos are not annotated, the evaluation is performed manually by sampling one frame every 30, or around one frame per second, in each of the videos. A detection was considered a hit when $\min\left\{\frac{b_i(o)}{b_d(o)}, \frac{b_i(o)}{b_r(o)}\right\} \geq 0.5$, where $b_d(o)$ is the detected bounding box returned by the proposed method of object o, $b_r(o)$ is the real bounding box, or the smallest box that contains o, and $b_i(o) = b_d(o) \cap b_r(o)$.

Local Database. The local database consists of two videos recorded using a fixed camera of an amateur game viewed from two different points of view. The results in Table 1 show that the detector provided very good results on this database. Figure 1 shows some images of the observed results. As evidenced by the results, the table detector is robust to scale changes caused by the perspective, as well as different lighting conditions. The detector usually presents good results, finding the whole table, with just a few failures of partial detections. The players are also usually correctly detected, even under varying conditions of movement.

UCF101 Table Tennis Shots. This database is composed of 15 types of videos, which remained after removing videos where the table color was not blue. As these videos do not present real matches and only one player, the structural

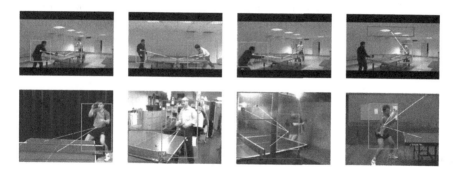

Fig. 1. Detection results for both databases. The first row shows the results for the local database, while the second for UCF101. The method works well even under changes of perspective and challenging lighting conditions. Even when only one player is detected and the structural properties are not used, the player and table are correctly detected among the possible candidates.

descriptor cannot be used, which means that an increase in the number of false positives is expected. The main interest of this database is therefore to check if the correct detection is also present among the false ones. If that is the case, then the correct detection could be found by using the structural descriptor later.

Some results are shown in Fig. 1 and are summarized in Table 1. As it can be seen, the players can be robustly detected even under the several changes present in this database. The table detector, on the other hand, was more highly affected by the changes. This is caused mainly by the large variety of table colors, as well as the very different lighting, which sometimes caused light reflections or shadows. It is worth noting that the tests were performed using only a single general color model, as opposed to learning a different model for each video, which would improve the results. Nonetheless, the detector showed satisfactory results detecting the table in more than half of the time, even under these conditions. As already mentioned, without the structural descriptor, sometimes other misdetections were present among the results, but the most important point is that the method finds the correct one.

6   Conclusion

We presented a framework to detect objects in videos. The detectors combine extraction of low-level features, temporal consistency and structural properties in order to obtain more robust results. They were tested on two databases containing table tennis videos: one created for this project and the challenging UCF101 table tennis shots, showing an average accuracy of over 75% for both table and player detection.

As future works, we intend to improve the detection of the table independently of its color. This could be done by using color quantization to segment the image and by searching for the region *between* [2] the players. Another ongoing research includes the use of action recognition in order to add more information to the process. This would work both ways, because the detection could benefit from information about the actions, as well as the action recognition step could be improved by better detection results.

Acknowledgments. The authors would like to thank FAPESP grants #2013-08258/7, #2012-09741-0, #2011/50761-2, CNPq, CAPES and NAP eScience - PRP - USP.

References

1. Almajai, I., Yan, F., de Campos, T., Khan, A., Christmas, W., Windridge, D., Kittler, J.: Anomaly detection and knowledge transfer in automatic sports video annotation. In: Weinshall, D., Anemüller, J., van Gool, L. (eds.) Detection and Identification of Rare Audiovisual Cues. SCI, vol. 384, pp. 109–117. Springer, Heidelberg (2012)
2. Bloch, I., Colliot, O., Cesar, R.: On the ternary spatial relation between. IEEE Transactions on Systems, Man, and Cybernetics SMC-B **36**(2), 312–327 (2006)
3. Bradski, G.R.: Real time face and object tracking as a component of a perceptual user interface. In: WACV, pp. 214–219 (1998)
4. Choi, W., Chao, Y.W., Pantofaru, C., Savarese, S.: Understanding indoor scenes using 3D geometric phrases. In: CVPR, pp. 33–40 (2013)
5. Dalal, N., Triggs, B.: Histograms of oriented gradients for human detection. In: CVPR, pp. 886–893 (2005)
6. Felzenszwalb, P.F., Girshick, R.B., McAllester, D.A., Ramanan, D.: Object detection with discriminatively trained part-based models. IEEE PAMI **32**(9), 1627–1645 (2010)
7. Gaur, U., Zhu, Y., Song, B., Chowdhury, A.K.R.: A "string of feature graphs" model for recognition of complex activities in natural videos. In: ICCV, pp. 2595–2602 (2011)
8. Isard, M., Blake, A.: CONDENSATION - conditional density propagation for visual tracking. International Journal of Computer Vision **29**(1), 5–28 (1998)
9. Lowe, D.G.: Distinctive image features from scale-invariant keypoints. International Journal of Computer Vision **60**(2), 91–110 (2004)
10. Matsushita, Y., Ofek, E., Ge, W., Tang, X., Shum, H.Y.: Full-frame video stabilization with motion inpainting. IEEE PAMI **28**(7), 1150–1163 (2006)
11. Morimitsu, H., Hashimoto, M., Pimentel, R.B., Cesar Jr, R.M., Hirata Jr, R.: Keygraphs for sign detection in indoor environments by mobile phones. In: Jiang, X., Ferrer, M., Torsello, A. (eds.) GbRPR 2011. LNCS, vol. 6658, pp. 315–324. Springer, Heidelberg (2011)
12. Nistér, D., Stewénius, H.: Scalable recognition with a vocabulary tree. In: CVPR, pp. 2161–2168 (2006)
13. Soomro, K., Zamir, A.R., Shah, M.: UCF101: A dataset of 101 human actions classes from videos in the wild. CoRR abs/1212.0402 (2012)
14. Wang, Z., Shi, Q., Shen, C., van den Hengel, A.: Bilinear programming for human activity recognition with unknown MRF graphs. In: CVPR, pp. 1690–1697 (2013)
15. Widynski, N., Dubuisson, S., Bloch, I.: Fuzzy spatial constraints and ranked partitioned sampling approach for multiple object tracking. Computer Vision and Image Understanding (CVIU) **116**(10), 1076–1094 (2012)

Robot Vision

Adopting Feature-Based Visual Odometry for Resource-Constrained Mobile Devices

Michał Fularz, Michał Nowicki[(✉)], and Piotr Skrzypczyński

Institute of Control and Information Engineering, Poznań University of Technology,
ul. Piotrowo 3A, 60-965 Poznań, Poland
{michal.fularz,piotr.skrzypczynski}@put.poznan.pl,
michal.nowicki@cie.put.poznan.pl

Abstract. In many practical applications of mobile devices self-localization of the user in a GPS-denied indoor environment is required. Among the available approaches the visual odometry concept enables continuous, precise egomotion estimation in previously unknown environments. In this paper we examine the usual pipeline of a monocular visual odometry system, identifying the bottlenecks and demonstrating how to circumvent the resource constrains, to implement a real-time visual odometry system on a smartphone or tablet.

Keywords: Mobile device · Visual odometry · Self-localization

1 Introduction

While many practical applications require to localize the user with respect to predefined objects or locations, such self-localization in GPS-denied indoor environments is still a challenging task that requires either an external infrastructure (e.g. WiFi base stations at known locations) or specific hardware platforms (e.g. mobile robots) being available to the user. However, recent advances to mobile devices like smartphones or tablets, make it possible to employ these devices for indoor self-localization. Embracing this opportunity we investigate the applicability of consumer-grade mobile devices as platforms to implement the monocular visual odometry for estimation of the user's egomotion.

The Visual Odometry (VO) methods estimate the trajectory of a camera by processing image frames taken at consecutive poses (i.e. positions and orientations) of this sensor, assuming no *a priori* map of the environment [14]. The VO methods can be implemented with either stereo camera setup, which enables to directly measure the scene depth, or a single camera, which makes depth information unavailable. The feature-based monocular VO methods that rely on salient visual features tracked over the consecutive images are well-established [5]. However, to be useful, the VO solution should be both precise and fast. This is hard to achieve on a mobile device due to the constrains imposed by the processing power, memory, and the operating system.

© Springer International Publishing Switzerland 2014
A. Campilho and M. Kamel (Eds.): ICIAR 2014, Part II, LNCS 8815, pp. 431–441, 2014.
DOI: 10.1007/978-3-319-11755-3_48

In this paper we evaluate the most important modules of a standard feature-based VO pipeline on the Android devices. Our aim is to make an informed choice of the particular solutions and computer vision algorithms for efficient implementation under the constrained resources.

2   Related Work

The approaches to VO in mobile robots range from dense, appearance-based methods that estimate the camera motion directly from the intensity values in the image, to feature-based algorithms that match sparse, salient features from one frame to the next. The appearance-based methods are more computation-intensive, and not robust to occlusions [14]. Because in navigation tasks the camera or robot trajectory has to be estimated in real-time, the practical approaches to VO in mobile robotics are dominated by the feature-based methods. The seminal work by Nistér *et al.* [9] defined the most typical framework for the feature-based VO, assuming unconstrained motion in 6 degrees of freedom (6-DoF).

Although the last decade has seen a substantial progress in practical VO implementations [5], very few VO or VO-like systems have been so far demonstrated working on actual mobile devices. The approach described in [12] besides the WiFi signal uses also the SURF [2] point features for image-based tracking of the user's pose, which is a simple form of VO. However, the results in [12] were obtained with a custom experimental setup rather than a real mobile device, thus avoiding the problems of limited computing resources. The Parallel Tracking and Mapping (PTAM) algorithm, which combines a VO-like, feature-based tracking of the camera with the structure from motion and bundle adjustment techniques for robust visual mapping has been implemented on a smartphone [7]. This implementation is targeted only for the iPhone devices, and offers only limited precision of tracking. In [11] an attempt to re-implement the full PTAM for the Android system has been made, demonstrating however only preliminary results for the camera tracking. Some very recent results [4] suggest that there is also a possibility to employ the appearance-based paradigm for a VO system working in real-time on a mobile device.

3   Visual Odometry: Structure and Algorithms

3.1   System Structure

The approach we consider in this work is aimed at obtaining a simple, feature-based VO system utilizing only the visual (RGB) data from a mobile device's camera. This VO system should run in real-time under the limited computing resources of a smartphone or tablet.

As the main idea of this paper is to demonstrate how efficient the particular VO pipeline components can be implemented on an Android device, we consider only the most simple incremental estimation of the sensor's trajectory. As we have a monocular camera, only the 2D-to-2D feature correspondences are used [5].

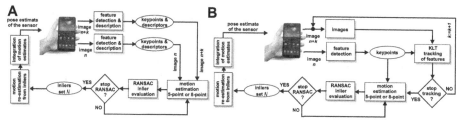

Fig. 1. Structure of a simple visual odometry system (without bundle adjustment) in two variants: using frame-to-frame matching (A) or tracking over several frames (B)

In the simple system we do not recover the 3D feature poses by triangulation, and do not perform windowed bundle adjustment to reduce the drift of the final trajectory. These two steps are considered as future work. The VO pipeline is proposed in two versions, which are depicted in Fig. 1. The difference is in the approach to establish the correspondences between the 2D features in the images. As we want to estimate the motion between the first image I_n and the last image I_{n+k} in a sequence of k images (k is considered to be small), we can simply match the detected photometric point features in I_n and I_{n+k} to obtain the correspondences (Fig. 1A), or we can detect the features only in I_n, and then track these points through the k images (Fig. 1B). In both versions the first step is to detect salient point features in the first image I_n. For the frame-to-frame matching version also the descriptors of these features have to be computed. Once the 2D-to-2D correspondences between I_n and I_{n+k} are established, the camera motion is estimated using either the minimal 5-point solver, or the 8-point solver within the robust estimation RANSAC scheme. When the 6-DoF motion is estimated, we re-start the pipeline with the last image as the initial frame of a new sequence. This way, computing the transformations for the consecutive short sequences of images, and then compounding the local transformations head-to-tail we estimate the whole trajectory of the mobile device.

3.2   Detection and Description of Features

The classic corner detectors, like Harris and Shi-Tomasi (GFTT) may be used to detect keypoints in VO, as corners tend to be well-localized in the image and repeatable. The more recent FAST point detector [13] is also more efficient in terms of computation. In contrast to those three corner-like detectors, the SIFT [8] and SURF [2] algorithms are blob-like detectors, closely related to their respective feature descriptors. Both are based upon the concept of scale-space, which makes them invariant with respect to the changing scale, rotation, and viewpoint.

To facilitate efficient matching of the salient point features between images the descriptors are used. They encode the appearance of the local neighborhood of each keypoint as a compact data structure. The aforementioned SIFT and SURF feature detectors have their own multi-scale descriptors. Both SIFT and SURF descriptor can be applied also with the corner-like detectors, but to preserve the computational efficiency one of the recently introduced low-complexity, binary descriptors optimized for speed may be considered: the BRIEF [3], ORB (Oriented FAST and Rotated BRIEF) or the very recent LDB descriptor designed particularly for mobile devices [17]. An interested reader can find a more comprehensive introduction to the detectors/descriptors available on the Android-based mobile devices in our previous work [10].

3.3 Feature Matching and Tracking

In order to determine the 2D points that represent the same 3D features of the scene in two or more images, it is necessary to find corresponding photometric features in these images. The matching features are then used to estimate the motion of the camera between the poses associated with the images. For that purpose the descriptors of keypoints in the images may be used. The similarity measure depends on the descriptor itself, it is the Euclidean distance for the SIFT and SURF, and the fast to compute Hamming distance for the binary descriptors.

An alternative to the frame-to-frame matching strategy is feature tracking. When features are tracked through a sequence of images, the keypoints are detected only in the first image, and then, their corresponding points are determined in the following images using a local search method. This task can be accomplished by using the well-established Kanade-Lucas-Tomasi (KLT) algorithm [1].

3.4 Motion Estimation with n-Point Algorithms

A n-point algorithm is a method that allows to estimate the relative camera motion from two views using n pairs of corresponding points. The classic solution is to use eight pairs of points, while the minimal solution for unconstrained, 6-DoF perspective camera motion uses five pairs of points [5].

The relation between two sets, $\mathbf{x}$ and $\mathbf{x}'$ of corresponding points from two images of the same scene is defined as $\mathbf{x}'^T \mathbf{F} \mathbf{x} = 0$, where $\mathbf{F}$ denotes fundamental matrix. When dealing with a fully-calibrated system (as in our case), the fundamental matrix is reduced to the essential matrix $\mathbf{E}$. For a monocular system, like the mobile device, the relationship between those two matrices is $\mathbf{E} = \mathbf{K}^T \mathbf{F} \mathbf{K}$, where $\mathbf{K}$ is the camera calibration matrix. The 8-point algorithm is based on the fact that essential matrix has 9 elements, but it is defined up to an unknown scale, so that 8 pairs of points are enough to find a solution using the SVD (Singular Value Decomposition) method.

However, a minimal solution is possible, which uses five pairs. This is possible due to the fact that the essential matrix contains five parameters – three for rotation and two for the direction of translation (the magnitude of translation cannot be recovered due to the depth/speed ambiguity). Practical solutions based on five pairs of points require solving various non-linear equations [6], and detailed description of those methods is beyond the scope of this paper.

In real-life systems the detection and matching of points between two images is done in an automatic way, which can introduce mismatches. To solve this problem the popular RANSAC scheme is used. The accuracy of the solution depends on the number of RANSAC iterations that was executed. The number of iterations k that has to be run to get the result with the probability p for n randomly chosen points and the probability of choosing an inlier ratio w is $k = \frac{\log(1-p)}{\log(1-w^n)}$. Therefore, the 5-point algorithm used within the RANSAC scheme results in fewer iterations performed than the 8-point version.

4 Experimental Evaluation

The experimental evaluation of the VO implementation was performed using mostly the Samsung Galaxy Note 3 smartphone with the Android 4.4.2 OS, and the slightly older Asus Nexus 7 tablet for some tests. Samsung Galaxy Note 3 is equipped with 3GB of RAM and quadcore Qualcomm Snapdragon 800 (max. CPU core frequency equal to 2.3 GHz). Asus Nexus 7 has 1GB of RAM and quadcore ARM Cortex-A9 Nvidia Tegra 3 T30L (max. CPU core frequency equal to 1.2 GHz). The image processing was done using the popular OpenCV library ver. 2.4.8. According to the conclusions drawn from our previous work [10], the image processing was implemented entirely in the C++ native code (NDK). The tests have been performed off-line, using two data sets containing images acquired in a scenario typical for indoor VO. A part of the experiments, mainly related to investigating the feature matching reliability and precision, was performed using the Freiburg University [16] data set, containing long sequences with very precise ground truth. Other tests were performed using the Poznan University of Technology (PUT) data set recorded using the Galaxy Note 3 smartphone mounted on a mobile robot [10].

4.1 Feature Detection and Description

The comparison of detectors and descriptors starts with the processing time analysis on the Galaxy Note 3. The evaluation was performed on 500 images taken from the `put/phone1` sequence. For this test the image processing was limited to a single thread. The obtained results are presented in Tab. 1.

Table 1. Computing efficiency of the selected point feature detectors and descriptors measured on the Galaxy Note 3 smartphone and the `put/phone1` sequence

detector type	GFTT	HARRIS	FAST	FAST	ORB	SIFT	SURF
descriptor type	—	—·	BRIEF	LDB	ORB	SIFT	SURF
aver. detection time [ms]	84.70	78.77	10.45	10.45	58.10	1084.79	1444.42
aver. no. of keypoints	790.72	265.14	1414.14	1414.14	499.65	477.21	1075.60
aver. description time per keypoint [ms]	—	—	0.025	0.035	0.18	2.60	3.10
aver. processing time for all keypoints [ms]	84.70	78.77	22.98	28.62	151.04	2384.81	2998.79

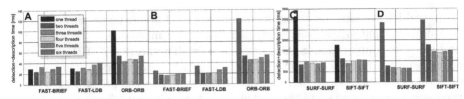

Fig. 2. Total feature detection and description time (500 points) for single-thread and parallel implementations of corner-like detectors with binary descriptors (A,B), and multi-scale detectors (C,D). Plots A and C show results measured on the Galaxy Note 3, while plots B and D measured on the Nexus 7.

The experiment involved evaluating the detectors finding corner-like point features (GFTT, HARRIS, FAST) that are recommended for tracking, and the typical detector/descriptor pairs used in VO systems based on feature matching. Additionally, the time needed for detection (tracking) or detection and description (matching) of 500 keypoints is presented in the last row of Tab. 1.

These results demonstrate that the SIFT-SIFT and SURF-SURF pairs, with the time exceeding two seconds are far too slow for real-time implementations of VO. What is surprising, is that SURF detection is slower than SIFT detection, but we believe that this situation is caused by the OpenCV default parameters used in each case. Also the results for FAST-BRIEF and its rotation-invariant version ORB-ORB are somewhat unexpected, as the ORB-ORB pair is 6.5 times slower than FAST-BRIEF. The new descriptor LDB is very fast, and challenges the very simple BRIEF. Among the features that are used in tracking (GFTT, HARRIS, FAST), the FAST detector is almost 8 times faster than the older algorithms. The single-thread implementation does not exploit the whole potential of the ARM architecture. Mobile devices like Nexus 7 or Samsung Galaxy Note 3 are nowadays equipped with 4 or 8 cores that can be used to speed up the data processing. Therefore, the parallel implementations of detectors and descriptors are investigated. In order to evaluate the possible gains of parallel implementations for N threads, each image frame of the size $(width, height)$ is divided into N subimages of sizes $(width, height/N)$. The images are divided into horizontal stripes to achieve a continuous memory accesses for each thread and therefore obtain faster processing. The keypoints in each subimage are also described in a separate thread. The influence of the parallel processing on the computing efficiency for the Galaxy Note 3 and Nexus 7 are presented in Fig. 2. In most cases, there was no significant increase of speed for the multi-threaded implementations, as compared to the single-thread, but in all experiments using two threads resulted in shorter computation time than in the single-thread. Only in the case of detector/descriptor pairs performing complex arithmetic operations, like SURF and SIFT, a significant gain from multi-threading is observed. This is also a result of using the subimages, as the detection is not performed on the highest level of the image pyramid. In case of the detector/descriptor pairs that are not so computation-intensive, the bottleneck for the multi-thread implementation is the common memory access. This was confirmed by repeating the experiment on a Galaxy Note 3 device with all the cores tweaked to run with the

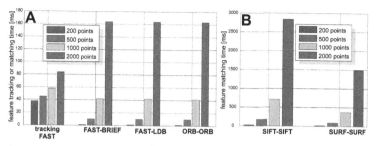

Fig. 3. Computation time per frame vs. the number of features for single-thread feature tracking or descriptor-based matching measured on the Galaxy Note 3 for the put/phone1 sequence. Parts A and B differ in scale to make the plot more clear.

maximal frequency. In that case, the percentage of CPU usage was measured to be around 50% for FAST-BRIEF in contrary to 95% for the SIFT-SIFT pair.

4.2 Comparing Tracking and Matching

Another important decision in the design process of a VO system is choosing between the tracking and matching processing flow. The first difference between both approaches is the scaling when it comes to the number of features. For tracking, there is a constant time taken for a pyramid creation used to find feature locations, but then features are tracked independently and therefore the time scales almost linearly with the number of features. In case of a matching, the number of operations needed to find matches between two sets of descriptors scales quadratically with the number of features as distances for all possible matches between features from both sets have to be computed. The experimental results that confirm this theoretical analysis are presented in Fig. 3. It is also essential to distinguish between matching based on binary descriptors and matching using descriptors compared with the Euclidean norm. Binary descriptors like BRIEF are faster as the Hamming distance operation can utilize special set of CPU instructions like ARM NEON. On the Android-based device matching of two sets containing 500 binary BRIEF descriptors is almost 10 times faster than matching of two sets of 500 features containing SURF descriptors. In the case of a larger number of features tracking is faster, but in the case of smaller number of features, matching is usually faster. But in most VO systems only several hundreds of features are enough to find a motion estimate and therefore we believe that 500 features choice combines the robustness of the VO system with the real-time requirements. For 500 features, it can be observed that matching using binary descriptors is faster than tracking, which is faster than matching based on the Euclidean norm.

Another evaluated improvement were the parallel versions of tracking and matching. In the case of tracking, the set of features is divided into even subsets, whereas features in each subset are tracked independently. In case of matching, the multiple threads are used to compute the distances between descriptors from both images and the best matches are found in a single thread. The results of

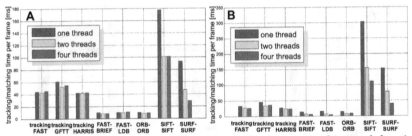

Fig. 4. Comparison of the time needed per frame for feature tracking and descriptor-based matching for single-thread and parallel implementations on the Galaxy Note 3 (A) and on Nexus 7 (B) with the `freiburg1/desk` sequence

the evaluation are presented in Fig. 4. Similarly to previous tests, any significant speedup can be observed only for algorithms that contain more complex mathematical operations, like matching using the Euclidean norm.

Besides evaluating the computing efficiency aspects of the matching vs. tracking choice, we investigate also the precision and robustness of the considered methods. To accomplish this, the ground truth information from the `freiburg1/desk` sequence was used to compute the essential matrix between two images [10]. Then, for each feature matched from two images, or a feature tracked from one image to the another, the Symmetrical Reprojection Error was used to determine if the pair is consistent with the ground truth (an inlier) or not (an outlier) [15]. The percentage of inliers in the total number of matched/tracked features was used as the measure of robustness. The successfull matching ratio is investigated for four different frame rates, imitating a VO system working at different speeds. In the plots presented in Fig. 5 the situations are presented, when all frames are used (A), or every 2nd frame (B), every 5th frame (C), and only every 10th frame (D) are processed. This corresponds to a VO system working with the maximal frame rate of 30Hz, whereas the plots with the skipped images correspond to processing with 15Hz, 6Hz, and 3Hz, respectively. In the case of processing every image, the inlier ratio is higher than 80% for all the considered solutions, with few sudden drops for images with significant motion blur. When smaller number of frames is used, the average inlier ratio drops significantly, which poses a challenge for the motion estimation block of the VO.

4.3   RANSAC with n-Point Algorithms

The remaining part of a VO system to test is the module estimating the motion from the matches of points found in consecutive images. As only a fraction of all matches is correct, the RANSAC procedure is used to remove the wrong matches and find the correct motion estimate. The implemented version of RANSAC estimates the number of iterations needed to achieve 0.99 success ratio assuming a known percentage of inliers. The 5-point and 8-point algorithms are evaluated within the RANSAC scheme in a single-thread and parallel implementations. In each case, the RANSAC is stopped if it cannot find the transformation in 5

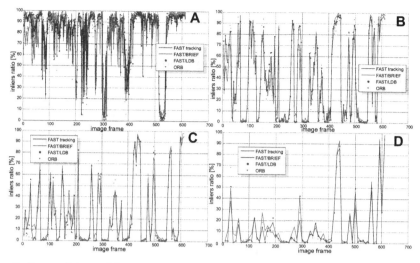

Fig. 5. Successful matching ratio at four different frame rates for feature tracking and three feature-matching-based solutions along the `freiburg1/desk` sequence

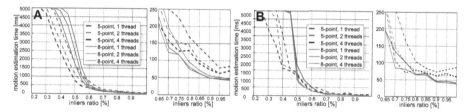

Fig. 6. Computing efficiency of the motion estimation in various implementations vs. the percent of inliers measured for the Galaxy Note 3 (A), and the Nexus 7 (B)

seconds. The results are presented in Fig. 6 for the two mobile devices used in our experiments.

From the presented results, it can be seen that it is usually impossible to find a correct estimate if the inlier ratio is below 40%. As the 8-point algorithm is based on SVD it's single call is faster than 5-point algorithm and therefore the 8-point algorithm performs faster in the case of high inlier rates. As the inlier ratio drops, it is getting harder to pick 8 correct matches for the 8-point algorithm, and thus the RANSAC with the 5-point algorithm is faster than the one using 8-point algorithm. Additional, parallel implementations allow to perform more RANSAC iterations in the same time. In that case parallel implementation of the 5-point algorithm allows to find a correct estimate in the case of low inlier ratio within reasonable time limit.

5   Conclusions

Presented evaluation suggest than in the case of Android devices the FAST-BRIEF pair outperforms other approaches in terms of time and provides robustness similar to the other detector/descriptor pairs. Additionally, the matching using binary descriptors is efficiently performed on the mobile platform. The total detection, description and matching process can be performed in approx. 35 ms. Combining the proposed solution with the 8-point algorithm the VO system is expected to work with the frame rate of 5 fps, providing that the inlier rate would be higher than 65%. This should be enough to estimate the egomotion using images with no significant motion blur and without sudden orientation changes. Unfortunately, there is no significant speedup, when parallel processing is used, as the memory access, not the CPU power is the bottleneck. Our future work will focus on evaluating a complete VO on Android-based devices.

Acknowledgments. This work is financed by the Polish Ministry of Science and Higher Education in years 2013-2015 under the grant DI2012 004142. Michał Fularz holds a scholarship for Ph.D. students specializing in majors strategic for Wielkopolska's development, co-financed by European Union.

References

1. Baker, S., Matthews, I.: Lucas-Kanade 20 Years on: A Unifying Framework. Int. Journal of Computer Vision **56**(3), 221–255 (2004)
2. Bay, H., Ess, A., Tuytelaars, T., Van Gool, L.: SURF: Speeded up Robust Features. Comp. Vis. and Image Underst. **110**(3), 346–359 (2008)
3. Calonder, M., Lepetit, V., Strecha, C., Fua, P.: BRIEF: Binary Robust Independent Elementary Features. In: Daniilidis, K., Maragos, P., Paragios, N. (eds.) ECCV 2010, Part IV. LNCS, vol. 6314, pp. 778–792. Springer, Heidelberg (2010)
4. Forster, C., Pizzoli, M., Scaramuzza, D.: SVO: Fast Semi-Direct Monocular Visual Odometry. In: Proc. IEEE Int. Conf. on Robotics & Automation, Hong-Kong (to appear, 2014)
5. Fraundorfer, F., Scaramuzza, D.: Visual Odometry: Part II - Matching, Robustness and Applications. IEEE Robotics & Automation Magazine **19**(2), 78–90 (2012)
6. Hongdong, L., Hartley, R.: Five-Point Motion Estimation Made Easy. In: Proc. 18th Int. Conf. on Pattern Recognition (ICPR), pp. 630–633 (2006)
7. Klein, G., Murray, D.: Parallel Tracking and Mapping on a Camera Phone. In: Proc. IEEE/ACM Int. Symp. on Mixed and Augmented Reality (ISMAR 2009), pp. 83–86 (2009)
8. Lowe, D.G.: Distinctive Image Features from Scale-Invariant Keypoints. Int. J. of Comp. Vis. **60**(2), 91–110 (2004)
9. Nistér, D., Naroditsky, O., Bergen, J.: Visual Odometry. In: Proc. IEEE Conf. on Computer Vision and Pattern Recognition (CVPR), pp. 652–659 (2004)
10. Nowicki, M., Skrzypczyński, P.: Performance Comparison of Point Feature Detectors and Descriptors for Visual Navigation on Android Platform. In: Proc. IEEE IWCMC 2014, Nicosia (to appear, 2014)
11. Porzi, L., Ricci, E., Ciarfuglia, T., Zanin, M.: Visual-Inertial Tracking on Android for Augmented Reality Applications. In: IEEE Workshop on Environmental Energy and Structural Monitoring Systems, pp. 35–41 (2012)
12. Quigley, M., Stavens, D., Coates, A., Thrun, S.: Sub-Meter Indoor Localization in Unmodified Environments with Inexpensive Sensors. In: Proc. IEEE/RSJ Int. Conf. on IROS, Taipei, pp. 2039–2046 (2010)

13. Rosten, E., Drummond, T.W.: Machine Learning for High-Speed Corner Detection. In: Leonardis, A., Bischof, H., Pinz, A. (eds.) ECCV 2006, Part I. LNCS, vol. 3951, pp. 430–443. Springer, Heidelberg (2006)

14. Scaramuzza, D., Fraundorfer, F.: Visual Odometry: Part I - the First 30 Years and Fundamentals. IEEE Robotics & Automation Magazine 18(4), 80–92 (2011)

15. Schmidt, A., Kraft, M., Fularz, M., Domagala, Z.: Comparative Assessment of Point Feature Detectors in the Context of Robot Navigation. JAMRIS 7(1), 11–20 (2013)

16. Sturm, J., Engelhard, N., Endres, F., Burgard, W., Cremers, D.: A Benchmark for the Evaluation of RGB-D SLAM Systems. In: Proc. IEEE/RSJ Int. Conf. on IROS, Vilamoura, pp. 573–580 (2012)

17. Yang, X., Cheng, K.T.: LDB: An Ultra-Fast Feature for Scalable Augmented Reality on Mobile Devices. In: Proc. ISMAR 2012, Atlanta, pp. 49–57 (2012)

Strategy for Folding Clothing on the Basis of Deformable Models

Yasuyo Kita$^{(\boxtimes)}$, Fumio Kanehiro, Toshio Ueshiba, and Nobuyuki Kita

National Institute of Advanced Industrial Science and Technology (AIST), AIST
Tsukuba Central 2, 1-1-1 Umezono, Tsukuba, Ibaraki 305-8568, Japan
{y.kita,f-kanehiro,t.ueshiba,n.kita}@aist.go.jp

Abstract. In this study, a strategy is given for automatically reshaping an item of clothing from an arbitrary shape into a fixed shape by using its deformable model. The strategy consists of three stages that correspond to the clothing state: unknown (before recognition), unknown to known (recognition), and known (after recognition). In the first stage, a clothing item that is initially placed in an arbitrary shape is picked up and observed after some recognition-aid actions. In the second stage, the clothing state is recognized by matching the deformable clothing model to the observed 3D data [1]. In the third stage, a proper sequence of grasps toward the goal state is selected according to the clothing state. As an instance of this strategy, a folding task was implemented in a humanoid robot. Experimental results using pullovers show that the folding task can be achieved with a small number of grasping steps.

Keywords: Robot vision · Clothes handling · Deformable model

1 Introduction

Domestic service robots and rehabilitation robots are expected to play an active role in graying societies, and thus it is becoming increasingly important for robots to autonomously handle daily necessities, such as clothes folding. Because of clothing's high deformability and complex self-occlusions, the techniques required for handling clothing are quite different from those required for handling rigid objects.

Recently, many studies on handling clothes have been conducted, such as those on skillful manipulation of a cloth [2][3] and on detection and classification of clothing [4],[5],[6]. Studies on automatic folding of clothing items are also becoming more common. Maitin-Shepard et al. [7] demonstrated that a robot can skillfully handle towels on the basis of corner detection by using multiple-view observation. However, extending this method to other types of clothing, which may have complicated shape variations and several types of characteristic points, seems difficult. Berg et al. [8] proposed a method of folding several types of clothing by assuming that the target clothing is neatly laid on a desk when the process begins. Although Miller et al. [9] eased the tidiness requirements of this

© Springer International Publishing Switzerland 2014
A. Campilho and M. Kamel (Eds.): ICIAR 2014, Part II, LNCS 8815, pp. 442–452, 2014.
DOI: 10.1007/978-3-319-11755-3_49

method, as a first step items still have to be flattened without self-occlusions. Flattening all parts of an item itself is not necessarily an easy task, as shown in some other studies (e.g., [5]) and requires extra procedures.

Because we exclude flattening in our strategy, it is desirable to recognize the clothing state while changing the grasping on items held in the air. Kaneko et al. [10] proposed a method that recognizes the clothing state by comparing the contour features (e.g., curvature and length ratio) of the observed data with models when clothes are held by two points in the air. The state of clothes held at two points, however, can vary tremendously because of the large number of two-point combinations. In addition, the detailed contour is difficult to extract robustly from real observations , which are highly sensitive to slight deformations of the clothing. Osawa et al. [11] and Cusumano-Towner et al. [12] proposed methods for estimating clothing state in a manner similar to the method proposed by Kaneko et al. [10] and showed a good recognition rate for several types of clothing. However, those methods require repeated grasping of the lowest point of a hanging item of clothing, which is time consuming and delays achieving the target state. In addition, reaching the lowest point with one hand while holding the item with the other hand might be impossible when the clothing is large. We[13][14] previously proposed a method that recognizes the state of a clothing item by using its deformable model and calculates the necessary information for grasping the item at any specific point, such as a shoulder. One advantage of our approach is that the overall configuration of the clothing item is considered through use of its deformable model. This is important both for handling the item without undesirable twisting of the item and for selecting the best action toward reaching the goal state.

In this study, we present a strategy for achieving a practical task: folding an item of clothing from an arbitrary shape into a fixed form on the basis of model-based recognition of the clothing state. In the next section, we introduce our complete strategy, which consists of the following three stages: actions to aid recognition, visual recognition of clothing state, and actions to complete a task on the basis of the clothing state. The first and second stages, which have been already presented elsewhere, are briefly explained in the same section. In Section 3, the key functions of the third stage and some methods to realize the functions are described. In Section 4, results of experiments with a humanoid robot are presented and discussed. Finally, in Section 5, current progress and future subjects are summarized.

2   Strategy for Folding Clothing

Fig. 1 shows the overall flow for reshaping an item of clothing from an arbitrary form into a fixed folded form. We treat "recognition of clothing state" as a core process of the strategy, because, once it is achieved, the desirable clothing shape can be positively led and traced. Hence, the total flow is divided into the following three stages:

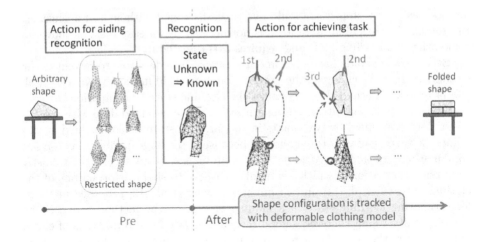

Fig. 1. Strategy based on model-driven analysis

I. Action for aiding recognition
II. Model-driven visual recognition
III. Action for achieving task based on the recognition

At the first stage, the target item of clothing is brought into the shape which makes the following recognition process easier and more robust[14]. In our methods, two types of actions are used for this purpose: restrictions on shape configuration and acquisition of abundant information about the item. For restricting the shape configurations, we adopt the strategy of grasping the rim of the target item of clothing after picking it from the desk. Through this action, the possible shapes are limited to the states as shown in "State x" in Fig. 2(a). For acquiring abundant information about the clothing item, we use 3D observed data taken from different view directions in an integrated fashion [1][15].

At the second stage, we use the model-based state recognition methods [13]. Fig. 2 shows the core idea of these studies. By simulating the physical deformation of the target clothing based on an approximate knowledge about the target, such as the type (e.g., sweater, pants), approximate size, and softness, possible 3D shapes of the clothing being held in air are predicted as shown in Fig. 2(a). Here, the clothing states are classified into "State 1," "State 2," ... according to the position in which the article is held. After observation, to consider the variation in the shape of clothing that can arise even when it is held at the same point, one representative shape of each state is deformed to better fit the observed 3D data. The state that shows the best fit to the observed data is selected as the correct state. Once the clothing model is fit to actual observations, the position and normal direction of any part of the target article of clothing can be estimated by checking the 3D data corresponding to that part of the model. This is useful in determining the action plan for further handling of the part. Fig. 2(b) shows an example of the calculated action plan for grasping

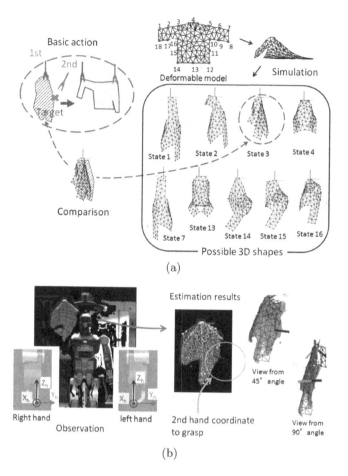

Fig. 2. Model-driven strategy of clothes recognition for automatic handling: (a) basic action and model-driven recognition; (b) calculation of action to perform the basic action; to grasp a specific part, the hand should approach the part from outside along the blue line with its thumb open in the direction of the green line

a shoulder part. The red, green and blue lines superposed on the left and right hands show the definition of their hand coordinates respectively. These lines are used for illustrating the position and orientation of the hand in all the figures of this paper. For example, in Fig. 2(b), the red, green and blue lines illustrate the position and orientation of the left hand at the point when it should close its fingers to grasp the shoulder part; the hand should approach the part from outside along the blue line with its thumb open in the direction of the green line.

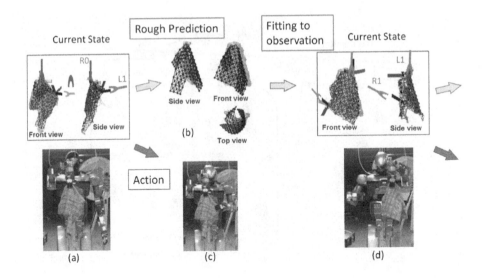

Fig. 3. Rough prediction and fitting to observations by deformable clothing model

3   Actions for Achieving Folding Task

After the recognition process, a proper sequence of grasps to achieve the goal task is determined according to the resultant clothing state. Execution of the sequence while keeping the clothing state known is done by repeating the rough prediction of the clothing shape and fitting the shape to the observations at each grasp change. Fig. 3 illustrates this core process. The model in Fig. 3(a) shows an example of the clothing state obtained by the recognition process. The part to be grasped next is qualitatively determined from the state, such as grasping rim position 37 to move from state 25. The position and pose of the hand coordinates necessary to execute this action are calculated as indicated by the red, green, and blue lines superposed on Fig.3(a). During execution of this action (Fig. 3(c)), the 3D shape after this action is predicted, as shown by the model in Fig. 3(b). Then, the model is deformed and fitted to the observed data, as shown in Fig. 3(d). This gives a new "current state," and the system is then ready for the next grasping step.

In this study, we implemented the proposed strategy for the task of folding a pullover. Folding can be realized by transiting the target clothing item through some shape configurations. The sequence of key states for folding a pullover is shown in Fig. 4(a): Body opened, One sleeve folded, Two sleeves folded, and Body folded.

3.1   Opening the Body

Since gravity is useful for opening clothing items with few wrinkles, we set a subgoal of opening a pullover in air (Key State 1 in Fig. 4). By allowing three

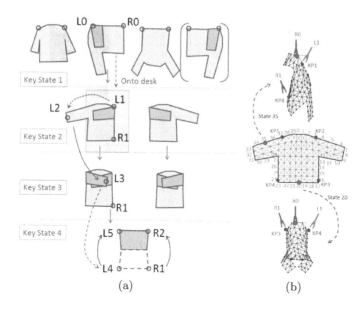

Fig. 4. Key states for folding a pullover: (a) folding action from S-B case; (b) automatic determination of opening action

types of opened states, S-S, B-B, and S-B (or B-S), the opening procedure can be realized by a small number of grasping steps from any initial state. Here S and B represent a shoulder and a corner of the bottom, respectively. The four red points in Fig. 4(b), $KP_i(i = 1,...,4)$, show the positions of parts S and B. The actions necessary to open the body of the clothing item can be systematically determined by selecting the pair KP_i according to the clothing state. In Fig. 4(b), two examples (states 20 and 35) are shown.

3.2 Folding on a Desk

For each of S-S, B-B, and S-B (B-S), the action sequence for folding the pullover can be determined in advance. Fig. 4(a) shows the sequence of the folding actions for case S-B.

During the folding process, two types of grasp steps are necessary. In Fig. 4(a), these are illustrated by the dotted lines and represented by the markers $L1 \rightarrow L2$ (grasping the tip of a sleeve) and $L3 \rightarrow L4$ (grasping a corner of the bottom). During the image processing for detecting the position and pose of the target part at each grasping step, the expected position of the target part is used to simplify the processing and obtain robust results. The details of the processes are as follows.

1. Detection of the tip of the hanging sleeve ($L1 \rightarrow L2$)

Before this process, the trunk of the item is placed at the edge of the desk so that the sleeve hangs down from the edge, as shown in Fig. 5(a). As a result,

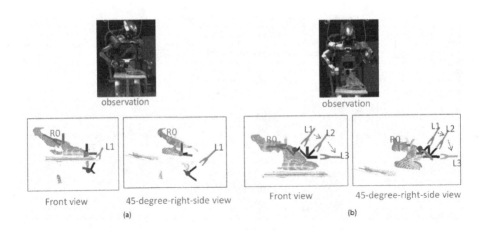

Fig. 5. Grasping actions during folding on a desk: (a) picking up a sleeve; (b) tracing a bottom line

the position of the tip of the hanging sleeve can be assumed to lie within a limited space and is robustly detected. Here, the extracted position of the sleeve tip and calculated position and pose of the left hand grasping the sleeve are superimposed on the front and side views of the observed 3D data and indicated by red points and red, green, and blue lines, respectively. Once the tip of the sleeve is grasped by a hand, the sleeve is folded by moving the hand in a circular trajectory whose center is on the edge of the desk (blue points in Fig. 5(a)).

2. Extraction of the 3D rim line ($L3 \rightarrow L4$)

Because the other corner of the bottom is held by the other hand (the holding hand) at this phase (e.g., R0 in Fig.5(b)), the corner can be grasped by sliding the grasping hand along the rim at the bottom. The rim can be detected by extracting the 3D boundary line of the region connected to the holding hand, as shown by the orange line in 5(b).

4   Experiments

We conducted experiments using two pullovers, Pullover A and B. Pullover B is softer than Pullover A. Eight experimental results are summarized in Table 1. In the experiments, we adopt the strategy of grasping the locally lowest rim of the hanging item first for restricting the shape configurations. After this first action, the pullovers were held by a tip of a sleeve (Nos. 1,4,5, and 7 of Table 1) or by a corner of the bottom (Nos. 2,3,6, and 8 of Table 1) . Fig. 7(a)–(d) shows one example (No. 5 of Table 1).

Then, the pullover is observed from multiple direction by the method proposed in [1]. During the process, the item is rotated around the vertical axis to be convex from the perspective of the camera automatically. In the cases where convex observation were not automatically obtained (Nos. 6 and 7), appropriate angles were manually input to continue the experiments.

Table 1. Experimental results for two pullovers (– means "no trial")

No.	Pullover	State	Recognition	Opening	Folding
1	A	8	◯	◯	◯
2	A	17	✕	✕	–
3	A	23	◯	◯	–
4	A	8	◯	◯	△
5	A	32	◯	◯	◯
6	B	17	◯	◯	–
7	B	8	◯	◯	△
8	B	17	◯	◯	–

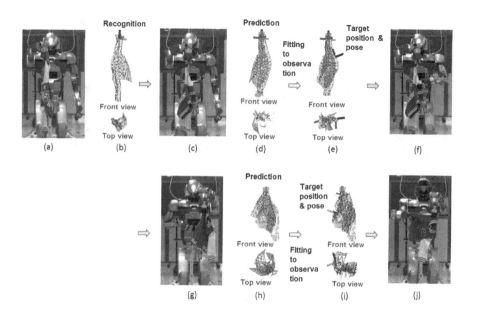

Fig. 6. Result of opening (Pullover B)

Once a pullover was observed from the side yielding a convex surface, the state of the pullover was successfully recognized and could be opened in most cases. Fig. 6 shows a case where Pullover B was successfully opened (No. 7 of Table 1). After the observation (Fig. 6(a)) was recognized as State 8, the model shape was fitted to the observed 3D data as shown in Fig. 6(b). Here, KP_2 and KP_3 were selected for the opening process. To grasp the shoulder part ($KP_2(Rim3)$) first, the item was rotated (Fig. 6(c)). Concurrently, the shape of the item after this rotation was predicted by rotating the current model shape, as shown by the model in Fig. 6(d). After fitting, this predicted shape was matched to the newly observed 3D data as shown in Fig. 6(e), where the position and

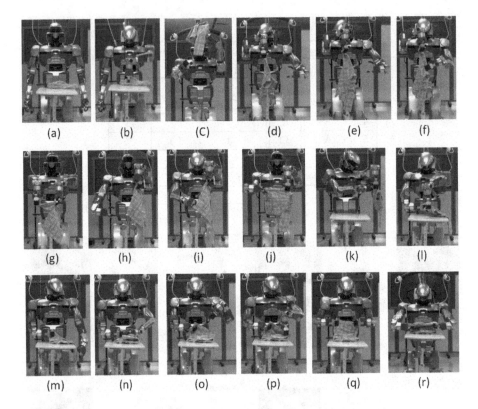

Fig. 7. Result of successful folding process (Pullover A)

pose of the hand to grasp the target part (rim position 3) was calculated as shown by the three axes illustrated as red, green, and blue lines superposed on Fig.6(e). After grasping the position according to these values (Fig. 6(f)) and releasing the sleeve from the right hand, a new observation was obtained (Fig. 6(g)). Here, again the process of rough prediction (Fig. 6(h)) and fitting (Fig. 6(i)) was repeated. As a result, $KP_3(Rim16)$ was detected and used to calculate the next motion for the right hand. Finally, the item was well opened in S-B mode, as shown in Fig. 6(j).

In the case of No. 2 in Table 1, although the correct state was selected, the clothing model failed to fit the surface. As a result, the estimation of the target part failed.

Fig. 7 shows an example of a successful folding process, from the first step to the last (No. 5). In the cases of No. 4 and No. 7, the folding procedure went well before the grasping of both corners of the bottom, at which time the robot failed in sliding its hand along the rim of the bottom.

5   Conclusions

We proposed a strategy for reshaping an item of clothing from an arbitrary shape into a fixed folded shape by using a deformable model to consider the overall configuration of the item. At each grasping step, the position and pose of the part to be grasped is determined on the basis of the corresponding part of the deformable clothing model, which is fit to the observed data. Through the experiments, we found that deforming the item to a desired shape is a key issue from a practical viewpoint. We showed the result with only one type of clothing (pullovers) in the experiments, but we believe that the proposed strategy is applicable to multiple types by changing clothing models. One of our future subjects is to enable handling of softer clothing items.

Acknowledgments. This work was supported by a Grant-in-Aid for Scientific Research, KAKENHI (22240019). We are thankful to Dr. K. Yokoi, Dr. Y. Kawai and Dr. K. Harada for their support in this research.

References

1. Kita, Y., Ueshiba, T., Kanehiro F., Kita, N.: Recognizing clothing states using 3D data observed from multiple directions. In: Proc. of International Conference on Humanoid Robots 2013, pp. 227–233 (2013)
2. Shibata, M., Ota, T., Endo, Y., Hirai, S.: Handling of Hemmed Fabrics by a Single-Armed Robot. In: Proc. of 2008 IEEE Conf. on Automation Science and Engineering, pp. 882–887 (2008)
3. Yamakawa, Y., Namiki, A., Ishikawa, M.: Motion Planning for Dynamic Folding of a Cloth with Two High-speed Robot Hands and Two High-speed Sliders. In: Proc. of IEEE Int'l Conf. on Robotics and Automation (ICRA 2011), pp. 5486–5491 (2011)
4. Yamazaki, K., Nagahama, K., Inaba, M.: Daily Clothes Observation from Visible Surfaces Based on Wrinkle and Cloth-Overlap Detection. In: Proc. the IAPR Conf. on Machine Vision Applications, pp. 275–278 (2011)
5. Willimon, B., Birchfield, S., Walker, I.: Classification of Clothing using Interactive Perception. In: Proc. of IEEE Int'l Conf. on Robotics and Automation (ICRA 2011), pp. 1862–1868 (2011)
6. Ramisa, A., Alenya, G., Moreno-Noguer, F., Torras, C.: Using depth and appearance features for informed robot grasping of highly wrinkled clothes. In: Proc. of International Conference on Robots and Systems, pp. 1703–1708 (2012)
7. Maitin-Shepard, J., Cusumano-Towner, M., Lei, J., Abbeel, P.: Cloth Grasp Point Detection based on Multiple-View Geometric Cues with Application to Robotic Towel Folding. In: Proc. of IEEE Int'l Conf. on Robotics and Automation (ICRA 2010) (2010)
8. van den Berg, J., Miller, S., Goldberg, K., Abbeel, P.: Gravity-based robotic cloth folding. In: Hsu, D., Isler, V., Latombe, J.-C., Lin, M.C. (eds.) Algorithmic Foundations of Robotics IX. STAR, vol. 68, pp. 409–424. Springer, Heidelberg (2010)
9. Miller, S., Fritz, M., Darrell, T., Abbeel, P.: Parameterized Shape Models for Clothing. In: Proc. of IEEE Int'l Conf. on Robotics and Automation (ICRA 2011), pp. 4861–4868 (2011)

10. Kaneko, M., Kakikura, M.: Planning strategy for putting away laundry - Isolating and unfolding task. In: Proc. of the 4th IEEE International Symposium on Assembly and Task Planning, pp. 429–434 (2001)
11. Osawa, F., Seki, H., Kamiya, Y.: Unfolding of massive laundry and classification types by dual manipulator. JACIII **11**(5), 457–463 (2007)
12. Cusumano-Towner, M., Singh, A., Miller, S., O'Brien, J., Abbeel, P.: Bringing Clothing into Desired Configurations with Limited Perception. In: Proc. of IEEE Int'l Conf. on Robotics and Automation (ICRA 2011) (2011)
13. Kita, Y., Ueshiba, T., Neo, E.S., Kita, N.: A method for handling a specific part of clothes by dual arms. In: Proc. of International Conference on Robots and Systems, pp. 480–485 (2009)
14. Kita, Y., Kanehiro, F., Ueshiba, T., Kita, N.: Clothes handling based on recognition by strategic observation. In: Proc. of International Conference on Humanoid, pp. 53–58 (2011)
15. Ueshiba, T.: An Efficient Implementation Technique of Bidirectional Matching for Real-time Trinocular Stereo Vision. In: Proc. of 18th Int. Conf. on Pattern Recognition, pp. 1076–1079 (2006)

Multiple Camera Approach for SLAM Based Ultrasonic Tank Roof Inspection

Christian Freye[✉], Christian Bendicks, Erik Lilienblum,
and Ayoub Al-Hamadi

Institute for Information Technology and Communications,
Otto von Guericke University, 39106 Magdeburg, Germany
{Christian.Freye,Ayoub.Al-Hamadi}@ovgu.de
http://www.iikt.ovgu.de/NIT

Abstract. This paper presents an approach of an autonomous measuring system for the wall thickness of tank roofs. It consists of a mobile robot, a multi-camera system and an ultrasonic sensor. A simultaneous localization and mapping with six degrees of freedom (SLAM-6D) is performed. The developed algorithms are optimized to work in manmade environments. Because of the great amount of line features in such environments, feature extraction is based on line segment detection. We propose a simple method for matching line segments in multiple images of three cameras. The correspondences are used to calculate 3D lines, which are used for localization. The accuracy of the system is evaluated by measurements on a prepared scene with unique markers.

Keywords: Robotics · Photogrammetry · Visual SLAM · Line matching

1 Introduction

Measuring the wall thickness of a tank roof is currently carried out by hand and at random. A complete monitoring of the tank roof is not possible, because the entering is only allowed on defined areas. An autonomous measurement system has the capability for a complete monitoring. It reduces the hazard of human examiners and guarantees the technical security at the operation of refineries. Furthermore, a complete overview of corrosion can help to plan repair work. According to the work described in [1], tracking of an ultrasonic sensor in 3D is aspired. To achieve the sensor-tracking, a visual SLAM algorithm is used for localizing the measurement system on a tank roof.

As shown in Fig. 1 there is a limited amount of landmarks, which can be used for localization on such tank roofs. Lines at the circumferential guardrail seem to be appropriate for this task. The robust detection and tracking of these features under outdoor-conditions is a great challenge.

In the field of robotics there are already a lot of different SLAM approaches available. In [2] laser range data is used. They extract different features like edges

© Springer International Publishing Switzerland 2014
A. Campilho and M. Kamel (Eds.): ICIAR 2014, Part II, LNCS 8815, pp. 453–460, 2014.
DOI: 10.1007/978-3-319-11755-3_50

Fig. 1. Overview of a tank roof with a yellowish circumferential guardrail

or curvatures from the scan and create a feature map of them. Nüchter et al. apply laser scan methods to create consistent 3D point clouds, using different error minimization techniques [3]. These approaches are widely explored and work well on indoor environments. However, in our case the bars of the guardrail provide only a few features, which would be detected by conventional 2D laser scanners. These bars have a round and smooth surface, so that incoming laser beams are scattered in different directions. Thus, a robust and accurate detection of the bars with a laser scanner is unfeasible and it would not be possible to create a consistent map of the roof top.

Other approaches work on monocular and depth images to create a map of the environment. Civera et al. [4] use an extended Kalman filter to estimate the camera motion and a sparse 3D map of feature points from an image sequence. Endres et al. acquire colored 3D models with a Kinect-style camera [5]. They take advantage of Random Sample Consensus (RANSAC) to estimate the transformation between the images. These approaches can use more features for localization. But depth cameras like the Microsoft Kinect have problems with infra-red light from the sun, so that it would not be adequate to use them outdoors. Furthermore, the range is too limited.

The proposed localization approach in our paper is based on line features in multiple camera views and their reconstruction in 3D. We present the development and evaluation of algorithms for feature extraction and SLAM in such an environment. Due to the special regulations, which apply on industrial used tank roofs, the SLAM problem should be solved without modifications of the roofs. Therefore, it is necessary to have a good contrast between the rail and the background. A colored rail as shown in Fig. 1 would be useful. We will investigate, if the feature detection and tracking is robust enough to guarantee a specified measurement precision. The remaining paper is structured as follows: First, the orientation concept is described in section 2. In section 3 the current experimental set-up and the results of the accuracy estimation are presented. The paper ends with a conclusion in section 4.

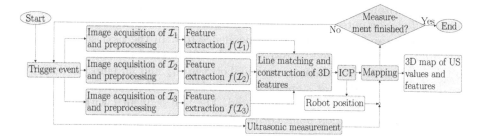

Fig. 2. Schematic representation of the measurement process

2 Orientation Concept

The process for localizing the measurement system and mapping is summarized in Fig. 2. It includes the consecutive steps of a measurement. Because common tank roofs are dome-shaped, a SLAM-6D approach is considered. Therefore, the images are preprocessed and line features are extracted. Corresponding lines are searched in the images and 3D lines are computed. With these lines, the intersection points for the Iterative Closest Point (ICP) algorithm are created. The movement of the robot is estimated with the ICP algorithm and the map of the tank roof is extended.

2.1 Image Acquisition and Preprocessing

The robot records the surrounding with a system of three cameras. Acquisition of the images $\mathcal{I}_1$, $\mathcal{I}_2$ and $\mathcal{I}_3$ is synchronized by a trigger signal. This guarantees the simultaneous acquisition of the images, which is essential for the matching of corresponding lines and their 3D reconstruction. To smoothen the edges of the guardrail, a 2D Gaussian is applied, whose parameter σ can be defined by the user. For the later operation, an automated parameter tuning is aspired. Due to the colored bars, a color filtering is also part of the preprocessing. Therefore the images are converted into the HSV space and a color segmentation is performed. Afterwards, the masked image regions are converted to gray scales.

2.2 Feature Extraction and Matching

Features are based on the line extraction algorithm proposed in [6]. It detects line segments in the images in linear time and provides sub-pixel accuracy, which is important for the following matching process.

Trifocal geometry of the involved cameras is applied. The needed internal and external camera parameters are known from the previous calibration [7]. In Fig. 3 the matching process on a rail-like structure is visualized. First of all, horizontal and vertical line segments are distinguished. The matching is explained for horizontal lines. For vertical lines $\mathcal{I}_2$ and $\mathcal{I}_3$ are processed in opposite direction.

For every horizontal line segment l in image $\mathcal{I}_1$ the epipolar line $\mathcal{E}_{13}$ of its center in image $\mathcal{I}_3$ is computed. Hence, every line segment in image $\mathcal{I}_3$, which intersects with $\mathcal{E}_{13}$ is a candidate for the correspondence to l. In the next step, epipolar lines in $\mathcal{I}_2$ are constructed in respect to these intersections, and additionally to the center of l. Now the intersections between $\mathcal{E}_{12}$ and all epipolar lines $\mathcal{E}_{32}^n$ are determined. In the last step the distances between these intersection points and the line segments in $\mathcal{I}_2$ are computed. The line segment $\hat{l}$ with the closest distance to an intersection point corresponds to l.

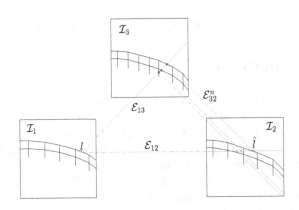

Fig. 3. The use of trifocal geometry to find correspondences

2.3   Construction of 3D Features

The obtained corresponding line segments l and $\hat{l}$ can be used to compute a line in $\mathbb{R}^3$. Firstly, the endpoints of the line segments (p_1, q_1) and (p_2, q_2) in $\mathbb{R}^3$ are calculated with known camera parameters. They are located on the rays from the projection centers o_1, o_2 towards the segment endpoints on the image plane. To obtain a 3D line, two planes

$$E_1 : \boldsymbol{n} \cdot \boldsymbol{x} = d,$$
$$E_2 : \boldsymbol{x} = \boldsymbol{o_2} + r\boldsymbol{u} + s\boldsymbol{v} \tag{1}$$

are spanned by o_1, o_2 and the endpoints (p_1, q_1), (p_2, q_2) of the line segments. With $\boldsymbol{n} = (\boldsymbol{o_1} - \boldsymbol{p_1}) \times (\boldsymbol{o_1} - \boldsymbol{q_1})$, $\boldsymbol{u} = (\boldsymbol{o_2} - \boldsymbol{p_2})$ and $\boldsymbol{v} = (\boldsymbol{o_2} - \boldsymbol{q_2})$. For further calculations, E_1 is given in normal form and E_2 in parameter form. The substitution of E_2 into E_1 results in

$$\boldsymbol{n} \cdot \boldsymbol{o_2} + r\boldsymbol{n} \cdot \boldsymbol{u} + s\boldsymbol{n} \cdot \boldsymbol{v} = d. \tag{2}$$

If $\boldsymbol{n} \cdot \boldsymbol{u} \neq 0$ the equation can be solved for s and inserted into the equation of E_2. The result is a linear equation, which represents the observed line:

$$g : \boldsymbol{x} = \left(\boldsymbol{o_2} + \frac{d - \boldsymbol{n} \cdot \boldsymbol{o_2}}{\boldsymbol{n} \cdot \boldsymbol{u}}\boldsymbol{u}\right) + t\left(\boldsymbol{v} - \frac{\boldsymbol{n} \cdot \boldsymbol{v}}{\boldsymbol{n} \cdot \boldsymbol{u}}\boldsymbol{u}\right). \tag{3}$$

In the next step, "intersection points" between the resulting 3D lines are computed. Because it is unlikely that two 3D lines intersect in a specific point, the nearest point between two skew lines is calculated. If two lines are approximately orthogonal and their distance is below a threshold d_l, the nearest point between these lines is included into the feature set. The threshold for the euclidean distance between lines is used to exclude "intersection points" between irrelevant lines. The resulting point set is used for the following ICP algorithm.

2.4   Iterative Closest Point Algorithm

For estimating the transformation the well known ICP algorithm is applied, which was first introduced by Besl and McKay in 1992. A comparison protocol and a modular ICP framework is presented in [8]. There are six stages of the algorithm:

1. Selection of features,
2. finding close points in feature sets F_{t-1} and F_t,
3. weighting of point pairs,
4. rejection of pairs,
5. assigning an error metric,
6. compute transformation that minimizes the error metric.

In [9] the comparison of different approaches for these six steps is presented. The algorithm was configured according to their results and the properties of our obtained data.

In the first step, all 3D points from the feature sets are selected. The closest points between the two sets are found by using a k-Nearest Neighbor (k-NN) algorithm with Euclidean distance. An additional weighting of the pairs is skipped, but pairs are rejected, if their distance is greater than a given threshold d_p. The sum of squared distances of the pairs is then determined as the error metric. To minimize this error metric a closed form solution is used, which was published in [10]. The result of that computation is a transformation from F_t to F_{t-1}, that minimizes the squared distance between the point pairs.

This process is repeated from step 2 until one or more of the following termination conditions are achieved: The absolute error falls below a threshold ϵ_{abs}, the relative error between two iterations is less than a threshold ϵ_{rel}, the iteration number exceeds an upper limit ϵ_{iter}.

The resulting transformation is applied to the old robot position at time $(t-1)$ to compute its new position and the location of the ultrasonic measurement value. The transformed point features from F_t are fused to a map of the environment, which is continuously extended while the robot moves along.

2.5   Mapping

At the beginning the first observation is inserted into map M. New observations are fused with the existing point set in M. If $||a - b||_2 < \epsilon$, where $a \in M$ and

$b \in F_t$, the points are averaged. Otherwise, the new point b is added to the map. That leads to a continuous expansion of the map.

To remove outliers from the map, every point $a \in M$ also holds a value c_a, which expresses its confidence. The more often a point is fused with an other the higher becomes c_a. With the threshold ϵ_{conf} the outliers are removed in continuous intervals according to

$$\forall a \in M : M = M \backslash \{a\}, \text{if } c_a \leq \epsilon_{conf}. \tag{4}$$

3 Experimental Results

Because of the strict security regulations and the resulting limited access to tank roofs on a refinery, it is difficult to get real images of the environment. Therefore, the actual experimental set-up is done in the laboratory. As seen in Fig. 4 a grid texture is attached on two walls. Additionally unique markers are applied, which are used for evaluation. The results of the line segment approach are furthermore compared to a Harris corner detector, which provides features for the SLAM algorithm. Because of the constitution of the ground, no ultrasonic measurements are recorded. Just the position of the ultrasonic sensor in the map is evaluated, while the robot moves along.

Fig. 4. Mobile robot with camera installation and visualized route

The actual hardware for the experimental set-up consists of three color cameras with a resolution of 2048 × 2048 pixels and objectives with a focal length of 16 mm. The three cameras are arranged in an equilateral triangle with an edge length of 600 mm. With an increasing distance between the cameras the accuracy of the 3D reconstruction could also be raised, but it is limited by the design of the measuring system. The robot has a diameter of 452 mm and is 245 mm high (without additional installations). The cameras are placed at a rack on the top of the robot in a height of approximately 300 mm to 900 mm off the ground.

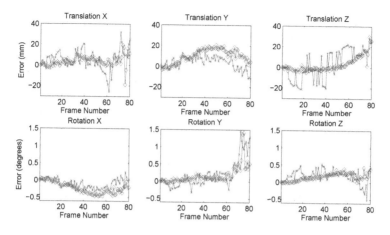

Fig. 5. Results of the accuracy estimation for localizing the robot and its ultrasonic sensor. Comparison of the "line intersections" ($\Diamond$) and the Harris corner points ($\times$).

The robot starts with a distance of about 4500 mm from the wall and moves 3000 mm in a slalom course towards the wall (yellow line in Fig. 4). At the same time, its position is estimated using three different feature sets (our method, Harris corners, unique markers). The results of our approach and the Harris corner detector are compared with the results from the marker detection. The markers can be detected very precise and they have an unique ID, so that a nearest neighbor search in the ICP algorithm is unnecessary. An error for incorrectly assigned point pairs can be eliminated. The remaining uncertainty is at least an order of a magnitude lower the expected measurement precision.

The algorithm was configured as follows: distance between lines $d_l = 30$ mm, within the ICP, point pairs are excluded if their distance $d_p \geq 1000$ mm. The termination conditions of the ICP algorithm are set as $\epsilon_{abs} = 3.0$, $\epsilon_{rel} = 1 \cdot 10^{-4}$ and $\epsilon_{iter} = 50$. The results of the robot localization are shown in Fig. 5. It represents the positioning error compared to the marker results for translation and rotation. We achieved a mean error of 13.7 mm (std. 0.17 mm), which is 0.46% over trajectory and a maximum of 33.9 mm with our approach. The Harris corner points obtained a mean error of 17.7 mm (std. 0.24 mm), which is 0.59% over trajectory and a maximum of 39.2 mm. This shows that the usage of more complex features lead to a robuster localization of the robot. Compared to the localization results in [4], our approach reaches a 0.24% better accuracy, but under laboratory conditions and with a shorter trajectory. The results suggest, that the combination of a multi-camera system and detection of line features on grid-like structures satisfies industrial requirements in terms of accuracy.

4   Conclusion

In this paper, we presented a method to localize a mobile robot on a tank roof and to create a map with 3D features of that environment. We consider, that the method is useful for the navigation of intelligent robot systems in this special surroundings. An established line detection technique was combined with the advantages of multi-camera systems to solve the correspondence problem and to create 3D features. Afterwards, we used the well known ICP algorithm to calculate the robot position within the map. The localization of the ultrasonic sensor reaches an accuracy of approximately 13.7 mm in our experiment.

It has been shown, that lines are appropriate features for robot localization, because they can be detected very accurate and robust. For future work, an iterative closest line approach will be followed to calculate the movement of the robot. This could help to raise the accuracy and reliability of the SLAM approach. The tests with our prototype were promising and the development of an outdoor system is aspired. Therefore, a GPS sensor could provide a basic, but inaccurate estimate of the position and movement of the robot. Furthermore, the localization in other man-made environments has to be investigated.

Acknowledgments. This work was funded by the German Federation of Industrial Research Associations (KF2188304WM2).

References

1. Bendicks, C., Lilienblum, E., Freye, C., Al-Hamadi, A.: Tracking of a Handheld Ultrasonic Sensor for Corrosion Control on Pipe Segment Surfaces. In: Blanc-Talon, J., Kasinski, A., Philips, W., Popescu, D., Scheunders, P. (eds.) ACIVS 2013. LNCS, vol. 8192, pp. 342–353. Springer, Heidelberg (2013)
2. Tipaldi, G.D., Arras, K.O.: FLIRT - Interest regions for 2D range data. In: IEEE International Conference on Robotics and Automation (ICRA), pp. 3616–3622 (2010)
3. Nüchter, A.: 3D Robotic Mapping: The Simultaneous Localization and Mapping Problem with Six Degrees of Freedom, 1st edn. Springer Publishing Company, Incorporated (2009)
4. Civera, J., Grasa, O.G., Davison, A.J., Montiel, J.M.M.: 1-Point RANSAC for extended Kalman filtering: Application to real-time structure from motion and visual odometry. J. Field Robot. **27**, 609–631 (2010)
5. Endres, F., Hess, J., Engelhard, N., Sturm, J., Cremers, D., Burgard, W.: An evaluation of the RGB-D SLAM system. In: IEEE International Conference on Robotics and Automation (ICRA), pp. 1691–1696 (2012)
6. von Gioi, R.G., Jakubowicz, J., Morel, J., Randall, G.: LSD: a Line Segment Detector. Image Processing On Line **2**, 35–55 (2012)
7. Tsai, R.Y.: A versatile camera calibration technique for high-accuracy 3D machine vision metrology using off-the-shelf TV cameras and lenses. IEEE Journal of Robotics and Automation **3**, 323–344 (1987)
8. Pomerleau, F., Colas, F., Siegwart, R., Magnenat, S.: Comparing ICP variants on real-world data sets. Autonomous Robots **34**, 133–148 (2013)
9. Rusinkiewicz, S., Levoy, M.: Efficient variants of the ICP algorithm. In: International Conference on 3-D Digital Imaging and Modeling, pp. 145–152 (2001)
10. Horn, B.K.P.: Closed-form solution of absolute orientation using unit quaternions. Journal of the Optical Society of America **4**, 629–642 (1987)

On Tracking and Matching in Vision Based Navigation

Adam Schmidt, Marek Kraft, and Michał Fularz[✉]

Institute of Control and Information Engineering,
Poznan University of Technology, Poznan, Poland
{adam.schmidt,marek.kraft,michal.fularz}@put.poznan.pl

Abstract. The paper presents a thorough comparative analysis of the feature tracking and the feature matching approaches applied to the visual navigation. The evaluation was performed on a synthetic dataset with perfect ground truth to assure maximum reliability of results. The presented results include the analysis of both the feature localization accuracy and the computational costs of different methods. Additionally, the distribution of the uncertainty of the features localization was analyzed and parametrized.

1 Introduction

Establishing point features correspondences across images in video sequence plays an important role in the visual navigation of robots. The correspondences can be used to estimate the transformations between the consecutive poses as in the visual odometry (VO) systems [1][2][3] or to update the environment model in the simultaneous localization and mapping (SLAM) [4][5][6].

The contemporary visual navigation systems use either the feature tracking or the feature matching approach. In the first case the position of the features on the new image is determined by finding the most probable displacement of the features within the local neighbourhood of their last positions. This approach is used in several visual navigation systems such as [3]. The more popular approach is based on finding the characteristic points on the analysed images, calculating the descriptor of their local neighbourhood and finding the pairs of the most similar descriptors. The examples of the systems using the feature matching paradigm include e.g. [5] and [7].

According to Fraundhofer and Scaramuzza [2] the tracking-based approach is usually more suited for small-scale environments and frame to frame tracking. The descriptor-based matching is generally used in larger environments where the displacement of the camera introduces significant changes to the features' local neighbourhood. In such cases the matching may be performed less frequently to compensate for the computational cost of the descriptor calculation and matching of the early descriptors such as SIFT [8] or SURF [9]. However, the introduction of the FAST detector [10] and binary descriptors such as BRIEF [11] or ORB [12] significantly changes this distinction.

© Springer International Publishing Switzerland 2014
A. Campilho and M. Kamel (Eds.): ICIAR 2014, Part II, LNCS 8815, pp. 461–468, 2014.
DOI: 10.1007/978-3-319-11755-3_51

Over the years, significant attention has been paid to the evaluation of different point features detectors and descriptors [13]. However, no similar research of the feature tracking algorithms has been performed. Moreover, to the extent of the authors knowledge, no study comparing the efficiency of the tracking and matching paradigms in the context of visual navigation is available.

This paper presents the evaluation of the feature tracking and matching approaches to the feature localization task. Moreover, the analysis of the features' localization uncertainty was performed. The synthetic, rendered data was used in the experiments guaranteeing the precision of the reference camera poses, which is especially important considering that the errors of features localization are measured in single pixels.

2 Methods

Feature matching and feature tracking are two alternative approaches to the problem of finding keypoint correspondences across a sequence of images. Feature tracking starts with finding points of interest in the initial image, and tracking them in consecutive frames by finding their correspondences using local search methods, e.g. correlation or gradient descent. Feature tracking performs best if the viewpoints in which the images were taken are not too far apart. Significant apparent feature motion caused by viewpoint change is usually associated with the deformation of the features' neighbourhood, making tracking significantly more prone to failure than matching.

Feature matching is based on direct keypoint-to-keypoint comparison rather than on local search. Each keypoint is assigned a unique descriptor computed based on the distribution of the image intensity function in the feature's neighbourhood. To match the features pairwise between consecutive images, a similarity metric is computed between their descriptors and the pairs with a smallest distance are considered to be matches. The descriptors are designed to cope with some degree of distortion of feature neighbourhood. This makes them better suited for finding feature correspondences whenever one has to deal with a wide baseline.

Historically, feature tracking had the advantage of being less computationally demanding, as the first robust detectors and descriptors were quite complicated both to calculate and to match [8][9]. With the advent of the recently developed binary descriptors [11][12], the barrier of computational cost being prohibitive in real-time applications was overcome.

The experiments involving feature tracking were performed using a pyramid variant of the widely known Kanade-Lucas-Tomasi (KLT) optical flow algorithm first proposed in [14] and extended in [15]. Tracking was initialized using the features detected using the FAST algorithm [10] known for its low computational cost.

The following algorithms were used for feature detection, description and matching: the FAST [10] feature detector paired with the binary BRIEF feature descriptor, the multiscale, L2-norm based SIFT [8] and SURF [9] detectors and descriptors, as well as the ORB multiscale binary detector and descriptor [12].

3   Experiments

The experiments were performed using the data from the ICL-NUIM dataset [16]. The dataset consists of video sequences from a synthetic environment with perfect ground-truth poses of the camera. During the rendering process special care has been given to simulate the artifacts usually present in the images registered by a camera. The synthetic data was used due to the required precision of the ground truth, as even small errors in the reference camera trajectory could corrupt the evaluation of the features localization.

The 'Living Room 0' sequence consisting of 1510 frames was used in the study. The most prominent 200 point features were detected on each of the first 1460 frames. Afterwards the detected features were localized on the following 50 frames.

In the case of the feature tracking approach, the points of interest were detected using the FAST detector. The KLT tracker was used to estimate the positions of the features on the consecutive images. Only the features that were successfully tracked on the i-th frame were analyzed on the $i + 1$-th image.

In the case of the feature matching, the features were detected and described using one of the following algorithms: the FAST-BRIEF combination, the ORB, the SURF and the SIFT. The descriptors of the features found on the i-th frame were independently matched against the descriptors of the features detected on each of the following frames, up to the $i+50$-th frame. The match was considered to be successful if the ratio of the distances between the second-best match and the best match was smaller than 0.8.

The experiments were performed on a computer with the Intel i5 processor (2.6 GHz) and 12GB RAM. The resolution of the analyzed images was 640×480.

The precision of the point features' localization on the analyzed frame was evaluated in the terms of the symmetric reprojection error. Consider $\begin{bmatrix} u_0 & v_0 \end{bmatrix}^T$ and $\begin{bmatrix} u_i & v_i \end{bmatrix}^T$ to be the position of the feature on the initial frame and the feature's estimated position on the i-th frame correspondingly. If R_i and t_i stand for the reference rotation and translation between the considered poses of the camera and M is the camera matrix. The fundamental matrix describing the epipolar geometry can be calculated as:

$$F = \left(M^T \right)^{-1} R_i [t_i]_x M^{-1} \tag{1}$$

where $[t_i]_x$ is the matrix representation of a cross product with the vector t_i. The parameters of the epipolar lines on both images can be calculated as:

$$\begin{bmatrix} a_0 & b_0 & c_0 \end{bmatrix}^T = F \begin{bmatrix} u_i & v_i & 1 \end{bmatrix}^T \tag{2}$$

$$\begin{bmatrix} a_i & b_i & c_i \end{bmatrix}^T = \begin{bmatrix} u_0 & v_0 & 1 \end{bmatrix} F \tag{3}$$

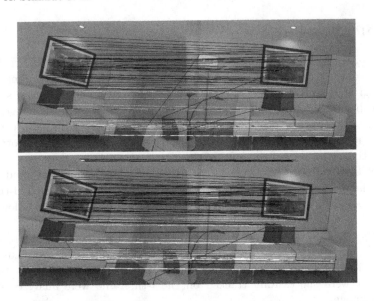

Fig. 1. Matching with FAST-BRIEF combination (top) and tracking (bottom). Matches with reprojection error less than 2 are marked white.

Finally, the symmetric reprojection error of the analyzed feature's localization is defined as:

$$d = max \left(\frac{|a_0 u_i + b_0 v_i + 1|}{\sqrt{a_0^2 + b_0^2}}, \frac{|a_i u_0 + b_i v_0 + 1|}{\sqrt{a_i^2 + b_i^2}} \right) \qquad (4)$$

Figure 2 presents the comparison of the analyzed approaches in various aspects of feature localization. Subplot (a) shows the average ratio of the features that were successfully localized on the consecutive frames. It is clearly visible that following the tracking approach results in the biggest number of maintained features. It is caused mainly by the fact that the tracking is performed on the frame-to-frame base and an exhaustive search of the features' neighbourhood is performed. In the case of the descriptor matching the most features are maintained by the FAST-BRIEF combination. The biggest number of rejected matches is observed when using the SIFT algorithm.

Subplot (c) shows the ratio of successfully localized features for which the reprojection error is smaller than 1 pixel. It is visible that using the KLT or SIFT gives the best results. The combination of the FAST and the BRIEF algorithms performs slightly worse, followed by the SURF and the ORB. The accuracy of different methods converges as the frames distance increases. If the reprojection error threshold is set to 2 the characteristics of all the methods but the SURF become similar.

It is worth noting that if the threshold is set to 1, the average ratio of correctly localized features exceeds 0.5 for the frame distance of over 20 frames. The same ratio is maintained for over 30 frames if the error threshold is set to 2. This means

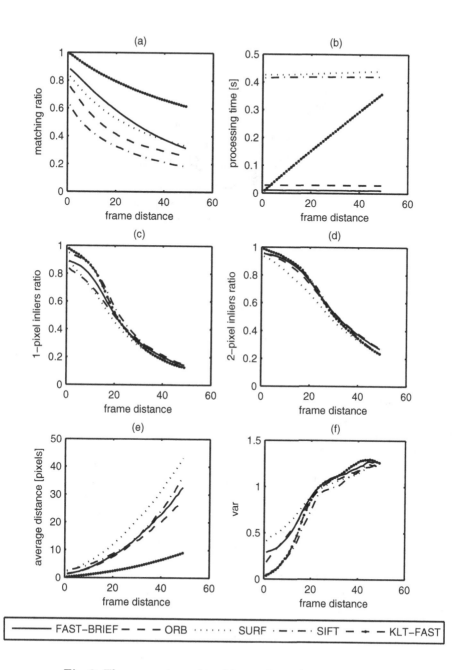

Fig. 2. The comparison of tracking and matching approaches

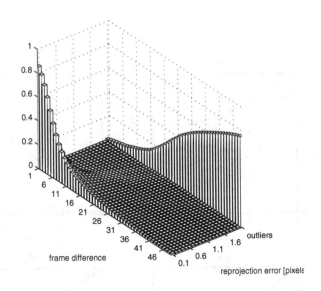

Fig. 3. Normalized histograms of the reprojection error for the KLT

that all the methods can be used for estimation of the camera displacements within a robust estimation framework and they do not differ significantly in the quality of the features' localization.

The biggest difference between the analyzed methods lies in the processing time as shown on subplot (b). In the case of the tracking approach the processing time increases proportionally to the number of analyzed frames. It is caused by the fact that the features are localized on every incoming frame. In the case of the matching the processing time is approximately constant as it comprises of the detection and description of features on only two images and their matching.

It is clearly visible that the matching using the FAST-BRIEF combination outperforms all the other approaches. The KLT is faster than the ORB if less than every fourth frame is analyzed. The SURF and SIFT require over 0.4[s] to match features across two frames. Such long processing time renders the usefulness of those two algorithms in a real-time system doubtful.

The experiments also allowed the estimation of the features' localization uncertainty. Figure 3 presents the concatenated, normalized histograms of the features' reprojection error. The values of the error were dividded into 20 regularly spaced bins between 0 and 2 pixels and the 'outliers' bin. Feature correspondences with the error bigger than 2 were considered outliers. The number of the outliers increases with the frame distance. This also explains the increasing average reprojection error observed in subplot (e) of Figure 2.

Currently, most of the visual navigation systems use robust estimation frameworks (e.g. RANSAC) to find the camera movement hypothesis supported by the biggest number of inliers. Therefore, only the uncertainty of those inliers needs to be parametrized. It may also be assumed that the features localization is not biased towards any direction. The shape of the normalized histograms suggests that the uncertainty of the features localization on the image can be modelled as an isotropic, additive 2D Gaussian noise. The distribution is considered to be zero-mean and defined only by the diagonal covariance matrix:

$$C = \begin{bmatrix} c & 0 \\ 0 & c \end{bmatrix} \tag{5}$$

Traditionally, the values of c are set to 1. However, they depend on the frame difference and can be estimated from the histograms. Subplot (f) of Figure 2 presents the values of the parameter c for all the considered algorithms. It is visible that the variance of the noise is the smallest if either the KLT or the SIFT was used. The larger variance observed in the case of the other methods is probably caused by the spatial interpolation (SURF) and non-maximal suppression (FAST and ORB).

4   Conclusions

This paper presents the comparison of the feature tracking and matching approaches in the context of visual navigation. The performed experiments clearly show that all the considered methods offer similar accuracy of the features localization. Surprisingly, despite the claimed robustness of the ORB algorithm w.r.t. the in-plane rotation and scale changes, it performed worse than the FAST-BRIEF combination. This is probably caused by the interpolation of features localization across different scales in the ORB detector.

Due to insignificant differences in the accuracy, the selection of the specific algorithm should be based on other criteria. If the processing time is crucial, which is the case in most visual navigation systems, the combination of the FAST detector and BRIEF descriptor is an obvious choice.

The BRIEF and ORB algorithms outperformed the tracking mainly due to the fact that only two frames are analyzed. However, the frame-to-frame analysis can be advantageous. The tracking can be stopped if the number of correctly localized features drops below an assumed threshold like in [3]. This is especially important in the presence of motion blur or rapid changes of the scene which can lead to an abrupt decrease in the number of correctly localized features.

Moreover, the analysis of the features' localization uncertainty was performed. The obtained results will be used in the visual SLAM system to parametrize the observations of the point features.

The future work will focus on two tasks. Firstly, the influence of the number of localized features on the processing time and localization accuracy will be assessed. Secondly, the performance of different feature detectors with the KLT will be evaluated. The obtained results will be used to select the optimal approach for point features localization in the visual SLAM system.

Acknowledgments. This research was financed by the Polish National Science Centre grant funded according to the decision DEC-2013/09/B/ST7/01583, which is gratefully acknowledged.

References

1. Scaramuzza, D., Fraundorfer, F.: Visual odometry: Part I the first 30 years and fundamentals. IEEE Robotics and Automation Magazine **18**(4) (2011)
2. Fraundorfer, F., Scaramuzza, D.: Visual odometry: Part II: Matching, robustness, optimization, and applications. IEEE Robotics & Automation Magazine **19**(2), 78–90 (2012)
3. Nowicki, M., Skrzypczynski, P.: Combining photometric and depth data for lightweight and robust visual odometry. In: 2013 European Conference on Mobile Robots (ECMR), pp. 125–130. IEEE (2013)
4. Strasdat, H., Montiel, J., Davison, A.J.: Scale drift-aware large scale monocular slam. Robotics: Science and Systems **2** (2010)
5. Zhang, Z., Huang, Y., Li, C., Kang, Y.: Monocular vision simultaneous localization and mapping using surf. In: 7th World Congress on Intelligent Control and Automation, WCICA 2008, pp. 1651–1656 (June 2008)
6. Schmidt, A., Kraft, M., Fularz, M., Domagała, Z.: Visual simultaneous localization and mapping with direct orientation change measurements. In: Gruca, A., Czachórski, T., Kozielski, S. (eds.) Man-Machine Interactions 3. AISC, vol. 242, pp. 127–134. Springer, Heidelberg (2014)
7. Lee, J., Cui, X., Lee, S., Kim, H., Kim, H.: Inha: Localization of mobile robots based on feature matching with a single camera. In: 2013 IEEE International Conference on Systems, Man, and Cybernetics (SMC), pp. 2765–2770 (October 2013)
8. Lowe, D.G.: Distinctive image features from scale-invariant keypoints. International Journal of Computer Vision **60**(2), 91–110 (2004)
9. Bay, H., Ess, A., Tuytelaars, T., Van Gool, L.: Speeded-up robust features (surf). Computer Vision and Image Understanding **110**(3), 346–359 (2008)
10. Rosten, E., Drummond, T.W.: Machine learning for high-speed corner detection. In: Bischof, H., Leonardis, A., Pinz, A. (eds.) ECCV 2006, Part I. LNCS, vol. 3951, pp. 430–443. Springer, Heidelberg (2006)
11. Calonder, M., Lepetit, V., Ozuysal, M., Trzcinski, T., Strecha, C., Fua, P.: Brief: Computing a local binary descriptor very fast. IEEE Transactions on Pattern Analysis and Machine Intelligence **34**(7), 1281–1298 (2012)
12. Rublee, E., Rabaud, V., Konolige, K., Bradski, G.: Orb: an efficient alternative to sift or surf. In: 2011 IEEE International Conference on Computer Vision (ICCV), pp. 2564–2571. IEEE (2011)
13. Schmidt, A., Kraft, M., Fularz, M., Domagala, Z.: Comparative assessment of point feature detectors and descriptors in the context of robot navigation. Journal of Automation, Mobile Robotics & Intelligent Systems **7**(1) (2013)
14. Shi, J., Tomasi, C.: Good features to track. In: 1994 IEEE Conference on Computer Vision and Pattern Recognition (CVPR 1994), pp. 593–600 (1994)
15. Bouguet, J.Y.: Pyramidal implementation of the lucas kanade feature tracker description of the algorithm (2000)
16. Handa, A., Whelan, T., McDonald, J., Davison, A.: A benchmark for RGB-D visual odometry, 3D reconstruction and SLAM. In: IEEE Intl. Conf. on Robotics and Automation, ICRA, Hong Kong, China (to appear, May 2014)

Biologically Inspired Vision
for Indoor Robot Navigation

M. Saleiro[✉], K. Terzić, D. Lobato, J.M.F. Rodrigues, and J.M.H. du Buf

Vision Laboratory, LARSyS, University of the Algarve, 8005-139 Faro, Portugal
{masaleiro,kterzic,dlobato,jrodrig,dubuf}@ualg.pt
http://w3.ualg.pt/~dubuf/vision.html

Abstract. Ultrasonic, infrared, laser and other sensors are being applied in robotics. Although combinations of these have allowed robots to navigate, they are only suited for specific scenarios, depending on their limitations. Recent advances in computer vision are turning cameras into useful low-cost sensors that can operate in most types of environments. Cameras enable robots to detect obstacles, recognize objects, obtain visual odometry, detect and recognize people and gestures, among other possibilities. In this paper we present a completely biologically inspired vision system for robot navigation. It comprises stereo vision for obstacle detection, and object recognition for landmark-based navigation. We employ a novel keypoint descriptor which codes responses of cortical complex cells. We also present a biologically inspired saliency component, based on disparity and colour.

Keywords: Biologically inspired vision · Stereo vision · Object recognition · Robotics

1 Introduction

Many types of sensors are being used for robot navigation. Some can be cheap, such as infrared and ultrasonic rangefinders [12], RFID [7,12] and GPS [10, 17], but others can be quite expensive, like laser rangefinders [13]. They allow robots to acquire information about the environment within certain ranges and depending on certain environmental conditions. However, such sensors are not always appropriate if we want to build a robot that can adapt to changes in the complex world. The use of cameras as sensors offers new possibilities. Vision can provide information about odometry and obstacles in the path of the robot, or find landmarks [5] and objects along the path. A robot can also detect humans and interact with them by understanding their gestures. The advent of low-cost RGB-D sensors has spawned a lot of interest since they allow to get reliable depth maps effortlessly if compared to stereo vision [2,8]. However, such sensors also have their limitations, like the limited range and the fact that they can only be used indoors.

© Springer International Publishing Switzerland 2014
A. Campilho and M. Kamel (Eds.): ICIAR 2014, Part II, LNCS 8815, pp. 469–477, 2014.
DOI: 10.1007/978-3-319-11755-3_52

In order to build robots that may be able to interact with a dynamic environment, a framework inspired by human cognition must be developed. This must integrate sensory information with a memory management model, with both short- and long-term memory components [16]. Concerning sensory information, we can model processes in the human visual system, such as visual saliency, Focus-of-Attention (FoA) [14], optical flow [6], local and global gist [11], stereo vision and object recognition [18].

In previous work [16] we developed a minimalistic vision-based cognitive SLAM system comprising visual saliency, object segregation and object recognition. The vision processes were integrated with a cognitive memory structure composed of short- and long-term memories. The first one has a small capacity, storing only the necessary for immediate navigation. The latter stores important information, selected from short-term memory, for longer periods of time in order to use it for global navigation. The system also integrates a task management system for building complex tasks from simpler ones.

In this paper we integrate biologically inspired vision processes and replace some previously used components which were based on computer vision: SURF keypoints and descriptors for object recognition and Fast Saliency [3] algorithm for focus of attention. With the integration of fast multi-core processors and high capacity batteries in laptops these biologically inspired processes are finally making their way into real-time mobile robotics. As main contributions in this paper we present new biologically inspired approaches for (a) keypoint descriptors, (b) stereo vision, (c) visual saliency and (d) object recognition. These approaches are based on complex cell responses obtained from a cortical V1 model [14,18]. However, the main goal of this paper is to address the feasibility of using an integrated visual framework in real time robot navigation.

The rest of this paper is organised as follows: Section 2 describes the visual processes: keypoint descriptors, stereo vision, saliency and object recognition. Section 3 presents the robot platform, tests and results. Section 4 addresses conclusions and discusses further work.

2   Biologically Inspired Vision for Robot Navigation

In this section we present a system for robot navigation which makes use of recent advances in modelling early cortical vision processes. Instead of SURF keypoints and descriptors commonly used in robotics, we developed a simple biological descriptor based on the responses of complex cells of V1 cortex which are also used for keypoint extraction [14]. We apply a biological stereo algorithm in order to improve obstacle detection and to eliminate the restriction of using artificial sandboxes. Disparity maps are combined with colour information to create saliency maps for object segregation. Finally, the novel keypoint descriptors are used to perform object recognition. In our tests we employed a Bumblebee-2 colour camera (BB298S2C-60) with a maximum resolution of 1024×768, a focal length of 6mm and a $43°$ horizontal field-of-view.

2.1   Multi-scale Keypoints and Biological Keypoint Descriptor

In cortical area V1 there are simple, complex and end-stopped cells [15], which play an important role in coding the visual input. They can be used to extract multi-scale line, edge and keypoint information: keypoints are line/edge crossings or junctions, but also blobs [14]. To use extracted keypoints for matching, we developed a simple binary descriptor which encodes complex cell responses according to a sampling pattern (see Fig. 1, left.) around a keypoint and compares them to the responses of the complex cells at the keypoint position. The use of these responses makes the descriptor very fast to compute because these are already calculated in the keypoint detection process [18]. Pairwise comparison of image intensities with similar sampling patterns has been successfully used in other binary descriptors such as BRIEF [4], BRISK [9] and FREAK [1].

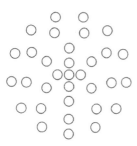

Fig. 1. Left: biological keypoint descriptor sampling pattern with 32 points radially distributed in 4 concentric circles. The radii of the circles are proportional to the scale $\lambda = 4$ of the keypoint. Right: stereo example. Top: left and right images. Bottom: filtered disparity map and binary obstacle map. In the disparity map brighter pixels correspond to closer regions and darker pixels to more distant ones.

We use a sampling pattern with 4 concentric circles, with the most distant circle having a radius equal to λ, where λ is the spatial wavelength of the Gabor filter used for modelling simple cells [18]. The smaller concentric circles have a radii of 0.2λ, 0.45λ and 0.75λ, respectively. Radial sampling patterns are commonly used in other binary descriptors [1,4,9]. We stress that we only apply one scale ($\lambda = 4$ pixels) in this paper in order to achieve real-time performance on a portable computer. However, we apply 8 filter orientations equally spaced on $[0, \pi]$.

At each sampling position we take the responses of the complex cells in all 8 orientations and compare each response with the response of the center cells with the same orientation. If the response of the center cell is larger, we code this with a binary "1". Otherwise, we code it as a binary "0". Since we use a total of 32 sampling positions and 8 orientations, each keypoint is coded by a 256-bit descriptor. Matching of two keypoints is done by simply calculating the Hamming distance between their descriptors.

2.2   Stereo Vision

Stereo vision is a fundamental process for robot navigation because it allows to detect open spaces, obstacles on its path and estimate the distance to those obstacles. Stereo vision is also useful for computing visual saliency. The stereo process employs the simple descriptors presented in Section 2.1.

In order to navigate and avoid obstacles, a robot only needs a coarse view of the obstacles and walls in front of it. A coarse disparity map can be calculated by downsizing the images captured from the left and right cameras. The algorithm is as follows: (a) resize the images to 160×120 pixels, (b) apply the descriptor previously presented to code every individual image pixel, (c) compare each pixel P in the left image to the next K pixels on the same line starting from the same position P, in the right image, and (d) using the Hamming distance, evaluate which of the K pixels is most similar to pixel P and use the horizontal displacement as the disparity value. Parameter K depends on the stereo camera used: we used $K = 150$. Since both descriptors and Hamming distances for matching are very fast to calculate, we can obtain a rough disparity map for real-time robot navigation. After calculating the disparity map we apply a median filter of size 5×5 to reduce noise due to wrong matches. In order to allow the robot to avoid obstacles and walls we threshold the disparity map and then apply a blob detection algorithm to locate nearby obstacles. This is illustrated in Fig. 1 (right).

2.3   Visual Saliency

Visual saliency is important for real-time vision, since it allows a robot to select important regions to process instead of processing entire images. Saliency maps are also useful for segregating objects from the background, reducing clutter and improving object recognition rates.

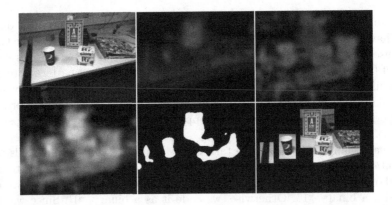

Fig. 2. Visual saliency example. Left to right, top to bottom: input image, colour based saliency, disparity based saliency, combined maps, thresholded map and interesting regions. Although the book is more distant, its distinctive colours make it an interesting region to process.

Our new saliency component combines colour with disparity. We build a stack of 6 retinotopic maps representing different channels in CIE L*A*B colour-opponent space. The CIE L*A*B model is based on retinal cones and provides a standard way to model colour opponency. The first three channels code the image in L*A*B colour space, thus represent white, green and blue. The other three channels are the complements of the first three channels, thus represent black, red and yellow.

After computing the retinotopic maps we apply blob-detection based on a stack of bandpass Difference of Gaussians (DoG) filter kernels with $\sigma_+ \in \{5, 10, 20\}$ and $\sigma_- = 2\sigma_+$. The same process is applied to the filtered disparity map after thresholding to get only the nearest regions. Finally, we sum the individual colour maps and the disparity map (Fig. 2). Since a saliency map does not need to be detailed, we compute it using the subsampled colour images for faster processing. After computing the final saliency map we threshold it and process only interesting regions for object recognition.

2.4   Object Recognition

For object recognition we selected a small set of objects to which we apply the keypoint extraction and description algorithms. Resulting keypoint descriptor arrays are then stored in the robot's memory for faster processing during runtime. During navigation, these descriptor arrays are matched to keypoint descriptors extracted from the images captured by one of the robot's cameras. Since we use binary descriptors, matching is quickly done by calculating the Hamming distances. When 50% of all descriptors of a certain object can be matched, i.e., having a Hamming distance smaller than 48, the object is confirmed. A matching example is shown in Fig. 3.

 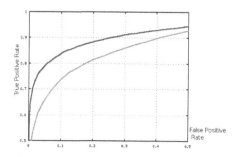

Fig. 3. Left: example of matching: the segregated book shown in Fig. 2. Right: comparison between our descriptor(green) and BRISK(blue) over 20000 patches.

In our preliminary tests we verified that our descriptors can be used for basic object recognition. We successfully used them to recognize 8 different objects (boxes, cups, book covers) under good lighting conditions. For object recognition we used $\lambda = 8$. For evaluation purposes we also used our descriptor for patch classification. We tested it on the Yosemite dataset. The graph on Fig. 3 shows a comparison between our descriptor and BRISK, which performs better. However, we emphasize that our descriptor uses half the bits that BRISK uses and has not yet been optimized in terms of redundancy, relevancy, coding and pooling.

3   Tests and Results

3.1   The Robotic Platform

To test the developed system we used a child-sized Pioneer 3DX robot, equipped with a Bumblebee-2 stereo camera, a PhantomX robot turret for pan and tilt movement of the camera, and ultrasonic and laser rangefinder sensors (see Fig. 4). The range sensors are only used for emergency collision avoidance, not for navigation. A structure has been mounted on the robot in order to give it more height, providing the point of view of a child with a height of 1.20m. The robot has been set up with ROS (Robot Operating System).

Fig. 4. Robotic platform used for testing

3.2   Test Results

For testing the stereo algorithm we placed the robot in a 60 meter long corridor and programmed it to go from one end to the other end and to avoid walls and obstacles, always trying to the initial orientation. Every time it detected an obstacle it move away from it. The corridor had varying lighting conditions, being dark in some parts, well lit in others with fluorescent lamps, which generate a lot of image noise, or with direct sunlight from the side. Along the corridor there were 7 obstacles with different sizes, shapes and colors, such as a table, a chair and cardboard and styrofoam boxes. During autonomous robot navigation we randomly placed ourselves in front of the robot. Other persons occasionally passed in front of the robot as well. In the middle of the corridor, it had a wider region with two pillars that the robot also had to avoid. We rearranged the obstacles in three different setups (A, B and C) and made 20 entire runs for each setup. The results can be seen on Table 1.

During sixty runs the robot ran into obstacles only 11 times. The major failure causes were: (a) moving obstacles in dark parts of the corridor (see Fig. 5); (b) navigating almost parallel to a blank wall due to the lack of texture and to the small FOV of the cameras; and (c) navigating in narrow spaces. Most of these problems can be easily solved by integrating the SLAM system that we previously developed which makes use of the pan and tilt system to build maps for local and global navigation. The stereo maps took an average of $0.085s$ to compute on a 2.4 GHz Intel quad core i7-4700HQ processor for the size of 160×120 pixels. For 320×240 it takes an average of $0.39s$. However, the smaller resolution proved to be enough for obstacle avoidance.

Table 1. Testing results of 60 runs in three different setups

Setup	Successful runs	Failed runs	Success Rate
A	17	3	85%
B	16	4	80%
C	16	4	80%

Fig. 5. Corridor navigation examples. Top, left to right: left and right camera images, disparity map and obstacle map. Bottom, left to right: robot detecting one of the pillars, robot detecting a person as an obstacle to avoid and screen of the computer showing the two images from the Bumblebee-2 camera and the disparity map.

4   Conclusions and Further Work

Our initial tests demonstrate that our biologically inspired system works quite well for vision-based robot navigation. Using the stereo algorithm, the robot was able to avoid the obstacles and walls in most testing runs. Visual saliency also enabled the robot to select interesting image regions for further object recognition using our novel keypoint descriptors.

Regarding visual saliency, we are working to extend it by including other cues, such as texture, shape and motion. Motion can be quite useful for avoiding moving obstacles or humans.

Although the keypoint descriptor proved to be good enough for the simple tasks used in our experiments, we are still improving it to make it competitive with state-of-the-art keypoint descriptors. Other pooling and coding approaches could yield a more robust and reliable descriptor based on complex cells from cortical region V1.

As further work we also intend to integrate the presented visual components into the cognitive robot framework that we have previously developed [16].

Acknowledgments. This work was partially supported by the Portuguese Foundation for Science and Technology (FCT) projects PEst-OE/EEI/LA0009/2013 and SparseCoding EXPL/EEI-SII/1982/2013 and by FCT PhD grant to author SFRH/BD/71831/2010.

References

1. Alahi, A., Ortiz, R., Vandergheynst, P.: FREAK: Fast Retina Keypoint. In: Proc. Int. Conf. on Computer Vision and Pattern Recognition, pp. 510–517 (2012)
2. Astua, C., Barber, R., Crespo, J., Jardon, A.: Object detection techniques applied on mobile robot semantic navigation. Sensors **14**(4), 6734–6757 (2014)
3. Butko, N., Zhang, L., Cottrell, G., Movellan, J.: Visual salience model for robot cameras. In: Proc. 2008 IEEE. Int. Conf. on Rob. and Automation, pp. 2398–2403 (2008)
4. Calonder, M., Lepetit, V., Ozuysal, M., Trzcinski, T., Strecha, C., Fua, P.: BRIEF: Computing a Local Binary Descriptor Very Fast. IEEE Transactions on Pattern Analysis and Machine Intelligence **34**(7), 1281–1298 (2012)
5. Dmitriy, Y., Postolsky, A., Grigoriy, P., Gennadievich, G.: Mobile robots navigation based on artificial landmarks with machine vision system. World Applied Sciences Journal, 1467–1472 (2013)
6. Farrajota, M., Rodrigues, J.M.F., du Buf, J.M.H.: Optical flow by multi-scale annotated keypoints: a biological approach. In: Proc. Int. Conf. on Bio-inspired Systems and Signal Processing (BIOSIGNALS 2011), Rome, Italy, pp. 307–315 (2011)
7. Hossain, M., Rashid, M., Bhuiyan, M., Ahmed, S., Akhtaruzzaman, M.: A qualitative approach to mobile robot navigation using RFID. In: IOP Conference Series: Materials Science and Engineering, vol. 53(1), p. 012064 (2013)
8. Biswas, J., Veloso, M.: Depth camera based indoor mobile robot localization and navigation. In: Proc. IEEE Int. Conf. on Robotics and Automation, pp. 1697–1702 (May 2012)
9. Leutenegger, S., Chli, M., Siegwart, R.Y.: BRISK: Binary robust invariant scalable keypoints. In: IEEE International Conference on Computer Vision, pp. 2548–2555 (2011)
10. Morton, R., Olson, E.: Robust sensor characterization via max-mixture models: GPS sensors. In: Proc. Int. Conf. Intelligent Robots and Systems, pp. 528–533 (2013)
11. Oliva, A., Torralba, A.: Building the gist of a scene: the role of global image features in recognition. Progress in Brain Res.: Visual Perception **155**, 23–26 (2006)
12. Peng, S., Dong, W.: Robot navigation system with RFID and sensors. In: Int. Conf. on Computer Distributed Control and Intelligent Environmental Monitoring, pp. 610–612 (2012)
13. Pyo, Y., Hasegawa, T., Tsuji, T., Kurazume, R., Morooka, K.: Floor sensing system using laser reflectivity for localizing everyday objects and robot. Sensors **14**(4), 7524–7540 (2014)
14. Rodrigues, J., du Buf, J.M.H.: Multi-scale keypoints in V1 and beyond: object segregation, scale selection, saliency maps and face detection. BioSystems **2**, 75–90 (2006)
15. Rodrigues, J., du Buf, J.M.H.: A cortical framework for invariant object categorization and recognition. Cognitive Processing **10**(3), 243–261 (2009)

16. Saleiro, M., Rodrigues, J.M.F., du Buf, J.M.H.: Minimalistic vision-based cognitive SLAM. In: Proc. 4th Int. Conf. on Agents and Artificial Intelligence, Special Session on Intelligent Robotics, pp. 614–623 (2012)
17. Tao, Z., Bonnifait, P., Frémont, V., Ibaez-Guzman, J.: Mapping and localization using GPS, lane markings and proprioceptive sensors. In: Proc. Int. Conf. Intelligent Robots and Systems, pp. 406–412 (2013)
18. Terzić, K., Rodrigues, J.M.F., du Buf, J.M.H.: Fast cortical keypoints for real-time object recognition. In: Int. Conf. Image Processing, pp. 3372–3376 (2013)

Author Index

Printed in the United States
By Bookmasters